Patrick McGilligan is o̶̶̶̶̶̶̶̶̶̶̶̶̶̶̶̶̶̶̶̶̶̶̶̶̶ aphers and historians. His previou̶̶̶̶̶̶̶̶̶̶̶̶̶̶̶̶̶̶̶̶̶ definitive and highly praised biographies of Jack Nicholson and of directors Robert Altman, George Cukor and Fritz Lang. He lives in Milwaukee, Wisconsin, with his wife and three children.

Further reviews for *Clint*:

'A biography that will make your day . . . A biography that says plenty, and then says plenty more . . . a compulsive trawl through the life and career of one of America's most enigmatic characters . . . You want gossip you can have gossip. But there's much more to McGilligan than gossip. Having written books on Cagney, Altman, Cukor, Nicholson and Fritz Lang, McGilligan's got this unauthorised film biography business off pat, and is a fair old digger . . . A comprehensive film biography rounds things off nicely and adds to the feeling that you're getting the full story here. And yes, the pictures are lovely.'

Maggie Pringle, *Daily Express*

'A thorough unpicking of that serape-like cover . . . McGilligan's book is the first substantial corrective that brings the legend down to a level of reality.'   David Thomson, *Independent on Sunday*

'Extremely well written, a compulsive read . . . a formidable array of evidence and on-record interviews. Above all, it's a sobering analysis of the mismatch between the shabby reality of a man's life and his shimmering public image.'   *Sight and Sound*

'Patrick McGilligan has the courage and the research to unmake Clint Eastwood's day.'
Garry Wills, Pulitzer Prize winner and author of *Reagan's America* and *John Wayne: The Politics of Celebrity*

'Adamantly unauthorised ... diligently researched but poisonously disaffected.'
Tom Charity, *Time Out*

'An engrossing, warts-and-all portrait of a Hollywood legend, his films, his marriages ...'
William Russell, *The Herald* (*Glasgow*)

'Clint Eastwood always nurtured the image of a family man far removed from the anti-heroes he plays on screen ... [McGilligan] exposes the real man – a violent, compulsive, sexual predator who cheated on his wife for 25 years and forced his mistress Sondra Locke to have two abortions ... [This] exhaustively researched biography by one of America's leading film historians exposes the violent, vengeful self-consumed egotist behind the Hollywood myth.'
Daily Mail

'Here are the facts ... and here are all Eastwood's women ... exhaustive.'
Nicholas Wapshott, *The Times*

'McGilligan's *Clint* provides the fuel to burn Eastwood at the stake.'
Philip French, *Observer*

'When you realise that Clint's life is a huge tapestry of half-truths and bullshit, the act of unpicking it becomes a noble quest ... In relentlessly peeling back publicity-department veneer, McGilligan's book makes morbidly entertaining, compulsive copy ... power-crazed egomaniac, insatiable womaniser, control freak, all Clint Eastwood's faults are here in loving detail ... Avoid if you can't handle the truth.'
Andrew Collins, *Empire*

'Unlike Richard Schickel, author of last year's fawning authorised biography, McGilligan tackles Clint with all guns blazing ... most writers have been intimidated by Clint's power ... the research is nothing if not thorough ... revealing.'
Daily Mirror

'Everything you know about Eastwood is wrong. Four years of tireless research allow McGilligan to smash every aspect of accepted Clint wisdom to smithereens, in a debunking as total and more shocking than Albert Goldman's *Elvis*, with the advantage of empathy with the star's artistry. Starting with his family tree – not blue-collar drifters, but bourgeoisie – Clint is revealed as a selective self-mythologiser on an epic scale . . . what elevates this above scurrilous gossip is McGilligan's equally investigative interest in Eastwood's films. Again, apparent truisms are upturned, and uncomfortable facts scurry beneath. The star's much-admired economy as a director is convincingly debunked as laziness, leaving most creative tasks to able underlings.'

Nick Hasted, *Uncut*

'Such is the power of the Hollywood publicity machine that it has taken until the twilight of his career for someone to really put the boot into the myth of Clint Eastwood . . . it's certainly a good read.'

FHM

'Entertaining and pointedly unauthorised biography . . . Anything you need to know about Clint? It's all here.'

David Graham, *Manchester Evening News*

PATRICK McGILLIGAN

Clint

THE LIFE AND LEGEND

HarperCollins*Entertainment*

An Imprint of HarperCollins*Publishers*

For Mom

HarperCollins*Entertainment*
An imprint of HarperCollins*Publishers*
77–85 Fulham Palace Road,
Hammersmith, London W6 8JB

www.**fire**.and**water**.com

This paperback edition 2000
3 5 7 9 8 6 4 2

First published in Great Britain by
HarperCollins*Publishers* 1999

Copyright © Patrick McGilligan 1999

The author asserts the moral right to
be identified as the author of this work

ISBN 0 00 638354 8

Set in PostScript Linotype New Baskerville

Printed and bound in Great Britain by
Clays Ltd, St Ives plc

This book is not authorized by Clint Eastwood

Contents

Acknowledgements

Permission to cite from the following unpublished manuscripts
is gratefully acknowledged:

Take Ten (The Life Story of Anita Lhoest) by Ria Brown
Who the Hell is Kitty Jones? by Kitty Jones
Clint Eastwood (Untitled) by Paul Lippman

An Oral History with Edward Carfagno
Interviewed by Barbara Hall
Beverly Hills, California: Academy of Motion Picture Arts
and Sciences, 1991

An Oral History with Charles Marquis Warren
Interviewed by Ronald L. Davis
Dallas, Texas: DeGolyer Library, Southern Methodist University, 1980

Photographs courtesy of the following individuals: Ria Brown, Robert Donner,
Geneviève Hersent-Koevoets, Ross W. Hughes, Harley R. Jones Jr, Jeremy
Kronsberg, Paul Lippman, Sondra Locke, Ted Post, B. Kenneth Roberts,
Megan Rose, Meredith Runner, John Saxon, Floyd Simmons, Lindy Warren
and Bobs Watson.

Organizations: Eddie Brandt's Saturday Matinee; Ray Cavaleri Talent
Agency; Department of Parks, King County, Washington; Las Vegas Tourist
Bureau; Linn County Historical and Genealogical Society; *The National
Enquirer;* Cinema–Television Archives of the University of Southern California;
the Wisconsin Center for Film and Theater Research; The Ronald Grant
Archive; Aquarius Picture Library; Popperfoto; Paul Sakuma/AP/Wide World
Photos; Pierre Gleizes/Gilbert Tourte/AP/Wide World Photos; Rex Features;
John Hayes/Associated Press.

Illustrations

Clint with Roxanne Tunis on the set of *Rawhide*. *Private Collection*

Roxanne Tunis. *Private Collection*

Get Yourself Another Fool!, one of Clint's '45s. *Private Collection*

All The Hits With All The Stars, Vol. 4. *Private Collection*

Clint making a guest appearance with Buddy Ebsen, Fess Parker and Danny Kaye. *Private Collection*

Jill Banner with Kitty Jones. *Private Collection*

Clint and Maggie with Ted Post and Roger Moore. *Private Collection*

Maggie and Jane Brolin. *Private Collection*

Kitty Jones's wedding. *Private Collection*

Clint and Maggie. *Private Collection*

Sergio Leone. *Photograph © The Ronald Grant Archive*

Clint with cowboy equipment on the roof of the Residence Palace Hotel, Rome. *Photograph reproduced courtesy of Geneviève Hersent*

Clint with French actor Philippe Hersent on the roof of the Residence Palace Hotel, Rome. *Photograph reproduced courtesy of Geneviève Hersent*

Clint with Steve Rowland and Bill Thompkins in Spain. *Private Collection*

The Italian language poster of *For A Few Dollars More*. *Private Collection*

Clint and Eli Wallach in *The Good, The Bad And The Ugly*. *Photograph © The Ronald Grant Archive*

Clint with Ted Post on the set of *Hang 'Em High*. *Private Collection*

Clint and Inger Stevens in *Hang 'Em High*. *Photograph © The Ronald Grant Archive*

Clint on the set of *Coogan's Bluff* with Don Siegel and Melodie Johnson. *Photograph © The Ronald Grant Archive*

Clint with Richard Burton in *Where Eagles Dare*. *Photograph © Aquarius Picture Library*

Clint and Jean Seberg relax off set while filming *Paint Your Wagon*. *Photograph © Popperfoto*

Paramount studio group photograph, 1969. *Private Collection*

Clint with Jo Ann Harris in *The Beguiled*. *Photograph © The Ronald Grant Archive*

Clint as *Dirty Harry*. *Photograph © Aquarius Picture Library*

Clint in Carmel at his own tennis tournament in the early 1970s. *Private Collection*

Clint with friends on the slopes in Aspen. *Private Collection*

Clint's 40th birthday party. *Private Collection*

Clint at home with Maggie, Bob Daley and Brett Halsey. *Private Collection*

Clint with Donna Mills in *Play Misty For Me*. *Private Collection*

Clint with Roxanne Tunis on the set of *Hang 'Em High*. *Private Collection*

Clint with Jeff Bridges and George Kennedy on the set of *Thunderbolt and Lightfoot*. *Private Collection*

Clint in *The Outlaw Josey Wales*. *Photograph © Aquarius Picture Library*

Alison and Kyle with the family dog. *Private Collection*

The 'forever' house. *Private Collection*

Clint with Sondra Locke. *Photograph © Aquarius Picture Library*

Clint with Jeremy Joe Kronsberg, James Fargo and Rexford Metz on the set of *Every Which Way But Loose*. *Private Collection*

Clint with Manis the ape. *Photograph © Aquarius Picture Library*

Clint as Bronco Billy. *Private Collection*

Clint with Sondra Locke and Dani Crayne. *Private Collection*

The house on Stradella Road. *Photograph reproduced courtesy of Sondra Locke*

Clint with Megan Rose. *Private Collection*

Clint becomes mayor of Carmel-By-The-Sea. *Photograph © Paul Sakuma/AP/ Wide World Photos*

Clint with Forest Whitaker at the 41st Cannes Film Festival. *Photograph © Pierre Gleizes/Gilbert Tourte/AP/Wide World Photos*

Clint directing *Unforgiven*. *Photograph © Aquarius Picture Library*

Clint with Jack Nicholson and Barbra Streisand backstage at the Oscars. *Photograph © Rex Features*

Clint with his mother Ruth, step-father John and Frances Fisher at the Oscars. *Photograph © Rex Features*

Kimber Tunis Eastwood. *Private Collection*

Clint with daughter Alison, drag queen The Lady of Chablis and John Cusack at the première of *Midnight In The Garden Of Good And Evil*. *Photograph © John Hayes/Associated Press*

int with Dina Ruiz at the première of *Bridges Of Madison County*. *Private Collection*

Clint © AP/Wide World Photos

CHAPTER ONE

The Tree of Clint
1930

The Man With No Name has a past as mysterious as his moniker. Dirty Harry had a wife once, but she is dead and barely mentioned in the films. The characters played by Clint Eastwood tend to suffer from haunting nightmares of preceding events, while existing only in the fast-action of the present. They materialize out of swirling mists, settle ambiguous, long-overdue scores – twirling their guns like magicians – and ride off into the sunset, or drive away in flashy cars.

Like the characters he plays Clint is secretive about himself, his past, his private life. Not so much secretive, more selective, but it's an act he performs well for the public. His memory is perfect on occasion, convenient on others. He likes to know, but *withhold*. The actor, as well as the characters he plays, prefers knowing something the audience doesn't.

The audience couldn't possibly know the family saga of the Eastwoods, which parallels the history of the United States. Clint himself probably does not know the full extent of it. In interviews, the screen star has treated his family tree in passing, only titbits useful to his image. (It is completely left out of Richard Schickel's authorized biography *Clint Eastwood*.) But the heritage is fascinating, the genes seep into his films, and the epic of the Eastwoods before Clint was born provides, here, a majestic overture to a life that is a triumphant, entirely American – if not entirely golden – success story.

For some, the opening music, to scroll behind the credits, will seem startling, something with carnival as well as jazz flourishes, lush strings as well as tinkling banjo, bits and pieces of disparate melodies and rhythms surprisingly integrated into a red-white-and-blue composition worthy of Copland or Ives.

1

It isn't quite true, as Richard Schickel wrote, that 'there are no Eastwoods in the Society of Mayflower Descendants', although that nicely burnishes the aura of an underdog. The first paternal forebear arrived in America early in the seventeenth century, and Eastwoods were among the early pioneers heading West. Originally Yankees, Puritans and Easterners, family relations spread out and pushed into New York, Ohio, Michigan, Virginia, Illinois, Louisiana, Kansas, Colorado, Nevada, California and Alaska, along the way inscribing their name in the annals of the Revolutionary War, early statehood struggles, the War of 1812, the Civil War and the Gold Rush. They chartered new towns, erected prairie churches, held local office, wore peacekeeping badges, accumulated land and property. They were a business-minded clan, and worked as farmers, teamsters, sloop-builders, store-owners, travelling salesmen, hotel and saloon proprietors, miners – and yes, very early on, the Eastwoods evinced a flair for show business.

Clint is like a seed nurtured in shadow that emerges as the pride of the forest, the tallest redwood. But success and prosperity marked his genealogy long before he was brought into the world.

The first American-born male with the surname was Lewis Eastwood, who was born more than a quarter-century before the Revolutionary War, in 1746, in Long Branch, New Jersey. Lewis's parents had come to the New World from England where the Eastwoods were respectable property owners who claimed antecedents dating back to the seventeenth century, from Dublin and Louth in Ireland.

Lewis lived a life that bore object lessons for future Eastwoods. A farmer and carrier (transporter of commercial goods), Lewis Eastwood moved about freely and resided for a spell in Allentown, New Jersey, as well as Goshen, Schenectady, Ballston Lake, Kinderhook, Catskill and Red Hook in the state of New York, living in certain places for several months only, while in others for years. His earnings were ploughed into land – an Eastwood penchant – and post-Revolutionary War optimism brought him to New York City, where he set up a tannery.

This was roughly in 1792. Apart from the tannery, Lewis Eastwood continued as the owner of a good-sized transport company. A New York City directory ranked him No. 103 out of 1200 carriers, indicating he owned a large number of carts. Cartmen dominated all intracity transport in New York in the early 1800s, and governed the trade and sale of furniture, mercantile goods, firewood, hay and food. In return for pledging obedience to municipal ordinances, cartmen were awarded licence monopolies, and therefore grew to accumulate considerable civic clout.

The upstart immigrant classes were rigidly barred from the cartmen's association, against whom there were constant complaints of price-gouging. Cartmen were generally aligned with the establishment party, the Democratic Republicans, in those days still the party of Thomas Jefferson, which did its best to limit the intrusions and regulations of governmental bodies. Although Clint would often tell interviewers, 'I'm the first in my family to ever make it', the cartmen were 'made' – and the earliest Eastwoods were closely aligned with privilege and power.

According to the *Encyclopedia of New York*, a cartman was 'easily recognizable by his white frock, farmer's hat and clay pipe'. The white-frocked Lewis Eastwood probably did little actual carting himself, while contracting for others to haul the merchandise. He lived successively on Eagle (later renamed Hester) and Henry Streets, both neighbourhoods of brick dwellings located in the Seventh Ward – what would become known as the Lower East Side – the city's most populous ward at the turn of the century. Both addresses were conveniently near the East River wharves and ferry terminals.

Also nearby was the Third Presbyterian Church, where the Eastwoods probably worshipped, for they were a churchly clan – one of the family characteristics, curiously, that would evolve to disappear in Clint. Lewis Eastwood shows up in documents pledging fifteen shillings for the salary of an Allentown, New Jersey, clergyman in 1784.

Lewis's ordered life began to crumble when his first wife died. Although it appears he married a second time, he was never again the same well-respected man. He took to alcohol and in his remaining years managed to go through 'the whole of his property', according to his son Asa. Lewis retreated to Allentown, near where he was born, dying there in 1829, his addiction to drink a caution to future family members.

Lewis managed to sire five children, including John, a builder of boats who lived in Sackets Harbor, New York; Enos, a sea captain who freighted oysters in Shrewsbury, New Jersey; and Asa, born in Allentown in 1781. Eastwoods had a fondness for Biblical names, which were common among the Puritans streaming to America.

Asa, who was Clint's great-great-great-grandfather, was the youngest son of Lewis, and the standout – thrifty, hard-working, societally-minded, endlessly adaptable to life's challenges. The Eastwoods believed in experience as the best teacher. Asa didn't finish his schooling, and learned carting as his father's foremost pupil. In 1800, Asa enlisted in the Navy, was assigned to the frigate USS *Constitution*, and served in the Tripolitan War between the US and the Barbary States, earning commendations for gallant conduct. New York City was his home port, and that is where he married Mary Doxsey, in Long Island in 1801, when she was nineteen and he just twenty.

After his marriage, Asa was offered an officer's appointment on a Dutch man-of-war, which he readily accepted. 'After fighting in all quarters of the globe for several years and undergoing all the vicissitudes of fortune, the youthful adventurer returned to New York to find his young bride patiently waiting for him,' according to one published account of Asa Eastwood's life, as glossy as some of Clint's later writeups. Asa could not have been undergoing vicissitudes for very long, since in 1802 he was granted a cartman's licence by New York Mayor Edward Livingston. 'These licences were secured for Mr Eastwood by friends while he was sailing the seas,' according to the published account, overlooking that parental influence guaranteed a place for Asa in the cartman elite. But early Eastwoods, too, preferred the 'self-made' mystique.

Longworth's New York Directory shows Asa following in his father's cartman footsteps while taking up residence on the Lower East Side. Several other Eastwoods, it appears from records, were in the remunerative cart business. But Asa wore many hats; he also operated a hotel and tavern near the docks – precursor to Clint's Hog's Breath Inn – and became the first Eastwood to mix heavily in politics. Like his father, Asa was a Democratic Republican, a prominent member of the Tammany Society (later to become notorious for its corruption), and the holder of several public offices.

As of 1807, Asa was listed as ensign in the city's light infantry. Soon, he would be appointed a lieutenant and recruiting officer. From 1807 to 1822, he acted as one of the city's unpaid constables, who were appointed by the mayor and charged with responsibility for suppressing riots, maintaining peace in the streets, and acting as officers of the court. The nation's first Dirty Harrys, the New York constables and marshals also lit street lamps at night, looked out for fires and guarded Potter's Field, the cemetery of paupers, from grave-robbing medical students. The mayor's appointees wore no special uniform apart from leather helmets, which is why they were dubbed 'leatherheads'.

'Other appointments followed thick and fast,' went one Horatio Alger version of Asa's life, 'and the former soldier of fortune became one of the solid politicians of old New York. With a hotel, a bakery, the old tannery, municipal and State offices and a position as a Federal collector to force the Quakers to make good back war taxes, Asa Eastwood soon became a wealthy man and a political leader of Manhattan.'

Reverses and setbacks were integral to the Eastwood mythology. After the war of 1812 Asa found himself 'at the bottom of the ladder', albeit still in possession of a barrel factory and other business operations. Metropolitan life was stressful, and Asa became the first Eastwood to heed the call of the wilderness – heading to upstate New York. Early in April 1817, he purchased a 100-acre farm in Onondaga County, then sailed to Albany on a flat-bottomed boat, from there traversing the 'roadless woods' for nine days, accompanied by his wife and family of three daughters and five sons, including a five-month-old baby boy.

'We were within three miles of our destination, when night overtook us,' wrote Asa Eastwood in his journal. 'It was dark, drizzly and cold, no road to be used. We drove by guess, my hired man and children in a wagon, my wife in a buggy and myself ahead, feeling out the way. It became pitch dark and the wagon upset in a huge mudhole. My first exclamation was, "My God, my children!" We finally got them out and used the wagon top for a tent. We made beds on a carpet and turned in hungry, cold and muddy. We had nothing to eat for man or beast. We made as good a fire as we could, lighting it from an old tinder box. The wolves howled at a fearful rate, the woods being full of them.'

Such family-centred suspense would never be replicated in a Clint Eastwood Western. For one thing, Clint's characters are rarely 'with wife' and they usually started their adventures further West, past the Mississippi, with the frontier already settled – the settlers needing six-gun protection more from human than environmental dangers.

The principal crisis for Asa and his household, however, was obvious upon arrival. Their new farm was located on the south bank of the Oneida, about a mile east of South Bay, and the Eastwoods, accustomed to urban, red-brick comfort, instead found a 'miserable shanty' in desperate need of rebuilding.

Neighbours gathered to help renovate the house, and the men added a spacious new wing while their spouses fed shifts of volunteers. Venetian blinds were fitted to elegant windows. Oak trees were burned to clear the land. Nearby Cicero buzzed with the gossip that a rich man had moved to town. One of the first things Asa Eastwood did was to join the local congregation.

Asa once said he was 'a jack of all trades and master of none'. Now he set about growing produce to take to market through the wood creek and Mohawk River, capitalizing on the proximity of Syracuse. He launched into selling cattle, horses and hay, entered briefly into a salt enterprise, and opened a household goods store to boot. However, being a man of high rectitude, Asa 'found that there was so much lying to be done in selling goods that I could not stand it', and he didn't enjoy the store management or farming chores. He felt the urge to return to New York City to tend to politics and investments. His wife would have plenty to do while he was away, with Mary Doxsey Eastwood delegated to oversee farm operations, rear eleven children, and when she had time to spare, earn a bit of extra money by weaving and spinning wool.

Under their mother's supervision, the oldest children chopped wood, raised crops, took care of the horses and stock. Asa was back in New York City by 1821, and for the next decade divided his time between the country and the city. In Onondaga County he served as a justice of the peace, and in New York he continued as a marshal. Such was his social standing in New York that he was made an honorary life citizen by an act of the Board of Aldermen, upon recommendation of then Mayor Stephen Allen.

He often boarded at Tammany Hall, writing his wife long letters crammed with practical advice. Bemoaning the fast-paced city life, Asa Eastwood declared he pined for his family and the bucolic existence. 'It is a positive fact that the beauties of New York is [sic] not equal to that of the banks of the Oneida,' he wrote. Coogan – the character played by Clint in *Coogan's Bluff* – shows himself a true descendant when he stands on a hill overlooking Manhattan skyscrapers and muses: 'I'm just trying to picture it the way it was – just the trees and the river before people came along and fouled it all up.'

In 1821, Asa was elected a delegate to a convention assembled to revise the State Constitution. In 1833, he was elected to the New York State assembly, representing Onondaga County. Although reared according to Jefferson's faith, by then Asa was drifting towards the Whigs. He had 'steadily opposed the encroachments of the slave power' and refused to follow the Democratic Party 'when it abandoned its old landmarks and fell into a mire of slavery and propagandism', according to one account. After voting for the anti-slave candidate, John C. Frémont, the first presidential nominee of the newly formed Republican Party in 1856, Asa switched political parties. Subsequent generations of Eastwoods – Clint included – would stick with the Republicans, upholding fundamentally conservative beliefs.

Mary Eastwood died in 1862, after sixty years of marriage to Asa, who outlived her to 1872, keeping in touch with his progeny by regular letter-writing and maintaining his daily journal until just a few days before his death. Asa's children had fanned out. Daughter Mary had married and relocated in Indiana, Lucinda went to Michigan, Samuel to Nebraska, and Elisha ended up in Louisiana – where he stayed a staunch unionist during the Civil War, and later became a well-regarded justice of the peace. But some Eastwood offspring evidenced scant wanderlust, and stayed in place in upstate New York. These included John, Benjamin, Nelson, Enos, William and Lewis, the latter figuring in this narrative as Clint's paternal great-great-grandfather.

Born in 1810 in New York City, when Asa lived on Front Street, Lewis Washington Eastwood was the third eldest son. One of the complacent Eastwoods, he proved content to live his life on an Onondaga County farm. He married Margaret A. Sullivan, fathered five children, and became the first of Asa's children to die, in 1863, in Cicero. His five scions included Asa Bedesco, the youngest, named for the patriarch, born 1846 in Cicero. Asa B. would turn out to be Clint's great-grandfather. Judging from census records, Asa stuck around for a while after his father's death, then became the first Eastwood to head West, between 1872 and 1879. By then he had already left farming behind for mining and engineering.

*　　*　　*

Cities are filthy and crowded. The beauty and solitude of the wilderness inspires. In his best Westerns, Clint's characters have no permanent home. They are fleeing, pursuing. They journey across the miles and years to wreak vengeance and leave their old, troubled lives behind.

The next available record finds Asa B. a miner in Nevada, before being listed as superintendent of the Hathaway Mine in Placer County, California, one of the counties lined up along the western slopes of the Sierras in central and northern California. This territory was one of the first overrun during the 1849 gold rush, and thereafter had been regularly mined and quarried by individual gold-seekers as well as big companies.

A mining background would run on both sides of Clint's family. In his films, the actor also shows a fondness for the milieu of boom camps and ore towns, even if his own relatives never quite struck it rich in the same way as does Pardner, the character Clint plays, who sings 'Gold Fever' in *Paint Your Wagon*. Less harmonious gold fever also injects excitement into the bloodstained plots of *High Plains Drifter* and *Pale Rider*.

The Hathaway Mine was located about three-quarters of a mile southwest of the town of Ophir, where Asa B. Eastwood supervised roughly thirty men whose job it was to explore a three-foot wide vein of ore that carried argentiferous galena, zinc blende, and pyrites containing copper, arsenic and iron. Like many an Eastwood, Asa B. kept up at least two residences – one, for work purposes, in a fruit growing and shipping hamlet called Newcastle, and a domestic dwelling in nearby glittering San Francisco.

When he died of pneumonia, on 2 April 1908, at age 62, Clint's great-grandfather would be eulogized by the *Placer Herald* as 'a most valuable citizen. Not only in a moral and patriotic sense, but in a business way ... He was a big, broad-minded man, honoured and respected.' The *Placer County Republican* agreed Asa B. was 'one of the staunchest citizens of Placer County. He was a thorough mining man and had lately worked hard to put the Hathaway Mine in perfect order for operation on a large scale. He was highly respected by all who knew him, as an honest, upright and straightforward man, and will be greatly missed by the community in which he lived.'

After the funeral ceremony, Asa B.'s remains were shipped for cremation on the No. 5 train to Oakland, which was, by 1908, the family hub – at least for that branch of the Eastwoods that had migrated West. Clint's great-grandfather left behind a wife, Mabel; a daughter who lived in Los Angeles; a son, Orlo, of Corte Madera in Marin County, and another son, Burr Eastwood, born in 1871, the youngest of Asa B.'s children and the one designated by fate as the grandfather of Clint Eastwood.

Mrs Asa B. Eastwood and her three children had settled down on Seventh Street in San Francisco back in the 1880s, when the bay city was blossoming into the major seaport and financial centre of the American Pacific Coast. Asa B., whose duties included the transport and sale of the ore and minerals dredged at Hathaway, spent regular time in San Francisco; perhaps the temperate climate was preferable for Mabel Eastwood and her children. No doubt, as a well-to-do gentle-man, Asa B. appreciated the high society.

By 1888, seventeen-year-old Burr and older brother Orlo were work-ing as stock clerks at Holbrook, Merrill and Stetson, a retail store, located at the corner of Market and Beale Streets, which had commer-cial ties to the mining companies. Pioneering importers and jobbers, Holbrook, Merrill and Stetson sold tinware, hardware, tools and machines, pumps, electrical goods, furnaces, stoves and ranges, housewares, and, later on, automobile accessories. Their sales amounted to millions of dollars annually.

The Eastwoods had salesmanship in their veins. Burr was promoted at Holbrook, Merrill and Stetson, and took up his own living quarters in 1900. That same year Burr married Jessie Anderson, one of four daughters of Matthew and Lois Anderson. It is the Andersons, immi-grants from Scotland, who provide the first cultural stirring on the Eastwood side of Clint's genealogy. Both Andersons were music teachers, and the mother passed on her German-made upright piano ('Grandma Andy's piano') to daughter Jessie. The piano occupied an esteemed position in Clint's home when he was growing up, and is said today to be still in the family, an heirloom in good working condition.

The first son of Burr and Jessie Eastwood, Burr Jr, was born two years after the marriage, in 1902, followed by a second son, Clinton, in 1906. Even for a family inclined towards crisp given names, Clinton was a departure, the first in Eastwood records. It seems reasonable to speculate that it was originally the surname of Helen Anderson, Jessie's mother, who was born in Vermont, from where the family originated.

Although Orlo soon left Holbrook, Merrill and Stetson to take a management job with the Mechanical Installation Company, Burr Sr was one of the stolid Eastwoods and would work for the same retail firm throughout his entire life. He was steadily employed by the company in its various incarnations for roughly forty years, rising up to become a department manager of Tay-Holbrook, which by the time of Burr Sr's retirement, in the early 1930s, had expanded to offices, plants and warehouses in eight cities.

Such was Burr Sr's secure position that he was able to move his family across San Francisco Bay, in 1908, to Piedmont, a small municipality then as now surrounded by Oakland. Piedmont, whose name derived from the Latin, meaning 'foot of the mountain', was a community of oak-dotted hills and sparkling streams with a spectacular view of San Francisco and the ocean. Banking, railroad, energy, investment, lumber and mining magnates who disdained the hustle and bustle of San Francisco were flocking to Piedmont. There they could raise their families in magnificent homes on rustic acreage with extensive gardens. 'Gasoline buggies' were beginning to appear in the recently incorporated city, an improved water system had been instituted, and electric lighting was being introduced to residences.

Burr Sr's first house on Bonita Avenue was on the Piedmont-Oakland border, yet nicely situated all the same. His wife's tragic death occurred there in 1925. Jessie Eastwood was just forty, the victim of complications from breast cancer. Burr's youngest son Clinton was almost twenty when she died, and certainly he would miss his mother; but he had already been taught to love music by this daughter of music teachers.

Clinton was 'kind of intellectually lazy' as a student, remembered one classmate, and he had a 'casual arrogance' about his good looks and his assured social standing. Clinton was a tall, handsome, solid athlete at Piedmont High, where he played football in the backfield. Family friends believe that he had an opportunity to attend college on an athletic scholarship. But he defaulted after a semester or two at Berkeley in 1925, and instead, following a family tradition, opted for the school of life.

Burr Sr swiftly remarried, in 1927, the same year his son Clinton exchanged vows with Margaret Ruth Runner. When Burr Jr was married, his nuptials made a splash in the local society pages; Burr Jr's bride was the socially prominent daughter of Dr M. O. Forster, president of the Indian Institute of Science of Bangalore, India, while the groom was reported as 'well known in the younger set' of Piedmont. Clinton was the unassuming one in his older brother's shadow, and when his wedding ceremony took place, the celebration was modest, and newspapers made no mention of the occasion.

The Runners were not as well known as the Eastwoods. Yet Margaret Ruth Runner, called Ruth, would bring a backbone of steel to the union. More than one person interviewed for this book said there was more than met the eye to quiet Ruth Eastwood. That was the case with many of the Eastwood women, who basked in the reflected glory of their husbands with gracious airs that masked their inner fibre.

Ruth's famous son, who dedicated his Best Picture Oscar for *Unforgiven* to his mother, sitting in the audience on the night of the awards broadcast, was sometimes more inclined to talk about his father in interviews. But it can be said with certainty that Ruth Eastwood exerted an equal if not greater influence on Clint – and that her half of the family tree brought impressive, colourful, sometimes quirky qualities to the lineage.

Clint's maternal forebears were among the first settlers of New England, where they organized their lives around land, community, authority and public worship.

William Bartholomew – the first recorded American ancestor on the Runner side of the clan – was the well-born son of a Burford, England, family. The first of a long line of American Bartholomews, the thirty-two-year-old William arrived from London in 1634, and set up shop as a merchant in Ipswich; later he would reside in Marblehead and Charlestown. In Charlestown cemetery he was buried adjacent to John Harvard.

William sired William Jr, probably the first Bartholomew born in the New World, in 1640 or 1641. William Jr wed Mary Johnson, and their son Andrew married Hanna Frisbie of Branford, Connecticut, moving to Connecticut some time before 1729. The family was thus well entrenched in America fifty years before the War of Independence.

The Bartholomews owned mills in Branford, and Andrew managed them until his father's death, thereafter owning and operating them in concert with his brother Benjamin. In his lifetime Andrew was able to amass large quantities of real estate in Branford, Wallingford and adjoining towns; he was well known locally for being active in church and civic affairs, and also served as commander of the area's volunteer military.

Andrew's son Joseph (born 1721) begat Andrew (born 1744), who married Rachel Royce of Wallingford. Residing in Wallingford on an extensive farm on the north road to Durham, Andrew was also a commander of volunteers, which explains why neighbours knew him as Captain Bartholomew. One chronicle of the Bartholomew genealogy states that he and his brood were (like Clint) 'of dark complexion and large size'. Said to be thrifty with his money (like Clint), he was nonetheless profligate where offspring were concerned. And among Andrew Bartholomew's ten children by two successive wives was one Noyes Dana Bartholomew.

Noyes Dana – Clint's maternal great-great-great-grandfather – was born in Wallingford on 2 April 1785. A Whig up to 1856, and like the Eastwoods, a staunch Republican Party member thereafter, 'he was an industrious, thorough farmer', according to one account of his life, 'who did his work in its proper season'. After taking part in the war of 1812, Noyes Dana Bartholomew moved, during Martin Van Buren's presidency, from Wallingford to Elmwood in northern Illinois, just west of Peoria. He took with him his wife, Elizabeth Hall, and his ten children, including three sons born in Wallingford, Luzerne (the eldest, born in 1812), Noyes Ellsworth (b. 17 June 1826) and Edward Franklin (b. 8 August 1828). Other Bartholomew relations followed.

Elmwood was an outgrowth of the planned route of the Peoria and Oquawka Railroad cutting across north central Illinois. In 1835, coal was discovered in nearby hillsides, and the prospects for burgeoning growth and development seemed attractive.

On 3 April 1838, four men – Noyes Dana Bartholomew and eldest son Luzerne, Calvin Cass and Frederick Kellogg – laid out the township of Newburg, three-quarters of a mile west of Elmwood. The Kelloggs were another founding family of Newburg, and Cornelia and Cordelia Kellogg were twin daughters (b. 1829) of Edward and Jane Kellogg, whose house and garden on North Street was one and a half miles from the Bartholomew farm. Close to each other in age and upbringing, the twin sisters would marry brothers Noyes Ellsworth and Edward Franklin Bartholomew, in 1848 and 1853 respectively.

The intermarriage of the Bartholomews and the Kelloggs more than qualifies Clint for the Mayflower Society. The first Kelloggs had arrived in America during the height of the Puritan emigration, from 1620 to 1640, with ample money, goods and stock. Myles Standish and Governor Bradford were direct ancestral relations; most US states can claim a Kellogg among their earliest pioneers and leading citizens. One famous descendant was W. K. Kellogg of Michigan, the king of breakfast cereal foods.

The Kelloggs and Bartholomews would erect Newburg's first school-house and Congregational church. Noyes Ellsworth Bartholomew would ship the town's first carload of cattle to Chicago. Oldest brother Luzerne built up 240 acres of land, which boasted a woollen mill, a treadmill, a windmill for pumping water and a slaughterhouse from which he barrelled pork to be shipped down the Illinois River to market in St Louis.

Newburg was small, with many citizens interrelated. 'Those were days of community interest when pioneering in Illinois meant sacrifice, hardship, loneliness, compensated only by promise of big return, of neighbourly love and sharing of one another's burden', according to one account of the Newburg pioneers. 'They were the days of the log schoolhouse, the spelling bees, and the singing schools and the little community church.'

Luzerne's wife happened to be Betsy Yale Bartholomew, a direct descendant of the Yale family of Connecticut, and a highly educated woman said to write both prose and poetry with facility. Luzerne himself was probably the most folkloric of the Runner ancestors. He was not only a farmer, machinist and inventor (his son John, in the early 1900s, would run the Bartholomew Co., maker of the 8 h.p., single-cylinder Glide automobile, also known as 'The Bartholomew'), but a brave adventurer. When the Illinois Jayhawkers, a company of men under various aggregations, decided to leave Illinois to quest for gold, Luzerne distinguished himself as one of their leaders. Yet another 'Captain Bartholomew', Luzerne served as guide to one contingent of fifteen covered wagons and twenty-one men striking out for the far horizon.

After leaving from Galesburg, Illinois, in April 1849, the Bartholomew-led group arrived at Salt Lake City in September, too late to explore the frigid northern route across the mountains. A tracker offered to take them by the Old Spanish Trail to the south. 'There was divided judgment about whether to continue westward or to winter in Salt Lake City because it was too late in the season,' according to Manley Ellenbeckan, a historian of the Jayhawkers. 'A previous Donner Pass winter disaster created the hesitation. At this juncture Luzerne and his brother Edward Franklin separated. Luzerne was among the minority group. He took the Bartholomew wagon No. 9 on the Lossen Route along the Humboldt River. They reached Sacramento on the third of November with all members of the party well and in good spirits.'

Luzerne's younger brother, twenty-three-year-old Edward Franklin, served as a driver for the teams who travelled via the Death Valley route, arriving in the Sacramento area later, in the spring of 1850. Edward Franklin would have good luck as a miner, while Luzerne soured on gold digging after washing out about ninety cents' worth of sparkling dust. Luzerne then chanced to meet a Sacramento River rancher whose cattle were mysteriously being preyed upon, and on impulse bought out the rancher's holdings. Luzerne was patrolling the range to investigate the mystery when he encountered the culprit: a grizzly bear. With a fellow forty-niner, a blacksmith, Luzerne rigged up a large iron cage with a deadfall door, and using venison as bait, captured the grizzly, reputed to be the largest seen in captivity up to that time. It was estimated as standing nearly 4'10" at the shoulder and weighing in at over 1900 pounds.

Showing instincts for exploitation that were pure Bronco Billy-like, Luzerne proceeded to name the grizzly 'Bruin' and freight it in a wheeled cage and then by boat across the isthmus of Central America, across the Gulf to New Orleans, then up the Mississippi back to Elmwood, where Bruin wintered, before being exhibited to the gawking public the following season, throughout the East and Canada. Later, Luzerne toured with the bear in P. T. Barnum's sideshows, and presented the animal in leading European cities. Later still, Bruin was displayed for tourists in Central Park.

An enriched Edward Franklin Bartholomew meanwhile returned to Illinois, got married, and set about the mundane responsibility of raising a family. The second of his four children, and eldest daughter, born in 1859, was Sophia Aurelia Bartholomew, Clint's maternal great-grandmother. Edward Franklin operated a general store, until being drafted as a 'wagon master' in the Union cause. He served in the cavalry for a year before a foot injury caused his discharge.

With the Civil War still raging, Edward Franklin laid plans to move to Linn County, Kansas, perhaps enticed by letters from fellow forty-niners who had migrated there. Uprooting to Linn, at that time, was tantamount to raising an abolitionist banner, since that county had long been a bloody battleground of the anti-chattel movement. The abolitionists had defeated the slavers in an 1857 election which declared Kansas a free state, but pro-slave raiders and activists were still fiercely contesting the issue. Rabid anti-slave crusader John Brown, and the equally rabid Col. James Montgomery, were Linn County heroes.

Early in 1863 a Bartholomew caravan set out for Mound City, Kansas, the county seat and a main junction for frontier sojourners. Indications are that Edward Franklin travelled first by way of St Louis to fill freight wagons with supplies for the opening of a new general store. His wife Cordelia and the children followed by train in the winter of 1863–4. By then Edward Franklin had purchased a one-room log house and a corral for cattle; he had set up a hardware and implements store, Bartholomew and Smith, on Third and Main. And business was brisk – newspapers tallied the steadily rising number of wagons churning up dust as they arrived from the East.

Older brother Noyes Ellsworth, a once well-to-do farmer whose business had been buffeted by the postwar depression, followed with his wife and children in 1866, driving 1,100 head of sheep. A third brother, Samuel Dana, also moved to Kansas. The Bartholomew brothers were founding members of the 1866 society that built the town's first Congregational church. Noyes Ellsworth acted as the church's first deacon and served in that capacity for twenty-four years.

In Clint's Westerns, the actresses usually play narrowly-defined, duty-bound supporting roles – saloon mistresses, frontier prostitutes, desic-cated farm wives. The real women from whom the movie star is descended led more complicated lives, and Edward Franklin's wife, Cordelia Kellogg Bartholomew, an exemplar of the line, cuts a striking figure in Linn County history.

Linn County had one of the first 'Women's Rights' associations, and Cordelia Bartholomew was among those who helped to organize what was probably the first women's club east of the Mississippi, the Ladies'

Enterprise Society of Mound City, which had as its goal the erection of a Mound City Free Meeting House for religious worship, educational meetings, scientific, literary and political lectures. Cordelia was one of the first presidents of the club.

'The association was composed chiefly of young matrons who had come from the comforts, cultures and refinements of civilized life to make homes in this raw new country,' according to *Linn County, Kansas, A History* by William Ansel Mitchell. 'With families of little children growing up about them – large families were then in vogue, a new baby born at least every two years – the matter of a new building for school, Sunday school, church, lecture-room, was of vital importance to them. Their husbands and brothers were interested in this work but life in the last year of the Civil War and even in the years closely following was too strenuous for them to undertake this work.'

Edward Franklin owned at least 180 acres on the southeast edge of Pleasanton, and records show that he engaged in constant land transactions. From 1874 to 1878 he also took on work travelling for an agency believed by relatives to be Wells Fargo. These travels brought him to Colorado, where in Oro City since 1860 there had been active digging for gold. Although the amounts of gold had begun to dwindle, sands from the placer mining were discovered to consist of lead carbonate with a high silver content, leading to the founding of the nearby boom town of 'Leadville'.

For nearly fourteen years the Bartholomews had behaved as leading citizens of Mound City. Yet in some Eastwood ancestors there was an itch that could not be scratched by conventional home life. In 1878, the year of Leadville excitement, Edward Franklin Bartholomew moved once again, this time to central Colorado. Upon arrival at Buena Vista, Edward Franklin bought a building from one Charles Claude ('C. C.') Runner, who had property and mining claims in the area. The other members of the Bartholomew family came by train a year later, arriving at Canon City, the end of the line. Edward Franklin met them, and by freight wagon transported them to Buena Vista, southwest of Denver. A photograph shows Edward Franklin at the reins of a wagon in front of the newly-named Bartholomew Bros Store on Gunnison Street.

Buena Vista was anticipating the spring of 1880, when construction of the railhead would pass through the town on its way to Leadville.

The Bartholomews pitched in to cut timber for railroad ties. Laying rails with them was C. C. Runner, who can be glimpsed in one vintage photograph, roughly 1880, with Edward Franklin's son Edward Albert Bartholomew (Sophia's brother), a Bartholomew nephew, and another man.

The Bartholomew Bros Store – jointly owned by Edward Franklin and brother Samuel Dana – hoped to capitalize on the fact that the Buena Vista depot loomed as a vital stopover. Bartholomew Bros advertisements in the Laffee County newspaper promised quality food and mining equipment, and 'an elegant stock of Fine Furniture, Crockery and housekeeper's goods on hand. We have the largest storeroom in town and can offer unparalleled inducements to purchasers.' Edward Franklin would eventually launch several auxiliary businesses, including a nursery for forest seedlings in nearby Pueblo.

C. C. Runner was one of the rascals of the dynasty – according to family lore, a rogue whose very presence beguiled people. He was related to another entrenched American family that harked back to Virginia in the 1600s. C. C. was born in 1857, probably in Virginia. Inevitably he fell in love with Edward Franklin's eldest daughter Sophia, and C. C. and Sophia were married in 1881, probably at the Congregational church in Buena Vista, where Samuel Dana Bartholomew, her uncle, had just been elected deacon. Their first child was born in Buena Vista, Colorado, on 17 February 1882: that was Waldo Errol Runner, Clint's maternal grandfather.

Homesick for where she had grown up, Sophia wished to return to Mound City. The young marrieds moved there shortly after the birth of Waldo, and their second son was born in Mound City in 1885. Mound City newspapers indicate that C. C. Runner quickly went into business for himself, opening the Wolf and Runner feed store and meat market. (Joe Kidd, one of the frontier characters Clint later played in movies, was a 'meat supplier' of the type essential to the Wolf and Runner enterprise.)

The Runners stayed in Mound City from 1882 to 1889, an eventful period. C. C. emerged as businessman, community personage, and local entertainer. The newspapers were full of both husband and wife: C. C., busy organizing the summer fair and chairman of arrangements for the annual Fourth of July celebration; Sophia, founder of the Library Club, and volunteering to lead diverse civic functions.

By far C. C.'s signal trait was his theatrical inclinations: he was both actor and musician. He is recorded as playing the role of Livingston in the popular play, *Streets of New York*, mounted in May 1884 by Watson's Independent Hook and Ladder Co. at the Mound City Opera House, in order to raise money for new fire uniforms. The impressed reviewer for the *Mound City Progress* made note, as latter-day critics would sometimes do in the case of Clint, how well the fictional guise suited the real-life person known to all: 'And the utterance of the words: "I cannot help you, I am penniless but I never felt my poverty until now," were eloquent and appropriate. Perhaps Mr Runner once had occasion to use such terms in his time in earnest.'

Perhaps because C. C. had a thousand-dollar-a-year 'sit' as travelling agent for a music house, he was also an available musician. C. C. is glimpsed in newspaper accounts providing organ music for a military drill performed by the Mound City Broom Brigade (May 1884), and as one of five accompanists for a grand ball to benefit the Bucket Brigade (also May 1884). Not only actor and musician, but he was also known as a dancer – enough of one, at least, that C. C. taught the terpsichorean art at one of three Mound City schools. As Eastwoods liked to combine business with pleasure, C. C. went so far, briefly, as to open his own Dancing Academy at Strong's Hall.

C. C. had many proverbial irons in the fire; it is a wonder such a fellow had time to sleep. He also opened the Oyster Lunch Room in the Hulland and Curry Building, where as a sidelight turkeys were awarded to Christmastime gamblers; and with a partner ran a brickyard that boasted the burning of 250,000 bricks in a forty-day span.

When 'two drunken Negroes' rampaged through the Oyster Lunch Room in early 1885, C. C. wrote an open letter to the newspaper, fuming about dereliction of duty on the part of the town marshal. Visions of C. C. strapping on a six-gun to take the law into his own hands are premature, however; for when the marshal responded, with his own open letter, he accused C. C. of contributing to the decaying moral atmosphere in Mound City by promoting, through his personal example, widespread drinking, smoking, swearing, gambling, and hunting on Sundays.

This embarrassing flap may or may not have stimulated C. C. and Sophia's return to Pueblo, Colorado, where, as of 1889 municipal records, they are again listed. The Runners would have two more daughters, and five more years of a not entirely happy marriage. Mining had given out, and C. C. had tried and did not enjoy the staid life of a merchant and upright citizen. Now he travelled regularly to promote an organ sold by a Pueblo music store, representing its virtues in public recitals given in the open air in nearby towns.

Sophia converted to Christian Science, which wasn't such a radical departure from Congregationalism, but according to relatives her fervent beliefs disrupted the family. At one point, following Christian Science dictates, she refused to call a physician for a seriously ill daughter, who later died. Religion held no allure for C. C., and fatherhood had outlived its glow. The Yukon gold rush sounded its siren call, and by 1898 C. C. could be found in Alaska in the company of a woman named Lizzie Burke. Sophia was so outraged by his desertion that she began to list him as 'dead' on official records. It is doubtful she ever laid eyes on her vagabond husband again. And when a son journeyed to Alaska to meet C. C. they must have had an unpleasant reunion because, returning, the son vowed to avoid any future contact with his father.

Up in Skagway, Alaska, C. C. and Lizzie Burke lived in the Fifth Avenue Hotel, appearing in city directories as owner and manager, respectively, for the next ten years. Burke eventually managed a chain of fourteen Alaskan hotels. A railroad running through Skagway provided the main entryway into the Yukon and much of Alaska, and gold strike flurries injected excitement and vitality into the town. The Fifth Avenue Hotel was the forerunner of Clint's present-day Mission Inn in Carmel; it appears to have been a first-class operation – one hundred rooms, all plastered, lighted by electricity and furnished with a system of electric call bells, private baths, hot and cold water, and dog kennels for miners to house the dogs that hauled their supplies.

At the height of the gold fever, Skagway listed a population of over ten thousand. By 1910, this had dwindled to around one thousand. By then, C. C. had fallen out with Lizzie Burke, and retreated to one of the last American frontiers, Los Angeles, California, where he would finish his life toiling obscurely for mining companies in the shadow of the fast-mushrooming motion picture industry. When C. C. Runner died in 1936, the signatory on the death certificate was one Val Burke, though by then C. C. had several close relatives in California, including a six-year-old grandson by the name of Clinton Jr. The likelihood is that Val Burke was an illegitimate son.

In July of 1903, Waldo Errol Runner – C. C. and Sophia's firstborn – had married Virginia May McClanahan, in a ceremony presided over by the pastor of the First M. E. Church in Pueblo, Colorado.

Virginia May was a product of the Pennsylvania and St Joseph, Missouri, Boyles and the Virginia McCorkles and McClanahans. The Boyles were related to the Beyls of Germany, who came to America in the mid-eighteenth century, and as Boyles in Virginia served as notable doctors, preachers and legislators. Virginia May was the daughter of Matilda, also known as Mattie Bell, whose husband was said to be the first medical doctor trained by Johns Hopkins University, who then practised west of the Mississippi; whose father was a county superintendent of public schools in Missouri; one of whose uncles was William Boyle, a pioneering lumberman of Indiana; and another of whose uncles was Henry Green Boyle, an early citizen of San Bernardino, also a lumberman, who built a sawmill and twice served as a representative in the California legislature.

The Boyles were rugged, righteous folk, who acted like some Clint screen characters. Henry Green Boyle, born a Methodist, was converted to Mormonism, and one day in the early 1840s, he chanced to meet a Virginia town constable, a notorious 'bad man' named Henry McDowel, who spoke ill of Mormons and taunted him. 'I did not want any trouble with him, & told him that I did not, but nothing but a row would Satisfy him,' he wrote in a diary.

After a heated exchange of insults, Boyle knocked the constable down. 'He got up,' wrote Boyle, '& I knocked him down the Second time after Strikeing him three times. I struck him in the face & eyes & mouth until the blood poured from him, but he managed to get up with me (for he was a Stout man, & weighed 180 lbs) & throwed me back over a chair into the corner of the counter among Some nail keggs & castings.

'McDowel was getting out his knife to use it on me, when I picked up an oven lid that happened to be near, & I Struck McDowel three times . . . This laid him out lifeless . . .

'I was not hurt a particle, but it was a long time before McDowel was brought to his right Senses. He did not speak for two days, & he did not get well for Six Months. Most all the people in the community were glad that I had used him up.'

The marriage of Waldo Errol Runner and Virginia May McClanahan would eventually produce three children: the first (Virginia Bernice, b. 1904) was born in Pueblo, Colorado, but the next two, Melvin (b. 1906) and Margaret Ruth (b. 1909), didn't come along until California, to where the Runners had moved by 1904.

This included Sophia Bartholomew, Clint's great-grandmother, who materialized in the Oakland City Directory in 1910, advertising her occupation as 'Christian Scientist practitioner' and stubbornly identifying herself as a widow, although C. C., her husband, was still very much alive and well. Her son Waldo worked for a time for the Southern Pacific Railroad, then as a clerk and accountant in the Oakland area, before emerging in the 1920s as an executive of the Gray Bumper Manufacturing Co., which built fashionable rear bumpers – racks that held spare tyres and a 'trunk' – for automobiles.

Although Waldo and Virginia May initially lived in Oakland neighbourhoods, they steadily improved their lot in life, and their 1920s address at 169 Ronada was situated in Piedmont about six blocks away from Burr Eastwood's home; not only did the Runners and Eastwoods have similar backgrounds in mining and business, but their children attended the same neighbourhood churches and mingled in school classes.

Clinton and Ruth Eastwood both went to Piedmont High School, although Ruth always made a point of emphasizing that she left the school before her senior year and in fact graduated from the well-known Anna Head School in Berkeley, a day and boarding school, established in 1888, which educated and trained young ladies in proper deportment. Although the Runners were Piedmonters, they could not really afford Anna Head's, yet Ruth was determined to go there for the social cachet, according to one relative, unlike older brother Melvin, who was content to stay in the Piedmont public schools. Also unlike Ruth, Melvin chose to continue his education and earned a college degree in engineering.

Pretty and petite Ruth, although she was smart, was not interested in college. She had one boyfriend who was more of an aesthetic type; but Ruth had her sights set on Clinton Eastwood, who was better known and liked – not to mention that the Eastwoods were higher up on the social ladder. One of the reasons Clinton didn't last long in college, relatives say, is that Ruth, two and a half years younger than her beau, was in a hurry to get married as soon as possible after she earned her high school diploma.

'I think Ruth chased the father rather than the other way around,' said one relative, who spoke on the condition of anonymity. 'I think Clint Sr was too self-satisfied to chase anyone.' Ruth was more the go-getter; not only did she pursue Clinton and clinch his affections, but relatives credit her – and the Runner family – with eventually making a success out of him. 'Some people are takers, some givers,' said one relative, 'and Ruth was a taker. I think that's where [her actor-son] Clint comes by it, naturally.'

Ruth's father Waldo had done a C. C. when Ruth was about sixteen, leaving his wife and separating from her geographically, moving down to Los Angeles. Virginia May Runner continued to reside in the Piedmont vicinity, but essentially Ruth Runner was left fatherless, just as Clinton, whose mother had died in 1925, was motherless. This common lack must have forged a bond between them, as well as influencing the relative strengths and weaknesses of their parental roles.

The Eastwood–Runner marriage certificate of 5 June 1927 shows that Ruth, eighteen, toiled as an accountant for an insurance company while Clinton was working as a cashier. The clergyman who presided over their exchange of vows was Rev. Charles D. Milliken, pastor of Piedmont's Interdenominational church. Three years later records show Clinton had joined the longstanding family tradition of being a salesman – of stocks and bonds.

Their first child, a whopping boy, was born on 31 May 1930, for some obscure reason at Saint Francis Hospital in San Francisco. 'He immediately assumed star status,' his mother explained in an interview for England's *News of the World* newspaper, 'by being the largest baby – 11 lbs., 6 oz. The nurses had lots of fun showing him off to the other mothers and named him "Samson" because he was so big.' His mother reminisced that, after two weeks in the hospital, when the new mothers gathered to learn how to change and feed their new charges, the biggest newborn in the ward earned his first starring role: as the nurses' 'diaper model'.

The boy – the evolutionary product of this slowly-steeped, richly rough-and-tumble, purely American past – was named Clinton Jr for his father. There was no middle name. Sometimes he was called 'Sonny' or, simply, 'Junior'. It was Clinton Sr who was first known to many of his friends as 'Clint', although today, the son with his father's name is recognized around the world by that single-syllable appellation. Some older acquaintances, however, still refer to the movie star, from long-ingrained habit, as 'Clinton'.

CHAPTER TWO

'The Shitty Years'
1930–1953

The motion pictures playing in Oakland and San Francisco, in the last week of May 1930, were preceded by stage acts and advertised as 'All Talking'. These included films by Clara Bow and Ramon Navarro, once 'All Silent' stars who would soon disappear from the screen, and *Free and Easy*, a hapless attempt by an already outdated genius, Buster Keaton, to adjust his comedy to the era of sound.

The Bay Area newspapers were full of bank robberies, narcotics raids, lurid homicides, Negro lynchings and spicy divorce cases. The more far-reaching news reflected the anxiety of a nation facing a technological revolution. Dispatches reported the first refrigerated vessels to ship Californian fresh fruit to the Far East, the first transcontinental use of a radio phone on an aircraft, US scientists' speculation about moon travel in the distant future. The Golden Gate Bridge, which would begin to traverse San Francisco Bay in 1933, was still a matter of fierce civic debate.

Although the Great Depression had walloped the Bay Area just as hard as the rest of the country, the coverage was scant and the mood upbeat in the local newspapers owned by conservative interests. While author Theodore Dreiser was quoted on page three of a San Francisco newspaper, saying democracy was a joke and Wall Street wielded the true power in America, page one was reserved for California's foremost banker, A. P. Giannini, reassuring readers that conditions were sound for a 'slow but sure recovery in business during the next few months'.

Nonetheless, in the State of California unemployment would rise to 28 per cent in 1932, and jobs were lost in manufacturing, shipping, sales and most sectors of the economy. In 1934, violent longshoremen's strikes culminated in a general strike that halted business in the Bay Area. Times were tough, and ordinary people were suffering.

Although the Depression was scarcely a lark for 'the Piedmont set', it was not as much of a factor in daily lives. Piedmont was a posh area, really an elite suburb of Oakland, so elite that it was rigidly segregated against blacks, Jews and Asians, until a Supreme Court ruling in 1948. If the Depression put a dent in Piedmont bank accounts, many kept up their expensive hobbies and country club memberships.

For forty years Clint's publicity stated – he himself emphasized in interviews – that his hometown was Oakland, whose working man's image added lustre to his archetypal triumphs. Probably, Clint said on one occasion, the reason why he called people 'asshole' so often in his films was because of his Oakland background.

For the first time, in his biography of Clint, Richard Schickel relocated Clint as a Piedmont citizen. The 1996 book conceded that the Eastwoods resided in a 'modestly shingled house' in Piedmont during the World War II years, although Schickel hastened to add the qualification that the house was 'close to the Oakland line, and it was that blue-collar port and industrial city, always invidiously compared to glamorous San Francisco across the bay, not conservative Piedmont, that would eventually claim his loyalty'.

Actually, when Clinton Eastwood Sr married Ruth Runner in 1927, both of their families were established Piedmonters. At first, the newly-marrieds lived at the Beacon, an apartment house one block off Lakeshore Avenue, a proper and sought-after address, about three-quarters of a mile away from – not quite inside the borders of – Piedmont. And later the Eastwoods moved to Woodhaven Way, a few blocks north of Piedmont limits. So it is true that Clint's childhood was lived on the fringes of Piedmont, and his earliest memories were mixed up with Oakland locales.

In 1933–4, the lowpoint of the Depression, Clinton Sr and Ruth disappeared from the area. Clinton Sr had been engaged as a salesman for East Bay Refrigeration Products before the worst period of layoffs. Now, according to Clint's publicity, Clinton Sr had to seek work any-where and in whatever capacity he could find it. 'The young family travelled in an old car, pulling all their possessions behind them on a one-wheel trailer,' went one of many accounts of the Eastwood misfortunes. This one-wheel trailer – 'a little two-wheeled cart' from another rendition – went up and down California roads passing shan-tytowns made up of flattened Prince Albert tin cans.

Clint's father was young and, unlike other Piedmonters, without a college degree or professional skills. Ruth's older brother Melvin had to bail the family out on more than one occasion. A University of Washington graduate, Melvin held high-paying jobs for international corporations and did well throughout the Depression; he had married into a wealthy family besides. After Clinton Sr lost his job, Melvin offered him employment in a refrigerator company in Spokane. Ruth estimated the family then lived in Spokane one year, though it must have been less. According to relatives, Clinton Sr was diffident about jobs and evinced no burning ambitions. He needed all the help and pushing he could get – from Melvin, older brother Burr, and especially from Ruth.

After Spokane, friends found Clint's father a job pumping gas at a Standard Oil station on Sunset Boulevard where it meets the Pacific Coast Highway, north of Santa Monica. The family could afford 'half of a double house' (in Richard Schickel's words) in Pacific Palisades, which permitted them to regularly visit the nearby beaches, where, one day, four-year-old Clint survived a near-death watery escape after being almost washed away by a high crashing wave.

The family spent roughly a year in Pacific Palisades, followed by a shorter stay in half a bungalow in mid-Los Angeles, a block south of Olympic on Curson Avenue, where the family was registered when Clint's sister, Jeanne, was born on 18 January 1934. On the birth certificate Clint's mother listed her trade as 'housewife', indicating that she had not worked outside the home since her marriage.

Jeanne is the forgotten, low-profile Eastwood. Although in later years Clint's sister would sometimes appear in public at events honouring her famous brother, she has never given an interview about him. Clint was only four years older than his sole sibling, and one might think they would be happy playmates. But curiously, as Clint has made it clear, the boy was not close to his sister in those growing-up days.

The gas station job petered out, and the Eastwoods had to push on. But the inspiring image of Clint reared 'in a mix of Okies also wander-ing up and down California searching for work', as Norman Mailer would phrase it for *Parade* magazine, can be forgotten, and Mailer forgiven for reading the same press clippings as everybody else. 'There was never any panic or desperation in these moves,' updated Schickel in his account. 'The elder Eastwood always had a job lined up before his family began packing. And Clint never felt unloved or abandoned at any time during this period.'

Mostly the Eastwoods stuck close to family job connections. They shuttled around between cities like Redding and Sacramento in the northern part of the state. Although the jobs were often white collar, Clint's father preached 'working-class values', as Clint liked to put it. Sacramento, the state capital, is where the Eastwoods turned up in 1936, then again in 1939; both times Clinton Sr worked as a bond salesman and both times the family dwelled at addresses followed by an 'h' in the city directory, indicating they were householders ('owners') in respectable neighbourhoods.

Towards the end of the 1930s Clinton Sr took a job with Shreve, Crump and Lowe, San Francisco jewellers, 'then controlled by the family of a young man with whom he had once played football', in Schickel's words. Shortly thereafter, reading the real estate section one day, Ruth chanced across an advertisement placed by one of her aunts putting her Piedmont home up for sale. 'We knew the house very well,' Clint's mother was wont to explain. 'Houses were not selling in Piedmont at all, so we bought it for very little down and very little a month.'

In all, the Eastwoods had moved around, taking jobs set up in advance for Clint's father, for less than six years. 'Those were shitty years,' Clint told the *Village Voice* in 1976, in the sort of language he varied to suit the venue. 'We weren't itinerant,' he told *Rolling Stone* at a later point. 'It wasn't *The Grapes of Wrath*, but it wasn't uptown either.'

Exaggerating 'the shitty years' was convenient for some interviews. But the Depression milieu in *Honkytonk Man* is mere window-dressing for the insistent tragedy of Clint's character, the self-destructive life of cowboy musician Red Stovall. The period atmosphere is thin and quick, mostly glimpses of Walker Evans-tintypes – like those Prince Albert shackvilles Clint says he noticed on the road between family stops.

By 1940, Clint's family was back, just south of Piedmont, living in the Ardley Avenue neighbourhood close to where Clint's great-grandmother, Sophia Runner, had lived out her final days. Other Eastwoods had never left the Piedmont area. Clinton's older brother,

Burr Jr, stayed at his Clarendon Crescent address throughout the Depression, prospering as manager of a stock-selling plan affiliated with California banks, and later, of Franklin Wulff Co. Clint visited often, and probably among relatives, Burr's daughter, Inez, Clint's first cousin, grew up closest to the future film star.

Another person Clint visited regularly in the 1930s was Ruth's mother, Virginia May Runner, the matriarch of the Runner clan after Sophia passed away in 1928. Grandmother Runner continued to live in the Oakland–Piedmont area until 1936 or 1937, when a series of moves took her into rural areas, further and further beyond the eastern outskirts of Oakland. Her other children lived outside the immediate area. Alone in life, Grandmother Runner could be counted on to dote on her first grandson.

'Occasionally times were so hard the family had to be separated,' goes one oft-repeated canard about the Eastwoods during this time. Clint was sent to stay at his grandmother's ranch up near Sunol for extended periods. It was Grandmother Runner who, according to accounts anxious to explain Clint's cowboys' skills, taught the young boy to ride and take care of horses. For his grandmother, the boy did ranch work, learning about values like duty and sacrifice. 'Grandma had more to do with my turning out the way I did than any educational process,' said Clint in one interview. 'She lived all alone and was very self-sufficient.'

Perhaps Grandmother Runner was a unique, independent spirit, but like other 'self-sufficient' Eastwoods, she did not lack for money and in fact had an inheritance, an allowance from her husband, and financial support from her son Melvin, increasingly prosperous as a globetrotting engineer. People say that Clint's mother, hearing anecdotes about Clint boarding with Grandmother Runner, was given to muttering that she couldn't remember him going there for more than a week or two, now and then. But it made for better publicity if it was for longer stays and if it was 'character-building'.

Clinton Jr was not quite ten by the time Clinton Sr found more lucrative employment as an insurance agent with Connecticut Mutual Life Insurance Co. When the war came along, because he was vulnerable to the draft, Clinton Sr also toiled as a pipefitter in the shipyards. By 1942, however, the economy had been reinvigorated by wartime needs, and the Eastwoods had rebounded. By then the family was listed at fashionable 107 Hillside Avenue, residing in a two-storey house with a big backyard that compared favourably with others on the block and was situated only a short walk from Piedmont schools.

The 'shitty years' were short, and truly over. Considering the times, it was a better than average middle-class upbringing. But the six years away from Piedmont almost robbed him of his entitlement. They were the Rosebud of his life story, the lost link with family and home, and perhaps the beginning of romantic imagination.

Strangely, for a family whose genealogy was sprinkled with church-builders and devout religionists, Clint doesn't show up in Bay Area baptismal or Sunday school records. All that moving around created another deprivation in this category.

Although later he would try to define himself as a morally complex hero in his films, Clint would have to admit that he didn't believe in God or subscribe to any special organized religion. He was not a churchgoer, even as a boy. When David Frost mulled over the subject of God with Clint in one of his prestigious television interviews, Clint grew mumbly, falling back on nature as his main spiritual source.

'Is it [religion] important to you?' asked Frost. 'God?'

'I take it in a personal way very much,' said Clint. 'I'm just not a member of an organized religion. But I've always felt very strongly about things, I guess. Especially when I'm out in nature. I guess that's why I've done so many wide open films out in nature. But religion is, I think, a very personal thing. I've never really discussed it to philosoph-ize out loud about it.

'I just kind of . . . you're sitting on a beautiful mountain, or in the Rocky Mountains, or wherever, and you . . . the Grand Canyon is something . . . and all of a sudden you can't help but be moved. An awful lot of time has gone by on this planet, and mankind's part of it was all about like that [snaps fingers]. And so you think, "How did that all come to be?" So you can go on for ever, within your mind, but it's fun to philosophize on it, as long as you don't, it doesn't drive you to jump off the cliff.'

When, in the early 1940s, the Eastwoods settled down at Hillside Avenue, the neighbourhood was up-market and the two-storey house picturesque, with Grandma Andy's piano in the living room and a set of barbells in the roomy backyard. In a few short years the family would graduate to even more spacious residences with backyard swimming pools. They were a family that thrived on a recreational lifestyle, playing tennis and golf at exclusive clubs (Clint earned pocket money as a caddy for a brief time). They even maintained a vacation cabin on a lake near Fresno.

Piedmont was the good life for an adolescent. There was a reservoir and streams where children swung off high, drop-off ropes, or fished for black bass and bluegills; the parks were perfect for hiking and camping. Everybody knew everyone else in the close-knit community, and kids in the neighbourhood could play 'kick the can' until dark.

Young Clinton ended up going to eight or ten schools, a statistic employed in interviews to emphasize those rootless, 'working-class' years of the 1930s. But all children in those days attended elementary, junior and high school, and in at least one case, the reason Clint left one school to enrol in another was delinquent behaviour.

Glenview (near Ardley Avenue), Crocker Highlands (named for the banking Crockers, who donated the site) and Frank Havens School (named for one of the Piedmont city fathers) – three of the grammar schools the boy attended – were all within a close radius of Piedmont. Havens was already a local institution, and one day, at Crocker Highlands, the tousle-haired boy sat for a class photograph with schoolmates that included Jackie Jensen, the future star outfielder for the Boston Red Sox.*

The Piedmont schools were ahead of the rest of the country in modern facilities, lesson development, even health and nutrition consciousness. Parents were urged to adopt vigorous fitness regimens for their children: that included plenty of rest, fresh air, outdoor play, and the fundamentals of a sound diet ('plenty of milk, vegetables, cereal, eggs, fruits and water', according to one school handbook).

Being the eldest and the male heir to the family name, Clint the boy was made to feel, as Francesca remarks in another context in *The Bridges of Madison County*, like a 'prince of the kingdom'. He was a lucky prince – lucky in his upbringing and environment, lucky in his looks and physical vitality. When he was little, his mother used to hold him up over the backyard fence and exclaim to neighbours, 'Isn't he

* The American League's Most Valuable Player in 1958.

handsome?' And he was as handsome as can be. Even before he turned a teenager, Clint, on his way to his ultimate height of 6'4", was already a head taller than most of the other youngsters his age. He was known throughout the neighbourhood as a long strider. He had unruly hair, twinkling green eyes and already that big, disarming grin. A grin that connected magically with people and lit up their faces as easily as his own.

Entering junior high, however, there were few other signs that set Clint apart from other boys. He was not alone in plying a paper route, delivering the *Oakland Tribune* to subscribers sprinkled along Piedmont Avenue. Clint was also involved in mowing lawns, bagging groceries, joining in Boy Scout activities, and collecting for the neighbourhood scrap metal drives that were an ongoing part of the 'war-at-home' mobilization.

If he was show business material, that was not obvious. Searching for the genesis of his profession as an actor, his mother has said that as a boy Clint sometimes fantasized his companions and acted out make-believe scenes with his toys. 'Clint enjoyed his own company,' said Ruth Eastwood. 'All his toys had personalities of their own. They conversed with him and acted out his ideas.' His mother recounted one anecdote – typical of many American childhoods, not only Clint's – about her son and a friend splashing ketchup blood on each other during their backyard cowboy games.

'Since I was almost always the new boy on the block,' Clint told *McCall's* in 1987, 'I often played alone, and in that situation your imagination becomes very active. You create little mythologies in your own mind . . .' One of the little mythologies may have been the over-done 'alone' bit: Ruth Eastwood has said that even she was unaware of it. So were the gang of friends the 'lone-wolf Clint' was very much part of, several of whom trailed along with him in life, from junior high school, some of them right to Hollywood.

Clint liked to say that one of his first brushes with acting occurred at Piedmont Junior High, where his father and mother had gone, as well as other Eastwoods. It was one of the area's enviable schools, adjacent to the high school, with a sprawling campus, modern pool and gym.

Unexpectedly, Clint had been selected by his eighth grade English teacher, Gertrude Falk, to perform the lead in a one-act play ('I guess to help me, because I was an introverted guy in class'). It was nothing momentous, just part of an English assignment. Harry Pendleton, one of Clint's pals, was also picked to play a part, and shared Clint's misgivings. To compound matters Mrs Falk announced the play was going to be presented in the auditorium for the Senior High.

He was 'so scared I almost cut school that day', he said on one occasion. Clint told *Playboy* in 1974 that the show was 'disastrous' and 'we muffed a lot of lines'. Harry Pendleton fumbled with his copy of the script concealed inside a newspaper, while Clint kept bumping into furniture on stage. Then they started loosening up and getting appreciative laughs. The whole ordeal was over in minutes.

For his authorized biographer, this provided 'a rare moment of recognition in his generally anonymous school career' in which Clint learned 'a little life lesson'. One of the lessons Clint had learned was, 'Never again!' Clint in another stage play would certainly prove rare, although already the pattern was established in his life, of fate picking out the tallest, handsomest guy in the crowd and offering him rare opportunity.

In all his many interviews Clint never mentions attending theatre or seeing any plays. Movies would always be his main frame of reference. Like everyone else Clint as a boy went to Saturday matinees and double-features, although he certainly didn't give any thought to film-making as a potential career, or art form. *The Grapes of Wrath, Snow White and the Seven Dwarfs, Gone With the Wind, Yankee Doodle Dandy* and *Sergeant York* – the movies Clint could name that had impressed him, in boyhood – were the big hits of the 1930s and 1940s that might crop up on anyone's list.

It wasn't until his stint as a contract player at Universal that he would catch up with many classic films at the regular studio screenings. There for the first time Clint learned the names of directors such as Howard Hawks and John Ford, to whom one day he would be compared (he slyly liked to compare himself with them). But Clint had to catch up on the subject of film history, and was quite capable, when playing the cinéaste, of praising director George Cukor for his luminous close-up of Greta Garbo in *Queen Christina* – when, actually, it was Rouben Mamoulian.

Music was one popular art that was definitely an Eastwood enthusiasm. Clint's father played guitar and sang in pick-up bands, entertaining at social events; Ruth Eastwood, who collected jazz records, sometimes joined in on mandolin. Clint grew up, like the characters in *The Bridges of Madison County*, listening to jazz and rhythm and blues on Oakland radio station KWBR. He started out with experimental noodling on the flugelhorn and clarinet, before gravitating to Grandma Andy's piano, imitating his mother's favourites, jazz giants Art Tatum and Fats Waller. Mostly home-taught, Clint would eventually be given a few piano lessons from a teacher who lived in nearby Berkeley.

Thanks to his mother's influence, Clint knew jazz, and in his teens, there would be fondly remembered Jazz Night concerts at the Oakland Philharmonic. Jazz was a hobby that evolved into a passion. Clint gave the impression that he was never happier than when lost in the music – 'his eyes reflecting the mesmerization of his mind', as a reporter for the *San Francisco Chronicle* wrote, observing the star at an Oscar Peterson show many years later, 'his concentration total, broken only between numbers for one or more incredulous expletives undeleted'.

But there was another reason why playing piano riffs afforded him such pleasure, which the buddies Clint ran around with appreciated, even way back then. 'If you can play an instrument,' explained Don Loomis, one of Clint's friends in school, 'you can score with girls pretty good. At least it gets the front door open.' 'I was such a backward kid at that age,' Clint told *Rolling Stone* in 1985, 'but I could sit down at a party and play the blues. And the gals would come around the piano, and all of a sudden you had a date.'

Clint's gawkiness was both authentic and affected. 'Rather than speak when he saw you, he'd raise his chin up and down in your direction – or hooking his thumb over his front pants, would point a forefinger at you,' noted Ross Hughes, a Piedmont neighbour. 'I've seen him swallow twice before he'd say something to a girl.'

Girls liked the shyness, no matter if it might be an act. Clint has admitted that he became sexually active earlier than most, losing his virginity at the age of fourteen. He'd only tell Richard Schickel, 'I had nice neighbours', leading his biographer to remark that 'that's all he will say about that momentous occasion. He was then, as he was to remain, terribly discreet – not to say secretive – about his sexual adventures.'

Not all that discreet, or secretive, strictly speaking. Clint's buddies always bragged about their girlfriends and sexual forays, and when among buddies Clint did the same. In Hollywood, too, the best buddies would find out about Clint's conquests, with all the salacious details, long before the tabloids.

From Piedmont Junior High Clint followed the accepted path to Piedmont Senior High School, at least from January 1945 to January 1946, when problems arose.

Records indicate that Clint was already indifferent to classroom education, and had to attend summer school brush-ups to maintain grades. Although well brought up, and socially advantaged, he was increasingly assuming the pose of a James Dean-type misfit, a rebel, which was, in a sense, the first persona the future film actor mastered.

It is not quite right to speak of young Clint, as so many articles do, as an introvert. Though at times a listening, low-profile type, he could also be surprisingly garrulous. It is not quite right to speak of him as a loner. The list of good friends from those days is long and includes Fritz Manes, Don Kincaid, Don Loomis, Jack McKnight, Harry Pendleton, Milt Young and more. They ran in a pack.

Clint was definitely not a joiner – not a team player, not the leader of his circle. Though he could play musical instruments, he balked at joining the school band. Though built like an athlete, he never stuck with school sports. The first incarnation of his publicity – the all-American phase at Universal – advanced the fairy tale that Clint was 'a star' on the high school basketball team', and this became an established nugget of his life story, carried down in permutations through the years in articles and books, appearing in even as authoritative and recent a source as *Current Biography* (*Yearbook,* 1989).

Clint didn't mind going along with this little charade in interviews – saying he played 'a little basketball' in school and 'some football in junior high'. It was flattering, standard movie-star publicity. But he didn't play enough of either basketball or football to get mentioned in the yearbooks. 'I didn't really get involved in team sports because we moved so much,' he informed *Rolling Stone,* though he didn't move at all after 1940.

Clint as a high school athlete is scoffed at by his oldest friends. About the only sports he wanted to play were the individualistic, middle-class ones of tennis and golf. 'Clint actually is a coordinated guy,' noted Don Kincaid. 'He's a good athlete. He could have been good at basketball, because he's so tall, but he just didn't seem to care about that.'

Teamwork was something that people would extol, years later, apropos of Clint's Malpaso organization. But, at Malpaso, the teamwork was one that delegated responsibilities, with Clint as the clear if reluctant leader, a situation echoed in many films where he played antisocial heroes thrust into crises that demanded action.

Some of his friends *were* athletes and active in the social clubs; others were the guys known to hail from the lower-rent neighbourhoods. These latter were proud to skip classes and compete with each other for pranks played on the teachers. Clint had a rare likeability, and was accepted by both groups, while only half-belonging to either.

Like his rich friends, he was able to afford Pendleton shirts and new Levi's. Unlike some – who drove 'better cars than my parents', in Clint's words – the teenage Clint had to make do with beat-up roadsters. While the rich friends were inclined to accept Clint because of his looks and social standing, the others embraced his rebel stance.

Already, during his first year in high school, it looked like his rebel pose was gaining the upper hand, although exactly why Clint exited Piedmont High School remains a mystery. Clint's early publicity promoted the whimsical idea that the teenager transferred to Oakland Tech to become a star of its superior drama department; as late as *Honkytonk Man*, his publicity releases were insisting that Clint 'consistently resisted the efforts of drama teachers at Oakland Technical High School to enlist him in school plays'. Even alumni began to believe the widely reported fable that Clint was a star, first, in high school plays. One Oakland Tech classmate of Clint's wrote to this author, responding to a query: 'I didn't know him [Clint] well personally, but of course he was quite well known throughout the school as the star of several of our class plays.'

This gets a big laugh from Clint's old buddies. The Piedmont High School drama department was excellent, even if the programme at Oakland Tech – where Clint ended up – was better. As a matter of fact, Oakland Tech had one of the outstanding drama departments in the city, if not in all of northern California, mounting an ambitious schedule of recycled Broadway plays, Shakespeare, annual pageants, children's theatre. But Sally Rinehart Nero, who taught English as well as eleventh and twelfth grade performing arts at Oakland Tech, insisted that Clint Eastwood was not in any of her classes or workshops. He never tried out for or acted in a single school play. Nero said she was tired of being asked about him by people who assumed from his publicity that he had been under her tutelage. 'Nobody remembers Clint,' Nero stated flatly.

The suggestion of the official biography that Clint left Piedmont because he had become 'acutely conscious that there were no blacks in Piedmont, no Asians, only one or two Jewish families' – that Clint had begun to learn contempt for such bigotry – also invites laughter from his oldest buddies. All of them white, middle-class boys, like himself.

Clint's departure from Piedmont schools had nothing to do with acting or racial consciousness, maybe a little something to do with girls, and probably a lot to do with his mounting delinquency problems. Many years later Ruth Eastwood would confirm to an Oakland newspaper that Clint left Piedmont High School because he was 'asked' to. 'Clint not only wrote an obscene suggestion to a school official on the athletic field scoreboard, but buried someone in effigy on the school lawn.' According to his mother, it was these incidents, on top of other school infractions, that prompted a Piedmont school official to firmly suggest her first-born might thrive elsewhere.

Oakland Tech would become part of the Blue Collar Clint mystique, reflexively mentioned in clipping after clipping, so that even as reputable a source as the *New York Times* could point out repeatedly in articles that the star 'was raised in a mixed neighbourhood in Oakland, California amid black, Asian and Mexican families' (17 October 1996) and attended high school in a neighbourhood 'that also produced Billy Martin, the baseball manager, and other Dirty Harrys' (24 February 1985).

The 'Technical' really belied the school's character. Oakland Tech did have shop and business classes, but also a full complement of arts, literature, language, science, civics, history and advanced mathematics courses. Its academic curriculum was challenging, it had an affiliation with the University of California, and the vast majority of the student body was expected to go on to college. It was a top-rated high school, although markedly different from Piedmont in that it boasted, among its two thousand students from Oakland neighbourhoods, a true racial and social mix.

As he approached his senior year, however, Clint had two priorities in life: 'fast cars and easy women', in his own words. He owned his first car even before he could legally carry a licence, driving it around on his paper route, according to an accepted Piedmont tradition. Then followed a series of Fords and Chevies. The lifestyle of his friends celebrated joyriding, drag-racing, making out with girls in automobiles.

Once in charge of his own film productions, Clint would be repeatedly drawn to stories constructed around his undying love for cruising around in cars, motorcycles or other vehicles – *Thunderbolt and Lightfoot, The Gauntlet, Honkytonk Man, Pink Cadillac, The Rookie* and *A Perfect World* among the obvious examples – all the better if the plot mandated a surfeit of chases and crashes.

What were his other pursuits? At Oakland Tech, Clint busied himself – not in drama, orchestra or sports – but in shop and auto mechanic courses. He took aircraft maintenance too ('Wartime aviation movies had stirred in him a romantic feeling for flight', wrote Richard Schickel). 'I rebuilt one plane engine and a car engine too,' Clint told *Crawdaddy* in 1978. 'I never had any dough so I could never afford anything very nice. I think kids go through certain times, in certain towns, where cars are their whole life. Cars first, chicks second.' After school, while some of his acquaintances played varsity football or studied to improve their grades, Clint, in his ducktail and leather jacket, would clock time at a local gas station where a pal worked, using the lube rack on his car.

Cars, girls, beer: Clint wasn't thinking about the far future. He and his friends were just hanging out – at Coffee Dan's where they listened to a young pianist named Merv Griffin, then a fixture on radio station KFRC; at a blues joint called Hambone Kellys in EI Cerrito; at the Omar, a pizza place in downtown Oakland, where Clint occasionally slid into the piano seat and played for 'pizza and tips' and 'the pizza was better than the tips'.

'I've heard him tell this story and I've told it a million times myself, so whether it gains or loses something by the repetition, I don't know,' recalled one of the gang, Fritz Manes, 'but Clint would actually play the piano until his fingers were bleeding.'

The tight group of buddies stayed relatively the same, while the girls came and went according to their lasting power. Wild parties with plenty of beer were the vogue. Clint had a voyeuristic streak, like the characters he plays in *Tightrope* and *Absolute Power*. One time, according to a buddy who asked not to be identified, Clint hid in a bedroom closet in order to watch his friend fornicate with his girlfriend; only Clint wasn't able to stifle his laughter, and burst out of the door right in the middle of the action.

Clint's first sexual experience was followed by many others. Already in high school, according to his official biography, Clint 'was beginning to have some idea of how attractive he was', and naturally that was combined with 'an even more urgent sense of how attractive certain members of the opposite sex were to him'.

According to Fritz Manes, Clint developed a hot and heavy relationship with one older Piedmont girl from a well-to-do family that socialized with the Eastwoods. 'It became an embarrassment to the two families,' said Manes. Their unspoken fear was pregnancy, and even though Clint made noises about being willing to get married he was barely keeping afloat in school. So both sets of parents acted decisively to break it up.

Nobody who knew the Eastwoods can figure out, in retrospect, how this unassuming family produced one of America's great screen icons, much less one with Clint's singular traits – among them, the Don Juanism that grew to dominate his private life.

Everyone felt that if ever there was a dream family to be born into, it was the Eastwoods. Clint's friends envied him his seemingly ideal home and happily married parents. Ruth they found untiringly sweet and supportive, and Clinton Sr was 'a helluva nice guy', in Don Loomis's words. Clint's father would even bring home an extra six-pack or keg of beer and turn it over to Clint and his buddies, no matter if they were under age. While both parents started out with social pedigrees, they did seem to work long and hard, they were always hospitable to Clint's friends and tolerant of their shenanigans.

After her children grew older, Ruth held a series of clerical positions, at one point working for IBM, while Clinton Sr didn't find his permanent niche until after World War II. He then took a job with California Container Corporation, a corrugated box company with three plants

on the West Coast – Los Angeles,
Washington. Clint's father started o
lowest level, as a trainee in a field n
Pooley, a fellow employee.

The looks of both Clinton Sr and Ru
who as he got older took on his own disti
Sr was tall, yet with a little more heft than (
similar grin and ambling walk, the same casu   You
wouldn't call him [Clinton Sr] an extrovert,' sa   n, a pulp
and paper mill executive who met Clint's father .   World War II.
'He wasn't an introvert. He was a low profile person. I never saw him
rattled. He was laidback.'

Corrugated boxes were the workhorse of the shipping industry, vital
to West Coast canners. Clinton Sr, started out servicing accounts in
the Oakland territory for California Container Corporation. At first
glance he was 'a plodder, not a charger', in Donald Pooley's words,
but Clint's father had the family luck. When a new parent company
took over in 1948, and redefined operations, many of the Emeryville
personnel quit or were fired. The college-educated ones, especially,
jumped to better jobs. 'One of the guys who didn't go along with the
programme was Clint Eastwood [Sr],' said Pooley. 'He was left. There
were all kinds of openings for him, because there wasn't anybody
there. I think he was made Sales Manager at that time.'

By then, Clinton Sr was in his early forties. He quickly adapted to
the pulp and paper industry, and developed a reputation as an efficient
sales manager, well regarded in the field for establishing a close rapport with his customers. As a salesman, however, Clint's father also
had an curiously recessive trait that would be reflected in the passive–
aggressive type of personality that took shape in his son. Clinton preferred the socializing that went along with his job, and liked to insulate
himself from the tough decisions.

'I found in making some sales calls with him [Clinton Sr] that he
was very friendly with people and they loved him, and incidentally he
would get the business,' recalled James Frew, who worked with Clint's
father later at Georgia-Pacific. 'But I was with him a couple of times
when he didn't get the business because he didn't ask for it. I'd go
and we'd have good times and everything. Finally I'd have to bore
in on the business and ask for the damn order. Which Clint [Clinton

to do. He never seemed to get around to it.'

was swiftly promoted by the new management to head the company's main plants in Seattle. That meant increased responsibility and a big hike in salary. It all happened very quickly, and by late 1948 or early '49 the Eastwoods had to hastily organize a move to Washington, taking fourteen-year-old Jeanne – who had continued in the Piedmont school system – while leaving Clint behind. Their son would dwell with Harry Pendleton's family, in an apartment complex on Oakland Avenue, while finishing off the weeks remaining in his final semester of high school.

The Senior Memories pages of the Oakland Tech high school annual for the 1948–9 class list Clinton Eastwood only for participating membership on the Senior Day and Senior Banquet Committees, obligatory assignments for graduating seniors.

In his senior year Clint was cutting classes regularly. Clint got kicked out of high school 'at least once, more than once probably', according to one of his friends. It was all innocent mischief, friends insist, nothing that crossed the line into criminality. Clint just preferred to skip out and idle with the guys rather than doze in class.

A slow bloomer in every regard, Clint was nearly nineteen by the time he graduated, in an era when some young people graduated at sixteen. *If* Clint graduated – friends aren't sure. 'Clint graduated from the airplane shop,' explained Don Kincaid, with a laugh. 'I think that was his major.' 'I don't think he was spending that much time at school because he was having a pretty good time elsewhere,' echoed Don Loomis. 'I think what happened is he just went off and started having a good time,' agreed Fritz Manes. 'I just don't think he finished high school.'

High school graduation records are a matter of strict legal confidentiality, but the Oakland Tech yearbook places Clint as a midyear graduate – January 1949. His class photograph shows him off in a jacket and tie and sporting a piled-high pompadour.

After graduation, Clint would continue to live with Harry Pendleton for a spell. It was probably in the spring that Clint and Don Loomis took a trip by car to Southern California to visit a mutual friend who had enrolled at California State Polytechnic University. Besides having lived in LA as a young boy, Clint had ventured down south several times before, on one occasion attending a Charlie Parker concert with friends.

This time he and Loomis took a walking tour of the campus in Pomona and discussed the pros and cons of academic life. They decided it held little appeal except for the social whirlwind. They then busied themselves in a weekend of partying, including a bash at a fancy place in Westwood with a swimming pool. Loomis always remembered how Clint sat down at a piano and began to tickle the ivories and the girls flocked around.

Somewhere along the line they met a girl who lived in Malibu and accepted an invitation to her house, where they partied up a storm. Later, coming back from that occasion in a car, they had to brake in the middle of the road to avoid hitting some horses that bolted in front of them. One of the guys in the car, who was from the neighbourhood, recognized the horses' markings. 'This guy stops the car and says, "Stop, I know who that horse belongs to," remembered Don Loomis. 'He gets out and grabs the goddamn horse. He told us it belonged to Howard Hawks, the producer-director. He took the horse back to Howard Hawks's house and gave it to him.'

That is when Clint Eastwood, still a teenager, first crossed the path of Howard Hawks, the director of classic screwball comedies and John Wayne Westerns. Over time this anecdote would be transformed into the same kind of folklore that did wonders for Clint's lacklustre stint at blue-collar Oakland Tech. 'That was Mr Eastwood's only meeting with Howard Hawks, one of the directors he most admires,' wrote Janet Maslin in a flattering *New York Times* profile, timed for a tribute to Mr Eastwood's directorial work at the Museum of Modern Art in 1993. 'He cites Mr Hawks, along with John Ford and Anthony Mann, as an influence on his own career.'

'I was no cineaste but I knew who Howard Hawks was,' Clint told Richard Schickel for his authorized biography, the author adding, for the benefit of untutored readers, that Hawks was 'the director of *Sergeant York* and countless other action movies treasured by young men of his generation because they were about fractious but good-natured males bonding and working together toward some common goal'.

Hawks, Ford and Mann were certainly an influence on Clint's publicity. According to Don Loomis, at the time Clint didn't say a word, he just stayed in the car and drank it all in – it was the *other* boy who knew Hawks and did the requisite rounding-up. According to Loomis, Clint, the young man from Piedmont who had eked his way through high school, didn't meet Hawks or have the foggiest notion who he was.

Before he headed north to Seattle to join his family, probably early in the summer of 1949, Clint bought a modified Peabody from Don Loomis. By then, Clint told *Crawdaddy*, he was already 'pretty much on my own anyway . . . drifting around'. The writer of the *Crawdaddy* piece, Robert Ward, added his own elegiac observations: 'There is a hint of loneliness in Eastwood's voice. Not self-pity, but something lost, something he missed in childhood: security, closeness. Clearly, he has fed off that loss.'

Judging from his school record, Clint was already that strange mixture of half-lazybones and restless driving force that would be manifest in his character later on. He had held a few summer jobs as a teenager – a haybaler on a farm belonging to Jack McKnight's relatives near Yreka; cutting trails and timber for the Forest Service near Paradise. But in the next year or so, wending northward to Seattle, he would roll up his sleeves and work more, at an hourly grind, than during any other time in his life.

Since the young man had few qualifications, the jobs were probably arranged through his father's connections in the pulp and paper industry. Clint toiled at one mill operated by the Weyerhaeuser Company in Springfield, Oregon, near Eugene, staying there 'maybe about a year, a year and a quarter', in his words; probably less, when the chronology is diligently reconstructed. As a lowly 'ship feeder', Clint was among those poling logs from the water onto the chain which led to the sawmill.

Springfield, Oregon is where Clint attended a show by Bob Wills and the Texas Playboys, who figure in *Honkytonk Man* and represent the more sophisticated side of his intermittent interest in country-and-western music. 'Unlike most country bands, they had brass and reeds and they played country swing,' the star told *Rolling Stone* in an interview, years later. 'They were good. It surprised me a little bit, how good they were. Also, there were a lot of girls there, which didn't surprise me at all. So I guess you could say that lust expanded my musical horizons.'

Springfield was in the middle of gorgeous Willamette Valley, but winter could be long and dank, and by spring Clint was ready to mosey on. A good guess is that he settled in Seattle in the late winter–early spring of 1950. Clint was already recorded in the 1948–9 Polk Directory as residing there with his folks. The Eastwoods had taken up quarters in a two-storey house on a quiet cul-de-sac in a comfortable, tree-lined neighbourhood, located on a ridge overlooking nearby beautiful Lake Washington.

A high school buddy, Jack McKnight, joined Clint in Seattle. Clint took several temporary jobs: at Boeing, inventorying parts; driving a truck for Color Shake siding; and the graveyard shift at Bethlehem Steel, where he could have rehearsed that speech from *Thunderbolt and Lightfoot*, the one in which Thunderbolt (Clint) rhapsodizes about a bank vault door which is 'stainless steel-faced – an inch-and-a-half of cast steel – another twelve inches of burn-resisting steel, and another inch-and-a-half of open hearth steel'. Technical know-how was an Eastwood speciality.

These experiences were short-lived, however, and summer is likely when Clint underwent initial training and worked briefly as a lifeguard. The Red Cross offered such a programme, and Clint picked up life-saving certification. It was a good thing, too, since his draft notice arrived in the mail and that certificate would prove invaluable.

Clint has said in interviews that he had made up his mind to go to college, intending to major in music at Seattle University. First, according to Clint, he had to enrol in a junior college and bring himself 'up to speed academically' before entering university. No doubt college *was* on Clint's mind, since matriculating students were exempt from Major General Lewis B. Hershey's August, 1950 public pledge to deliver '300,000 within 90 days' for the burgeoning war in Korea.

Those well-bred college youths got all the breaks. Clint phoned the draft board, and pleaded for a delay in his case. No such special treatment was accorded. Clint was obliged to return to California for induction. A few days before that was to take place Clint showed up in Oakland, drinking bitterly.

The reception and processing centre for draftees culled from the Western states, Fort Ord, was located on nearly 30,000 acres spread across several sites in the Monterey Peninsula, close to the communities of Monterey, Pacific Grove, Carmel and Salinas. The different subinstallations and diverse topography, which ranged from the rolling plains and sand dunes of the bay to the rugged hills of the East Garrison area, had made the base especially valuable as a staging area for infantry training during World War II.

By September of 1950, the Korean War was in full cry. North Korean forces had invaded South Korea on 25 June, capturing Seoul. The United Nations, prodded by the United States, had entered the war on behalf of the South Koreans, while China was poised to join the North Korean cause. United States forces, the bulwark of the UN 'police action', had, after early mishaps, cut the North Korean invading force in half by converging from the north and south. Now, freshly trained soldiers were needed for General Douglas MacArthur's drive northward back to the 38th parallel.

By the thousands raw recruits arrived at Fort Ord, where they had to be hammered into fierce fighters for the army's famous Sixth Division. All around the recruits, in headlines and on loudspeakers, the propaganda demanded more backbone and less wishbone in the life-or-death struggle against Communism.

The vast majority of men who passed through Fort Ord at the height of the Korean War did so rapidly, and were then channelled into urgent overseas assignments. A draftee at Fort Ord knew himself to be directly in the pipeline for battle. Clint was one of the few among his circle of friends who, in fact, waited to be drafted. Others had volunteered and several among them wound up seeing action in Korea.

Clint probably arrived at Fort Ord in the fall of 1951. Luck was inevitable for him. The people who worked for the star on his film productions in later years in Hollywood even had a phrase for the phenomenon: 'Clint's luck'. Privately, Clint would admit to believing in his own willpower, and his belief in his ability to *will* good luck to happen.

The recent lifesaving credit on his résumé was lucky in that it qualified him to apply for a position on Fort Ord's Division of Faculty – teaching swimming. The faculty audition was Clint's first casting call: candidates had to present themselves before a staff committee and give a rehearsed talk on any subject which they felt qualified to teach. Many of the prospective instructors were college graduates. But Clint was a good swimmer, and his audition was impressive.

He was appointed a life-saving instructor whose job it also was to help oversee operations of Fort Ord's swimming pool. There were some obvious privileges involved in faculty status: first and foremost, faculty members were yanked from the 'replacement stream'. There was opportunity for advancement and recognition without threat to life or limb. Because of their teaching responsibilities, faculty were also granted a rare measure of independence and freedom from more mundane army duties, such as KP ('kitchen police'). And their communal living quarters, in a separate building, were a notch above those of the average recruit.

Clint was already on the Division of Faculty when Wayne Shirley, a World War II veteran, arrived at Fort Ord in early 1951. They roomed together on the second floor: Shirley in a non-com's room, Clint relegated to one of the bunks. Shirley taught first aid, and sometimes worked alongside Clint, finding him 'an excellent instructor'.

Shirley's observation is that the army has a deserved reputation of straightening some people out, and this includes Clint. Fort Ord cultivated skills Clint didn't even know he had, some of which amounted to a surprising rehearsal for Hollywood. Faculty, for example, had to memorize and practise their spiels, and lecture with poise in front of constantly changing audiences. There were also film projection courses and a certificate of know-how required for each faculty member, because classes entailed regular showings of 16mm training films. And army leadership wasn't bad preparation for film directing: more than once, later in life, Clint would sentimentally compare his crew and film production to a military-type operation. 'It's a little like a platoon,' Clint would say. 'I guide the platoon where it has to go.'

'I think Clint liked to be on stage and be centre stage,' noted Wayne Shirley. 'In his job he had to understand what he was talking about, he had to have rapport with his audience, he had to relate to people and interact with them, and he had to learn all the techniques of interaction and the different methodologies of instruction. I think all of this helped him get his head together as to what he was going to do later on in his movie career.'

At the same time that Clint was an outstanding teacher, according to Shirley, he preserved the attitude of a layabout. He didn't like to shine his shoes or straighten his bunk; the dustballs would gather in mounds under his bed. He didn't like being called on to serve as a 'dummy' for first aid demonstrations, though one of the tacit obligations of faculty was to pitch in when any colleague needed assistance. 'He'd rather be sitting around on the bench in the office,' recalled Shirley.

Fort Ord was a self-contained small city: not only mess halls and barracks, but first-rate hospital facilities, sports and recreation centres, shops and stores, theatres and auditoriums. Hollywood studios had a special relationship with branches of the military, with Universal Pictures probably having the most active support programme at Fort Ord. New movies were often premiered on the base before nationwide release, stars attended and signed autographs, and the base had several theatres which changed the featured bills two and three times weekly. (Clint probably picked up spare change as occasional projectionist, one way the faculty training came in handy.)

Since it was an all-purpose processing centre, anyone from Hollywood who was drafted into the army started their tour of duty at Fort Ord, and many show business people ended up there, usually in Special Services, which organized the base's continuous schedule of entertainment and sports events. It was one of Clint's lucky strokes that the athletics division of Special Services interfaced with swimming pool operations, and therefore that the swimming instructor interfaced with Hollywood.

The Hollywood performers conspicuous in Special Services included Norman Bartold (he had a part in 1952's *She's Working Her Way Through College*), former child actor Bobs Watson (he had appeared in *Boys Town*), Martin Milner (an up-and-comer with five screen appearances 'in the can', including a bit in *Destination Gobi*, which would be premièred on base while he was still at Fort Ord), and young David Janssen (just starting out at Universal, but on the road to eventual fame in TV's *The Fugitive*).

Janssen and Milner emceed the weekly variety shows and playlets that entertained local civic organizations as well as Fort Ord soldiers. They also crafted instructional films for army field forces. Although Clint had a nodding acquaintance with the Special Services troupe, he didn't know Janssen or Milner intimately at the time, despite the fact that the trio were often referred to in subsequent publicity and articles as 'friends' who nudged him along towards Hollywood. 'I really didn't know Clint that well,' said Martin Milner. 'The three of us had a career afterward, so they just sort of lumped us together.' 'If we did lay eyes on him [Clint],' echoed Bobs Watson, 'we didn't know him at the time.'

Clint has said that Norman Bartold (later given a small part in *Breezy*) was encouraging. David Janssen might have flattered his chances too, since Janssen was always on the lookout for someone who was 'camera material'. But as Martin Milner pointed out, Janssen himself was just starting out, and 'having trouble holding his own career together at that point'. Again, as in high school, Clint never actually joined or participated in Special Services; it was as though he were watching and waiting, biding his luck: watching those talented, handsome guys in Special Services, who seemed to have all the girls flocking around them, and who had a life that seemed more fun even than faculty.

Musicians were also part of Special Services, and Fort Ord a surprising hotbed of jazz. A steady stream of established names such as Billie Holiday and Lionel Hampton made base appearances; nearby clubs in Monterey and other ocean towns hosted up-and-coming artists like Gerry Mulligan and Chet Baker; San Francisco, with well-known jazz spots like the Blackhawk and Facks, also beckoned. 'That particular year, 1952, changed my view of jazz for ever,' composer André Previn, who was in the army band in San Francisco and also exploring jazz nightlife, wrote in his memoirs.

Among the young musicians doing army time was Lennie Niehaus, an alto saxman who had served as an arranger and soloist with Stan Kenton. Niehaus's combo regularly played in Fort Ord's Junior NCO Mess, four nights a week from '1900 hours' to closing, while gigging other places on the base and at different jazz havens on the Monterey peninsula. 'He [Clint] used to be a bartender in the NCOs' club where I would be playing with my quartet or my octet,' remembered Niehaus in one interview. 'At weekends I'd play in a club near Monterey and he used to come in and I'd see his long, lanky body, feet on a chair, drinking a beer and listening to me play.'

Clint didn't get to know Lennie Niehaus very well either. But he couldn't fail to notice that the musicians, like the Hollywood actors, were also their own bosses. The musicians slept late, avoided the grunge work, even lived off base, sometimes in communal houses where they had all the booze and partying they could handle.

One of the advantages of being faculty was free time to roam the surrounding vicinity, which included some of America's most spectacular coastline and best-known golf courses, especially Pebble Beach on Carmel Bay, which offered unrivalled greenery, peppered with trees and shrubs, bordered by the blue Pacific. Every winter, Bing Crosby held his annual celebrity 'Pro-Am' tournament on the Monterey Peninsula, alternating rounds between the Monterey Peninsula Country Club and the Pebble Beach course. Before heading off arm-in-arm to the links, Crosby and Bob Hope would make their annual foray to Fort Ord, headlining a show at the Soldiers' Club.

For the first time Clint would visit Carmel-by-the-Sea, known as Carmel, the seaside community just south of Monterey, murmuring to himself, 'Some day I'd like to live here.' For the first time he would visit the Mission Ranch, a cluster of buildings on the outskirts of town, next to the Mission San Carlos Borroméo, in those days housing a Fort Ord Officers' Club. He might not have said to himself, 'Some day I will own this place,' but some day, in fact, he would.

Later on in his Hollywood career Clint would epitomize military machismo in films like *Where Eagles Dare* and *Kelly's Heroes*. What little 'backstory' there was to some of his characters would consist of mentioning that he was a decorated veteran. His morality might lapse in *Thunderbolt and Lightfoot, Heartbreak Ridge* or *Absolute Power*, but the script reminded audiences of a once-heroic record in the Korean War. Well, Clint never got sent overseas, and in fact stayed 'permanent party' at Fort Ord throughout his two years of service. Army heroes, like others of the characters he played, were more of a fantasy projection, or wish fulfilment.

'He was a long, tall, easygoing guy with a nice grin,' said Wayne Shirley. 'I still like him in a way but there are some things you need to know about Clint.' In the first place, according to Wayne Shirley, he was a womanizer who wouldn't quit. Secondly, while some members of the swimming committee were swept up into the pipeline for the Far East, Clint was dead scared that he was going to have to go to Korea.

How did Clint manage to avoid the Korean conflict? In part, Shirley thought, it was because he 'kept a low profile and did his job'. The swimming instructor was promoted by degrees up to corporal, and his instructional course was even awarded special merit citations ('like four-star movie reviews', as Clint put it in one interview).

High school friend Don Loomis posited another theory: he recalled hearing from Clint that the swimming instructor was romancing one of the daughters of a Fort Ord officer, who might have been entreated to watch out for him when names came up for postings.

Chasing girls was the number one pastime for many guys on the installation. There were plenty of WACs and female volunteers, and also reputed prostitution in Seaside and other adjacent towns. On Monday mornings, Clint would let everyone know of his weekend exploits, one time regaling his wide-eyed bunkmates, Shirley remembered, with descriptions of a particular nymphomaniac who had managed to tire him out.

Although Clint was generally less talkative when discussing relationships on the record, he occasionally let slip. Speaking, in 1987, about the obsessive relationship between a fan and a disc jockey in the first film he directed, *Play Misty for Me*, Clint told *US* magazine about one of his Fort Ord love affairs. 'I had a similar experience when I was nineteen, with a gal who was maybe twenty-three, where there was just a little misinterpretation about how serious the whole thing was.' In 1998, speaking to the London *Times*, the star elaborated: the woman was a Carmel schoolteacher, 'someone stalking me and threatening to kill themself'. It would happen more than once in Clint's life: 'a little misinterpretation' between him and women he bedded.

Skirt-chasing figured in the most celebrated episode from Clint's army life, when, in the fall of 1951, he survived a dramatic plane crash. Clint had taken a weekend pass and returned home to Seattle on a naval reserve plane. Bunkmates in faculty knew from what he told them that he was keeping a prearranged tryst up north.

After his leave was up, he hitched a ride back on a two-seated Douglas AD-1, a Navy attack bomber, that departed from Seattle for Mather Air Force Base near Stockton. 'Everything seemed to go wrong from the start,' remembered Clint in one newspaper interview published contemporaneously with the incident. The oxygen system 'snafued', the intercommunications system failed, the visibility worsened.

Because of the faulty radio, the pilot, Lt F. C. Anderson of San Diego, was unable to receive proper landing instructions. Then, when gas ran out he had to belly-land at dusk 'about five miles north and two miles out of Point Reyes', according to contemporary accounts. Especially in the wartime atmosphere of fear and paranoia about possible enemy sabotage, the incident made headlines in the Bay Area newspapers. Clint's misfortune was page one of the 1 October 1951 *San Francisco Chronicle*.

In his book Richard Schickel noted: 'It is not a trip that Clint has discussed in much detail in the past', overlooking the fact that the earliest CBS hand-outs for *Rawhide* told the anecdote, in part to promote Clint as 'one of the best physically conditioned actors in Hollywood'. Clint's authorized biography said: 'He has usually skimmed rather quickly over it in interviews, lest it be mistaken for a heroic adventure. It was not – but it was suspenseful and shaping.' Six pages are then devoted to the 'suspenseful shaping'.

According to newspaper articles at the time, the two servicemen managed to eject from the sinking craft into life rafts, after which they made their way in cold water, paddling towards shore in the gathering darkness. Later on it would be reported in articles and books that Clint had to swim three or even four ('those four miles were not too tiring') miles to safety. Ruth Eastwood, Clint's mother, stretched this to 'seven' miles in one of her rare press interviews, although if Norman Mailer can be forgiven for swallowing the bunk, mothers above all should be allowed to stretch the truth.

The *San Francisco Examiner* headlines were 'Swimming Teacher *Paddled* [author's emphasis] 2 Miles After Plane Crash'. 'Actually I had my life raft with me most of the way in,' Clint told the *Examiner*. 'I got dumped three or four times but I managed to hang onto the raft. I had to do some swimming though.' The pilot also had a Mae West; indeed the *Oakland Tribune* reported that *both* passengers had life jackets, as well as rafts, although this is contradicted in other reports.

The escape from death, aided by a lifeboat and maybe a Mae West or two, was covered with a scintilla of humour in the *Fort Ord Panorama*, the base newspaper, which featured a cartoon lampooning the incident. The article told in detail how Clint and the pilot had to take off their shoes to paddle their lifeboats, which they tried to hold together, approaching shore. 'The two men, on the rafts for about three hours, were separated by the current,' reported the *Panorama*. When Clint's lifeboat hit the surf close to shore, the raft capsized, and that is where the real swimming came in.

Lt Anderson washed up near a ranch west of Inverness. Clint made it to the Marin County shoreline and, shoeless, had to walk a reported seven miles before stumbling in on a Point Reyes radio station. When Wayne Shirley spotted Clint soon after, he was limping up the stairs to Faculty quarters. After recounting his experience, a grinning Clint conceded that the swimming wasn't the worst of it. 'What really got me was I had to walk for miles on a gravel road. My feet are killing me!'

Another part of the anecdote that was understandably left out of publicity versions is that Clint was trying to stretch a three-day leave past its mileage limit. Partly for this reason, according to Wayne Shirley, there was supposed to be an official army inquiry into the incident, but – Clint's luck – it never happened. 'He thinks it possible,' wrote Richard Shickel ingenuously, 'that he was never sent to Korea because the army wanted to keep him conveniently available for the investigation into the crash.'

The same editions, ironically, that covered Clint's escape from watery death carried relevant war bulletins. The 23rd Regiment, Second Division of the US Army, was then making repeated, costly assaults up the jagged slopes of 'Heartbreak Ridge' on the Eastern Front of Korea. Thirty years later, Clint, otherwise engaged at the time, would turn to 'Heartbreak Ridge' in one of his more jingoistic films.

After the plane-ditching, another whole year would pass, during which time neither army inquiry nor Korean call-up intruded on Clint's routinized life. The 1952 presidential campaign would mark the first election he was eligible to vote in; like previous generations of Eastwoods, he registered Republican and cast his ballot for Dwight Eisenhower.

Towards the second half of his army stay Clint was granted even more freedom as a dividend of faculty tenure. To bouncer, bartender and projectionist, he now added seasonal moonlighting for the Spreckles Sugar Company near Salinas. He gave off no hints to people of any screen destiny – he surely didn't realize it himself yet. How a Fort Ord swimming instructor really made the transition to Hollywood is another Clint mystery never quite clarified by all the publicity and interviews.

For much of his career the pat version of events was that a visitor from Hollywood noticed Clint at Fort Ord for the same reason that his English teacher picked him to play the lead in an eighth grade skit: his good looks. Feverish publicity brains may have cooked up the story – it was the male equivalent of Lana Turner being discovered on a barstool at Schwab's. Clint's very first publicity release at Universal, dated 18 February 1955, claimed, 'Eastwood was discovered by director Arthur Lubin during filming of *Francis Joins the Wacs* at Fort Ord last spring.'

The first CBS Television press release for *Rawhide* elaborated on this tale: 'A Universal–International film company was shooting on location at Fort Ord, California. An enterprising assistant director spotted the six-foot four-inch youngster on his way to join a chow line and told him, "After you're through, drop over to the set. I want you to meet our director." Clint did so, and the director was so impressed with Eastwood's good looks and the way he read a brief scene that he asked Eastwood to call him at Universal–International as soon as he got out of the service.'

The official biography modifies this anecdote. There the key figure is reported to be not a director, nor an assistant director, but a man named Chuck Hill, someone stationed at Fort Ord who encouraged Clint to come to Los Angeles. After their army stints, they kept in touch; Clint enrolled in the same college as Hill, who then took a job at Universal. One day Chuck Hill sneaked Clint onto the studio prem-ises and introduced him to a studio cameraman named Irving Glassberg, 'who saw in him a good-looking young man of a sort that had traditionally done well in the movies', in Richard Schickel's words.

Hollywood fan magazine correspondent Earl Leaf – the first person ever to interview Clint – didn't mention Chuck Hill or Irving Glassberg. Leaf knew Clint well, they partied with the same crowd in the 1960s. According to an account by Leaf, Clint went through a brief period in Hollywood sitting 'for hours on a Schwab's drugstore stool in a tight sweater' waiting to be discovered *à la* Lana Turner. The break-through came when 'he met an alluringly seductive blonde telephone operator at U-I studio who took quite a fancy to him' and consequently 'sneaked him into the studio', steering him to the head of casting.*

* This 'phone operator' was also mentioned as being helpful in the first CBS press release announcing Clint in the cast of *Rawhide*.

The 'alluringly seductive blonde' might be an embarrassing detail nowadays, although more than one of Clint's lucky breaks had a blonde lurking in the background. Or the assistant director angle might be embarrassing, if the man who first approached the stud material standing in the Fort Ord chow line happened to be a homosexual.

To Arthur Lubin, the versatile Universal contract director at the height of his commercial success in the early 1950s, Clint was obvious 'beefcake'. Actually, Clint had left Fort Ord by the time Lubin filmed *Francis Joins the Wacs* there; and to the best of Lubin's recollection, someone took him to meet Clint at a Los Angeles gas station where he was working. That is how they met. Maybe that person was Glassberg and maybe Glassberg *did* introduce Lubin to the handsome young man, feeling the two would click automatically.

In interviews and publicity the anecdote would vary, with Clint trying to minimize the 'good looks' that continued to enhance his luck. 'I was the kind of guy the studios didn't want in the 1950s,' he said more than once. Like a Piedmont upbringing, the God-given benefits would tend to soften the self-made, tough-loner mystique. But by the time Clint left Fort Ord, in the late spring of 1951, he had already been sighted in the mess line by someone with studio connections and the chain of events was set in motion.

'Very few people really get to know Clint,' the actor's first wife, Maggie Eastwood, once told Hollywood columnist Rona Barrett, a remark echoed by Clint's closest friends and associates. On the one hand, Clint in 1953 seemed a laid back, almost aimless guy, as much of a plodder as his father; on the other hand, he had slow fires burning inside.

One of Clint's high school buddies returning from Korea was Don Kincaid, who started attending the University of California at Berkeley on the GI Bill in January 1953. Because Clint was still at Fort Ord, it was only natural for him to drive up and visit Kincaid when he had leave time. Since Kincaid was dating a young woman from Alpha Delta Pi, the nation's oldest and most prestigious college sorority, he hooked Clint up with a sorority sister named Margaret Neville Johnson, known as 'Maggie'.

Although 'we hit it off right away', Clint was a man accustomed to hitting it off right away with women, and not so smitten that, when discharged from Fort Ord, he didn't return to Seattle for the summer.

Maggie was scheduled to graduate from Berkeley in June and then return home to Altadena, an unincorporated community in Los Angeles County, northeast of Pasadena. Maybe they would meet up again in the fall, when Clint voiced hopes of enrolling in a Los Angeles area college.

Up in Seattle, Clint had the not very secret agenda of wooing a girl – or two. This is probably the summer when he served longest as a beach lifeguard. By now he had so much experience that he taught other would-be guards at the annual training session at Beaver Lake. Among the newcomers was a husky guy named Bill Thompkins, who would become his closest friend, following Clint to Los Angeles.

Ronald Reagan liked to speak of 'my beloved lifeguarding' (Garry Wills argues that Reagan's summer beach job taught him 'stability, discipline, an authority recognized and not resented'). Gary Cooper and John Wayne and not a few other screen stars also clocked valuable time as lifeguards. An essay could be written about the lifeguard rite of passage as good training for striking the right pose in Hollywood.

Lean and tall, stripped to his trunks, lolling in his chair or pacing the sand, Clint carved quite a figure at Kennydale Beach in Renton, where he was assigned. 'He was a nice-looking young kid, well-built,' said George D. Wyse, the athletics supervisor for King County, who hired Clint. 'He drew quite a gang of young ladies around him.' 'There are stories,' added Penny Wade, chief of budget and personnel for King County Parks nowadays. 'He never had to bring his lunch. He never had to do any of the normal duties like beach clean-up, because all the girls would do it for him.'

Later on, Clint would scribble 'Little Theater in Seattle' under 'Previous Experience' on his first employment form at Universal, and that may be one way in which he whiled away the summer nights of 1953. One of his earliest profiles reported the interesting detail that 'to please a girl he dug, he joined a Little Theater group, which infected him with a crazy itch to act and he was soon heading south to try pot-luck in Hollywood'. If anything, it was curtain-pulling, or passing out programmes. The part about trying to please a girl was true, however, and the crazy itch was scarcely for acting.

Clint soon left Seattle because, as he told only a few friends, he had 'knocked up' his young girlfriend. Her parents knew Clint's parents and both sets of parents were scandalized. Clint thought getting married might be the answer, but her parents were dead set against a lifeguard without any obvious abilities or education.

Because Clint was cash-poor, he had to extract a loan from his parents to underwrite a possible abortion. Once again Clint's parents cushioned a crisis for their son, and gave the necessary funds. So Clint handed money over to the woman and left for LA.

In later years Clint liked to portray this episode, to the very few people who ever heard of it, as personally devastating. He indicated he never got over this regrettable experience. The woman left behind in Seattle would always be the 'true love' stolen away from him by life's unfair circumstances. It crushed his heart.

Was the 'crushing' part true? One could never tell with Clint if he was speaking from the heart or trying to evoke sympathy.

The Seattle vanishing certainly inaugurated a pattern for Clint of loves and families left behind. Clinton Sr and Ruth were disappointed in their son. So it was then partly to assuage his parents that Clint made the commitment to get serious about his future.

Clint picked up his romance with Maggie in Los Angeles, where she was working for Industria Americana, a small company that exported auto parts; and where he got a job managing an apartment house which he then moved into in Beverly Hills. He signed up for classes on the GI Bill at Los Angeles City College. Nights, he worked at a Signal Oil gas station.

Clint and Maggie had known each other intermittently for less than a year when he surprised her with a marriage proposal. When she flew up to Berkeley in October to attend the annual Berkeley–USC football game, she announced her engagement at a chapter house luncheon where they passed around a box of chocolates to celebrate.

Indicative of the bride and groom's social standing, the society pages in San Francisco and Oakland newspapers carried items reporting the engagement, with cameo photographs of the bride-elect. Clint, described as 'formerly of Piedmont', was said in one announcement to be studying at UCLA and in another, as enrolling at Berkeley come September. Later announcements corrected this 'local publicity' with the less impressive fact that Clint was attending Los Angeles City College. 'His prep schooling was received at Piedmont High,' the papers also noted inaccurately.

It was a fast-paced engagement. A week before Christmas, 1953,

Clint and Maggie were married in South Pasadena by a Congregational minister, Rev. Henry David Grey. They honeymooned briefly in Carmel, and then moved in together at Clint's residence at 427 South Oakhurst Drive. Harry Pendleton, who served as Clint's best man, was one of several buddies who had recently made a similar marital plunge. Marriage seemed the thing to do, and pleased Clint's parents.

CHAPTER THREE

Clint's Luck
1954–1959

Los Angeles City College, located at the corner of Vermont Avenue and Santa Monica Boulevard in Hollywood, offered enrolment to anyone, regardless of whether they had graduated from high school. The GI Bill assured Clint of subsistence benefits.

One of LACC's strengths was its well-known Theater Arts Department which prided itself on high professional standards. LACC was considered the best college in town for acting, a place where studios even sent their contract players. Over time, LACC launched a number of students into impressive careers, including, among those immersed in the programme in the 1950s, Kim Novak, Robert Vaughn and James Coburn.

Once again, however, Clint had little to do with a first-class dramatics programme. Instead, following in family footsteps, he enrolled in LACC business classes. School records show that Clinton Eastwood was a student during the fall 1953 semester, which ran from September to February; then Clint re-registered for the spring, 1954 term. But he changed his mind at the last moment, withdrawing before the start of classes.

By April, whether owing to army contacts or the assistance of an 'alluringly seductive blonde', Clint had made it past the front gates of Universal and been signed to a short-term player's contract.

In the spring of 1954, the headlines in *Variety*, the venerable show business weekly, told a sad tale of decline and disarray in the motion picture industry.

United Paramount Theaters, largest of all the exhibition chains, reported that it had finally reduced the number of theatres once owned by the company, in partnership with the studio, from 1,424 in 1949, to 669 in 1954. Late-1940s court rulings had forced this and other divestitures on the major producers, weakening their domination.

Salt of the Earth, a low-budget, pro-labour film produced by a small group among the hundreds of Hollywood personnel blacklisted for alleged Communist sympathies, was in the news, being picketed by American Legion and the International Alliance of Stage and Theatrical Employees members at its New York City première. House Un-American Activities hearings continued, with names of Reds and pinkos listed regularly in industry trade papers. When *From Here to Eternity* lost the grand prize at the Cannes Film Festival that spring, *Variety* ascribed the decision to 'rumours' that 'Commies in the 14-man jury' were punishing Hollywood by withholding the award.*

The public was reported to be riveted by NBC's live broadcasts of the McCarthy–army hearings. Nightly television was ruled by CBS, under the leadership of Bill Paley; audiences were staying home to watch top-rated shows starring Jackie Gleason, Red Skelton, George Burns and Gracie Allen, Lucille Ball and Desi Arnaz – all of them refugees from the big screen. Walt Disney had just signed a seven-year programming deal with ABC-TV hailed by *Variety* as the 'first major step in the long-anticipated wedding between the major motion picture studios and the television networks'.

Reported obituaries that spring included Auguste Lumière (co-inventor of the first motion picture camera), Ernest Vajda (a Hungarian-born writer for Ernst Lubitsch and Greta Garbo films) and Will Hays (the first enforcer of America's Production Code censorship).

Old Hollywood was passing away. Divestiture, the blacklist and the novelty of television were taking a toll on the studios in cutbacks, slashed payroll, operating costs and diminished production. A New Hollywood inevitably would rise from the ruins of what people like to call the Golden Age, but only after two decades of turmoil.

Universal, the perennial underachiever among film companies, was doing better than most in riding out the difficult times. For years the studio had thrived on a low-budget formula: Abbott and Costello

---

* The winning film, incidentally, was Japan's *Gate of Hell*, written and directed by Teinosuke Kinugasa.

comedies, Deanna Durbin musicals, Westerns and horror. Universal's reaction to the calamitous slump of the early 1950s was to embrace ever more fervently the verities that had always delivered at the box office. Abbott and Costello were now in decline (their best writers, ironically, blacklist victims) and Deanna Durbin had retired, but the studio still churned out Westerns and horror.

The company's survival strategy:

1. Build cheap unknowns into popular stars.
2. Exploit colour photography and outdoor scenery, especially with Westerns.
3. Make 'gimmick' pictures such as the Francis and Bonzo mule and chimp series.

Like so much of Universal's philosophy, these would also be adopted as paradigms for Clint's career. He would start out as the definitive 'cheap unknown'. At home in Westerns, he would become Hollywood's only post-Sixties cowboy star. And Clint would share the screen, in two of his most successful vehicles, with an orang-utan.

In 1950, acting coach Sophie Rosenstein, who was married to actor Gig Young, had formulated the Universal Talent School, an 'emoting university' for young acting aspirants, that was intended to incubate new stars for the future. As many as sixty hopefuls were interviewed by the Talent School staff each month; only ten would earn an audition, two or three advance to screen tests, and maybe one survive to be invited to join the prestigious programme, which paid up to $150 weekly. The 'new talent', who numbered from twenty to thirty at any given time, were enrolled in dramatics and other classes, while providing cheap bodies for smallish parts and remedial chores for Universal productions.

The first prerequisite was attractive looks. The women in the classes invariably included some girlfriends of producers as well as the winners and runners-up of the annual Miss Universe contest, which was sponsored by the studio. It didn't matter if Miss Germany never progressed in her language skills beyond, 'I must learn to keep my head cold' – i.e., 'I must learn to keep cool' – she, Miss Japan, Miss Sweden and other beauties in their swimsuits were granted Talent School contracts.

The men usually had some experience, although looks were just as important for the men, and they all knew it. Clint would not be the only tall and handsome one in the group. And he was closer than some to the category of a beauty contestant since he was probably the only guy who hadn't studied acting before joining the programme. Clint surely realized this; he even had a characteristic greeting for the other fellows, kidding about their beefcake status: 'Hi, Meat!'

Universal contract director Arthur Lubin recollected that when he first met Clint, he was struck by such a specimen: 'so tall and slim and very handsome looking' – and immediately offered to arrange a screen test for him. Lubin was vague concerning the precise circumstances of their first meeting, but he clearly remembered Clint's anticlimactic audition. 'He was quite amateurish,' remembered Lubin. 'He didn't know which way to turn or which way to do anything. I said, "Don't give up, Clint. I'll suggest that you go to the dramatic school on the back lot.'

Lubin was able to arrange a try-out contract for Clint. Dated 26 April 1954, the contract called for Clint's 'exclusive services as an artist in motion pictures, personal appearances, and stage, radio and television productions'. It offered only a twenty-week guarantee, paying $100 a week, but with built-in extensions up to six months. The form Clint filled out stated that he had no previous show business experience (except the aforementioned 'Little Theater in Seattle'). It also sweetened the truth by stating he had completed one year of college. Strangely, for a fellow said to have considered studying music in college, the form indicates that Clint didn't play any musical instruments. Perhaps that was an indication of his actual skill level, and the extent to which tales about his youthful prowess have been embellished by friends.

The employment form also attests that Clint's agent at the time was none other than Arthur Lubin himself. Lubin placed the young unknown under his personal management, giving the contract director a percentage of any salary or fees Clint might earn. His fellow contract players knew nothing about Clint's unusual pact with Lubin, which gave the director more than one reason to promote his handsome protégé's welfare.

There would be additional tests for studio talent coaches to assess Clint's aptitude. Shortly after signing, the new contractee was obliged to perform in front of staff members opposite a young actress, 1950s pin-up Myrna Hansen. The choice of material, although standard, couldn't have been more disastrous: Clint played Alan Squier, the Leslie Howard disillusioned intellectual from *The Petrified Forest*. 'Clint, a pure American, was the last person in the world to make an Englishman,' recalled Lubin wryly.

Fortunately, his looks saved him again. A woman, one of the staff who reviewed the camera test, thought he was exceedingly handsome, according to Lubin. The woman proposed another scene, 'a simpler form of presentation', in Lubin's words. 'The choice was to make a test in the complete nude, with just a jockstrap,' recalled the director. 'I questioned it, and they said, "You'll see, he has a magnificent body, a wonderful smile. If he doesn't know how to act, we'll teach him."' This time all Clint had to do was answer simple questions about himself which Lubin lobbed at him from behind the camera. 'That's all he did,' Lubin said, 'and that's all he was *able* to do.'

'When the film was finished and developed,' Lubin continued his account, 'I was called in to look at it and I thought it was wonderful. I said, "He might not be able to talk, but at least he looks good standing there in nothing." To make sure that this lad who tried so hard to be an actor had some chance, I made an arrangement for all the secretaries in the studio to come to a screening and see the test. They oohed and aahed and were delighted to see a man with such . . . shall we say, "possibilities".'

In a curious way, this G-string breakthrough would also become part of the Universal tradition adopted by Clint. It's amazing how many times in his films he finds the excuse to doff his clothing. Clint likes bathtub scenes (more than once, concealing a pistol under the suds); he likes to pump iron and jog and perform other workouts in front of the camera; he's comfortable in swimming trunks, underwear, even occasionally in the buff (albeit, glimpsed prudishly from the rear). Clint is a man's man in all of his films, but with a Brigitte Bardot, narcissist's streak.

The outstanding success stories of the Universal Talent School were Rock Hudson and Tony Curtis who, though established figures by the time Clint joined the programme, still dropped by classes occasionally. After completing his army stint, David Janssen was back under studio contract and in the programme. Others in the 1954–5 classes who would develop their potential and later go on to some degree of fame and fortune included Grant Williams (the 'Incredible Shrinking Man'), Mamie Van Doren (the so-called 'poor man's Marilyn Monroe'), Allison Hayes (the 'Fifty-Foot Woman'), Rex Reason (a leading man of second-tier features), William Reynolds (later the co-star of TV's long-running *The FBI*), Mara Corday (a sultry, low-budget leading lady), Barbara Rush (star of Nicholas Ray's *Bigger Than Life*) and John Saxon (a former male model who developed into a brooding actor with a long, eclectic career).

Students were expected to be punctual, showing up 'nine to six' five days a week, plus half days on Saturdays. They had to work hard in the classes, which were held in a converted bungalow at the back of the lot, where there were offices, a rehearsal hall, and an additional room for dance and exercise with a hardwood floor and mirrors for *barre* work. Acting workshops were held daily, dance and singing were scheduled regularly. Diction was tutored individually. Horseback riding, which took place on Wednesdays and Saturdays, made it a goal to teach all of the young men and women not to look too terrible on a horse – in case they were needed for a Universal Western.

Applying oneself counted. If Clint didn't always score high marks for his expertise, he won approval for his determination and likeability. And he was recorded as doing well from the outset.

One of his earliest summary reports from the Talent School staff stated: 'Clint has been with us just one month. Our experience with him so far is excellent, as he gives promise of being one of the most conscientious boys we have ever had in our roster of contract players. He is refined; ambitious and cooperative. He is an extremely likeable boy who has gained admiration from his associates by his good nature and eagerness to learn.'

If was easy to like Clint, it was tough to figure out how to cast him. To possess, in person, the seeming qualities of a young Gary Cooper – Universal secretaries quickly had dubbed him 'Coop' – was one thing. In person Clint was soft-spoken, amusing, natural and sensitive-seeming. Performing in front of people, he was cold, stiff, awkward. His raw appeal was hard to transfer to performance, either in classes or on the screen.

'He [Clint] seemed like a kind of hayseed,' remembered friend and fellow Talent School actor John Saxon, 'thin, rural, with a prominent

Adam's apple, very laconic and slow speechwise.' Actress Elayne Hollingsworth recalled: 'He was terribly, terribly young, a sweet, shy boy, and nobody dreamed what was going to happen to him.'

In class, one of the drama coaches coined the term 'Plus-X' to describe the magnetic quality that bona fide movie stars projected. In person, everybody could agree, Clint seemed a *potential* Plus-X. But in performance, he barely registered as an 'X'. Playing an Englishman in *The Petrified Forest*, he was an 'X-minus'. Playing himself – dressed in skimpies and supplying side-of-mouth comments – inched him back towards 'Plus-X'.

He was difficult to peg. 'It's funny,' said actress Kathleen Hughes, another contract player, 'I have much more vivid memories of some of the other people.' The new trainee certainly wasn't up to being a leading man. He lacked creative imagination in the improvisations. He wasn't ever as funny on cue as he was on the sidelines. Though he would emerge a ladies' man off camera, he failed to impress in class, when delivering romantic dialogue.

In May 1954 Clint would have his first real audition, trying out for a bit part in *Six Bridges to Cross*, a film about the Brink's robbery that would mark the debut of Sal Mineo. But director Joseph Pevney rejected him for any role. With others from the Talent School, Clint then would perform scenes from *Brigadoon, The Constant Nymph* and *The Seven Year Itch*, early in the summer of 1954, showcasing his abilities for the casting department. None of these in-house auditions landed any commitments. The fault wasn't entirely Clint's. One of the constant complaints of the Talent School administrators was that they had difficulty getting studio producers to take the programme seriously.

In the beginning Clint would have to mark time, just as they all did, doing unheralded looping and 'wild' voices on *Bengal Brigade* (in May 1954), *Sign of the Pagan* (June), *Smoke Signal* (August), and *Abbott and Costello Meet the Keystone Kops* (September). Dispensing off-camera ad libs and muttering 'peas and carrots' as one of many in the chorus was valued experience in the Talent School curriculum. It might also instruct a future director in the nuances of postproduction.

Arthur Lubin was busy finishing *Francis Joins the Wacs* (Clint's very first looping assignment, early in May), so in late July it fell to another Universal contract director to make the historic gesture of scheduling Clint's big screen debut. That director was Jack Arnold, and the film

Revenge of the Creature, about a dangerous Gill-Man in the Amazon jungle. This was a sequel to *The Creature from the Black Lagoon*, which had just been released in the spring and was still drawing crowds in second-run theatres.

Clint would have one scene as a young, white-coated lab technician, Jennings, who assists the doctor (John Agar) trying to research the scaly monster. Clint's cameo would be memorable, however, because of a laboratory rat hiding in his character's pocket.

JENNINGS: Doc, there were four rats there in that cage when I changed my lights. Now there's only three. It's my considered opinion that rat number four is sitting inside that cat.
(Closeup of a black and white cat, with three white rats, in a wire cage.)
CLETE: Are you sure you fed them all this morning?
JENNINGS: Here! I always feed them.
(He puts his hands in the pockets of his lab coat, and produces a white rat from one of them.)
JENNINGS: Uh-oh. What're *you* doing here?

Interestingly, here, in his first public exposure, Clint was already advertising his affection for animals and small, helpless creatures. This, one of the most over-publicized 'facts' about the actor, turns up in countless interviews and articles, and inevitably will find its way into any conversation with friends or colleagues about Clint. Apparently it is a Clint truism, or 'Clintism'.

Rats in pockets would also turn up in *Escape from Alcatraz*. Pet dogs and squirrels on park benches and other cute animals were guaranteed cutaways in Clint films. But the very first one, the laboratory rat in *Revenge of the Creature*, was in the original script. Did this Clintism originate in boyhood, as is often claimed, or did it, perhaps, start here, in *Revenge of the Creature*? One thing that quickly became clear about Clint is that as an actor he was always borrowing from other people's ideas of him. And when something clicked for Clint, it was absorbed and integrated into the persona.

Though much of *Revenge of the Creature* was shot at the Oceanarium in Jacksonville, Florida, Clint's work was done on Stage No. 16 at Universal, all in one day, on Friday, 30 July 1954. The day started at

8:30 a.m., with the rehearsing of principals (i.e., not Clint). Clint would not step in front of the cameras until 12:30 p.m. First the director shot the 'master' of Clint and John Agar, which was followed by individual close-ups; then, between 12:45 and 1 p.m. the director photographed the interplay between Clint and the lab rat. A one-hour break for lunch was followed by another hour of 'over-the-shoulder shots'. Clint was done with everything by 3:30 p.m.

'I remember Clint very excited,' reflected Floyd Simmons, another Talent School actor, 'and telling me over and over how he handled his scene. It was a cute little scene that he hoped would attract some attention. We had seen *Wings* in class, and he kept comparing it to the Gary Cooper scene where Coop had to sew a button on his jacket. That was the most memorable thing in the movie to some fans – a good-looking young guy having trouble sewing on a button.'

Subsequently, Simmons saw other evidence of Clint's love of small creatures. One day, Clint found a weak or injured sparrow and carried it around in his pocket all day, Simmons recalled, nurturing the bird between studio classes. An incredulous Simmons kept imploring him to let the sparrow go. All day long Clint kept feeding the sparrow little bits of bread with milk while talking baby talk to the bird. At the end of the day, Simmons remembered, he asked Clint what had happened to the sparrow, and Clint said the little creature had finally recovered, 'gotten feisty' and just flown off.

'I was so touched by his tenderness towards creatures like that,' said Simmons, 'in contrast with his later projection of a ruthless killer – bam, bam, bam – bodies all over the place.'

Clint's single day of work on *Revenge of the Creature* would be typical of his insignificant appearances in 1950s films. And during his brief stint as one of Universal's stars of tomorrow, Clint would never utter more lines of dialogue than he did in his screen debut as Jennings, the technician with a lab rat in his pocket.

To be closer to the Universal lot, Clint and Maggie moved over to the Villa Sands at 4040 Arch Drive off Ventura Boulevard near a busy intersection in Studio City.

The Villa Sands was one of those U-shaped, two-storey apartment complexes built around a central swimming pool. The apartments were small, but the rent was $125 a month, steep in those days, reflecting the convenient proximity – a long walk, or a short drive – to the Universal studio location. Living there were other contract players and a general run of interesting people. Hollywood celebrities were always dropping by too, it seemed. For one thing, the Villa Sands was well known as a spot for swimsuit layouts. People like Anita Ekberg, memorably captured in a leopardskin bikini, were forever being photographed there, sunning themselves by the pool.

It was a friendly, communal place. After work someone was always tacking a note over the mailboxes announcing where – in whose apartment – dinner was 'first come, first served' that evening. The designated host would mix drinks and toss burgers on the grill for everybody. The Villa Sands neighbours got to know each other pretty well.

Gia Scala and Lili Kardell were two Talent School actresses with apartments there. Clint was chummy with both of them. Lili was dating Aly Khan and James Dean at the same time, people recollect, and sometimes Dean, the hottest actor in Hollywood, would come screaming up in his Porsche to collect her for a night on the town.

Bob Donner, who became one of Clint's close friends, was a gregarious shipping clerk, just out of the navy. Another young man just starting out was low-key, sandy-haired Bob Daley, a Chicago native who had grown up in Texas and California and had graduated from UCLA. Daley was toiling in Universal's budgeting department, where he was learning to break down a script into projected production costs. Bill Thompkins, Clint's brawny lifeguard friend from Seattle, came to visit and then lingered on, at first crashing with Clint and Maggie, later finding his own Villa Sands digs. Fritz Manes, Clint's high school confederate, was stuck in the Marines at Camp Pendleton in Oceanside, but drove up regularly for long weekends.

Floyd Simmons, the ex-University of North Carolina star athlete and two-time Olympic decathlon bronze medallist, had been recruited by Universal and signed to a contract just one month after Clint. Simmons, who would become another of Clint's closest friends during this period, spent most of his free time at the Villa Sands, though he lived a couple of blocks away, in an apartment complex near a walnut grove. Clint, an early riser, would walk to the studio past his place some mornings, scoop up a walnut and crack it against the door as a way of waking Simmons up.

All of them, in their mid-twenties, were trying to figure out life. They were determined to work hard, do their best, have fun. Clint was just one of the bunch, hardly the ringleader. Many of them were, like him, leaving chequered youths behind, adapting to marriage, learning new occupations. 'Clint was a regular guy when I knew him,' remembered one Talent School friend, Race Gentry, 'struggling like everybody else.'

They were a straight-arrow crowd, their lives virtually untouched by drugs or bohemianism. A good time was an impromptu picnic, a luau on the beach, drinks and casual conversation at a jazz joint. Shelly Manne's Manne Hole was one after-hours hangout. Pianists Paige Cavanaugh and George Shearing were playing steadily in the Los Angeles area. Scatman Crothers was also gigging around town.

All of them enjoyed body surfing, and nothing beat heading down to San Clemente on the weekend for an entire day of riding the surf. Life was never so idyllic as when hours were spent lazing at the beach and watching for the perfect wave.

While they sprawled on the sand waiting for the clouds to burn off, Bob Donner would amuse them by reading Hedda Hopper's gossip out loud in the Hollywood columnist's affected manner. Clint told his Villa Sands friend more than once he had real 'thespian potential', but Donner shrugged off the compliment. Afterwards, heading back to Los Angeles, they'd make a point of stopping at Knott's Berry Farm for pie and milk.

Nobody had much extra money, and sometimes it seemed they lived purely on pie and milk, burgers and beer. Clint was not a huge drinker, but he drank; people remember how he always seemed to be nursing a beer. It became a virtual cliché in his movies – Clint nursing a beer – a prop for an actor who liked to have something in his hands. Off camera too, when directing, Clint sometimes carried a beer around.

He and Maggie lived simply. They were both into health food, and sometimes a meal would consist only of fresh fruit and vegetables, yogurt and cottage cheese. But Clint was hardly jesuitical about his diet. Occasionally, friends remember, he took a trip downtown to a certain place that trafficked in inexpensive horsemeat, and then this future icon of Oscar-winning Westerns cooked up his speciality – horse steaks.

Pretty, slender Maggie took jobs as a model, and she was the main breadwinner for long periods, providing the couple's steady income. For a while she worked as a fitting model for Rodeo Drive couturier Chuck Waldo, who designed the well-known 'Caltex by Waldo' swimwear line. 'Maggie was different from the other models,' Waldo remembered, 'because she was more plain, more quiet, more understated. She was more the housewife type of person that you'd meet than what you'd expect of a model at that time.'

Annually Waldo presented his new collections at lavish shows at the Towne House opposite Bullock's on Wilshire. 'I remember Maggie was a little in awe of putting on the first two-piece swimsuit with a bare midriff,' said Waldo. Later Clint would remember the fashion designer who made Maggie look sexy when filming *The Eiger Sanction*, and he would ask Waldo, then working at Universal as a costumer, to create alluring outfits for his female co-stars, Heidi Bruhl and Vonetta McGee.

Through Betty Jane Howarth (a.k.a. Betty Jane Howard), one of the actresses in the Talent School programme, Maggie found occasional work as one of the lovelies decorating the background of Jimmy Durante's television shows. Betty Jane was Durante's paramour, and lived in a house supplied to her by Durante, where she hosted festive social occasions sprinkled with Hollywood luminaries as well as Villa Sands denizens. Clint's ability to mingle with all types made him a guaranteed hit at Durante's parties; the beefcake actor and the Schnozz would strike up an unlikely friendship.

Although Maggie herself toyed with acting, most people say that her single burning ambition in life was to be Clint's wife. In those days they seemed perfectly partnered, kindred in many ways while at the same time meshed opposites. Clint was Mexican beer, Maggie was white wine. Clint favoured crudity in jokes and casual conversation, Maggie was always pushing classiness. Clint was laid-back, Maggie sharp-edged.

Maggie was every bit Clint's equal in sociability. Clint's laid-backness was not only charming, but a wall that served to separate him from people. He was always so earnest and engaging, yet that friendliness was also practised and cool. Behind the dreamy smile was a certain quality hard to pinpoint. Hard to penetrate. It was a guard for the restless intensity that few people besides Maggie could really claim to know.

His face was a tabula rasa. Especially when Clint was acting shy or taciturn, people could read anything – their own thoughts – or nothing into his blank look. When Sergio Leone magnified Clint's face and lingered long on it without any dialogue he emphasized the same, enigmatic, walled-off effect. What was pleasing and beguiling off-screen was mesmerizing in extreme close-up.

The first time Clint's old high school buddies met Maggie, they were intimidated by her, because it appeared as though she had bewitched and captured Clint. It took them and others a little time to see that things might be the other way around. It took a little time to realize that his passivity in the relationship was also a form of power. He liked her to boss him around; but it was she who was always adjusting to *his* needs.

His seemingly stable marriage ought to have warned other women off, but even this appeared to work to his advantage. Other women had to accept the fact that he was married, and that was part of the arrangement. And if one didn't, well, there was always another woman standing in line for somebody who looked like Clint.

The women were pledged to secrecy. But Clint himself was known to be incorrigible about other women and upfront about it, at least with his buddies, upfront about his extramarital adventures. 'We shared a lot of those confidences,' recalled Floyd Simmons. 'It was kind of like a game. How did you do with that girl? The gal who came in for the test.'

Clint might ask an actress to meet him after work across the street from Universal at a bar called The Keys, just to run through lines. Then he'd bide his time. Or he'd stand around at a party hemming and hawing, doing his aw-shucks, hands-in-the pockets routine. That usually worked like magic, and also put women in the position of aggressors. Clint was not hesitant about making the moves on someone, but he also liked it when a woman picked up on his tacit signals and initiated the seduction.

Clint had funny names for things – cute little animals were 'tweak-a-beaks', babies were 'googles'. Many of the women who appealed to him were 'little dollies'. The tall young man had the preference, noted by his buddies, for 'pixie types': Peter Pan women with small breasts and flat bottoms. Short and lean, a little scruffy, with angular features that to some evoked a female variation on Clint himself.

Sometimes, however, they were physical opposites. Clint did what he pleased with a rich variety of women. His taste was broad as well as egalitarian. Just as important as looks, Clint liked his girlfriends to be 'interesting', often intelligent and surprisingly assertive to the point of bossiness. He liked them to 'mother' him – up to a point – making him favourite snacks and giving him all kinds of advice, personal and professional.

The women came from all walks of life but were rarely public personalities. It is a longstanding Hollywood tradition for famous actors and actresses to fall in love with each other and have a torrid romance during a film production, but, in his career, Clint would contrive to have very few leading ladies equal to his own stature. Even in early Hollywood years Clint preferred the anonymous 'little dollies' who could be trusted to keep quiet. And if any of the 'little dollies' made noises about having fallen in love with him, Clint was quick to remind them of his happy marriage. And quick to move on.

His buddies were habitually recruited for conspiratorial roles in his furtive love stories. Clint's perpetual pursuit of – and success with – women drove some of the friends to insane envy; others were mystified. 'Clint had something going on I wasn't aware of,' reflected Floyd Simmons, 'something charismatic that I couldn't put my finger on. He attracted attention – not anything poignant, but just people coming over and saying hello, and gals hanging around him. I never could understand that because he didn't seem to be doing anything. It was all kind of a nervous demeanour.'

Clint couldn't always use his own Villa Sands flat (with its blank walls, lack of posters and books, which was pure Clint, not Maggie). Floyd Simmons' nearby place was convenient for afternoon trysts, no matter if it made Simmons feel guilty about Maggie. Clint himself seemed guilt-free. The next day, after having used Simmons' apartment for one of his midday romps, Clint would be lying around the Villa Sands swimming pool behaving as sweet as could be with Maggie, hugging and kissing her. Appearances aside, Clint's friends learned who had the upper hand in that marriage.

'The first year of marriage was terrible,' Clint would tell one interviewer a decade after his marriage to Maggie. 'If I had to go through it again, I think I'd be a bachelor for the rest of my life. I liked doing things when I wanted to do them. I did not want any interference . . . One thing Mag had to learn about me was that I was going to do as

I pleased. She had to accept that, because if she didn't, we wouldn't be married.'

Sometimes his behaviour was extremely covert, sometimes it all transpired within shouting distance, as when busty Jayne Mansfield, who used to hang around the Villa Sands, showed up at one Halloween party. Dazzling some – appalling others – she wore long red undergarments. Clint disappeared from the merriment for a while, and later made a point of boasting to a friend that he and Mansfield had sneaked away and hit it off in the laundry room.

Did Maggie totally accept this failing of Clint's, or was she bamboozled? Mutual friends could never be sure. There were many such escapades and close calls with Maggie, but the betting among all the guys was that Clint – however amateur as an actor, he was already a master of duplicity in his private life – managed to keep his wife guessing and in the dark.

Meanwhile, throughout 1954, Clint made strides in Universal classes.

He got particularly high marks on horseback, riding the narrow winding trails up in the mountains above the studio. He started out in the beginner's group – evidencing how little horse-riding he must have done up at his grandmother's farm – but by fall had progressed to 'advanced horsemanship'. The running mounts and trick vaults he practised were the type later featured in a circus run by a fellow named Bronco Billy.

His singing was mildly promising. 'His singing quality seems quite pleasing,' one of his teachers reported. 'He is very enthusiastic.' His dancing was iffy, however, and therefore Clint didn't offer very much 'musical potentiality' for the studio's song-and-dance productions, according to the Talent School report of September 1954. However, as one instructor wrote, 'His attendance is good and he tries very hard.'

Charlotte Hunter, head of the studio dance department, liked Clint and appreciated his humble demeanour. In dance classes Clint and the other 'meat' were taught the fundamentals of ballet right alongside the leotarded ladies. Men as well as women were encouraged to practise leaps and pirouettes as a way of achieving agility, grace and balance. Concentrating on posture, body mechanics and self-control would help them move with strength and fluidity; in a gunfight scene for a Western, for example, it might enhance their poise and attitude.

Even when he wasn't signed up for a class, Clint used to stop by now and then and watch Charlotte Hunter teach exercises and routines to Universal players. 'I think he was interested in everything.' Hunter explained. 'He was just a learner.'

Every year, using the lavish studio resources, the dance department staged a Christmas musical for children of Universal employees and executives. For Christmas 1954 Clint agreed to play the small part of a scarecrow and perform a little dance on stage. According to Charlotte Hunter, Clint did it to be gracious and for the experience, however unimportant. 'It was so dear of him to do that,' Hunter recalled, 'because some of the students were aspiring to do more, and didn't want to be in the show.'

There were also annual New Talent Shows, in which the young contractees would tread the boards of Universal's famed *Phantom of the Opera* stage, enlivening their rehearsed skits and musical numbers with studio costumes and props. Scouts and casting directors from the other major studios were invited, and a handful of luminaries could be counted on to dot the audience – actress Jane Russell and director Douglas Sirk, or important talent agents like Henry Willson, who represented Rock Hudson.

Perhaps diction was the biggest hurdle for Clint, more so even than song or dance. The contractees were entitled to individual coaching from Dr Daniel Vandraegen, a UCLA professor who specialized in correcting inherited bad speech. Vandraegen's goal was to achieve a solid American twang, where possible, in people's inflections.

In those days Clint spoke with almost a sibilant whisper while at the same time evincing a slight, nervous stutter. 'Voice work must improve – projection not good,' read Dr Vandraegen's first report on Clint. The reports did improve, but not dramatically, and Universal grew to consider Clint's weak speaking voice a detriment.

In time that would prove another weakness which Clint was able to convert into a strength. The writers of *Rawhide* were the first to take the stutter into account – Rowdy was always hemming and hawing. Later in movies, playing tough guys with no names, Clint would turn this limitation into an advantage. He got into the habit of pushing his soft words through clenched teeth, and then institutionalized his rasp in films like *Heartbreak Ridge* and *Unforgiven*.

Self-improvement in general was the goal of the Talent School. One staff member was delegated to teach etiquette and interaction with the general public. She gave little lectures exhorting everyone to keep their nails clean and always to dress neatly as befitted a screen star. Not all of the lessons adhered; and after all, she was a schoolmarmish type who rubbed some of the guys, off on a more rebellious tangent, the wrong way. 'I can still see Clint holding his mouth laughing,' recalled John Saxon.

The studio publicity department worked overtime to create some kind of persona for each young contractee, while monitoring their fan mail. Universal publicists instructed the contract players how to behave in the course of a press interview, and studio staff members tirelessly orchestrated fan magazine and newspaper layouts. The Talent School actors and actresses were sent out on mini-promotional tours for new films – even those in which they didn't appear – in order to give them press experience.

Publicity was part of the profession, from Clint's earliest training, 'one of the inventories of our trade', according to drama coach Jess Kimmel. The selling of image and persona was an accepted deception related to the art of acting. Learning to convince reporters went hand in hand with convincing oneself. Clint was a natural at publicity: photogenic and at ease. His good looks, charm and friendliness made for instant relationships with the press. One of the supreme accomplishments of his career, no matter what one might think of his acting and films, would be his publicity.

Half the time Clint was told that he evoked a young Gary Cooper; that comparison shows up more than once, expressly stated, in the official class reports. Other times, people compared him to a tall, rangy James Dean, especially with Clint's preferred garb of T-shirt and slacks, and with his high forehead and unruly hairdo like Dean's. Both comparisons pleased Clint. But Clint wasn't James Dean any more than he was Gary Cooper, and when Clint met the widely admired rebel-star, one time, the encounter was less than momentous.

Clint had stopped by to visit Lili Kardell in her Villa Sands apartment where James Dean happened to be lounging on a sofa. Lili introduced them. Dean didn't jump up, just sort of slouched forward and languorously lifted his hand up to say 'hi'. An annoyed Clint grabbed Dean's hand and yanked him to his feet, saying, 'Goddamn it, fellow, stand up when I speak to you.' This was followed by one of Clint's slow, kidding smiles.

One of the highlights of the acting classes was the occasional 'celebrity lectures'. Rod Steiger came by one day. He impressed them as a Stanislavskian poseur, answering a question with forty seconds of rumination, staring off into space and stretching out each syllable of every word. Steiger was trying to be more Method than Marlon Brando. Clint and his Talent School friends, on the sidelines, could barely contain their laughter.

'It's effective,' one of his friends argued. 'It gets attention.'

'If a dog licks its belly,' countered Clint, 'it gets attention.'

The great Brando, known as the leading exponent of the Method, also visited one day. Everybody looked forward to the moment. Brando turned out more likeable than Steiger, answering questions deferentially, and later posing for a publicity photograph with all of the students: the goateed Brando, front and centre, was seated on a high stool, with everyone else flanked around him. Clint, in sports shirt, slacks and tennis shoes, was not important enough to be identified in the caption sent out by the studio press department, though he stuck out, looming a head taller than the others.

Still, Brando's Method was not likely to end up as Clint's. 'Clint's own attitude towards getting theoretical or intellectual about acting was not very strong,' recalled John Saxon. 'Basically, I can almost hear him now, forty years later, saying, "I think you should just be yourself." And that's actually what he might have said.'

The Method, intriguingly, was an unstated component of the Universal programme, and figured to a substantial degree in Clint's training in the 1950s. Clint has claimed that the first acting teacher he encountered was George Shdanoff, a disciple of Michael Chekhov, and a leading Stanislavskian theoretician and mentor. Clint says he actually attended some of Chekhov's lectures at Shdanoff's studio. That may or may not be true.

Universal contractees were generally conversant with the Method, however. They were urged towards a course of serious study, and expected to read Sophie Rosenstein's *Modern Acting: A Manual* and Richard Boleslavsky's *Acting – First Six Lessons*, as well as Stanislavski's *An Actor Prepares*, the sacred text of the discipline. Not only Rosenstein, but her successor drama coaches were all stage thespians schooled in

Stanislavski's approach. After Rosenstein died in November 1952, Estelle Harmon took over the position of head coach, and after her, temporarily – around the time Clint joined – a veteran actress named Katharine Warren.

Harmon was instrumental in setting up the Talent School regimen, which she dubbed the 'Harmon Guide to Acting'. It leaned heavily on Stanislavski's theories about 'the inner life of an actor' while, more accessibly for studio purposes, teaching an 'on-camera approach' that emphasized practical techniques for enhancing performance and relating to the lens. Sometimes the students would actually emote on soundstages in order to get comfortable with the presence of camera equipment, but more often, the drama coach would position herself where the camera might stand, holding a viewfinder in front of students while they practised in order to teach them the requisite level of camera interaction.

Helpfully, for an actor later noted for his on-screen tight-lippedness, 'nonverbal communication' was one of Harmon's emphases. 'Reaction lessons' were a vital part of the curriculum. One person would be assigned to speak their lines off-camera, while a listener 'practised' the over-the-shoulder shot. 'Reactive' acting was crucial to the film-making process and the factory system. Clint was a natural for such techniques, and in his career he would adopt terseness amd mysterious silences into his persona.

'We did work to be sure that when the camera came in to look at an actor's eyes, or at subtle facial reactions, there was real thought process going on,' said Harmon, 'so "truth" would come over on camera.

'For years people thought that stage acting was more difficult than film acting, and in some ways it certainly is. But in film acting there are major problems that make excellent work difficult. Example: Acting out of continuity, or what I call "instant emotion". In a stage performance, you usually won't reach your major crisis or climax scenes until an hour-and-a-half into the play. Whereas you may be called to work at eight a.m. for a film, and that's the moment in the script when the baby dies. Of course, shooting out of continuity, it might even be a scene before the baby is born. So there is certain "inner work" an actor must learn to do, both in order to learn how to act out of continuity and how to achieve instant emotion.

'In addition, "instant relationships". Again, a play might be in rehearsal for at least three or four weeks before it formally opens, maybe more than that if there are out-of-town tryouts, and maybe more than that if it's a repertory company where the actors have worked together for years. Whereas in film you meet with strangers whenever you walk on a set. "John Smith, this is Mary Jones, and she is playing your lover. Now, get into bed." I remember Bill Bixby saying to me once, "At least there ought to be an exchange of money!"

'That means actors have to develop techniques for believable, instant relationships. We had specific exercises for that. Let's say the assignment was "love". Actor A must look at Actor B and try to complete this sentence honestly. "I love you because . . ." and then Actor A must verbalize why he loves Actor B. It might be an external thing: "Because you have beautiful, blonde hair." It might be a substitution: "Because you remind me of my sister." It might be an inner thing: "Because your eyes look kind." If Actor A verbalizes it, Actor B can say, "Yes, I believe you." Once that idea is located in Actor A's mind, no matter what else is going on in his mind, when he approaches Actor B, in character, that little extra idea is there. So he doesn't have to work so hard to pretend to love – or hate, or fear – because that little extra truth is there for him to work with.'

Screen acting required constant adjustments to different types of shots: extreme close-up, medium shot, long shot. Therefore the contract players had exercises to practise the 'size' of their communication with the camera; and they were drilled differently, if the 'message' was being communicated by body or face alone. The focus, in classes or on soundstages, was always the close-up; whereas it might be okay to 'act' the intensity of a close-up in a coliseum-style long shot, it didn't make any sense to do it the other way around. Therefore, achieving the close-up was paramount.

'Another problem for the film actor is "matching",' explained Harmon. 'Whether an actor gives a performance in, say, medium close shot or long shot, it has to match his performance in the other shots, or the editor will have a horrific time. The students had one exercise in which they had to do the same short scene, a half page say, three times – with everyone watching, concentrating on the physical matching. Which, incidentally, trained them not to do too much, because if they improvised and floundered with their hands, they would find it almost impossible to repeat themselves every single take.'

This film-friendly coursework, as compared with Brando's Method, was perfect for an actor like Clint, teaching him, from the outset, to understand and explore his limitations . . . as strengths. In Universal acting classes, he would learn to stress the non-verbal and simple solution in a scene, which in Clint's case would give him a long-term edge over Brando's high-flying intuition. Doing 'less' minimized acting, minimized reacting. Clint would build a career out of minimalism – and of exploiting his enigmatic face in close-ups.

Although Clint would rarely resort to shedding his skin and 'becoming' someone other than himself – disappearing into his role in *White Hunter, Black Heart* would be almost singularly adventurous in his career – at the same time he could justifiably claim to be versed in the Method. And he had clever ways of incorporating the Method into his film productions. For one thing, he would frequently choose co-stars and second leads, who were Method, or East Coast types, against whom, Clint well understood from this early training, his distinctly 'non-acting' style stood out in contrast and relief.

None of this, of course, was manifest in 1954–5. Clint was hardly conspicuous in acting classes at Universal. While people recall his easygoing quality in one-to-one situations, they struggle to remember his 'on-camera' highlights, or noteworthy class moments. Clint was, nearly everyone agrees, green and self-conscious.

He was a quick read, however; memorizing lines came easy for him in those uncomplicated days. And he had the likeable capacity to shrug off failure. His self-confidence seemed to come from acceptance of his flaws. Clint *laughed* about his flaws.

One of his relative strengths was playing 'anger'. One day in class, Clint was portraying a husband abandoning his wife. He performed the improvised scene with Betty Jane Howarth, his rage building up so menacingly during the improvisation that Howarth was reduced to tears. The residual anger was a hidden side of the real Clint that close friends noted; it would always be a plus in his acting, even if he grew to rely on it too much in films.

Floyd Simmons said that, ironically, where Clint really sparkled was in 'little comedic pieces', the sort of amusing vignettes that would provide breathers in his later action-heavy films. Strangely, Clint in his career would make few out-and-out comedies, as if he didn't trust that ingratiating side of himself. But 'cute' comedy was definitely a side of

Clint. 'It is hard to describe him as being cute,' explained Simmons, 'but he did cute things with girls, ad libs or kissy-muzzling things, that would get a laugh out of the class.'

Clint had his own ways of 'licking his belly'. When he wanted to be, he was low-profile; other times he contrived to stand out. Simmons remembered taking Clint along to several Olympic functions as his guest. 'I was always embarrassed about him there,' Simmons said. 'He had no social skills. He'd kind of meet someone and look away. No "Hi, how are you . . . glad to meet you . . . what's your name?" None of that. Yet other times he was very charming. At parties he was always popular, laughing and kidding.'

Once, Simmons remembered, he and Clint were walking through the Universal gym when they noticed Charlton Heston, with a towel wrapped around him, relaxing after a work-out. 'I said hello and passed on, then noticed that Clint was no longer beside me,' recollected Simmons. 'He was back there speaking to Heston. I turned around and heard him say, "Are you Chuck Connors?" "No, I'm Charlton Heston." "Oh, I thought you were Chuck Connors." I was amazed. It was embarrassing. Then he walked off. I wondered then, and I still wonder today, did he do it on purpose? Was he trying to make an impression? Or was he maybe trying to level him off?'

The front-office's appraisal of Clint, as inscribed in the Talent School reports, was optimistic, even after he had been under contract for several months. 'He has both intelligence and understanding, and his feeling for dramatic values is unusual considering he has had no experience other than what he is getting now. He is one of the most cooperative and interested boys in the group. It should be understood, however, that he needs experience, continued work, and general seasoning.'

In the fall of 1954, meanwhile, there occurred an important staff change: drama coach Katharine Warren was succeeded by Jess Kimmel, a former stage manager for José Ferrer. Kimmel's major innovation was to introduce fencing and boxing as adjuncts to the physical training for the men. But Kimmel's ascendancy also meant increased visibility for assistant coach Jack Kosslyn, who took over more of the acting instruction.

Kosslyn, from Brooklyn, had trained on the GI Bill at the left-wing Actors Lab in Hollywood, and was even more influenced by the Method than his predecessors. He too had taken classes from and felt in the debt of Michael Chekhov, whose books he recommended to serious practitioners. Kosslyn's main teacher had been George Shdanoff (if Clint ever attended a Shdanoff workshop, it's news to Kosslyn).

One of the techniques Kosslyn – and Shdanoff – strongly advocated was 'visualization' exercises, which helped an actor 'concretize' a characterization by focusing on a distinct mental image; also the 'psychological gesture', which helped an actor convey his 'inner self' through physicality. Both would be useful to Clint, who came to Kosslyn already believing in willpower and his own well-being.

Clint and Kosslyn felt an immediate kinship. They became oddly-matched friends – the short, intense, opinionated Method expert from Brooklyn and the tall, soft-spoken raw recruit from northern California. A nurturing teacher, Kosslyn would move into the Villa Sands and become one of the first to shower Clint with encouragement.

More significant than Jack Kosslyn to Clint's future was Arthur Lubin, although the director who had him under personal contract was hardly far-sighted about his protégé's chances. 'He [Clint] always had his good looks,' recalled Lubin. 'We never thought much of him as an actor, but he *was* charming.'

In the first week of September 1954, Clint worked for almost three weeks in Lubin's production of *Lady Godiva of Coventry*, and then in February he had another longish stint – four weeks – in one of the films in the 'Talking Mule' series, *Francis in the Navy*, playing Jonesy, a sailor, for which he was paid $300 a week. Producer Stanley Rubin, who thirty years later was to play a pivotal role in the making of *White Hunter, Black Heart*, was unaware that Clint was paying a percentage of his salary to the person who cast him in the part. Lubin merely brought Clint in for the requisite interview, and Clint made an impression. Producer Rubin thought 'his look was perfect for one of the young naval officers in the story – tall, slender, very Waspish'.

In *Lady Godiva* Clint was barely recognizable in medieval costume, however, and in *Francis in the Navy*, playing a naval chum of Donald O'Connor, his part stayed minuscule and his dialogue inconsequential.

Lubin, with his built-in incentive as Clint's agent-manager, always tried to wangle extra time for Clint on the shooting schedule and a more generous weekly (as opposed to daily) rate of renumeration.

Lubin tried to give Clint as much luxury time as possible off the lot; the locations were not too distant in those days – in the case of *Francis in the Navy*, cast and crew simply trooped off to the navy yards in San Diego. But Clint savoured location work, Lubin understood, because he was able to carry on with women outside of wife Maggie's purview. 'Women loved to work with Clint,' said Lubin. 'He was a real masher. He was not what I would call, in those early days, a great lover for his wife. He like to go on location and leave her behind.'

Betty Jane Howarth preferred to describe Clint's 'mashing' passively: 'The extras chased him. You can only stand so much temptation. I wouldn't say he gave in to it, but he staggered a little bit.' 'Passive' worked for Clint, professionally and personally.

Maggie was suspicious of Clint when he went on location, according to Lubin, so Mrs Eastwood often manoeuvred to be brought along. A Clint tradition was inaugurated: although locations were his inviolate turf, Clint also knew the wisdom of setting time aside, on out-of-town film sets, for Maggie to visit – days carefully blacked out in his mind – so that he could coordinate his surreptitious love life accordingly.

During his time at Universal Clint seemed to ping-pong mostly between Arthur Lubin productions and films of fellow contract director Jack Arnold. Clint spent more calendar time with Lubin, but the more memorable films would be those directed by Arnold. Another Jack Arnold horror film was *Tarantula!*, with Clint playing a squadron pilot, his face shrouded by gear, who fire-bombs a giant hairy spider in the desert.

PILOT: (crackle, crackle) ... dropping napalm – follow in order ... (crackle, crackle)
(We see another bomber peel off, through the pilot's cockpit window.)
PILOT: Here goes ...
(The pilot's plane swoops down on the magnified spider.)

He managed two days of work on that one. The part wasn't much, but *Tarantula!* remains one of those tacky cult classics whose appeal has grown over the years, as compared to the unspectacular *Lady Godiva* or the unutterable Talking Mule vehicles. Jack Arnold was, like Lubin, a notoriously fast director, a one-take craftsman whose on-schedule efficiency might have rubbed off on Clint long before he ever met Don Siegel. *Tarantula!* would warrant a nod from the star, thirty years later in the film, *The Rookie*. The character played by Lara Flynn Boyle is watching a newscast on television, when she realizes from an image flashed on the screen that she is in the presence of a murderer; nervously switching channels, she alights on a sequence from the 1955 feature in which a giant arachnid claimed billing over Clint Eastwood.

Clint would turn up on the screen less than most of the other contract players, and sometimes he was barely visible. He darts by in several Universal pictures shot in 1955, including a few that have eluded the very best reference books. In May 1955 he put in four hours on 'A Time Remembered' (released as *Never Say Goodbye*), playing another white-coated technician who delivers one line of dialogue. In June 1955, Clint put in a single day of emoting on *Away All Boats* (watch closely for him on the bridgehead). In August, another day was notched on *Pillars of the Sky*. Both these latter vehicles starred the studio's bread-and-butter lead, Jeff Chandler.

One day of shooting was all it took, also, for Clint's maiden Western foray – uncredited as a ranch hand – in 'Law Man' (a.k.a. *Stars in the Dust*), filmed late in August 1955. 'If he played any role,' director Charles F. Haas struggled to recall, 'it must have been tiny, because I have not the slightest memory of him in that context.'

The parts Clint performed in acting classes were just as forgettable, with Clint just as earnest about them. All weekend, down in Palm Desert, where he took getaway trips with Maggie, Floyd Simmons and the television actress Kathy Adams – who married the Western novelist Louis L'Amour in 1956 – Clint would be carrying around his single-page, ten-line 'side' crumpled up in his hand, trying out endless permutations of his readings. It got to be a joke; he did it so relentlessly, they had to beg him to shut up.

Where Universal really utilized Clint and the other apprentice talent was for inexpensive looping and dubbing sessions. Universal records indicate Clint was among the nonentities contributing to *Purple Mask*, *Kiss of Fire*, *Ain't Misbehavin'*, *The Spoilers*, *To Hell and Back*, *Square Jungle*, *Backlash* and *The Benny Goodman Story*.

From behind the scenes, however, Clint was able to observe each stage of film-making and monitor the progress of every Universal production. Along with other members of the Talent School he enjoyed a crash course in film history. Every Wednesday the contract players gathered in a screening room to watch *A Place in the Sun* or the latest film starring Rock Hudson, an actor whose development particularly fascinated them because he was an alumnus. After the screening, Jack Kosslyn would lead the class in a wide-ranging discussion, which focused on the calibre of the performances but also took into account the writing, direction and overall pictorial values.

Clint was green when it came to film history too, noted Floyd Simmons. 'I'd already had knowledge of those movies as a kid,' said Simmons. 'I remembered the actors and the character actors. Clint had no knowledge of those people. It was like a completely new thing. He never expressed anything in discussions, he didn't display any knowledge, and I think it's a genuine assessment on my part that he really didn't know.'

By the end of the summer of 1955 Clint was making 'definite progress', according to Universal records, and his outlook at the studio appeared rosy. Late that summer, in fact, the young actor asked for and was granted a two-week leave to vacation with Maggie in Yellowstone Park. His six-month option was coming up, but Clint felt confident of renewal. It was all the more shocking, therefore, when he returned from vacation to learn that his option had been declined and his contract dropped.

In September of that year, Universal made the decision to release three players: Miss Ceylon, Miss El Salvador and Clint Eastwood. The blow was made all the worse by the fact that Clint's best friends, including Floyd Simmons, were among those whose contracts were extended. Clint's internship terminated on 25 October 1955.

Quite apart from the financial implications (losing his weekly paycheque), the worst of the blow was psychological. Clint, to whom everything in life came easy, felt uncustomarily defeated. He confided his demoralization to dance teacher Charlotte Hunter, who tried to cheer him up by exhorting him to believe in himself.

Ironically, it appears from studio records that the decision to drop Clint was purely budgetary, part of the general cutbacks the studio had been staving off for years. If none of the Universal staff were willing to go out on a limb to predict Clint's surefire future, all of them did seem to genuinely like him. Joan McTavish, who supervised the Universal talent development programme at the time, said Clint was 'a wonderful human being', whose enormous potential was simply overlooked by the studio.

Clint himself entertained the suspicion that a studio higher-up had taken a personal dislike to him. He decided, according to one friend, that Robert Palmer, the Universal executive in charge of casting, was the man who might be to blame. One day years later, when Palmer came by to apply for a job at his Malpaso company, Clint took pleasure in turning him down. 'I showed that son of a bitch . . .' he told a friend, although there was no real evidence Palmer had spurred Universal's decision.

Universal would always loom in his psyche; it was a place that evoked sharply mixed emotions. Certain people from the Talent School crowd – Brett Halsey and Dani Crayne – would remain nostalgic acquaintances for years, while others – Betty Jane Howarth and Mara Corday – he would help out financially, more than once, with small parts in his film productions. Clint's days as a 'star of tomorrow' were happy days, among the happiest of his life, but they were also full of bitter disappointment.

Failure spurred Clint to redouble his efforts and his determination to succeed.

The first change in plans was Arthur Lubin. The director had been so intimate with Clint that to some their relationship raised eyebrows. Not only did the homosexual director give Clint a boost in films, but they held long, private dinners together, and Lubin took Clint with him on out-of-town trips. Clint seemed comfortable among Lubin's entourage of handsome young men. Lubin bought him suits, helped him learn how to comport himself in public, even proffered financial loans.

Clint's closeness with Lubin – not to mention the profusion of beefcake publicity poses early in Clint's career – has led some people in Hollywood to speculate that Clint might have dallied sexually with men in the 1950s. But there is no evidence that Clint was ever anything but a raging heterosexual, and Lubin certainly never had any carnal knowledge of Clint. Even he wondered, however: Clint was so-o-o good-looking. 'I knew him well,' Lubin mused late in life (he died at age 93 in 1995), 'yet I never knew for sure . . .'

There is rich irony in this vaunted man's man – whose later films would take occasional potshots at homosexuals – 'bearding', early in his career, for a gay gentleman. At one point, according to Lubin, Maggie actually asked him if he were trying to steal her husband. He assured her he wasn't. 'She was jealous, not only of me but also of every woman or man who came near him,' explained Lubin. 'She treasured him.'

It was probably Maggie, whose instincts and advice were invaluable to Clint in the early years, who convinced the actor to sever his contractual relationship with Lubin. According to Lubin, Clint simply decided to 'renege' on their two-year-old agreement. He insisted that his deal with Lubin was legally dubious. Lubin said letters arrived from lawyers representing Clint, threatening to sue if their pact was not dissolved.

One thing Clint never discusses is his financial and legal affairs. So who sent the threatening letters to Arthur Lubin? Probably a man named Irving Leonard, whom Clint had hooked up with towards the end of his contract days at Universal.

Leonard was a former Washington, DC cost accountant who had turned his bookkeeping gifts towards handling finances for Hollywood celebrities. Leonard would succeed Lubin as Clint's personal manager and also bring Clint into Gang, Tyre & Brown, a Los Angeles law firm that specialized in film industry clients. A small firm, Gang, Tyre & Brown was nonetheless influential in Hollywood, and never more so than during the blacklist decade of the 1950s, when Martin Gang, the firm's senior partner, was one of the busiest among those brokering deals for repentant ex-Communist film figures.

Clint also lost little time in acquiring new publicity representatives. The husband and wife team of Ruth and Paul Marsh were headquartered in the same Taft Building on Hollywood and Vine as Irving Leonard. A small but respected agency that had opened its doors around 1950, the Marsh Agency handled all types of Hollywood clients – actors and actresses, writers, directors and producers – and local accounts, many restaurateurs for example. Like everyone else they paid a lot of attention to the booming field of television, and actors Richard Long (soon to break through on TV's *Big Valley*) and Adam West (soon to become TV's Batman) were on their list.

Betty Jane Howarth, a Marsh Agency client, introduced Clint to Ruth Marsh. Although he was basically unemployed and making very little money, he agreed to pay five per cent of his earnings to the Marshes in return for their services. They had their work cut out for them, since Clint was one of their true 'unknowns'. But Ruth Marsh thought Clint had 'star potential', and besides she found him extremely personable.

Although Clint and Arthur Lubin parted ways contractually, they managed to stay cordial. The mild-mannered Lubin wasn't one to carry any sort of grudge, and shortly after Clint's dismissal from the Universal talent programme he handed Clint his biggest part to date, a 'featured' role in a Ginger Rogers–Carol Channing Western comedy called *The First Traveling Saleslady*, which was to be directed by Lubin for RKO.

Ginger Rogers was playing a former corset retailer, and Carol Channing was a saloon singer, the two of them selling barbed wire out West. Clint played a recruitment officer for Teddy Roosevelt's Rough Riders. Clint's character was a decent man – and so was Clint, thought Lubin. So Lubin put Clint in uniform, encouraged him to adopt a spurious Texas accent, and gave him scenes flirting with Carol Channing.

After *The First Traveling Saleslady*, Clint would be tapped for a fleeting part as a rescue pilot in yet another Arthur Lubin production, *Escapade in Japan*, and still later, in the early 1960s, he would make minor television appearances for his first Hollywood benefactor. But after Clint's career began to really take off, silence ensued between them for years. 'As time went on, he forgot Arthur Lubin,' said Lubin in 1994, sadly.

But the director had played an indisputable role in launching Clint. Clint himself acknowledged this in a phone call to Lubin which took place shortly after he received his *Unforgiven* Oscar. Lubin said he hadn't spoken to Clint for years when the phone rang one night, and it was Clint. 'I said, "Congratulations on your great success." He said, "Some time we must have lunch together." I was amazed.' They never did have that lunch, but Lubin was touched by a gesture that seemed to wipe away the debt.

Without Arthur Lubin, however, Clint's acting opportunities very nearly dried up.

Clint looked in vain for contract work at Warner Brothers, Paramount, and Twentieth Century–Fox. At Fox, Clint performed an audition from Sidney Kingsley's play *Detective Story*, a scene very different from the one he had improvised with Betty Jane Howarth – this one with an 'eponymous protagonist', in Richard Schickel's words, pleading with his estranged wife to return to him.

'Clint had studied the entire work carefully and correctly understood this figure to be a hard and inward man, not used to begging for anything, virtually strangling on the words he was compelled to speak. Clint's auditor, the head of the studio's talent programme, disagreed entirely with this interpretation. He told Clint that he and his wife had recently come close to divorce, and that he had gone out and bought her a mink coat, dropped to his knees when he presented it and pleaded for forgiveness.

'Clint was astonished. Such behaviour was entirely beyond his ken. And so were confessions for a stranger. "I was thinking, 'Boy, this guy's pussywhipped' . . ."'

Although Clint had Irving Leonard to advise him financially, he had to look around for the right talent agent to jump-start his flagging career. He took what he could get and was represented, in rapid succession, by the Kumin–Olenick Agency in 1956 and by Mitchell Gertz in 1957. Olenick was well known for signing co-op deals with East Coast agencies, and Gertz, who ran a small agency with a preponderance of youthful clients, was an old-time mover and shaker with a cigar. Importantly, Gertz concentrated on the mushrooming field of television, where Clint had not exhausted his welcome.

Actually, Universal had presented Clint first on national television. Clint's small-screen debut had come live on NBC on 2 July 1955, in a little-remembered programme called 'Allen in Movieland'. Steve Allen's coming to the studio to play Benny Goodman in the jazzman's life story was the springboard for the show. Although the programme's stars were Allen, Benny Goodman, Tony Curtis, Piper Laurie and Jeff Chandler, the show was also designed to shine a light on lesser-knowns on the Universal payroll. Clint's negligible bit included portraying an orderly in a re-enactment from *Bright Victory*, with Rex Reason and Grant Williams in the bigger parts.

His earliest TV roles did not expand much in size. For a segment of television's *Reader's Digest* series, broadcast on ABC in January 1956, Clint played a hotheaded army officer who inveighs against negotiating with the bloodthirsty Cochise. Clint had a meatier part the same year, as one of two motorcycle gang members prodded into troublemaking by a café owner on a *Highway Patrol* episode, also telecast on ABC.

The 'White Fury' instalment of the *West Point* series featured Clint as a cadet who goes skiing with a friend and gets embroiled in an emergency rescue. That was shown in 1957, the same year Clint could be spotted, fleetingly, in an episode of the highly-rated, prime-time series, *Wagon Train*. Nineteen-fifty-seven was also the year Clint had a fair-sized role in *Death Valley Days* as a gold rush prospector who is luckless and on the verge of suicide until a letter arrives from Maine informing him that he has inherited a family fortune.

Audiences could follow Clint, lean and hard as a knife, wearing another uniform as a Navy lieutenant in a 1958 segment of *Navy Log*. And in 1959 he would have his most substantial guest appearance in a top series, awkwardly cast as a cowardly villain, intent on marrying a rich girl for her money, in *Maverick*. This modest, pre-*Rawhide* highlight of Clint's career was once again directed by Arthur Lubin.

Prime-time, network exposure was the rare plum. Clint's appearances were usually on syndicated shows, not major series. Typically he worked a day or two, got paid scale for his efforts. Critics had little reason to note his midget parts.

Luckily for him, Maggie remained in demand as a model, and probably both their families helped out with loans. Clint took day jobs – digging pools with Bill Thompkins, Bob Donner and a third friend, George Fargo. But these jobs were periodic and never seemed to last long. 'One day I got fired,' George Fargo told *Life* magazine in 1970, 'and the boss looked over and saw Clint unbuttoning his work shirt. "What're *you* doing?" the guy asked Clint. And Clint just said very casually, "Well, George is my friend, he hasn't got a ride home." And he quit, just like that.'

The years 1956–8 were spent largely idle and lolling by the Villa Sands pool, flirting with Texas starlet Kathryn Grant – before she married Bing Crosby – and other women. The day would be broken up by a visit to Vince's Gym. Clint had arrived in Los Angeles long and lean but a little soft in muscle definition; now he went to work building himself up, especially in the arms and shoulders. One of the reasons why Clint loved to wear T-shirts, friends say, is that he was especially proud of his sinewy arms.

Keeping fit, looking attractive and staying young were basic to his psychology. Although actors in those days were not encouraged to get 'overly pectoral', in Floyd Simmons' words, Clint had been a regular at the Universal gym, ironically remembered as much for his steady presence there as for his emoting in films or in class. 'I only remember Clint in the [studio] gym, when I was exercising,' said Rex Reason. 'There was Clint, pumping away with weights, and I was doing the same.'

In the meantime Clint would stick by Jack Kosslyn, or maybe it was Kosslyn who stuck by Clint. When, in the mid-1950s, the Talent School programme fell apart at Universal, Kosslyn opened his own workshop and theatre called the Mercury Stage on Cole Avenue. It was a small place with a slightly elevated proscenium stage, where twelve to fifteen students acted scenes for group criticism, and where, occasionally, the group would mount full-scale productions to be attended by scouts, agents and casting directors. Such was its intimacy that actors felt, almost, like being 'on camera'.

Kosslyn's classes met several times a week, and for a long time Clint was a dutiful participant. The other students included Nick Adams, Irish McCalla, Jamie Farr and other up-and-coming performers. Kosslyn had more than one face: he was a stern father figure when necessary, but to many he was also a low-key, intensely caring friend who, after class, was always willing to step out for coffee and conversation.

It was a very fluid format. Kosslyn was always trying to persuade actors to stretch themselves – to 'counter-cast' themselves. He would ask students to play a scene imagining a soft – or steel-hard – object inside them, defining their characters according to that imagined object. He'd stress subtext, the deeper meaning of a scene, while at the same time emphasizing surface 'focus'. He would put an empty Coke bottle on stage and ask students to look at the bottle for a couple of minutes, then whisk it away and go around the room asking each of them to describe it in detail.

These voluntary classes actually stretched over a longer period of time than those which Clint first attended, mandatorily, at Universal. And people say the habitually out-of-work actor sometimes burst forth in the workshop, showing surprising range and ingenuity, especially when playing scenes of festering rage or violence.

'We did improvisations', said Jamie Farr, who later gained fame as one of the stars of television's *M*A*S*H*. 'Clint was quite good. He's a pretty big fella, and I'm a little guy, and I remember there was this one improvisation we did where we had an altercation. It got a little bit physical. You know how Clint likes to talk through clenched teeth. He was really getting into the part. He grabbed me, really got carried away. He was actually beginning to hurt me. I kept saying, "Clint, Clint! It's me, Jamie! Snap out of it!"

Some friends insist Clint was dead serious in his approach to acting, while others believe he was only taking classes because it was the thing to do: it was lip-service to the game. Years later Clint himself said, revealingly, that 'really, it [acting study] was sort of a pseudo-intellectual thing, a fad that people were going through at the time'.

'I think he was acting at being an actor,' asserted Fritz Manes. 'I think he was kidding himself because it was an easy way to make a living. It was his way of looking like he was busy while not really having to do too much. He saw the film industry – he's never admitted this – as the greatest escape from reality. Not reality the way an actor looks at having to work; reality as in, "You mean you get paid for doing this stuff?"'

The 'shittiest years' were probably 1956–8. When in July 1957 *TV Guide* published a profile of a promising newcomer named Jeanne Baird, a participant in Jack Kosslyn's classes, the article featured photos of Baird with 'Cliff Eastwood' – in one of the photos, rehearsing an acting scene for class; in another, 'Cliff and Jeanne' are seen spending 'an inexpensive evening at a Hollywood jam session'. There was no further background on 'Cliff', no mention that he might be married, no follow-up correction that he was actually Clint Eastwood. Such were the depths of his obscurity.

Clint's self-assurance often unravelled even in the best of times. There were rumblings and eruptions, back in the 1950s, that close friends couldn't help but notice.

One night Clint, Maggie, Floyd Simmons, his date, and another couple, went to Trader Vic's for dinner. After dropping the others off at the entrance and parking the car in the back, Simmons approached the front door where an ominous scene was unfolding. The three women were crowded behind the two men – Clint and the other man – their path blocked by a gang of young Latinos in leather jackets.

The Latinos were taunting the men, with the offensive remarks building into a confrontation.

'Just as I walked up, Clint, according to my total recollection, pushed the other guy aside and said, "Let me talk to that little son of a bitch," or something to that effect. One of the Latinos had a silver pistol and it was stuck right in Clint's face. I was ready to hit the deck. The adrenalin was going like crazy. These are the words Clint said: "Go on and pull the trigger, you little son of a bitch, and I'll kill you before I hit the ground." We were all amazed. The guy with the gun said, "Well, fuck you, man, we're leaving," and backed off. They had a complete turnaround. Clint's fierceness astounded me. That evening was far better than anything out of *Dirty Harry*.'*

Clint owned a second-hand Austin-Healey with a top that sometimes went up – sometimes didn't. Floyd Simmons had splurged for an MG. Clint was territorial about his cars, and sometimes more reckless when behind the wheel of other people's vehicles.

One time Clint and Simmons, travelling in Simmons' MG, pulled up to back into a parking space on a Hollywood side street. Another driver zipped in front of Simmons, who was driving, and beat him to the space. Perfectly normal – except that Clint jumped out of the car and started to berate the other driver. Then Clint climbed up on top of the other guy's car and started jumping up and down on the hood. The driver, flabbergasted, not to mention terrified, started his engine and drove away. Afterwards, Clint laughed about it. 'I guess I showed that son of a bitch,' Clint told Simmons.

It was brave play-acting. But at times Clint's violence was more than posturing, and the subliminal resentments and aggrievedness boiled over. One afternoon, according to Fritz Manes, Clint and he were in a bar down on Highland Avenue. Manes, a hotshot Marine, was in uniform, and that plus Clint's unusually long and wavy hair drew the attention of a bunch of sailors, who swaggered over to them and said something ill-advised about Hollywood faggots. Manes said something right back, and a free-for-all ensued. One of the guys made the mistake of yanking Clint up by his coat, and punching him in the face.

'I don't know whether you've ever noticed – he's had them capped

---

* This scene is played out, with remarkable similarity to how it is described above, between Clint and Don Stroud in *Joe Kidd*.

now – but in his early pictures his two upper front teeth are broken,'
remembered Manes. 'By the time the police arrived ten minutes later,
two of the five sailors had to go to the hospital. The cops came, the
shore patrol came. Clint literally almost killed these guys.'

Manes ended up with a concussion, Clint's mouth was badly cut.
When they finally returned to the Villa Sands, Maggie wanted to know
what had happened. It caused constant tension in their marriage that
Clint insisted on spending an inordinate amount of his free time
hanging out in bars with 'the guys'. Sometimes it really wasn't 'the
guys', but Clint hated accounting for his time to Maggie anyway and
sometimes deliberately told her nothing, just to rattle her. Now he
informed Maggie that he and Fritz had been screwing around on the
diving board and fell in, against the concrete side of the pool.

Tension in the marriage wasn't helped by the fact that Clint wanted
his apartment to be perpetually available as a crash pad for his friends.
Although Manes was still stationed at Camp Pendleton, he would
monopolize Clint's couch whenever he visited Los Angeles. This time
Manes had been there for several days in a row when Maggie started
nagging at Clint. What was he doing all day when she wasn't around?
Where was he running around to all the time? What was Fritz Manes
doing, staying here with them for so long? Clint finally became fed
up. 'He just turned around and cold-cocked her,' recollected Manes.
'Just decked her – knocked her right flat on her ass, clear from the
living room into the bathtub in the bathroom. I got out of there. I
left.'

Although Maggie was the vulnerable one, she could also be just as
strong-willed as Clint. Clint liked someone to organize his life, and
she was the organized one – always drawing up endless shopping lists
and reminders for errands and chores. It was Clint's job to take out
the garbage, and he *hated* taking out the garbage. Once, arguing about
the garbage, Clint struck Maggie, she confided in a friend. When the
friend confronted Clint, he claimed Maggie hit *him* first. 'Still, that's
no reason to hit a woman!' the friend insisted. 'You want me to stand
there like some asshole and take the beating?' answered Clint, who
liked to be mothered but refused to be 'pussywhipped'.

One of the simmering tensions in their marriage was that Clint
didn't get along very well with Maggie's parents. Maggie's parents
belonged to that unfortunate club of people who were slow to

recognize Clint's 'star potential'. Friends say Maggie's parents thought their sorority-girl daughter might have done better than Clint for a husband.

Another, more painful tension was that Maggie wanted to have children, and for some mysterious reason couldn't sustain a pregnancy. After a few years of marriage, the couple began to see fertility doctors, and for a while Clint was a familiar sight at the Villa Sands, on his way to the clinic with a vial of sperm tucked under his arm, gamely keeping it warm. To his buddies, however, he expressed diffidence about fatherhood, though he was happy to have children if it would give him any peace with Maggie.

All this time Clint continued to enjoy himself on the side with his little dollies. One sporadic girlfriend may have been the woman who helped Clint get his Universal contract. Clint met Jane Agee when she was a secretary at Universal. Although an 'alluringly seductive blonde', Agee, from Texas originally, made a great pretence of being Clint's buddy – just one of the guys – able to curse and drink as well as any man. Close friends believe Cint and Jane Agee were sexually involved on and off over the years, and that at one point in the early 1960s Clint drove Agee down to Tijuana for an abortion. A bossy, difficult woman, almost witch-like in the spell she cast over him, Jane Agee would last as long, however, as any in the ladies' auxiliary that was Clint's.

By 1959, Clint's acting career was in truly desperate straits. He couldn't seem to land any decent parts. 'Every day I felt like someone was coming up to me with a big wet towel and slapping me right in the face with it,' Clint remembered. Forty years later, the taste was still fresh in his mouth. 'It was a difficult period,' Clint told *Cosmopolitan* in 1997. 'People say I "play anger" well. I just remember how many no-talents passed judgment on me back then.'

He read reports about a worldwide talent hunt to play aviator Charles Lindbergh in a new 'biopic' director Billy Wilder was making – *The Spirit of St Louis*. 'I auditioned for it; hundreds of guys did. But they ended up picking Jimmy Stewart who just put on some make-up to make himself look younger. So much for the worldwide talent hunt.'

Clint scored a walk-through as a flyer without significant dialogue in *Lafayette Escadrille*, a French flying squadron picture which turned out to be the less-than-epic swansong of director William Wellman. And he won his biggest screen role to date in a regulation Western called *Ambush at Cimarron Pass*, shot in nine days for Regal Films Inc.

Sporting a brush-cut, Clint played an ex-Reb still loyal to the Confederacy whose troop of renegade soldiers surrounds a squad of blue-coats searching the frontier for gun-runners. Both parties are trapped in a pass by Apaches. There's a lot of the usual 'You're a lousy Reb,' 'No, you're a lousy blue-coat' dialogue, as well as some rather brutal touches. Clint, playing a hotheaded coward who undergoes the requisite change of heart, is not terrible, nor is the film especially bad.

But Clint was feeling 'really depressed', and thinking of quitting the acting profession. He viewed *Ambush at Cimarron Pass* as 'sort of the low point of my movie career'. When it turned up at a neighbourhood theatre, he and Maggie went to see it. 'It was *sooo* bad,' Clint said. 'I just kept sinking lower and lower in my seat. I said to my wife, "I'm going to quit, I'm really going to quit. I gotta go back to school, I got to start doing something with my life.'

Clint went through the motions of shopping for a new agent – and considered switching drama teachers. He auditioned for a workshop taught by former Universal coach Estelle Harmon, reading a monologue from Arthur Miller's *All My Sons*. 'I thought he had wonderful commercial potential and artistic potential in the sense that he did nothing phony, even then,' said Harmon. 'I thought he had a wonderfully honest, very virile quality about him.' Harmon observed that 'his mood wasn't very good in those days because he had been discouraged'. She gladly agreed to accept Clint in her class, then was surprised when she never heard from him again.

Floyd Simmons recommended that Clint sign with his agent, Bill Shiffrin. Shiffrin had a number of young, muscular-type actors under contract including Vince Edwards (later TV's Ben Casey), ex-Olympian Bob Mathias and Bill Smith (who would pit his physique against Clint's many years later in *Any Which Way You Can*). Shiffrin was a hard-nosed guy – later one of the few to stand up publicly against the merger of Universal and MCA. He was respected for giving his clients individual attention.

Shiffrin had a hand in Clint's biggest break. It's one of those stories – like the plane ditching or the Fort Ord 'discovery' – that has been told in dozens of articles, with endless permutations. Apparently

Shiffrin told Clint that CBS was casting an hour-long Western series for television. The lead was supposed to be in his forties, but there would be other recurring parts. Armed with this knowledge, Clint decided to head over to NBC, ostensibly to visit a friend of his, Sonia Chernus, a story editor who, like so many others in Clint's world at the time, first encountered him at Universal.

A Los Angeles native, Chernus was a UCLA graduate. Starting in the film studios as a secretary at Warner Brothers in the early 1940s, Chernus worked her way into a position as a reader and story editor for Arthur Lubin. Her eagerness about short stories featuring a talking horse spurred the *Mr Ed* television series. Chernus' unusual credit on the screen read, 'Format Developed by Sonia Chernus'.

The ever-industrious Lubin was at CBS in 1957 and 1958, and in the process of developing the *Mr Ed* series. According to Lubin, Chernus had a lifelong crush on Clint, and would have gone to the ends of the earth for him. Clint was talking to Chernus, having 'coffee or tea or something' at the canteen in the CBS basement, when an executive in a blue suit passed by and spotted the tall, formidable-looking Clint.

Floyd Simmons tells about the time he and Clint were having lunch in the MGM commissary, when on the way out Simmons stopped to say hello to a group of influential people. He started to introduce Clint to one production executive, when Clint interrupted him 'in a loud, offhand way – these are the words – "C'mon Simmons, let's get the hell out of this slop shoot." I was embarrassed and as he was leaving I turned back and apologized. About a couple of days later, the guy asked, "By the way who's your friend? What's with him?" Putting it all together, there were a lot of calculating things all along . . . appearing to be a kind of bumpkin.' Clint had *ways*.

Now the blue-suited CBS executive asked Clint, 'How tall are you exactly?' 'And I thought,' Clint told *Crawdaddy*, 'why does he care how tall I am?' Clint told his height (6'4") and then thought to mention that he was an actor, 'but I wasn't very enthusiastic because I figured "Screw it," I'd had it. The guy says, "Well, could you come into my office for a second?" and meanwhile my friend is behind me motioning, "Go, go!"'

His practised ambivalence again worked its magic. The blue-suited executive was Robert Sparks, and Sparks took Clint into an office and introduced him to another guy 'wearing old clothes. Looked like he'd just been pushing a broom in the back room,' recalled Clint. 'I didn't know whether he was going to sweep under the chair or what.'

The old-clothes producer was Charles Marquis Warren, the creator of the impending hour-long Western series. 'So, anyway, I was being very cool, and I just casually asked him, "What's the lead like?" And he says, "Well, there's two leads, and one is a young guy in his early twenties." My agent wasn't bright enough to find that out. So I started perking up, straightening out the wrinkles in my T-shirt, you know – I was just wearing Levi's – and finally the guy said, "Well, we'll get in contact with you." I kind of halfway wrote it off, because I figured once they'd seen *Ambush at Cimarron Pass*, that'd be the end of it.'

By the time he got home, that not-bright-enough agent, Bill Shiffrin, was on the phone informing Clint he was scheduled to test tomorrow for the old-clothes producer. 'I say, "Can I get to the scene ahead of time?" and they say, "No scene, we're just going to ask you questions." I thought, "Oh hell, that's the worst kind of test you can have." I never could read that well. I couldn't read scripts out loud. If I knew the lines, I was fine, but I wasn't a great reader.'

When Clint went back to CBS, Charles Marquis Warren did have a scene prearranged for him to read. It was one of Henry Fonda's monologues from *The Ox-Bow Incident*, the classic William Wellman Western. 'I think, "Holy shit, there is no way I am going to learn this, no way in the world I am going to learn this dialogue,"' Clint told *Crawdaddy*, 'But there were three transitions in it, so I just picked out the three points I wanted to make and took out everything else.

'So I got up and came in, and I started going ... and the guy is looking at me really strange. I was playing it rather well, at least I felt like I was ... I was believing it, I thought. I did it again, twice, and then I finished and he looked at me coldly and said, "Okay, we'll call you." (I found out later he was a writer and he didn't want his words tampered with.) So I go into the dressing room and take off this Western costume, and as I'm leaving I hear this other guy doing it word-for-word, letter-for-letter, and I said, "Well, that's the end of that." So I walked out and I wrote that one off.'

A week later, however, Bill Shiffrin called and Clint had got the job. He would play a cowboy named Rowdy. Before Clint came along, a young actor named Bing Russell, who had worked for Charles Marquis

Warren in films, had been the inside candidate for Rowdy. But, according to Clint, telling the anecdote in a way that reflected positively on him, 'the guy who projected all the tests for the wheels who came in from New York and LA was an old army buddy, and he told me that the wheels didn't know what the dialogue was, and didn't care. They were just looking at all of us, and what happened was that one of the wheels pointed at me and said, "That guy," and all the other little wheels said, "Yeah, that guy, that guy. I agree, J. R. He's absolutely perfect."'

But the road to television glory was still strewn with potholes.

Charles Marquis Warren had been working his way up the ladder in Hollywood since 1934. Besides work as a scenarist he had paid his dues as a writer for the pulp and slick magazines, as a songwriter and amateur historian, even as a novelist who had a best-seller to his credit. After a stint in World War II as a navy commander, he became a specialist in Westerns, with *Little Big Horn* the first of several low-budget features he wrote and directed, in 1951. Its modest virtues vaulted him into television.

A onetime all-Maryland football player, Warren had met F. Scott Fitzgerald back East and become something of a Fitzgerald cultist, leading to a career that mixed literary pretensions with more than a whiff of machismo. Warren was a hard man, a heavy drinker. His various TV series, which tried to blend Western authenticity with Fitzgerald-like literariness, would reflect the strengths and shortcomings of their creator.

Westerns seemed to dominate American television in the 1950s, and one of the standouts was *Gunsmoke*, Warren's brainchild for the 1955 season. Not an immediate hit, *Gunsmoke* built a steady following and continued on the air for twenty years, eventually becoming the longest-running prime-time dramatic series in US history. Thanks to *Gunsmoke*, Warren was the golden boy of CBS president Bill Paley, who in 1957 had prevailed upon Warren to create another popular Western for the network.

It so happened that one of Warren's last films, before going over to television, was *Cattle Empire*, about an iron-man trail boss and the vicissitudes of a cattle drive. A longtime Warren associate named Endre Bohem, who had come to America from Hungary in 1938 and worked in various capacities in Hollywood for twenty years, was the co-writer of *Cattle Empire*. And around the time of Clint's audition, Warren was sharing office space with Bohem, who was indispensable to him as his story editor.

Warren and Bohem had taken a cattle-drive script by Les Crutchfield, which had been floating around CBS corridors, and turned it into a prototype for a cattle-drive series. Warren wanted to call the series 'The Outrider', a pet title of his that was always getting rejected by muckamucks, but the network preferred *Rawhide*, an unabashed steal from a totally unrelated Tyrone Power Western dating back to 1950.

Warren and Bohem worked out the characters and continuing plotline with Robert Sparks, who was in charge of programme development. For verisimilitude Warren had drawn on the diary of a real-life trail boss named George C. Duffield, who, with three hundred head of cattle, made the journey from San Antonio, Texas to Sedalia, Missouri in 1866, the year in which the series was set. The stories would stick to the cattle drive, with the drovers pitted against the harsh elements and even harsher human nature.

In the beginning they would shoot all the interiors on studio soundstages – those saloon and Main Street scenes and endless pages of the trail-drivers sitting around the campfire eating beans and drinking coffee in front of painted skies. The 'beeves' (as the drovers affectionately referred to their four-footed charges) would be photographed in stock shots of an annual round-up in the Southwest, with smaller herds, required for close-ups, available at ranch locations near Hollywood.

Clint would play the second in command, the likeable ramrod Rowdy, a variation of the part Montgomery Clift had played opposite John Wayne in the ultimate cattle-drive movie, *Red River*. Scenarist John Dunkel, working on early *Rawhide* episodes, was visiting the office one day and speaking to Endre Bohem when Charles Marquis Warren rushed in, flushed with excitement. 'Wow! You know, I just got a great name for the sidekick,' said Warren. 'I'm going to call him "Rowdy".' Recalled Dunkel: 'We both kind of shook our heads and said, "All right. That will probably work."'

Another actor, as unknown as Clint, would get the top job of trail boss. Eric Fleming, like Clint a California native, only had limited

Broadway experience. Besides Clint and Eric Fleming, there would also be a scout, a cook, a cook's helper, and a couple of grizzled cowhands who always stayed the course, no matter what. Pete, the scout, would be played by Sheb Wooley, an effortless actor and country musician whose best-known hit was the cross-over novelty song 'The Purple People Eater'. Wooley had acted in *High Noon* but he was also a Charles Marquis Warren regular with appearances in *Little Big Horn* and *Hellgate*. Two stunt men from *Cattle Empire*, Steve Raines and Rocky Shahan, would cross over into the *Rawhide* ensemble as Scarlett and Quince. The cook's helper, Mushy, would be played by James Murdock.

The comedy-relief part of the cook was actually cast and filmed with a Chinese actor, but after the pilot episode, his scenes were junked. Paul Brinegar, also from *Cattle Empire*, was then recruited. A journeyman actor, Brinegar would inherit the part of his life as Wishbone, the bewhiskered curmudgeon whose coffee is endlessly badmouthed by the drovers. Wishbone, like Rowdy, was never written out of the series and, thanks to his reliable warmth and humour, his role would only grow over time.

The music over the credits was a lucky strike. Dimitri Tiomkin, who had scored many films, including *Tension at Table Rock* for Charles Marquis Warren, supplied the music, and Ned Washington came up with simple lyrics. 'Roll 'em, roll 'em, roll 'em, keep those dogies rollin' . . .' Warren was happily surprised when Robert Sparks persuaded the network to splurge $5,000 on pop stylist Frankie Laine, who crooned the hell out of the song. A generation of Americans would grow up knowing one of television's most familiar theme songs, and a number of them would name their boys 'Rowdy' – or even 'Clint'.

In the summer of 1958, CBS started filming a half dozen episodes, still uncertain of what the precise flavour and format should be. The network had not decided whether the episodes would be a half-hour or an hour. Warren kept pushing for *Playhouse 90*-type portentous themes. Though the series had been announced with some fanfare, behind the scenes the network really couldn't decide whether to commit its resources to the new Western, and, in fact, when the fall 1958 schedule was formalized *Rawhide* was missing.

'I thought, "Oh my God, my career is going to sit there on the shelf," ' Clint told one interviewer. 'I remember I was up for a part at

Fox after that and I asked them if I could show one of the episodes I had the lead in, and they said, "No, we don't want to show it to anybody," and I thought, "My career is going to sit in the basement in tin cans at CBS."'

It was a nerve-wracking period. Clint developed hives. Fritz Manes remembered, one evening, his friend smashing his fist down in frustration and clearing the table at a restaurant. The paramedics had to be called to the Villa Sands in the middle of the night for psychosomatic hyperventilating. Three or four times this cool, manly star – capable of facing down a group of punks – woke up, all knotted into a ball, unable to breathe, convinced he was experiencing fatal chest pains.

At Christmas, Clint and Maggie headed north on a train to spend the holidays with friends and relatives. (By now the Eastwood family had moved from Seattle back to Piedmont.) A telegram caught up with the train, saying that *Rawhide* had been approved for the winter schedule after all, and Clint was to report to work after the New Year. 'So Mag and I did a little champagne trick and yelled a lot and shouted a lot of profane things.'

CHAPTER FOUR

The Rowdy Years
1959–1964

Eric Fleming was five years older, an inch or two taller, and twenty pounds heavier than Clint. A World War II veteran, he looked solid and mature – the trail boss type. Billed first, his character was the series' lead and dominated all the early episodes, with the plots revolving around the tough, maverick decision-making of Gil Favor.

Yet Clint, the second lead, thought of himself as every bit the star. '*My* show', is how he referred to *Rawhide* among friends. The tension between Gil Favor and Rowdy Yates, a staple of the series, was echoed by the subtle rivalry between the actors off camera.

On the very first day of shooting in Arizona in 1958, the trail boss and ramrod had a legendary, unscripted showdown. 'When the noise [between them] became intolerable, they retired behind the wagons and had at it,' reported *TV Guide*. Clint later denied that he and Eric Fleming had engaged in a fistfight, but the scuttlebutt was otherwise. Clint was always careful publicly to express respect for Fleming, especially after the star's tragic demise. Yet a line was drawn with that early altercation.

It helped Clint's edge in the rivalry that key people behind the scenes thought of him, regardless of his actual age, as 'the Kid'. In their minds he was indivisible from Rowdy. People often made the mistake of thinking Clint was the characters he played.

Charles Marquis Warren used to say privately that Clint reminded him of his younger brother, who had been killed in action in Italy during World War II. Both were tall and handsome. Both had sun-streaked hair. Both were shy. Clint even pronounced 'quarter' as 'korter', just like Warren's brother had. 'Even Clint does not know this,' explained Lindy Warren, the widow of *Rawhide*'s creator. 'I doubt if Charles mentioned it to anybody outside the family. He told the story to me only a couple times over the years, since any reference to his brother made him very emotional.'

Hilda Bohem, the widow of story editor Endre Bohem, agreed Clint's boyishness was crucial to his casting. 'They hired Clint because he had such a wonderful smile. It's sort of ironic when you realize that he built his movie career on never smiling at all. In those days he just had this delicious, boyish grin, and it made you feel good just to look at it.'

Endre Bohem and Paul Brinegar, who played Wishbone, adopted less of an older-brother and more of a fatherly attitude towards the actor playing Rowdy. 'You felt that Clint sort of needed a protector,' explained Hilda Bohem. 'Endre fathered him. Between Endre and Paul Brinegar especially, Clint was sort of looked after.'

The 'kid-brother feeling' was built into Rowdy's characterization. From the first segments, Rowdy was the callow, hotheaded one – 'new as they come, but he's got the makings', in Wishbone's words. Brash with gunplay, tongue-tied with women, always deferential to 'Mr Favor'. That too was a Charles Marquis Warren touch; close friends called him 'Bill' but the producer insisted on being addressed by cast and crew as 'Mr Warren'.

The character of Gil Favor would ossify while Rowdy grew with the show. Partly it was more fun to write for 'the Kid'. 'I kind of fell in love with [Clint's] character and made it mine,' explained John Dunkel, who wrote seven episodes for the debut season and then continued writing for the series throughout its entire run, one of the few original scenarists to do so. 'I wrote an awful lot of things that were really slanted entirely toward him. Rowdy started out as a supposedly young kid and really developed as a character, and that was partly because of Clint's strengths as an actor.'

Partly it was because Eric Fleming had debits. He was a torturous actor: all slow burns and rolling eyebrows. 'Fleming was stiff,' noted writer Charles Larson. 'We were always told not to make the speeches in his scenes with other people too long. We had to write in short breaks in the other person's speech so Fleming would have a line. If he just had to stand there and react, he felt jumpy. He didn't know what to do.'

Personally, Fleming was also problematic. Later, Charles Marquis

Warren made no bones about describing the actor as 'a miserable human being' – not only a lousy performer, but a colossal egotist.

Others, more sympathetically, saw Fleming as a gentle, troubled soul with mixed feelings about being stuck playing the same part over and over on television. It was Fleming who was the genuine loner. From a broken home, he had not seen his father since he was a boy, when his parents divorced. As a young man, an accident had caused damage to his face; the reconstruction gave him a look of moulded plastic. He had odd habits, like eschewing hard-soled shoes and walking around in his bare feet.

Vain as well as insecure, genuinely quirky, Fleming managed to endear himself to friends, but he lorded it over most people. On the *Rawhide* set, Clint was the democratic one who hung out and made pleasant with people, while Fleming tended to disappear into the solitude of his trailer.

When Charles Marquis Warren quit, or was fired, after *Rawhide*'s first season – he was a martinet with the tendency to burn his bridges – the tilt in favour of Rowdy was already underway. The torch of producer was passed to Endre Bohem, who was second to no one in his detestation of Fleming, and the second season launched with 'The Incident of the Dead', where for the first time Clint delivered the opening soliloquy. 'I'm Rowdy Yates, ramrod of this outfit . . .'

That episode was Rowdy's 'strongest showcase on the series to date', according to Hank Grant of the *Hollywood Reporter*. Wrote Grant, one of those film industry columnists who only spoke well of Clint in print, into the 1990s: 'He [Clint] did acquit himself ably, appearing as he did in practically every scene in the hour.'

Although Gil Favor had started out as the more admirable figure, Solomon-like in his wisdom, increasingly on the show he revealed a monotonous disposition 'like ten miles of bad trail', in Rowdy's words. More and more it would be okay if the pigheaded Mr Favor disappeared for the entire episode – the trail boss, someone would casually mention, was off riding ahead on a vague errand. Endre Bohem had to plan instalments like 'Incident of Dragoon Crossing' in the third season, with two versions of the script: one with Gil Favor absented from the plot, and another with the character making a cameo appearance in the opening 'frame', before being whisked off-stage with a somewhat absurd manifestation of 'brain fever'. The end of the segment then would be an inside joke, Mr Favor returning to the trail drive after all manner of events and asking, 'Anything special happen while I was gone?'

Eric Fleming, who felt the programme was beneath his talent, was increasingly temperamental, increasingly happy to be eased out of plotlines. 'He was perfectly willing to take time off,' said Paul Brinegar. 'He was glad when he was written down in an episode.' Clint was glad to fill in. Fleming remained the star; he got the bulk of the fan mail. But Clint rose in people's estimation.

It is somehow characteristic of Clint's lucky life story that, except for that first fistfight, nobody remembers him forcing this dynamic, whereby gradually he would eclipse Eric Fleming. Favourable things just sort of happened to Clint. He had fate on his side, along with those seeming all-American qualities that enabled people to view him, in person or on the small screen, as a boy-next-door, a wished-for son, or 'the Kid'.

It was true that there was plenty of Clint in the raw, sweet, underachieving Rowdy, but also true that the actor playing the role turned thirty years old in 1960. Rowdy was too young, too cloddish for Clint to feel too comfortable with the part. 'The Idiot of the Plains' is how he referred to him in later years. He especially didn't like the Dirty Harry type name, which mocked his character's toughness. Although boyishness was a key element in his casting, he disliked the juvenile overtones. Clint felt he was more intricate than Rowdy, according to Paul Brinegar. 'Here Clint was in his twenties, playing a teenage type – he was very unhappy with that,' said Brinegar.

Clint may not have been college-educated. Maybe he didn't speak any language other than English, had never travelled outside the continent, didn't read that many books. But the actor wasn't really tongue-tied around women and he did have a cold, tough streak. And if he wasn't book-smart, Clint was as shrewd-minded as they come, even if it took confidence, success and fame for that shrewdness to manifest itself.

One of Clint's far-sighted shrewdnesses was the team of management experts he began to assemble, from the earliest days of *Rawhide*. As important to his career as any acting mentor or director, they would lay the foundations for his long-term security.

In the late 1950s, when Clint sorely needed representation, he couldn't seem to find the right talent agent. Having learned *not* to rely on one, he dispensed with an agent altogether, soon after landing the *Rawhide* series. Bill Shiffrin, who had made the TV deal, lasted only a short while, then he was jettisoned. Shiffrin was followed by Lester Salkow, another agent with ties to Universal, who represented Clint from 1961 to 1963.

By then, with *Rawhide* an acknowledged hit, the real bargaining power had shifted to Irving Leonard and Frank Wells, who was Leonard's as well as Clint's attorney. A young lawyer, Clint's age, Wells had inherited the actor's portfolio at Gang, Tyre & Brown. Unlike Clint, Wells was well educated, a Stanford graduate and Rhodes scholar. Also unlike Clint, he was a Democrat. Like Clint, however, he was from the WASP establishment, an avid athlete, passionate about tennis, skiing and mountain-climbing. To some, Wells even evoked Clint physically – tall, lean, handsome, chiselled features.

During the ebb and flow of agents, Leonard and Wells took over the negotiating of Clint's contracts. Together they pioneered unique clauses, including structuring Clint's earnings to avoid paying undue taxes. Some of his salary was deferred; the *Rawhide* paycheques from CBS would be guaranteed for years into the future.

At first the actor earned roughly $750 per episode, excellent money in those days, although it was a toss-up over who was more reluctant to spend any of it: Clint or Irving Leonard. Leonard had backed Clint and carried him with small loans and advances in bleak times. Not only for this reason, Clint believed wholeheartedly in his business manager, whom he referred to as a second father. Leonard was someone in the Eastwood family tradition who stressed savings, prudent investment and long-range consolidation. He specialized in creating trust and pension funds for his clients. And above all, Leonard was wily about devising imaginative contract perks and bonuses – the per diems and extras that would increasingly be seen by Clint as indispensable icing on the cake.

Leonard's clients were expected to turn over their entire salary cheques to him and then let him handle one hundred per cent of their business transactions. Notoriously frugal, he then doled out personal allowances to clients that were strictly enforced. Clint, whose thriftiness had been legendary among his friends dating back to high school, would grow only more thrifty as time went by. And he loved the fact that Leonard was a pit bull about money, more of a tightwad than him.

In those days there was still some question as to who was the boss of his money, but Clint liked mother hens who fussed over the details of something for him. On any special expense or unbudgeted purchase he was expected to consult Leonard. The actor would loyally phone his business manager to propose, for example, trading in one of his cars for a new one – and what model. Clint was crazy about cars, and once he became a fixture on television the vehicles he owned began to add up. The fanciest of them stayed out of view; for interviewers and public occasions Clint affected déclassé trucks and jeeps, but even these vehicles were generally outfitted with all the expensive and up-to-date accoutrements, with, as director Ted Post pointed out in an interview, 'everything you could possibly imagine'.

One side effect of Leonard's growing authority was that Maggie sacrificed power in the marriage. She had always done the finances. Now, Leonard usurped that function entirely. Clint and Leonard had a 'good cop–bad cop' routine going with the family purse strings: Maggie had to twist Clint's arm to get money out of him. Now Clint could use Leonard, when he felt like it, to turn Maggie down. And among Leonard's special services, sources say, were the double set of books he kept for the actor, so that Maggie wouldn't spot any of his periodic trinkets for girlfriends.

Clint and Maggie continued to live inexpensively, more inexpensively than his salary and fame warranted. They left the Villa Sands and bought a home in Sherman Oaks off Beverly Glen. But it was only a modest, hillside ranch house, albeit with an extra room, a small swimming pool and a scenic outlook. The house had a peculiar non-personality – as one journalist visitor reported, it was 'bereft of all the usual untidy impedimenta of everyday living, stripped to bare essentials as one would strip a race car' – gradually remedied when Maggie quit work and applied her taste to interiors. Increasingly, her art, her touches and preferences would decorate the household. One of her fortes was dark, moody portraits. People speculate that the production 'look' of Clint's later films was influenced by the visual style of Maggie's paintings.

The Eastwoods thought of the Sherman Oaks place as their

'Hollywood house'. Weekends, they house-hunted for something more permanent up in Monterey County. Land and houses were safe investments from Clint's point of view. Irving Leonard wasn't so sure. Clint always bought more land than was reported, and often the lots went under the name of other people or paper corporations. Early in the 1960s the actor was quietly buying up Monterey County parcels. One of his first purchases was the 279-acre Mal Paso property, located along Highway 1 south of the Carmel Highlands near Garapata.

Leonard's clients included many other top television names of the Sixties. The lead horse in his stable, and a silent investor in his banks and orange grove developments, was *Maverick* star James Garner. Others included Roger (*77 Sunset Strip*) Smith, Van (*Green Hornet*) Williams, George (*Route 66*) Maharis, and Roger (*Maverick*) Moore. Several *Rawhide* regulars – including Eric Fleming and director Ted Post – would also wind up under Leonard's management, sometimes at Clint's behest.

It was a small world, a pocket of Hollywood, the TV screen elite. Especially with the film industry suffering losses and a leadership vacuum at the major studios, small-tube stars reigned supreme. Irving Leonard's extended family all knew each other, worked with each other, partied at the same places, co-invested in the same properties and businesses.

'You have to keep selling yourself,' Clint attested in one of his earliest published interviews, from 1959. 'You have to run around peddling a commodity that is you. You have to believe in yourself the same way a salesman believes in a vacuum cleaner. It's hard, but if you don't, nobody else will recognize what you're worth. Humility in Hollywood is something you can afford only when you're a star'.

Good publicity was as critical as good financial and legal counsel, although Clint, even after finding his niche as Rowdy, was very Clint-like about publicity: strangely diffident about self-promotion, while at the same time highly aware and involved.

Throughout the run of *Rawhide*, he actually had two publicity representatives: a CBS staff member who cranked out the 'canned' articles about Clint, highlighting the Depression era Oakland upbringing, the all-American high school days, the Fort Ord plane crash; and, on retainer, the husband and wife duo of Paul and Ruth Marsh.

The Marshes did yeoman work on his behalf. Ruth Marsh, who had signed Clint, had an 'older-sister' feeling about him. She found Clint handsome and magnetic and thought he had a big future, even when he was a struggling nobody.

It was hard to get the press interested in writing about a television actor, but Clint didn't 'sit' on the Marshes, demanding coverage. He didn't particularly read or critique the articles about himself. Still, Ruth Marsh thought it was important to keep his name before the public, and she pushed him; she was one of those people who worked harder, were more ambitious on his behalf, than he appeared to be for himself.

The Marshes prided themselves on their constructive relationships with the local, Los Angeles-based columnists, with the fan magazines, and with people who toiled primarily for the trade papers. They were on positive terms with Hedda Hopper and Louella Parsons, the two queens of show business gossip who were happy to drop Clint's name into their nationally syndicated columns. They were close friends with James Bacon of the Associated Press, Vernon Scott of United Press International, Hank Grant at the *Hollywood Reporter*, Army Archerd at *Variety*, and Bill Schallert and Cecil Smith at the *Los Angeles Times*, all of whom met Clint and who could be counted on to carry items about him. The world of critics and journalists who covered the Hollywood scene was a small one, then as now, and these were important relationships at the time. Thirty years later they were still important relationships: Scott, Grant and Archerd, particularly, were still at their key posts in the 1990s, their 'mentions' picked up and recycled by countless other entertainment reporters.

The same boyishness that worked for Clint as Rowdy usually conquered the press. Clint knew well his country-boy charm, and he played that tune for all it was worth. The shrewder he became in his life and career, the more country-boy he acted sometimes. Years later, he was capable of giving the wink to barroom buddies, before heading off to interviews: 'I'm going to give them a little of my Gary Cooper . . .'

Clint was perfectly at ease and fluent during interviews, said Ruth Marsh. He knew when and how to turn on the warmth and humour. Journalists felt an intimacy with him.

Local 'breaks' were one thing, national 'breaks' were harder to come by. Years later, when Clint received his first retrospective at the Museum of Modern Art in New York City, he appraised the honour thus: 'It wasn't one of those promotional things. No campaigns, no ads, no fake gold medals.' But it *was* a campaign: a slow, lifelong one, and if the Marshes couldn't land an important magazine cover, it wasn't for lack of trying.

One of the few venues the Marshes could count on was *TV Guide*, which comprehensively covered prime-time television programming, and therefore had a vested interest in reporting on the popular new series of *Rawhide*. Clint's first exposure in that venerable weekly magazine came in August 1959, before the second season.

There was Clint stripped to gymwear, and photographed doing push-ups on lawn furniture. He advised readers to keep in shape by doing 'push-ups during the commercials' of *Rawhide*. He expounded on physical fitness, warned against carbohydrates ('especially rich desserts'), advised proper rest, an optimistic outlook, plenty of fruit, raw vegetables and vitamins, skipping beverages loaded with sugar, avoiding alcohol in excess, and 'most important, see your doctor for a physical check-up'.

Clint told *TV Guide* he kept in tip-top shape by working out with a friend on Saturday mornings along the Los Angeles River. 'We run as hard as we can for a hundred yards, then walk for a hundred, then trot for a while, then walk again.' Clint was in such good condition, *TV Guide* noted, 'he could make a living as a stunt man if necessary'.

When, along with Eric Fleming, Clint made the cover of the same magazine in 1961, the inside, full-page photograph showed Clint limbering up on the *Rawhide* set by doing a handstand with his shirt off. Clint liked these shirt-off angles, according to the Marshes, which is one of the reasons why they developed into a staple of his coverage. Frankly, the Marshes found it hard to come up with other angles. Clint didn't have any fascinating hobbies, for example. And each story couldn't be about Clint Eastwood the budding star, when he really didn't seem to be budding outside TV.

They fibbed now and then, circulating items about how Clint was 'in demand' for such and such a film. In reality, Clint wasn't in demand – wasn't getting phone calls for major projects. So it was partly by default that Clint's publicity focused on his physical prowess; partly by default, too, that journalists were invited to write about his happy home life.

Fan magazines visited the couple at their Sherman Oaks house, and the happy-marriage articles began to stack up. There were photo lay-outs of the picture-perfect couple, Clint and Maggie, both svelte in swimming suits, her cutting his lank hair or helping him learn his *Rawhide* lines. 'With *Rawhide*, everything changed,' reflected Maggie in one interview years later. 'Before we knew it we had some money, a house with a pool, and were forever posing for pictures as Holly-wood's latest young and exciting couple.'

The 'happy home life' publicity had a subtle loophole: Clint, in interviews, liked to stress his penchant for privacy and his deep need to spend time alone. This may have been intended for the general public, but it also washed over his marriage with convincing effect: Maggie wanted to believe that her husband 'just needed to be alone', even if, in reality, Clint was incessantly out and about with other women.

His buddies certainly knew about the other women because he con-tinued to use their houses for his 'nooners', which is how some of them referred to Clint's midday rendezvous. His publicists also knew, ironically, and wrung their hands over it. And even some journalists knew or suspected the truth about the marriage.

Of course many of the women Clint was involved with also knew he was married. But Clint sometimes took that particular morsel of information for granted. Unlike the 1950s, he no longer hastened to tell women that he was happily married. 'He didn't *act* married,' said one woman, who dated him in the 1960s, 'I'll tell you that.'

Another woman, after club-hopping for a few months with Clint, was invited to his house for the first time. She went, thinking she would be attending a soirée. The woman who answered the door astonished her, introducing herself as Clint's wife and exclaiming, 'I've been hearing all about you for weeks, and finally I get to meet you!'

Having never heard of Mrs Clint Eastwood, the woman nearly keeled over. She went through the whole evening with her heart pounding in her ears. Later that night, after she went home, Clint turned up at her place only to find the door locked. When she wouldn't answer the door, Clint kicked it in. When he asked her what was the big problem, she said he had never told her that he was married. 'What?' replied a furious and seemingly genuinely amazed Clint. 'Don't you read the fan magazines?'

* * *

It took only three weeks in 1959 for *Rawhide* to reach the Top 20, according to the national ratings system long administered by the Nielsen organization. In May, CBS made an intelligent move, rescheduling the Friday night show so that it aired a half-hour earlier, from 7:30 to 8:30 p.m, thereby guaranteeing the family audience that would grow up watching Clint. There the series was firmly anchored for the next four years, up to and including the 1962–3 season. For several years *Rawhide* would hover high in the ratings, although it peaked at No. 6 during the October 1960–April 1961 tracking period.

The *Rawhide* years were undoubtedly the most gruelling time of Clint's life. At first, from late July until April, they filmed six days a week for an average of twelve hours a day. The cast members were all grateful when, after the show became entrenched, Eric Fleming made the demand to knock off at 6 p.m., and they could all do likewise.

It wasn't log-lifting or labouring at a steel furnace. Much of the day was spent resting between set-ups, waiting for the camera and lighting. But for Clint, it was vital seasoning. If Fort Ord finished off high school, and Universal was the college from which he never quite graduated, *Rawhide* provided Clint with an honorary degree. And it gave him a permanent feeling of ease in a Western.

The series was not only extremely popular but well respected. It never achieved Emmy stature – it was never even nominated – but four times *Rawhide* won the American Heritage Award as the Best Western on television, and several times the Writers' and Directors' Guilds found individual episodes worthy of best nominations.*

In peak form, the series was brutal and naturalistic. Its situations were sometimes apocalyptic: parched plains, anthrax, gypsy curses, steers with the word 'Murder' carved into their hide. The historical sidelights educated. The moralizing was on target. The cast clicked.

More often, the bulk of the episodes were contrived and preposterous, hardly television's best, then or in retrospect. The stories veered away from genuine tragedy, and the comedy was predictably mild, silly. The directors ran the gamut. One of them worked so fast they nicknamed him 'Cut–Good–Print', or CGP for short. The job of the

---

* Clint had his only brush with an Emmy in 1973, when he appeared as one of the guests on *The Merv Griffin Show*, and that episode of the talk show was nominated as 'best' in its category.

Rawhide director was, admittedly, 'to convert shit into ice cream', in Ted Post's words.

Good or bad episode, Clint's presence was a dependable one. Rewatching the series nowadays, one is struck by the fact that Rowdy – Wishbone too – were the real backbone of the series and the most ingratiating actors in their roles.

By degrees the ramrod revealed his complexities. Rawdy took to calling Mr Favor by the less obsequious and sometimes half sarcastic 'Boss'. Episodes revealed that he had spent time in a Yankee prison, and that his sympathies still lay with the Rebels – an idea Clint would carry over into films. Although Rowdy never claimed 'a real, Sunday kind of girl', he flirted with a few of the guest stars and more than once got embroiled in heavy romance (not for the first time, however, until episode thirty-nine of the second season).

Clint started out in the series almost mannequin-like, swively in his movements, awkward in his speech. The scripts came up with endless reasons for him to whip off his shirt and display his rippling physique. Clint had as many stock gestures as Eric Fleming, and was forever rubbing his nose and scratching his cheek, or combing fingers through tousled hair while preparing to launch into dialogue.

More than a few people thought laidback Clint just didn't work hard enough. That he coasted on his looks, was resistant to emotional demands. Directors such as Gene Fowler Jr said outright that Clint was 'lackadaisical' in his attitude. Tommy Carr, one of the series' most prolific helmsmen, echoed that with his remark that Clint was 'lazy'. The laziness, said Carr, went beyond Clint's attitude. 'He always cost you a morning,' said Carr in one published interview. 'I never started a day with Clint Eastwood in the first scene, because you knew he was gonna be late, at least a half hour or an hour.'

Or he might cost an afternoon. Karen Sharpe, an actress who appeared in two or three *Rawhide* segments, thought Clint's womanizing might explain why certain people felt he was 'lazy' in his professionalism. Ironically, considering his physical-fitness spiels, Clint's energy tended to flag after lunch, according to Sharpe's observation. She presumed that Clint's lunchtime disappearances into his trailer with a regular girlfriend had something to do with his extreme nonchalance on the set. It was nonchalance that, sometimes, translated into downright sleepiness.

'She [his girlfriend] had some kind of job that made it look like she had to be there every other day,' said Sharpe. 'It didn't seem to me that she had any job in particular other than being with him at lunch. They would have lunch and then I guess go make love, and then he'd be too tired to do the scenes in the afternoon. That's how I interpreted why we almost had to coax him out of his chair sometimes, to play scenes.'

In one instance, Clint even admitted to Sharpe that he was too darn weary to bother to work on improving a scene. The actress had got into an argument with one of the *Rawhide* directors, disagreeing vehemently with him about the interpretation of her character. Clint, standing by, said nothing, and she lost the argument. Later a sheepish Clint sidled up to her. 'I think you were right,' Clint admitted. 'If I wasn't so tired, I probably would have stood up for you, because I like your ideas very much.'

But series work could be a grind, and other people believe that the best performance of Clint's life may have been as the constantly evolving Rowdy. Ted Post, one of Clint's most empathetic directors on the series, disagreed that the actor was lazy, at least on those frequent occasions – more than two dozen episodes – when Post guided him. 'At that time he was highly intelligent, very sensitive', said Post. 'He listened. I liked him very much. I really loved him. He, to me, was a young man truly struggling to master the craft of acting, trying hard to understand it'.

A veteran of live television, Post had forged his reputation doing *Schlitz Playhouse, Studio One* and *Ford Theater* shows in the early 1950s, before embracing Westerns with work for *The Zane Grey Theater, Gunsmoke* and *Wagon Train.* Post was another of those intense, Method-trained East Coast types that Clint had a tendency to cling to, professionally. Since Post was also a longtime acting teacher, he and Clint often talked seriously about acting and how to 'attack' difficult scenes.

Clint was proud of his training, recalled Post, often citing Jack Kosslyn as his mentor. When Clint paid Paul Brinegar a compliment one day, it was to say that Kosslyn thought Brinegar the most truthful actor on the series. The maxim of Kosslyn's Clint relished quoting was his tabula rasa philosophy. 'Don't just do something, *stand* there,' Clint'd say, then after a pause: 'Gary Cooper wasn't afraid to do nothing.'

Clint's affected style became so 'non-actorish' that at times it even annoyed fellow cast members and faithful friends like Brinegar. 'I never expected him [Clint] to be as big as he is,' noted Brinegar. 'I always felt that he underplayed too much. There is such a thing as being "too strong", but he certainly never was that in *Rawhide*.'

By degrees the glib self-assurance Clint had always evinced off camera began to manifest itself on screen. It was on *Rawhide* that the actor first introduced and began to perfect the slouched stance, the slow burn, the half-feral smile and – in moments of crisis – the vein that bulged like a continental divide in the middle of his forehead. As Rowdy's participation in plots grew and varied, Clint began to demonstrate surprising authority, precision, mocking humour and emotional nuance.

Rowdy could be fiery and righteous in a segment like 'Incident of the 100 Amulets', in which he fought off a town mob. He could be sensitive and fatherly, helping a little boy to reunite with his long-lost father, in 'Incident of the Night Visitor'. He could fake a pretty believable drunk scene in 'Incident on the Road to Yesterday'. He could get the solo spotlight as a hunted man in 'Incident of the Running Man' and turn the episode into a virtual mini-film starring himself – with nary a sighting of Mr Favor, Wishbone, or the thundering herd.

Rowdy was hardly loquacious, but not really terse. In an episode like 'Incident of the Promised Land', which was directed by Ted Post, Clint – wounded and stripped to the waist – could deliver a moving monologue about the hardships of frontier life.

This is all hindsight perspective: Clint didn't get noticed much as an actor at the time. Publicist Ruth Marsh witnessed Clint's performance in one of the better-than-average episodes and complimented her client. 'I didn't know you had it in you,' she told Clint. She never forgot his almost outraged response. 'I've got a lot *more* inside of me!'

A young man struggling to master – not just ramrodding, but the craft of acting – made for some memorable television. Although Eric Fleming's fan mail never flagged, Clint's picked up, especially from teenage girls watching *Rawhide* in its early time slot. Most of Clint's subsequent roles would be variations on the two most famous: the Stranger With No Name and Dirty Harry. Rowdy was every bit as much of an accomplishment.

* * *

Oh, and somewhere along the line, Rowdy picked up a guitar and strummed and sang 'A Drover's Life' to relieve plot tedium. Then, in episode 105, 'Incident of the Pitchwagon', he stood on a saloon stage and softly sang 'Beyond the Sun' in a low throb which drew the rapt gazes of men in the audience and had the ladies squealing.

Thus Clint launched his musical career. People who have extolled Clint's predilection for jazz usually ignore the less adventurous half of his split musical personality, as a country-and-western enthusiast. If jazz appealed to the frustrated musician in him, country appealed more to the frustrated vocalist. Clint was quite capable, when having had too much to drink, of climbing up on the stage of the Palomino Club and duetting with Sheb Wooley on 'The Purple People Eater'. He wasn't earthshaking as a singer, but in the right context he was moderately effective.

The actor had learned from Universal the added value of musicianship, and he probably saw singing as corporate diversification. Young, hunky stars were half-expected to crash the Top Ten charts in the late 1950s and early 1960s, and fresh from his singing debut on *Rawhide* Clint would go into a recording studio and cut his first album, on the Cameo label, in late 1959. It was called *Cowboy Favorites*.

He had a tour to plug the album, and advice from record promotion experts in New York. They wanted to change his look so that he resembled either 'a juvenile delinquent or better yet, way far out, with the short-jacketed continental suits with no pockets and skin-tight pants'. He declined the advice, and the pants that 'weren't pants. They were leotards.' As he later told Associated Press columnist James Bacon, 'I refused to believe that I had to look like a fop in order to sell records.'

The song list included one or two classics – a Bob Wills composition ('San Antonio Rose') and Cole Porter's 'Don't Fence Me In' – as well as two Sheb Wooleys. Although professionally crafted, Clint's delivery was whispery, and in spite of the publicity tour – his first nationally – the LP didn't generate enough sales to materialize on Billboard's Hot 100.

Over the course of the 1960s sporadic attempts would be made to revive Clint's musical career, with occasional singles keyed to *Rawhide*'s popularity (including the ballad 'For All We Know' in 1961 and a signature tune called 'Rowdy' in 1963). Cameo producer Kal Mann attended one recording session in 1963, where Clint taped a selection for the compilation album *All the Hits with All the Stars, Vol. 4.* Afterwards Mann went up to the actor and told him, frankly, he would never make it big as a singer.

'I know,' said Clint with a smile. 'But I'm going to make it big *somehow.*'

It was typical of Clint that even while he hated to be too closely identified with the character of Rowdy he might be ranked first among the *Rawhide* cast in maximizing opportunity out of show-related appearances. Musical interludes spiced up the Rowdy-and-Wishbone act that Clint and Paul Brinegar – sometimes joined by Sheb Wooley – put together for the off season, late spring to early summer, touring rodeos, state fairs and festivals. Their full-page advertisement in the 1962 *Amusement Business Cavalcade of Fairs* offered them 'available individually – as a duo or group'. The festival circuit was surprisingly remunerative – they could make as much as $15,000 for a single date. It was fun, it was positive publicity, Clint looked on it as extra money that he could tuck away, and it was another of his infinite excuses for travelling.

Brinegar was also a boon companion on the first trip Clint made out of the US, travelling to Japan in February and March of 1962. *Rawhide* ran on Japan's NET network from 1959 to 1965, and for a time the show, dubbed into Japanese ('I guess it is much better than my English,' Clint joked in interviews), was a number one sensation.

Eric Fleming also came along on the one-week trip, sponsored by Suntory Products. The trip made headlines in Japan, news akin to the Beatles coming to America. Up to eight thousand fans greeted the *Rawhide* trio at one airport. The three actors visited Hakone, Nara, Kyoto and Osaka, drawing crowds that were so huge, wherever they went, that public parades in their honour had to be cancelled at the request of the police.

Interviews and press receptions evidenced their disarming camaraderie:

'How good are you as gunmen?' one Japanese reporter asked.

ERIC FLEMING: Eastwood is really fast to pull his gun out of his holster, but his control is not so good. I am slower, but my control is perfect.

CLINT EASTWOOD (laughing): We use only imitation guns for the shooting. How can you say your control is perfect?!

PAUL BRINEGAR: When it comes to baking biscuits, I am *much* faster than the other two.

'Are you really good at handling cattle?' was another query.

FLEMING: Anybody can be good at it if they practise it for four years.
EASTWOOD: I would like to handle three thousand women instead of cattle.

Clint was always smiling and throwing kisses, reported the press, although he was not as popular as Eric Fleming in Japan, either. Fleming drew fans from all generations, according to Japanese accounts, while Clint was most popular with the teenage girls. Although the *Rawhide* actors were introduced to well-known Japanese actresses and brought together with Geisha girls, the press made a point of stating that rather than disappoint their fans they behaved throughout their trip like gentlemen.

At the end of the week of publicity events, Clint missed a day of activity because he came down with a cold. He stayed in his hotel, according to accounts, ordering presents for his mother and wife. His wife had become known to Japanese fans, and indeed the trip had been preceded by a broadcast interview with Clint and Maggie, from their home. Maggie, in a kimono, served green tea to the interviewer, and she and her husband spoke of their love for each other.

Why then didn't Maggie Eastwood accompany her husband on his journey to Japan? 'Because the company didn't invite her,' Clint told one Japanese interviewer. The actor was more blunt later with an American fan magazine. 'To tell you the truth,' Clint told *Photoplay*, 'I just didn't want her along. I felt like going myself.'

Eric Fleming, sitting with Clint during the Japanese interviews, chipped in with this observation. 'It is because,' Fleming said, 'he put more weight on his friends than his wife.'

Eric Fleming was right: Clint did spend a lot of time running around with buddies, hitting the bars or the golf courses or dropping in at other houses for impromptu parties.

For a time Clint, Bill Thompkins and George Fargo formed a Three Musketeers. Fargo was a friend of Robert Mitchum's, hoping to be a film producer one day, but meanwhile operating as a swimming pool contractor. Fritz Manes or Bob Donner sometimes augmented the trio. Chill Wills, whom Clint had met as the voice of Francis the Talking Mule, was an occasional add-on, and the Mitchum brothers – Bob and his younger brother John – also proved available for the occasional escapade.

Clint and Robert P. Eaton, Lana Turner's fifth husband, were running-around pals, and when Lana was off on location her house was open range. One tight-knit group of TV's leading men – mainly cowboy stars – hung out at another Hollywood house set aside for after-hours bacchanalia. It was dubbed 'The Playhouse', and although it was unclear who owned The Playhouse, a safe bet is that they all chipped in lease money. Clint was part of that crowd which included Brian Keith, Jim Arness and Chill Wills.

Everybody seemed to know a beautiful blonde torch singer by the name of Kitty Jones, and wherever she sang Clint and pals were sure to show up. Jones had come to Hollywood from Texas. When, in the early 1960s, she sang at an intimate club called Riggio's – next to Don the Beachcomber's on McCadden Place – people flocked around. Smoothly handsome Robert Lansing from TV's *Twelve O'Clock High* would be there, arm in arm with Jo Heims, the future writer of *Play Misty for Me*. Eric Fleming was then dating Kitty Jones's roommate, and they'd be off in a corner, whispering over drinks. Lansing enjoyed sitting in on drums, and Clint liked to get up and sing 'My Romance'.

'Clint liked to sing,' remembered one of the Riggio's regulars. 'Although he was really quite a bad singer, everybody loved it because here was the star of *Rawhide* getting up to do a song, and then all the other television stars used to sit in too.'

The various houses that Kitty Jones lived in became Clint's favourite hideouts, according to sources. A supremely good-natured hostess, Jones would throw almost nightly parties when she wasn't singing (often, 'rent parties'). She was known for cooking up chicken gizzards for all the hungry cowboy stars, and there was no better spot in Hollywood to meet any and every gorgeous actress or would-be actress, all of them her friends.

When, later, Bill Thompkins became one of Jones's endless succession of roommates, sharing her house on Cahuenga Boulevard, people knew the door swung open around the clock for Clint.

Cahuenga was close enough to CBS in Studio City, where *Rawhide* was then being shot – a convenient drive-by for Clint's 'nooners'.

One of Clint's wild flings was Jill Banner, a friend of Jones's. A chestnut-haired, blue-eyed looker, Banner, whose real name was Mary Kathryn Molumby, was a starlet born in the state of Washington, whose first role was in the low-budget horror comedy *Spider Baby*, made in 1964, which has a cult following nowadays. Banner palled around with actress Peggy Lipton, soon to make a splash in TV's *Mod Squad*, and assiduously collected star relationships – partying with Elvis Presley and Marlon Brando as well as Clint. She was only a teenager. One of Clint's friends warned him about her age, but he said, 'Oh, she's older than she looks.' Everybody knew that this actor, now well into his thirties, liked his girlfriends 'under twenty-one'.

Banner's career as an actress did not go very far, although in 1967 she had a showy part in *The President's Analyst*. (Some sources place her, later, among the unbilled cast of Clint's film, *The Beguiled*.) She was quoted by fan magazine correspondent Earl Leaf, in an article describing Kitty Jones's parties ('rap sessions, beer busts, fun and games'), affirming that 'nobody ever made me laugh as much as Clint did. He and his buddies were like a pack of wild college comedians, always horsing around, cracking jokes, telling risqué jokes, rough-housing and teasing the girls.'

Clint's and Elvis's circle overlapped with other ladies. One stripper girlfriend of Elvis was also a Clint conquest. Her height made her notorious: she was only 4'8". Another of his girlfriends, later on, handled reptiles while doing an erotic gyration on stage. 'Clint was into, once in a while, a stripper, a dancer, somebody in a show,' according to Kitty Jones's reminiscences in her unpublished book, *Who the Hell is Kitty Jones?*

'When he looked at you, his eyes seemed to drink you in,' noted one female acquaintance, who knew Clint in the 1960s. 'We called it "the Look". You can see how he became a director, because his eyes really *directed* you. You felt under a spell. I used to have a picture on my wall with him looking at me that way. But I can't tell you, honey, how many other women in this town have that same picture. After a while, I'm sorry to admit, you came to realize that Clint looks at all women that way.'

Some, like the diminutive stripper, were quick affairs; others were long-timers, accepting of his marriage, content to see Clint period-ically. One lover during the late 1950s and early 1960s was the former national swimming champion, Anita Lhoest, whose Hollywood career had peaked in 1950 with her appearance opposite Johnny Weissmuller and Buster Crabbe in the Jungle Jim movie, *Captive Girl*. Clint saw this blonde beauty when it happened to be convenient under the strict code of secrecy that the actor demanded and with the understanding that he was happily married.

However, Clint seemed to have little compunction about bringing some of the 'other women' into Maggie's proximity. After working behind the scenes on TV's *Batman* show, the 'alluringly seductive blonde', Jane Agee, had married actor James Brolin, whom Clint knew and with whom he was friendly. Jane Brolin worked hard to become one of Maggie's best friends, becoming a frequent guest at the Eastwood home. The two couples often went nightclubbing together. Mutual friends out on the town were made nervous by their suspicions that Clint had a sexual relationship with more than one woman at the table. 'We hated her [Brolin] because Maggie didn't realize she was sleeping with Clint too,' said one friend of both couples during the 1960s.

When Hollywood failed to satisfy – when Maggie's suspicions grew suffocating – there were distant getaways for Clint. *Rawhide* had its occasional 'location' forays. San Francisco was a major stopover, especi-ally after Kitty Jones moved there for two years in the mid-1960s; Clint could always claim to be 'visiting my family'. Golf and skiing afforded frequent buddy-trip excuses, while Las Vegas – Reno, too – were entire cities devoted to games and pleasure, where Clint loved to amuse himself.

In the fall, during the first years of *Rawhide*, Clint made an annual expedition to Las Vegas, along with a carful of buddies, appearing with other television cowboys at the National Fast Draw Tournament at the Hotel Sahara. Apart from public relations, this meant partying and connections in America's fun capital. Among celebrities whom Clint mingled and partied with there, were Frank Sinatra and his Rat Pack. Among the women Clint avidly romanced in Las Vegas was Keely Smith, the deadpan casino-lounge singer married for a time to jazzman Louis Prima. Clint pursued Smith during Quick-Draw Days – and then saw her furtively for years after.

*   *   *

Now that Maggie was no longer modelling, she played a lot of tennis. When she wasn't socializing with her friends, she was a stay-at-home in Sherman Oaks. The Eastwood house became her domain, and the guest list for the parties there usually reflected her preference among the married couples and agreed-upon friends – Sonia Chernus, Chuck Waldo, Bob Daley, the Marshes, Bob Donner and wife Cissy Wellman (William Wellman's daughter).

Although, to outsiders, Maggie seemed unawares – or willing to put up with Clint's philandering – she was suicidal at times, wondering where he was. She'd drive by houses, hoping to catch him. Close friends felt that Maggie was a doormat for Clint. She seemed dependent on his whim and afraid to speak to him about important issues, especially money.

The tension between them was now so palpable at times, that some people thought it verged on love–hate. 'While I was at their house, working on a scene or two to see what we could do on it,' said director Ted Post, 'she came in and said something and he blew. Very strong. I was embarrassed. My ears shut. I didn't want to hear it. I usually didn't see that in him. But he was a walking volcano who had his hand on the cover on top to hold it down. Sometimes it just oozed out between the fingers.'

The press was supposed to furnish alibis to the public, just as Clint's friends provided alibis to Maggie. And most journalists cooperated. Clint understood that the Hollywood press, especially in this polite era, liked to be gulled. One friend asked Clint how he dared to show up in clubs and restaurants with some of his girlfriends, without getting 'fingered' in a newspaper column. 'It's better to show up with them in public,' Clint explained, 'than to hide, as then people really think you're trying to hide something. This way I can always tell them "I'm casting", or that it's business.'

Sometimes the normally cooperative press balked. According to Ruth Marsh, pleading as well as pressure tactics were necessary to keep the lid on Clint's affairs and misbehaviour. On occasion the discrepancies between the image and the truth leaked into print.

Even the generally respectful *TV Guide* had to take note of the 'walking volcano' side of Clint's personality. In 1961, *TV Guide* had published an adoring cover story on Clint, describing him as an 'amiable young giant'. Only a year later, a less enamoured article in the same periodical would describe the *Rawhide* ramrod as having a 'cloak of boyish amiability' underneath which lay 'not so much a man as an explosion'.

The television magazine reported one incident, which occurred during Clint's trip to Indianapolis over Memorial Day 1961, when a woman walked over to the actor's table in a nightclub and 'in an apparent bid for attention' – no other explanation as to why – misbehaved. The woman dumped a drink over Clint's head, prompting him to pursue her out the door, picking up drinks and flinging them at her all the way to her car.

The press took note of Clint's rages, which could be triggered by almost anything. He liked things to go easy, look easy. That included marriage.

The 1962 *TV Guide* article was one of the first to take a closer look at the 'happy marriage' image and reassess the Eastwood union as a potential minefield, explaining that in Clint's world 'almost everything seems in some strange way expendable. This might almost be said to include his family. Clint's longtime press agent – a woman [Ruth Marsh] explains: "His wife, Maggie, is crazy about him. And he about her. But Clint is the kind who does what *he* wants when he wants to do it. *She* does the adjusting." '

Maggie's true goal – motherhood – seemed relegated to the back burner in these interviews. When Clint might become a father was a surprisingly open subject. 'I like women,' Clint told *TV Guide*, 'always have. Maggie? She's got a few marbles. Kids? We keep putting them off. I don't feel I have a duty and – well, I am not so egotistical as to think I have to have something in my image.'

At a time when Maggie was still trying desperately to become pregnant, however, other Clint girlfriends had more success. Only Clint's closest buddies knew about swimmer-actress Anita Lhoest, whose affair with the actor continued. In fact, according to her biographer, Lhoest at one point became pregnant with Clint's child, but went ahead and had an abortion without consulting him. She believed that Clint was firmly married and knew that parenthood was a burning issue between him and Maggie.

Clint's most intense relationship during this period was undoubtedly his romance with Roxanne Tunis. Tunis was an exotic-looking brunette from Pennsylvania who had studied dance with Martha Graham in

New York. A road show brought the dancer to Los Angeles, where she appeared among the chorus and as one of the crowd in major films, including George Cukor's *Let's Make Love* and Alfred Hitchcock's *The Birds*. She was also one of the dancers in *West Side Story*. But Tunis aspired to serious acting, and to billed roles. To this end, she became another student of Jack Kosslyn's.

A mutual friend, another dancer, introduced her to Clint, and after hitting it off and sleeping together one night, she and the *Rawhide* star forged a long-lasting bond. Besides being pretty and shapely, Tunis was a spiritual person and an early proponent of meditation with an unshakably serene outlook on life. Her personality had a soothing effect on Clint, and her apartment in Studio City became a repeated 'escape'.

Maggie might have spotted Tunis whenever she happened to visit the *Rawhide* set, since Clint helped arrange for his girlfriend a unique seasonal contract as a 'double', dancer and bit-part actress. Tunis was a dancehall girl in saloon scenes, and even a stand-in for short actors – Mickey Rooney, in one episode. She was on the show for five years, because Clint wanted her on the set, even when she wasn't scheduled for scenes.

All the better, say sources, for Tunis to nurture Clint through his periodic anxiety attack episodes. According to sympathetic friends of Tunis, lunchtimes, when they'd disappear into his trailer – people suspected they were making love – what she'd really be doing was massaging Clint's neck to relieve tensions, while rehearsing Rowdy's lines.

Some cast and crew members, knowing that Clint was married, were embarrassed that the actor felt obliged to parade Tunis in front of them. Others, however, grew comfortable with her constant presence, and felt sympathy with Clint. Clint's tenseness and 'anxiety attacks' were laid at Maggie's doorstep; Clint's marriage, scuttlebutt had it, was a strained and unhappy one.

Clint didn't mind giving off such hints. When, more than once, cast members kidded a sleepy-eyed Clint about having had 'a hard night in the sack with the old lady', meaning Maggie, he'd exclaim, 'Don't make me barf!' Although most of their life together was covert, Clint was not shy about advertising his affections for Tunis in restaurants and clubs. When it came to more public events, Clint had to veto her presence at his side. But then Eric Fleming, for one, was available to help out with the charade, and it was Mr Favor drafted to stand in for Rowdy as Tunis's date.

All during the Rowdy years, sources say, Clint went over to Tunis's house frequently after the day's work on *Rawhide*. They made love and then he was fed supper, before heading home.

Maggie has never commented publicly on Clint's extramarital relationships, the full extent of which did not begin to become known until after their divorce, in the mid-1980s. One of the few times Maggie alluded to the subject in print, she explained her attitude stoically. 'I was never very realistic about some things. I used to always hope for the best. I wanted to protect myself. I wondered about it but I didn't dwell on it because it would probably have driven me insane. I just preferred to hang in there . . .'

The people who have known Clint the longest debate amongst themselves whether he was always the same Clint, as his publicity emphasizes, or whether during this period, the years of *Rawhide* recognition and success, he began to change. Even those acquaintances who feel that he has been the same Clint since boyhood concede that he is a person with hidden dimensions and depths. The public knows the altogether relaxed and congenial Clint, but there is also the private, more complicated Clint. Besides offering sometimes stark contrast to the public image, the other Clint provides the underpinning for the cold, hard characters he often plays in films.

The Clint who has been endlessly promoted as being 'loyal to close friends' was especially helpful to aspiring actor-buddies during the initial years of *Rawhide*. He finally talked Bob Donner into taking a stab at acting; Donner enrolled in Jack Kosslyn's class, and then Clint arranged it so Donner would get his first job, a small part, on the 'Incident of the Running Man' episode of *Rawhide*, in 1961. Donner went on to have a substantial acting career, chiefly on television, as a semi-regular on *The Waltons* and *Mork & Mindy*. 'If ever anybody changed someone's life, Clint changed mine,' Donner says today, gratefully.

Bill Thompkins was another fortunate. After picking up work as Clint's stand-in on *Rawhide*, his frequent camera cutaways stretched into a regular gig. Thompkins became a continuing character, a drover dubbed 'Toothless'. (Thompkins had false teeth which he removed to play the part.) Most people agree that the former Seattle-area life-guard was probably Clint's best friend in the late 1950s and early 1960s.

But it might be said there sometimes seemed a pattern to whom Clint assisted and why. Bob Donner would act in only one Clint East-wood film, *High Plains Drifter*, before their paths separated. Mutual friends still wonder, in low tones, why Geoff Lewis got all the jokey parts later on that Donner could just as easily have managed. And Thompkins' adoration of Clint counted; once he became beholden to Clint for *Rawhide*, he quickly went from being a friend to a gofer, right down to schlepping Clint's luggage.

A fellow like Floyd Simmons, more in Clint's category in the looks and ambition department, couldn't hitch a ride. Simmons tried every means possible of getting Clint's attention for *Rawhide* parts, but received no encouragement. Clint didn't seem to hear his entreaties; Clint was always preoccupied with himself, his own status.

One day playing golf, Simmons was startled to hear Clint explain that he had to break off their game and make a call to his agent. 'You mean Bill?' asked Simmons, referring to Bill Shiffrin – the agent whom Simmons had recommended to Clint. 'Yeah, my agent,' responded Clint, not missing a beat. 'Suddenly, he was *his* agent, not our agent,' recalled Simmons. To Simmons, Clint had a tunnel vision that was focused narrowly on himself, and a stealthy way of expropriating things in his own name.

Already, by the third season of *Rawhide*, the Hollywood trade papers were reporting that Clint was bored with the series and anxious to break free of his Rowdy straitjacket.

'Calm on the outside and boiling on the inside,' is how Hank Grant described Clint in his 'On the Air' column in the July 1961 *Hollywood Reporter*. Clint claimed the network had reneged on its promise to let him pursue extracurricular acting. Grant relayed Clint's vow to walk off the series 'unless CBS makes good the promise they made when he signed on' to let him make appearances in other films and TV shows.

'I haven't been allowed to accept a single feature or TV guesting offer since I started the series,' Clint was quoted as claiming in the *Hollywood Reporter*. 'Maybe they really figure me as the sheepish, nice guy I portray in the series, but even a worm has to turn sometime. Believe me, I'm not bluffing. I'm prepared to go on suspension, which means I can't work here, but I've open feature offers in London and Rome that'll bring me more money in a year than the series has given me in three.'

Indeed he *was* bluffing, and the Hank Grant column was but a ploy to hike up his salary. Clint had no 'open feature offers', according to Ruth Marsh, nor did he particularly *want* any. He filled only a handful of 'guesting offers' on television, among which were two appearances as *himself*, Clint Eastwood, on *Stump the Stars* and *Mr Ed*.

The *Mr Ed* episode was more than the usual cameo. The script had Clint poking fun at himself as a new neighbour of Mr Ed's, who gets drafted into directing Wilbur (Alan Young) and his wife in a love scene for a community theatre production. 'Mr Ed Meets Clint Eastwood' was directed by Arthur Lubin, but the job was set up, according to Lubin, by Clint admirer Sonia Chernus, co-writer of the segment.

Indeed, Clint stayed pretty contented with *Rawhide*, until the 1963–4 season when the show slipped out of the Top 25. By then, producer Endre Bohem had been replaced by Vincent Fennelly, who had surrendered after a couple of years to a tag-team of producers handpicked by the network – Bernard Kowalski and Bruce Geller.

New regulars like Charles Gray had been introduced – lasting one season – to fill in for Eric Fleming's unpredictable absences. Novelty subjects had begun to dominate. The guest stars (the programmes biggest-budget item at $10,000 a shot) became more important. Established performers like Lon Chaney Jr, Mercedes McCambridge, George Brent, Mary Astor, Ralph Bellamy, Barbara Stanwyck, Ed Wynn, Eddie Bracken, Burgess Meredith and Dean Martin all joined the cattle drive at one time – sometimes more than once, no matter if anyone in the television audience happened to notice – giving illustrious example to the workaday cast.

'When the show was good, which it often was,' *TV Guide* would later analyse, 'it filled the screen with the look and feel of the life of a cowboy, depicting it not at all in sweetness and light, but in sweat and grime and the sight and sound of milling cows.' But *Rawhide* was not consistent, it lost focus, its freshness and popularity suffered.

Not only did Rowdy increasingly upstage Mr Favor, Clint's character had begun to borrow some of the trail boss's solemnity and tough veneer. The original balance between the two characters was upset. Rowdy may have developed into a more interesting character, but the totality of the show suffered. This is one lesson from *Rawhide* that Clint didn't learn: in his films, he would habitually draw attention to *his* character at the expense of co-stars.

A smell was in the air in late 1963 when the offer came through to Eric Fleming to star in an Italian-made Western called 'The Magnificent Stranger', to be filmed in remote Spain. But the money wasn't much, and Fleming had big eyes. He was determined to extract lavish concessions when his *Rawhide* contract came up in 1964. He intended to blaze his name in prestigious, big-budget Hollywood movies. He wasn't going to toil overseas in some nothing horse opera made during the off season.

Through Irving Leonard, Eric Fleming passed the offer on to Clint.

The story of how Clint ended up starring in the 'spaghetti Westerns', which transformed his career, has as many versions as other fateful events in his life.

Sergio Leone liked to be very specific about his casting acumen: the director said he had been urged by Claudia Sartori, a young woman working in the William Morris Agency in Rome, to watch episode ninety-one of *Rawhide*, 'Incident of the Black Sheep', which had been dubbed, for his benefit, into Italian. He was meant to concentrate on Eric Fleming. 'What fascinated me about Clint, above all, was his external appearance,' explained Leone. 'I noticed the lazy, laidback way he just came on and stole every single scene from Fleming. His laziness is what came over so clearly.'

Actually, the opportunity to star in 'The Magnificent Stranger' had already been rejected by James Coburn, Charles Bronson, Richard Harrison and Frank Wolfe – the latter two, Americans living in Rome with marquee value in Italy – as well as the ruggedly handsome star Leone probably courted most energetically, Rory Calhoun, with whom the director had worked on *The Colossus of Rhodes*, his first feature.

The Leone version of events is fishy for another reason. According to Ruth Marsh, it was she, and not the William Morris Agency, who brought up Clint's name, mentioning the television actor to Filippo Fortini, an agent in Rome, while visiting Italy on a vacation. She knew Fortini, not an important agent but an honest and capable one, because he represented actor Philippe Hersent, the husband of writer Geneviève Hersent, who acted as the Italian intermediary of the Marsh Agency.

Ruth Marsh's sole motive was to provide the *Rawhide* star with an off-season job. She sympathized with Maggie, and knew that when Clint took off on his motorcycle with idle time his wife became desperately unhappy. Marsh believed that if Clint was busy in front of a camera, he was less likely to be partying or chasing a girl somewhere.

Fortini said that if Marsh could provide him with a reel from *Rawhide*, then he would take that reel to Jolly Film, which, in partnership with Munich and Madrid film companies, was backing the first production of a little-known director named Sergio Leone. Back in the US, Ruth Marsh and Maggie conspired to manoeuvre past Irving Leonard, who didn't want to pay for the 'duping' of a *Rawhide* reel, much less its overseas delivery. According to Marsh, Leonard thought Clint's fate was to be trapped on television, because of his limitations and his thin, papery voice.

The publicity agent and Clint's wife scraped the money together, and sent the reel to Fortini. He took it to Jolly Film, and Leone was inveigled to sit down and watch the reel. When the script of 'The Magnificent Stranger' arrived in America, however, the role *was* offered to the series lead, Eric Fleming. When Fleming said no, Irving Leonard forwarded the script to Clint. Clint's initial reaction was similar to Fleming's. Hell no, he was already in a Western. Clint would rather spend the off-months improving his golf game. Leonard urged him to at least give the Western script a read.

This was when Clint was again in the process of shuffling agents. Irving Leonard had quid pro quos with the William Morris Agency. Tall, pasty-faced Leonard ('Lennie') Hirshan, one of the rising lights of the agency, was encouraged to visit the *Rawhide* set and shake hands with Clint. Clint was urged to sign with the agency, even as Claudia Sartori in Rome coaxed Leone into watching the episode again – this time for Clint.

In America, about ten pages into reading the script, according to Clint, he recognized elements of Japanese director Akira Kurosawa's samurai film *Yojimbo*. Clint thought the dialogue was 'atrocious' but the storyline 'intelligently laid out' with distinctive humour. He learned that, in Italy, Sergio Leone was considered a promising talent. 'I was tired of playing the nice clean-cut cowboy in *Rawhide*,' Clint would say later on, with the advantage of 20–20 hindsight. 'I wanted something earthier.'

The script opinion of Maggie, the Berkeley English major who was rooting for her husband to take the offer, was a deciding factor: 'Clint says I'm good at spotting the woman's angle to a story, and I liked this one of the loner,' Maggie was quoted in one interview. 'Women want to be looked after and protected, and a man who can dominate the scene, handle himself against the odds, has instant appeal to women.'

Irving Leonard reminded Clint, 'You will have money and a vacation, all right?' It may have helped Clint to make up his mind that Roxanne Tunis had become pregnant, in the fall of 1963, and a prolonged absence from the US, at the very moment when Tunis was due to give birth to the child he had helped conceive, might be wise.

Along with Sandy Bresler from the William Morris Agency – who at that time also represented a young unknown named Jack Nicholson – Irving Leonard negotiated the terms. Filippo Fortini was cut out of the deal. History was rewritten so that the William Morris Agency would receive the credit. Clint's agreement called for $15,000, coach air fare for one and expenses for eleven weeks' work. The pay-out was less than the actor's annual TV salary, but even so, this job would add up to eternal gratitude to Eric Fleming and unswerving loyalty to the William Morris Agency.

Leone had never met Clint, nor did he speak to him directly prior to his arrival. Leone didn't even dare to meet the American at the Rome airport when Clint arrived the first week of May. Clint was met instead by Marsh Agency publicist Geneviève Hersent, a few Italian journalists, and Leone's assistants. 'I went to the airport with [assistant director] Mario Cavano to pick up Clint,' said dialogue director Tonino Valeri.* 'Sergio was too scared to come with us. Although he said the contrary, Sergio could not speak English at all . . . he didn't want to make a fool of himself.'

'I will never forget the first impression that Clint made on me when he got out of the plane,' added Valeri. 'He wore jeans and he was holding one of those old-fashioned cloth suitcases. He went straight

---

* Valeri would later direct another noteworthy 'spaghetti Western', *My Name is Nobody*.

to Mario Cavano, whom he mistook for Sergio. He was very embarrassed when we managed to tell him that none of us was Sergio.

'We brought him back to the hotel where he would be staying. When he met Sergio later that day, it was actually Clint who showed Sergio many of the Western items that he was later to wear in the film. Clint took out the following things from his suitcase: a poncho, a cowboy hat, a leather bracelet and the Indian leather cases with two serpents. Sergio liked them a lot and he decided to use them in the film.'

Leone's recollection of their first meeting was more flattering to himself: 'He [Clint] arrived, dressed with exactly the same bad taste as American students. I didn't care. It was his face and his way of walking that I was interested in. He didn't talk much, like in *Rawhide*. He simply said, "We are going to make a good Western together."'

The thirty-four-year-old television star would have his first European vacation while making his first starring movie. Clint thought 'The Magnificent Stranger' probably wouldn't amount to much, but he had managed to squirrel away enough money that if and when *Rawhide* was cancelled he was pretty sure he wouldn't ever have to work again.

Sergio Leone didn't bathe properly. He was maniacally cheap. He had gross appetites that turned him into a fat, truculent bear over time. He treated people terribly and had an ugliness in his psyche that was mirrored in his films. Yet most of the world's critics would agree that he was one of the cinema's visionary film-makers, in spite of the fact that his output over thirty years was limited to only a handful of titles.

In 1964, Leone was almost as unknown in Italy as in Hollywood. The son of a well-respected Italian director, he had worked obscurely as an assistant to Hollywood directors Raoul Walsh, William Wyler and Robert Aldrich on the Roman scenes of international co-productions. The foreigners seemed as fixated on gladiatorial epics as Leone, an Italian, was enamoured of the American genre of Westerns. 'While I organized chariot races, battles between triremes, and explosions on galleys,' mused Leone in one interview, 'I was silently dreaming about Nevada and New Mexico.'

After getting *The Colossus of Rhodes* under his belt, Leone set his sights on making a Western that would blend 'not only Carlo Goldoni [one of Italy's greatest writers of comedy, their equivalent of Molière], but the traditions of Sicilian puppet theatre, commedia dell'arte and the picaresque novel as well' to the 'dying American genre'.

He had met the scenarist Duccio Tessari during the making of *The Last Days of Pompeii*, which Leone co-wrote in 1959. One day three years later, Leone knocked on the door of Tessari's Rome apartment. 'What are you doing today?' Leone asked. 'Nothing,' said Tessari. So they went to see *Yojimbo*.

Although they weren't always candid about it, Leone and Tessari borrowed their basic storyline from the 1961 Japanese film. Leone even went so far as to write to Akira Kurosawa and ask for permission to adapt the script of *Yojimbo*, which Kurosawa had written in collaboration with Hideo Oguni and Ryuzo Kikushima. If the working title of Leone's proposed project hadn't alerted the Japanese film-maker ('The Magnificent Stranger' being an obvious play on *The Magnificent Seven*, the American Western derived from another well-known Kurosawa film) the letter certainly did.

Kurosawa asked for $10,000, and Leone might have paid, but Jolly Film withdrew the offer, thinking the sum too high. Nobody would ever see the picture outside of Italy anyway. 'Why do we have to spend $10,000 on Kurosawa while spending only $200,000 on the entire film?' the film's producers, Harry Colombo and George Papi, reasoned. Kurosawa would subsequently sue, and the resulting litigation would delay Clint's stardom in America. When the issue was finally settled, Kurosawa would receive *all* the Japanese profits from the Sergio Leone Film. And this was a country where Clint was *already* popular.

Although Leone never actually sat at the typewriter, he was nonetheless a splendid raconteur who acted out all the parts of a story, while his collaborators hashed out the fine points and inconsistencies. The morning's work would frequently start off, according to Tessari, with Leone exclaiming, 'Last night I dreamed three words. You must put this idea in the film . . .' Tessari would declare himself baffled. 'What kind of scene will this fit into?' 'That is not my problem,' the boss would announce imperiously. 'That is *your* problem.'

In their script of 'The Magnificent Stranger', a lone, expert gunfighter rides into a Mexican border town fought over by two greedy gangs. He takes money from both factions, and incites the rivalry between them. After much double-crossing, death-dealing and a climactic bloody showdown, only the mysterious stranger is left alive.

The director grandly visualized each sequence and even the pre-

Above: One of many schools he attended: Clint (front row, third from the right) poses for his class picture at the eminently proper Crocker Highlands. At far left, slightly behind the first row, sits Jackie Jensen, a future Most Valuable Player in major league baseball.

Below: Clint (back row, second from left) at a Red Cross lifeguard training session in Beaver Lake, Washington, probably in 1954. Same row, second from right, is his best friend Bill Thompkins, who followed Clint to Hollywood and appeared on *Rawhide*.

Left: Wedding Day:
Clint and Maggie, 1954.

Below: Salad days in the
1950s: this pool party is not
at Arch Drive but at a nearby
place. That's Clint (far left,
back to camera) talking to a
beautiful woman, and
Maggie (v-neck swimsuit,
seated centre) keeping an
over-the-shoulder eye on her
good-looking husband.
Good friends Bill
Thompkins, Robert Donner
and Bob Daley are among
the crowd.

Clint and Maggie, all smiles, on the beach at San Clemente.

Lazy days at the beach: Bill Thompkins, Robert Donner and Clint.

Arch Drive friends and neighbours: Maggie and Clint with fellow Universal contract players Floyd Simmons and Lili Kardell.

Director Arthur Lubin, Clint's booster and benefactor, clowns with Carol Channing on the set of *The First Travelling Saleslady*.

Donald O'Connor, a talking mule, and Clint in a typically miniscule role in *Francis in the Navy*, whose director, Arthur Lubin, was also Clint's agent.

Physical fitness was part of the regimen for contract players. Here Universal athletics instructor Frankie Van shows Clint and other 'New Talent' how to box.

Above: The Universal drama school had occasional guest visitors: Marlon Brando gave one highly publicised 'lecture'. Drama coach Jess Kimmel is next to Clint (centre), and the others assembled include Dani Crayne, Colleen Miller, John Saxon, Mamie Van Doren, David Janssen, Barbara Rush, Gia Scala, Leigh Snowden and Grant Williams.

Below: Another on-and-off girlfriend was former swimming champion Anita Lhoest.

Above: With the flea-budgeted Western *Ambush at Cimarron Pass*, Clint (fourth from right) felt he had hit rock-bottom.

Below: Along came producer Charles Marquis Warren (seen here with Clint and Eric Fleming) to pick a Rowdy for *Rawhide*. He chose Clint, and the rest is Hollywood history.

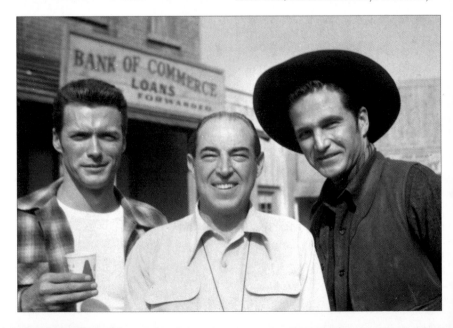

Right: When the dynamic between Mr Favor and Rowdy – Eric Fleming and Clint – shifted, the show's popularity began to suffer.

Below: Rowdy gets a dab of make-up on the set.

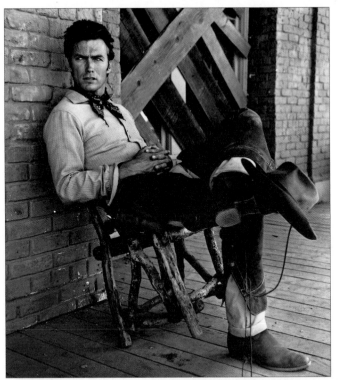

Left: From the beginning Clint thought of *Rawhide* as *his* show, and eventually it was. Floyd Simmons photographed his friend between takes one day, and captured a hint of the ambivalent and steely persona that would one day eclipse Rowdy.

Below: *Rawhide* was popular in Japan, which was Clint's first foreign conquest. He, Eric Fleming and Paul Brinegar made a publicity trip there in 1963. He sent this postcard to Maggie, who stayed behind.

ROWDY YATES (CLINT EASTWOOD)

GIL FAVOR (ERIC FLEMING)

RAWHIDE

★洋酒の寿屋 提供 TV映画・《ローハイド》

posterous ones would come alive when he acted them out. Luciano Vincenzoni, who succeeded Tessari as screenwriter of the second and third 'spaghetti Westerns', said that he never would have approved of the childish scene in *For a Few Dollars More* where the two bounty hunter rivals, Clint and Lee Van Cleef, dare each other to fight by scuffing each other's boots; except that, in person, Leone made him believe in it.

Both scenarists, Tessari and Vincenzoni, said most of the best ideas were Leone's. Leone was a rule-breaker. He wanted to push Western clichés beyond accepted limits. His bad guys were rotten to the core, but the heroes were also dark and unpredictable. The women were Madonnas or whores, mostly whores. It was a macho world. Everything revolved around greed. All of the violence was graphic in the extreme, almost cartoonish.

In his initial script Tessari had dubbed the mysterious stranger 'Ringo', a homage to John Wayne's character in John Ford's *Stagecoach*. Leone made Tessari delete the name (the character, who became popularly known as 'The Man With No Name', is referred to fleetingly as 'Joe', but only at the very end of the film.) 'Not a name,' Leone insisted, 'not a past, not a future, only the present.' The mysterious stranger wouldn't even shoot his gun like a Hollywood cowboy. 'Not to shoot fast – like a machine gun,' noted Tessari, 'that was also Sergio's. He would shoot *slow*.'

From the beginning, the 'look' of the mysterious stranger was crucial. It is said that when Leone finally settled on Clint, he announced, 'That face – with a cigar.' And a cowboy hat. 'The truth is,' Leone explained in one interview, 'that I needed a mask more than an actor, and Eastwood at that time had only two expressions: with or without a hat.'

Although Leone often claimed credit for Clint's costume – especially the Spanish poncho, about which there remains doubt – Clint was convincing when he said, on repeated occasions, that he had made a special trip to Mattson's, a sports shop up on Hollywood Boulevard, to purchase a pair of black Levi's – 'bleached them out, roughened them up' – and that he collected his boots and spurs, guns and holsters from the *Rawhide* stash. At Western Costume, he picked out a low-brimmed hat.

A curious thing about Clint's career is that his Western costuming has always been as striking as his dress for contemporary films has been nondescript. The actor's everyday garb (T-shirt, jeans) was as impersonal as it was casual. But Clint dressed in the world of his forefathers with more individuality. On *Rawhide*, Rowdy's get-up seemed moulded to his body: neckerchief and chaps, a perpetually sweat-stained chequered shirt and leather vest, a pale hat with a wide brim. The series costumer, Glenn Wright – he might have helped out with Clint's Italian ensemble – would become one of the few *Rawhide* personnel to go to work for Clint when the actor formed his own production company. Wright would contribute apt costuming for Clint's latter-day Western films, while he would always seem considerably hampered, in the Dirty Harry series and other Clint vehicles, by the actor's bland preferences in modern dress.

The script forced the cigar on Clint. The health-conscious actor wasn't a smoker, and on screen wasn't always credible as one. Clint hated the terrible cigar smell. But he acknowledged the value of cigars to the character's mystique, and ironically, cigars would be one of the things that Clint took away from his experience with Leone. Clint would end up carrying around cigars – or cigarettes – in a surprising number of his films. No matter if his characters rarely inhaled, cigars (like bottles of beer) were another one of those cosy props without which Clint felt incomplete.

All the better if the cigar provided a further rationale for the Man With No Name to be tightlipped. This was something about which Leone and Clint were apparently in accord, each for their own reasons. Right away in the US, once he accepted the role, Clint launched into pruning his dialogue, according to director Ted Post. On *Rawhide*, the cast had got into the habit of tinkering with their 'sides' when necessary, and this would become a mixed asset in Clint's career: the focus on his own scenes sometimes a virtue, even when the rest of the script needed work.

Clint, like many non-writers, didn't often start with the blank page. He needed someone else's work to attack, removing what he considered excess verbiage and adding Clint-touches: Clintisms. While paring things down is a time-honoured strategy in film-making, in Europe as in Hollywood, it might also be considered a defensive strategy for an actor such as Clint, insecure about loquacity or emotional revelation.

While Tessari insisted that Clint's editing was minimal – 'the final film was exactly one hundred per cent the same as the script; when I thought to ask him his opinion of the script, his answers were always "yes, no, maybe"' – Clint remembered differently that the original script had 'endless pages of dialogue' about the character's background.

'I wanted to play it with an economy of words and create this whole feeling through attitude and movement,' said Clint in retrospect. 'It was just the kind of character I had envisioned for a long time – keep to the mystery and allude to what happened in the past. It came about after the frustration of doing *Rawhide* for so long. I felt the less he said the stronger he became and the more he grew in the imagination of the audience.'

All the script issues were resolved by the time the first interiors were filmed at the Cinecittà studio, on the outskirts of Rome, and before the company left for Spain early in May. The communication between the director and his American star was, in the beginning, awkward. Only gradually did the relationship develop into trust and respect, and even then, 'more from Clint to Sergio, than from Sergio to Clint', in Vincenzoni's words.

Leone could only speak a couple of words of English, and as for Clint, he knew '*ciao*' and '*arrivederci*'. Leone's brother-in-law, who had been in the diplomatic corps in America, acted as translator, and a multilingual assistant accompanied Clint on location. Much of the time Leone had to make himself understood by mine and gestures, but everybody says the director was a remarkable mime. 'The funny thing was we had a translator on the set but Sergio spoke in Italian and Clint understood perfectly what Sergio said,' said Tonini Valeri. 'The translator translated but Clint understood *before* the translation. He understood perfectly because of the movement of Sergio's hands, of his face, and it was always very clear. There was no need to explain it in English.'

Unlike much of everything Clint had previously done, he would clutter his handsome visage with a grubby beard (evoking Toshiro Mifune in *Yojimbo*), an omnipresent cigar and a sloping cowboy hat. The actor would be grudging with the smile that had made Rowdy so winning on American television. Above all, for the first time Clint would play a character who was cold, fierce, morally ambiguous.

It was fate picking the perfect persona. 'His [Clint's] personality was very quiet and he was very, very intelligent,' said Luciano Vincenzoni. 'But Clint was cold personally. Although I know the stories that he is a warm person, he was always very cold. Sergio taught him coldness [on camera],' Vincenzoni continued. 'But it was easy. Clint understood immediately. He is exactly the mysterious guy with the cigarillo. In life.'

Sergio Leone cast as Clint's main antagonist, the leader of the Rojo family – one of the warring clans – an Italian thespian with a reputation for intensity. Gian Maria Volonté had a background in Shakespeare and radical theatre. Cameraman Massimo Dallamano, who would later graduate to directing, was chosen to inaugurate 'the comic-book colours, the sharp depth, the exotic angles, the sweaty-close flesh land-scapes, and the slow-paced kinetics of Leone's Techniscope world', in the words of Robert C. Cumbow, in his book *Once Upon A Time: The Films of Sergio Leone*. To compose the score, Leone turned to Ennio Morricone, who had contributed the musical backgrounding for an earlier 'spaghetti Western', *Duel in Texas*.

'As soon as I got into his [Morricone's] flat,' remembered Leone in one interview, 'he announced to me that we had been to school together. I thought it was a bluff. Not at all. He showed me a picture of our class in our fifth grade, and I could verify that we were both in it. That was nice, but not enough for me to hire him. I told him frankly, "Your music for *Duel in Texas* was extremely bad. It was like very bad Dimitri Tiomkin." To my great surprise, he approved of my words: "I totally agree with you. But I had been asked to compose very bad Dimitri Tiomkin. I did it. I have to survive."'

Morricone stayed behind, working in Rome on the music, while the cast and crew travelled to Spain. Exteriors were to be shot near a small village in the rugged southern province of Almería. Almería had mountains, flatlands and desert that could stand in for the American Southwest. Scenes for *Lawrence of Arabia* had been filmed nearby.

This was before tourism and first-class hotels. Most of the company boarded with local residents. The food was basic, the toilet facilities primitive. The workday lasted twelve hours. The set was hot and dusty, perpetually swarming with flies.

The Italian trade journals had announced that Clint was a 'Western consultant' to the production, but this was just window-dressing. Clint later said he was able to dissuade Leone from dressing some of the actors in coonskin caps. Although there were no coonskin caps, authenticity would not be a hallmark of Leone's films, or Clint's. The most important thing was plenty of horses and costumes and guns and blood.

The actors came from everywhere. The extras and stunt men were gypsies that Leone hoped would pass as Mexican faces. Half the technicians spoke Italian and the other half spoke seemingly every language in the Western world, except English.

Cast members could utter their lines in any tongue they pleased. In the peculiar tradition of Italian film production, which had to accommodate non-Italian actors and cross-border distribution, Leone planned to dub everything later for both Italian and foreign-language audiences. Mickey Knox, an American refugee from the Hollywood blacklist who lived in Rome, was a good lip-syncher and would help with the dubbing. Even with Clint, one of the few speaking English, the dubbing was sometimes a problem; Knox was a good lip-reader too, but there were usually numerous takes, the camera was sometimes far from the faces, and then nobody remembered what had been said.

Leone was a sight, clomping around the set in ten-gallon cowboy hat and boots. Clint, when he wasn't on camera, was of course in T-shirt and jeans. He woke every morning before six and ran for several miles before photography started at eight.

The cast and crew rarely saw him for breakfast or dinner; and at night, Clint stayed aloof, usually heading up to his room. One evening Leone tried to arrange a party with flamenco dancers, Tonino Valeri remembered, but Clint made only a perfunctory appearance. He seemed to be 'very concentrated always' on himself and his work.

Volonté was an intellectual and a militant Communist, conversant in English, who tried out his ideas on his co-star. He attempted to draw Clint into a discussion about the political situation in Italy versus the US but only got about thirty seconds into his spiel. 'I don't know your position,' Clint told him, 'and I don't know your people.'

While Leone was busy setting up the lights or handing out instructions for a complicated scene, Clint would sit, reading *Time* magazine, which he had delivered to him on the set, from cover to cover. Or when delays stretched on, he would go into his lazy routine, appearing to doze off; he even might curl up in a car for a catnap.

'When we were working together, he was like a snake, forever taking a nap five hundred feet away, wrapped up in his coils, asleep in the back of a car,' said Leone. 'Then he'd open his coils out, unfold and stretch. This attitude he had – slow, laidback and lazy – was what he maintained throughout the film, and, when you mix *that* with the blast and velocity of the gunshots, you have the essential contrast that he gave us.'

The low-budget production had persistent cash-flow problems, however, and Leone had to stop photography more than once to wait for paycheques or revenue lagging from Rome. There'd be heated arguments on the set between Leone and unpaid crew members, with Clint on the sidelines, pretty much left scratching his head.

One time Clint came out of his trailer for a scene and found the set-up eerily deserted. 'Only the big arc lamps standing there like Spanish vultures.' The camera crew, in arrears, had deserted Leone. 'Maybe I hurt too easily inside,' remembered Eastwood. 'I used to flare up at the drop of a hat, until I learned better. I made a decision – I told them they could find me at the airport. Fortunately, Sergio caught me before I left the hotel. He apologized and promised it wouldn't happen again.'

When in his awake-mode, Clint could be a watchful guy, observing Leone and what was happening around him. Film critics reflexively cite Clint's directorial debt to Leone, the first – arguably only – great director the actor ever worked under; but as usual, Clint borrowed only what he felt useful. Indeed, it might be said he picked up more as an actor – in his persona – than from Leone's visual style, or camera techniques.

There would be little of Leone's bravura aesthetic in Clint's Malpaso films. The emphasis on long, adoring takes, extreme close-ups, the rapid back-and-forth cutting within a scene, the poetic visualization of Leone's cinema, would be largely absent from Clint's streamlined style. Clint griped once in an interview that Leone harboured David Lean-type pretensions, a comment that revealed as much about him as Leone.

Clint would certainly borrow from Leone's 'operacization' of stories, or the manner in which the director heightened the impact of his films with characters of exaggerated good and evil, primal emotions, violent impulses. There was an unprecedented body count in Leone's 'spaghetti Westerns'. In one scene from *A Fistful of Dollars* the Rojo gang shoots at people stumbling out of a house on fire, gunning victims in the back, the face, the groin – the effect on the audience ultimately numbing. That particular scene ends with a defenceless woman being riddled with bullets. In the US, Sam Peckinpah was still a few years away from *The Wild Bunch*. Critics looking for the seeds of wanton bloodshed in future Hollywood film-making needn't look any further.

Making his own films Clint would endlessly imitate those shootouts and death tolls. And Clint the star always had to be invincible amidst the ultraviolence. Dozens upon dozens would fall from his well-aimed gun, with Clint emerging – even in the overpraised *Unforgiven* – with nary a scratch. At least Leone made his no-names suffer (when the Rojos capture the mysterious stranger, Clint gets his worst, bloody-pulp beating). In his own films Clint's 'suffering' was usually minimal. It was 'Leone-lite'.

There were few memorable roles for actresses in a Sergio Leone film. Women in Leone's world were cheap sluts or filthy backstabbers, and the director took particular relish from cathartic moments in which they got shot, raped or punched in the face. 'Sergio told me one day,' commented Vincenzoni, "If an actor had to say I love you to a woman, I wouldn't know where to put the camera."'

Clint was obviously liberated by Leone's vision of a handsome engigma whose moral ambiguity was light years away from Rowdy. The post-Leone Clint would also state very few I-love-you's on camera. And few American stars would encounter as many prostitutes on the screen. Rape or kinky sex became obligatory to his plotlines, and Clint's characters would take perverse pleasure in punching lesbians in the face. Through Leone, Clint had stumbled on a dramatic subtext that appealed to him.

Cast and crew stayed on location in Spain for nearly eleven weeks, during which time Maggie came over for a visit. The Eastwoods found time to tour the Iberian peninsula and visit sites in Toledo, Segovia and Madrid. People remember the twosome, sitting together on the set, reading their individual copies of *Time*, turning pages in the hot sun. The space between their chairs seemed a gulf.

'What surprised me a lot is that they did not look, nor act, like a young couple,' said Tonino Valeri. 'Not that they seemed to have any problems, but they were very formal towards each other. They never kissed, embraced, or even held each other's hands. She was a very beautiful woman, reserved. I would say that she looked sad.'

One of the reasons Maggie looked sad, friends say, is that she still had not been able to conceive a child.

When filming was completed, Clint returned to Rome, and there Leone gave him a Mercedes that had been promised as a bonus to his contract. Nothing made Clint's day more, and this shiny prize, Leone claimed, once belonged to the Vatican. So Clint's Mercedes was a hand-me-down from the Pope.

The efficient Morricone had finished his composition of whistles, cracking whips, horses' hooves and guitar twangs, backed by a soaring chorus, that would inspire Leone during the postproduction, and make the film's soundtrack one of the most recognizable of all time. 'The Magnificent Stranger' went into the editing room, however, with the director and Jolly Film having no real idea how the film would turn out. No idea that it would revolutionize Westerns and forge an international star. Their hopes were modest as Clint said goodbye and returned to Hollywood.

CHAPTER FIVE

The Greening of Clint
1964–1969

While Clint was absent from the US, Roxanne Tunis gave birth to Kimber Lynn Tunis, at Cedars of Lebanon Hospital in Los Angeles, on 17 June 1964. The baby's father on the State of California birth certificate is Clinton Eastwood Jr.

In the recent authorized biography of Clint, the tale was still being spun that Clint didn't even realize the dancer–actress was pregnant, until after the baby had been born. Then Tunis 'simply disappeared from his life for a time', explained Richard Schickel. 'It perhaps says something about the nature of their relationship that he did not inquire too deeply into the reasons for her withdrawal. In his mind at the time this was yet another of his casual affairs, if perhaps a little more affectionate than most.

'Arrangements were made. There was never any question of his supporting the child. But as things worked out over the years, there was not much chance of his seeing her frequently, either. Roxanne for a time reunited with her estranged husband, whom Clint says he never met, and then moved about a good deal. His own career kept him away from Los Angeles for long periods of time, and he and Maggie were spending more and more time in Carmel, too. In any case, Clint says, Roxanne did not press him to spend more time with them. He saw their child when they all happened to coincide in Los Angeles.'

The facts of Kimber's birth are more complicated. According to close friends of Roxanne Tunis, Clint not only knew about the pregnancy, but wanted to have a baby with his mistress. The *Rawhide* actor would often stroke Tunis's tummy and ask, 'How's my little Rowdy coming?' When she became pregnant, Clint was ecstatic, according to

Tunis's friends. Although Clint sometimes brought up the possibility of marriage, Tunis didn't want to be the cause of his divorce, and so the sensitive issue was always laid aside. The baby would remain their secret, and they would continue to have, in effect, a 'secret marriage'.

The baby was given the last name of Tunis to protect her privacy and Clint's image. But Clint fed the bottle to the baby on lunch breaks from *Rawhide*, and went strolling with Tunis and the baby in their neighbourhood (after peeking out and making sure the coast was clear). Indeed, Tunis's friends say that Clint continued to see her as often as before in the years immediately following the birth of Kimber, taking Roxanne out to bars and restaurants and shows.

It was an enduring part of her appeal that Tunis never made any claims, monetary or otherwise, on Clint. Any financial support that the actor proferred for his daughter was appreciated (and Clint was always 'generous', close friends of Tunis insist).

What happened to Bill Thompkins supplies additional proof that Clint knew about the baby. Clint's best friend, Thompkins was the only American to have accompanied the actor to Spain for the Sergio Leone Western. Again Thompkins functioned as Clint's stand-in, while also taking a small role in the film as a member of the Rojo gang.

But Thompkins had scruples about Clint's relationships with 'other women', and thought that having a baby with Tunis was going too far. On location in Spain he made the mistake of speaking up, taking Maggie's side. That crossed a line with Clint, and Thompkins was banished from Clint's life. Weeping, apologetic phone calls had no effect. 'Toothless' henceforth was dropped from the *Rawhide* cast, and Thompkins left Los Angeles, moving back to Seattle to start over in life. Several years later, in 1971, Clint's onetime close friend perished in a road accident in Coupeville, Washington.

'When Clint was pissed off, nobody could change his mind about anything. He dismissed Bill as if he had never existed,' according to Kitty Jones in her unpublished autobiography *Who the Hell is Kitty Jones?* 'When I asked, "Did you hear that Bill Thompkins was killed in an auto accident?" he said coldly, "Yes, I heard." Not another word was said.'

People didn't pester Clint about what happened to Bill Thompkins – why his buddy had vanished from Hollywood. Even if they didn't know about Clint's out-of-wedlock baby, they did hear that Thompkins had transgressed somehow. Even at this early stage of his stardom, they understood that what Clint giveth, he could also take away.

'I built my whole life in this town,' explained one friend of Clint's, who, although she knew about the Tunis baby *and* Bill Thompkins, kept silent, 'and I had friends I wanted to keep. Relationships that were personal as well as professional. I worried that Clint could destroy me in one second with everybody. One word, and he could kick me to the kerb. It wouldn't just destroy one relationship, it would destroy all of my relationships.'

George Fargo would succeed Bill Thompkins as Clint's stand-in, until Clint became a star and then Fargo too fell foul of Clint. According to friends of Fargo, Clint took umbrage when Fargo tried too hard to interest him in a script he was hoping to produce. Clint cut Fargo off, wouldn't return his phone messages. Fargo later, in 1981, died suddenly of a stroke. Long excluded from the star's life, Clint's other best friend from the 1960s was a disillusioned man, according to mutual friends.

Fargo was succeeded for the early 1970s by Kitty Jones's husband. Then he was replaced by Buddy Van Horn, who had the longest run in the job. Clint didn't often stray outside his own clique, and even the stand-ins formed an inbred genealogy.

Maggie, who wanted nothing so badly as a child of her own, never gave any hint that she knew about Roxanne Tunis's baby. Some of Maggie's closest friends knew about Kimber, but these people never told her. Maggie, they believed, preferred to remain in the dark. She preferred to idealize Clint: one friend tells of a side trip she took with Maggie in Italy, when Clint was filming his 'spaghetti Westerns' overseas. They visited the museum in Florence that displayed Michelangelo's statue *David*. Maggie circled the magnificent sculpted torso again and again, exclaiming, 'Doesn't it remind you of Clint?'

Now Maggie's house-hunting weekends up in the Monterey Peninsula took on the added poignancy of escaping from Hollywood's wagging tongues. The first home the Eastwoods leased up north was in the lower-rent section of Pebble Beach near the Pacific Grove gate. Since the early 1960s they had spent as much time as possible up there, and in Carmel. These two communities, about a hundred miles south of San Francisco, were scenic enclaves for wealthy people. Pebble

Beach was for industrialists and their wives, while Carmel, originally a bohemian writers' and artists' refuge, had evolved into a quaint place dominated by antique shops, art galleries, restaurants and real estate brokerages.

While Clint scouted out parcels of land that he could buy cheaply and quietly, Maggie took a long time to pick out a site on which to build what the fan magazines dubbed the Eastwoods' 'forever house', along Pebble Beach's famed seventeen-mile drive.

Meanwhile, *Rawhide* limped into its seventh season. Clint and Eric Fleming's seven-year contracts were coming up for renewal, but Rowdy's fan mail had begun to overtake Mr Favor's, and Eric Fleming was behaving as contrarily as ever. 'When Eric would act up,' remembered director Ted Post, 'Clint would walk away.'

How many times could Mr Favor shout, 'Keep pushing! Keep pushing!' How many times could Rowdy exclaim, 'You hammerheads!' The drovers didn't seem to notice that the plots repeated. The leads got amnesia, fell in love, were falsely arrested, quit the drive in disgust, mixed it up with an endless variety of shifty jaspers encountered on the trail; nor was it too much to cross paths with a stranded troupe of ballerinas.

> ROWDY: Just what besides girls are those?
> GIL FAVOR: Ballet dancers.
> ROWDY: I've seen belly dancers at the Turkish Delight saloon in San Antone.
> GIL FAVOR: Ballet, not belly.

Most of the cast members, curiously, showed higher professional ambitions than Clint. Eric Fleming, Sheb Wooley, Steve Raines, Charles Gray and Paul Brinegar all wrote or sold scripts for *Rawhide* and other network programming. One of Fleming's constant bellyaches was that he intended to prove himself as a writer and director.

Not Clint, whose career goals were still low-key and voiced, if at all, only rarely and to a few friends. He did show interest in the technology of film-making, and poked his face into the editing room on occasion; he inquired about different lenses and lighting equipment. But he was making good money as an actor, and he was a waiter and a watcher – a surfer dreamily watching the waves – not a long-range planner.

Later, Clint would make the claim that, towards the end of the series, he coaxed the *Rawhide* producers into letting him try some camera shots. At one point they were planning to film a stampede from the sidelines. 'I'd like to take an Arriflex, run it on my horse and go right in the middle of this damn thing, even dismount or whatever. But let me get in there and really get some great shots because there are some beautiful shots in there that we're missing.' When they finally gave him a camera, he said, he filmed the stampede to his heart's delight; probably resulting in one of those brief, whirling, hand-held scenes of the sort Clint favoured in later films – the equivalent of jazz breaks in what was otherwise a conventional visual style.

Later too, Clint would make the claim that he had sounded off to the brass about directing an entire episode. 'I wanted to direct, way back when I was doing *Rawhide*. I'd been assigned to direct an episode, but the network CBS reneged, because someone on another series had gone way over schedule and way over budget – so they sent down a memo saying that no one who acted in the series could direct.'

The Clint-directed episode never happened. Paul Brinegar, as close to Clint as anyone among the cast, didn't recollect that it ever came up openly as an issue. Nor did Wishbone recall the time when Rowdy carried a camera into the middle of a herd. When that happened, it was an inconspicuous occasion, the footage then incorporated into 'some trailers and various coming attraction things', in Clint's own words.

Over in Rome, as the 1964–5 television season opened, Sergio Leone was showing the final cut of his Western to associates. Duccio Tessari remembered, 'I said to Sergio, "Very good film," but nobody had any expectations.' Partly to distract Kurosawa, Leone changed the title of the film from 'The Magnificent Stranger' to *Per un pugno di dollari*, or *For a Fistful of Dollars*. American-sounding names were concocted for the credits to corral Western fans: Leone became Bob Robertson (a homage to his father, Bob Roberti), Morricone became Dan Savio and Gian Maria Volonté, John Wells.

Still, when Leone went to the Sorrento movie market, he could not find a major distributor. No one wanted to take a chance on a faux-Western by an unknown director with a nobody star. So *Per un pugno di dollari* was first shown in a month generally considered dead

(September), on an opening day considered weak (Friday), in a small theatre, with little advertising, in one city. 'The only advantage was that the theatre was very close to the railway station, and so many travellers and salesmen went to see it,' according to one authoritative account. 'After two or three days which were really bad, the word started to spread, and on the following Monday the theatre was full of people. Just on time, because the film was about to be cancelled for the rest of the week.'

Although Italian critics 'ignored' the film or 'gave it extremely bad reviews', according to this account, its grassroots popularity spread. In Italy alone, *Per un pugno di dollari* would end up grossing more than three billion lire (roughly $4 million), before fanning out to other European countries, where it met equivalent success.

Clint, who hadn't even been alerted to the film's revised title, was obliged to read about the box-office phenomenon in the Hollywood trade papers. An 18 November 1964 review in *Variety* praised 'a James Bondian vigor and tongue-in-cheek approach' that was sure 'to capture both sophisticates and average cinema patrons'. The critic, who proved a sage, predicted that *Per un pugno di dollari*, whose title, when shortened into English, became *A Fistful of Dollars,* would emerge 'the sleeper of the year'.

Because the Kurosawa lawsuit frightened US distributors, *A Fistful of Dollars* would not be glimpsed in US theatres until 1967. That made it hard for Clint or anyone else in Hollywood to credit what was happening. 'Not only was there a movie prejudice against television actors,' Clint said years later, 'but there was a feeling that an American actor making an Italian movie was sort of taking a step backward.'

Nonetheless, with *Rawhide* increasingly shaky, Clint could feel reassurance in the fact that Leone had already proposed a follow-up film.

Convinced that Jolly Film was withholding his share of the profits, Sergio Leone had sued his producers to extricate himself from his contract. His new producer was Alberto Grimaldi, the Neapolitan who founded the Produzioni Europee Associate (PEA) film company. Grimaldi, who in his career served many great Italian film-makers – Pontecorvo, Bertolucci, Pasolini, Fellini – made a deal that gave the director an upgraded $350,000 budget for his next production as well as a sixty per cent stake in profits.

Leone also acquired a new scenarist in Luciano Vincenzoni. Leone had been assistant director on the first film Vincenzoni had written, *La Grande Guerre*. This time, together with his brother-in-law, Leone had concocted a story that would bring back the Mysterious Stranger as well as create a new character for Gian Maria Volonté (whose character had met his demise in *A Fistful of Dollars*). Though he usually took co-script credit, Leone needed Vincenzoni for the hard work of actual writing. 'Sergio was ignorant like a rock,' said Vincenzoni. 'He never read a book in his life. He never even read his own ID. But he had a great sense of and passion for movies.'

Vincenzoni whipped up the screenplay for *Per qualche dollaro in più*, or *For A Few Dollars More*, inside of nine days. The script had bounty-hunter Clint pursuing Volonté, a drug-addicted cutthroat planning to rob an impregnable bank; a third lead, a rival to the Mysterious Stranger, was an almost elegant bounty hunter rival dubbed 'Colonel'. That role was earmarked for Lee Marvin, but when Marvin asked for a few dollars too many, it was inherited by a journeyman actor named Lee Van Cleef, whose evil-eyed presence had made him a fixture in Hollywood Westerns since 1952.

To hear the Italians tell it, Van Cleef was through with acting – down and out, recovering from detox therapy, unemployed, almost a bum. He had turned to art, was working on a painting for a $30 commission. As soon as Sergio offered him $50,000, he took off his apron. 'When do we start?' Along with Clint and Volonté – and later, Eli Wallach – no further proof would be required of Leone's casting genius.

There was never any question that Clint would return to play the same part in the second 'spaghetti Western'. In Italy – and other European markets, where *A Fistful of Dollars* was also performing strongly – his face had become instantly recognizable. A feature story went over the wire services quoting Sophia Loren as saying Clint was 'the biggest male star in Italy'. He even had his own nickname there: Il Cigarillo.

This time Clint would receive first-class airfare and $50,000, albeit still without any percentage of profits. 'I'll come over and do the film,' Clint supposedly told Leone after this offer was made, 'but please, I beg of you, one thing only – don't make me put that cigar back into my mouth!' And the director is said to have replied, 'Clint, we can't leave the main protagonist at home. The cigar is playing the lead!'

After reading the script, according to Vincenzoni, Clint phoned him and said, 'Luciano, maybe we can try to fix my dialogue.' Clint's ideas, mostly in the category of vernacular and how to reduce the verbiage, were 'very good', recalled Vincenzoni. 'At the time, I understood, and not because I am a magician, that this guy, besides our little spaghetti Western, one day or another would become a star. I knew. His personality was very quiet, but when he volunteered one line it was precise.'

The second 'Dollar' film would again be shot in the late spring and early summer, during which time Clint was on his annual vacation from *Rawhide*. Initial scenes again would be photographed at Cinecittà in Rome, then, as before, the company would head for Spain, working on a budget twice as luxurious as for the first production.

Clint and Vincenzoni became friends. When in Rome, Clint used to go over to Vincenzoni's house for pasta. When the Italian writer had four or five guests coming, Vincenzoni said, he prepared one pot of water, maybe a pound of pasta. When Clint came, he'd cook two pounds – one for Clint and one for the other guests. 'Clint used to eat big amounts, but he was always skinny and strong,' recalled Vincenzoni.

Funny thing, Vincenzoni recalled, but there were always many 'interesting people and beautiful girls' stopping by his house. 'The moment that Clint came in, I would be in the kitchen, and suddenly everyone would stream into the living room. "Oh," I thought, "Clint is here." You felt the vibration of the man. The Clint personality.

'I never saw him as a playboy with a girl, however,' Vincenzoni added. 'I never saw him over-acting [with a woman]. He was always talking very softly, like he does in the movies. Never asking a question – always *responding* to a question.'

The first time Clint came to Rome, he had been an anonymous fellow. 'But this time,' he told a Hollywood columnist, 'I was mobbed. I'd walk down the Via Veneto and people would come up and ask for my autograph. I was wined and dined and treated like a king.'

Besides Vincenzoni, Clint socialized with Hollywood émigrés. He spent time with Brett Halsey, another ex-Universal contract player having a fling at Italian stardom, and with Halsey's wife Heidi Bruhl (who appeared as the foxy wife of one of the doomed climbers in *The Eiger Sanction*). He was glimpsed at sidewalk cafés in the company of

Woody Strode, the former black football star best known for roles in *Sergeant Rutledge* and *Spartacus*, with whom Clint was acquainted from a *Rawhide* segment.

He was also sighted by the press with various female companions, including Japanese actress Reiko Osada. But his publicity, overseen by Ruth Marsh's Italian representative, took pains to present him as happily married; and once again Maggie came to Europe for a time – ten days in Rome, and another ten in nearby Grottaferrata.

On the set in Spain, Clint behaved the same as before – focused and aloof. Once again, he was glimpsed reading *Time* between shots and hunkering down into a car seat during long waits. 'It was a way of concentrating himself,' explained Vincenzoni. 'Actually, many times he *played* like he was sleeping. He closed his eyes because he didn't want to be bothered by Sergio or by people wanting an autograph.'

Now Clint knew Leone's drill. The persona of studied cool was in place. Volonté's brutal and tortured performance would better that of the first films, while Lee Van Cleef, as the gunslinger whose seniority is resented by the Mysterious Stranger, provided a counterpoint – to Clint's nonchalance – of courtliness and witty élan.

For a Few Dollars More has its crude, objectionable elements: an eighteen-month-old baby and mother are gunned down in the bloody first reel. And the dubbing in a Sergio Leone film was always idiotic, the words never quite matching the lips.

But the film's structure was extremely clever, and Clint was never better than in *For a Few Dollars More*, trying to keep his poise while under pressure from competing killers. And Ennio Morricone would serve up another of his memorable soundtracks of whistling, shouting, church bells and twanging guitar. The second 'spaghetti Western' may not boast the grandiose action, lavish scope and expensive spectacle of *The Good, the Bad and the Ugly*, but scene for scene the film stands on its own as riveting entertainment.

For a Few Dollars More would, even more than *A Fistful of Dollars*, cement Clint's breakthrough in America. Because he was fluent in English, it was Vincenzoni who brokered the first North American distribution deal with United Artists. He and Leone dragged UA executives Arthur Krim and Arnold Picker to a 'super-cinema' in Rome, where they could observe audiences virtually pushing and shoving to get past the turnstiles. 'Inside it was an orgy of laughing, screaming and yelling,' remembered Vincenzoni. 'When the United Artists people came out, they said, "How much?"'

Vincenzoni asked for $1 million guaranteed and fifty per cent of the profits, outside of Italy, France, Germany and Spain; of which, Vincenzoni himself retained a percentage, according to his arrangement with Leone. English-language and other rights were sold for what was then a sky-high price of $900,000. When, soon after, the principals gathered to sign the contract in a big hotel suite, it was Arnold Picker who thought to ask, 'What are you going to do next? Because we would like to cross-collateralize.'

Leone said nothing. Alberto Grimaldi hemmed and hawed. Vincenzoni improvised something. 'I don't know why,' he recalled, 'but the poster came into my mind – *Il buono, il brutto, il cattivo*. "The Good, the Bad and the Ugly." It's the story of three bums that go around through the Civil War looking for money.' Arnold Picker said, "Great, how much will the film cost?" There was no book, no screenplay. Just three words.'

Replied Vincenzoni: '$1,200,000 maybe.' Enthused Picker: 'It's a deal.'

Even before the 1965–6 season, *Rawhide* was on the chopping block. The onetime Top Ten-rated programme had bottomed out at number forty-four.

Radical changes had to be made, if the programme was to survive. Network executives mulled whether to switch over to colour photography; that was the prime-time trend, but it also meant a substantial investment – and a longer-term commitment to the show.

The network programming head, James Aubrey, had made a preliminary decision to axe the series. When Aubrey himself lost his job in February, the new regime gave *Rawhide* a reprieve. Executive vice-president Mike Dann told a high-level meeting that it didn't matter what Aubrey thought, CBS Chairman William Paley loved the show.

Only there had to be drastic changes. Trail boss Eric Fleming would have to be unceremoniously dumped. 'They were paying me a million dollars a year,' was the reason Fleming gave *TV Guide*. (That showed 'an insouciant disregard for fact', the magazine felt obliged to point out. 'Fleming earned a measly $220,000' per season.)

The show would also dispense with James Murdock as Mushy and Sheb Wooley as Pete. A 'veddy English' drover (David Watson, a young pianist and singer) and an African-American (Shakespearean actor Raymond St Jacques, who had never appeared in a Western before), as well as a quasi-marquee name (John Ireland, well known to fans of John Ford and Howard Hawks Westerns), were added to the dwindling troupe of regulars that included Quince, Wishbone and Rowdy.

Clint claimed he first heard that Rowdy was being promoted to trail boss in a newspaper clipping forwarded to him in Rome. Was he pleased with the news? 'Why should I be pleased?' Clint was quoted in the press. 'I used to carry half the shows. Now I carry them all. For the same money.' The money was a sore issue with the actor. 'CBS just said to go to work. There was no talk about more money or anything. In the first show of this season, they don't even explain how Rowdy Yates is promoted from ramrod to trail boss,' Clint complained to the *Los Angeles Times.*

The network appointed a new producer, Ben Brady, who had been crucial behind the scenes of two hit series: *Have Gun Will Travel* and *Perry Mason.* Brady flew to Rome to spend a week assuaging Clint. Brady recalled that Clint did not venture any suggestions as to his character or the new format. It may be that the actor was simply dismissive of the producer species; Clint's natural dislike of anyone telling him what to do had been reinforced by perpetual, top-of-the-line changeovers on *Rawhide.*

In the brief interim it took for Clint to return to America and for the series to resume, things worsened. The network announced that the popular Sheb Wooley would return to the series, then backpedalled on that announcement. Ben Brady, not enjoying himself, decided he'd rather leave the creative continuity to someone else. The dependable Endre Bohem was wooed to come back; one of Bohem's wildest ideas was to move the whole show to Hawaii, adding *paniolos* to the cast. After thinking it over, however, Bohem decided he was better off away from the grind, and so the daily reins of running the show were turned over to the series' last producer, Robert Thompson.

The network had hedged support for so long that there weren't any colour stock shots of the cattle by the time the fall season rolled around, so black-and-white was a *fait accompli.* Adding insult to injury, the show was pushed into a new time slot on Tuesday nights opposite the gritty World War II series *Combat*, which attracted the same heavily male audience and was just entering the Nielsen Top Ten.

TV Guide wryly noted that the subtitle of the revamped *Rawhide* should have been 'How to Revive a Dead Horse'. Paul Brinegar was one person angry about the changes and willing to be quoted about his feelings: 'Utter shock. They have decimated the cast.' Steve Raines, who played Quince, had written scripts over the years; now he told the press that the newly conceived ones loomed as 'mediocre'.

The *Rawhide* cast started its eighth and final season with the veterans feeling as though they had overstayed their welcome. It definitely seemed odd, with Gil Favor gone and Rowdy in charge. 'I remember an episode or two before the last show, Raymond St Jacques and I were talking and we agreed the show was finished,' said Paul Brinegar.

Rawhide without Eric Fleming lasted just thirteen episodes. The last one aired in January 1966. By then, Clint was more than eager to leave the series and Rowdy behind. In Italy, where the second 'spaghetti Western' had proved as popular as the first, he had two more jobs lined up. Maybe now Hollywood would sit up and take notice.

Irving Leonard was able to negotiate an $119,000 severance from CBS, for the unfilmed remainder of seventeen episodes. 'No one, I would venture not even Paley by then, shed many tears at the [show's] demise,' recalled producer Robert Thompson. 'The show had more than run its course by then.'

Producer Dino De Laurentiis flew Clint to New York City, booked the actor into a first-class suite and squired him around in a limousine while convincing him to star in a non-Western production opposite De Laurentiis' wife, actress Silvana Mangano.

De Laurentiis knew his man: he offered Clint $25,000 for a quick and easy role, or $20,000 and a brand-new Ferrari. Clint accepted the Ferrari, realizing, as he liked to tell friends, that he would save ten per cent of agency fees on the luxury sports car.

The Ferrari-wooing (along with *Rawhide*'s plummeting fortunes) persuaded Clint to head for Rome in late February, there to shoot *Le Streghe*, or *The Witches*, a five-part anthology film with Mangano, a star beloved in Italy. Each segment would be guided by a different Italian director.

The production would be staged in De Laurentiis' studios Rome. Vittorio De Sica, whose neo-realist triumph *The Bicycle Thief* had electrified postwar audiences, was tapped to direct Clint's episode, the final one of the film. Called 'A Night Like Any Other', the segment was only nineteen minutes long, with a buttoned-down Clint, in thick, dark glasses, locked into a stale marriage. His wife desires flowers, compliments, an evening out at the movies – they debate whether or not to go and see *A Fistful of Dollars* – but Clint prefers to stay home, drink whiskey, nod off to sleep.

Whenever Clint's character dozes, his wife's fantasies come alive. Her husband becomes a dream dance partner, gliding around like Fred Astaire; a dream sex partner, diveboarding into bed. The husband is too sleepy for conjugal duties; so in the wife's fantasies Batman, Flash Gordon and other superheroes materialize to pleasure her. The story climaxes with her striptease in a theatre packed with screaming men, as a despondent Clint is imagined shooting himself atop a high rise.

The episode sounds fascinating, but it isn't, it's dreary. Clint does not appear comfortable in either the real-life or fantastical scenes. And no other screen performance of his is quite as 'un-Clintlike'. When *The Witches* was released in the US, the *New York Times* disparaged it as 'throwaway De Sica'.

Clint's instalment of *The Witches* only took a few days to shoot, however. Afterwards he stopped off in Paris to promote the première of *A Few Dollars More*, where director De Sica, accompanying him, 'introduced' Clint to the French press as 'the new Gary Cooper'. *A Fistful of Dollars* had been a huge hit in France, and Clint was already well known there (in some Paris theatres, the film had been shown with English dubbing).

It was probably here, his first time in Paris, that Clint met Pierre Rissient, the passionate cinéaste and press attaché who would prove such a boon to his career. It was probably here, too, that Clint had his brief fling with Catherine Deneuve, the exquisite blonde beauty of French *nouvelle vague* films. This affair was one of Clint's better-kept secrets. He had enough respect for Deneuve, one of the première actresses of her generation, to keep the details to himself.

Clint then had only two months in America before returning to Europe for the third 'Dollar' film, *The Good, the Bad and the Ugly.* Leone and Vincenzoni had collaborated on the script, which once again

...ysterious Stranger; Lee Van Cleef as a new
...less fortune hunter; and the two of them tangled
...ng Mexican bandit named Tuco. All three are seeking
...ne of Confederate gold. Whereas the first film had focused
on Clint, and the second on Van Cleef, the third story in
Leone's informal trilogy would cast the spotlight on Tuco, a character
originally written for Gian Maria Volonté.

That may be why Clint played hard to get. After reading the script,
he said to Leone, 'In the first film, I was alone. In the second, we were
two. Here we are three. If it goes on this way, in the next one I will
be starring with the American cavalry.'

According to Leone, Clint was worried that he would be upstaged
by Tuco. 'Even if Marlon Brando were to play that role,' Leone assured
Clint, 'he would actually be working for you when you are not physically
on the screen.'

At one point, negotiations broke off. Clint's publicist, Ruth Marsh,
interceded with the actor, urging him to commit himself to *The Good,
the Bad and the Ugly*. The William Morris Agency was furious that Marsh
had become involved. Also furious was Irving Leonard, who was already
jealous of the publicist's sway with his client. Leonard wanted to farm
out Clint's publicity to another firm, for which he would expect some
payback.

The first two 'spaghetti Westerns' still had not been released in the
US, however, and Clint could not count on any other offers. He
wanted the security of the third 'spaghetti Western'. But his show of
reluctance enabled the William Morris Agency to hike his fee up to
$250,000, in addition to ten per cent of the profits in the western
hemisphere. Another Ferrari was thrown in to sweeten the deal, which
on top of his years of solid *Rawhide* earnings, would make Clint a very
rich man.

But Irving Leonard had his revenge. He stipulated that the Marsh
Agency had to be let go. Clint patiently explained to Ruth Marsh that
when his business manager, in concert with an important agency like
William Morris, insisted he drop her, he had to obey. Some years later,
Ruth Marsh tried to contact Clint about resuming his publicity, but
was blocked from any contact with him. Her letter was answered by
attorney Frank Wells, whom she had never met, telling her to cease
any communication.

This kind of internecine fighting over a star and his bank account is hardly unique in Hollywood. But it was beginning to be a pattern with Clint, that people behind the scenes competed for his friendship and loyalty, hoping for a piece of the action. He seemed to encourage this, to enjoy the jockeying for his favour. And invariably Clint preferred the 'power relationships' to the less powerful ones.

In later years Ruth Marsh occasionally bumped into her onetime client and friend at industry functions. She thought he was terrified of meeting her gaze. 'Remember me?' she'd ask. 'Give me a hug.' He'd then give her a hug. But she felt Clint didn't really want to remember her, or the common past they shared.

After a brief period, Clint's publicity was taken over, starting in 1965, and handled for many years, by Jerry Pam of Gutman and Pam, one of Hollywood's high-profile firms. In time that function would be taken over entirely by the even more high-powered – and free to Clint – publicity machine of Warner Brothers studio.

When Gian Maria Volonté passed on another Sergio Leone production, the director approached Eli Wallach, whose scene-stealing had proved a highlight of *The Magnificent Seven*. Wallach, a well-respected actor who worked on Broadway as often as in films, had never heard of Leone, and thought an Italian Western sounded suspiciously like Hawaiian pizza. After watching two minutes of one of the 'Dollar' films, Wallach got up and told the projectionist to shut it off. He said yes to Leone. Director Henry Hathaway took a trip down to Western Costume with Wallach to help him pick out the hat, knee-length chaps and braces he would wear in the film.

Initial photography was launched at Cinecittà in Rome in mid-May of 1966, including the opening scene between Clint and Eli Wallach – the vignette of Tuco being captured by the Mysterious Stranger and forcibly taken to jail. Although this was the third time Clint and Leone had worked together, an interpreter was still on hand to translate the Italian director's more arcane commands and gesticulations.

'It was really a necessity since Sergio was incapable of uttering a single word in English,' said Tonino Delli Colli, the cameraman of *The Good, the Bad and the Ugly*. 'He pretended that he could speak the language. He could read it, but was never able to speak it. Sometimes to make fun of him, I asked him, "Sergio, what did he [Clint] say?"

and Sergio would answer very rudely, "What the hell do you want to know?"'

The first two 'Dollar' films had flaunted coarse, gaudy colours. Delli Colli, who worked with Pier Paolo Pasolini, Lina Wertmuller, Franco Zeffirelli, Roman Polanski, Louis Malle and other top-echelon filmmakers in his long, brilliant career, was part of the classier package for *The Good, the Bad and the Ugly*. Fast at capturing available light, Delli Colli could be counted on to lend dazzle and painterly elegance to the subject matter. Director Leone kept the cameraman hopping with his art-history-style instructions. 'I want the next scene to look like Vermeer, with light slanting in from the side!'

After Rome, Spain's plateau region, Burgos in the north, would stand in for the Deep South, with the Western scenes once again scheduled for Almería. The film would boast several elaborate set-pieces: a town under cannon siege, a sprawling prison camp, and a Civil War battlefield. For the climax, an especially memorable set-up, a few hundred Spanish soldiers were deployed to build a cemetery of several thousand gravestones, arranged in a circular pattern in order to evoke an ancient circus maximus. Leone asked Ennio Morricone to compose music for that scene, a three-way gunfight between Clint, Lee Van Cleef and Eli Wallach, that would suggest 'the corpses were laughing from inside their tombs'. Leone planned the photography – hypnotic whirling interspersed with static close-ups – to give audiences the impression of a visual ballet.

Clint and Eli Wallach flew into Madrid together, and Clint talked Wallach into driving the rest of the way to the location, long hours by car. They would also live together in local places for part of the filming schedule. Wallach remembered Clint warning him that hard work and few luxuries awaited them on location, but otherwise his co-star was not idly discursive with someone outside his customary sphere. 'Clint was the tall, silent type,' said Wallach. 'He's the kind where you open up and do all the talking. He smiles and nods and stores it all away in that wonderful calculator of a brain.'

By the time they set up the cameras, Morricone had already come up with the basis of the musical score: the separate motifs, reminiscent of the earlier 'Dollar' films, which tease and circle and eventually join into a rhapsodic fugue. Leone, seeking inspiration in Spain, would play the music incessantly over the course of filming.

Just before a shot Clint and Eli Wallach would talk over their lines. There was never very much rehearsal with Leone, and Clint wasn't big on rehearsal either. He, Wallach and Lee Van Cleef were the only actors speaking English anyway. Some of the others were merely shouting numbers out loud. Because it was not 'direct sound', Leone knew he could tinker with the dubbing later on. Sometimes the script girl was off camera feeding lines to the non-professionals who had trouble remembering them. Sometimes, too, stage hands would be crouched in a corner of the set arguing about soccer scores. The actors, struggling to concentrate, would have to yell at them to shut up.

It was amazing to Wallach how the scenes with number-shouting amateurs gelled. All his years in the Method, and the amateurs came off fine in the footage. As for Clint, juggling bits and pieces of character out of continuity was easier if the emotions were kept simple and clear.

'Clint had one gift', remembered Wallach. 'He *listened*. I remember doing a film with Steve McQueen where he said, "Take away the dialogue. I just want to react. I don't want to act." Clint did that extremely well. He was a consummate screen actor. He knew when and how to act, and he didn't overdo it. He gave time for what I was feeding him to sink in, and then he responded."

There were signs that Clint had settled in, felt more comfortable. There was less of the *Time* magazine routine, the hunkering down in cars and trailers, more of Clint practising his golf swing between shots. Now the actor was beginning to speak openly about heading into business for himself and making his own movies as a producer or director. Eli Wallach thought to himself, 'That'll be the day.'

There were also signs that Clint had reached the end of the line with Leone. The Italian director seemed to enjoy torturing Clint with the little cigars that made the actor sick. 'After two or three takes he would say to Leone, "You'd better get it this time because I'm going to throw up,' recalled Wallach. The endless number of angles and takes that Leone thrived on, the actor merely tolerated; they were the building blocks of the director's visual mastery, but Clint also saw them as time- and money-consuming.

Yet Clint was relatively at ease during the filming, and optimistic about life after *Rawhide*. He had developed a sense of humour about Leone, whose excesses exasperated everyone. The repetitive takes, the endless waiting for light, the finicky attention to details, these had the effect of amusing Clint, who must have felt in his gut that he would never again have to put up with such nonsense.

One day – a story they all liked to tell – a bridge was going to be blown up. It was probably the film's most costly scene, not only wrecking the bridge, but paying for the time of the hundreds of Spanish soldiers who were standing in for the Civil War armies. A military officer was working with a special effects man to wire the bridge as everybody waited for the signal to be given that the scene was properly prepared, and that the lighting was okay with Leone and Tonino Delli Colli.

Clint and Eli Wallach, who were not supposed to be in the master shot, had retreated to a hilltop, with Clint practising his putting. 'I know about these things,' he cautioned Wallach. 'Stay as far away from special effects and explosives as you can.'

Leone was down below with an eyeglass glued to his face, waiting for the clouds to sail past the sun. Three cameras were set up: a slow-motion, a wide lens, a third one for closeups. The special effects man told the Spanish officer that he could trigger the explosion. The signal was to be, 'Vaya!' But when the special effects man turned to a crew member and told him to run over to one of the cameras and turn the motor on, he made the mistake of saying: 'Vaya!' The Spanish officer heard the signal and launched the explosion. Leone was still gazing up at the sky when the bridge blew up.

The special effects man hastily jumped into a car and drove away. Pandemonium everywhere. A dismayed Leone simply announced, 'Let's go eat,' and fortunately, nobody had been hurt. But it took the crew several days to rebuild the bridge before the director could blow it up again, all of this at considerable added expense.

Up on the hilltop, Clint observed the incident with his toothiest grin. 'There, you see what I mean?' the actor said to Eli Wallach, before following through on a swing.

Nineteen sixty-six was also marked by the death of Eric Fleming, who was swept to his death and drowned in Peru on 29 September. Fleming was in the midst of filming a two-hour telefilm for ABC when his canoe overturned on the Haullaga River in remote jungle country, some three hundred miles northeast of Lima. He was only forty-one years old. According to Richard Schickel's book, Clint was shocked, and 'in his mind, Fleming's death seems to have put a blunt and indelible period to this phase of his own life'. The executor of Eric Fleming's estate, incidentally, was Irving Leonard.

In the US, *The Good, the Bad and the Ugly* suffered time-saving cuts. As Sergio Leone put it, 'They took away twenty minutes to make people go and buy popcorn.' The result was to diminish the weight of Lee Van Cleef's character; though Clint stayed central, some of his scenes were also abbreviated (including a fling with a prostitute, shown only in Europe). Tuco – thanks to Eli Wallach's grandstanding – wound up as much the star as Clint. On Wallach's grave-stone it well might say, 'The Ugly'.

Clint's three 'spaghetti Westerns', or the 'paella trilogy', as they were dubbed by some critics, would not be shown in America until January of 1967. United Artists' big-city marketing strategy was unusual for a Western and especially for a foreign-made film, much less a foreign-made Western. The three Leone films were touted as James Bond-type entertainments, and according to trade paper reports, supported by 'an ad budget several times more than anyone expected us to spend on a foreign-made Western', in the words of a UA company spokesman. Bookings were arranged for the nation's finest theatres – the Pantages in Los Angeles, the Music Hall in Boston and the Oriental in Chicago – as well as numerous regional playdates.

A Fistful of Dollars opened in January, *For a Few Dollars More* in May, and *The Good, the Bad and the Ugly* made its debut during the Christmas season. Clint did a month-long publicity tour, including a stopover in London to meet members of the press.

By the third 'Dollar' film there was remarkable word-of-mouth to complement the publicity and advertising. The most successful of the three films, *The Good, the Bad and the Ugly*, would eventually collect over $8 million in rental earnings.* It wasn't until *The Outlaw Josey Wales*, ten inflationary years later, that Clint's Malpaso Productions routinely began to earn over $8 million rentals.

Yet many of the initial US reviews for the three Sergio Leone films were harsh. This would be turned into a cornerstone of Clint's myth-

---

* Rentals are the amount theatre owners pay a motion picture company in order to exhibit the film; it is from this amount that the film's profits are determined.

ology: that from the beginning he has fought an uphill battle for recognition with American film critics.

Judith Crist thought *A Fistful of Dollars* was cheapjack, *Newsweek* said the second 'spaghetti Western' was 'excruciatingly dopey', while *Time* derided *The Good, the Bad and the Ugly* for its comic-strip values and wooden acting, especially Clint's. Renata Adler in the *New York Times* rejected the crowning production in the 'paella trilogy' as 'the most expensive, pious and repellent movie in the history of its peculiar genre', while even *Variety* regarded *The Good, the Bad and the Ugly* as 'a curious amalgam of the visually striking, the dramatically feeble and the offensively sadistic'.

At the same time the 'spaghetti Westerns' did impress some key tastemakers. Sergio Leone's innovative visual style was acclaimed, and Clint's refreshing presence duly noted. Sergio Leone's trilogy found a partisan in Andrew Sarris – the dean of American auteurists – who thought the films original (as well as derivative), darkly humorous as well as consciously poetic. Bosley Crowther and Vincent Canby of the *New York Times* were two other critics who found merit in the three Leone films, with Canby praising 'Eastwood's fathomless cool'. Early champions of Clint also included Hollis Alpert, Gene Siskel, *Time* magazine, and the *Los Angeles Times* despite some caveats.

For a while there was loose talk of a fourth 'spaghetti Western' furthering the exploits of the Mysterious Stranger. Leone even made a trip to Los Angeles and offered Clint the part of Harmonica, the gunfighter played by Charles Bronson in *Once Upon a Time in the West*. 'But their meeting did not go well,' Richard Schickel reported in his Clint biography. 'Leone particularly (correctly) loved the movie's opening sequence, in which three gunfighters await the arrival of Harmonica at a train station and engage in much memorable and subtly satirical Western business. Somewhat to Clint's impatience, he focused on the entrapment of a fly in a pistol barrel by the figure who was played in the film by the iconic Jack Elam. "It took him fifteen minutes to get past that part," he says, and he remembers asking, "Wait a second, where are we headed with this?" But Leone was not to be hurried . . .'

After Leone – and Don Siegel – Clint would make a habit of avoiding strong-minded directors, who might impose their methods on him and push him to work as an actor. After all, Leone was a kind of intense Tuco in the flesh, who as the creator of the trilogy was bound (and determined) to upstage the fathomlessly cool Clint.

Later, after directing Robert De Niro in *Once Upon a Time in America*, Leone would endeavour to compare Clint to the other actor, widely regarded as America's finest. 'The first [Clint] is a mask of wax. In reality, if you think about it, they don't even belong to the same profession. Robert De Niro hurls himself into this or that role, putting on a personality the way someone else might put on his coat, naturally, and with elegance; while Clint Eastwood hurls himself into a suit of armour and lowers the visor with a rusty clang. It is precisely that lowered visor which composes his character. And that creaky clang it makes as it snaps down, dry as a Martini in Harry's Bar in Venice, is also his character.

'Look at him carefully. Eastwood moves like a sleepwalker between explosions and hails of bullets, and he is always the same – a block of marble. Bobby, first of all, is an actor. Clint, first of all, is a star. Bobby suffers. Clint yawns . . .'

But it wasn't just the US critics who failed to unite in praise of Clint. Although United Artists publicity claimed that 'American producers are now lined up bidding for Eastwood's services,' that was hardly the case. *The Good, the Bad and the Ugly* was finished in June 1966. Almost a year then went by while Clint performed English-language dubbing and looping, and cooperated with publicity chores.

It was a long, hard year. Clint went in for interviews on other films, but mainly he set his hopes on one of his own projects, with United Artists underwriting one of the scripts that he carried around with him. But his name was still a gamble, and it was a slow process of choosing the right property and convincing people. 'On occasion I'd run into him, and he was very, very angry, frustrated and alienated,' remembered Ted Post.

One of the scripts was *Hang 'Em High*, a cross between *Rawhide* and Sergio Leone. Writer Mel Goldberg and producer Leonard Freeman had conceived of this Western in 1966, intending it either as a feature or TV series pilot. Freeman had produced *Mr Novak* on television; he was also the creator of *Hawaii Five-O*. When, in 1967, *Hawaii Five-O* received network go-ahead, Freeman and Goldberg got busy on the series and forgot all about *Hang 'Em High*. But Freeman's agent, George

Litto, ran into Irving Leonard at dinner one night, and mentioned the script. Leonard said it might be right for Clint. Freeman and Goldberg had barely heard of Clint, whose 'spaghetti Westerns' were just heading into release. In fact, they thought his name was 'Clint Easterwood'.

Although Irving Leonard was receptive, the William Morris Agency acted noncommittal. Clint's representative there was now Leonard Hirshan, but one of the jobs Hirshan and the agency performed for Clint was to keep people at bay. In this case, someone at William Morris actually tried to *discourage* Leonard Freeman by telling the writer–producer not to get his hopes up – that Clint had 'ten or eleven' better scripts in the hopper. The agency itself was pushing for Clint to appear in a studio project, a big-budget Western called *MacKenna's Gold*, which would take the safe route of including Clint among a cast of other stars. But Clint, unconvinced, was withholding his approval.

A stubborn George Litto spoke to Irving Leonard again and learned that Clint liked the *Hang 'Em High* script, but harboured some criticisms. The writers were given to understand that Maggie was the truly enthusiastic party. Litto pushed for a meeting with Clint to find out if they could resolve his objections. Goldberg remembered that they waited in Irving Leonard's new offices in Century City, an hour past the appointed time, until finally Clint showed up. The writers then got their first look at the prospective star.

'He walked in the door, alone, and physically he looked like he was about seven feet tall,' recalled Mel Goldberg. 'He was offered a seat. He didn't want to sit down. He stood in the corner in a cowboy hat and he didn't say anything. Finally, I said, "I understand you have some reservations about the script. I'd love to hear about them."'

It was a curious thing about Clint and scripts that he often had very little to say about them. If he responded to a draft, he might go ahead and film it with bare-minimum revisions. In Hollywood, where revision is an accepted if arduous part of the preproduction process, this trait is almost singular. It might show Clint's bedrock confidence, or a *lack* of confidence in the writing process, and an unwillingness to struggle with the demands of collaboration with other people.

On *Hang 'Em High*, Clint had only one niggling complaint: that scene before the first hanging, where the hero is attacked by his enemies? Clint said he had a feeling that scene shouldn't transpire in a saloon. He had seen too many other Westerns where that type of scene took place in a saloon.

Freeman and Goldberg looked at each other. They couldn't believe their ears. After all this time, that was the only hurdle? What about the 'ten or eleven' better scripts?

On the spot one of the writers winged a suggestion. The fight didn't have to take place in the saloon; they could introduce a whore into the story, and Clint's character, feeling pent-up because of the impending executions, could sweep her into bed. After they have their romp, *then* Clint could head downstairs to the bar and *then* the attack could ensue.

A long silence from Clint, who liked whore scenes. 'Clint,' Freeman prodded, 'what do we tell William Morris?' Finally, the actor spoke up. 'Tell them we've got a deal.'

Clint's character's name was Cooper, meaning he was a decent, complex Gary Cooperish sort of guy. In a sense *Hang 'Em High* would provide audiences with their last glimpse of the Clint once thought to be a possible successor to Coop. A last glimpse of Rowdy, too; the script even opened on a *Rawhide* riff, with Cooper cradling a 'dogie' in his arms and ferrying it across the Rio Grande. Cooper's wrongful lynching and the tumbleweed wagon that brings him to jail are also straight out of the TV series. *Hang 'Em High* borrowed swatches from Sergio Leone too – there is the cigarillo Cooper is always smoking, even a mock-'spaghetti Western' soundtrack.

The plot had Cooper accused by vigilantes of a cow baron's murder, lynched and left for dead – all before the opening credits conclude. After Cooper manages to survive and get himself acquitted, he pins on a badge and becomes a Count of Monte Cristo cowboy seeking vengeance on his enemies. However, Cooper is humanized by doubt and a woman's affections. Insiders say that Clint's wife thought the romantic relationship was particularly well done in the screenplay; such softhearted interludes were lacking in the 'spaghetti Westerns'. (The love scenes, incidentally, would give Clint something else he liked: his requisite shirt-off time.) At the end, Cooper finally can't bring himself to avenge his hanging; in fact, the final member of the lynching party, when hunted down, commits suicide!

Clint's deal called for $400,000 in salary, plus a remarkable twenty-five per cent of the *net* proceeds. The ingenious Irving Leonard extracted a clause for additional dividends off the top of 'rentals' in Italy, where Clint's name was guaranteed to bolster attendance. This clause – unprecedented in Hollywood annals – positioned Clint as an American star whose foreign box-office would always be as vital to his overall success as his US popularity. Equally important, *Hang 'Em High* was set up as a co-production between United Artists and Malpaso, Clint's new production company. Named for 'a river on my property'* up in Monterey County, in Clint's words, Malpaso was another clever business concoction of Irving Leonard's.

Malpaso was structured so Clint couldn't lose. The trade papers published articles about the actor's 'unique formula for getting rich' by controlling the stock in a company in which he was a principal office holder, and also a bankable commodity that was under exclusive contract to and hired out by Malpaso. According to these accounts, Clint's salary and percentages would guarantee him upwards of $1,000,000 per film, spreading 'the tax bite with arrangements for deferred payments'. In most instances he – through Malpaso – would control script, director, major casting.

The mastermind of the Malpaso set-up, Irving Leonard, was the company's president (and, still, Clint's 'business manager'). There were mixed signals, during this initial, post-Leone phase, that Clint was feeling his way, still hesitant, in some ways, as an actor. No question, however, no matter who was company president, who made the major production decisions.

Old-timers Robert Aldrich and John Sturges were both in the running for director. United Artists production chief Arnold Picker preferred a veteran. Clint insisted on his old friend Ted Post, with whom he felt secure. 'He wanted him,' remembered Mel Goldberg, 'because there were a lot of talk scenes in which he had to act. He said the few things he did on *Rawhide* that he was happy with were directed by Ted Post.'

Post's reputation was as an 'actor's director'. Although his experience was concentrated in theatre and television, he had also directed two features, *The Peacemaker* and *The Legend of Tom Dooley*, both of them

---

* Actually, it is officially a creek – Malpaso Creek – about five miles south of Carmel in the Carmel Highlands.

Westerns. Clint could count on Post to be conscientious about the script, too. Together, they whittled down Clint's dialogue. As with much in his life, Clint would develop a tidy philosophy to explain this acquired habit. 'If the hero talks too much,' he liked to say, 'it weakens him.'

Being attuned to actors, director Post was also instrumental in the casting. He phoned Inger Stevens, who was stirring up interest in films after stardom on television in *The Farmer's Daughter*. 'Who's Clint Eastwood?' she asked. 'He's the *Rawhide* guy,' Post replied. Post gave her a sales pitch about Clint and the 'spaghetti Westerns'. 'Okay, who's Sergio Leone? . . .' She had to meet Clint to be persuaded.

'Well, as you know,' explained Post, 'Clint's not intimidating in any way. She began to like him. She began to like him very much as the days went on. Then, very, *very* much, etcetera. When we got to the love scene [in *Hang 'Em High*], they had already found their way together. At the end of the picture she came over to me and said, "Anytime you do a picture with Clint and there's a part in it, call me."'

The supporting cast was filled out by Pat Hingle, Ed Begley, Bruce Dern, Dennis Hopper, Ben Johnson, James MacArthur and other well-respected actors. Post would give each of them defining moments – condemned man John McIntire, for example, asking for a chaw of tobacco before being hung. Casting like this didn't come along in many other Clint films, and even when it did, the performances didn't achieve the same level.

In June of 1967, the company started filming in the Las Cruces area in New Mexico, including some scenes shot at the nearby White Sands national monument. After location work in the Southwest, the production returned to MGM for interiors.

One early crisis concerned the original cameraman, whom they all felt had to be replaced. But United Artists disagreed with Ted Post's substitute choice. Clint backed Post, bucking both the studio and producer Leonard Freeman. And Clint got his way.

Freeman, determined to safeguard his interests, had been set up contractually as the film's producer, with Irving Leonard listed as 'associate producer'. Ted Post had been imposed on Freeman as director, but the writer–producer showed up on the set intent on watch-dogging the script. Clint didn't like anybody second-guessing him, or the director, and one day early in the filming, he warned Freeman off. 'Clint's very quiet about it,' explained Post. 'He just took him aside one day and said, "You come on the set again and confuse the actors etc. with your opinions and feelings, and you're gonna face an empty set." He [Freeman] never showed up again.'

The real power rested with Malpaso, and the less-confrontational Mel Goldberg was appointed Freeman's proxy. Goldberg said that when Clint ventured a script idea, it was usually specific to his character, and usually terrific. In a barroom scene, where Cooper confronts one of the mob who had tried to hang him, the script gave Cooper 'five brilliant lines of dialogue', in Goldberg's words. Only five were too many for Clint.

Before the scene was shot, according to Goldberg, Clint came to him and said, 'Part of what I did on the "spaghetti Westerns" was to smoke this stogie. There's nothing wrong with these lines, but can I cut them? Can I do this instead? When I walk in and the guy says his first line, "Don't hassle me etc.", I'll take out the stogie and stick it in his drink. No more dialogue. That will get his attention. When he looks at me, I'll pull down my bandana to reveal the hanging scar, and let them know who I am.'

They filmed it – Clint's way, sans dialogue – which was better. Sometimes, however, Clint's way was just to step aside. When the film was completed, Ted Post and Leonard Freeman clashed anew in the editing room. Editor Gene Fowler Jr said Clint was rarely around to offer any input. The release version of *Hang 'Em High* still has a scene in it that Post hates: 'The shooting of Clint at the bar – Leonard Freeman made a Warner Brothers gangster scene out of that. The amount of shots that were poured into Clint, and he lives! That's a laugh!' Exaggerating his character's invincibility might have originated with Sergio Leone, but Clint didn't hesitate to appropriate it.

In the end, *Hang 'Em High* added up to an artful Western with a thought-provoking morality. It would be Clint's last merciful film for many years. The star claimed, for publicity's sake, that with *Hang 'Em High* he had fashioned an 'anti-capital-punishment' statement, but director Ted Post was largely responsible for the sensitive humanism; especially later, when, as Dirty Harry, he turned judge, jury and executioner, Clint's claim seemed empty.

Hang 'Em High pleased critics at the time, ('A Western of quality, courage, danger and excitement,' enthused Archer Winsten in the

New York Post). Already there was a solid Clint bandwagon of US reviewers. Although the star's long march toward critical respectability is half publicity myth and half defensive psychology, it may be that the barbs which bothered Clint the most were those he remembered best; there were people like Howard Thompson of the *New York Times* who, while complimentary towards the film, made a point of remarking upon the lead's 'glum sincerity' as an actor.

Hang 'Em High took off at the box-office when it was released in July of 1968. In Baltimore, the film registered an opening day total of $5,241, 'the biggest UA opening day in history, including all the [James] Bond films,' according to *Variety*, while Cincinnati, Cleveland, Detroit, Oklahoma City, Chicago, New York and Philadelphia reported similar results. *Hang 'Em High* would debut at number five on *Variety*'s weekly survey of top films, and 'literally went into profit two weeks after release', according to Mel Goldberg.

Variety reported that United Artists regarded the film's success 'as payoff for its investment in the Eastwood "mystique" for close to three years'. The show business weekly mused: 'How long the Eastwood cult will last, or how long the violence theme can be milked, or how successful opposition to it will be, is anybody's guess; but it's obvious that, for the present, Eastwood's name on the marquee is box-office.'

Clint already had another film completed by the time *Hang 'Em High* was in theatres.

United Artists was an unstable, slow-moving company, however, and so the door had swung open for the new star elsewhere. Although Jennings Lang, the onetime talent agent who wooed Clint to Universal, was famously persuasive, it wouldn't have taken much for the actor to gravitate back to the studio. Universal was a rock-solid company in a business that was quaking in the 1960s; many of Clint's relationships stemmed from his contract days there; and his ego would benefit from a triumphant return to the studio that once rejected him.

Not unimportant, Universal more than doubled Clint's salary to $1 million for his next film. His contract with the studio was also 'non-exclusive', and Malpaso, which 'owned' Clint, was permitted to set up joint ventures with other film companies.

Jennings Lang had worked for MCA before it took over Universal

and was forced by the government to get out of the talent representation business. He was a storied go-getter. As the former executive in
charge of television for Universal, he was well aware of the name Clint
Eastwood. In fact, *Coogan's Bluff* had also originated as a television
project when, early in 1967, the first-draft script was written by Herman
Miller. Miller and Jack Laird, who did a revised draft, were old *Rawhide*
hands. In fact, Herman Miller had been a story editor of the series
during its ill-fated final season, though he was acquainted with Clint
only in passing.

Although Herman Miller was quickly left behind in the succession
of writers, his name would survive on the screen and as creator of the
hit television series (*McCloud*) that would be spun off from the original
concept. The concept was a 'Rowdy-Goes-to-New-York' sort of *policier*,
following an unsophisticated Southwestern cowboy–detective assigned
to extradite a criminal suspect from Manhattan. Changing the projected television show into a feature film attraction mandated changes:
a 'name' cast; real locations for added scope and allure; heightening
the sex and violence quotient to accommodate America's contemporary mores.

Who ought to direct his second American film? Clint was tentative.
Initially he focused on two television directors with *Rawhide* credentials.
It was Jennings Lang who moved to act as matchmaker between Clint
and Don Siegel, a Universal contract director. Lang had once been
Siegel's agent; Siegel thought Lang 'genial, friendly and full of fun, a
most likeable chap', albeit undeniably 'tricky' on occasion.

Apparently Clint did not know very much about Siegel, who was
from Chicago, but Cambridge-educated. He had been kicking around
Hollywood since 1934, when he started out as an assistant librarian at
Warner Brothers. Siegel had worked his way up as a cutter, insert
director, montage expert. As a director he had notched more than
twenty feature credits since 1946 – including classic science fiction
(*Invasion of the Body Snatchers*) and hardboiled crime films (*Riot in Cell
Block 11, The Lineup*). Atlhough Truffaut and Godard had championed
the intelligence of his work in French film magazines, Clint hadn't
seen any of Siegel's movies, nor for that matter was Siegel more than
dimly aware of the hard-charging Clint.

'Jennings Lang was selling Clint on Don and Don on Clint,' recalled
Dean Riesner, the 'finishing writer' on *Coogan's Bluff*. 'Clint said, "I

want to see something Don has done." Don got uppity about that and said, "I want to see something that Clint has done." So we had to go watch Clint's pictures while Clint was watching ours.'

With Universal came not only the script but the almighty studio apparatus that would always be underplayed in Clint's mythology as an 'independent'. Accompanied by Universal's head of casting, Siegel was flown up to Carmel for a top-level meeting with the star. Although in the meantime Clint had viewed three Don Siegel films and pronounced them satisfactory, Siegel was already feeling resentful, having to be auditioned by a newcomer. Until he met and was charmed by Clint. 'After two martinis, during which time we discussed dames, golf, dames, the glorious weather, etc.,' according to Siegel, the two hit it off, and a natural partnership was born.

Another writer, Howard Rodman, was enlisted for a revised draft. As they were already behind the studio's wishful schedule, Clint and Siegel went to New York – then the Mojave desert – scouting locations, while Rodman holed up, writing against the clock. Rodman produced a new version inside of a month, but after copies went to Jennings Lang, Richard Lyons (the studio's designated line producer) and Leonard Hirshan, the phones lit up. Lang informed Siegel of the bad news. The start date was off. Clint wanted a meeting, accompanied by his entourage – his agent, lawyer, business manager. And entourages are born to dislike everything, thought Siegel.

The next morning Jennings and Siegel greeted Clint and entourage. The star disarmed everyone with his un-Hollywood outfit: sneakers, Levi's, sports shirt. However, 'no one shook hands', according to Siegel. 'Everyone waited for Clint to speak.' When Clint finally did give voice to his thoughts, what he said was, 'I hate the script.'

Siegel felt almost relieved. He would be glad to abandon the troublesome project. 'I feel that the writer has gone away from the original concept,' elaborated Clint. Siegel pointed out that there had been at least seven versions of the script. How many had Clint read? Only one, said Clint. Siegel told him that it was only fair for him to read them all before deciding to junk the hard work. 'Shit,' Clint said, but went home and read them. The scenario he had read first and liked, it turned out, was the original Herman Miller one.

This experience is often mentioned by Malpaso insiders to explain why Clint resists developing successive drafts of a script. But 'the first one is always the best' was also a rationalization that justified the star's preference for moving fast and cheap.

The next day, according to Siegel, he and Clint found themselves 'lying around on the floor surrounded by pages from the various drafts by the four writers', working with scissors. By the end of the day, they had nearly thirty pages with scribbled instructions for bridges between scenes.

After that, Siegel decided they needed the proverbial 'fresh writer'. Enter Dean Riesner, who had met Siegel several years back on a tele-film starring Henry Fonda, called *Stranger on the Run*. Riesner, whose father had been a comedic actor and director closely affiliated with Charles Chaplin, started out at Warner Brothers as a scenarist in 1941, under the *nom de plume* Dean Franklin. A favourite of Siegel's, Riesner had a proven ability to cure ailing scripts. The writer was also malleable – his motto: 'It's only words' – as well as tough and iconoclastic. Like Siegel.

Riesner patched together a new version of *Coogan's Bluff* to carry to his first meeting with Clint. According to Riesner, who ended up working for Clint on more films than any other writer, the star was never very specific about what he wanted from a script. 'He was deliberately vague,' explained Riesner. 'He just wanted it *better.*'

One day, years later, when they were working on another film, Clint surprised Riesner with the remark, 'Maggie liked your script.' 'That's the only thing like that he ever said to me,' said Riesner. 'Not "I liked the script" but "*Maggie* liked the script." He wasn't too effusive about scripts.'

Riesner *thought* Clint liked his scripts, but the actor had already raised to an art form the practice of maintaining his silence, while allowing others to fill in the blanks. Scenes in his films were akin to those silences; purely visual, they appeared to reflect the contemplative nature of the non-verbal man. Critics could be expected to fill in the blanks, crediting Clint. For example: the long opening sequence of *Coogan's Bluff*, with Coogan stalking a suspect in the desert, is played virtually without dialogue. 'Eastwood's work on the screenplay had ensured that this was a totally visual scene,' wrote Michael Munn in *Clint Eastwood: Hollywood's Loner*. Except this exact scene existed in the original Herman Miller script, before Clint had anything to do with the project.

Riesner and Clint had an early 'bad moment', in Siegel's words, when, at their first meeting, Riesner dared to criticize one of the star's pet scenes: Coogan 'banging Linny Raven, a young girl, in the hope that she would take him to her boyfriend'. Riesner thought it was a stupid scene, not particularly logical or attractive in terms of Clint's character. 'Clint thought otherwise, losing his temper,' remembered Riesner.

'His face went white,' said Riesner. 'He gave me one of those Clint looks. He hemmed and hawed and sounded very dangerous, like a bomb about to explode. He didn't really make a threat like "You're finished!" but I got a feeling I shouldn't have said anything.'

Siegel had to step in, take Clint aside, persuade him to apologize. 'He did apologize and he was very Clint about it,' said Riesner, 'hesitant and sincere.' Riesner went to work, feeling hesitant himself. He was supposed to turn out a final draft inside of a week. Inevitably it took longer, and there were further additions and changes. 'Before we finished shooting,' said Siegel, 'the script would look like a rainbow – blue, green, yellow, pink pages with a few white ones scattered in between.'

Siegel, through Universal departments, handled the first-rate casting: Lee J. Cobb would play the gruff New York police lieutenant who is dismissive of Coogan; Don Stroud would play the wacko criminal he is chasing; Susan Clark would play the probation officer who falls for Coogan; Tisha Sterling (daughter of actor Robert Sterling and actress Ann Sothern) would play the drugged-out girl involved with Stroud; and bit parts would be filled by old-timers Betty Field and Tom Tully.

They started filming in November of 1967 while Riesner was still rehauling the script. His final draft would be a compilation of Miller's best stuff with scenes from the other versions, blended with his own enhancements. Riesner recalled that Clint was very clear in story conferences about being 'sick of nice Hopalong Cassidy heroes and all that malarkey'. He wanted to come off as a 'heroic bastard', in Riesner's words. The star especially liked the scenes where he pushed women and punks around, according to Riesner.

After their initial set-to, Clint and Riesner got along fine. One day, Clint took the scenarist aside and told him about an unusual story he had optioned: his character would have a one-night stand with a psychopathic stalker. The script was called *Play Misty for Me.* Maybe Riesner would consider doing a rewrite? Clint was thinking of directing the film. 'It didn't really sound that great to me,' said Riesner, who told Clint he was interested, 'but I had a feeling that Clint was going to happen.'

Coogan's Bluff hardly proved an ideal shoot. They worried about the weather in New York, where the weather was fine; and they didn't worry about it in the Mojave Desert, where it snowed. Jennings Lang showed up on the set in New York, and was booted off by Siegel, whose antipathy towards producers would reinforce Clint's. Both Tisha Sterling and Susan Clark balked at performing certain scenes according to the director, and had to be read the riot act by Siegel, always backed to the hilt by Clint.

During one rehearsal, Siegel suggested that as Julie (Susan Clark's character) crosses behind a sofa where Coogan is sitting, he should pull her down and give her a fervent kiss. After which Julie breaks free – announcing 'Dinner!' – picks up a bag of groceries and heads for the kitchen. The actress, Susan Clark, took umbrage at the blocking. 'Susan disliked my suggestion quite strongly,' recalled Siegel. 'She felt that I was making Clint too macho and overemphasizing the kissing, etc.'

CLARK: It's too obvious.
EASTWOOD: It's obvious you don't know what you're talking about. Let's shoot it, Don.

Final interiors were photographed on Universal soundstages just before Christmas. The frenetic scene at a hippie-filled discotheque – dubbed 'The Pigeon-Toed Orange Peel' – was crammed with dancers and extras in various stages of nudity – 'groovy types, various freaks, boys with boys, girls with girls, men with women, dancing madly on thick glass squares of constantly changing coloured lights', in Siegel's words.

Siegel supervised the final cut of the film. *Mise en scène* was one of his strengths as a director. The narrative drive, economy of storytelling, the ingenuity of the montage (the fight scene at the airport, all implicit, furious blur) would be missing from those Malpaso productions that merely emulated Siegel's fast, efficient philosophy. *Coogan's Bluff* ended up running some 94 minutes; Clint's films would average out at over two hours. Yet *Coogan's Bluff*, when seen today, seems impressively crammed with detail, nuance and energy.

One thing Clint learned from his first collaboration with Don Siegel was the value of a top-flight crew. Set designer Alexander Golitzen had been on the Universal lot when Clint was a contract player, and met him then. Typical of the old-fashioned Hollywood art directors whom Clint would utilize to offset a personal weakness – decor and design – Golitzen would go to work at Malpaso. The crew members Clint inherited from Siegel and recycled into future films also included *Coogan's Bluff* stuntman Buddy Van Horn and cameraman Bruce Surtees. Surtees was the camera operator racing to keep behind Coogan during the motorcycle chase scene – which has Coogan pursuing Ringerman (Don Stroud) through the park surrounding the Cloisters monastery – the first of numerous cycle and car chases in Clint's oeuvre.

Nineteen sixty-eight was capped by the birth of Kyle Clinton Eastwood on 19 May.

With the worldwide popularity of the 'spaghetti Westerns' and the success of *Hang 'Em High*, Clint was no longer a Man With No Name. Now and forever, the press knew his name and was thrilled to interview him. The 'happily-married angle', left over from a previous publicity incarnation, was freshened. *Modern Screen*, interviewing Maggie and Clint on location in London where Clint was busy filming *Where Eagles Dare*, endeavoured to explain 'How They Had a Baby After 14 Childless Years'. At first, mentioned Maggie, there had been 'the question of money'. Then, after *Rawhide*, there ensued several years where she tried without success to get pregnant. 'For the childless, these are difficult times,' sympathetically observed *Modern Screen*, 'times when a husband and wife begin to wonder: which of us is to blame?'

Maggie had suffered a lingering bout of hepatitis, then a miscarriage, all the while time was passing. 'Hope and heartache alternated for them, month after fruitless month.' They even explored the alternative of adoption. Finally another pregnancy resulted.

In London for the month of April, Clint and the exceedingly pregnant Maggie spent time with the Burtons (Richard and Elizabeth) on their yacht moored on the Thames. When the filming dragged on, Maggie had to return to California for childbirth, ahead of Clint.

Clint phoned 'practically every night', according to *Modern Screen*. On the day she felt labour pains, Maggie was driven to the hospital by a friend. Kyle was born on a Sunday in St John's Hospital in Santa Monica. Clint came home the following Friday.

Although 'not the kind of man to gush with excitement, or even to pass out cigars', in the words of *Modern Screen*, Clint admitted to being a proud papa. 'The real Clint and the character he created in the "Dollar" flicks – "spaghetti Westerns" as he dubbed them – are poles apart,' the magazine assured readers. 'He lives, and has always lived, quietly. He drives around the country home in Carmel in a pick-up, he shuns parties, and when not working he likes to laze around in the sun, not even harming a fly.'

Clint wasn't lazing around the hospital or home for very long, however, since he already had another acting obligation. The fallow period immediately following the 'spaghetti Westerns' was succeeded by one of his busiest, and most varied, with contracts signed for several shared leads that, later, more smug stardom might disdain. According to close friends, Clint already had one eye cocked on John Wayne, who was the country's reigning box-office champion; Wayne worked hard, often more than one film a year, and Clint would have to work just as hard to overtake him.

Where Eagles Dare was calculated to cement Clint's standing in England and Europe, and to expand his repertoire beyond Westerns. Although his salary of $850,000 was less than his established rate, Clint could make it up in percentages.

Clint liked to play the occasional heroic spy or soldier, and this part was opposite Richard Burton at the peak of Burton's drawing power. However, the script, by Alistair MacLean, based on a novel of his commissioned by the film's producer, Elliott Kastner, was 'terrible', Clint declared in one interview. 'All exposition and complications,' said the star. So Clint began to scratch out his dialogue. 'Pretty soon I realized I had no dialogue left.'

'We sat down one day over in Austria,' Clint ventured to explain on another occasion, 'and the subject of why we were doing the film came up. [Director] Brian [G. Hutton] pointed to Richard Burton. "Because he's doing it." I pointed to Burton and said, "Because he's doing it." The thing was, we all knew Richard was doing it for the loot.'

There was loot to go around in the big-budget film. The story was about a World War II squad parachuting into a Gestapo castle that is nestled in the mountains and reachable only by cable car. Burton was the squad's commander and Clint the fearless right-hand man. There are people who like the film, but Clint doesn't really register in the sombre, murky atmosphere, and Burton's talent was squandered.

Clint's next project would also have the added insurance of box-office names, although it couldn't have been more unalike. Surprising some in Hollywood, Clint signed to sing a starring role in *Paint Your Wagon*, Lerner and Loewe's gold rush musical, which had originated during the Broadway season of 1951. His part of Pardner didn't even *exist* in the original show, and had been built up with Clint in mind. He would play a 'moral' and 'green' Rowdy type, a peaceable ex-farmer from Michigan who forms a partnership with a grungy, boozing, cussing gold miner.

Lee Marvin was Paramount's choice for the grungy, boozing cuss and Jean Seberg was Malpaso's approved casting for the leading lady. By July Clint had to be up in a fork-in-the-road called Baker, Oregon, where the sets were being built. The Hollywood trade papers noted that the redoubtable Irving Leonard had extracted a half million dollars in salary for his client's musical comedy debut – before percentages and other fillips – to be paid out in annual fifty-thousand-dollar increments.

In Hollywood history there have been few fiascos to compare with *Paint Your Wagon*.

All the horrors descended. Weather wreaked havoc on the locations and outdoor sets. Director Joshua Logan was unstable and constantly rumoured to be on the verge of replacement (*Paint Your Wagon* would spell the end of his Hollywood career). The 'super-budget', which besides accommodating the star salaries had to absorb hundreds of chorus and extras along with the film's extravagant 'earthquake' climax, would rise above $20 million.

But the worst horror may have been the miscast stars. The only intriguing element of the story – two husbands and one wife in a G-rated *ménage à trois* – was created for the film version by Lerner, after he had split up from Loewe. Seberg, playing the double-duty wife, was a sophisticated actress with a facility for projecting wild innocence on the screen. Born in Iowa, she had made a second home for herself in Paris after her Hollywood debut as Joan of Arc in Otto

Preminger's *Saint Joan* and Preminger's equally disappointing follow-up, *Bonjour Tristesse*. A starring role in Jean-Luc Godard's *nouvelle vague* hit *A Bout de Souffle*, or *Breathless*, along with a second marriage to novelist Romain Gary, had recharged Seberg's career in Europe.

She would prove distinctly uncomfortable in her hapless part, however; and although Lee Marvin, one of Hollywood's premier heavies, cast against type, seemed more at ease in his, he played to the rafters, blasting Clint's mild mannerisms off the screen.

Clint's singing is one of the all-time cringing embarrassments. Incredibly, he was awarded *four* songs to sing. One of them, 'I Still See Eliza', was an established hit that had been sung in the original show by Ben Rumson, the Lee Marvin character. Nobody in the film version is named Eliza, however, so Marvin covers this discrepancy by asking, 'Hey Pard, is that the name of your girl?'

Another song was particularly thankless, with Clint strolling in the woods as he warbles, 'I talk to the trees, but they don't listen to me . . .' The mood was conveyed by a gauzy long shot for pastoral effect. Clint's pale voice, when put to the test of Nelson Riddle's lush scoring, proved barely serviceable.

Later Clint would point to *Paint Your Wagon* as inspiring his low-cost, no-nonsense approach to producing his own films. But his $50,000 annuity was part of the inordinate budget, and no matter what the critics eventually said ('a monument to unparalleled incompetence' was how Rex Reed described the film when it was released in August 1970), the man who played Pard probably had fond memories of the shoot for at least one reason . . . maybe why he took the role in the first place.

Clint was always interested in the actresses and leading ladies who populated his films. His friend from boyhood and later, the producer of a number of Malpaso films, Fritz Manes, said that sometimes Clint would emerge from a casting conference and exclaim about an actress he had just encountered, 'Oh, that shit's hot! Did you see the way she was looking at me? I could have that in a minute!'

'The little head was always thinking for the big,' Manes explained. 'If you look at the films [that Clint stars in], you can see recurring women [players]. These are usually the ones brought back because it was a good piece of ass last time.'

The pattern was long established with Clint that location work meant a respite from marriage. On *Hang 'Em High*, he had a fling with Inger Stevens; on *Coogan's Bluff*, according to Dean Riesner, who held script meetings after hours with Clint in his hotel, 'I'd leave his suite, and I'd be going down the hall and there'd be some girl coming down the hall from the opposite direction and heading into Clint's room.' Added Riesner: 'There were always a bunch of girls around him, I'll tell you that. Gals from the office, gals around the set, gals in the picture. He's a pretty good man with the ladies.'

The little dolly on the *Paint Your Wagon* set, at least up in Oregon, was Jean Seberg. Off screen, she was another of Clint's blonde gamine types. She looked a little like Maggie, with full lips, prominent cheek-bones and an aura of feverish androgyny.

Seberg's affair with Clint has been well documented. Mexican novel-ist Carlos Fuentes (another of her lovers) refers to it in his *roman à clef, Diana: The Goddess Who Hunts Alone*. Film-maker Mark Rappaport made it a caustic focal point of his 'pseudo-documentary' *From the Journals of Jean Seberg*. Biographer David Richards reported it in depth in his authoritative book, *Played Out: The Jean Seberg Story*, published a few years after Seberg, just 40, died, a probable suicide, in 1979.

In his authorized version of Clint's life, Richard Schickel treats the affair coyly. He quotes Clint as saying that he and Seberg were 'close buddies' up in Oregon, which comment is followed by one of Clint's studied pauses, then – 'I really liked her a lot' – another pause, then – 'I was kind of nuts about her.' According to Schickel: 'It was her fragility and vulnerability that attracted him, a sense that this was a woman who needed protection, as both her professional and personal histories seem to prove.'

Clint and Jean Seberg took long motorcycle rides together whenever they were not obliged to be on camera. Her marriage to Romain Gary happened to be conveniently on the rocks. Clint's 'I'm-happily-married' line might have been a little time-worn, but he had the advantage of being able to update that with the recent news of fatherhood.

Indeed, Maggie showed up on location with three-month-old baby Kyle, making her brief, ritual visit to one of her husband's sets. Seberg disappeared from Clint's side, while none-the-wiser Maggie expounded for the press.

'I want Clint to get better acquainted with his son,' Maggie informed one fan magazine correspondent. 'He really hasn't gotten a good look at him lately. What with the new picture starting so soon after the last one, Clint managed to get into town only once or twice. The last time he got back from location, it was night. Kyle was asleep, and Clint just got a glance at him in his crib. That's pretty rough on a new father.'

After Maggie left Oregon, Clint and Seberg's relationship faltered. 'Given their other commitments,' the Clint–Seberg romance 'could only be a thing of the moment,' wrote Schickel. *Played Out: The Jean Seberg Story* states plainly that the Clint–Seberg romance tapered off in October, when the production was forced to quit Oregon and retreat to Hollywood soundstages. 'Dropping temperatures and the threat of early snow sent the company back to the Paramount lot, where No Name City was partly reconstructed at additional expense,' according to David Richards.

'Once they got back to Paramount,' Jerry Pam, Seberg's Hollywood publicist (also, at the time, Clint's), is quoted in *Played Out*, 'it was as if Clint didn't know who she was. Jean couldn't believe that he could be that indifferent to her, after everything that had gone on in Baker. She was a very vulnerable woman, and it was a terrible trauma for her.'

Seberg never publicly identified Clint as the man who broke her heart, but *Played Out* notes that she confided 'her disappointment' to a few friends, and then made apparent reference to Clint a year later in a newspaper dispatch from Rome, in which she admitted her affair with a man who was 'the absolute opposite' of her husband, 'an outdoor type'. She said her confidence in this person turned out to be 'misplaced'.

'It's always a bit of a shock to discover that people aren't sincere,' Seberg said.

In his book, intended to reflect Clint's perspective, Schickel added a sorrowful postscript: 'In the years that followed' their affair, the actress's 'unhappiness and confusion deepened, and after a decade of troubled relationships she died of an overdose of sleeping pills.' This not only minimizes any betrayal of Maggie, shortly after the birth of Kyle, but overlooks the fact that Seberg's 'decade of troubled relationships' started with her Clint romance during *Paint Your Wagon*.

CHAPTER SIX

Blue-Collar Clint
1970–1973

The decade began with two unexpected deaths. Shortly before Christmas 1969, Irving Leonard passed away at age fifty-three. Clint's long-time business manager – the president of the actor's company and producer of the first Malpaso films – had supervised Clint's contracts and cannily organized his financial affairs.

Friends say they have never seen Clint as devastated as he was by Leonard's death.

An old friend was recruited to replace Leonard in the Malpaso operations. Since Arch Drive days, Bob Daley had worked at Ziv and Desilu, first as an assistant director and then as a unit manager, on series such as *The Untouchables, Ben Casey* and *The FBI*, gradually working his way up to a position as co-producer of Doris Day's television programme. For Malpaso, Daley would become the consummate backroom man, handling all the production arrangements with finesse. He would negotiate for scripts and cast, put the crew together, scout locations. Although sensitive and literate, his artistic input would be limited, however. Nor would he ever wield Leonard's overall power.

Irving Leonard's last will and testament indicates that the man who used to loan Clint sums of money to tide the actor over now represented only a small number of clients, of whom two were paramount: James Garner and Clint Eastwood. The will states that with the approval of these two clients, two green-shade bookkeepers in Leonard's employ, Roy Kaufman and Howard Bernstein, would assume the reins of the accountancy. The new entity, Kaufman and Bernstein Inc., would continue to handle Clint's portfolio, with Kaufman, a veritable human computer, in charge. It would be his challenge to trump Clint in the thrift department.

The will gives clues as to the investments and holdings about which Clint has always been genuinely secretive. Leonard's will states that Clint already owned roughly five hundred acres of Carmel Valley woodlands, with a fair market value estimated, at the time, at half a million dollars. He also owned approximately one hundred and eighty-five acres of land south of Carmel whose worth was estimated at several hundred thousand dollars. 'Much of this [property] would make ideal ocean-view homesites,' one Monterey County newspaper reported, when the land was originally purchased.

Clint also owned a participation in several business interests including Label Gun Inc., Summa Corp. and Eastlen Enterprises. Leonard's pooled investments for his clients favoured real estate, office development and shopping centre ventures.

In numerous ways Clint's world was a closed one. Apart from a few television actors like Alex Cord and George (*Route 66*) Maharis, Irving Leonard's other clients in 1964 were people closely associated with Clint, or Malpaso. And Leonard's will had been drawn up by his attorney, also Clint's – Frank Wells of Gang, Tyre & Brown – whose influence with Clint, now that Leonard was gone, would grow.

In his book Richard Schickel makes the curious statement that Clint bristled under his long-term commitment to Universal because that studio made choices for film subjects that were 'generally unimaginative and often vexed' by poor scripts, by inept studio-appointed producers, and by indifferent handling of the product in the marketplace.

Universal (through Jennings Lang) did come up with most of the subjects. For that reason, the studio can be held responsible for a period of work, 1969 to 1973, that would have to rate as one of Clint's most varied and risky. Nor is it fair to blame only the studio for the imperfect scripts. Once Clint agreed to a project, he (and Don Siegel) exercised latitude over the script, and any blame for the results was partly theirs.

The real issue with Universal was autonomy. Irving Leonard had made only one mistake: Malpaso's deal with the studio was fifty-fifty, with Universal the arbiter of important disagreements. Universal was still an old-fashioned, controlling studio, and Jennings Lang was very much an activist, as a producer. As Clint's fame grew, so did his resentment of studio input and authority.

The issue with the first Malpaso co-production of the 1970s was autonomy – and a star that tempted the focus away from Clint. *Two Mules for Sister Sara* was a story about an American mercenary who gets mixed up with a whore disguised as a nun, both of them aiding the Juarista rebels during the puppet reign of Emperor Maximilian in Mexico. Budd Boetticher's script had been optioned by Martin Rackin, a journeyman screenwriter who had turned writer–producer in the 1950s.

Rackin annoyed Siegel and Clint from beginning to end. He tried to leave his stamp on the script revisions; he tried to cut costs; he pushed to shoot on location in Mexico, with an indigenous supporting cast and crew (this would lead to the hiring of an internationally renowned cameraman, Gabriel Figueroa, who had worked on Luis Buñuel and John Ford films). Siegel thought Rackin a nuisance, and Clint's official biography would describe him as 'an almost parodistic version of a Hollywood operator – all gold chains, sunlamp tan and tough talk'.

Maybe Boetticher was a little-old fashioned; his last screen credit dated back ten years. So Rackin hired Albert Maltz, the onetime blacklisted member of the Hollywood Ten, to give the script a fresh rewrite with obvious 'quotes' from Sergio Leone's *oeuvre*. Clint was the Mysterious Stranger all over again, this time in Mexico. The approach of Maltz's script was less brutal and more sardonic, however – 'Leone-lite'.

Early on, the script had been sent to Elizabeth Taylor, who was pencilled-in as the leading lady, and also to Clint; this was in London, back during the filming of *Where Eagles Dare*. Liz playing opposite Clint was a box-office mirage that whetted everybody's thirsts. When Don Siegel visited England to loop some lines for *Coogan's Bluff*, he met Clint and Liz, and was enlisted as the preferred director.

This chronology is important because Clint was signing contracts left and right, consolidating his Hollywood status by aligning himself with other big stars in big-budget projects. Six months later, after the double-barrelled successes of *Hang 'Em High* and *Coogan's Bluff*, *Two Mules for Sister Sara* might not have seemed as bright an idea, but Clint had already committed, and was caught up in the momentum.

One of the problems, in the meantime, was that Liz had been struck from the cast. Nobody can recall the precise reasons. Siegel said in his memoirs that the actress insisted on shooting in Spain, where husband Richard Burton was scheduled for his next film. Siegel and Clint were amenable, but Rackin and the studio said no. The trade papers reported, alternatively, that Liz had made impossible demands and, furthermore, that her health was unstable. In any case, Shirley MacLaine proved available, and Universal and Rackin both lobbied for her casting.

After making her debut in *The Trouble With Harry*, MacLaine had been nominated for three Oscars over the next fifteen years. One of her acknowledged fortes was playing sentimental whores and floozies. But Siegel and Clint were unenthusiastic about MacLaine, partly, they said, because Sister Sara was supposed to be Mexican. Although everyone had been prepared to accept Liz as a Mexican, MacLaine's pale, freckle-faced mien ('the map of Ireland', in Siegel's words) called for eleventh-hour rewrites to provide her character with some kind of American background.

The problem, once the production finally began shooting in Mexico in February 1969, was not MacLaine's un-Latin looks or thespian abilities, however. The problem was that she was a strong-minded free spirit who didn't mesh well with Siegel.

To be fair, it was not an easy shoot for MacLaine. She had to perform in nun's habit under a blazing sun that often pushed the mercury to 100 degrees–plus. The company hired a peon to follow her around with a big, shady umbrella. Nonetheless, the actress suffered severe sunburn and at one point came down with a case of double pneumonia. The actress also had difficulty riding the mules that were integrated into the storyline, in scene after scene. Her problems wore on everybody's nerves.

On top of everything, MacLaine, according to Siegel, was a 'nightbird' who didn't always show up on time for her morning calls. More than once MacLaine and the director disagreed about a scene and fenced with words, while Clint held his tongue on the sidelines. Time came for a showdown, towards the end of the location schedule, and the distaff star stormed off the set. Siegel decided he would simply quit. He thought MacLaine 'talented but hoydenish'. The director was just about to pack his bags when there came a knock on his hotel room door. MacLaine had arrived to apologize. Siegel wrote in his memoirs: 'From that moment on, she was a doll.'

Clint is strangely passive and in the background of these MacLaine–Siegel battles. And the actress says virtually nothing about co-starring with Clint, in her own memoirs. MacLaine is one leading lady whom Clint never has boasted about bedding. Like Siegel, he seems to have regarded her with respect and not a little trepidation.

The cast was headquartered at a magnificent hotel in Coyococ, a small town about thirty miles from Cuernavaca. Published sources indicate Clint kept busy during his off hours wooing other women: actress Susan St James was one visitor to the set, and another Clint girlfriend was reportedly 'flown in to Coyococ from the Bahamas'. Buddies say that Clint also 'entertained' at least one lady journalist among the members of the press flown in to tout the forthcoming film.

Clint was by now a prize interview, and the years when he had to scrounge for newspaper mention or magazine coverage were over. The press – because Clint was 'ill at ease about their presence and innocent about their needs', according to Richard Schickel – were steered toward the star's love of animals. There was one scene in *Two Mules for Sister Sara* which called for Hogan (Clint) to cut off the head of a rattlesnake, then hand the writhing creature over to a discomfited Sister Sara (MacLaine). He did as required, but very reluctantly, according to location interviews. As Clint told one journalist, 'I guess I have too much of a reverence for living creatures.'

This 'reverence' could reach absurd lengths. Another on-set anecdote described the filming of a scene, which was interrupted by a large moth flitting madly around the set. The moth appeared to be trapped and dazed by the huge arc lamps. 'A member of the crew immediately chased after it, trying to swat it and stamp on it,' chronicled one journalist who witnessed the incident. 'Eastwood flew into a rage. "Leave it alone," he yelled at the startled moth hunter. "They need killers like you in Vietnam," Eastwood told him, and then, gently cupping his hands around the moth, guided it to safety.'

Back at Universal, after shooting the final interiors, Siegel wrangled with Rackin over the editing. Rackin was known for muttering, 'Lose the battles, win the war.' According to Siegel: 'The war he won on *Two Mules for Sister Sara* was that he, not I, did the final editing. It's a limited victory, however, because if you cut the picture in the camera, shoot the minimum and get to do the first cut as Alfred Hitchcock or

I do, then there isn't that much leeway in the editing, unless the producer orders more film shot.'

When *Two Mules for Sister Sara* was released in the summer of 1970, one of the most flattering reviews emanated from the *New York Times*, where Roger Greenspun wrote, 'I'm not sure that it is a great movie, but it is very good, and it stays and grows in the mind the way only movies of exceptional narrative intelligence do.'

That is the way it still looks: a film that 'stays and grows in the mind'. It was a transparent Sergio Leone imitation, but a clever one. The unique thing about *Two Mules for Sister Sara* – it would have been just as unique for Leone – was the standoff between a tough guy and an equally tough lady. Like the actress who played her, Sister Sara was no pushover. She smokes her own cigarillos, swigs whiskey before breakfast, acquits herself admirably in the fight sequences. Shirley Maclaine's more intimate scenes with Clint were delightful sparring matches without any clear victor. A dynamic of genuine equality usually worked to force Clint into alertness.

One scene, Clint commented some years later, boasted his best-ever acting. It is the one where Sister Sara must get Hogan drunk in order to extract an arrow protruding from his shoulder. As he sings a ditty about a Protestant parson, she lights gunpowder to cauterize the wound and shoves the arrow out the other side of his flesh. Clint was never held to higher standards than in the Don Siegel films; but Shirley MacLaine was one-of-a-kind, and her performance raised the stakes.

'It's hard to feel any great warmth for her,' Don Siegel remarked about Shirley MacLaine some years later. 'She's too . . . unfeminine. She has too much balls. She's very, very hard. You have the feeling that if you talk gently to her, she'll ridicule you.'

Although a bridge is blown up and there is an all-out battle at the end of the film, *Two Mules for Sister Sara* is really a two-character story. MacLaine's relative stature can be measured in the equal dialogue, the divided screen time, the number of close-ups. MacLaine was also billed above Clint, the last time that would happen in his career. It would be twenty-five years before *The Bridges of Madison County*, before Clint would again risk a leading lady who might overshadow him. Too bad.

*   *   *

The actor only had a few months off before he headed to London and Yugoslavia in July 1969, honouring another prior commitment, a film called *Kelly's Heroes*, with Clint as one of a larcenous band of Americans who play hooky from the war to steal a fortune in bullion from the Nazis. *Two Mules for Sister Sara* had taken four months to shoot, with the costs creeping above $4 million; *Kelly's Heroes* would prove an even more problematic experience and occupy Clint in Europe for most of the rest of the year.

Such a dragged-out schedule was probably the worst debit. Once Clint seemed, like his father, a contented plodder; full-fledged stardom had come almost as a surprise, rather late in life. Approaching forty, the actor seemed increasingly fired by mortality and impatience. 'I can't stand long locations or production schedules,' Clint told *Action*, the Directors Guild of America magazine, in 1971. 'Once you get moving, I don't see any reason to drag your feet. During production, I can function much more fully and efficiently if I move full blast. Maybe it's because I'm basically lazy.'

Unfortunately for Clint, nothing seemed to move full blast during the filming of *Kelly's Heroes*. The schedule called for filming in Yugoslavia with logistics that involved hundreds of extras and scenes utilizing explosives and dangerous special effects. There seemed endless travail: sets burning down, weather turning bad, more than the customary bumps, even for an expensive, complicated, overseas production.

The film had the same director as *Where Eagles Dare* (Brian G. Hutton), the same cameraman as *Two Mules for Sister Sara* (Gabriel Figueroa). And it had one of the all-time loopy casts: Telly Savalas (pre-Kojak, and coming off as cool, composed as Clint), Don Rickles (a comic relief hustler), Donald Sutherland (a hipster in uniform) and Carroll O'Connor (a puffed-up commander dishing out medals and asides).

Clint was Kelly, whose interrogation of a Nazi colonel captured behind enemy lines sets in motion the perfect caper. With an ever-multiplying number of cohorts, Kelly must slog through miles of German soldiers to break into a bank vault. At the climax is one of those 'spaghetti Western' moments that abound in Clint's cinema, with the Good (Clint), the Bad (Savalas) and the Ugly (Sutherland) advancing in lockstep on a German tiger tank on the street of a small European town. Ennio Morricone had provided the kidding music for *Two Mules for Sister Sara;* here the Lalo Schifrin soundtrack 'borrows' from Morricone.

Clint is excellent in the film, the resolute leader and wary ally of Savalas, Sutherland, Rickles et al. But on- as well as off-camera dissatisfaction with the oddball troupe was hinted at in Clint's subsequent verdict on the production. 'Our styles were inconsistent,' Clint explained. 'People off on different trips. No cohesion'.

Clint tried to stay happy during the never-ending shoot by tooling around the European countryside on the 750 c.c. B11 Norton motorcycle he had purchased in England during *Where Eagles Dare.* By November, however, the filming had dragged on for too long. The star was fed up. When the company returned to London, Clint took time for interviews to promote *Paint Your Wagon,* then balked at staying a few extra days to perfect some things for *Kelly's Heroes.* 'The shot footage was scheduled for shipment to Paris, and Clint declared that he was going to be on the same train with it,' wrote Richard Schickel. 'He had given all that he could to this endless enterprise, had a date to celebrate Thanksgiving there with some friends, and that was that.'

The World War II film was the last non-Malpaso deal to which Clint had agreed. Again, the chronology is important, because Clint didn't have sufficient clout to overrule MGM when it came to decision-making. The executive in charge of MGM, James Aubrey, had presided over the long run of *Rawhide* while at NBC, before trying to cancel the series. So he and Clint were not exactly endeared to each other.

Indeed, while on the set of his next film, Clint engaged in a screaming match with Aubrey over the phone. *The Beguiled* lost Clint's services for a day, according to Don Siegel, while the star sat in his trailer, surrounded 'by agents, lawyers, accountants and other advisers', doing his best to pressure Aubrey into a different final cut. The original script had been clearly 'anti-war', Clint later explained, but that message was blunted by the studio with a version that accented the comedy. The star regretted losing a particular scene where he and Savalas summed up 'what the war had done to them'.

But was this really the issue? In the film Kelly does have a few lines of 'serious' subtext, revealing that he once had been a gung-ho lieutenant, until he was handed orders to attack the wrong hill and accidentally wiped out half a company of his own GIs. This is a tossed-off scene, however, and the rest of Clint's characterization, all of the performances, slouched towards comedy. In the end people 'on different trips' made for an exceedingly entertaining vehicle, and Clint's dislike of the film seems out of proportion. *Kelly's Heroes* holds up still, playing endlessly on television nowadays.

'He had, as well, a purely practical complaint [to lodge with Aubrey],' noted Richard Schickel in his book, 'that "creeping" release date. If it was held to, *Kelly's Heroes* would open in many major markets virtually day and date with *Two Mules for Sister Sara*. "Why should I open across the street from myself?" Clint asked Aubrey.'*

When, later on, Clint was able to break free to make his own military films, *Firefox* and *Heartbreak Ridge*, he would strive to present war as a sober, manly business. The latter did try for some broad comedy, and fell flat. Neither film would be cluttered by anti-war sentiments of the sort which Clint felt cheated out of in the case of *Kelly's Heroes*.

Almost immediately, in the winter of 1969–70, Clint and Don Siegel launched into planning for their next film. To this day, the unusual production that resulted, *The Beguiled*, is ranked by many, French critics in particular, as a veritable masterpiece.

It started, as did most of the projects during this period, with Universal's initiative. Again, it was Jennings Lang who saw, in the 1966 novel by Thomas Cullinan, a possible bold departure for Clint. He gave the book to the actor, who passed it on to Siegel with the remark that he had stayed up all night reading the strangely compelling tale of a wounded Civil War bluecoat, a beguiler given sanctuary in a Deep South finishing school for young ladies, who are eroticized by his presence.

Clint would demonstrate, with this and future film properties, that he liked stories where nubile females gazed upon him with adoring eyes. A young nymph follows him around, misty-eyed over his noble suffering, in *Honkytonk Man*. One of the subplots of *Pale Rider* is the sexual rivalry over Clint's character that is carried on between a teenage

---

* That is exactly what happened: *Two Mules for Sister Sara* and *Kelly's Heroes* both played theatres during the mid-summer of 1970. Each earned approximately $1.5 million. Ironically – something Clint couldn't have anticipated – he had a third film in release that summer. *Paint Your Wagon* had been playing in movie houses for almost a year, and more than doubled the ticket sales of *Two Mules for Sister Sara* and *Kelly's Heroes*, ultimately, with nearly $7 million gross.

girl and her mother. And the film version of *The Beguiled* would open audaciously with Clint planting a passionate kiss on the lips of a thirteen-year-old girl (a scene *not* in the book).

Once Clint and Siegel agreed to team up again, the script toil started, again with Albert Maltz, the veteran of *Two Mules for Sister Sara*, working on four drafts of the script, all the time Clint was in Yugoslavia on *Kelly's Heroes*. Julian Blaustein, assigned by the studio as producer, flew to London in November to meet with Clint and discuss the project. He made the mistake of telling the star that he felt the part really belonged to a younger, more innocent-seeming man, thus offending Clint. The character in the book was a young soldier, just twenty; Clint was on the verge of forty. So what?

Blaustein was promptly shunted to the sidelines, and thereafter had almost nothing to do with the project. Siegel took over as producer, although the film was still officially 'a Jennings Lang production'. Lang had second thoughts when the script drafts failed to impress him. So did Clint. It was Siegel who then stuck with the writing, and eventually shepherded into existence a shooting scenario that satisfied everyone.

The book had been written in the first person, telling the story of Johnny McBurney, or McB (Eastwood), through the shifting viewpoint of a succession of young ladies who fall for his seductive lies. Siegel saw the tale as 'strange and fierce, like the novellas of Ambrose Bierce'. Albert Maltz, who couldn't quite figure out the attraction of the novel, said he wished he had the talent of Ambrose Bierce. 'Pull off the masks of these innocent, virginal nymphs, and you will reveal the dark, hidden secrets of wily manipulators,' Siegel exhorted him. 'I don't agree,' Maltz said, 'I believe in people.'

This exchange summed up one of the major themes of Clint's films. Rip off the masks of women and they are revealed as murderous harpies. Females on whom Clint bestowed the gift of his body came back at him with weapons, not only in *The Beguiled,* but in his next film, *Play Misty for Me*, and also in *High Plains Drifter*, *The Eiger Sanction* and *The Rookie*. *Sudden Impact*, *Tightrope* and *Absolute Power* would explore related terrain: sex, violence, vengeance. In Don Siegel's words, one of the motifs of *The Beguiled* was 'the basic desire of women to castrate men'. As even Richard Schickel conceded, Clint possessed 'retributive fears' where the fair sex was concerned.

When Maltz failed to deliver on the 'nymph-ingredient', in Siegel's words, Irene Kamp, whose screen credits included *Paris Blues* and *The Sandpiper*, was approached. Working closely with the director during the month of October 1969, she tried to add Southern touches to the script and to humanize the female characters. One of her lasting contributions was to make Hallie, the black cook, young, beautiful and *also* attracted to McB. In the novel Hallie was an older, more clichéd Southern mammy.

But Siegel and Clint were displeased with her version too, and the final polish was handed over to Claude Traverse, Siegel's longtime production associate. Traverse went uncredited on the screen, and Maltz, unhappy with all the changes, took the pseudonym 'John B. Sherry'. Siegel insisted Irene Kamp had not done enough to warrant credit, but she thought otherwise and the Writers Guild agreed. She also disliked the final form of the script and took the pseudonym 'Grimes Grice', the name of an uncle.

By the time *The Beguiled* was set to begin photography, in April 1970, the screenplay was a solid one, however. Remarkably, considering the ordeal of rewrites, it ended up following closely the plot and characters of the original novel.

Siegel was able to employ, over studio qualms, the production designer he wanted (Ted Haworth). He was able to arrange a non-studio, out-of-state location (the Belle Hélène Plantation near Baton Rouge, Louisiana). He had his choice of cameraman; Bruce Surtees would be promoted from operator, and begin to cultivate the dark, moody low-lighting that would earn him the sobriquet of 'Prince of Darkness'.

Early on, Jennings Lang had campaigned for Jeanne Moreau to play the headmistress Martha Farnsworth, whose tortured psychology dictates the increasingly macabre turn of events. But that glamorous possibility somehow fell through the cracks. As Siegel stated in his memoir, 'As far as the women in the picture were concerned, the studio didn't care about who we had in it as long as we had Clint.'

They instead got Geraldine Page, a (frequent) stage and (less frequent) screen actress, a well-known exponent of the Method who came with respectability but without taxing the budget.* (Nor did she have

---

* 'I thought Geraldine Page was out of my league, being a big star on the Broadway stage and all,' Clint explained in a later interview, 'but when we started *The Beguiled* she told me she was a big fan of mine on *Rawhide*.'

any particular cachet with film audiences.) The other leading parts went to Elizabeth Hartman (Edwina), Jo Ann Harris (Carol), Darlene Carr (Doris), Mae Mercer (Hallie) and Pamela Ferdyn (Amy).

Faraway location work meant relative independence from the studio – and as usual for Clint, fresh romantic prospects. Jo Ann Harris was one of those 'new faces', busy on television but virtually unknown on the wide screen, whom Clint tended to favour in his films. (He could justifiably claim to have discovered them; also they possessed egos more pliant than 'names'.) Harris was playing a seventeen-year-old with a crush on Clint's character, and their on-screen relationship was echoed in the affair that transpired between them off camera. Their love affair would grow so heated – continuing after the location – that friends were gulled into thinking she might be the one, finally, to break up the Eastwood marriage.

Siegel and Clint had the script they wanted, the cast and crew, the production appointments. They had the editing to themselves. Siegel gave the film a different, languorous rhythm, opening with sepia photographs to evoke Matthew Brady and to set the artistic mood, a technique Clint later would copy in *The Outlaw Josey Wales.*

The studio questioned the ending – McB fatally poisoned by the women – but Siegel and Clint stood firm. Everyone fretted about the gruesome amputation scene in which Clint has his wounded leg sawed off by the bloodthirsty females. Both scenes were also in the book, however, and the amputation, though it remained excruciatingly graphic in the film, would suffer only minor diminution.

The allusive title was debated right up to release. Behind the scenes on these productions where Clint departed from the norm, there was often as much anxiety as firmness. How could Siegel and Clint alert his usual following that this was a Clint Eastwood vehicle, yet not the actionfest for which staunch fans were already programmed? Memos were written, proposals debated – 'A Nest of Sparrows', 'The Beguiling Bastard' and 'Johnny McB' (the latter two might communicate a 'stronger appeal to men and connote Western-action at a much higher level', according to studio correspondence) – before the film harked back to the title of the novel.

Pierre Rissient, the Parisian cinéaste and press attaché who represented American screen personalities passing through the French capital, was also a Don Siegel enthusiast. He wanted to take the finished film to the Cannes Film Festival in the south of France and stage its première there in order to attract the attention of critics. Clint 'loved the idea', according to Richard Schickel, because 'he craved this kind of recognition'. But Hollywood had a history of skittishness about Cannes, and Universal, which controlled the marketing and distribution of the film, said no.

Then the studio proceeded to release *The Beguiled* in 'stupid' fashion, in Siegel's words, with inadequate publicity and misleading advertising. And as a 'result of their ineptitude' the picture never earned a profit. It grossed less than $1 million.

Actually, the studio tried, and tried hard. *The Beguiled* opened in a handful of cities in the last week of April 1971, and did modest business before opening 'wide' in twenty-five theatres in Los Angeles and another thirty in New York. Because it was then playing in some fifty-eight theatres nationwide, *The Beguiled* zoomed to number two on *Variety*'s chart of top-grossing films. But this was an illusory ranking, principally reflecting the film's surge over the previous week's statistics: seven of the Top Ten films had higher earnings.

The nation's number one film, *Sweet Sweetback's Baadasssss Song*, by comparison, would eventually quadruple *The Beguiled*'s revenue. A low-budget film without the benefit of studio advertising or distribution, *Sweet Sweetback* was playing in only twenty-one theatres in April 1971 – in those days before quadriplexes, there were fewer first-run venues – whereas *The Beguiled*, thanks to Universal's marketing clout, was playing in more US theatres than any other film in the Top Fifty. Yet the audience numbers fell off, *The Beguiled* began to lose playdates, and within two weeks the film dropped off the Top Fifty, for ever.

'Maybe a lot of people just don't want to see Clint Eastwood's leg cut off,' snorted Jennings Lang in one interview. Clint's opinion was not so very different. In one interview, he volunteered that his regular fans didn't want to see him 'emasculated'. In another he mused that maybe playing a 'loser' was the problem with *The Beguiled*.

'Dustin Hoffman and Al Pacino play losers very well,' Clint said. 'But my audience likes to be in there vicariously with a winner. That isn't always popular with the critics. My characters have sensitivity and vulnerabilities, but they're still winners. I don't pretend to understand losers. When I read a script about a loser I think of people in life who are losers and they seem to want it that way. It's a compulsive philosophy with them. Winners tell themselves, "I'm as bright as the next person. I can do it. Nothing can stop me." '

Compulsive, downbeat losers – what a drag. Clint thought of himself as a winner. It would be many years before he would venture to play another 'loser' who is killed off in one of his films.

But Pierre Rissient in Paris maintained his enthusiasm for *The Beguiled*, and paved the way for its reception in France by arranging for important critics from *France Soir*, *Nouvel Observateur* and *Figaro Littéraire* to see advance screenings and spread the word. Rissient was well suited to his job: like many Parisian film enthusiasts, he wore several hats. He was a reputable expert (with his byline in film journals) as well as press agent. He circulated widely, in France and elsewhere. He could credibly praise a film's artistry while being paid to promote it.

Rissient did such a good job that he would remain on Clint's payroll as his European press spokesman for two decades. Siegel attended the Paris opening (*Time* magazine, profiling the director for the release of *Coogan's Bluff*, said Parisan film fans regarded him as 'a bit like Picasso'). The notices in the French press flew right out of the director's mouth (*Paris Match*: 'strange and fierce, like the novellas of Ambrose Bierce'). In France, Clint, already attached to the legend of Sergio Leone, would also end up inheriting Don Siegel's cult.

The French recognition of *The Beguiled* would also serve the 'triumph-over-adversity' theme that was becoming integral to Clint's publicity. To wit, America didn't appreciate the film, and it took the French to see its merits. Partly as a result of this underdog mystique, *The Beguiled* continues to enjoy a reputation nowadays as one of Clint's best.

Its reputation is perhaps exaggerated. Looking at the film nowadays one is struck by the unusual source material as well as by the studied, atmospheric quality of Siegel's directing. But, though he strives mightily, Clint doesn't quite meet the expectations of his role. McB called for a complexity and abandon that the actor was unable to deliver. Clint's great strength may be his mysterious cool. But his flaw has always been the reverse: his inability or unwillingness to open a window on to his soul.

McB was more interesting than a mere 'loser'. *The Beguiled* required Clint to reveal himself as a charming fraud and devious womanizer. Clint's later comments on the film indicate how the star rationalized these defects in his own mind. 'You know,' Clint told Richard Schickel, 'he's [McBurney] totally justifiable. What guy wouldn't try to save his life in a situation like that?' Then continuing, 'With seven girls hauling you around on a stretcher say, "Hey well, I'll grab a little nookie while I'm here and who cares." '

The other unexpected death to occur in the early 1970s was that of Clint's father.

Clinton Eastwood Sr had left the employ of the Container Corporation in the early 1960s, when he either accepted early retirement, or was eased out after a new management took over and promoted others over him. Whichever it was, Clint's father was quickly snapped up by the rival Georgia–Pacific, which gave him a made-to-order executive position and the challenge of opening the door to big-volume suppliers for its expanded corrugated box and paper operations. Clint's father was the perfect ambassador for Georgia–Pacific, a man who knew all the potential buyers and who was well liked by everyone for his good humour and easygoing manner.

Some of his new clients dubbed Clinton Sr 'Rawhide' after his famous son, and Clint's father was unabashedly proud of 'Junior' for making it big in a profession about which admittedly he had expressed scepticism. Clint's father gave no hint to associates of any show business flair of his own – although he loved to dance, for example, and was always the last one to leave a party. 'We used to say, "Where the hell did Clint get his acting?" ' said Al Naudain, who was instrumental in recruiting Clint's father to Georgia–Pacific. 'Because Clint the father was not an actor in any sense of the word. He was a good problem-solver. He was a man trained at and good at facts, a walking encyclopedia of the specifications and nitty-gritty' of the paper box field.

By the end of the decade, Clint's father had made enough money to retire. He and Ruth Eastwood were living on Bird Rock Road in Pebble Beach where Clinton Sr was a familiar figure on the greens. Dressing for a day of golf on 21 July 1970, Clint's father never came out of the bedroom. When Clint's mother went in to check on him, she found him gripped by a heart attack. Clinton Sr died within minutes. He was only sixty-four. Burr Sr, his father, had lived to the ripe age of ninety-two, so the news came as a shock. Clint himself made phone calls informing all of his father's business colleagues.

The star had just finished *The Beguiled* and was in the midst of preparing *Play Misty For Me* when his father died, and he took a few weeks off, dropping out of circulation. Friends say that when he returned he was imbued with a greater sense of urgency than ever before – about work – but also about his health. No longer would he occasionally drink hard alcohol. Now 'health food' became a near-obsession. And everyone speaks of his speed and efficiency while filming; it was partly because 'his life is in a hurry', in the words of James Fargo, who worked with Clint on eight films.

Clint was always dedicated to his own well-being, but now, on top of rigorous daily exercise, he began to seek out and adopt farther-out remedies for looking and staying youthful. Although he had turned forty before his father's death, his roles would continue to belie his age, flaunt his 'youth' and fitness, accent his sexiness.

'His father's death was completely devastating to him,' said Fritz Manes, 'because it was the only bad thing that ever happened to him in his life. Everything else was always taken care of, or always worked out fine at the end of the day. He couldn't understand this. It was a personal thing to him – something personal that had been done to *him*. He couldn't get over it for a long time, and he damn near collapsed.'

Irving Leonard's last deal, before he passed away, had been for Clint to make his directing debut on *Play Misty for Me*, a film which would stress his love of jazz and give him another foray into the realm of sexual psychosis. Clint had had the script under option for several years, before finally letting it go to Universal, which then absorbed the costs. It was Leonard who advised Clint to waive his usual star fee and accept a gross percentage, which in the end turned out to be a much higher payment than if he had taken an 'acting-plus-directing' salary.

It became another one of those scripts with blue, pink, yellow and green pages, but Dean Riesner was still around to make sure the mixing of colours was harmonious. The script was originated by Clint's longtime friend Jo Heims, a former model, fashion illustrator, dancer and actress, who moved to Hollywood from the East Coast in the 1950s. Starting over as a secretary at Universal, she became acquainted with Clint. Clint has made a point of declaring that he and Heims – short and thin, casual and scruffy, she looked a little like the lead character she later created for *Breezy* – never had any sexual relationship. But sources insist otherwise: Heims, although she was hardly misty-eyed about Clint, was a 'periodic' for the actor over the years.

Two of the early Clint films critics praise the most – *The Beguiled* and *Play Misty for Me* – benefited from a female writer's point of view. The original treatment of *Misty* set the story in Los Angeles, however, and Clint wanted to shift the locale to Carmel, where he felt comfortable and where he intended to shoot scenes at the local radio station, in familiar bars and restaurants, at friends' houses. So Heims was usurped, although she would stick around to write one other script for Clint. Only on one other Malpaso production would there be a female scenarist; this deficiency would be reflected in the stolid masculine perspective of film after film.

Heims' story featured a jazz disc jockey named Dave, who has a casual fling with a woman named Evelyn, one of his listeners. She is the one who has been calling the radio station late at night and asking him to play her favourite song, 'Misty', the signature tune of jazz pianist Erroll Garner. When Dave tries to call off the affair, the female fan becomes increasingly possessive . . . until she turns into a crazy murderess.

Clint pretty much left Riesner alone on the re-writing. Throughout the summer of 1970, the scenarist concentrated on changing the script for Carmel locations. Sonia Chernus, in her capacity as Malpaso's story editor, was the one who pushed for a bigger subplot involving Dave's relationship with a conventional sweetheart, named Tobie. This was necessary both to augment the sparse story-line and to show that Dave was a 'good guy'. 'I don't remember a lot of the story conferences,' Riesner said. 'Clint either trusted me, or he was so gentle in his remonstrances that they didn't strike me.'

Evelyn had to be cast perfectly. Clint's friend Cissy Wellman urged him to watch Jessica Walter's performance as a frigid Vassar graduate in *The Group*. Walter, who had mostly acted in theatre and on daytime television, would turn out to be an inspired choice for Evelyn, giving the most indelible performance of any actress in a Clint film. The 'nice' girlfriend, Tobie, would be played by Donna Mills, another TV performer, who came with a recommendation from Burt Reynolds. And Don Siegel agreed to play the bartender in whose tavern Dave first meets Evelyn.

Subconsciously, Clint once said, Siegel might have been around 'as a buffer' for the first-time director. With *Play Misty for Me* the mentor would pass the torch of directing to the pupil. More than symbolically: Clint's crew was one that Siegel had assembled, including editor Carl Pingitore and cameraman Bruce Surtees, the latter Siegel alumnus, especially, someone who would contribute greatly to Clint's visual style.

The filming started in Monterey in September 1970. It would be tempting to make the observation that the passing of Clint's father influenced the look and feel of a subject already dark and reckless. Certainly it appears that Clint, more the novice than ever again, threw himself intensely into the preparation and planning, as would not always be the case with future Malpaso productions. 'I compared all the shots in my mind,' Clint said, 'laid everything out, made notes to myself, looked at film . . .'

Even his acting approach was more meticulous than usual. Clint decided to use videotape 'to judge his own performance' during the shooting of *Play Misty for Me*, *Variety* reported, 'but hasn't used it on subsequent films', albeit adding, 'for a particularly taxing role, he might use the vidtape procedure again as a double check.'

Clint had seen jazz pianist Erroll Garner at the Concord Music Festival in 1970 and obtained the rights to use his beautifully romantic tune in the film. It was Garner who came up with the idea to redo the vintage recording with modern shadings, a notion that Clint would carry over into future soundtracks. Impresario Jimmy Lyon also gave Clint permission to shoot portions of *Play Misty for Me* at the Monterey Jazz Festival – window-dressing in the story, but a joyous highlight of the filming.

Clint first heard the song, 'The First Time Ever I Saw Your Face', which is used to underscore Dave's romantic scenes with Tobie, on the radio late one night. The song had been recorded by Roberta Flack on her debut album, which was languishing in stores. Clint tracked down the master recording and, according to insiders, was offered ownership of the song for $10,000, or one-time rights only for $2,000. 'Good old Clint, a man with fishhooks in pocket, took the latter position for the least amount of money and wound up making a song famous that earned millions,' recalled a friend. The song, which became heavily identified with the film, was issued as a single and shot to number one for six weeks.

Clint's publicity exploited the fact that the filming came in anywhere from $40–50,000 under its $1 million budget – and four or five days ahead of schedule. Clint, whose publicity treated him as a working-class star, was beginning to metamorphose into Clint, the fast, economical, blue-collar director. It may or may not have been strictly true this first time around, but this virtue would be greatly exaggerated over the years to come. And it wouldn't be long, in fact, before Clint eschewed the care and preparation he underwent as a first-time director, and developed an opposite, 'shoot-from-the-hip' philosophy of film-making.

Pierre Rissient, who had connections with film festivals, did his job by arranging for an October 1971 première showing of *Play Misty for Me* and the first 'mini-retrospective' of Clint's work at the San Francisco Film Festival. Starting, cautiously, small, and close to home, Clint's first appearance at such an event was hardly a roaring success. Some questions from feminists in the audience were hostile. Clint was 'nervous and not very talkative, and became rather defensive when several people dealt him ticklish questions', reported Dennis Hunt in the *San Francisco Chronicle*. Although Clint had just been named the world's biggest movie star by *Life* magazine, Hunt professed scepticism that the first-time director was deserving of any retrospective. 'After examining several hours of samples of his work,' wrote Hunt, 'one can only conclude that the majority of the world's moviegoers have questionable taste.'

But Clint didn't give up easily in his career, and he didn't give up on film festivals. And when *Play Misty for Me* was released in November, the reviews were encouraging. *Variety*, Jay Cocks in *Time*, Andrew Sarris in the *Village Voice* and Archer Winsten in the *New York Post* were among those who praised the film and Clint's direction.

Play Misty for Me is treated almost like a classic by Clint's fans nowadays, and it does have Hitchcockian virtues. Clint's visual knack is undeniable; he has an instinct for camera placement. Tracking shots, hand-held camerawork and aerial photography would become trademarks of his style. And *Play Misty for Me* has all the production gloss provided by the top-calibre crew inherited from Don Siegel.

But looking at the film today, there are embarrassing moments that Hitchcock wouldn't have tolerated. Dean Riesner did his best, but there was rarely enough time or money for script development on a Malpaso project. The love story between Dave and Tobie, especially, plays as hackneyed. The Roberta Flack number is a throwback to 'I talk to the trees . . .': Half fuzzy long shot and the rest close ups of pretty flowers. Dave and Tobie's big moment of lovemaking takes place in a forest with the two of them rolling around under a waterfall. (Donna Mills said Clint brought out cognac to warm them up during the takes.) The scene isn't awful, just a cut above collegiate.

Clint is exceptional in his scenes with Jessica Walter, where her pathology keeps him and the audience on nerve-wracking edge. As in *The Beguiled*, it was Clint's powerlessness that was different and fascinating. It would have been a more provocative film, however, if Dave was a habitual romeo who caused Evelyn's breakdown by his cavalier treatment. Instead, the case is stacked against her, with the film eventually exposing her as a berserk mental patient. Clint has said that the script originally appealed to him because it was about 'the misinterpretation of commitment'. But Dave's guiltlessness meant that the film would fall short of being very profound.

When, in 1995, Clint was announced to receive the Academy of Motion Picture Arts and Science's special Irving G. Thalberg Memorial Award, given for high achievement by an individual producer, he told *Variety* that, 'In the old days producers were knowledgeable on all aspects of film-making, plus they were the presidents of the company.' Nowadays they were not as capable. 'Don Siegel used to say, "The trouble with producers is that they don't know what they do," ' Clint added sagely.

Play Misty for Me was a watershed in his career, his first directing job and the first Malpaso film without a studio-appointed overseer. But Malpaso, seen by many as bravely 'independent' of Hollywood, was, in many ways, Hollywood incarnate. Like Clint, it was half a mirage of good publicity.

From the beginning Clint has striven to present Malpaso as a kind of Mom-and-Pop company, dedicated to efficiency and elimination of excess. Only a handful of employees, only a bare-budget overhead. 'I've got a six-pack of beer under my arm, and a few pieces of paper, and a couple of pencils, and I'm in business', said Clint in one interview.

Only a handful of employees meant a small continuing payroll. And in the entire history of Malpaso you could count on one hand the people who would share in the company profits.

Apart from Bob Daley, the president of Malpaso as well as producer of Clint's films, the continuing staff *was* small, and in the beginning included Sonia Chernus and Jack Kosslyn. Chernus was the head of the so called Story Department, which consisted mostly of herself; Chernus dutifully read scripts, but the scripts came from outside Malpaso, and in-house stories were not developed. Jack Kosslyn became a kind of combination talent scout and acting coach for Clint, although he didn't stay on salary between films. The only person who could be counted on to be in the office on a daily basis, besides Bob Daley, was Clint's secretary, who organized the star's schedule and handled his official communications.

Clint's secretary, in 1970, was Carole Rydall, who later married Don Siegel. One of the important aspects of her job was to fend off 'outsiders'. Although unvaryingly gracious to fans when out in public – he almost never refused to sign an autograph – Clint liked to be walled off, in the office, from people he didn't know or trust. His series of secretaries scored their highest marks for screening people. Indeed, 'Clint the cautious', as he was dubbed by some insiders, was generally 'out' to anyone who wasn't famous or who he wasn't already in business with, and the only phone calls he could be relied upon to take were from the 'Jewish mafia' (as he sometimes put it) of his agent, attorney and accountants.

The secretary's trick was to mention the name of the caller loud and clear, and then Clint, often listening with one ear, either gave her the acceptance sign, which was rare, or waved her off. Sometimes Clint's technique was to wave her off, only to make a point of returning the call minutes later, depending upon the status of the caller.

The well-known cameramen and production designers and editors who worked on more than one Malpaso production also went off salary between films. Clint was shrewd about who he picked to head these 'departments of one', choosing people with talent who would also assume all the creative responsibility without asking for much input from the boss.

Bruce Surtees, for instance, would guide the camerawork of more than a dozen Malpaso productions, returning to the fold again and again, and becoming, by the 1990s, the only link to the first regime. Surtees had several cachets with Clint: he had come up under Don Siegel and he was also the son of Robert Surtees, a three-time Oscar-winning cinematographer of Hollywood's Golden Age. The Surtees lived in Carmel, and were part of the Carmel clique. Although an unassuming guy (Surtees had 'zero presumption, zero arrogance and the love and determination to do something good', in the words of production designer Ted Haworth), Clint valued him highly – and paid him as well as he ever paid anyone who worked for Malpaso.

All the other Malpaso cameramen would also come, directly or not, from the Surtees professional tree. Frank Stanley (who would shoot *Breezy, Magnum Force, Thunderbolt and Lightfoot,* and *The Eiger Sanction*) had been the elder Surtees' assistant. Rexford Metz (who photographed *The Gauntlet* and *Any Which Way But Loose*) had hung out in Haight-Ashbury in San Francisco with Bruce Surtees back in the late 1960s, and then became an informal protégé of Surtees' father. Metz, an award-winner as a documentarist, and another member of the small band of friends, a former barber named Jack Green, did aerial photography, advertising and second unit work for San Francisco-based productions. Jack Green would stick around long enough, after working obscurely behind the camera for roughly fifteen years, to be promoted and then photograph almost as many Malpaso films as Bruce Surtees.

The 'Prince of Darkness' aesthetic, which grew to be recognized as the house style, was sometimes striking, sometimes pushed to extremes. Clint resisted bright or 'fill-in' lighting; it took more time and money, and anyway he preferred scenes shadowed with darkness. It became another component of his 'shoot-the-rehearsal' philosophy of supposed spontaneity and realism. If the low lighting didn't flatter some of the leading ladies, well, the cinematographers understood that, at least, the boss benefited from the shadows that concealed his accumulating age lines.

The aerial photography background they all had in common was significant because Clint loved planes and helicopters; he loved establishing shots from the air, sweeping photography of coastlines and buildings, the camera swooping under bridges, dizzying angles from hairy heights. Clint had learned to pilot a helicopter in Oregon during the long shoot of *Paint Your Wagon*. In time he would purchase his own plane and copter. His plane then could be designated as a 'camera ship' and leased back to Malpaso for production use. He could also lease the copter to himself for aerials. In Hollywood, where such is common practice, Clint outdid people in maximizing his dollars.

*   *   *

Clint was already thoroughly rich by 1971, the year he plunked down a cool one million dollars for twelve acres of prime oceanfront property along Pebble Beach's famed seventeen-mile drive, a coastline that was inhabited principally by America's captains of finance and industry. Maggie planned to devote herself to overseeing design and construction of their home on the property. One of the Eastwoods' nearest neighbours would be the talk show host and former lounge pianist Merv Griffin.

Having lived in the area for several years, the Eastwoods were already fixtures on the local scene. And most of their closest friends up in the Carmel–Pebble Beach area had nothing to do with show business, at least until they met Clint. The star had a whole different set of buddies up there, for drinkathons and afternoon sports; his closest friends were Ken Green (from his high school days at Oakland Tech), tennis pro Don Hamilton, and new net partner and kindred spirit Paul Lippman. These three comprised his Celebrity Tennis Tournament committee for Fourth of July weekends for several years. Later, there arose another group of friends (mostly golfers), locally dubbed 'the barnacles' – because they clung to Clint, competing for invitations to play golf or drink with him. Friends knew Clint hated to enter any public establishment alone; he almost always had a 'barnacle', or someone there to meet him.

Lippman had Oakland schooling, Fort Ord, and Los Angeles City College in common with Clint, although they met first at the Carmel Valley Racquet Club in 1966. A journalist who had started his career as a sports writer with the *San Francisco Examiner*, Lippman later wrote people-oriented features and travel articles for national magazines. Starting with his natural pairing with Clint as novice tennis players, they developed a close friendship. 'Hell, we were so bad, nobody else would play us,' Lippman joked in an interview, 'but we had a lot of laughs . . . and many beers!'

Maggie would have been an 'A' player on any tennis club's ladies' roster, but Clint wasn't too serious about the game and only played for fun. Some of his matches with Lippman went on for hours. 'The scores would read like, 21–19, 17–19, and 1 quit!' remembered Lippman. 'We were often in the bar getting a beer before the last lob had come down.'

Clint playing doubles with Maggie was always vastly entertaining for opponents. Although Maggie had a high boiling point, Clint knew how to set her off, and it would happen predictably when they paired on the courts. A superior singles player, extremely competitive, Maggie would rather not 'partner' Clint, and only did so, on occasion, in the 'friendly', after-singles mixed matches at the Beach Club on Sundays.

'One blown point on the part of the big cowboy,' said Lippman, 'and it was not uncommon for her to yell, "You wimp!" and if it meant the game or the match, it invariably went, "You fucking wimp!", loud enough for everyone in the club to hear. "Wimp" always was her favourite and final putdown of the superstar, and he would take a lot of "wimps" before he'd blow, finally telling her, "Aw shut up, Mag," or, if he was really mad, "Aw, fuck off, Mag," after which he generally would stalk off in the middle of the play. He then would grab a buddy and go for a beer, but usually would get over the indignity quickly and, somehow, they would show up for dinner or a party that evening, warm and friendly.'

Tennis – golf, too – was always an excuse for beer busts and partying. Often the Eastwoods were hand in hand at parties attended by other couples, with Clint seeming the dutiful husband. At the same time, Clint was known by close friends to be a 'runner', according to Lippman, at least when out of Maggie's eyesight. Because Carmel (where Clint preferred the clubs and bars) was basically a small town, his behaviour became even more of an open secret up in Monterey County than it was in Hollywood.

It was during the filming of *Play Misty for Me* that Clint and Lippman started talking about opening their own bar, 'a place where we would like to hang out', as Clint put it. Lippman had quickly been drawn into Clint's orbit professionally as well as personally. Although Maggie and Bob Daley comprised the 'court of last decision' on Malpaso scripts, Lippman began to be asked his opinion, and to make line-editing suggestions, word and phrase changes that Clint adopted. Like other Clint friends, Lippman would also make a fleeting appearance in one of his films, playing one of the 'assholes' in *Play Misty for Me*.*

After *Play Misty for Me* wrapped, Clint and Lippman started searching

---

* Lippman and Clint's friend George Fargo were in the 'interference' scene out front of the Sardine Factory in Monterey, where Clint and Jessica Walter are having a fierce verbal battle. Fargo hollers, 'Need some help, lady?' And Walter screams back: 'Get loss, assholes!'

for 'their bar', the place that later would become known as the Hog's Breath Inn. Clint insisted on a funky, English-pub-type name. 'Something far out,' Clint declared, 'something that's never been used.' The third partner was Walter Becker, an established Carmel restaurateur. During the first meeting of the partners in the overgrown courtyard that was to become 'the Hog', Clint laid down the primary rule of their *modus operandi*. 'By God, our wives aren't going to have anything to do with this place, understood?' Lippman and Becker nodded their assent, thinking they could get the message across to *their* wives; it was headstrong Maggie they were worried about.

The two 'yes' men from southern California, Roy Kaufman and Howard Bernstein, looked over the site and thought it had potential for earnings, but Bruce Ramer, who had succeeded Frank Wells as Clint's attorney, balked. He insisted that the Hog wouldn't be a money-maker and that Clint's name shouldn't be exploited. Clint won him over, up to a point, on the condition that Clint invest only an initial $20,000, taking just a third of 'the action', and without his name ever appearing on any of the necessary bank loans. Or (Lippman never was sure), was Ramer's reticence just another overly cautious strategy of Clint's, limiting his monetary risk and investment?

Herb Caen, the widely read columnist of the *San Francisco Chronicle*, was an old friend of Lippman's from newspaper days and already a Clint fan. In his column, he advance-hyped 'the Hog' as the soon-to-be '*in*' spot in Carmel, serving a rare combination of health food and booze', but the three partners didn't anticipate the swarms that descended on the place after its opening in 1972. When the US Open golf tournament came to Pebble Beach, 'Clint's place' found itself wall-to-wall with bodies. 'Little old ladies around Carmel, who at first were horrified by even the thought of the name, came to love the place,' said Lippman. Clint's drinking buddies, the 'barnacles', moved in permanently.

'I will say that Clint was a vital partner in business,' recalled Lippman. 'He was good on operational input, conserving money, of course, and public relations on the right nights. There were times when he knew that just a walk-through would have every tourist in town there in an hour, and that always helped.'

There was more than one reason for frequent walk-throughs. The 'crew', mostly beautiful young people, twenty-one to twenty-five, generally had that fresh-scrubbed all-American look, and some of the wait-resses were so pretty they could have auditioned for movie parts. A few did wind up 'auditioning' for Clint, according to Lippman. 'He [Clint] told me early on that my "casting couch" looked even better than his,' said Lippman, 'then he proceeded to polish off – one of his favourite terms – a few of the choice morsels. Hell, most of them were fifteen to twenty years younger than him!

'I had to terminate three pretty good waitresses in the first few months of operation; not because they went to bed with Clint East-wood, but because they either talked about it all over the premises, or came in the next day acting like they owned the place. A fourth waitress continued sleeping with him on a regular basis, but I didn't have to fire her because she didn't talk about it; she wanted to be an actress. And she got a speaking part in *The Eiger Sanction* while still a waitress!'

According to Lippman, Clint didn't have to stray too far from the 'Hog trough' for lovemaking, as he had an apartment two doors down, on the third floor of a new building, where old and new girlfriends – ladies from the Carmel tourist shops and sundry passers-through – were known to meet him for 'nooners', or five-in-the-afternooners; and 'he wasn't adverse to nailing them in his pickup parked nearby on Dolores Street, a dark thoroughfare leading to the Carmel Mission, only most of these goggle-eyed girls weren't looking for the Mission'. Clint often was gone for only minutes, then would come back into the Hog and joke about the action to buddies.

'He seemed to get a "bang" out of this kinkier side of himself and he rarely concealed it, often gloated about it,' Lippman said. 'I'm frankly surprised that he didn't pick up every social disease known to man, but the worst he could count was an occasional catch of crabs. Consequently, we kept a bottle of Pyrinate A-200 in the office medicine cabinet at all times, the only thing in the whole cabinet.' Lippman remembered he once asked Clint about his good fortune in escaping other social diseases, and he answered with his patented smirk: 'I take a lot of vitamins.'

As usual with Clint, the trysts came in all colours, shapes and person-alities. The relationships lasted for an hour, months or years. Although he still favoured small or slight women – the onetime 'little dollies' Clint was now more likely to call 'squirts', 'shrimps' or 'spinners' – a couple of the Hog's Breath waitresses the star dallied with were 'big gals in the six-foot-one and -two range with bustlines that would make Dolly Parton pout', according to Paul Lippman. 'I had several of those tall beauties, and they were especially good for seeing over and working through the big crowds on major event nights, carrying the trays too high for any normal person to reach or bump, so, when Clint saw these tall gals all lined up at the bar service window, he smiled and said, "Christ, it looks like you've got the LA Lakers working tonight!" Then he proceeded to "polish" the one older gal, a former hooker, I know because she later told me, and that went on for quite awhile because she didn't talk about it – only to me.'

Although the restaurant was notorious for attracting beauties, the 'barnacles' came up with a trash-term for the star's occasional preference for less lovely pick-ups, calling them 'Clint's dogs'. The loveliest ladies didn't always connect with Clint, and sometimes the best imaginable come-on lines didn't work; alternatively, sometimes the least likely succeeded.

One time the actor was in San Francisco with Lippman when they met a cute squirt on the street who looked up at the big cowboy star and sniffed, 'Oh, you're Clint Eastwood . . . I hear you're a bum lay!' Said Lippman: 'Clint, very stunned and at a total loss for words, stretched his neck muscles mightily, as he always did when stuck for a quick response, then finally managed, "Well . . . uh . . . where did you hear that?" To which she pertly answered, "Oh, it's all over town." *That* worked,' Lippman allowed, 'as Clint, after a few more neck strehes, invited her back into the club to have a drink and discuss the matter, then spent the night at Sausalito's Alta Mira Hotel trying to prove otherwise.' Lippman buttonholed her in the morning and asked her if she still thought Clint Eastwood was 'a bum lay', and she held out a flat hand, palm down, and wiggled it.

It didn't help a candidate if she was 'mature', i.e. Clint's age. The 'barnacles' had a standing joke: if a girl was over twenty-one, she was over-the-hill for Clint. One time he started out on an arranged date with a thirty-nineish boutique owner, who spent part of the evening boasting about her daughter, a teenager. 'You should meet my daughter, a knockout,' etc. Clint eventually would make the smooth switch from mother to daughter; not only with Mom's permission, but with her encouragement.

Waking up the next morning in adjoining motel rooms, Lippman heard through the walls the shrill blare of a TV set featuring Donald Duck and Scooby-Doo. Afterwards, he and Clint discussed the matter, and Clint said the teenager had been 'superb' in bed, which was one of his classic morning-after assessments. 'Succulent,' he added, invoking another of his favourite carnal descriptions, '*absolutely* succulent.'

Lippman cautioned Clint about her age. 'We'd better make it *eighteen*,' Clint said, now wary, according to Lippman, 'the word, any word, would get out'. But what do you talk about in the morning with a girl that young? Lippman wanted to know. 'We don't talk,' came the sly reply, 'we watch cartoons.'

During this period of initial superstardom, the early 1970s, Clint was more than ever 'possessed by the demon sex beast', in the words of one of his lady friends, and Maggie, busy with construction of their 'forever house', looked the other way. Mrs Eastwood was admired for her stoic single-mindedness (a 'saint' in the eyes of many). The rationale behind her stoicism, people thought, was simple: 'I've got him. He's my husband. I am Mrs Clint Eastwood, and as long as he doesn't embarrass the children or me, that is the way it will be ... until he runs out of gas and comes home for ever.'

Although the Universal films did okay at the box-office, none of Clint's post-Sergio Leone films had cracked the annual Top Ten box-office earnings lists. But *Hang 'Em High* and *Where Eagles Dare* had performed particularly well, and the 'spaghetti Westerns' continued to earn money in rerelease, sometimes as triple features. Already, 1971's *Current Biography* would estimate the aggregate gross of Clint's films, worldwide, at $200 million. And already, in July of 1971, Clint would be trumpeted by *Life* magazine as 'the world's favourite movie star'. ('No kidding', the headline of *Life* added, rightly surmising that many would be sceptical.)*

This was before *Dirty Harry*. Jennings Lang was also responsible for bringing this project to Clint's attention. It was Lang who first showed

---

* The *Life* article hit on all the Clint publicity points: his loyalty and privacy, his love of cold beer, how women flocked to his side, and how, beneath all the fame and fortune, he was still a humble, simple man whose everyday language was uncomplicated.

Eastwood the script, written by Harry Julian and Rita M. Fink, about a New York cop, Dirty Harry Callahan, determined to stop a psychotic killer by any means necessary. The script was taken under option by Universal. But Clint was temporarily overbooked after the 'spaghetti Westerns', and the option lapsed. The rights wound up at Warner Brothers.

Clint's move from Universal to Warner Brothers is usually presented as an instance of a growing film-maker determined to acquire more independence and control over his work, and that is true up to a point. It is also true that in mid-1969 Warner Brothers–Seven Arts was acquired by Steve Ross's Kinney Service Corporation. The film studio had just suffered its worst losses in history ($52 million) and was considered practically moribund. The most lucrative asset of the deal, for Steve Ross, was Warner's thriving popular music label.

Heretofore Kinney Service Corporation had been known for its parking-lot and funeral-home businesses. Ross, a former slacks salesman without any experience in show business, was determined to resurrect the studio's once-glorious film operations. His choice to head production was brilliant: onetime NBC executive John Calley had distinguished himself as a producer for Filmways from 1960 to 1969, with such acclaimed films as *Topkapi*, *The Loved One* and *Catch-22*. In late 1969 Calley picked Frank Wells, Clint's longtime lawyer, as his new West Coast vice-president for financial affairs.

The new Warners management was expected to keep the current film programme afloat while structuring the future viability of the studio. That meant developing long-term relationships with the next generation of Hollywood stars. Calley was noted for his benevolent relationships with film-makers, and Wells had Clint's trust. The man who for fifteen years had written all of the star's contracts now began to court him to come to Warner Brothers.

The first step down this road was *Dirty Harry*, which by 1970 had ended up in the 'active' file at Warners. Frank Sinatra had been involved in the project for a while as its prospective star, with Irving Kershner slated as the director. But Sinatra grew unhappy as the script drafts multiplied, and eventually he would withdraw from his commitment (reportedly because of a 'hand injury'). During the shooting of *Play Misty for Me*, Frank Wells contacted Clint – as if they had ever been out of contact. In December of 1970, the trade papers published initial announcements that Clint next would star in *Dirty Harry*, the first joint Malpaso production with Warners, with Bob Daley producing.

Don Siegel would have to be loaned out by Universal: no problem. Dean Riesner agreed to do a rewrite in time to schedule principal photography for the summer of 1971.

The original setting of the script had been Manhattan. Because Clint had already done one cop film in New York, they decided to switch the locale. San Francisco, a city Clint loved and with which Siegel felt comfortable, emerged as the obvious choice.

Again, real-life locations helped guide the rewrite. Siegel and Clint caught the television broadcast of the last San Francisco 49ers football game in Kezar Stadium, and that suggested an eerie showdown in the empty, floodlit arena between Harry and Scorpio, the psycho killer – 'a Greek amphitheatre-like setting between two immense forces: evil and rage against evil', as Fuensanta Plaza put it in her coffee-table book *Clint Eastwood–Malpaso*. Isolated Mount Davidson Park, with its giant concrete cross, would serve for the brutal scene where Harry is trapped and beaten up by Scorpio. The railroad trestle crossing over Sir Francis Drake Boulevard would be used for the film's thrilling climax, when Harry jumps onto the roof of the school bus full of children that has been hijacked by Scorpio.

Although John Milius had been involved in earlier revisions, everyone agreed that the original script by the Finks was the best. Riesner said he believed that even Dirty Harry's signature dialogue, 'Do ya feel lucky, punk?' came from the Finks. With his growing feeling for Clint's tough-guy persona and his respect for Siegel's strengths as a director, Riesner made his final touch-up more ambiguous both in its toughness and humour.

Clint said that from the beginning he discerned a 'sadness about him [the Dirty Harry character], about his personal life' that attracted him as an actor. This 'sadness' was depicted in Riesner's script only in passing, with a reference to Harry's wife, whose death has been caused, before the film begins, by a drunk driver. *Dirty Harry*'s most affecting moment probably occurs in the scene where Harry warns the wife of Chico, his wounded partner, 'This is no life for you two.' And she asks him, 'Why do you stay then?' Harry answers, 'I don't know. I really don't . . .' In this, his first Dirty Harry vehicle, Clint was truly enigmatic: not only a loner on the beat, a man without any love in his personal life.

The film had to have a credible villain, someone as loathsome as Gian Maria Volonté. Siegel discovered the actor who would play Scorpio, Andy Robinson, in an off-Broadway play called *Subject to Fits*, inspired by Dostoevsky's *The Idiot*, in which Robinson played the epileptic Prince Myshkin. Clint went to see the play, stayed until the intermission, concurred with Siegel. Robinson's long-haired and epicene appearance made him look like a weird hippie-gone-sour. He would make a perfect foil for Clint.

Others in the cast: Harry Guardino as a police supervisor (a circumscribed role that minimized Guardino's talent); Reni Santoni as Harry's picked-upon partner Chico; John Vernon as the mealy-mouthed Mayor; and John Mitchum (Robert's younger brother) as the overweight cop DiGiorgio, who trailed behind Harry and supplied comedy relief.

Glenn Wright, Clint's costumer since *Rawhide*, would give Harry a brown-and-yellow checked jacket to wear that made Clint the embodiment of 'square' values, with his sidekicks Chico and DiGiorgio in virtual knockoffs. 'All of Harry's partners looked up to him,' explained Wright. 'They were almost a casual shadow of him.'

Bruce Surtees was back for atmospheric photography that would build his reputation as one of the best of the new-generation cameramen. Siegel's editor was again Carl Pingitore, and Lalo Schifrin, who had worked on *Kelly's Heroes*, would supply a jazz-tinged score. Schifrin, born in Buenos Aires but educated at the Paris Conservatoire, was the first composer with big-band background to work on one of Clint's films. Although a classically trained pianist, he also knew the bebop style. After moving to New York in 1958, Schifrin had played with Dizzy Gillespie, then subsequently, from 1962 on, he worked almost exclusively in Hollywood. An accomplished *pasticheur*, Schifrin would end up composing four out of the five Dirty Harry soundtracks.

The filming began in April 1971. It was not an uncomplicated production. There were dangerous stunts, car flips, those aerial shots of the city that would become a Dirty Harry trademark. Much of the photography took place at night, which Bruce Surtees relished. Surtees eagerly framed hand-held shots while lying on his back, or shot from atop flagpoles, functioning in virtual darkness or harsh glare.

When, on one occasion, Siegel fell ill with the flu, Clint, wanting to keep things moving, stepped in to direct himself in the scene where Harry behaves callously to a man threatening to leap to his suicide from high above an intersection. The man was played by Buddy Van Horn, Clint's double in action scenes, later to be his 'double' as director.

One tense night, according to Siegel, the director and Clint exchanged sharp words, their argument interrupted by Surtees, close to tears. He had his own camera difficulties with which he was struggling to cope. As Siegel turned to reassure Surtees, he sensed Clint's anger immediately dissipate. He then felt on his cheek a gentle kiss. 'As I slowly turned around, I caught a glimpse of Clint's back,' wrote Siegel, 'headed quickly for the exit doors to the street. I'll never forget his consideration and kindness.'

People say Siegel and Clint – their success intertwined – were never closer personally than at this point in time. But there may have been some distance between them on interpretations of the film.

Clint said in later interviews that he had realized right from the outset of the project that *Dirty Harry* contradicted the 1966 Miranda vs. Arizona decision of the US Supreme Court, which protected criminal suspects by assuring them they would receive a 'Miranda warning' of their constitutional rights before any interrogation by police. This ruling was generally regarded as a victory for liberals and the bane of law-and-order conservatives. Dirty Harry was a character who gladly bent the Miranda rules, and Clint's dialogue excoriated mushy academics, stupid prosecutors and judges, inept government officials. Universal had offered the project to the more liberal actor, Paul Newman, at one point. Newman rejected it, citing his political qualms. 'Well, I don't have any political affiliations,' Clint had said to Jennings Lang, 'so send it over.'

The film had pointed scenes that crossed the boundaries of decency and justice: jokes about Harry's all-encompassing bigotry, Harry taking his arrest of Scorpio a little too far in the brutality department. The most notorious example was the scene in which Harry's hot-dog lunch is interrupted by an ongoing bank robbery. Coolly and efficiently, Harry pulls his gun and breaks up the robbery, never mind car crashes and innocent bystanders darting for safety. Still munching on his hot dog, Harry approaches a bank robber sprawled on the pavement slowly inching towards his weapon. Harry points his pistol at this criminal suspect – an African–American.

'I know what you're thinking,' says Harry, rather matter-of-factly. 'Did he fire six bullets or only five? Well, to tell you the truth, I kinda lost track myself. But seeing how the '44 Magnum is the most powerful handgun in the world, and that it would blow your head clear off, you got to ask yourself – do I feel lucky today? Well, do ya, punk?'

The punk doesn't feel lucky and he doesn't go for his gun, but this scene, as even Clint said he realized, was a depth charge in the context of American politics. There was ample news coverage, in 1970–71, of cases where local and federal police had overstepped their authority by entrapment and obstruction of justice and even outright assassination. Often enough the criminal suspects (like the bank robber in *Dirty Harry*) were African–American. Black Panther Party members went to court in Oakland, New Orleans, Chicago, New Haven and New York City, and earned mistrials or acquittals.

If the police were being challenged on the streets and in the courts, the United States government was losing the Vietnam War. Clint himself said, in later interviews, that his Dirty Harry character helped quench people's thirst for 'vengeance', which the actor linked to 'a great feeling of impotence and guilt' over two national crises: Vietnam and Watergate, the scandal that drove President Nixon from office (albeit, Watergate did not occur until later, in 1972).

The cops, the government, the armed forces were losing. America needed a hero, a winner. In *Dirty Harry*, Clint not only found a contemporary persona to equal the Man With No Name, he also found one that seemed to embody a resurgent America. The line between actor and self, which Sergio Leone had maintained as a mystery quotient, appeared to dissolve.

The culminating – still provocative – sequences of *Dirty Harry* were the inspiration of Don Siegel: the school bus hijacked, Harry leaping from a bridge atop the bus, the bus crash, chase and then ultimate face-off with Scorpio. The killer holds a Luger to the head of an innocent child. Harry shoots and manages to wound him. That is when Harry taunts Scorpio with the reprise of 'Do ya feel lucky . . . ?' This time, when the criminal reaches for his gun, Harry fires first, finishing him off.

Clint said later, defensively, that he found a measure of resignation in that instant when Harry pulls the trigger, which defined for many people *Dirty Harry*'s simple-minded solutionism. If so, that internal sigh is all but invisible. He certainly appears to do it coldly.

The scene had a telling postscript, which Siegel and Clint debated during the filming. After Scorpio's 'execution', a disgusted Harry yanks off his badge and skips it into the water of a nearby sump. At first, Clint didn't care for this conclusion. It was a copout. He didn't play characters who were losers. Nor did he play 'quitters'.

Siegel argued with him. 'You're *not* quitting. You're rejecting the bureaucracy of the police department, which is characterized by adherence to fixed rules and a hierarchy of authority.'

EASTWOOD: I still feel I'm quitting by throwing away my badge.
SIEGEL: You're wrong, Clint. You're rejecting the stupidity of a system of administration, marked by officialdom and red tape.

Siegel came up with a compromise bit of action: 'Harry draws his arm back as if to throw the badge into the sump. Suddenly, he pauses, as he hears the faint distant wail of approaching police sirens before the audience hears it. Then, with something close to a sigh, he puts the badge back in his pocket...' By the time they got around to shooting the coda of the story, however, the star had come around to agreeing with Siegel's point of view. In the film, Dirty Harry does rip off his badge, quitting in disgust.

They might have left out Harry quitting if they had guessed that *Dirty Harry* was going to inspire such profitable sequels. Clint was already a golden goose, but while in production nobody seems to have realized that *Dirty Harry* was going to turn out to be as bountiful an egg as *A Fistful of Dollars*. But when it was released in December of 1971, the film quickly shot to number one at the box-office. Its eventual $53 million gross would almost triple the revenue of any of his previous American films and help make Clint, for the first time, in 1972, the top moneymaking star in Hollywood.

While some critics hailed *Dirty Harry* as a superior cop thriller (Jay Cocks in *Time* wrote that Clint gave 'his best performance so far – tense, tough, full of implicit identification with his character'), others focused on the film's veiled politique and decided that Clint flirted with a fascist message by ennobling a ruthless vigilante cop who expressed contempt for the courts and the legal bureaucracy.

Newsweek dubbed *Dirty Harry* 'a right-wing fantasy'. A widely quoted freelance article in the Sunday *New York Times*, penned by a Harvard student, defined the film as glorifying 'Nietzschean policemen' who were 'without mercy'. Even *Variety* diagnosed the new Clint vehicle as 'a specious, phony glorification of police and criminal brutality', with 'a superhero whose antics become almost satire'.

The review that gnawed the worst was Pauline Kael's in the *New Yorker*. Kael described *Dirty Harry* as 'a remarkably single-minded attack on liberal values, with each prejudicial detail in place'. Kael added: 'When you're making a picture with Clint Eastwood, you naturally want things to be simple, and the basic contest between good and evil is as simple as you can get. It makes this genre piece more archetypal than most movies, more primitive and dreamlike; fascist medievalism has a fairy-tale appeal.'

Kael had already proved a particular thorn in Clint's side (she had taken on his 'spaghetti Westerns' and denounced them as 'stripped of cultural values'). As one of the most widely read and influential film essayists in America, Kael had many devoted readers and followers of her views. The term 'fascist' stuck for a while.

'The long-term effects of her piece were slightly more ambivalent,' commented Richard Schickel in his authorized biography of Clint. 'Interviewers kept asking him [Clint] about it, and anyone attempting a critical overview of his career was obliged to conjure with it. Even now, when he is the beneficiary of one of the most astonishing reversals of critical fortune in movie history, a majority continues to hold with Kael. Yet it could be as well argued that this contempt has had a goading effect on Clint.'

Clint was hissed by feminists, a few times in the Bay Area. At the Oscar ceremonies that year, protesters outside carried signs reading 'Dirty Harry Is A Rotten Pig'. Siegel and Clint didn't like being labelled pigs or Nazis. They might have confessed to a film not entirely conscious of its hidden meanings; instead they insisted that *Dirty Harry*, consciously or otherwise, didn't imply fascism of any sort.

The writer who wrote the film, and the director who orchestrated it, both were, ironically, liberal Democrats. They knew they were making 'a pro-cop film', in Dean Riesner's words, but they didn't overanalyse the implications. Nor did Clint. 'Not once throughout *Dirty Harry* did Clint and I have a political discussion,' said Siegel.

Siegel, the true liberal, was particularly stung. As *Dirty Harry* was being released, his interviews would describe Harry as 'a bitter bigot'. Later, the director would modify that, pointing out that he deliberately created a scene for Harry with an African-American medical intern, and another one mocking the detective's biases (with Harry ticking off his equal-opportunity detestation of Limeys, Micks, Hebes, Dagoes, Niggers, Hunkies and Chinks). This, said Siegel, ought to tip people off that Harry was more 'a tease' than a bigot.

Clint sometimes did seem bitter. 'Jesus,' the man who played Dirty Harry told the *Los Angeles Free Press* in 1973, 'some people are so politically oriented, when they see cornflakes in a bowl, they get some complex interpretation out of it.'

Clint's oft-stated view was that Harry was obeying 'a higher moral law'. 'People even said I was a racist because I shot black bank robbers at the beginning of *Dirty Harry*,' he complained to New York City's *Village Voice* in 1976. 'Well, shit, blacks rob banks, too. This film gave four black stunt men work. Nobody talked about that.

'So first I'm labelled right-wing. Then I'm a racist. Now it's macho or male chauvinism. It's a whole number nowadays to make people feel guilty on different levels. It doesn't bother me because I know where the fuck I am on the planet and I don't give a shit.'

Clint would probably accept 'I don't give a shit' inscribed on his tombstone. He liked to expound on 'the rebel lying deep in my soul' and being 'the outsider'. He preferred to be associated with Oakland, not Piedmont. Malpaso was a fiercely autonomous operation, according to publicity dogma; not an appendage of Universal or, later, Warner Brothers. As an actor who eschewed subtext, he couldn't credit any unconscious urges in his persona. Clint's entire image was *anti*-Establishment. Imagine being labelled a Republican, a right-winger, even a latent fascist!

December 1971, the month *Dirty Harry* was released, was also the month Richard Nixon declared he was a candidate for re-election for the Presidency. As part of Clint's disingenuousness about *Dirty Harry*, he sometimes liked to play down the fact that he was a longstanding Republican. Clint had backed Nixon and thereby lent his name to issues for which the Dirty Harry character stood as a perfect symbol. In California, he had supported the two gubernatorial campaigns of Ronald Reagan, who made public statements about wanting to give police a free hand to mow down anti-war protesters.

Clint hadn't been particularly visible during Nixon's 1968 presidential drive (he hadn't yet achieved full-blown star status), but he did supply money to the campaign and with Maggie attended at least one official dinner intended to reward celebrities and big donors with the chance to brush elbows with the President and Republican leaders.

Depending on the interview situation, Clint sometimes preferred to describe himself as a political moderate, liberal on some issues (e.g. civil rights), conservative on others (against government spending and too much 'freeloading'). Indeed, Clint said, he had voted for Nixon in 1968 mainly because he perceived President Johnson's Vietnam bombing pause as a cynical election ploy. Clint insisted he too was *against* the war. 'But I'm not among the people who say let's stop Vietnam, zap!' Clint explained, 'If you're going to stop it, I'd like to say, "Here's a constructive way."'

It is true that under President Nixon the troop levels declined, as did American casualties. Nixon's 'constructive' way to win the war, however, was to authorize stepped-up incursions into Laos and Cambodia, and to carpet-bomb Southeast Asia to force Hanoi to the bargaining table. Even before Watergate – Nixon's Dirty Harryish over-riding of laws from the Oval Office – there had been congressional calls for the President's impeachment on grounds of 'high crimes' against the Vietnamese people.

Nixon in 1971 was a figure as divisive as Dirty Harry. However, a stubborn-minded Clint told Tom Shales of the *Washington Post,* shortly after the release of *Dirty Harry,* that he was supporting Nixon for the second time around because the President was a 'tough man' needed for 'where the world is going'. Throughout the 1972 election campaign, Clint would stand shoulder to shoulder with other Hollywood luminaries, albeit most of the rest white-haired, who came out publicly for Nixon. During the 1972 election Clint made substantial donations of money and free time, and made appearances at Committee to Re-Elect the President (CREEP) fundraisers. Clint appeared on one campaign poster with such other Nixon endorsers as Green Bay Packer quarterback Bart Starr and basketball giant Wilt Chamberlain.

Clint and Maggie were conspicuous at the star-studded 27 August 1972 reception for Nixon at the Western White House in San Clemente, California. That is the night when Nixon, in his welcoming remarks, noted, 'I like my movies made in Hollywood. This is something that is typically American ... something that means a lot in presenting America to the world.' John Wayne, Frank Sinatra, Charlton Heston, Lawrence Welk, Jack Warner, Dick Zanuck, Jack Benny, Jimmy Durante and Zsa Zsa Gabor glittered among the Hollywood guests. Scatman Crothers sang to entertain the crowd. 'Some of those there observed that it was the greatest concentration of mature stars in history,' declared Hugh Sidey in *Life*, 'beating even the Academy Awards night.'

Clint, reportedly, was even made an honorary 'delegate-at-large' to the Republican national convention in 1972. Nixon was said to be a huge fan of Clint's, and the President had a standing order to rush each new Clint film to the White House screening room.

But a delegate-at-large didn't have to attend the convention, and when President Nixon rewarded Clint with an appointment to a governmental panel on the arts, his actual obligations were equally light. That was fine with Clint, who liked the occasional Republican gesture, but could hardly be counted a deep-dyed activist.

Shortly after the August 1972 San Clemente get-together, Nixon announced that Clint had been selected for a six-year term on the National Council of the Arts, an advisory body to the National Endowment of the Arts, which consisted of the Endowment chairman, Nancy Hanks, and twenty-six presidential designates charged with advising the chairman on federal funding for arts programmes. Clint's appointment made the screen actor an unlikely cultural bedfellow with such other prominent figures on the board as dancer–choreographers Judith Jamison and Edward Villela, classical pianist Rudolph Serkin, writer Eudora Welty, and painter Andrew Wyeth.

According to Richard Schickel, Nixon's selection of Clint was 'a typically Nixonian gesture of contempt for liberal opinion'. But according to sources inside the National Endowment, Clint was not even Nixon's first choice. That was actor Cesar Romero.

The National Council had been set up to represent various arts constituencies in the debate over government funding for the arts. Gregory Peck and Charlton Heston were the film industry's first members on the panel, and replacements had to be found when their six-year terms expired. California's state Republican Party pushed the name of Cesar Romero – then in his mid sixties – because Romero had campaigned vigorously for Nixon and raised substantial sums of money for him. The President was about to go along with the appointment of Romero, until Charles McWhorter, his advisor on the arts, vehemently stated the case against him. Romero was a second-rater, argued McWhorter, and Nixon, who wanted to go down in history for his arts support, would be remembered for choosing a guy who played the Joker on the *Batman* TV series.

Clint's name was advanced as a substitute. Since actress Rosalind Russell, an articulate liberal, was the other Hollywood nominee, Clint balanced the equation. It didn't hurt that Michael Straight, the deputy chairman to Nancy Hanks, who was in charge of panel recommendations, loved Clint's films, and himself had written novels about the West. Clint was the kind of celebrity they wanted, one who 'resounded nationally', in Straight's words.

Once appointed, the actor proved 'a voice for the smaller American arts', especially jazz, according to Richard Schickel's book. 'Populist that he was,' wrote Schickel, 'he felt that "man-in-the-street, woman-in-the street" projects, work that didn't attract much upscale interest, needed encouragement.'

The truth, as minutes for the National Council of the Arts attest, is that Clint rarely attended meetings and rarely said anything. Twice he spoke up for the record:

Seattle, Washington, 1–4 May 1975: 'Mr Eastwood felt it was important to consider when and to what extent the Endowment should help groups not performing up to par to improve their operations, and when it was time to stop assistance. He also hoped that special attention would be paid to jazz and other community groups which cannot raise private funds as easily as some other organizations.'

Washington, DC, 14–16 May 1976: 'Clint Eastwood suggested that the time taken for presentations such as that given at this meeting by the Public Broadcasting Service should be kept limited. The Chairman and other Council members agreed . . .'

Clint's position was largely honorary anyway. All of the organizational work was performed by staff. According to Michael Straight, as important as anything they might say or do at meetings, it was the job of the celebrities on the panel to mingle with Senators and congressmen at parties, and 'create a bonding with the agency'.

Even so, Clint's participation record was poor. Though officially a member of the National Council of the Arts from 1972 to 1978, the star attended precisely five meetings out of the roughly twenty-four held during that timespan at various locations around the country. (Some appointees kept perfect attendance.) Indeed, according to one National Endowment source, Clint's lack of attendance and involvement grew so conspicuous that he was quietly asked to resign before the end of his six-year term.

More than a few times, Clint has articulated his philosophical attraction to the Western, conjuring up a clumsy marriage of Dirty Harry vigilante justice and Malpaso independence, blended with the nobility of a legendary Sherwood Forest outlaw.

'Westerns,' he mused on one occasion, 'a period gone by, the pioneer, the loner operating by himself, without benefit of society. It usually has something to do with some sort of vengeance; he takes care of the vengeance himself, doesn't call the police. Like Robin Hood. It's the last masculine frontier. Romantic myth, I guess, though it's hard to think of anything romantic today. In a Western you can think, Jesus, there was a time when man was alone, on horseback, out there where man hasn't spoiled the land yet.'

Clint's next production, *Joe Kidd*, was just such a 'loner' Western. Based on an Elmore Leonard treatment, the story had been optioned by Jennings Lang, who brought it to Clint's attention. Sidney Beckerman, who had functioned behind the scenes of *Kelly's Heroes*, had a deal with Universal; he would act as producer, in partnership with Malpaso. In early 1971, Leonard went to work on a full-blown script.

Considering the people involved, hopes were high. Leonard was a hard-nosed novelist who had provided the stories for other exceptional Westerns (including *3:10 to Yuma*, *The Tall T* and *Hombre*). The director was veteran John Sturges, who had been among the early candidates for *Hang 'Em High*. But Clint was oddly reticent in such auspicious company, even though as star (and *de-facto* co-producer) he was the boss.

According to Elmore Leonard, the original treatment had focused on a character inspired by a fiery land-grant leader from the 1960s named Reies Lopez Tijerina, who wore a big chihuahua hat and was at one time a follower of Robert F. Kennedy. In a much-publicized incident, Tijerina and his supporters had stormed a New Mexico courthouse in 1967 (the original title of Leonard's treatment was 'The Sinola Courthouse Raid') and taken hostages, while demanding that land be returned to the Hispanic people.*

Leonard's original intention was to treat the Tijerina character – called Luis Chama in the film – as a glory-seeking egomaniac. Clint's role was that of a former frontier guide who is hired by a ruthless land baron, Frank Harlan, to stalk Chama. When Robert Duvall was cast to play Harlan, however, the part had to be built up for Duvall to loom a villainous match for Clint. And the characterization of Chama fell by the wayside. He became more of a stock figure, with his motivations half-baked.

Clint's old friend John Saxon, who portrayed Chama, thought this happened because 'Clint needed to be the hero. This character didn't need to be smeared, but they smeared him just so it would be clear who the hero was. They tainted him with self-serving and cowardice.' Once, addressing a meeting of Nosotros, a Latin-American actors' organization opposed to stereotypes, Saxon actually apologized for playing such a dubious character.

In any event, the three-way relationship between the main characters developed poorly. Elmore Leonard thought that happened partly because everybody – Clint included – surrendered authority to director Sturges, on whom they all conferred an aura, owing to Sturges' credits as director of such vintage Westerns as *Gunfight at the OK Corral* and *The Magnificent Seven*. 'I think we were all in awe of Sturges,' said Leonard.

Sturges presided over the story conferences, sometimes drooling from the side of the mouth. It only later occurred to them that the director was a boozer and in the downhill stages of his career. Sturges would occasionally dictate a scene intended to be a highlight, and then

---

* It was on 5 June 1967, that Reies Lopez Tijerina and his band of armed men invaded a courthouse in Tierra Amarilla in the northern New Mexico county of Rio Arriba, shooting up the place, kidnapping a newsman and deputy, wounding two officers. The 'courthouse raid', intended to force land-grant concessions on behalf of New Mexico's impoverished Hispanic population, later became a famous courtroom case.

exclaim, 'That's movies!' Producer Sidney Beckerman kept rewriting Elmore Leonard's dialogue after he turned it in, according to Leonard, and then Leonard tried to change it back before the secretary could type up each new draft.

There weren't that many story conferences anyway, Leonard recalled. Clint was 'the easiest guy in the world to get along with'. The star–producer had little enough to say about the niceties of the story. Clint mainly watched over his own role.

There was one scene, Leonard recalled, that sparked more than the customary debate. In this particular vignette, Joe Kidd was confronted by an armed faction. Clint thought he should whip his gun out and wave it around when standing up to the bad guys. 'I don't think you need to have your gun out,' opined Leonard. 'But my character has not been presented as a gunfighter,' insisted Clint. He turned to the director for support. 'Don't you think I need my gun out?' Clint asked. 'No,' John Sturges said. 'Why not?' the star demanded to know. 'Because,' Sturges replied phlegmatically, 'the audience knows who you are. They've seen all your pictures.'

That appeared to settle it. However, when the picture was finished, Leonard, watching that telltale scene, couldn't help but notice that Clint had his gun out.

Don Stroud, who had played the wacko criminal in *Coogan's Bluff*, joined the cast to play one of the wackos of *Joe Kidd*. Lalo Schifrin would contribute his most 'spaghetti Westernish' score, while Bruce Surtees, another returnee, would perform photography chores.

Down in Old Tucson, where they shot initial scenes in November of 1971, another production, *The Life and Times of Judge Roy Bean*, was just wrapping up. Some of the cast and crew overlapped at the local hotels and restaurants. But Clint said later he never crossed paths with John Huston, the director of *The Life and Times of Judge Roy Bean*, whom he would later impersonate in *White Hunter, Black Heart*.

They filmed the outdoor sequences near June Lake, east of Yosemite National Park. They didn't have an ending, however. They had all been counting on Sturges to wave his magic wand, but he never did, and the right ending had eluded all the story conferences. One day on location, producer Bob Daley made a joke about having a train crash through the barroom at the climax, and everybody took the joke seriously. Everybody loved the idea. Clint always preferred a spectacular *deus ex machina* – some kind of a big-bang finale – with plenty of bodies piling up around him.

To be fair, Clint might have been distracted, throughout the filming, by a mysterious illness. He started with the flu, then sprouted apparent allergies. Rumours persist that the Western star had developed an allergy to horses; Clint says, 'cats'. Whichever it was, the illness had the symptoms of a bronchial infection, worsening to the point that Clint began to suffer a recurrence of his debilitating anxiety attacks. He had his worst anxiety attack ever, according to sources, and felt he was dying. Fears for him were bad enough that Clint's illness leaked into print in the gossip columns.

Although his paramour from *Rawhide* days, Roxanne Tunis, had become a Transcendental Meditation practitioner, Clint had only paid polite attention to TM before this incident. His illness coincided with driving daily to the set, however, with Stella Garcia, the main actress in the film. She was listening to TM tapes by the same Maharishi who had tutored the Beatles. When *Joe Kidd* wrapped up filming, Clint went straight to Tunis and arranged to undergo TM instruction. Then he began a habit of briefly meditating – mornings and nights – from which he has never strayed.

This 'miracle cure' was so effective, it inspired Clint to send others to Roxanne Tunis for TM tutelage: Burt Reynolds, even Roy Kaufman and Howard Bernstein. According to close friends, to this day Clint has never suffered the same degree of high anxiety.

From even the worst films Clint usually salvaged people or ideas that he could incorporate into his future agenda. Three of the people behind the scenes, working for John Sturges, were production designer Henry Bumstead, editor Ferris Webster and assistant director James Fargo.

Bumstead and Webster were seasoned craftsmen of the type that Clint employed to assure the professional look of his films. Bumstead, a leading art director since the late 1940s (Oscar-nominated for Hitchcock's *Vertigo*, and winner of Academy Awards for *To Kill a Mockingbird* and, the same year as *High Plains Drifter*, *The Sting*), would execute designs for the dream-like Western setting of Clint's next film, *High Plains Drifter*, and then disappear from Malpaso for almost twenty years before returning for *Unforgiven*. Ferris Webster's long career as a cutter dated back to the 1940s; he spent many years at MGM, and was

Oscar-nominated for his work on *The Blackboard Jungle, The Manchurian Candidate* and *The Great Escape.* Although Webster had been closely associated with Sturges for over ten years (he edited *The Magnificent Seven*) he would jump to Malpaso and edit Clint's next fourteen films. James Fargo, typical in his own way of the younger, hardier breed of individuals drafted to perform spadework for Clint, would continue on *High Plains Drifter* and then, after various Malpaso jobs, rise higher than most, to director.

At the same time, old friends did not always fit into new schemes. John Saxon's experience with Clint on *Joe Kidd*, the first time they had worked together since drama classes at Universal in the 1950s, was revealing. Much that could not have been predicted had happened to the two of them in the intervening time: Saxon had had an early brush with stardom, but then struggled for a clear screen identity and now played mainly colourful secondary and supporting roles in films and on TV. Both had gone to Italy to make features, though Saxon had not done as well there as Clint. Whether Saxon had got his part in *Joe Kidd* directly at Clint's say-so, he was never sure.

'I think Clint looked back on that [Universal] period with a sense of nostalgia,' recalled Saxon, 'but he wanted to be appreciated for now. We spent some time together, and it was okay, but it wasn't really fluid. I remember the first time we had a scene together he was very nervous, as if he hadn't considered himself a good actor during the time when we started out. In the old days I was probably considered the more adept one. Now he was the star, and I sensed a desire to be accepted.'

Saxon made missteps. He and Clint had dinner one night, 'and I think he picked up the tab, and I don't think he was too happy about that'. Then, at the end of the filming, Saxon was asked to come back for an additional day of photography because the director had neglected to obtain a closeup considered vital to the final cut. 'I think Clint was trying to get me to do it for nothing,' remembered Saxon. 'We weren't talking about a lot of money. Under my contract, my day would have been something like $1,000. I said, "Why should I do it for free?" and I don't think he liked that either.'

The past represented a gulf between Clint and certain old friends. The last time Saxon saw Clint was a few years ago, by chance. He walked up to him with the old friendliness and said, 'Hi, Meat!' Clint acted aloof. 'He was over whatever the nostalgia was, and there was no great desire to rekindle friendship,' said Saxon.

In the four-year span from 1968 to 1971, Clint had appeared in the somewhat astonishing total of ten films. 'Eastwood Topples John Wayne' was the headline in the *Motion Picture Herald* in 1972. But Wayne, who reigned as number one at the box-office twenty times in his half-century career, had only one film in release in 1972, *The Cowboys*. Whereas Clint not only had the spillover from *Dirty Harry*, his other 1972 vehicle, *Joe Kidd*, also did exceedingly well; there was additional ticket residue from both *Play Misty for Me* and the still-popular triple-bookings of the 'spaghetti Westerns'.

Clint's impressive productivity and shrewd marketing acumen were always stealth factors in his career. His box-office ranking often benefited from him having more than one film in theatres within a given year. Plus he always manoeuvred to release his films in the summer or at Christmas, the two biggest seasons for Hollywood.

High Plains Drifter was Clint's next film. Coming towards the end of Clint's first cycle of stardom, it was another Western, and a benchmark as the first one Clint himself directed. Once again it was Universal who had the property in hand, a short treatment by Ernest Tidyman, who had earned the equivalent of a Triple Crown for *The French Connection*: a Best Screenplay Oscar, a Writers Guild plaque, an Edgar from a mystery writers' organization. Between Tidyman and Dean Riesner – hired to rewrite Tidyman – the final script would be better than *Joe Kidd*'s, filling plot holes with black humour and allegory. One of the ideas Clint had taken away from his experience with Leone was 'mixing in a little allegory with the action'.

Actually, the film ripped off Leone in more than one category. The story was about another Mysterious Stranger arriving in a brooding Western town where the populace shares a craven secret. Although the townspeople hire the stranger to defend their town against three dastardly parolees bearing a grudge, they don't seem to recognize him as their former sheriff, who once before survived their treachery and greed. The stranger deputizes a dwarf, paints the town red and renames it 'Hell'. Soon it's hard to tell which – the evil cowboy trio, or the town – are more the object of his contempt.

It was another cigar-in-mouth part for Clint, with three swift, bloody killings in the first reel alone. His character has one of those convenient shirt-off scenes in which, once again – as he did for Sergio Leone in *The Good, the Bad and the Ugly* – Clint dodges bullets while bathing. And he undergoes one of those recurrent slow-motion nightmares that haunt Clint in film after film – evoking some painful, incriminating episode in the past (in this case, a man being whipped to death by three shrouded villains).

The women are treated badly of course. In the opening scene, Clint's character drags a foul-mannered female into a barn and then brutally rapes her; she begins to enjoy the experience, and later on Clint is forced to make love to her one more time. There has to be a decent woman around for Madonna–whore contrast, in this case an older, married hotel keeper who observes Clint's hard-hearted behaviour from the sidelines – half appalled, half aroused. When Clint's character makes a rape joke, she attacks him with a knife. (Maybe she has seen *Play Misty for Me.*) Shortly afterwards, the two find cause to jump into bed together, if for no other reason than because, in Judith Crist's words, Clint is always presented as 'God's original gift to the ladies'.

On the shores of Mono Lake near the High Sierras, Henry Bumstead created an eerie set. Again with Bruce Surtees behind the camera, the filming of *High Plains Drifter* took place in the summer of 1972. Dee Barton, a drummer, trombonist and arranger with Stan Kenton, had first orchestrated the jazz score for *Play Misty for Me*; now he was asked to write the music for *High Plains Drifter*, deliberately evoking Clint's Italian Westerns, 'without sounding exactly like Morricone', in Barton's words.

Paul Brinegar from *Rawhide* and Bob Donner from Clint's Arch Drive past had small parts, and were never again glimpsed in a Malpaso film. Marianna Hill and Verna Bloom played, respectively, the thankless roles of whore and Madonna. Geoffrey Lewis, a rubber-faced actor, had his first and perhaps best part in what would become a cottage-industry career as Clint's sidekick, playing the leader of the evil gunmen.

Lewis has a good death scene, dying while shouting out, 'Who are you?' Nobody learns Clint's identity for sure until he rides out of town at the end of the story, after extravagant killings and destruction. He rides past the name of the former sheriff being chiselled onto a tombstone. Even attentive viewers might not have noticed the real-life names of directors Brian G. Hutton, Sergio Leone and Don Siegel coyly emblazoned on three of the graves. 'I buried my directors,' Clint told interviewers jokingly.

Even disapproving critics had to admit the star–director was becoming 'amazingly proficient', in the words of Jon Landau, writing in *Rolling Stone*, 'framing shots with spontaneous, natural beauty, tracking with expressive fluidity...' Landau added: 'It is only in his thematic shallowness and verbal archness that this film falls apart.'

Other critics thought Clint's directing was as derivative as it was expressive, and the thematics not so much shallow as downright ugly. Arthur Knight in *Saturday Review* found that Clint had 'absorbed the approaches of two of his former directors, Sergio Leone and Don Siegel, and fused them with his own paranoid vision of society'.

The gravestone names at the end of *High Plains Drifter* were not merely a joke. With this film – its professionalism assuring his future as a director, its brisk box-office consolidating his stardom – Clint indeed buried Sergio Leone and Don Siegel. Leone of course had long been left behind. As for Siegel, early on in their partnership he had realized that Clint was going to be a superstar. They had reasons to work well together, and Siegel always made sure they clicked. Siegel was very good at annoying producers. But he wasn't going to annoy someone like Clint, whom he genuinely liked. The director always pretended he wasn't impressed by Clint, said Dean Riesner, but he *was* impressed. 'I remember I looked out the window once and saw Don running down to Clint's bungalow,' said Riesner. 'He'd stroll in front of me, but he would run when he thought it was safe to run.'

But Siegel and Clint had started out on shared footing, and Siegel understood, even as it was happening, that Clint would grow to overshadow him. By 1972, the balance of power had shifted permanently and the relationship was changed. 'It surprises me,' Siegel told a magazine some years later, 'that he [Clint] is not more interested in a greater variety of roles.' But Clint wasn't, and *Dirty Harry* would be their last real collaboration.

The year 1972 was also marked by the birth of Clint and Maggie's second child, a daughter. Alison, no middle name, like Clint, was born at St John's Hospital on 22 May, a couple of weeks earlier than her expected due date and just a short time before the start of photography for *High Plains Drifter*.

'Not quite willing to believe her good luck at getting what she wanted,' reported the *Monterey Peninsula Herald*, 'Maggie more than once asked, "Are you sure it's a girl?" Clint, the strong and silent man of mystery, said nothing, but looked like the cat that ate the canary, said Maggie.'

Clint still appeared the loving husband and attentive father (he 'even changes diapers' was one of the admirable traits floated in articles). He made well-documented public excursions with his wife. Maggie was his date on Oscar night in early 1973, for example, when Charlton Heston didn't materialize, and Clint had to wing it as a presenter. Clint and his wife came arm in arm to Republican Party functions; they could be counted on for Carmel area charity functions; in the early 1970s, they jointly hosted Clint's Celebrity Tennis Tournament in Pebble Beach.

Behind the façade, however, the marriage was in deep trouble. Clint had a 'one-more-notch-on-the-belt' philosophy about women: later on in life, in one of his interviews, he would compare his attitude to cigarette addiction.

Now more than in previous years, cracks in Clint's façade were hinted at by articles in the fan magazines, which were increasingly sceptical of the official publicity. Earl Leaf was one fan correspondent who had known Clint since the mid-1950s. He wrote in *Rona Barrett's Hollywood*, 'Though he [Clint] never ceased loving and caring for Maggie, he hasn't made a secret of the free-living sexy side of his life around other women, especially young free-thinking chicks.'

'Why They Call Clint Eastwood the Worst Husband in Hollywood' was the headline of another article in *Modern Sereen*.

Roxanne Tunis was still in the star's life – and frequently in the background of his films. She was given menial parts so that she could be with Clint on the set. (Assuring her anonymity while at the same time limiting her fee, she was *never* billed.) There are many unpublished photographs of the two posing affectionately in costume.

In the early 1970s, however, Tunis declared herself a full-time follower of 'a higher spiritual path', and told Clint she didn't want the karmic responsibility of poisoning his marriage. She and her daughter Kimber soon moved to Denver where Kimber entered private school. There, according to sources sympathetic to Tunis, mother and daughter saw Clint on his regular skiing trips, probably more often than before.

'I love being horizontal,' the hippie girl, Breezy, would boast in Clint's next film. An admirable quality in a young woman, evidently, and other horizontal ladies seemed endlessly abundant when Maggie wasn't around. There was Inger Stevens on *Hang 'Em High*, Jean Seberg on *Paint Your Wagon*, Jo Ann Harris during *The Beguiled*. The actress who played his girlfriend in *Play Misty for Me* was another co-star who was linked to Clint, according to sources for this book. Donna Mills has insisted otherwise: 'I liked him a lot, but he was married and we were very proper,' she told Fuensanta Plaza for *Clint Eastwood– Malpaso.*

Maggie still made scheduled visits to most of the sets, however, so Clint's affairs and arrangements had to be masterly, sometimes almost hair's-breadth. One friend recalled going to the airport with the actor to see Maggie and his children off after their visit to a *Thunderbolt and Lightfoot* location. After his family departed, Clint checked his watch and glanced at the airport monitors. They only had to wait a short while before greeting a plane with Keely Smith stepping off into Clint's arms.

Clint also had intimate relationships with certain journalists. Although Clint liked to say that he was 'never particularly "in" with the press', he was a dedicated activist where journalists and critics were concerned. Acutely aware that 'a lot of them [US critics] put my films down', the movie star was also aware that if a critic or journalist liked him *personally*, they might like his films better.

Only a handful of US film critics were 'purists' who saw and wrote about films in relative isolation from the industry. Many also interviewed the stars and wrote feature articles about their lives and careers, quoting their subject at length. Clint had learned to be at his best in such one-to-one interview situations, pouring his charm over people who might critique his films later.

Clint took critics golfing, skiing and to jazz clubs – he took them up, later on, on his private copter with the star himself piloting. Clint was receptive, very early in his career, to invitations to critics' seminars. Those Hollywood journalists whom Clint liked, and those who liked him back, were treated with 'exclusive' interviews with the star and hot-ticket invitations to visit his on-location sets. These favourites could be counted on not only to write expansively for their 'home' newspapers or magazines, but also to freelance auxiliary pieces in other publications.

Jay Cocks of *Time*, film critic for one of America's two most influential weekly news magazines, was one of the passers-through on the set of *High Plains Drifter*, visiting his fiancée, actress Verna Bloom, who was in the cast. After Cocks gave *Dirty Harry* 'the only positive review in a major publication', in Richard Schickel's words, he followed up with listing the film as one of the year's Ten Best. The critic was then casually drafted into Clint's social circle. When, speaking to *Playboy*, Clint felt obliged to list 'the better, more experienced reviewers' who had liked his films, he mentioned Cocks, along with fellow New York-based critics Andrew Sarris, Vincent Canby and Bosley Crowther.

It might be too hard on Verna Bloom to say that Cocks's wife-to-be should have refused a role in *High Plains Drifter*, or the later one Clint awarded her in *Honkytonk Man*. Such apparent conflicts of interest might be perfectly acceptable among film critics, although lawyers and judges recuse themselves for less. Cocks went on to review other Clint films in *Time*. No doubt he was an articulate ambassador for Clint with critics' organizations.

Bridget Byrne was also a Clint ambassador. She covered the entertainment scene and reviewed movies for the *Los Angeles Herald Examiner*, the Hearst-owned daily newspaper regarded as 'second' to the city's more widely read *Los Angeles Times*. Her movie reviews, interviews and articles were carried over the wire services for other Hearst newspapers.

Byrne met Clint for the first time at a Las Vegas press junket to promote the release of *Where Eagles Dare*, back in 1969. Elizabeth Taylor and Richard Burton were expected to show up; they didn't, Clint did. Although the actor was then a relatively unknown quantity to most of the hundred journalists, he was in his element, hesitating over the more probing questions, all the better if the questioner was a pretty woman.*

---

* This is the press conference, incidentally, at which one journalist noted that Richard Burton, Clint's co-star in *Where Eagles Dare*, had just finished a new film (*Staircase*), in which he dared to portray a homosexual hairdresser. Would the macho Clint ever consider playing a gay character on the screen? 'Only,' Clint replied, 'if I was sure I could convince people I was merely acting.'

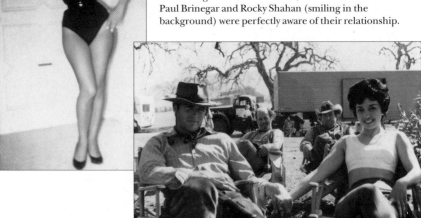

Clint led a 'double life' with Roxanne Tunis (left), a dancer with whom he kept up an intense romance – and fathered a child – despite his marriage to Maggie. He got Tunis a continuing contract on *Rawhide*, where cast members like Paul Brinegar and Rocky Shahan (smiling in the background) were perfectly aware of their relationship.

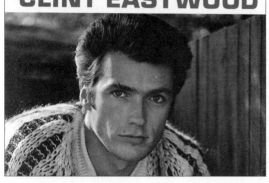

GET YOURSELF ANOTHER FOOL!
FOR YOU-FOR ME-FOREVERMORE
STAR OF RAWHIDE
CLINT EASTWOOD

Left: Clint seemed to have different, more modest ambitions than the rest of the *Rawhide* cast. For a while he tried singing and was touted as a prospective teen-idol. This was one of his '45s.

Below: Record companies tried various formulas with him, including packaging him with other 'singing stars', like Merv Griffin, later Clint's tennis partner in Carmel.

ALL THE HITS
WITH
ALL THE STARS
VOL. 4

JIMMY DEAN □ MERV GRIFFIN
CLINT EASTWOOD □ CHARLIE GRACIE
PEGGY KING □ BILLY SCOTT
DENISE DARCEL □ THE SKYLINER

BUMMING AROUND
STREETS OF GLORY
DRESSIN' UP
SWEET DARLIN'
SIERRA NEVADA
DOES HE REALLY LOVE ME
A MILLION BOYS
DORMIR
EVERYONE BUT YOU
THE TOWN OF NEVER WORRY

wyncote

Clint was game for any sort of singing: he is seen here making a guest appearance with Danny Kaye and other TV cowboys, including Buddy Ebsen from *The Beverly Hillbillies* and Fess Parker of *Daniel Boone* fame.

Above: Clint engaged in many other affairs, including a fling with young actress Jill Banner (star of the low-budget *Spider Baby*), seen here with friend Kitty Jones. Jones's house was a magnet for parties and a drop-in spot for Clint's 'nooners'.

Below: There were more public nights on the town with Maggie and mutual friends, including (at left) director Ted Post and fellow television star Roger Moore. Note that Clint was still drinking the occasional glass of hard liquor in those days.

Joint birthday party for Maggie and Jane Brolin (at right). Close friends suspected Clint was sleeping with both of them. The cake reads: '21 My Ass.'

Kitty Jones's wedding: Clint, Kitty Jones, her husband Dick Lee, and in the back row, Maggie, James and Jane Brolin. Lee would become Clint's stand-in in the 1970s.

Snapshot of Maggie looking adoringly at Clint in the 1960s.

Left: Italian director Sergio Leone (seen here in 1984) could only communicate with his American star by gestures and stock phrases, but the 'paella trilogy' made Clint an international name.

Fresh off the plane in Rome, Clint clowned on the roof of the Residence Palace & Hotel with cowboy equipment and actor Philippe Hersent, the husband of Geneviève Hersent, the Italian representative of his American publicist.

Right: A night out on location in Spain with Steve Rowland – the son of MGM director Roy Rowland, an American actor also trying to make a career for himself in Europe – and Bill Thompkins, soon to be banished from Clint's retinue. The women are unidentified.

The Italian-language poster for *For a Few Dollars More*, nowadays a collector's item. The 'spaghetti Westerns' triumphed first in Italy and then swept Europe, making Clint a film star, first, outside the US.

Above: The final
showdown, a
visual ballet of
gunfighting, with
the 'good'
(Clint), the 'bad'
(Lee Van Cleef)
and the 'ugly' (Eli
Wallach).

Left: Old friend
Ted Post, whom
he trusted from
Rawhide days, was
Clint's choice to
direct his first
American
Western, *Hang
'Em High.*

It is a truism that US film critics tend to be predominantly male. The fact that they are predominantly white males may have more than a little to do with Clint's extraordinary appeal among the best as well as the worst of them. Unusual for being a woman, from England, ten years younger than Clint, Byrne was a beautiful blonde of the type that appealed to the star. 'Some people thought we looked right together,' Byrne said. 'Some people thought we looked alike. I looked a bit like Sondra Locke.'

Byrne was one of the people privileged to visit the set of nearly every Malpaso production during the early 1970s, whipping up anticipation for the next Clint vehicle. On the set of *The Beguiled*, for example, she interviewed Don Siegel extensively; then, according to Siegel's memoirs, she turned around and narrowed the focus of her article on Clint, praising his simple virtues: his work ethic, his pleasantness, 'how he represented the best in American men'.

In an interview, Byrne said she had no professional qualms about the close friendship that developed between her and Clint. As she explained, the relationship never influenced her critiques, except 'it may have affected me in the sense of my feeling that I had a bit more insight'. Byrne occasionally doubled as a sports reporter for the *Los Angeles Herald Examiner*, and 'I don't see any difference in, say, reporting on a tennis match. I was the tennis writer for a number of years. I'm not going to change the score [in my reporting] because I'm sleeping with the guy.'

Byrne noted that she arrived at a decidedly jaundiced opinion of *Dirty Harry*, and in her review complained that 'the twists and jumps of the script don't bear too close inspection and Siegel doesn't allow us time for thought'. The director called her up to complain about the critique, and Clint told her she didn't know how to appreciate the film. But if Clint took offence at her comment that 'the star is at his best when he's too out of breath to speak', he might have consoled himself with Byrne's observation that Siegel had photographed the star as though he were a distinctive piece of architecture, 'savoring and revealing the driving tension beneath the long, lean lines. Eastwood has never looked so right since his early days.' (Byrne's review of *Magnum Force*, the sequel, was studded with words like 'great', 'wonderful', 'witty', 'warm', 'touching'.)

Clint's friend Fritz Manes said the star regarded his periodic affair with Byrne as a win-win situation: Clint would show up at the Malpaso office after one of his rendezvous with Byrne, and announce that the review was 'in the bag', in Manes's words. Nor was Clint shy about boasting about the mechanics of their lovemaking.

Although their relationship has never been reported, Byrne insisted that it was widely known among Los Angeles's film journalists. 'I don't think it's a deep, dark secret that at some point he and I knew each other beyond the [usual] thing,' Byrne said. 'Most people who know me and know Clint know we had some sort of relationship at a certain point in time, but to make anything major out of it would be of great insignificance.'

She was *not* in love with Clint, Byrne emphasized, nor he with her. The star was always very considerate, and she regards him as a friend to this day. He made the gesture of meeting her parents, and she herself met Maggie on several occasions.

She had no idea what Maggie knew about her and Clint. Clint never spoke much about Maggie, although Byrne had the clear impression that his marriage was unhappy.

Bridget Byrne would drop out of the rotation around the time Sondra Locke entered Clint's world. Still a Los Angeles freelancer covering the film scene, Byrne refused to confirm on the record any additional details of their acquaintance. 'Clint is kind to animals, I can tell you that,' Byrne did say. 'I was with him once in Carmel when we saw some ducks crossing the road, and we did stop the car and try to rescue them.'

Just before *Joe Kidd* was released, Clint phoned Elmore Leonard and asked him if he had any other script ideas that might be right for him. *Dirty Harry* was making an awful lot of money worldwide, said Clint, but he didn't own as big a piece of the take as he would like. 'Do you have anything like *Dirty Harry*,' Clint asked, 'only different? A guy with a big gun, but he doesn't have to be in law enforcement. That same kind of character . . .'

Elmore Leonard had one idea and told Clint the story of an artichoke farmer who wouldn't surrender to a criminal syndicate trying to squeeze his profits. A little time passed before Leonard sent over twenty-five pages of outline. Clint read it, and declined. Leonard always believed he had made a big mistake – he had located the story up around Castroville, near Carmel. 'What I thought,' said Leonard, 'is that Clint'll love this because he can go home from work, not knowing he didn't *want* to go home.'

Castroville became Colorado, artichokes became watermelons, and Clint's part went to Charles Bronson, who starred in *Mr Majestyk*, the 1974 film that eventuated. Clint would never find another cash cow as lucrative as the Dirty Harry series, and when the sequel was made the star would make sure he got a bigger percentage.

Meanwhile, the star-director turned his attention to a script about love blossoming between a middle-aged man and a teenage girl. Jo Heims had written *Breezy* for Clint to play the starring role of realtor Frank Harmon – a bitter divorcée living alone – who is propelled into a relationship with a free-spirit with the metaphorical name of Breezy. Thinking of Clint's avowed love for animals, she even gave Harmon a dog, a German wirehaired hunter that is rescued from a road accident. 'I understood the [Frank Harmon] character,' explained Clint in one interview, 'and she kind of wanted me to play it. I said, "Jo, I don't think I'm the right age." ' Clint, taking a psychological step back from the character, chose to direct only. Instead William Holden, twelve years older than Clint, was approached to play Frank Harmon.

For the part of Breezy, Clint interviewed a number of young actresses. Sondra Locke was one. The blonde actress from Shelbyville, Tennessee, had earned a Best Supporting Actress Oscar nomination for her screen debut as a small-town Southerner in 1968's screen adaptation of Carson McCullers's *The Heart Is A Lonely Hunter*. She knew Jo Heims casually and was alerted to the casting call by her. Locke went over to Universal and met Clint for the first time. She didn't actually 'audition'. They just chatted. 'I thought the same as probably most people think, after meeting him,' Locke remembered. 'I perceived him as, "Gee, what a really nice guy. He's so unpretentious. Here he is, this big star, but he's really just this kind of accessible, a hang-out guy." '

Born in 1947, Locke was too old for a character that Clint wanted as youthful as possible to emphasize the May–September disparity. Jo Ann Harris, who had been intermittently involved with Clint since *The Beguiled*, believed that she was the front-runner in Clint's heart. But

Harris was in for an unpleasant letdown. Clint made her audition for the starring part – one of his ominous signals – then switched his allegiance to someone else. That tolled the end of their relationship.

The 'someone else' was another pixie type, Kay Lenz, the daughter of show business parents, who had a long show business résumé. Except for a small part in *American Graffiti*, however, she was new to films. Once again, Clint opted for someone whose background was mainly in TV. A thin, long-haired brunette, Lenz's 'Junior Miss' looks belied her age: she was twenty. According to sources, although Clint had refused to star as the middle-aged man who falls in love with Lenz on screen, off camera he became infatuated with the actress.

'I knew about Kay,' said one old friend of Clint's, who visited the set. 'I can remember watching him direct her in a scene where she was supposed to look sexy or vulnerable. He'd take her face and stroke her mouth and jaw, saying, "Soft! Soft!" Because she had a kind of mouth that jutted out at you. He kept saying, "Soft! Soft!" He was very, very gentle with her. I knew something was going on.'

Breezy began shooting in November of 1972, one of the few Clint films to avail itself of LA locations. Bruce Surtees, by now in demand on more prestigious projects, yielded the camera duties to Frank Stanley, the first of four films Stanley would photograph for Malpaso. The filming was quick, with publicity boasting Clint under schedule (three days) and under budget (under $1 million).

The reported budget didn't ever reflect Clint's fees and percentages. It certainly didn't reflect much retooling of the script. Maybe Clint owed Jo Heims a favour, after having taken *Play Misty for Me* away from her and handing it over to Dean Riesner. Clint said he was originally attracted to *Breezy* because it offered the thematic 'rejuvenation of a cynic', but the thinness of the story, the ordinariness of the dialogue, cried out for rewrite. Clint was always in a hurry, however, and script drafts took time and money.

The script wasn't entirely at fault. Paradoxically, with Clint, quick directing often translated into deadly pacing on the screen. Lenz, who turned out a fine actress in her career, had ample opportunity here, but was charmlessly adrift in her scenes. (She and the film's other hippies are all plastic anyway.) Holden was okay, but his character – a cynic with a 'black cloud' over his head – is turned into a grinning fool by love.

Lenz and Holden have one of those 'walk-on-the-beach' scenes with a Michel Legrand background song, 'The morning is a friend of mine . . .', reminiscent of Clint's tree-talking ditty in *Paint Your Wagon*. Then there is some tasteful, soft-focus, flickering sex of the type that passes swiftly and unmemorably in more than one Clint film. Even with William Holden as his emotional stand-in, the tone of the romantic scenes is guarded. 'For a work exploring such a potentially explosive – and, to many minds, scandalous – sexual encounter, it is not a very sexy movie,' conceded Richard Schickel in his book. 'Once again, Clint was too polite in his eroticism.'

Polite in eroticism, veiled as a personal work. Maggie, however, could scrutinize the film and take note of Harmon's ex-wife – depicted as a troublemaking bitch. Wives in general fared badly. One of Harmon's friends complains, 'My wife doesn't turn me on like she used to,' and when Harmon explains the reasons for his marital breakup, he notes, 'I just stopped loving her . . . All the things that I dug about her suddenly turned me off.'

Perhaps the most revelatory moment of *Breezy* occurs after Harmon is forced to realize the May–September incongruency of his affair with the hippie teenager. He decides to toss her out of his life. 'I can't cope!' Harmon explains. Imagine this plaintive line of dialogue coming from Clint, and one can understand why he didn't play the part.

Breezy might be seen as the star's attempt to speak to his own inner fears about ageing, while offering a mawkish defence of his continuing dalliances with younger women. The film did not set audiences or critics on fire, however. In Clint's career, nothing would rival it as a flop. Released in November 1973, *Breezy* barely cracked *Variety*'s list of current Top Fifty films, before disappearing from the weekly rankings. It was not widely booked then or thereafter, and was not made available in video until 1998.

Twenty years would go by before Clint dared to direct – or star in – another love story.

There was one member of the Eastwood family actually living a true-life love story.

Just after *Breezy* was completed, two years after the death of her husband, Clint's mother, Ruth Eastwood, entered into a second marriage with John Belden Wood.

The bridegroom, a widower, hailed from a prominent Piedmont family, which 'appropriately made a fortune in wood (lumber, that is) and once owned a hill and an estate, appropriately called Woodland Hill, that is now partially in Lafayette and partially in Orinda', according to a Bay Area society columnist. Wood was associated with a San Francisco investment firm. Although he had been socially acquainted with Clint's mother for some years, their romance really started a year earlier, in Hawaii, at the fortieth wedding anniversary celebration of mutual friends.

Their wedding with a Hawaii theme was held in the chapel of the Robert Louis Stevenson School at Pebble Beach in October 1972. Clint, a pragmatist about love, was happy for his mother – he beamed, escorting her up the aisle. The extended Eastwood family was there, with Maggie looking slender and radiant. Four-month-old Alison, among the grandchildren present for the occasion, was held by her nurse.

CHAPTER SEVEN

Clint's Weather
1973–1976

Soon after *Breezy* finished shooting, Warners announced that Clint would reprise his role as Detective Harry Callahan in a sequel to *Dirty Harry* with the tentative title of 'Vigilance'.

Great film-makers, when tackling a sequel to one of their works, are naturally concerned with continuity and deepening the story line. In the case of the Dirty Harry series, continuity meant the same location (San Francisco), one or two of the supporting cast, and not much else. If anyone expected an answer as to how and why the detective had rejoined the force, after chucking away his badge in *Dirty Harry*, they were disappointed. If anyone remembered the sad, bitter Harry who dominated the first film, they were surprised by the new breed. In *Dirty Harry*, Harry was alone in life, grieving the loss of his wife. In *Magnum Force*, Harry would become sexier and acquire a young girl-friend, one of those 'squirts' that barely reached up to the star's shoulder, not to mention a bevy of other 'pretty girls begging for his body', in the words of Paul Zimmerman of *Newsweek*, who was among critics panning the sequel.

If the first film was ambiguous and complex, the second sought ways to be more pleasing and plain-spoken. Children could hug a warmer, fuzzier Harry. And there was effort to make the first film's rightist politics more palatable. Clint liked writer John Milius's suggestion to wrap the plot around a rogue clique within the San Francisco police bent on the systematic extermination of criminals. Translation: there are worse cops than Dirty Harry.

Milius, a gun aficionado and political conservative, was in the early stages of a flamboyant career. After USC film school, he had become a scenarist for Roger Corman and then in the early 1970s wrote two major films, *The Life and Times of Judge Roy Bean* and *Jeremiah Johnson*. He had worked on early drafts of the first *Dirty Harry*. Apart from his main plot contribution to the sequel, however, his script was an intentional retread. 'Do ya feel lucky?' would be repeated in the opening credits, and Clint would get a scene, eating a hot dog and foiling an airplane hijacking, to remind audiences of one of the highpoints of *Dirty Harry*.

When Milius ran out of ideas or time – he was on track to direct *Dillinger* – Clint turned to Michael Cimino, another relative newcomer, who had been brought to his attention by the William Morris Agency. Cimino agreed to revise the shooting script, but he was a hired-hand, and director Ted Post would also have to contribute some remedial writing, when filming commenced in late April 1973.

'Vigilance' would be changed to *Magnum Force*, in deference to the long-barrelled Magnum .44 which Detective Callahan liked to flourish. Post, who had served Clint honourably during *Rawhide* and then directed *Hang 'Em High*, would guide the camera, with Frank Stanley hired for photography and Lalo Schifrin for music.

Hal Holbrook would play Clint's establishment antagonist, who turns out to be in cahoots with the vigilantes; young actors David Soul, Tim Matheson, Robert Urich and Kip Niven (David Niven's son) would portray the 'death squad' cops.

Director Post would learn that Clint was no longer the young Rowdy-type struggling to master the acting craft and learn from his elders. *Dirty Harry* had clinched his claim to be the hottest movie star in the world. Now as the de facto producer of *Magnum Force*, as well as a director in his own right, Clint seemed to enjoy crossing swords with Post.

First of all, Clint resisted the director on his performance. Post reminded Clint that he needed to substitute intensity for volume. 'You don't want to come off as a ham,' Post warned the star. But Clint liked vein-bulging scenes. He felt he knew better how to act crowd-pleasing characters.

One contretemps arose over the director's call for a 'second take' on a minor scene. Clint, standing by and observing impatiently, said the take was fine; he didn't want to waste any more money. The director thought a mistake had been made in the 'master' or 'establishing set-up', and he told Clint, 'I'm calling the shots here. Otherwise you direct the picture.' In front of everybody, the star had to back down. When the 'dailies' showed that Post had been right, and indeed there was a glitch in the 'master', Clint made an apology. 'I knew that was the kiss of death,' said Post. 'He got very tough with me after that.'

Clint's 'penny-pinching' on behalf of the budget – really, on behalf of his own bonuses and percentages – had already reached the point where optional takes and retakes were looked upon as extravagances. According to Rexford Metz, who worked on several Malpaso productions, twice as director of photography, 'Clint's got a lot of great ideas, but at the same time he's – lazy's not the term I think of – it's the wrong term. But he won't take the time to perfect a situation. If you've got seventy per cent of a shot worked out, that's sufficient for him, because he knows his audience will accept it'.

On *Magnum Force*, Post was chagrined to learn that Clint had dropped 'two very important scenes' from the schedule without consulting the director. The star said he wouldn't authorize the scenes, according to Post, because of the expense and time entailed. One of these set-ups came at the climax, and amounted to an elaborate long shot showing Harry on his motorcycle as he squares off against one of the killer-cops. Post still regrets losing the shot.

There seemed to be a ritual involved in Clint letting his old friend know which one of them had risen up in the world to become the final arbiter. Sitting in on the editing, Clint disagreed with Post and made side-of-the-mouth comments that denigrated his long experience. 'A lot of things he said were based on a pure, selfish ignorance,' remembered Post, 'and showed that he was the man who controlled the power.'

Magnum Force couldn't hope to be anything other than derivative and schematic. Most critics disapproved when it was released in December 1973. Frank Rich in *New Times* called it 'the same old stuff', while Nora Sayre in *The New York Times* said the film was 'a muddle of morality'. Pauline Kael's comments harshly targeted the star: 'Clint Eastwood isn't offensive; he isn't an actor, so one could hardly call him a bad actor. He'd have to do something before we could consider him bad at it. And acting isn't required of him in *Magnum Force* . . .'

Clint could laugh all the way to the bank. He was at the height of his charisma, and knew he could carry a weak film on his strong shoulders. Audiences responded to his innate likeability as much as his toughness. *Magnum Force* went on to gross $58.1 million in the US alone, more than even *Dirty Harry*, Clint's biggest box-office ever . . . until the next Dirty Harry vehicle came along.

The sequel did have one memorable line: 'A man's got to know his limitations,' muttered repeatedly by Dirty Harry. This became an American byword, endlessly parroted in articles and speeches. Although the line was often quoted about Clint himself to express the star's essential humility, by the mid-1970s, it was clear to some people that the opposite was true. 'By *Magnum Force*,' said Post, 'Clint's ego began to apply for statehood.'

Post believes that Clint 'made my career an impossibility' by not correcting the general impression around Hollywood that the star himself was responsible for all the best stuff in *Magnum Force*. (It was becoming part of Clint's mystique that even when he wasn't directing one of his films, he was the one really directing.) Post, who had been loyal to Clint during the Rowdy years and who did a capable job under trying circumstances, wonders what the star said about him, when asked. Post couldn't seem to get referrals; he would be relegated to television for too much of the rest of his career.

Post has no documented proof of this. Richard Schickel thought it 'highly unlikely; it is not the way Clint does business'. But if it wasn't a pattern with Clint, and if the list wasn't a long one of writers, cameramen, directors and others who have struggled to prove themselves outside Malpaso, Post's claims could be more easily dismissed. There was a word around the production company for such ex-friends and ex-employees dismissed from Clint's purview. They were 'non-persons' who no longer existed in Clint's world.

Clint's next film was an anomaly in several respects. It originated as a William Morris Agency 'package'. The best role in the film wasn't (for once) the star's. The first-time director, who also wrote the screenplay, came from outside Malpaso ranks; furthermore, he stayed independent, thriving on his own after his experience with Clint.

Leonard Hirshan – known to some as 'the smiling jackal', though he wasn't a big smiler – was, like many of the longest-lasting people in Clint's retinue, a treasured foot soldier. Malpaso insiders say that Clint liked Hirshan especially because the agent was always at his desk at William Morris and therefore answered the phone whenever Clint called. Clint liked people to be 'available'. Hirshan was also appreciated as a glad-handing advance man, at Clint's side whenever the star made public appearances.

Most importantly, Hirshan acted as a buffer for people trying to get to Clint. Usually, his job was to say no. Although Hirshan read scripts and made recommendations, that was not really his greatest value to Clint, and it was uncharacteristic for him to originate a Malpaso project.

Someone at the William Morris Agency other than Hirshan came up with *Thunderbolt and Lightfoot*; that someone was Stan Kamen, the consummate dealmaker who had bypassed Hirshan to become head of the agency's motion picture department. Kamen had a client, Michael Cimino, who had tailored a script for Clint. An episodic 'road' movie teaming up a bank robber and a young drifter, the script had a big part for an actor under the age of forty. Jeff Bridges, the son of Lloyd Bridges and one of Hollywood's most engaging new personalities, fresh from his Best Supporting Actor nomination for *The Last Picture Show*, was also a William Morris client. Why not bring Clint and Jeff Bridges together on Cimino's script, and triple the commission?

This was the period of time, during the mid-1970s, when the major studios were at their most indecisive and vulnerable. The talent agencies had picked up the ball and were pushing films 'packaged' with people from their client lists. Sometimes the results turned out disastrous – *Lucky Lady* with Liza Minnelli, Gene Hackman and Burt Reynolds, was one notorious misfire – but in this respect, too, *Thunderbolt and Lightfoot* would prove an anomaly.

Cimino was under forty, though he was notoriously vague and stingy about biographical data. According to his entry in *Who's Who in America*, Cimino claimed to be born in 1943, but 'other sources suggest dates three or four years earlier'.

The oldest son of a music publisher, Cimino was educated at private schools, but liked to brag about hanging out with 'tough characters from less advantaged backgrounds', according to his profile in *Current Biography*. A Yale graduate with a fine arts master's degree, he had entered the motion picture industry through the back door in New York, directing industrial documentaries and television commercials. His first feature credit was the 1971 script, along with two collaborators, for *Silent Running*.

Cimino wrote for Clint the part of Thunderbolt, a Korean veteran turned bank robber who is trying to stay one step ahead of vengeful ex-members of his old gang, as he searches for a stash of money left behind from a previous heist. Bridges would play Lightfoot, a con man who bonds with Thunderbolt during escapades on the road.

The script had many unpredictable twists and turns, but Cimino correctly diagnosed what would appeal to Clint with the sentimentalized buddy-buddy relationship between the two lead characters. Clint's own, first-billed part was a charming loser who ultimately proves one of life's winners. Thunderbolt would have the kind of scenes Clint liked: drinking brew, noodling on the piano, talking about weapons and cars. The character's a sly softie at heart; with his last change, Thunderbolt even buys schoolchildren ice cream cones. Young ladies roll over for him, naturally. And he and the other fellows in the story have a good ole time discussing sexy women and 'cocksucking' and how guys really prefer ladies with tight butts.

Clint loved Cimino's script, but Cimino was refusing to sell it without himself attached as the director. As a director Cimino was a long shot, but Clint agreed to meet him, and they hit it off. Cimino had intellectual pretensions, but he also identified with tough guys. He knew and loved Westerns and presented himself as an unabashed Clint fan.

In addition, Cimino was a short, goony guy, who looked like a Geoff Lewis-type Clint-sidekick, 'more like a garage mechanic', according to one magazine profile, 'than a director'. That may have helped their instantaneous rapport. 'I was an unexpected personality to him,' said Cimino. 'He thought a different type of person had written the script.'

First, there was the little matter of *Magnum Force*. That script needing 'juice' was already in preproduction, and it was typical of Clint to latch on to the first writer to walk through the door. Cimino wasn't over-eager, but he executed a quick draft. *Thunderbolt and Lightfoot* was further postponed when Malpaso looked for studio financing. Frank Wells at Warner Brothers hesitated to back such an offbeat (offbeat for Clint anyway) production. Wells would have cause to regret that decision, and in the future he would be more of a pushover for Clint's projects.

Clint still had high-up friends at United Artists, which was continuing to profit off the Sergio Leone trilogy; so *Thunderbolt and Lightfoot* was set up there, announced as the first of two Clint films intended as UA releases, with Malpaso co-producing.

The casting coup was George Kennedy as the brutal Red, Thunderbolt's ex-friend, although solid performances would also be registered by Gary Busey (one of the hit men) and Catherine Bach (skinny blonde fling). Geoffrey Lewis was on hand to play the dimwitted Goody, Red's sidekick, and composer Dee Barton, editor Ferris Webster and cameraman Frank Stanley were also on point behind the scenes, helping first-time director Cimino and supplying the necessary 'comfort factor' for Clint.

The production notes state that director Cimino and producer Bob Daley were the ones who scouted the picturesque Northwest locations that so enhanced the film. Years later, promoting *The Bridges of Madison County*, Clint enjoyed likening himself to the itinerant *National Geographic* photographer he portrays in that film, reminiscing about the days when he used to drive around in his pick-up truck scouting the countryside. The truth is, many of Clint's movies were deliberately shot on familiar terrain, and he *hated* the scut work of scouting. Already those days were long behind.

According to the production notes, Cimino and Daley roamed ten thousand miles of Big Sky Country in Montana, before selecting areas around Great Falls, including the small towns of Ulm, Hobson, Fort Benton, August and Choteau. The small-town faces, the ruddy buildings, the wide-open landscape, would contribute to the natural beauty of the film. Other weapons in Cimino's directorial arsenal – extreme close-ups and chaotic jump cuts – would make him look like the avatar of an American 'New Wave'.

Principal photography took place from July to September 1973. With Clint not directing, little publicity emanated from the set. Cimino gave few interviews during this production, and, following the later controversies of *The Deer Hunter* and *Heaven's Gate*, he became even more press-shy. Although, on occasion, Cimino stated his gratitude to Clint for making possible his directing debut, he didn't often enlarge on the subject.

According to sources, however, Cimino was already a perfectionist who shot a high number of takes, a habit that later got him into trouble on more expensive films. The 'day shoots' of *Thunderbolt and Lightfoot* stretched into darkness, and Clint was driven to distraction.

Cimino didn't often tell the story of Clint cutting him short one day by informing the director that he was going home on Saturday, wrapping up all of his work, so Cimino had better have all the footage 'in the can' by then. But that is what happened. Clint was a seemingly easy-going man for whom the hands on the clock were always moving.

Yet here, for Cimino, playing a character of puzzling, contradictory qualities – a man, like himself, at once carefree and driven – Clint was never better suited to a part. He was never more in command of that country-boy diffidence he liked to project, and his performance as Thunderbolt reminded sceptics that he could act.

The film was really Jeff Bridges' showcase, however, and more than a handful of critics thought Bridges stole the show. Bridges, who has carved a spectacular career out of playing hollow hunks, ended up giving a dark, uninhibited performance as the not-so-happy-go-lucky drifter whose dream is to make the big score and buy a Cadillac. Dolled up as Clint's 'date', Bridges is unforgettable during the bank heist at the film's climax, a sequence which begins as high suspense and veers towards comedy and tragedy.

If there is one film of Clint's from the Seventies that stands up to repeated viewings, it is *Thunderbolt and Lightfoot* – a consummate caper film, a disquieting buddy-buddy story, a rich acting and character contrast. So why did Clint never do anything quite like it again? Was it because he realized he had been upstaged? Was it because, then as now, the film was seen by most critics as distinct from Malpaso, 'a Michael Cimino film'?

One possible reason, one-time Clint friend Paul Lippman explained, is that the star had forthrightly tried to answer a criticism of his work by casting someone like Jeff Bridges. Not the simplistic 'anti-establishment' figure of his publicity, Clint already had one eye fixed on the Academy Awards. When Bridges was Oscar-nominated, however, Clint 'fumed openly', said Lippman. 'Not so much because Jeff had been nominated – Clint would never show such prejudice in public – but because the Academy had passed *him* up.' Clint had felt *Play Misty for Me* was Academy Award material; he thought his own performance in *Thunderbolt and Lightfoot* was Oscar-worthy.

Former United Artists executive Steven Bach, in *Final Cut*, his book about the costly failure of *Heaven's Gate*, offered another possible reason for Clint's disappointment with *Thunderbolt and Lightfoot*. When the film was released in the spring of 1974, it returned 'rentals of a solidly profitable level to the company' which translated into 'a respectable, if not spectacular, hit for Eastwood'. The $32.4 million gross, down from the stratosphere of *Magnum Force*, upset Clint. Bach noted 'some unpleasantness between Eastwood and UA over the company's handling of the picture', with the actor swearing 'he would never work for UA again'. Nor was the second Malpaso film in the ballyhooed UA deal ever brought to fruition.

Clint's next production, *The Eiger Sanction*, was based on a spy novel by Trevanian that was widely regarded by book reviewers as a witty and intelligent thriller.

Again, it was Universal and the unsung Jennings Lang who steered the property towards Clint. Bought by Universal in 1972, the year of its publication, *The Eiger Sanction* had been bequeathed to the Richard Zanuck–David Brown production unit with Paul Newman slated as the star. The hero of the novel was Jonathan Hemlock, a college art professor who agrees to return to his former occupation, paid assassin, for one last 'sanction' – in return for the payment of a rare Pissarro. Besides being an art collector, Hemlock is also an expert mountain climber. The 'sanction' is contracted by a shadowy counterintelligence agency, and the professor is expected to perform the ruthless deed, ultimately, while scaling perilous Mount Eiger in Switzerland.

Once again, Paul Newman stated certain qualms, deciding to withdraw from the project because of 'his commitment to non-violence', according to co-producer David Brown. So the producers approached Clint. 'Yet Clint, too, abhors violence,' Brown assured readers of his autobiography, *Let Me Entertain You*. 'He is a peaceable man by nature, with a decidedly intellectual streak in his film philosophy. There is a morality footnote in all his films. You may have to dig, but it's there. He'll tell you where.'

It was already a pattern with Clint that some producers were happy to surrender their supervising authority to him. They would gain in box-office returns whatever they lost in other areas. So Zanuck and Brown faded out of the decision-making.

The earliest script drafts had pleased no one. One of them was by Trevanian himself, then a University of Texas professor, under his real name of Rod Whitaker. Now, in February 1974, Clint made a long-distance phone call to novelist Warren Murphy, who lived in Connecticut. Murphy had never written a film script before, and he hung up on the operator announcing the call. 'Marooned in a snowstorm, feeling morose and weak and weary, I was in no mood for joking phone calls from friends,' Murphy recalled. 'The truth was – and is – that I don't watch television, never saw *Rawhide*, and rarely go to movies and I barely knew who Clint Eastwood was.'

After a second call was put through, Murphy realized that it really *was* Clint Eastwood calling. Talking with Clint, Murphy quickly decided he liked the star because he was so down-to-earth, so funny and gracious. 'He asked me if I had read Trevanian's book, *The Eiger Sanction*. I said no. He asked if I had ever written a screenplay. I said no. He asked if I could write a screenplay. I said, "If it has words in it, yes." He said, "I knew if I asked you enough questions, you'd eventually say yes."'

Murphy asked him, 'Why me? – and Clint said he had read a couple of my books and "you write novels as if you were writing screenplays", which I guessed was a compliment.' Since it isn't often that someone mentions Clint as a reader of books, it raises the question, what kind of books was Murphy writing that Clint was reading? Although Murphy would later win multiple awards from crime writers' organizations, at the time of *The Eiger Sanction* he was known primarily as the co-creator and continuing author (with Richard Sapir) of *The Destroyer* series, a multi-volume pulp paid-assassin series, with individual titles like *Death Check* and *Slave Safari*.

After dutifully picking up a copy of *The Eiger Sanction* and reading the book, Murphy decided he agreed with Clint's assessment that the plot was exciting but the tone of the book was off-putting. 'I found much of the book offensively smart-ass patronizing to readers,' Murphy said. But he accepted the scriptwriting job. He had to work fast because the option was expiring. Occasionally consulting Clint by phone, Murphy wrote the scenario over the next month, armed only with *The Eiger Sanction* paperback and 'a book I got from the library on "How to Write a Screenplay".'

One thing Clint wanted changed was that 'Hemlock was kind of amoral', in Murphy's words, and he wanted him made more heroic. He wanted Hemlock's participation in the mountain 'sanction' motivated by IRS pressures as well as by the desire to avenge his buddy's death. Clint's script ideas, Murphy said, were 'eminently sensible and it occurred to me that Eastwood knew a hell of a lot more about how a story was constructed than Trevanian did'.

Actually, the shooting script pretty much followed Trevanian's story, with all of the main characters intact, except for trivial substitutions. It was the *tone* that changed, from sophisticated to ... pulpy. After delivering the script in late March, Murphy went to Hollywood for his first face-to-face with Clint. 'By now, of course, I knew more about Eastwood's film persona as killer of men,' Murphy said, 'so I was kind of surprised to walk into his office at Universal the first time and find he was just finishing his twenty morning minutes of transcendental meditation. Then, during a story talk with him and Bob Daley, Eastwood walked around the office, catching a fly in a paper cup and then releasing it out a window.'

They talked about final revisions – 'most of them actually pretty minor', in Murphy's words. Indeed, according to one Malpaso insider, Clint startled Murphy by declaring, 'Okay, let's shoot it.' Murphy protested, 'But Clint, this is just a draft. I'd really like to go through it and make a lot of improvements.' Clint said, 'No, no, let's go to work.'

Murphy did remember one crucial detail of their meeting. 'In conversation, it came up that Clint wanted to do this film – which was pretty far removed from his other work – "because I don't want to do the same thing every time",' Murphy recalled Clint saying. 'I also got the impression that he just wanted to go climb a mountain. As I told him, that's because "you're not all there". To his credit, he understood the reference and the joke.'

The revised script was approved a month later, with filming scheduled for August.

The character descriptions in Trevanian's book provided the casting blueprint. George Kennedy, inherited from Michael Cimino and *Thunderbolt and Lightfoot*, would play the robust, gregarious Big Ben Bowman, Hemlock's friend, but also his secret adversary. Jack Cassidy would portray the nefarious Miles Mellough, who is decidedly less of a swish in the novel ('tall, brilliant in his physical trim', wrote Trevanian, 'he pulled off his epic homosexuality with such style that plebeian men did not recognize it'). And who would play lady spy Jemima Brown (erudite African-American with 'taut bottom' and flecks of gold in brown eyes)? Although casting directors and outside consultants were available for talent searches, this one called for personal detective work.

Clint and Bob Daley took a trip to Las Vegas, inviting Warren Murphy along to watch a dinner show and inspect a nominee. 'I won't mention her name,' said Murphy. 'Afterwards, he asked me what I thought of the girl and I said she had an ass like Cleon Jones.* He seemed to agree and cast somebody else.' The 'somebody else' was the sexy actress Vonetta McGee, who had just finished *Thomasine and Bushrod*, a Bonnie-and-Clyde-type 'blaxploitation' Western.

Ladies with taut bottoms were one associative link between *Thunderbolt and Lightfoot* and *The Eiger Sanction*. But the real reason Clint wanted to make the film, as screenwriter Murphy discerned, was to climb a big bad mountain.

In Trevanian's book, Jonathan Hemlock is said to be too old, at thirty-seven years of age, to attempt such a foolhardy act as scaling the Eiger. Clint would be forty-four by the time filming started. Again and again in his preferred roles, Clint would defy the reality of his age and attempt to appear 'forever young'. Now, because he was said to be a stickler for 'motion picture realism', in the words of the film's official publicity, Clint was going to head for the Swiss Alps, there to climb the dreaded North Face of the Eiger.

What could the studio and producers say except, hey, what a great idea! Clint went ahead and contacted Mike Hoover, a professional climber from Jackson, Wyoming, who had made mountaineering films, including one, *Solo*, which two years earlier had been Academy Award-nominated for Best Short Subject. Hoover agreed to act as a technical advisor and as a mountaineering cameraman on the slopes. First, Hoover would take Clint through a crash course in climbing at Yosemite.

Hoover was a tall, sculpted man like Clint, and the two of them struck up a fast rapport. For three days, Hoover took Clint along established routes, climbing over rocks and hills, preparatory to braving the arduous climb of Lost Arrow, a 1200-foot chimney and detached spire. The success of this climb firmed-up Clint's confidence

---

* Superstar left-fielder for the New York Mets, who cut off Baltimore Oriole Dave Johnson's drive to end the 1969 World Series in victory for his team.

and convinced Hoover that it would be possible to photograph the star high up on the Eiger.

Hoover began to assemble a team of experts to accompany the expedition. Not all of them thought three days in Yosemite was sufficient preparation for the daunting prospect of one of the most rugged peaks in the world. 'You're out of your fucking mind,' Dougal Haston, the Scottish director of the International School of Mountaineering, reportedly told Clint in one tense meeting. Haston was one of a small number who could claim to have climbed the North Face – twice before; his partner, American Alpinist John Harlin, was one of the dozens who had died there, in 1966.

'Eiger' translates as 'ogre' in German. One of the nicknames for the mountain was '*mörderwall*', or 'killer wall'. Trevanian wrote, 'Though not as high as the famed Matterhorn or other mountains of the world, the North Face of the 13,041 foot Eiger is considered to be one of the most challenging climbs any man can make.' The North Face was a steep frozen field consisting of crevices and gullies, ice and blowing snow.

After an advance team headed by James Fargo had travelled ahead to scout the earthbound locations, the company arrived in Grindelwald, Switzerland, in mid-August 1974. The filming would start on the mountainside, to take advantage of the relatively mild late summer weather. Therefore the final and climactic sequences of *The Eiger Sanction* were the ones scheduled to be photographed first. Hemlock is climbing with a quartet of men, one of whom is a mole assigned to kill him. He must identify and strike his enemy – or is the whole assignment some kind of evil ruse?

Cast and crew would hole up for the duration at the Kleine Scheidegg Hotel, which had been built before the turn of the century, at the base of the mountain. Principal photography would start under gorgeous skies and temperate weather. Malpaso insiders call this 'Clint's weather', a phrase which corresponds with Clint's luck.

Although Richard Schickel made the amusing argument that Clint chose to film on the actual mountain because he preferred close-knit operations – therefore he could 'limit cast and crew to a daring handful' – that was hardly the case. Apart from a dozen reputable mountaineers from England, Germany, Canada and Switzerland, there was also a Hollywood contingent. And the publicity grind never rested: people were there whose job it was to snap photos of the star dangling from the mountainside.

This vanity exercise had its first dose of un-Hollywood reality on the second day of photography, 13 August.

Clint didn't really climb, per se. Everyone in the company, including Clint, was transported by helicopters from the base of the mountain to the North Face. The Eiger has a cog-train tunnel all along the inside of the face with periodic windows that are used to discard tunnel rock, and, for some scenes, Clint would hang out of the windows to give the illusion of climbing. Still, the heights (up to 12,000 feet) were terrifying, and the professionals would later profess admiration for Clint's courage.

Several people mentioned one incident: while filming a scene, Clint's rope slipped, and the actor plummeted down the mountainside before the line caught. When he hauled himself back up, he launched into a retake, without the slightest hesitation.

One of the climbers hired to assist the film crew was an Englishman, David Knowles, twenty-seven, who held the Royal Humane Society's highest award for bravery for his part in a mountain rescue in Glencoe, Scotland, in December 1970. Knowles was helping with the climbing and photography, while also doubling for the actors.

All during that second day the company had worked on a scene in which Hemlock and the others are threatened by a rock slide. By the mid-afternoon the light was beginning to fade, so filming was halted and the helicopters began to relay everybody back to base. Mike Hoover grabbed a handheld camera and rappelled down to a ledge to obtain some last-minute rock slide shots from the point of view of the climbers. Knowles accompanied him, deflecting the rubber rocks which were being hurled at them from above by another mountaineer, keeping them from striking the lens.

One of the constant dangers of the Eiger was crumbling rock and loose scree, which according to legend, was the 'ogre' shedding its skin in annoyance at the puny humans who dared to scale it. The tiniest clatter might be the only warning of a deadly slide, snowfall, or full-scale avalanche. Now, as Hoover and the others packed up their gear to quit for the day, they heard real rocks crashing down towards them.

The first reports of what happened came via two-way radio, which kept the company back at the hotel in contact with the climbers. 'It was around 7 p.m. when the distress call came in,' according to one account. ' "There has been an accident . . ." The combined American–Italian crew stood about at the ready, but somewhat dazed, wondering who had been hurt. Was it Eastwood, the only novice climber in the group?'

Hoover had managed to cling to the mountainside, escaping with a pelvic fracture and bruises. Feeling a heavy weight, he glanced up and discovered Knowles 'on top of me – hanging upside down – dead.' Clint, with the other members of the company, was close by in a safe spot.

It was too late, even, to claim the body, and Knowles's body was left where it had fallen until the next day. That evening, the climbers held an informal wake. 'Clint considered cancelling the production,' wrote Richard Schickel in his book. 'The climbers, however, urged him to go on. They knew the risks of their trade, ran them habitually, and felt that moviemaking added nothing to them. For his part, Clint came around to the view that aborting the production would render Knowles's death – not to mention all the hard and dangerous work that had preceded it – meaningless.'

The news of Knowles's death was sent out over the wire services. Some people thought the tragedy had been unnecessary. Frank Stanley, the film's cameraman, believed that the photography could have been accomplished just as well inside a studio, or in the lower regions, except for the egos at stake. Clint's publicity would hammer home the point of bypassing 'lesser and safer mountains' and avoiding 'studio process shots in order to capture the climber's sense of giving himself to the mountain, loving it as he hates it, and to create on film the chilling spectacle of men dwarfed by one of nature's most awesome creations'.

But Frank Stanley believed: 'The need for doing it [filming on the mountain] I could never understand. We weren't going to the moon, or inventing the Salk vaccine. We were making a motion picture. After all, we're in the business of creating illusions.'

Other disturbing things happened on the Eiger shoot, which were muffled by Malpaso and never reported. Although Clint had the benefit of fitness and special training, not all of the crew he brought along from America were as well-conditioned. With Knowles dead and Hoover temporarily out of action, the Hollywood camera team, including Frank Stanley, were obliged to help out with some mountain area filming.

As a corollary to his 'Fountain of Youth' obsession, Clint preferred not only to cast himself opposite overly youthful actresses but to surround himself, behind the camera, with stand-ins and stunt men and other specimens of pulchritude who could be counted on to stay the course of his style of fast and furious film-making. 'Clint loved the macho guys,' explained cameraman Rexford Metz. 'He loved the guys who rolled and flipped cars, shot "aerials". He gets off on that kind of action-energy stuff.'

The older Malpaso regulars were sometimes let go ('not rehired', in company parlance) in unceremonious fashion, while younger men benefited from Clint's perception that they were in tip-top physical condition. According to cameraman Rexford Metz, it certainly helped his climb up the ladder of the Malpaso organization. Explained Metz: 'Clint's whole thing with me was, "You're athletic, you'll get into a helicopter, you'll climb a mountain, you're in good shape, you're Mr Macho, one of the guys."'

One time, during the production of *Every Which Way But Loose*, Metz suffered a major accident. While skiing, he fell and 'just tore the shit out of my knees. I showed up on the set on crutches. Clint's face fell. It wasn't, "Oh, my god, can you do the picture?" It was, "What *happened* to you?" I said, "I crashed skiing." He said, "Great! Let's go to work." It was like, "That's cool, you hurt yourself doing the right thing."'

Metz (who shot the Totem Pole sequence) and Jim Fargo ('who had never climbed before', in Hoover's words, 'but quickly learned the basics and ended up doing anything from make-up to assistant camera') were two who acquitted themselves admirably during *The Eiger Sanction*: they would be promoted. Director of photography Stanley, who had shot three previous Clint films, would fail in the macho department and be demoted to the status of a 'non-person', his name struck from Malpaso's rolls.

The avuncular Stanley made the mistake of being overweight, not anyone's idea of a man's man. When Stanley first glimpsed the Eiger, he felt a nervous twinge. His pride at having come up with special equipment and a new camera stock for *The Eiger Sanction*, and his feeling that he was about to make a breakthrough in his career, was offset by the anxiety he felt when Clint said the Hollywood contingent might have to fill in a little, up on the mountain.

'I never dreamed that's what I'd be doing,' remembered Stanley. 'You know how it goes. He's up there hanging from ropes, so you figure you owe him this. He's taken you over to Switzerland . . . and up you go.' The director of photography didn't dare to utter any protest, when he and members of his crew were airlifted to high locations.

Typical of the whole operation was a camera manoeuvre, involving a helicopter, that really worried Stanley. In the scene where Hemlock is dangling from the centre of the North Face, a helicopter was assigned to zoom in close enough for a tight shot of the star's face. Only they had trouble satisfying Clint, and had to try the shot again and again. 'The biggest objection to that shot,' said Stanley, 'was the fact that they could never get close enough to show that that was Eastwood himself doing it [the climbing]. You might think it was *not* Eastwood.' It was vainglorious, thought Stanley, because the shot could be done just as well, and with complete safety, as a studio insert.

Something happened to Stanley – he suffered an accidental fall. Dangling from a rope, the line gave way, or he lost his footing – then dropped ten feet, scaring the hell out of himself. He didn't realize that he had sustained a bad bruise until the next morning, when he woke up, feeling disoriented. He tried to stand up and fell over on his left side. His left side had gone numb. Taken to a nearby hospital, Stanley was confined to a bed while doctors tried to figure out what was wrong. The cameraman exhibited all the classic symptoms of a stroke.

His crew consulted Stanley, lying in bed. His trusted operator was able to supervise the rest of the mountaintop photography. And Clint kept the cameraman on payroll, though he never visited him in the hospital. Although he couldn't walk, Frank Stanley knew he had to hurry to get out of bed and return to work. 'I realized if I folded up in the show I'd probably never get a job again,' he explained, some years later.

He got himself into a wheelchair in time for the Zurich sequences, and then back in the US, he virtually relearned to walk. Stanley recovered to oversee the Monument Valley scenes and the others set at Hemlock's eastern seaboard college and home. These latter were filmed in Carmel area locations, including the Hog's Breath Inn.

Speaking, years later, of Clint's methods, Stanley said the director was a 'very impatient' man who 'doesn't really plan his pictures or do any homework, truthfully. He figures he can go right in and sail right through these things.' Clint was just as impatient as an actor, said Stanley, especially in an action picture when directing himself. For example, Clint was always 'blowing his lines', recalled the cameraman. 'It's very hard for him to say more than four lines consecutively.'

And, said Stanley, no matter if Clint forgot his lines, he would insist that the camera pick up the dialogue just where he had left off, without going back and starting the lines over. It was the cameraman's problem to choose different angles and make the 'pickups', or transitions, work. Notorious for doing his acting scenes with multiple pickups, according to Stanley, Clint had an ironclad belief that everything could be fixed in the editing room. Nobody among his fans would notice the incongruities.

There are people, like Stanley, who swear that Clint shirks the memorizing of his lines, and others, such as Richard Tuggle, who wrote *Escape from Alcatraz* and directed *Tightrope*, who insist that the star's habit of *appearing* to fumble for his lines is a personal style. 'It's hard to explain,' said Tuggle. 'I seldom remember him not knowing his lines. But it's as if he *almost* forgets them. When you see him, sometimes in his movies, it is as if he is almost hesitating for the right words, because he's been able to forget them, and then, like a normal human being, think of the words to say.'

Although Clint liked low lighting, according to Stanley, the star also had 'an instinct for the key light' – an unerring instinct for 'nosing himself into position', in Stanley's words. One scene with muted lighting in *The Eiger Sanction* was the lovemaking between Hemlock and Jemima Brown, which in the film is the usual 'soft jazz' elegy to Clint's prowess as a lover. That scene was shot towards the end of the schedule in Carmel, with only Stanley and a small crew present, besides Clint and Vonetta McGee.

Everything was deep shadows, hand strokes, close-ups of flesh. Clint and his lady co-star were on a bed that had been slightly elevated so that the camera could frame them from unusually low angles. The two were cross-lit from behind. Stanley remembered how he called out the blocking as he and his crew moved the camera around to photograph the scene from every possible perspective. The cameraman couldn't help but notice that Clint and his leading lady were not really listening to him. They were carrying on intensely on their own.

Finally, the crew had shot over one thousand feet of film, which was more than Clint's standard coverage. 'I was kind of embarrassed to say anything,' remembered Stanley, 'but finally I said, "Clint, you know we ran out of film about five minutes ago." So then he broke off . . .'

Although he never totally recuperated during the production, Frank Stanley courageously finished *The Eiger Sanction*. But he felt, and others confirm, that Clint grew short with the cameraman. The star acted upset with the cameraman for being out of condition physically and for having suffered such a strange accident at the Eiger. In effect, it seemed, Clint blamed Stanley!

Stanley was another person who came to believe that his failure to please Clint haunted his career. The director of photography had started *The Eiger Sanction* 'looking forward to a brilliant future', and now felt that he couldn't catch up with rumours around Hollywood that he 'had a heart attack, or was inept'. 'Frank's feeling in private was worse,' said one close friend. Stanley believed that Clint said unfair things about him to other people; according to this friend, 'Clint hated anybody who was weak.'

Stanley would remain debilitated, emotionally as well as physically, for several months after the filming. Time passed before he started over again at 'ground zero' on a television movie of the week; more time before he resumed his status as director of photography on films, including *Car Wash*, *The Big Fix* and *10*. He never worked for Clint Eastwood or Malpaso Productions again. But the experience of the Eiger never left him. Giving seminars at a photography institute in later years, Stanley would break down weeping as he recounted memories of the filming of *The Eiger Sanction*.

All the publicity was full of Clint's boldness and bravery. James Bacon could report in his widely read column that *The Eiger Sanction* was 'without question the most hazardous film ever made and directed by a superstar'.

'I just got involved deeper and deeper,' Clint told Bacon. 'There was no turning back. At first, I was going to use a double but a double can only think of the stunt. He can't think of the characterization.'

'What's the most exciting part of filming on the Eiger?' asked Peter J. Oppenheimer of *Family Weekly*.

'The helicopters,' replied Clint.

'What intrigues you so much about film-making?'

'It lets me do all the things I wanted to do as a kid, and get paid for it – drive fast cars and motorcycles; ride horses and now, climb a mountain.'

Partisans of the film might extol the gorgeous scenery. But the problems that arose on the mountain mandated a foreshortened climax and the obvious compensation of 'process shots'. The earlier climbing scenes, with Hemlock and Big Ben scaling the Totem Pole, a 640-foot high, 18-foot in diameter spire on the Navajo Reservation in Monument Valley, were more exciting, and, by far, the simpler achievement.

Clint's bad movies told as much about him as his good ones. What humour and chilling ambiguity wasn't ironed out by the screenplay of *The Eiger Sanction*, Clint, as star and director, further deflated. The leaden tone of the movie is pervasive.

Clint's villains and romantic conquests are pushovers. The book flattered Hemlock by describing him as a lover nonpareil to whom warm-blooded ladies were 'attracted by his arctic aloofness, which they assumed concealed a passionate and mysterious nature'. Like Clint, Hemlock prides himself on 'controlling' his love life. Blonde students hit on him (the camera darts up skirts and crossed legs), but he can pick and choose. Hemlock's interracial love affair with Jemima Brown is straight out of the book. And the Indian beauty named George (played by Brenda Venus), whose job it is to sweat the spy–professor into shape, was also in the novel. It was Clint, however, who lobbed the ad lib at her, 'Screw Marlon Brando!'*

'I wish I'd written it,' said screenwriter Murphy.†

---

* Referring to the 1972 Oscars and Marlon Brando's Best Actor Oscar. Brando did not appear at the Academy Awards that year and refused the honour voted to him by his peers, sending to accept the trophy, a woman who wore Native American garb and read a political statement on behalf of Indian rights.

† Later in the film, George goes to bed with Hemlock, and while sleeping with him, tries to inject him with a lethal concoction. She is another 'castrating woman' – à la *Play Misty for Me*.

Hemlock in the book is a genuine sophisticate, a connoisseur of wine and martinis who dabbles with a hookah. But Clint lacked the savoir-faire of a James Bond and preferred to cultivate his Joe Average image. No matter how professorial the part he played, Clint would find a chance to call someone an asshole.

Most critics grimaced when *The Eiger Sanction* was released in May 1975. *Playboy* described it as 'a James Bond reject'. Andrew Sarris wrote, 'None of it [the story] made any sense to me.' No doubt it irked Clint that America's handful of female reviewers were the most disapproving. Judith Crist, who vied with Pauline Kael in her detestation of Clint's movies, wrote in *New York* magazine that the film was 'a total travesty' with Clint 'badly in need of a director'. The insightful Joy Gould Boyum, holding forth in the *Wall Street Journal*, noted that in order to make its manliness more emphatic, 'the film situates villainy in homosexuals, and physically disabled men'.

Trevanian himself, an early loser when his script was rejected, appended a footnote to one of his later novels, excoriating the filmmakers for having carried out a folly in which 'a fine young climber was killed' and damning Clint's film of his book as 'vapid'.

In-house, Frank Stanley may have been one of the scapegoats for the failure of *The Eiger Sanction*, but Universal was blamed as the worst culprit. Not for channelling the property to Clint in the first place – no, for mishandling the distribution of the film and thereby hurting its potential revenue. *The Eiger Sanction* would gross only $23.8 million, down, even, from *Thunderbolt and Lightfoot*.

Frank Wells had been aggressively wooing Clint, and owning the Dirty Harry licence unto perpetuity made Warner Brothers mighty attractive. Wells and Clint had a tendency to do business on the tennis courts, or ski slopes. Now they went skiing at Bear Lake, and Wells, knowing the star was disgruntled, laid out some inducements.

The studio would pledge itself to major initiatives on Clint's behalf: peak numbers of prints, record floors for exhibitor bids, saturation bookings, unprecedented ad-pub budgets, junkets and other media incentives, Oscar campaigns for each Clint film. Each Malpaso production would have a studio-based 'Campaign Plan Manager' as well as regional publicists working overtime to hype the films, based on an approach approved by Clint. Joe Hyams, the head of Warners' publicity department, who dated his association with the studio back to 1960 and who had been handling public relations in Hollywood since 1947, would become, in effect, Clint's personal, full-time evangelist. (He jokingly introduced himself, sometimes, as 'Vice President for Clint'.)

Wells was more than willing to let Clint get heavily involved in his own publicity, advertising and marketing. In the future, a small outside agency, operating under Malpaso's aegis, and consisting principally of Bill and Charles Gold, two brothers from New York, would design posters, print ads, teasers, trailers, and radio and television spots for Clint's productions. Another small agency, Western International Media, would advise Clint on TV and radio placements. Although Warners would exercise final say over strategy and budget, Clint would be a partner in orchestrating the promotions.

Clint could count on Frank Wells to behave in laissez-faire fashion about the actual film-making. 'The guy [Clint] had a story sense about his persona that nobody else had,' Wells said once. And he could count on his old friend and attorney to be laissez faire about financial matters.

Wells, beloved by many who knew him, was famously generous. When out on the town, he would often arrange for bills to be slipped discreetly into his pocket while people sipped their after-dinner cappuccinos. 'Wells reportedly wrote cheques for thousands of dollars to numerous eateries around town,' *Variety* noted on the occasion of Wells's death, 'to avoid the embarrassment of deciding who would pick up the cheque'.

Clint, contrarily, almost never picked up the bill. He could look forward to dining out forever on Malpaso and Warner Brothers credit cards; and whenever he ventured out in public, alone or with friends, if the bill wasn't put on a company credit card, he would invariably be 'comped' (treated complimentarily, without being charged). Restaurateurs knew his psychology and were nonetheless grateful for the glamour of his presence. 'I have known Clint for twenty-three years,' said one lady friend, who spoke on condition of anonymity, 'and I have eaten with him in restaurants and places all over Los Angeles and the Valley, and I can tell you I have never seen him pay for a meal. He isn't going to, he doesn't have to, and they know he isn't going to when he walks in the door.'

Frank Wells, who with Irving Leonard had instituted many of Clint's contract perks, could be counted on to approve many more with Warner Brothers. He understood Clint's thriftiness and preoccupation with being 'comped'. Back in 1970, for *Dirty Harry*, Wells had approved per diems (out-of-pocket cash for daily expenses) of $1500 weekly for the star, or at least $21,000 additionally over the course of the fourteen weeks of photography. (Director Don Siegel's was half that amount.)

As some people knew, Clint would go a long way around the barn to avoid actually *spending* his per diems. The ready cash was set aside as part of Clint's hoard. One lady visitor to his Carmel house, doing a little cleaning up there in the 1980s, noticed stacks of dusty per diem envelopes – thick with $100 bills – hidden away in a closet. When this woman, with whom Clint was romantically involved, mentioned the cache, asking if Clint wanted her to do some organizing of the funds, Clint freaked out and dived into the closet to make a quick inspection of the money. Later, he congratulated this lady friend on the fact that none of the money appeared to be missing, while mentioning that in future he intended to find a safer place for his cash bounty.

Important to Clint was Wells's vow that the plush Warner Gulfstream 3, twelve-seat corporate jets would be put at his beck and call. Clint would never again have to pay to fly somewhere. Even executives would be 'bumped' in favour of the studio's top star. Although Clint did eventually buy his own private plane, nobody who knows him thinks he paid for it with his own money. New athletic equipment, house renovations, wardrobe (although minimal in Clint's case), could easily be tucked into one of his film budgets.

It was Clint – on Frank Wells's watch – who would pioneer the dubious 'product placement' that has become epidemic in Hollywood nowadays. Malpaso was one of the first companies to work out agreements with Puma, GMC, Dos Equis and other corporations to spotlight their merchandise in Clint's films. Every year, a truckload of athletic shoes would be delivered to Malpaso, and Clint would take boxes of them home. Every year, GM would sign over its 'dollar a year' cars and trucks to Clint, which were then used for on- and off-camera purposes (e.g. loaned to lady friends), in return for having the GM trademark blazed across screens. The protracted opening shot of *Any Which Way You Can* featured the hood ornament of a GMC Jimmy General tractor truck; GMC insignia would also figure in the emotional climax of *The Bridges of Madison County*.

When the 'dollar a year' was up, Malpaso would buy the loaned-out vehicles at reduced cost and then lease them out. There were hundreds of 'picture cars' over the years. One 'picture car' was sacrosanct, however, and that was the one Clint drove in each film, which he usually made a point of driving home afterwards.

No 'comp' was too petty for Clint, people say. Warners' annual Thanksgiving gift of a fresh-frozen turkey to company big shots would evolve into a ritual for Clint. The star couldn't be counted on to buy his own turkey. Each November, as Thanksgiving approached, Clint would peek out of his office, asking, 'Has the turkey arrived yet? Call so-and-so on the lot and see if he has *his* turkey yet...' One year, according to Malpaso insiders, a crisis arose. It didn't look as though the turkey was going to arrive on time and Warners executives, made aware of Clint's mounting anxiety, had to book an open seat on a commercial airliner for the frozen bird, so Clint could get his free turkey, and then make a show of bringing it to someone, usually his mother.

Wells was one of Clint's best friends. And his arguments added up. Clint was certainly ready to leave Universal.

In September 1975, shortly after the underwhelming release of *The Eiger Sanction*, Malpaso relocated to a Spanish-style building on the Warners lot in Burbank, just a short walk from executive offices. There Clint would remain for the next quarter of a century, the only major star of Hollywood's post-1960s era to keep a continuous relationship with the same film studio over such a lengthy period of time.

Wells was a believer in Clint and his luck. His triumph was not only in bringing Clint permanently over to Warners, but touting the star as a modest 'independent' while, in the background, the studio acted as a high-powered corporation on his behalf. Warner Brothers films would rise from the ashes, partly on Clint's shoulders. Even with the star's steadily rising salary, perks and percentages, it was the best deal Frank Wells ever made.

Because of Frank Wells, Warner Brothers, from the outset, did have a more auspicious view of Clint, both as actor and director, and his first production under the new Warners–Malpaso arrangement, *The Outlaw Josey Wales*, was trumpeted by the studio as a thematic commentary on America – 'a major Bicentennial Celebration release'.

The Outlaw Josey Wales was that rarity of rarities: a project discovered and launched from within Malpaso's own story department. For six years, that department had consisted only of Sonia Chernus working under the supervision of Bob Daley. Chernus dutifully piled up, sifted through, incoming scripts. Her position was considered, in-house, almost a gratuity; in general, people thought Clint didn't value her strong opinions. And usually the projects that came from unsolicited channels were doomed to be rejected.

Imagine everyone's surprise when Sonia Chernus and Bob Daley joined to champion a Western that had come in, unbidden. Daley had been touched by the author's covering letter – later described by Clint as 'such a reaching-out kind of thing' – and read the book. So did Chernus. The lead character, Josey Wales, was a Southerner who refuses to surrender his arms after the Civil War ends, and leaves a bloody trail as he is chased across the Southwest by a posse. Daley and Chernus liked the story, and thought it perfect for one of Clint's Westerns.

The novel had been privately published in 1972 as *Gone to Texas*, then reissued and retitled *The Rebel Outlaw: Josey Wales*. Its author was Forrest Carter, who promoted himself as an uneducated, self-taught Indian poet who was storyteller in council to the Cherokee Nations. The revelation didn't come until 1976 – after filming – that the author was actually Asa Carter, a onetime virulent racist, anti-Semite and supporter of Ku Klux Klan type politics. Clint knew only that he too liked the book. Not only was he looking for another Western, but the star liked to play underdog Johnny Rebs.

Clint liked the story enough that he invested a trifling amount of his own money in obtaining the screen rights. Usually, as he explained in one interview, his ownership deals with Warners were 'split' roughly equally. For this one, Malpaso advanced the 'front money', with Warners exercising a 'negative pick-up', meaning the studio agreed to assume all production costs, 'long before we even finished the film'. Although this amounted basically to the same thing – Warner Brothers underwriting the film's reported $4 million budget – it gave Malpaso the advantage of 'ownership'.

The official Malpaso version of events is that Sonia Chernus lobbied for the chance to break the book down into an outline and treatment, showing how the Western novel might be adapted for the screen. Or, considering what happened later on, it may be that Chernus was asked to do the writing as part of her job as story editor, since Clint was always entreating his employees to do 'a little extra' and 'comp' their efforts.

Chernus's draft must have been enough for Clint's – and the studio's – commitment. Then Clint went shopping (he never went shopping very far) at the William Morris Agency, where he found a writer–director who appeared to be in the mould of Michael Cimino. Philip Kaufman, born in 1936, had attended Harvard Law School, had written and directed *The Great Northfield Minnesota Raid,* a well-regarded, modernist Western, and lived far away from the industry limelight in San Francisco.

Kaufman went to work on a shooting script that would follow Chernus's adaptation and remain faithful to Forrest Carter's novel. The major characters (the tagalong Cherokee chief, Navajo squaw, old settler woman and her daughter) and main incidents of the novel would be preserved in the film. Clint would have many of the same character traits as Josey Wales in the book, right down to spitting tobacco juice on the upturned faces of his victims (declaring, 'Buzzards got to eat, same as worms').

Kaufman magnified the regulators chasing Wales, and also the various betrayals that fuelled many a Clint characterization – the death of Josey's wife and children at the beginning of the story (murky flashback); the Reb turncoat who facilitates the massacre of Josey's men. Kaufman also purged much of the lingo affected by Josey ('Reckin'' and 'thisaway', 'hoss' for 'horse', 'ye' rather than 'you') which some people might consider authentic; lingo that would have put tougher rehearsal demands on the star.

Although Kaufman, like Michael Cimino, would say very little afterwards about working with Clint, he did state in one interview that he had 'chosen the cast, picked the locations, determined the look of the film, [and] the wardrobe' before principal photography. But Kaufman liked to take his time with creative decisions, and he took a little longer than Clint was used to. When James Fargo, Bruce Surtees and Fritz Manes were dispatched to scout locations in the Southwest, they couldn't get Kaufman to leave his scriptwork. He was busy 'improving' scenes and dealing with the casting. By this time in his career Clint would probably have rather gone to church on Sunday than scout a location – by this time his personal scouting was limited to Polaroids or sketches – and when the star had to be dragged out of the office to nail down a particular river site, insiders heard the first rumblings of trouble.

It was Kaufman who had the inspiration of casting Chief Dan George, who had scored an Oscar nomination for his supporting role in *Little Big Man*. The Chief would play Lone Watie, the wry old Cherokee who accompanies Josey on his quest for regeneration. Chief Dan George, then in his mid-seventies, was memorable in the film, and more than held his own in scenes with Clint. In their first scene together, Lone Watie lays an ambush for Josey, who nonetheless sneaks up on him.

LONE WATIE: They said a man could get rich on reward money if he could kill you.

JOSEY WALES: Seems like you was looking to gain some money, here.

LONE WATIE: Actually, I was looking to gain an edge. I thought you might be someone who would sneak up behind me with a gun.

JOSEY WALES: Where'd you get an idea like that? Besides, it ain't supposed to be easy to sneak up behind an Indian.

LONE WATIE: I'm an Indian, all right. But here in the Nation [Indian Nation] they call us the civilized tribe. They call us civilized because we're easy to sneak up on. The White Man has been sneaking up on us for years.

The casting of the lead actress also stirred trouble. The character of Laura Lee, the daughter of the pioneer woman who joins Josey's motley band of followers, would not use up very much screen time. In the novel, she actually *marries* Josey Wales, but Clint was never going to end up domesticated in one of his films. The important thing was, Laura Lee had to be played by a young beauty; the book speaks of her straw-coloured hair and 'eyes of startling blue'. Clint took an interest in young beauties.

Sondra Locke's agent had been notified by Malpaso to send the actress over for a second chance at a part in a Clint film. Okay, so her long, flowing hair was more blonde than strawberry, and her eyes were not blue, they were hazel; she was young enough to play the part, however. And she was a squirt-type beauty, with sharp facial features that evoked Clint's own: wide eyes, a prominent nose, a high forehead.

A foot shorter than the famous star, the actress was a wiry 5'4", 102 pounds.

In the eight years between her Oscar-nominated debut in *The Heart Is a Lonely Hunter* and *The Outlaw Josey Wales*, Locke admittedly had not set Hollywood on fire. She was never very career-minded. Between 1968 and 1976, the actress had played roles in several film and television productions, with her best part probably coming in 1971's *Willard*, a horror feature about rats that was popular enough to mandate a sequel.

But the fact that she had once been nominated for an Academy Award was not lost on Clint, Locke believes. Most of his friends knew that the Oscars loomed in Clint's psychology. He'd bring up the subject by informing people that someone like him would never be nominated in any category, and, he liked to add, nor did he really care. 'I will never win an Oscar and do you know why?' Clint liked to aver. 'First of all, because I'm not Jewish. Secondly, because I make too much money for all those old farts in the Academy. Thirdly, and most importantly, because I don't give a fuck.'

Yet Locke was a link to that possibility. 'I think one of the things that appealed to him about me was that I had this reputation as an artistic and intelligent person,' said the actress. 'Clint had not had that imprimatur. It was like I was the small company and he was the big corporation, and he was taking me over because I had a good business profile and what he was going to do was incorporate me into the parent company.'

Locke was content with a low-key career. She was bookish, an indoors person, a child in spirit. When she went to interview for *The Outlaw Josey Wales* she was still under thirty, seventeen years Clint's junior. This time, they had an instant 'connection'.

'The nature of our attraction was almost archetypal,' recalled Locke. 'I admit I suffer from a childhood of never having had a father figure. I was a woman of intelligence with professional stature, yet at the same time I was a little girl who wanted a daddy. He was so big and powerful and handsome and everything just went his way. And I was really the archetypal female, adoring and all that. He needs that, but he wants to control and cocoon it, in the same way that Malpaso is a giant cocoon. He's very good at cocooning people, and he's very good at choosing the people he does cocoon.'

Clint had spurned Sondra Locke the first time but now felt she was right for *The Outlaw Josey Wales*. Kaufman hesitated – and hesitated. It wasn't that Kaufman didn't want Locke for the part, it was that for him rumination was part of the process. Clint waited and waited, sending off his coded signals, which Kaufman didn't acknowledge, until finally Clint phoned Locke's agent on a Saturday, and made the decision himself.

A short time later, scouting the final locations, Kaufman confided in Fritz Manes. 'That's the worst thing anybody's ever done to me. He cut my balls off.' Manes advised Kaufman, 'Well, you should tell him that. The only way to deal with Clint is to assert yourself.' But Kaufman decided discretion was the better part of valour, and Locke was a *fait accompli*. 'If he had confronted Clint,' noted Manes, 'Clint would have backed off, because Clint's basically a coward when it comes to confrontation'.

The film would have Bruce Surtees as director of photography and Ferris Webster as editor. Jerry Fielding was hired to compose the musical score. Fielding, a journeyman West Coast bandleader and arranger, a veteran of composing for such successful television shows as *You Bet Your Life* and *Life of Riley*, had first distinguished himself in film with Academy Award-nominated work on *The Wild Bunch* and *Straw Dogs*, both directed by Sam Peckinpah. Prior to 1992 and *Unforgiven*, *The Outlaw Josey Wales* would be the only Malpaso production besides *Thunderbolt and Lightfoot* and *Bird* (Best Sound) to receive *any* Oscar nominations – for Jerry Fielding's elegiac music.

Photography began in mid-October 1975 in Arizona, Utah and Wyoming locations.

Right away, Clint wasn't happy with the dailies. But the real reason he grew restless is that Kaufman's methodical pace was anathema to him. The introspective Kaufman made Clint nervous, pacing around in his leather cowboy hat like Sergio Leone, studiously weighing his options and framing his shots. Kaufman had a slightly off-centre vision of the film, whereas Clint's was straight down the middle. Totally intimidated by Clint, Kaufman bent over backwards to please the star, but that wasn't the way to go with Clint. Soon, according to sources, Clint began subtly to ride him.

Another reason Clint was grumpy was the unresolved Sondra Locke issue. Although Kaufman's wife was on location with him, the director who initially had balked at casting Locke now found himself nursing a crush on the actress. One of the first nights on location, Kaufman asked Locke to go to dinner with him and discuss her characterization. No sooner had this 'date' been arranged than Clint phoned and also asked Locke to dinner. The actress felt she had to say no to Clint, because she had already said yes to Kaufman. But she could tell when she hung up the phone that Clint was upset. Didn't Kaufman realize the star had a kind of *droit du seigneur*?

Thereafter a kind of bizarre competition over Locke developed, which Kaufman had no hope of winning. The director might have commanded her undivided attention during the days, but after his first miscalculation Clint launched into a seductive overdrive and monopolized the actress's evenings. Starting with their first night out, Clint and the actress began sleeping together. 'We were almost living together from the very first days of the film,' said Locke. 'Clint told me all the typical things about his marriage. "I would have left Maggie years ago ... but she got sick with hepatitis ... but we don't really have a relationship of consequence. It isn't happening anymore."'

Kaufman then made a fatal miscalculation while shooting the scene where Laura Lee (Locke) is nearly raped by the Commancheros. Smitten as he was by Locke, who loses part of her blouse and bares a breast in the scene, the director let the camera run on a bit too long for Clint's taste. Even after the scene was obviously over, the overexcited Kaufman kept yelling, 'Action! Action! Action!' Clint, standing on the sidelines, said, loud enough for others to hear, 'I think the word you want is *cut!*' 'What?' asked a momentarily confused Kaufman. 'Cut!' yelled Clint, and of course the cameras stopped rolling. 'Aw, right, I mean cut!' the director added irrelevantly.

Two weeks went by of this thrust and parry. Clint and Kaufman were oil and water. The incident that finished Kaufman, however, is referred to in Malpaso circles as 'The Beer Can Incident' (like one of those *Rawhide* titles). Weeks earlier, Kaufman, Bruce Surtees and Fritz Manes had scouted alkaline dunes for the scene where Josey Wales rides out of the sand with a white flag streaming from his rifle. After a hard day, they had stopped and were drinking beers, when Kaufman looked around and declared the spot perfect for the evocative quality he was seeking. The director drained his beer, pushed his can down in the sand, and announced, 'I'm marking the spot.' The time of day – 'magic hour', at dusk – would be perfect, too. That is when he would capture the magic in his mind.

Cut to a few weeks later, when the day's photography had wrapped early, with Clint already in an edgy mood. Kaufman came up to him, wringing his hands, and asked if they might get that particular shot of Josey riding up out of the sand dunes. 'You want to shoot the fucking thing?' asked Clint. 'Let's go.' Kaufman organized two station wagons, a camera truck, a horse trailer. Clint, Kaufman and Fritz Manes piled into the first station wagon with a driver, but Clint made a point of sitting next to the driver, with the director and Manes stuck in the back seat like children in the doghouse.

They drove and drove, and they drove some more. Clint kept muttering, 'Where the fuck are we going?' Kaufman, his spirits sinking, didn't really know. Finally, Kaufman announced that he could tell exactly where they were by that mountain over yonder. 'You guys wait here! I'll be right back. I'm positive this is the place!' The director jumped out of the car and marched off across the dunes, looking for the elusive beer can.

They waited and waited, and then waited some more. Kaufman didn't materialize. Finally Clint asked, 'What time is it?' Then, 'Well, shit, the sun's going to go down and we're not going to get the shot!' He got out of the car and told Bruce Surtees to get the goddamn camera out. He told Manes to get the fucking horse and rifle ready. He told Surtees that he was going to circle out around and then ride back in, coming over the dunes, and that he was only going to do it once so there would be no hoofprints to erase for a second try. 'Just yell when you're ready and check the framing,' Clint said.

Surtees yelled, Clint rode out, circled around and then rode back in, as the camera whirred. Clint called 'Cut!' and then they loaded everything back into the cars and trucks. Clint turned to Manes and said, 'Fritz, you wait for Kaufman.' Everybody left.

Manes and the driver waited and waited, then they waited some more. Finally from the opposite direction in which he had disappeared came a bedraggled-looking Philip Kaufman. He had his cowboy hat off and was scratching his head as he ploughed towards them. Coming up to Manes, Kaufman said, 'You know, it's really weird. I can't find that beer can.' Manes informed him, 'That's the least of your problems.'

Although Kaufman was crushed ('like a little kid', said Manes) that Clint had gone ahead and shot the scene without him, still he didn't confront the star. Instead, the director made a point of going up to Clint soon after viewing the dailies and praising the exquisite shot. In private, Clint kept complaining, 'What kind of a wimp is he?'

A couple of days later, the company moved over to Kanab, Utah, and a couple of days after that, on Friday, 24 October, Kaufman was fired. Typically, someone other than Clint was obliged to execute the dirty deed, and the actual firing was delegated to producer Bob Daley. Clint hid out in his hotel room until Kaufman had been driven to the airport, and then on Monday, 27 October, he took charge as the new director.

Back in Hollywood, an uproar ensued. The leadership of the Directors Guild of America was furious that an actor had been allowed to fire a director, especially a star who was also an executive in the production company; especially after the original director had completed all the preproduction and launched photography. A clause in the DGA contract was intended to preclude such a thing from happening.

More than once in his career blue-collar Clint had played fast and loose with the unions. Going off to locations was partly a way to avoid union add-ons; hiring his own extras and his crew members as bit actors was another way of avoiding set fees.

This time the violation was glaring. Warner Brothers was under heavy pressure to find some compromise resolution. Clint refused to budge, however, and up in Utah – where the union was impotent – filming continued. Eventually, it was the DGA that backed down, although Clint was forced to pay a symbolic penalty (reportedly in the neighbourhood of $60,000, and no doubt underwritten by Warners). The Directors Guild had to save face by instituting a new clause, known informally as 'the Clint Eastwood rule', which created a stiffer fine and mandated taking away a director's membership card, next time a producer discharged a director and then replaced him with himself.

James Fargo, associate producer on the film, thought that Clint didn't really want to direct *The Outlaw Josey Wales*. The star wouldn't have been shy about saying so, said Fargo, if he had. And it was tough for him to discharge Philip Kaufman, because it disrupted the all-important mystique of a smooth, easygoing operation. 'Clint always wanted everybody else to be laidback and relaxed,' explained Fargo, 'except he wasn't. He was always a little uptight, it seemed to me. He appeared on the surface to be laidback and easygoing, but there was always an anxious feeling underneath.'

If, initially, Clint hadn't wanted to direct *The Outlaw Josey Wales*, 'once Clint got into it', recalled Fargo, 'he enjoyed it'. But this sequence of events would repeat more than once with Clint – with directors fired after they had done crucial preparation.

Clint's method of directing was evolving into an articulated philosophy. He was shrewd about putting into words a 'shoot-from-the-hip' approach that sounded groovy in interviews. 'I like to swing with what's happening,' he'd say, making himself the equivalent of a jazz improviser. From jazz, critics could extrapolate, making the leap to realism, arguing that Clint's 'shoot the rehearsal' attitude lent his films 'a fresh, improvisatory, realistic flavour', in the words of Peter Biskind of *Première*.

Clint liked to work cheap (no matter that all the money wasn't reflected in the reported budgets), fast and loose (like cars and women), with scripts that didn't have to be polished to a glow (often first drafts). He preferred to leave the design and preproduction to others. He looked for collaborators who were subordinates. As the years went on, the crew might even block scenes with stand-ins before the director arrived. Clint preferred to walk onto the set and take a look at everything for the first time, and then shoot and print, preferably the first take, going for the spontaneity and the feeling of unfamiliarity and the 'realism'.

'It's a painful period and I'm not looking for any vindication at all, particularly in the press,' writer–director Phil Kaufman was quoted in *Films and Filming*, one of the few times he has spoken out about what happened between him and Clint. 'I felt *Josey Wales* was an epic film that needed certain styling. You don't start a film by placing a camera arbitrarily. You have to think about every shot in relation to the totality of the film, and how one scene isn't going to cut with another. Directing a movie isn't getting one shot after another depending on what looks good at the moment.'

Clint's philosophy *sounded* okay, but it couldn't really be applied to *The Outlaw Josey Wales*, which, thanks to Phil Kaufman's script and planning, showed more forethought than the standard Malpaso production. Clint in frontier apparel was already iconic, evoking not only his own ancestral past but America's manifest destiny. The motifs of historical vengeance and flight from civilization gave his Westerns an emotional undertow that the films set in modern times too often lacked. Critics warmly embraced *The Outlaw Josey Wales* when it opened in August 1976, and nowadays Clint's Bicentennial Western is widely considered one of his deepest, most personal works.

One of the reasons why *The Outlaw Josey Wales* found acclaim, however, is that Frank Wells had made good on his promises and the formidable Warner Brothers advertising and publicity departments had swung into action on Clint's behalf. Starting with *The Outlaw Josey Wales*, the massaging of critics and support of Clint film events more institutionalized by the studio. Each new film of Clint's would have its expensive promotional campaign, gala press parties and giveaways, arranged visits to set locations. Each new release would be heralded by 'exclusive' interviews with Clint.

Before *The Outlaw Josey Wales* was released commercially, Clint would take his new film to Sun Valley, Idaho, to show the film to two hundred academicians and film critics who had gathered at the Sun Valley Center for the Arts and Humanities for a six-day conference entitled 'Western Movies: Myths and Images'. Jay Cocks and Richard Schickel were among those present, along with old-time directors such as King Vidor, William Wyler, Henry King and Howard Hawks – names Clint would increasingly link with his own. Later, the Warners publicity department flew seventy members of the national press to Santa Fe, New Mexico for a barbecue and the world première of *The Outlaw Josey Wales*, followed by interviews with Clint, Sondra Locke and others.

A film critic who tells you that his attitude towards a film isn't softened by a junket – all expenses paid to a glamorous location, a private session with the star – is a film critic with one eye blind. In the early 1970s, Hollywood had begun to cut back on such junkets, partly because major East Coast newspapers – including the *New York Times*, *Washington Post* and *Boston Globe* – began to question the ethics of these love-fests.

But with Clint and Warner Brothers leading the resurgence, junkets made a comeback. The two main Los Angeles newspapers and Arthur

Knight of the *Hollywood Reporter* were among the invitees at Sun Valley, and also among those rhapsodizing over *The Outlaw Josey Wales* in their reviews. Clint's Western would crop up on *Time*'s prestigious, annual Ten Best listing.

When the carrots didn't work, it was out with the stick. Clint didn't read critics very assiduously, but now and then one really bugged him. He encouraged certain buddies to write poison-pen letters to the worst of the breed. One, in San Francisco, 'my own hometown yet', in Clint's words, got several letters from a Clint pal, pretending to be an average moviegoer. 'The hated critic only had to call one day,' recalled Paul Lippman, 'and Clint jumped into his car at a moment's notice and drove from Carmel to San Francisco to appear at a class the critic was teaching at a local college. He was very fair with Eastwood thereafter.'

Another 'hometown' critic, Judy Stone of the *San Francisco Chronicle*, was among those who gave *The Outlaw Josey Wales* a more equivocal notice. (Again, America's sparse number of female critics – Joy Gould Boyum, Judith Crist and Pauline Kael among them – were overrepresented among the negative opinion.) Stone commented in her review that at least the film showed some offbeat humour, no doubt owing to Phil Kaufman's script. She was astonished to receive a sharply worded letter from Clint accusing her of writing in praise of her pals. Stone, in fact, barely knew Phil Kaufman (she would later use Clint's letter as an excuse to seek him out and cultivate his friendship). If Stone wasn't so busy flattering Phil Kaufman, Clint's letter stated, the film critic would notice that it was really Clint who had the offbeat sense of humour.

John Wayne and Clint had been friendly enough when they met at Republican occasions and celebrity tennis matches, but Wayne was one person not wild about Clint's half-traditional, half-nouveau Westerns. Wayne dropped off the annual exhibitors' Top Ten list of box-office stars in 1976, the year of *The Outlaw Josey Wales*, and he never regained his lofty perch. Earlier in the 1970s, Wayne reportedly sent a letter to Clint, focusing on *High Plains Drifter* and attacking Clint's Westerns as being the antithesis of what the American frontier – and the American people – represented.

More than once, in interviews, Clint volunteered his reaction to

Wayne's critique. 'It's [*High Plains Drifter*] just an allegory, and it wasn't intended to be the West that's been told hundreds of times over by many players, about pioneers and covered wagons and conflict with the various Indian nations. *High Plains Drifter* was a speculation on what happens when they go ahead and kill the sheriff and somebody comes back and calls the town's conscience to bear. There's always retribution for your deeds.'

Wayne's letter would be interesting to quote from, but the text has never been released. And Clint made a point of telling interviewers that he 'never answered' it.

Just as, early in his career, Clint had been compared to Gary Cooper, now he was more often mentioned as Hollywood's post-Sixties answer to John Wayne, a fading hero. Clint bristled at comparisons to Wayne, or comparisons to anybody. He learned to enunciate an anti-John Wayne philosophy of Westerns – a philosophy defined less by what it stood for than what it stood *against*. And not only in the case of Westerns; the Marine Corps advisor on *Heartbreak Ridge* recalled watching a scene being filmed in which Clint's character shot an enemy soldier in the back, killing him, and then Clint telling him, by way of explanation, 'John Wayne wouldn't shoot a man in the back. But I'm *not* John Wayne.'

There were many generational differences between Clint and John Wayne. One, not often dwelled upon, is that Wayne subordinated himself to top-ranked directors, working more than once with Raoul Walsh, Henry Hathaway, Howard Hawks and especially John Ford, hardbitten taskmasters who helped mould his image and talent. These associations were part of Wayne's wisdom, accounting in his career for a dozen films that will always be regarded as classics.

Clint, after Sergio Leone and Don Siegel, now after Phil Kaufman, would never again surrender himself to any director who might dominate him. He didn't want to work that hard as an actor, and he didn't want to work according to someone else's methodology. Clint had chances to 'branch out'. Around this time he was offered the role of Willard, later played by Martin Sheen, in Francis Coppola's *Apocalypse Now*. 'I hate the thought of spending weeks in the Philippines,' he told a Carmel newspaper.

Director Ted Post tried to mend fences with the star by offering him the part of the platoon leader eventually played by Burt Lancaster in the Vietnam War film, *Go Tell the Spartans*. 'I just don't feel it's for me,' is all Clint would say, turning Post down. Later still, Clint would reject the role of an American journalist engulfed in the Cambodian War in *The Killing Fields*, saying it would be misleading to his fans; and that it was a terrible idea for a West Coast WASP to play an East Coast Jewish reporter.

He didn't say if salary terms had anything to do with his turndowns (*Go Tell the Spartans* was a low-budget operation). Nor did he say anything about the politics of these films, with their caustic views of the Southeast Asian conflict. 'I asked Clint if he was turning it [*Go Tell the Spartans*] down for political reasons,' said Ted Post, 'and he said, "No." Although he's very political, he never says he doesn't like something for political reasons.' That was another way in which Clint and John Wayne were different: Wayne supported the Vietnam War openly, taking his lumps for it. The pro-Nixon Clint made his endorsement of the war tacit, and refused to be pinned down.

Philip Kaufman wasn't the only victim of *The Outlaw Josey Wales*. Jack Kosslyn, mentioned repeatedly in Clint articles as an example of his loyalty to old friends, was another. Clint's longtime acting teacher was playing a small part in the production as well as serving as dialogue coach. Kosslyn had worked on Clint's films for six years, doing several tasks – casting, coaching, script touch-ups and acting bits – for one, chronically low, lump salary. Complaining about 'low salary' was frequently the subtext of any falling-out with Clint, although Malpaso people learned to come up with other explanations for the sudden deficiencies of someone once touted as indispensable.

Kosslyn, according to inside sources, was treated in a particularly mysterious fashion. The drama coach was plagued by a series of cruel pranks played on him by unknown persons during the filming. When he complained to Clint personally, the star brushed off the incidents, and then for the first time took issue with Kosslyn's job performance. Once warmed up, Clint lectured and excoriated his onetime acting mentor for several minutes, without once looking into Kosslyn's eyes, all the while skipping stones into a nearby pond.

The real reason it happened, say Malpaso insiders, is that Kosslyn had dared to make an implicit criticism of Clint, one day on the set, urging the star to try another take of a scene that he had performed inadequately. In the olden days, that would have been acceptable; indeed that was partly why Kosslyn was employed, as a 'second set' of eyes. But times were different, and Kosslyn had crossed an invisible line.

Kosslyn wasn't 'fired'. He was simply 'not rehired'. Hoping it was all a misunderstanding, Kosslyn phoned Bob Daley when the next Malpaso production was announced, only to be told there wasn't any slot for him. He never saw or heard from Clint again.

Sonia Chernus was another person loyal to Clint who suffered an unexpected reversal. She insisted that she had done enough work on *The Outlaw Josey Wales* to warrant a co-script credit. Chernus's actual contribution may have been arguable, but she wanted to qualify for Writers Guild benefits and a pension. Clint thought Kaufman deserved sole credit, and besides, that might placate the displaced director.

Chernus is described by most people who knew her as a sometimes difficult, opinionated woman, one type to which Clint curiously gravitated. Now, however, her insistence on a formal credit irked Clint. When she took the issue to a Guild grievance committee, according to sources, she was officially awarded co-credit. Clint could do nothing but comply by putting her name on the screen. But around this time, Clint raided Chernus's office, complaining about the piles of scripts and manuscripts that had gone unread. Then, shortly after, Clint asked the story editor to vacate her office and to review all future properties 'part time' from her home.

According to insiders, Chernus's workload and status dwindled. The worst thing about what had happened to her, Chernus told friends, was that she felt cut off from Clint personally. Most of her subsequent contact with the star was by telephone.

One could never be sure how important she really was to Malpaso operations, then or before. But Clint did keep Chernus on salary for the remainder of her life – at Maggie's behest, people say. Chernus had stayed close to Maggie, and thought of herself as an unofficial aunt to Kyle and Alison. In 1990, when Chernus fell gravely ill, Clint showed his fondness for the woman who had helped him get his break on *Rawhide* by visiting her at least once in the hospital and holding her hand on her deathbed.

Clint's blossoming relationship with Sondra Locke meant the time was past when friendship with Maggie was any insurance. It was a pattern that the revolving door of women in the star's life ushered in all kinds of tensions, professional as well as personal. Bob Daley, for me, was slow to realize that Locke was not going to do the usual disappearing act. And Clint's producer, who felt strongly about Maggie and the kids, had other reasons to look over his shoulder.

Fritz Manes, who had known Clint since junior high school, had ambitions at Malpaso. Manes had done impromptu stuff for other film productions, but now, after seventeen years of selling air time in television, and after a recent stint selling yachts in Sausalito, he was ready to make the full-time Hollywood plunge. Manes was hired by Clint to serve as Daley's assistant producer. Daley informed Manes, 'I feel like I've just hired my replacement,' but it was a hollow joke in Clint's world.

When not in Hollywood, Clint continued to cover all his stops with long- and short-running affairs known only to a few – certainly not to Maggie, much less Sondra Locke.

He had a yen for a husky, red-haired '21' dealer, who worked at one of the big hotels in Las Vegas, and a brief romance with an African-American cocktail waitress with a formidable bustline who worked at the Tropicana. Another busty '21' dealer from Reno moved to Carmel primarily because of Clint and became a regular in his 'backup stable', living not far from his family home. Although wary of the *haute monde*, the star also had a one-nighter, in the mid-1970s, with Joan Hitchcock, a flamboyant jetsetter well known in San Francisco polo circles, not the least because Hitchcock boasted publicly about having had an affair with John F. Kennedy.

The interviews with Maggie had begun to taper off. Certainly the 'happy-marriage' publicity, which had thrived for fifteen years, was no longer operative. Journalists visiting Clint's wife now usually focused on their 'forever house' in Pebble Beach.

The design and construction of this fan-shaped home, situated on a dozen prime acres of rock and cypress bordering the ocean, consumed nearly seven years of time, putting added pressures on a marriage already under strain. A solid wall of glass fronted the Pacific. Inside, twelve thousand square feet boasted four bedrooms, a studio for Maggie, a sunken living room featuring multiple fireplaces. There was also a sauna, jacuzzi, a gym, a projection room. The siding was done in redwood, the ceilings in Douglas fir. Maggie had coordinated the colours in rusts, greens, blues.

Clint – reluctant to keep pouring money into the house, diffident over details – endlessly delayed decisions over tiles, or switchplates for lights. By the time the $8000 redwood door swung open for the house-warming in 1976, Clint was already involved with Sondra Locke. Maggie didn't get the news until a few years later.

'Given Clint's long and frequent absences,' Richard Schickel was at pains to explain in his biography, 'the house became very much Maggie's project. That troubled him. He started to feel cut out of her consultation with designers and builders. As he began to see it, he was the one working hard to pay for a lifestyle growing ever more expansive, and he felt his wishes and opinions were being ignored.'

One particular sore point, said Schickel, was the placement of a shower head. 'The one in the master bathroom was, he thought, too low for a man of his height,' according to the authorized biography.

Clint wasn't eager to head to the Philippines (or anywhere else) to make a film based on a literary classic because he already had the next Dirty Harry ready to go on more amenable home territory. The orthodox theory of Clint's career is that the star had to rotate his personal films with the occasional Dirty Harry in order to satisfy Warners, but Clint was already worth, conservatively, $100 to $200 million by 1975. He wanted to continue the Dirty Harrys, because he – not just the studio – wanted to make the easy money. There is no case on record of Clint lobbying for a project which the studio turned down.

Early in 1975, Gail Morgan Hickman and S. W. Schurr, two former Oakland High School students who were fans of Clint's films, delivered a 110-page 'spec.' script called 'Moving Target', to Paul Lippman at the Hog's Breath Inn in Carmel. Lippman read it and passed it on to Clint, saying the storyline had potential but the script needed a Hollywood rewrite. Clint passed it on to Bob Daley, and eventually they decided in favour of the project. Because Clint leaned towards cheap, young writers, they sent the script back to the Oakland duo, who took a long time with their revisions and returned 'Moving Target' in worse shape than originally.

'This was a case of the ever-conservative Clint outsmarting himself,' Lippman said, 'for he had lost at least six months of production time, knocking him out of the number one box-office position. He was making at least two pictures a year regularly up to that time, and the few thousand dollars of rewrite money cost him dearly, at least in stature.'

The original story had pitted Harry against a Bay Area Symbionese Liberation Army-type terrorist group* with the climactic standoff taking place on Alcatraz Island. Screenwriter Stirling Silliphant, who followed the Oakland amateurs, had written one episode for *Rawhide*, but had never met Clint, except maybe in passing. However, the Oscar-winning scenarist of *In the Heat of the Night* had worked harmoniously with director Don Siegel back in the 1950s on another San Francisco crime movie, *The Lineup*, and Silliphant was currently executing a rewrite on Siegel's upcoming film, *Telefon*. A call came to Silliphant from Clint. The Siegel connection conferred reliability, and besides Clint was never one to look far afield for writers.

Silliphant was living in Marin, California, when the phone rang. No agents or intermediaries were involved; indeed all story conferences would be with Clint alone, and the screenplay written precisely 'to his measure and suggestion'. Clint introduced himself over the phone, asking simply, 'You got any ideas for a third Dirty Harry?' Remembered Silliphant, 'I did a hard-disk number in my head which would have put IBM out of business and in less than a nanosecond I said, "Yes, Mr Eastwood, I do." He said, "I can fly up. When can we have lunch?" "Anytime," I said. "Okay, tomorrow."'

They met at a restaurant both of them knew in Tiburon, by Seal Rock, overlooking Angel Island. 'Moving Target' was barely mentioned. Nor did the star explain why he chose Silliphant to be the 'fresh writer'. 'He never said,' recalled Silliphant, 'but I suspect that he was pleased that I had jettisoned southern California and that I was living in the Bay Area and that I knew the turf. It certainly helped in my writing the script'.

The idea Silliphant had, which he outlined to Clint, was a simple one. Dirty Harry needed a different kind of partner, 'one of the world's primary underclass', a female of the species. She would be assigned

* The Symbionese Liberation Army, very much in the headlines in 1974, were an ill-fated, left-wing Bay Area terrorist gang wanted for the kidnapping of newspaper heiress Patricia Hearst and a string of other violent actions. A manhunt to capture them ended in Los Angeles with a nationally televised police shoot-out.

to team up with him to defeat the gang of terrorists. 'Can you imagine,' Silliphant teased Clint, 'the absolute horror – it's truly Conradian – of Dirty Harry being saddled with a *woman* as a partner?'

According to Silliphant, 'His eyes began to dance as he played with the concept.' (Clint didn't mention that he had just turned down a truly Conradian project: *Apocalypse Now*.) 'The emphasis,' Silliphant told Clint, 'is on the character relationship, the slowly evolving relationship of trust which develops between you and your female partner, how it opens you up as a human being and you begin to shed all the sexist shit human beings are burdened with and, in the end, she gets blown away and you go fucking rampage crazy – big shoot-out at the end – and Dirty Harry's a different man than he was at the top of the show.'

'Finally,' said Silliphant, 'he said he liked it.' Clint liked the big shoot-out stuff and didn't mind loose talk about how a film was going to open him up as a human being.

Through late 1975 and early 1976, Silliphant worked on the third Dirty Harry. He knew in advance that 'minimalism in dialogue went with the territory'. When, in February 1976, he delivered his draft – retitled *The Enforcer* – Clint liked it, but all that relationship stuff worried the star. 'He felt it still needed more narrative drive, that maybe I'd put too much into the relationship and not enough into the bread-and-butter stuff that would pull in Clint Eastwood fans.'

So Dean Riesner was brought back to fold the bread-and-butter stuff of the original draft back into the relationship one. Silliphant, the 'relationship writer', was let go. 'I wasn't happy about this,' said Silliphant, 'but I liked him [Clint] so much.' Indeed, he liked Clint and respected his winning ways so much that Silliphant's opinion, in retrospect, was that this star, reputed to be an 'action guy', could also have made it as a 'a tenured professor of philosophy at a university'.

Bob Daley was quoted in the *Hollywood Reporter* as saying that Riesner would put the 'Eastwood touch and magic' on the script. Riesner knew his business, and did his best to marry the two scripts. Without Don Siegel around to mediate the process, however, the 'action' and 'relationship' halves didn't quite mesh. The film would need a lot of help from the casting. Clint would need a strong actress to play the novice cop, Kate Moore, whose teaming-up with Detective Callahan is dictated by the department's equal opportunity initiatives. According to Stirling Silliphant, it was he who recommended the husky-voiced actress Tyne Daly, who was another Don Siegel connection – she had just been hired for a bit in *Telefon*. Daly's best-known previous exposure was in a TV 'Movie of the Week'. She met Clint, and they got along.

Initially, however, Tyne Daly turned down the role – *three* times. 'I thought the woman was just there to be made fun of,' the actress told a reporter afterwards, 'to be the butt of all the jokes.' But Clint had committed himself to the idea of a distaff partner, and he hated rejection, so Daly was permitted to go through the script, making suggestions for her character. As a result, there were last-minute rewrites. *The Enforcer* was one of the most written and *rewritten* scripts Clint ever tolerated.

The leading lady was able to influence a major change in the scripted relationship between her character and Clint's. The original concept, Tyne Daly later told columnist Marilyn Beck, was that Clint and his female cop partner were 'seriously involved [romantically]' with each other. Researching her role by speaking to actual cops, the actress realized that if a policeman and woman did fall in love with each other they would have to act quickly to acquire new partners. 'Otherwise, you're putting yourself and him in jeopardy because you're not operating at peak efficiency,' said Daly. 'Audiences will see that there's the beginning of a feeling between the characters [in the film],' added Daly, 'but nothing more. It would have been wrong the other way.'

Another last-minute surprise was that Clint himself would not be directing. James Fargo, of increasing value behind the scenes, was promoted to director. Although Fargo had voiced his ambitions on several occasions, he learned the news in typically low-key fashion. At a birthday party for Fritz Manes at Malpaso, Clint took Fargo into Bob Daley's office and asked casually, 'Who are you going to get as your assistant?'

According to Fargo, Clint immediately allowed him to interact with Dean Riesner and to involve himself in the shooting script. The final, two-pronged story would have Dirty Harry suspended for insubordination, San Francisco's mayor kidnapped by the terrorists, and ultimately Harry and Kate, his partner, storming Alcatraz, where the mayor is being held hostage. In the end, true to Silliphant's suggestion, Kate would be killed.

According to director Fargo, Clint didn't hover on the set – 'some days he wasn't even in San Francisco'. *The Enforcer* was the rare production where Clint 'wasn't that impatient', remembered Fargo, 'basically because he was having the affair with Sondra' and therefore the star was distracted, and happy to surrender his usual authority.

Principal photography took place in Bay Area locations in the summer of 1976.

Director Fargo said that Clint was 'not comfortable with a lot of dialogue', so they made sure to go through the script and eliminate some of the lines. 'I blame a lot of that on Sergio Leone,' explained Fargo. 'Leone told Clint, "Don't talk, just look." So if you give Clint a long speech, watch him, he'll start to get nervous. He's more comfortable with confrontational and action scenes. He's great with that sort of stuff. But when he's doing something where he has to really show his emotions, or open himself up, he gets a little uncomfortable.'

Asked if a director can push Clint to try something different in a scene, Fargo replied, 'You can push him a little bit, not much. He has his own way of doing things.' What happens if he is pushed too far? 'Nothing really,' said Fargo. 'He [Clint] just doesn't do it.

'As I told him lots of times, especially on *Every Which Way But Loose*,' continued the director, 'Just give me a look. Clint does the greatest double-takes in the world. If you watch *Loose*, you will notice that is a lot of what he is doing in that film.'

Clint increasingly prided himself on 'winging' his dialogue in some scenes: especially barroom scenes. According to director Fargo, the star believed that any problems resulting from improvisation could be fixed in the editing room. Trivial mistakes in continuity or lighting were something his audience wouldn't even notice.

It didn't always work out that way, and Fargo pointed to one integral scene in *The Enforcer*, the 'getting-to-know-you' scene between Harry and Kate that took place in a bar. Clint insisted on improvising. Fargo warned him that matching the dialogue in the editing room later on would be difficult. Bending to Clint, Fargo filmed the scene with two cameras. They filmed a half dozen takes, no two of them identical in content.

In the cutting room, however, editor Ferris Webster nearly had a coronary. It was impossible to match the 'pickups' in the conversation. Clint came in, watched the footage, told the editor and director to fix the scene any way they could. They tried, but finally even Clint had to admit that it didn't splice together. Fargo had to throw it out and concoct a new scene, more carefully scripted, which took place outdoors on the patio of a fish restaurant. This time Clint carefully followed his lines.

Since Clint didn't like to rehearse, sometimes while 'winging' scenes he would also step out of the 'sight lines' and out of focus. To some cameramen, this is an unpardonable sin. But Clint didn't like to redo shots; he said the audience would recognize his voice, they didn't have to see his face. 'That was a kind of philosophy too,' said cameraman Rexford Metz. 'Not really a negative, but it adds up over time.'

Much of *The Enforcer* script added up to incredible nonsense. The militants were not faceted, not even interesting as caricatures (Pauline Kael noted that 'their real crime is that they're homosexual'). The relationship scenes between Clint and Tyne Daly were the better written and acted, and the acknowledged highlight of the film.

There was tension in their verbal fisticuffs but also better-than-average Clint comedy. Daly's tough, affecting performance fore-shadowed her eventual breakthrough on TV as a lady cop in *Cagney and Lacey*. All the more affecting since her character is killed off at the end. Then Harry goes berserk and . . .

Everyone sings the efficiency of Clint's film-making, but it often seems that every shot makes it into the final cut. *Magnum Force* timed out at 124 minutes. *The Eiger Sanction* clocked in at 125. *The Outlaw Josey Wales* droned on at 135 (Richard Corliss, writing in *New Times*, thought the film was at least a half hour too long, 'a situation I would remedy by shaving a second or so off almost every shot'). Not the least of director James Fargo's accomplishments was in making the quickest-moving Dirty Harry. In spite of all the script padding, the curtain rang down on *The Enforcer* after a brisk 95 minutes.

Clint was hardly uncorked as a human being (the *Harvard Lampoon* would name him 'Worst Actor of the Year'). But a number of film critics responded appreciatively to the novelty of a female partner for Dirty Harry. Even Pauline Kael, who detested the film, thought Daly's casting was 'one smart move'. Kael wrote, 'It's such a warm perform-ance that Eastwood's holy cool seems more aberrant than ever.'

Indeed, Jean Hoelscher in the *Hollywood Reporter* sounded the first inklings of a critical trend when she wrote, 'One thing for which

Eastwood certainly deserves credit remains his lack of ego when casting his female leads: He is not afraid to work with excellent women.' Marjorie Rosen, echoing Hoelscher in the feminist *Ms.* magazine, wrote that Clint and Malpaso had fashioned 'a heroine of steel and gut and innocence'. The 'feminist Clint' augured a remarkable turn in the star's mythology, which even Clint could not have predicted when he said yes to Stirling Silliphant.

Tyne Daly herself was not sure how unique and positive it all was. The excessive violence of the film bothered the lead actress. A mere five persons had been killed in the first *Dirty Harry*. *Magnum Force* would double that number and add one for eleven, including a pair of dead nude blondes, a particularly gratuitous swimming pool massacre, and one notably gruesome murder by Drano. In *The Enforcer*, the senseless carnage added up to fifteen or sixteen bodies (thanks, in part, to a one-shot, disposable bazooka), prompting Janet Maslin in *Newsweek* to observe, 'The gore has become so gratuitous that Harry has begun to look like a trigger-happy fool.'

A Hollywood columnist caught up with Tyne Daly after a screening, and the shaken actress confessed, 'I hadn't added them up before that, and it kind of gave me a bad feeling.'

'We live in a violent society,' Clint told the *Los Angeles Times* in an interview on the subject of screen violence. 'Newspapers don't put it on the back pages. Those who would censor violence would have to censor the Bible and Shakespeare. Nobody would go to the movies and see the routine work of a policeman, an officer going door-to-door, the drudgery. It's the highlights they want.'

Defending himself, the star switched the attack to director Martin Scorsese and one of the landmark films of the 1970s. 'I think films can go overboard on violence,' said Clint (the newspaper's reporter, Lee Grant, adding parenthetically, 'he should know'). 'But *The Enforcer* doesn't. We don't use slow-motion violence, for instance, or lingering blood squirts. Harry is a hero to the everyman, middle America, the working guy who'd like to tell his boss where to put it. He is a functioning police officer. I'd question a film like *Taxi Driver*, where the hero is mentally ill.'

Regardless, *The Enforcer* filled theatres and wound up surpassing *Dirty Harry*, grossing almost $60 million in the US – $100 million, counting overseas. It was Clint's biggest moneymaker up to that time.

CHAPTER EIGHT

The Sondra Years
1976–1978

Sondra Locke was not very conspicuous during the preproduction of *The Enforcer*. The few times writer Stirling Silliphant glimpsed her he had the impression 'she was strictly along as Clint's current girlfriend'. Most nights during filming, if Clint didn't have to make an appearance in Pebble Beach, he stayed with Locke in rented apartments in San Francisco and Sausalito.

At first, the new relationship was kept quiet, and people were slow to realize that the actress was much more than a casual fling for Clint, partly because those who understood the situation best were deep inside Malpaso and Warner Brothers.

As late as the spring of 1977, the Los Angeles newspapers were reporting that 'Clint is looking for someone special to co-star with him in his next film, *The Gauntlet*', which was touted as a 'contemporary action–adventure drama and policeman–prostitute romance'. According to press accounts, the reason Clint was 'having so much trouble finding the right actress is that she's got to be believable as a veteran of the Las Vegas wars, but still have a certain soft femininity'.

Dennis Shryack and Michael Butler were the writers of *The Gauntlet*, which had a plot trigger similar to *Coogan's Bluff*. Clint would play Ben Shockley, an over-the-hill cop who has to transport a prostitute from Las Vegas to his home state of Arizona. The prostitute is witness to a pending case. The routine assignment turns into a dangerous mission when an assortment of bad guys try to eliminate them both.

Shryack was a former talent agent whose agency once represented Butler, the son of veteran Hollywood scenarists Jean and Hugo Butler. Shryack and Butler had teamed up as writers, and in 1976 sold their first screenplay, *The Car*, to Universal for $300,000 plus fifteen 'points'

– i.e. fifteen per cent of the film's net profits. They were also advanced $55,000 for the soft-cover novelization. This deal, whopping by the standards of the time, rippled through the film industry, and made the writers the hot duo in town.

When Warners purchased *The Gauntlet*, the studio topped the first script's price-tag by $200,000, also guaranteeing the writers fifteen profit 'points' and $100,000 for their novelization. One of the things Clint told Shryack and Butler at their first meeting is that he never would have paid so much money for script. And nobody at Malpaso received 'points' besides Clint. Even when it wasn't his own money, Clint winced.

Warners had earmarked the project for Clint, with Barbra Streisand pencilled in to give the expensive property 'double' indemnification. Of course the first thing to go, once Clint was involved, was the whole 'age' angle. Although the star was in his mid-forties, Clint was not ready to be coaxed into playing 'over the hill'. Substituted was a sketchy backstory indicating that Ben Shockley was something of a bungler; the lowly extradition assignment might be his last chance to do a job right.

The second thing to go was Streisand, although Shryack and Butler certainly didn't have Sondra Locke in mind to play Gus Mally, the prostitute. They met with Clint several times before her name was even mentioned; they were outside the loop, didn't have the foggiest notion that Clint and Locke were involved romantically. Or that Clint, wearing one of the fishing-hat disguises he affected out in public, visited Locke on the location of her next film project in Arkansas and promised her a terrific part in his new production.

Even after learning Locke was going to play the part, they were slow on the uptake. 'The only reason I ever knew that there was something going on between him and Sondra,' said Dennis Shryack, 'is that I went to Vegas on location and we were all staying at the Jockey Club. I'd never seen Sondra in person. To me, she has a hard edge on the screen. She had never done anything for me on the screen. God, I saw her in the lobby of the Jockey Club one day, and I saw she had a vulnerability, a very interesting, waifish quality.

'The next day I was on the stage where we were shooting the blowing up of the whorehouse. Clint was busy directing, setting everything up, and I kind of sidled over to Sondra, and was just talking to her. It was obvious, I suppose, that I was trying to hit on her. Fritz [Manes] pulled me aside about an hour later and said, "Unh-unh."

'Now dissolve and we move to location in Phoenix, where I bring up to location my soon-to-be second wife, who very much resembled Sondra Locke. I introduced her to Clint, and he came on to her in a very overt yet very subtle Clint way – to the point where you just knew that if he had said, "Meet me in an hour . . ." she'd have said okay. Then he gave me a little look and walked away, and I always felt that was payback.'

Sondra Locke thought she was in love with Clint (and Clint was in love with her). She was thrilled to have a starring part, even if it was Clint who decided what that part would be: a veteran prostitute, albeit college-educated and with a 'certain soft femininity'.

Again, she would be nearly raped in one scene. The actress would undergo variations of sexual assault in *The Outlaw Josey Wales*, *The Gauntlet*, *Bronco Billy*. She would portray another sex hustler in *Any Which Way But Loose*. In *Sudden Impact*, she would reverse fields, playing an avenger of rape. These characters, over which the actress exercised little control, were more Clint's projections than hers.

The rest of the cast was soon announced: notably Pat Hingle, from *Hang 'Em High*, as Clint's friend, a police higher-up, and the Judas on the force. Rexford Metz was promoted to director of photography. Clint would be the director as well as star when *The Gauntlet* began shooting on locations in Nevada and Arizona in April of 1977.

Part of the publicity hook of the film was that Clint, although playing another tough, disenchanted cop, wouldn't gun down a single person. Not that there wouldn't be plenty of gunfire and violence: a helicopter would crash into high-tension wires; a prefab house would collapse under a hailstorm of bullets; a protracted climax would show the hijacked bus, captained by Clint, being shot at by hundreds of policemen.

Richard Schickel thought the overkill of gunfire and violence was a stylistic triumph and a thematic motif. 'An analogy to Vietnam is inescapable,' the authorized biographer said of the film's house-exploding scene. Schickel also managed to draw comparisons between *The Gauntlet* and *It Happened One Night*, *The African Queen* and *Gunga Din*.

The writers themselves were a little surprised at the exaggerated violence, which wasn't in their original scenario. 'The recurrent visual motif of over-the-top destructiveness in *Gauntlet* was entirely Clint's idea and appears in no script,' recalled Michael Butler. 'My initial reaction to it – the incessant fusillades that destroy the house, the cars – was dismay. But of course he was leading up to the relentless barrage which the police direct at the bus later on. So I would say that Clint has a gift for large bold strokes.'

Not all of the large, bold strokes were on the screen. Some were in Clint's publicity. Warner Brothers had taken the idea of Clint as a fast, economical director, and begun to elevate it to dogma. As more than one Malpaso insider pointed out in interviews, the schedule on Malpaso productions was now deliberately exaggerated in order to promote the Clint image. 'He [Clint] schedules pictures long so he comes in early,' said cameraman Rexford Metz. The workday wasn't even a particularly long one on a Clint film. 'We never had a schedule that was a killer,' added Metz. 'We'd work eight or nine hours, ten hours max, even on location.'

For example, according to Metz, a sequence would be scheduled that took place in a car with only three actors – Clint, Sondra and one of the house players. The production log of *The Gauntlet* would set aside seven days to shoot only a few pages of dialogue! 'We'd shoot it in three or four days, and all of a sudden we'd be three days ahead,' remembered Metz. 'In the worst scenario in the world you can't get hung up in a car for seven days with three people talking. We were always a week ahead.'

Another thing that kept the schedule moving was Clint's feeling that 'the spontaneity of the first performance and unfamiliarity with the surroundings gave a performance that was more realistic than the one that was polished,' in Rexford Metz's words. This, too, became part of the Clint mystique. But since he didn't like to discuss their characterizations with them, actors weren't always made aware of Clint's philosophy, and the first take is hardly everyone's best performance. Compare Pat Hingle in *Hang 'Em High* (directed by Ted Post) with Pat Hingle in *The Gauntlet* or *Sudden Impact* (directed by Clint); in the latter two films, the veteran character actor is on 'automatic', without much help from the director.

Clint's credo, which he wielded whenever necessary to fend off unwanted suggestions to slow down and ponder a scene, was, 'If the audience is thinking about *that*, then the movie's over.' Sondra Locke remembered hating her 'home' set for *Sudden Impact* – the paintings, the objects, the bedspread in her bedroom – and complaining, 'They're all wrong for my character.' The star looked at her as if pained. 'If they're looking at that . . .' Clint said. 'He said something like that *every* time I tried to get him to pay attention to some detail,' said Locke.

The 'contemporary' films were always particularly 'fast'. One morning in Las Vegas, cameraman Metz recalled, he noticed an actress on the set, preparing for her brief moment of glory in a Clint film. She was watching the lighting crew block the scene with stand-ins, while waiting for the director to speak to her and tell her what to expect. She asked Metz what her 'coverage' was going to be, wanting to raise her 'energy level' when the focus was intimate. The cameraman warned the actress to do her best no matter what, the first time she found herself in front of the lens. 'That might be the only shot you get,' Metz said. She was horrified, because the script had led her to believe there would be close-ups, or at least follow-up angles. Sure enough, Clint arrived, the cameras rolled, and the scene was all over in a single take – a 'master shot', with the actress's 'energy level' all but irrelevant.

The 'gun-and-go' method of film-making also had the effect of reinforcing the house style of dark, grainy lighting. Sondra Locke would be made to appear increasingly harsh and angular in successive Clint films. Rexford Metz would struggle to make the actress look as attractive as possible, but there could only be as much 'fill-in lighting' as Clint's fast schedule would allow. 'It was kind of tough on the ladies,' the cameraman noted.

When characterization was stripped away, when violent special effects were emphasized, when story points were trampled over and the plot boiled down to cars, cycles and choppers, *The Gauntlet* became a sort of live-action Road Runner cartoon, albeit 'Eastwood isn't so artful a director as cartoonist Chuck Jones,' as Richard Corliss put it in *New Times*, and the story moved 'as fast as Elmer Fudd'.

Sometimes Clint's timesaving shortcuts were obvious. And, for example, story logic suffered: the ending of *The Gauntlet* – with the bus carrying Ben Shockley and Gus Mally ringed by hundreds of policemen firing their weapons – was the film's third major shoot-out. That scene had been envisioned in the script in slow motion, but Clint, who had inveighed against slow motion in print, made a decision against the trendy special effect. Dennis Shryack, visiting the set, tried to make an argument on behalf of it. 'Peckinpah has done slow motion to death!' growled the director, cutting him off.

The scene only *seemed* like slow motion, since it was overlong – like the two other shoot-outs in the film. As usual, Clint seemed to have shot every syllable and comma of the script, and the editor seemed to include every frame of footage he shot.

The stupidest thing about it was that the bus's tyres were supposed to be blown out and the vehicle was supposed to churn up asphalt as it ploughed forward. But Phoenix didn't want its downtown streets torn up, and nobody at Malpaso focused on the issue until it was too late. Then, rather than shoot the bus from an angle that avoided any glimpse of the tyres, Clint photographed the scene in such a way that *obviated* the problem. The sides of the bus exploded and shattered as it rolled forward, its undamaged wheels turning round and round.

When *The Gauntlet* was previewed, audiences yelled out, 'Shoot the tyres, idiots!' When Don Siegel was treated to a rough cut, he added another caveat. 'I'd like to have seen a shot with four or five hundred dead cops lying on the street,' Siegel cracked. With all those bullets spraying around, wouldn't the police have massacred themselves?

Since the leading lady's part was uniquely shaped to complement Clint, the part of Gus Malley, coming at the height of his romance with Sondra Locke, was probably the actress's meatiest opportunity in a Malpaso film. Never mind the silly scene where she and Shockley 'meet cute': a punching match – she punches him; he punches her back.* Her early scenes were the best, although ultimately Gus Malley became just another Clint sidekick. By the time Gus is faced with Shockley's plan to storm city hall in a bus, she is reduced to muttering, 'The whole idea's insane.'

Yes, some of the film's ideas were foolish, bordering on insane. The producer, Bob Daley, was rumoured to be grumbling that *The Gauntlet* was one of the worst films he had ever seen. Clint demanded loyalty

---

* Later, Clint reiterates his willingness to slug a woman when, during Locke's near gang-rape, he fends off attackers and punches one of the biker chicks in the mouth. Then he pushes the offending tough-gal off a moving train – take that, John Wayne!

from employees and he confronted his old friend. 'No, that's not true,' Daley told Clint, 'it's one of the "ten worst", but not *the* worst.' Daley meant it as a joke, but such humour didn't sit well with Clint. Daley had been acting strangely lately, making a lot of curious remarks. It was as if his heart wasn't in his job any longer. It was as if he didn't realize that he was on the slippery slope.

Warner Brothers slotted *The Gauntlet* as the studio's major Christmas offering for 1977. But Clint thought the studio botched the early previews (mistakes in scheduling brought in an older audience offended by the film's violence and adult language). The star threw a tantrum. A Warner Brothers executive lost his job, and Clint threw himself into the marketing, coming up with a painting by the celebrated illustrator Frank Frazetta, which he brought back from the East in another of his expensive new cars, a Ferrari. That artwork became the centrepiece of the film's advertising campaign, featuring a menacing bus, a muscular Clint, a bosomy Locke.

Reviews of the film were generous. As David Ansen of *Newsweek* wrote, 'You don't believe a minute of it,' but 'at the end of the quest, it's hard not to chuckle and cheer.' Clint was developing into a 'fairly stylish action director', the critic wrote.

Sondra Locke's acting earned some of the better notices. Tom Allen in the *Village Voice* thought Locke provided 'the most natural, unaffected performance of the year by any young actress'. Arthur Knight in the *Hollywood Reporter* wrote that the actress hadn't given 'this persuasive a performance since her debut in *The Heart Is a Lonely Hunter*'. William Wolf of *Cue* magazine didn't much like *The Gauntlet*, but he felt that Locke was 'an exceptional actress' who showed 'guts and vitality'.

One of the supreme ironies of her association with Clint was that Locke helped to raise his level of critical recognition. The belief that Clint could guide a strong female performance had started with Jessica Walters and caught momentum with Tyne Daly. But it reached its height with Locke.

Many critics, because they liked Clint in person as well as on the screen, strove to find artistic merit in his films, even though there emerged a basic contradiction between the films they supported and those which audiences loved. The audiences wanted the omnipotent Clint, while the critics preferred the uncharacteristic films in which

Clint found himself powerless or defeated. In 1977, moviegoers were still in the midst of a decade-long love affair with the heroic, justice-dispensing Clint, and *The Gauntlet* would end up grossing $54.1 million, ranking as one of the year's Top Ten hits.

Some interviews, coinciding with the release of *The Gauntlet*, continued to paint the Eastwoods as a 'happy couple' (Richard Schickel, *Time*), but most interviews with Maggie had long since tapered off, and this was already a sadly outdated view.

Casting Sondra Locke was one way for Clint to spend time with the actress. When they weren't working together, they had complicated logistics. They were always shuttling around, staying in different places. From the beginning with *The Outlaw Josey Wales* they had played a shell game of houses and hotel rooms.

Maggie and the children lived in Pebble Beach, so nearby Carmel was, at first, hostile territory for Locke. During the editing of *The Outlaw Josey Wales*, which took place largely in Clint's suite of offices above the Hog's Breath Inn, the star installed his lover in a hotel in the vicinity and then eventually rented a house for her. One time Locke was caught alone in the editing suite, waiting for Clint, when the doorbell rang. She looked out of the fish-eye before opening the door, and spied Maggie leaning in to peer inside. Locke ducked. That is the closest she ever came to meeting Clint's wife.

In Hollywood, Clint and Locke skipped around, spending time at the house the actress shared with her husband Gordon Anderson (when he was out of town) or overnights at the small but well-appointed apartment (it included spa, kitchen, bedroom and dressing quarters) behind Clint's inner office at Malpaso. (This was rarely glimpsed by journalists commenting on the company's spartan premises.)

The Sherman Oaks house had become a *pied-à-terre* for Clint when Maggie was up in Pebble Beach, which was now nearly always. But Clint had to be careful, in case Maggie phoned or made an unexpected appearance. After *The Gauntlet* wrapped in the summer of 1977, however, that began to change. Locke virtually moved in, and people thought Clint was heading into the open about his relationship.

Indeed, the 13 February 1978 issue of *People*, which was timed to promote *The Gauntlet*, featured Clint and Locke on the cover with a smiling Clint gazing pensively into Sondra's eyes, giving her 'the Look'.

Inside, *People* reported the widespread speculation that Clint and Locke were 'more than just co-stars'. 'Everybody would love for us to say, "It's all true, we're madly in love,"' the actress was quoted. 'But people will believe whatever they want to believe. Even if it were true – which it isn't – I certainly wouldn't talk about it'.

People might have overdone it, since Clint felt obliged to fire off a letter, denouncing the magazine's appetite for 'adolescent titillation'. But it was too late. Maggie, who read the magazine off a supermarket rack, knew 'the Look' when she saw it. Usually unflappable, she was especially angered by Clint's reference to his female co-star as a 'princess'. 'I cast it [*The Gauntlet*] a little off,' the star was quoted by *People*. 'Good casting would be to make her a princess – she is a princess. But to cast her as a hooker – that's the twist.'

As someone who avoided confrontation, Clint might have put off for ever telling Maggie about his romance with Locke. He had to nudge her in print, and she had to discover it on a newsstand, then have the details confirmed for her by friends who had been holding their tongues.

Clint's wife wasn't completely taken by surprise, however. Her husband had been showing up arm in arm with Locke at parties in Carmel, some of which were attended by their mutual friends and at least once with Kyle and Alison in tow. No longer could Maggie stand the public humiliation, which now was national. She called an attorney.

It was in late January that Marilyn Beck picked up the buzz and carried in her Hollywood column a 'world exclusive' to the effect that Clint was going to separate from Maggie after twenty-five years of marriage. Clint, now that he had goaded Maggie into action, felt torn. A prolonged divorce fight would be nasty, not to mention expensive. Until things were sorted out, therefore, Clint would attempt to stifle the gossip. He picked one of his preferred venues to rebut the mounting speculation.

Clint had cultivated Herb Caen's friendship on the Dirty Harry shoots. Now the San Francisco newspaperman quoted Clint's Dirty Harry-like response to the Marilyn Beck report in his *Chronicle* column: 'Mizz [sic] Beck, or whatever you call her, reports that I am "unavailable for comment". Well, I have a comment. Marilyn Beck is an a——e. You can print that.' Caen himself added this supportive postscript: 'No, I can't. This is a family paper, as the Eastwoods are still a family family.'

Caen was in Clint's hip pocket, while *People* and Marilyn Beck were diligently trying to perform their jobs as members of the Fourth Estate. Members of the press who did not abide by Clint's rules of reportage and publicity found themselves on his shitlist. *People* would sometimes be treated frostily, almost like a tabloid, in the future, while Marilyn Beck was added to the roll of Clint's enemies.

Actually, Marilyn Beck was correct. Maggie had faced Clint down in private on the subject of Sondra Locke, and Clint had admitted, yes, he was in love with the actress. Locke herself found out about that showdown in anticlimactic fashion. One day at the Sherman Oaks house, she found Clint packing a huge suitcase. Where was he going? He told her that Maggie had pleaded with him to take one, last, promised vacation to Hawaii with her and the children. She hoped they might yet 'save the marriage'. Clint assured Locke that he was still in love with her, and that he was only going along on the trip with his family because Maggie was so 'emotionally fragile'.

When Clint returned from Hawaii, however, he surprised Locke by informing her that Maggie was going to file for a legal separation, *not* a divorce. 'This puzzled me,' wrote the actress in her autobiography, *The Good, the Bad and the Very Ugly*, 'because those were not actions of a woman who had given up a relationship entirely.'

Then as now, Sondra Locke defies easy categorization, and one of the aspects of her life which may be most mystifying to the public is that all along, during her love affair with Clint, she was married to another man. How could that be?

She was an unconventional spirit from a small Southern town, who had grown up alienated by her own provincial upbringing. Going on twelve, she met an imaginative boy named Gordon Anderson, the same age as her, who was 'crunching through snow in wooden shoes, wagon-hauling a fat cocker spaniel that was draped in strings of Christmas balls', according to one published account. They became soulmates, dreaming partners. One thing they both dreamed of was leaving Shelbyville, Tennessee, and going to Hollywood.

Anderson, originally from Arkansas, was an aficionado of the theatre who threw himself into local acting and directing projects starring his best friend. According to an early profile of Locke in *Look* magazine, Anderson helped teach her to cry on cue by advising her to listen to 'sad-happy circus music' and to think of the death of a pet dog. 'He made her reflect on her strange other selves before two angled mirrors, cultivated her taste for "anything that's not real but makes you think it is".'

Locke's family took offence at the influence Anderson exerted over her. Locke, rebellious and determined, moved in with Anderson's family and shortly thereafter, following high school graduation, the two friends were married. Locke then cut off all communication and ties to her own family, a situation that held for many years.

Anderson spent time chasing acting parts in New York, while Locke, between itty-bitty jobs as a model and in commercials, worked as a typist at WSM-TV Nashville. Back home one Sunday, Anderson read an article in the *Nashville Tennessean* about a nationwide talent hunt for a teenaged girl to play a lead in the planned Warner Brothers film of Carson McCullers's novel, *The Heart Is a Lonely Hunter*.

They drove to Nashville, where the resourceful Anderson filched a copy of the Carson McCullers novel from a college library, and then back to Shelbyville, where he proceeded to make up Locke in the tomboyish part. He thinned and braided her hair, painted freckles on her nose, created a scab on her knee. He taped her breasts down. Although she was twenty-one, they would lie about her age, lowering it to seventeen, closer to the scripted character. Locke always looked younger than her years anyway.

Anderson then drove Locke to the regional auditions, three hundred miles away in Birmingham, Alabama, where a thousand aspirants had gathered to face a studio casting scout. She did well in this round, and Anderson threw her back in the car and drove to New Orleans, there to meet the film's director, Robert Ellis Miller, and to audition again along with hundreds of other girls who had survived the initial tests.

Back in Shelbyville, the two waited. A week went by, then Warner Brothers sent Locke a ticket to New York City for a final audition. Everyone who encountered her thought the amateur had a unique quality. Happy-sad. Tough but delicate. A cold angel. The cockiness of a naif. Darkness mixed with light. Hard to pinpoint.

She did get the part, and those qualities transmitted wonderfully in her performance as Mick Kelly, the sensitive small-town Southern girl whose outlook on life is transformed by the deaf-mute played by Alan

Arkin. Her character in *The Heart Is a Lonely Hunter* was closer to her true self than anything she would ever play for Clint.

Although Locke was just the latest in a long line who had fallen for Clint, she had scant knowledge of his history with women. She believed Clint when he told her that he was unhappily married and that he never would have stuck by the marriage this long if it wasn't for the children. She read into his studied silences the idea that they had a golden future together, all the more so once he managed to break away from Maggie. If, by 1978, Maggie was beginning to seem a stubborn hindrance, her own husband did not present any kind of obstacle.

Locke's marriage to her childhood friend had endured. Gordon Anderson had long since given up acting and taken up the carving of speciality figurines. The townhouse he and the actress lived in together in West Hollywood was cluttered with their collections of rare fairy tale books, Art Nouveau, precious dolls and cherished antiques.

Like Clint's marriage, Locke's relationship with her husband was the opposite of what it appeared, however. For, although Anderson had been Locke's first real sweetheart, that was back during youthful days in Tennessee, and shortly after coming to Hollywood with her, Anderson had arrived at the realization that he was homosexual. He had lived as a homosexual for years, and by the time of *The Outlaw Josey Wales* was involved in a longstanding relationship with another man.

Locke and her husband did not engage in sexual relations. Theirs was a classic 'show marriage' as well as a deep, abiding kinship, a mutually satisfactory arrangement that allowed him to live discreetly and her to live according to her lights.

They remained alter egos. They regarded themselves as very much a family unit. It was one of the benefits of her arrangement with Anderson that Clint could send Locke home to her husband. She was happy to go, hated to be alone at night when Clint wasn't in town, officially continued to share her husband's address.

Of course Clint knew very well that Anderson was gay. Locke *told* him right away, after they first slept together. Clint accepted that. Anderson and his companion were in fact invited on location to visit the set of *The Gauntlet*, where the star took them aback by asking some curious questions – Had they both been having fun, cruising the Las Vegas bars? Over time, however, Clint would grow friendly with Anderson and his gay friends, to the point where they were included in holiday plans and sometimes invited along with him and Sondra Locke on short trips.

However, the public did *not* know that Locke's husband was gay, which lent an aura of mystery to Anderson's passivity, even as Clint seemed to take over his wife. Nor, in spite of any gossip she had heard, did Maggie know for sure. She only knew what Clint told her.

One of Clint's ingratiating moves was to involve the 'squirts' in his productions. One cute, young crew member, whom Clint doggedly pursued on the set of one of his films, described in an interview how disarming it was that the famous director would consult her on the forthcoming day's camera angles. Similarly, camera equipment was bestowed on Frances Fisher, on location in Alberta, Canada, and she was encouraged to shoot footage for a documentary or ad campaign for *Unforgiven*. Other ladies were passed scripts.

Her enemies claim nobody before or since has had as much power as Locke; that her intimacy with Clint conferred a unique ability to influence his decisions – a power she was not loath to exercise. Locke insists she had little influence. Rather she was a pawn in the Malpaso game, particularly useful to Clint when he needed to deflect responsibility for controversial policies, such as the wave of hirings and firings that would shortly rock the company.

'I was always really involved with whatever film he was thinking of doing,' Locke said, 'not because he felt he needed my help, that's for sure. We always talked a lot about scripts and the films. In fact, as I look back on it, that's most of what we talked about – the work. He was always interested in my opinions on everything. In general, he only takes your advice if he agrees on it. He can hardly ever be *persuaded.*'

Locke may have exerted her greatest influence in coaxing Clint into making two comedies that were seen as a quirky change of pace for him during the brief Democratic era of President Jimmy Carter. *Every Which Way But Loose* and *Bronco Billy* were different from preceding Clint films in their good humour and lack of bloodshed. The former was a genuine box-office phenomenon, while the latter film is still regarded as one of Clint's most artistic, personal works as actor and director.

The actress says she lobbied for both projects because they aligned with her then rose-coloured view of Clint. 'I thought of Clint in some ways as this innocent, kind of sweet, little boy, with an introverted nature,' said Locke. 'I thought that part of him was very much like the character in *Bronco Billy*, and that he saw himself that way too. At least that is what he preferred to project, especially off screen. But what I thought was shyness turned out really to be an inability to connect.'

Clint needed convincing on *Every Which Way But Loose*, and inside Malpaso there were sharp differences of opinion. The people who backed a winning turn of events in Clint's world could expect rewards, while others might receive a comeuppance.

Every Which Way But Loose arrived at Malpaso in roundabout fashion. Jeremy Joe Kronsberg had come out to Hollywood from Denver in 1958, gone under contract to 20th Century–Fox as an actor, then struggled as a journeyman songwriter, writing songs recorded by Steve Lawrence and Bobby Vee, among others. A lifelong physical fitness devotee, Kronsberg had worked out at Vince's Gym in the 1960s, and lifted weights in the same room as Clint, although he didn't know the actor personally.

Turning to screenwriting in 1976, Kronsberg wrote his first script called 'The Coming of Philo Beddoe', a rowdy, good-natured road story loosely based on a real person he had heard tales about: a truck driver with a pet monkey who had a reputation as a phenomenal bare-knuckle fighter. Kronsberg peppered the script with his own songs, including the device of a radio blaring constantly in the background with Greek-chorus-type lyrics commenting on events in the story.

Originally, Kronsberg wrote the truck driver's pet as a gorilla, until he discovered that gorillas were not very tractable. After talking with Dr Geoffrey Bourne of the Yerkes Primate Laboratory in Georgia, he got hooked on the idea of an orang-utan. Dr Bourne turned him on to Joan and Bobby Berosini, who supervised the circus act at MGM Grand in Las Vegas. Clint was far from his thoughts. 'The [Clint] movie before mine [*The Gauntlet*] appalled me,' Kronsberg said. Kronsberg wrote 'The Coming of Philo Beddoe' 'with someone like Burt Reynolds in mind'. And the script had been turned down by 'at least forty-seven people' in Hollywood before Clint's name came up, almost parenthetically.

Kronsberg's wife shared a film buff friend with Judy Hoyt, Clint's current secretary at Malpaso, whose husband Bob, having won a Best Sound Oscar for the editing of *Jaws*, now hankered to become a full-fledged producer. The film buff friend thought if Bob Hoyt read the script and liked it, Judy might walk the project into Malpaso and coax Clint into showing it to Burt. Bob Hoyt did like the script, and his wife did bring it into Malpaso, but that is not exactly how events panned out.

Fritz Manes recalled that he read the script and immediately championed it as an allegory about himself and Clint. 'It was Clint and me without the monkey, the two of us when we were growing up,' said Manes, 'almost an identical relationship.' Bob Daley expressed some scepticism, which would be held against him in the long run, while advising Clint to make up his own mind. Clint did so, with Sondra Locke reinforcing the star's enthusiasm. Clint announced that 'The Coming of Philo Beddoe' would be his next film.

Later, *Variety*, chronicling the film's success, would report that Clint's 'manager, attorney, agent and producer all advised against the comedy', but except for Bob Daley these others counted for little in creative decisions. And Clint's endorsement of the project would later be touted as a risk-taking departure by some film critics, although among the Hollywood press it was also widely regarded 'as a cynical attempt to muscle in on the Burt Reynolds good-old-boy drive-in trade', in the words of *Look* magazine. Reynolds had just had a runaway hit with *Smokey and the Bandit*, a 'good-old-boy' movie to which 'The Coming of Philo Beddoe' bore similarities.

The higher-ups at Warner Brothers also required some convincing. Head of production John Calley entertained doubts, although Frank Wells listened to Manes's sales pitch and decided that it might just make a funny movie. Wells, like a good lawyer, nonetheless thought it best to present all the facts to Clint. Warners commissioned survey-takers who went out in the field to ask members of the public, 'Would you go to see Clint Eastwood in a comedy with an ape?' Boxes of print-out results were brought into a top-level meeting attended by Clint, Manes, Daley and the experts. The presentation began. Daley was hedging, saying the survey showed valid qualms, when Clint, who didn't like meetings anyway, got up and walked out the door.

The debate continued, but nobody had any doubt that Warners

would bankroll the movie. By now, Clint walked on water for the studio. The film was put on the schedule for mid-April to shoot on locations in Los Angeles, Albuquerque, Santa Fe, Taos and Denver.

The unwritten etiquette in Hollywood was to reward the finder of a project with a credit and at least a token fee (if not additional salary), but that etiquette didn't always prevail at Malpaso. Bob Hoyt reportedly asked for too much – $100,000 – and an associate producer title. However, Hoyt hadn't signed any contract with Kronsberg, and with Manes and Daley jockeying for position inside the company Clint didn't think he needed another producer. 'So Clint told Bob Hoyt he would give him no title, $25,000, and if he wanted to take some time off from Universal and come over to Malpaso and see how a movie was made, okay,' remembered Manes.

There was bitterness all round, and eventually Judy Hoyt felt obliged to leave her post at Malpaso and go to work elsewhere to pacify her husband, who later settled with Clint for a sum that insiders say was much lower than the star's original offer.

An orang-utan named Manis, trained by the Berosinis of Las Vegas, would play Clyde the ape. Sondra Locke would portray Lynn Halsey-Taylor, the country-and-western barroom singer who flirts with Philo Beddoe but then mysteriously rejects him and vanishes on the road. Geoffrey Lewis was preordained as the dimwitted Orville, who buddies up with Beddoe. Orville's kooky girlfriend would be played by Beverly D'Angelo, and his even kookier mother, whose main goal in life is renewing her lapsed driver's licence, would be played by Ruth Gordon.

The octogenarian Gordon had won the Best Supporting Actress Oscar for *Rosemary's Baby* the year Sondra Locke lost in that category. She would bring to the film her own zany brand of comedy, well-established in such films as *Where's Poppa?* and *Harold and Maude*. The actress was probably the inspiration of Phyllis Huffman, who would function on Warner Brothers' behalf as Clint's casting director for over twenty years. Huffman's modest credit on Malpaso productions disguised her responsibility for the 'discoveries' credited to Clint by some critics.

Since Clint hated auditions, it was Huffman who usually narrowed the list of possible co-stars and winnowed the 'unknowns', videotaping their auditions and interviews. Clint just watched the tapes of the top candidates. In justification, he once explained, 'Basically I can't interview actors. I've been in their position myself. I've been there too many years of my life, sat with producers who didn't know their ass [from a hole in the ground] and had no idea what they were looking for. So I just can't put actors through that, and I hate to build up people to think that they're really close to something and then have to turn them down.'

James Fargo, who had not worked on *The Gauntlet*, was invited back to Malpaso to discuss 'The Coming of Philo Beddoe'. Clint felt comfortable with Fargo. He thought he'd done a good job with the sometimes humorous repartee between him and Tyne Daley in *The Enforcer*. Fargo, who was proud of having introduced a few gags into that film, now urged Clint, 'Use your double takes. Use your eyes. Have fun with it.'

Rexford Metz would continue in place as the director of photography, with Ferris Webster editing. Jeremy Joe Kronsberg had written the script so that his musical lyrics were integral to the continuity, and Dee Barton was hired to compose the music for his songs. Down in Memphis, Barton, who had scored *Play Misty for Me*, *High Plains Drifter* and *Thunderbolt and Lightfoot*, supervised a prerecording of the soundtrack.

Another reason Clint felt he didn't need Bob Hoyt around is that he had already acquired an 'associate producer' in Jeremy Kronsberg, who had driven a hard bargain. The hard bargainers did best with Clint, and Kronsberg had managed to extract a percentage deal on the picture; nobody thought the grosses would reach inordinate heights. The scenarist also angled to keep half of the music publishing rights and royalties.

Clint liked mirror images of himself, and he and Kronsberg hit it off personally at their first meeting at Malpaso. Both wore T-shirts and jeans. They bench-pressed close to the same amount – 250 pounds. The idea of Kronsberg as a struggling Tin Pan Alley type appealed to the frustrated musician in Clint. Clint even liked the fact that Kronsberg refused to be rushed into making up his mind. He announced that he was going off to the desert to meditate before signing his contract with Malpaso.

In the script Philo Beddoe had been written as being twenty-nine years old. Clint was closing in on fifty. Kronsberg kidded the star, 'I'm going to make him older ... I'm going to make him thirty-five.' But typically, Malpaso's preproduction focus had not been on script development, and the only rewriting Kronsberg did before filming was to make one of the two police officers in the story into an African-American. In the end Clint and company went out on the road with 153 pages of shooting script, which – because one page of shooting script equals roughly one minute of screen time – loomed as unwieldy.

It was a very picaresque continuity to begin with, taking Philo Beddoe and colourful companions in and out of bars, fistfights and slapstick jeopardy. All the time a dewy-eyed Beddoe is chasing an elusive country singer, he himself is being pursued by two grudge-bearing lawmen and a cartoonish Hell's Angel type motorcycle gang.

Kronsberg knew some of the scenes had to be trimmed or dropped, but he was little consulted once the cameras were turned on. At first he didn't mind. He was perfectly content in his role as associate producer, and, another deal-sweetener, he also had a featured acting part as one of the 'Black Widow' motorcycle gang. In his spare time Kronsberg was happy to hang out around Rexford Metz, picking up camera pointers. And whenever he had a complaint, he'd just knock on Clint's trailer door and say, 'Clint, we have to talk!' – launching into things 'nobody in their right mind would say to Clint'.

Kronsberg said Clint would often ad lib his lines, and not always for the better. 'He would say things that I thought, because comedy is so specific, changed the "reading" and blew the punchline,' said Kronsberg. 'It wouldn't work, or you'd lose the joke.' Kronsberg believed he was merely being helpful in reminding Clint about certain omissions, or the intended 'tone' of a scene. He'd actually grab the star by the elbow and walk him away, whispering his consultations. 'He'd look at me like I was crazy,' said Kronsberg. 'As a matter of fact, he was very gentle, all things considered.'

One improvisation really bothered the writer, however: When a snake crosses the black policeman's path, Kronsberg had written that the cop exclaims in horror, 'You are UGLEE!' Instead, the actor playing the part made a tired joke, 'Feet, don't fail me now!' – a riff on an old Mantan Moreland line.* Clint thought it was very funny.

---

* Donald Bogle in *Toms, Coons, Mulattoes, Mammies and Bucks* says it was Moreland himself who thought up his own great exit line [in the Charlie Chan films], 'Feets! Do your stuff!'

Later negative reviews would point to this line as an example of redneck humour bordering on racism.

Clint would always have some trouble transplanting the warm, comic side of his personality, which everyone knew in private, onto the screen. In person Clint could be freewheeling, his humour scatological, almost goofy at times. On screen his comedy often came across as forced and calculated. He liked to fall back on the kind of adolescent slapstick prevalent in *Every Which Way But Loose*: people tripping into horse dung, villains kicked in the balls, tits and ass jokes (Beverly D'Angelo holding up two cantaloupes at a roadside stand and asking, 'Want some melons?').* *Any Which Way You Can*, the sequel to *Every Which Way But Loose*, which Clint himself crafted from start to finish, would have the running joke of an orang-utan defecating in squad cars.

It says something that the comic highlight of Clint's career would be playing straight man to an arboreal anthropoid ape. The eleven-year-old orang-utan, Clyde, proved a natural ham who posed a sly, unpredictable presence on the set. Clint rose to the challenge. The camera was allowed to grind on, while Clyde went through his loose-limbed paces, doing outrageous things nobody could have anticipated; Clint reacted with his slow burns and double takes.

The script transgressions mounted, until there was a major brouhaha towards the end of filming. Director James Fargo, driving with his wife from Taos to Denver, tore out a chunk of pages in order to remain on schedule. 'The one thing Clint never wanted to do was go over schedule,' explained Fargo. But Kronsberg believed characterization and continuity had been sacrificed, and he complained vehemently.

By now, however, Kronsberg had proved himself 'a pain in the ass', in his own words. In Denver – which, to make matters worse, was his home town – the actor-writer-songwriter-associate producer was barred from the set. Fritz Manes, the *other* associate producer, delivered a message from Clint: 'You're ruffling feathers. Cool it.'

Kronsberg believed his true enemy was Manes, who was jealous of Kronsberg's equal title and easy access to Clint. Malpaso was like an Italian court with all the intrigues, thought Kronsberg, with Clint feeding on the attention. Kronsberg went over to Clint's trailer one more

---

* To be fair, the 'melons' joke was in Kronsberg's original script. Clint thought it was hilarious.

time and knocked. Clint looked shocked to hear of such a misunderstanding and assured the writer, 'Jeremy, you aren't banned ... enjoy
yourself!' Clint had a tendency to back down in person – everybody
knew that.

Scenes continued to be altered, shortened, dropped. Lines were
improvised. Kronsberg had learned his lesson, so he protested less.
'But when I saw the picture previewed at the end, I had a strange
feeling,' said Kronsberg. 'Because I knew it was mine, yet it wasn't
quite right. Some of the changes were better than what I wrote, but
some of it bothered me. I knew it wasn't what I wrote *exactly*. I was
stunned by what I saw, but I have to say I was even more stunned by
the success of it.'

Maybe Jeremy Joe Kronsberg's pesky behaviour didn't have anything
to do with Clint's decision to junk the songs the scenarist had written
for the film. Maybe Kronsberg owning half the rights and royalties of
the music didn't figure into the decision either. Maybe it was purely
an artistic decision on Clint's part.

But on paper, the move to rerecord the entire soundtrack of 'The
Coming of Philo Beddoe' looked like an aesthetic retreat and a canny
business move. Clint had passed on buying 'The First Time Ever I Saw
Your Face' outright for *Play Misty for Me* and then forfeited huge profits;
he wasn't going to let that happen again.

Snuff Garrett had been around Hollywood and the music business
for twenty years. He had known Clint in passing since *Rawhide* days,
and he was also buddies with Burt Reynolds. Bruce Ramer, Clint's
lawyer, had been Snuff Garrett's first lawyer in Hollywood. Clint and
Garrett shared the same law firm, which was now Gang, Tyre, Ramer
& Brown.

Garrett was one of the movers and shakers at Liberty Records in
the 1960s. In his career he would write or produce fifty Top Ten
country-and-western recordings and have many other hits that crossed
over into pop. Garrett was as close as you could come to a guaranteed
hitmaker, and he was Clint's kind of no-bullshit professional: a 'let's
do it now and do it fast' guy.

Garrett was up on his ranch in the San Fernando Valley when,
without prelude, there came a phone call from Clint. Clint (whom
Garrett dubbed 'CE') asked the music producer to come over to

Warners to discuss some work on his forthcoming film. Garrett had never done any movie work; he was intrigued, and hurried right over.

'We sat in his office and CE played me some tapes,' remembered Garrett, 'music that someone had recorded for the film he was doing, *Every Which Way But Loose*. He said, "I'd like to get your opinion of it." I listened to it and said, "You ain't got no hits in there." He said, "Could you do better than that?" I said, "I could do better than that, standing on my head." He said, "Well, you got about three weeks. Get on it." '

On a handshake they formed a partnership. Clint had managed to find another way of maximizing his profits. 'CE never directly, to my knowledge, owned any of the music to his pictures until me,' said Garrett. 'I got him into that.'

Snuff Garrett went to work with his stable of writers, crafting catchy tunes with chart potential. One of them, titled 'Every Which Way But Loose', was written by Garrett and his team, but the phrase itself came from one of Jeremy Joe Kronsberg's jettisoned lyrics. Clint liked the phrase so much he borrowed it as the film's new title. Warner Brothers records wanted one of its contract artists, Eddie Rabbitt, to break into the pop charts, so Rabbitt, a musician whose entrenched MOR ('Middle of the Road' in radio station parlance) status defined the shift that Garrett's score represented, was drafted to record the film's theme. Other country music personalities whom Garrett recruited for the soundtrack included Mel Tillis, Charlie Rich and Hank Thompson.

Clint was 'the most open, easy-to-work-with person on the face of the earth', in Garrett's opinion. The star deferred to the music producer's knowledge and experience. The only time they had any friction during their long relationship was when Garrett voiced concerns over whether Sondra Locke could sing her part.

Locke's character had three songs in the original script. Although Garrett liked the actress immensely (his affectionate nickname for her was 'Lock 'n' Load'), he realized that Locke wasn't a professional singer, so he did his best in the recording studio to help her through her numbers. Phil Everly of the Everly Brothers, a friend of Garrett's, coached Locke vocally, while adding harmony and a bridge to the most musically challenging of her songs, 'Don't Say You Don't Love Me No More'.

After a day and a night of struggling to get Locke's notes down,

Garrett felt beaten. The following morning Clint showed up. Garrett took him aside.

'Look, I'm really having a tough time,' Garrett told Clint. 'She's really having trouble with the song. We're on a schedule and the songs are pretty easy, but it's hard for her to sing them. I don't know what we can do. Maybe we should have her lip-sync . . .'

'I want Sondra to sing it,' said Clint tersely.

'Okay,' said Snuff, 'but we'd better load in some supplies because we're going to be in here for a while.'

Clint said nothing more. 'He just give me that CE look and the bones in his neck stretched out and he just turned and walked out. Bob [Daley] followed him out, and I walked back into the control room and said, "Hey boys, pack it up. I think we're at the end of the hunt. It's over." But there wasn't a word said, except what I said. I was pretty down and I sat around with all the guys in there, expecting to be fired.'

Bob Daley came back in a few minutes and walked Garrett out of the recording booth. 'Let me tell you something,' Daley assured Garrett. 'There aren't many people that Clint totally trusts. He totally trusts you. You do it however in the hell you want to do it. You've got Clint's blessing.'

That was it. Locke came in later in the morning, and they managed to finish her numbers, albeit slashing her solos to two. Later, during the 'Clint period' of her career, for a 1982 telefilm, the actress would again be urged by Clint to play a vocalist, a famous one in this instance, jazz-based balladeer Rosemary Clooney. 'Singing was more Clint's ego than mine,' Locke said. 'I had no business being a singer, but he wanted me to be one, especially since it was clear he couldn't be one himself.'

The astonishing success of the unassuming *Every Which Way But Loose* took everyone, including Clint, by surprise, but there were also good reasons for it.

The first single of the soundtrack, the title tune by Eddie Rabbitt, was released in late November, to precede distribution of the film. It shot to the top of the country charts, advertising the upcoming film while serving its purpose of introducing Rabbitt to wider audiences. The recording peaked at number thirty on pop lists. The title song would be followed by Charlie Rich's 'I'll Wake You Up When I Get Home', also a number one country hit. Snuff Garrett had delivered, and a Clint film never had a better promotional tie-in.

Garrett, an astute businessman like Clint, had other ideas that complemented Warners' promotional strategies. On Garrett's advice, before the film's release, the *Every Which Way But Loose* album had been previewed before a gathering of country music deejays, record distributors, storeowners and members of the film and music business press, all flown to Dallas for a party.

Terry Semel, Warner Brothers' former head of distribution, had just been promoted to chief operating officer. Robert A. Daly (no relation to Clint's producer Bob Daley) was made Semel's second in command. Also promoted was Barry Reardon, who became the studio's distribution chief in charge of dispensing the film's estimated $5 million advertising–publicity budget. These new Warners executives were not 'creatives' like John Calley, or onetime attorneys like Frank Wells; they were primarily salesmen, and under their salesmanship the marketing and promotion of Clint would soar to new peaks.

Initially, the big-budget *Superman* had been slated as the studio's major Christmas release for 1978, with *Every Which Way But Loose* relegated to a secondary status. But Clint complained to the new sales brass, especially since his films had a tendency to open with impressive numbers but, according to trade papers, 'sag in the dog days of early January'. Responding to Clint, the new executives 'came up with the most detailed release strategy yet for an Eastwood picture', in the words of *Variety*.

There would be unprecedented money set aside for local and network television spots, newspaper and magazine space, intensive radio advertising. *Every Which Way But Loose* would be booked to open simultaneously in 1,246 situations, including many small-town and rural venues, one of the biggest 'saturation bookings' in film industry history, touted in the trade press as the second biggest simultaneous screening of any film since *Star Wars*, which actually opened in fewer theatres.

Too bad if leading critics scorned *Every Which Way But Loose*. Even *Variety* opined, 'This film is so awful it's almost as if Eastwood is using it to find out how far he can go – how bad a film he can associate himself with.' Charles Champlin, holding forth in the usually sympathetic *Los Angeles Times*, called the film 'lumpy and skewbald'. In *Newsweek*

David Ansen wrote that *Every Which Way But Loose* was a 'plotless junk heap of moronic gags, sour romance and fatuous fisticuffs'.

Too bad, because Clint and Warners would enjoy an exceedingly Merry Christmas regardless. Partly this was because audiences had to choose from among some of the most dispiriting alternatives in memory. Among the joyless yuletide releases of 1978 were *Uncle Joe Shannon* (advance hype hoped it would prove a Rockyesque sleeper), *Brass Target*, *Paradise Alley* (directed by Sylvester Stallone), *Force Ten from Navarone*, *Oliver's Story* (the limp follow-up to *Love Story*), *Same Time, Next Year*, *The Brinks Job*, *California Suite*, *Lord of the Rings*, the remake of *The Invasion of the Body Snatchers* and two of the all-time letdowns, *King of the Gypsies* starring Eric Roberts, and *Moment to Moment*, romantically pairing the unsexy team of John Travolta and Lily Tomlin.

These holiday films failed studio expectations. Turned off by the non-competition, moviegoers swung over to Clint, who seemed to be entertaining packed crowds in practically every theatre. *Every Which Way But Loose* – and *Superman* too, which ended up almost doubling the $123.5 grosses of Clint's film – set coast to coast box-office records for Warner Brothers. The novelty of a gunless Clint playing for yuks with an orang-utan drew people in. His charm – his personality at its loosest and most winning – did the rest.

Bedtime for Bonzo, another film with a monkey co-star, had been one of Ronald Reagan's biggest hits too. Although Malpaso figures show that *Every Which Way But Loose* topped off at $123.5 million grosses in the US, Jeremy Kronsberg – in a position to know because his contract guaranteed a portion of the revenue – estimated the film eventually earned in the neighbourhood of $200 million worldwide.

Considering its reported costs – $4.5 million (omitting the star's salary) – it amounted to 'Clint Eastwood's most successful picture' ever up to that time, according to *Variety*. Taking into account today's inflation in production costs and ticket prices, it probably still is.

CHAPTER NINE

The Feminist Clint
1979–1980

Clint and Maggie never issued any formal statement about their marriage, but by the time *Every Which Way But Loose* was in theatres, their union of twenty-five years was effectively over.

Maggie's lawyer, Jack Miller of San Francisco, was quoted in the press as saying that Clint seemed more interested, temporarily, in a separation than divorce. Maggie was reportedly demanding fifty per cent of Clint's share of earnings of any films produced before their breakup, which would include *Every Which Way But Loose*. The lawyer estimated Maggie's share of Clint's latest film profits to amount to roughly $7 million; in other words, after his salary, Clint stood to collect $14 million in *Loose* percentages. This was before the release played out in theatres, *before* TV and video revenue.

Film dividends were one bargaining chip in the divorce negotiations; land and houses were others. Forced to move out of the Pebble Beach house, Clint had to find another 'forever place'. In late 1978, he did just that, purchasing from the widow of Bing Crosby, Kathryn Crosby, whom Clint used to flirt with back in Arch Drive days, the one-thousand-acre Rising River Ranch in Burney, located in northern California's Shasta County. The price was said to be close to $2 million dollars. Shortly after the purchase was finalized, Clint began to buy up available surrounding property. And Sondra Locke began to involve herself in the redesign of the main house, with Clint assuring her it would be theirs for ever, together in retirement.

She and, later, Frances Fisher too, said Clint would almost undergo a metamorphosis whenever he arrived at the Rising River Ranch. Locke said Clint would stop at the front gate and pick and smell the sage.

'Clint would get like a little boy,' the actress was quoted in one interview. 'That was the best part of Clint.'

When Clint was in Los Angeles, however, the two stayed in Sherman Oaks. Because she sometimes found herself alone there, Clint insisted upon buying her a gun.

Even though Locke moved in her belongings and tried to furnish the Sherman Oaks house with her own art and mementoes, she felt strange, living in a place that remained decorated with large-sized photographs of Maggie and the children. Clint was resistant to any more purchases; resistant to a new house – after all, they had Rising River Ranch. Finally he gave in. 'Go shopping for one,' Clint finally told Locke.

Purely by chance, there was no part for Sondra Locke in Clint's next film production, which would feature an almost exclusively male cast playing inmates of a maximum-security prison.

Escape from Alcatraz was based on the true story of Frank Lee Morris who, along with John and Clarence Anglin, made a daring escape from the island prison in 1962. The three inmates dug through walls with spoons, constructed papier-mâché dummies as decoys in their cells, and made from old raincoats a raft in which to cross the treacherous waters of San Francisco Bay. The three convicts were never seen again and prison officials believed they drowned, although legend holds they survived.

In 1963, J. Campbell Bruce wrote a non-fiction book called *Escape from Alcatraz: A Farewell to the Rock*, a history of Alcatraz and of the numerous attempts by prisoners to escape the prison site. A film buff named Richard Tuggle, a Florida native then living up in San Francisco, bought Bruce's book off a tourist stall after taking a tour of the facility. Tuggle had been working as an editor of a professional health magazine, but he also nursed ambitions to become a movie writer. Fascinated by the 1962 incident, Tuggle sought out the book's author and negotiated an option on screen rights to the material. Tuggle proceeded to write a script using Bruce's factual coverage.

Tuggle arrived in Los Angeles on the first day of March 1978. Because he was an admirer of an earlier Don Siegel prison drama, *Riot in Cell Block 11*, Tuggle submitted his screenplay to that director through Siegel's agent, Leonard Hirshan – who was also Clint's. The

William Morris Agency forwarded the script to Siegel, and the director immediately thought of Clint as the escape ringleader, a felon with the high IQ of 137.

Alcatraz Island had been an historic lighthouse and military fortification before it became a federal penitentiary in 1934, and was a familiar landmark to Clint. (The Bay Area site could be glimpsed from Piedmont elevations.) Tuggle's script had only that single setting, which had also figured prominently in the climax of *The Enforcer*.

After reading *Escape from Alcatraz*, Clint stated his willingness to star in the film if it was directed by Siegel *and* produced by Malpaso. There was only one hitch: Siegel preferred that it be 'A Don Siegel Film'. Clint didn't want any confusion as to who was the ultimate boss. He insisted on producing. But Siegel outmanoeuvred Clint by doing something he rarely did – paying $100,000 of his own money to buy the script – so he was firmly in command with the ownership rights.

The two friends had a falling-out over this issue, and partly for that reason Siegel took the property not to Warner Brothers, its natural steward, but to a rival studio: Paramount. There, production bosses Michael Eisner and Jeffrey Katzenberg welcomed the project with open arms, and there Siegel began to scrounge for another star in time to begin shooting in the fall, after the tourist season was over.

All the feasible names appeared to be sewn up, however. Paramount was eager to woo Clint away from Warners, and furthermore, the studio understood that Clint offered box-office insurance on a potentially downbeat subject. In August, Eisner took Siegel aside and persuaded him to give in to the star. The director made an appointment for a beer and sandwich with Clint over at Malpaso. He was made to wait an hour and forty-five minutes, according to insiders, but Siegel was an eminently practical man who knew when to swallow his pride. When the meeting was over, the relationship had been patched up, Clint was back, and *Escape from Alcatraz* was a 'go'.

Now they had to move fast. Siegel and Richard Tuggle worked minimally on a revision and because of the quick scheduling, without much input from Clint. Not much changed, except for a few scenes trimmed for length. 'When Clint likes something,' recalled Tuggle, 'he doesn't want to mess with it. He believes in his instincts. If he likes a script, he doesn't want to screw it up. He is less interested in changing the script than anyone I know.'

Less than six months had passed from the time Tuggle arrived in Hollywood to the start of filming, in September. Bruce Surtees was back as director of photography. Patrick McGoohan, known to TV audiences for his recurring roles in *Secret Agent* and *The Prisoner*, was hired to play the Captain Queeg-like prison warden, while Fred Ward and Jack Thibeau would portray the inmate-brothers who join Clint in the escape.

Alcatraz had been a national park since 1972, a popular sightseeing attraction. On location, the film-makers had to cope with the rules and regulations of the Department of Parks and Recreation Commission, and with the occasional intrusions of gawking visitors. They also had to cope with cell blocks, long in disuse, that badly needed repair. Paramount paid roughly half a million dollars to restore the crumbling facilities, but some interiors had to be replicated and those scenes photographed later on studio soundstages.

There had to be adjustments between Siegel and Clint. The rivalry between them, which had waxed and waned over the years, created a subtle layer of tension. Siegel had wanted Clint as the film's star, but now the star had marquee as well as co-producer clout. (The compromise credits would eventually read 'A Malpaso–Siegel Film', with Malpaso listed first.) No question that Clint outranked Siegel; that his importance had surpassed that of the veteran director.

In their earlier films together, Siegel was less beholden to Clint. Screen time was more balanced among all the characters. The director had a point of view, an ironic distancing, independent of 'the star'. Here Siegel's camera would fixate more on Clint, lingering on the big-money face. Everything else seemed subsidiary, short-shrifted.

The film's prison 'atmosphere' would be cursory, its pretensions to reality Hollywoodish. Except for a few modern details, the supporting characters would be at home in a vintage Warner Brothers movie starring Cagney or Bogart. Wolf (played by Bruce M. Fischer) is a goon on the prowl for a sex-punk; Doc (Roberts Blossom) is the doomed inmate who paints pastorals; English (Paul Benjamin) is the African-American librarian with a limp who learns about racism from the white star; the Anglin brothers (Ward and Thibeau) are . . . well, inter-changeable. Patrick McGoohan has a serviceable moment or two, but his character's impotence is underlined in the scene where Clint is permitted to call him an asshole.

It's all so pat. It's revealing that director Siegel, who took pride in his montage and in presiding over his editing, left *Escape from Alcatraz* before the end of postproduction, reportedly because he was behind schedule on his next film. Clint then supervised the final mix, ending up with a timed cut of 120 minutes – easily the longest and least taut of those Don Siegel films starring Clint.

Richard Schickel reported that there were 'some problems with the director's cut' that Clint felt obliged to fix. One was the ending: Siegel's final shot took place inside the cellblock, with the guards discovering the trio were gone. That left it up in the air whether the escape had succeeded.

Clint hated for his characters to die. He had consulted with fitness expert Jack LaLanne, who assured him that no one could swim those frigid waters without specialized training. Nevertheless, it was Clint's decision to append the footage, which sweetened the ending for audiences: searching for the escapees, the warden notices a flower, a chrysanthemum the prisoners have left behind on the far shore, a defiant symbol of their triumph.

After the Dirty Harry knockoffs and the orang-utan outing, however, US film critics were ready for a fresh Don Siegel–Clint Eastwood reteaming, and probably they were nostalgic for those prison films of yesteryear. *Escape from Alcatraz* earned the best notices of probably any Malpaso production of the 1970s when it was released in December of 1979. Stanley Kauffman in the *New Republic* called it 'crystalline cinema'. Frank Rich, in *Time*, said the film evidenced 'cool, cinematic grace', while Charles Michener in *Newsweek* hailed Don Siegel as a 'classical storyteller'.

Rewatching *Escape from Alcatraz* today, one is struck more by the film's compromises and calculations, its slackness and star-worship. By comparison, *Riot in Cell Block 11* seems a minor masterpiece. Siegel, who wrote extensively about the making of virtually every film he was associated with in *A Siegel Film*, his lively and articulate memoirs, offered only a plot synopsis of *Escape from Alcatraz* and then, surprisingly, little else. Although he always stayed friendly with Clint, he never directed him again. In later years, according to some friends, Siegel, watching from the sidelines, occasionally muttered his distaste for what the star had become.

*   *   *

Clint's appeal continued strong with audiences. *Escape from Alcatraz* had a spectacular opening nationwide and broke house records before tapering off. The film would eventually gross some $34 million domestically, way down from the usual Clint stratosphere, though not at all bad for an overlong, studied drama without much action.

Clint liked to boast to interviewers that *Alcatraz*, with its $8 million budget, had cost $10 million less to make than *Apocalypse Now*, in which he had spurned participation; and *Alcatraz* made more money, especially for Clint. According to the *Hollywood Reporter*, Paramount eventually paid out $1,985,000 in 'net points' to two of the film's contractual participants, likely Richard Tuggle and Don Siegel. Additional monies were paid out to 'gross players attached', probably only Clint. Reportedly the star was paid fifteen per cent of the worldwide revenue *in addition* to all his other fees.

Although most of the reviews focused on Siegel's directorial ingenuity, Clint also scored acting points. Already a 'Clint emotes!' syndrome – like 'Garbo talks!' – was at work, whereby the slightest variation in his Man With No Name or Dirty Harry guise warranted extravagant praise from critics who applauded the star for stepping out of his formulaic persona. Making a stark film about a jailed man stirred such plaudits.

More than one critic commented on the audacity of the film's opening sequence, where the middle-aged star is strip-searched and photographed from the rear in the buff as he is escorted to his cell. How bold that was of Clint to bare himself at his age! Never mind that it was one of the most ponderous set-ups in the film: theatrical lighting, portentous close-ups, a mean jailer barking a welcome.

Off camera, the star nearing his fiftieth birthday was more than ever preoccupied with his appearance and well-being, and open to increasingly radical and experimental measures to ensure the prime conditioning that had blessed his life.

Although, around this time, Clint denied published reports that he had undergone a face-lift, the actor was engaged in other surreptitious activities to keep himself attractive for the public. He secretly entered into a comprehensive programme to bolster his health, forestall ageing, promote longevity. The 'life extensions' plan Clint embraced was intended not only to heighten the star's healthy appearance but to serve his needs of fluency and ease in interviews and at public gatherings.

It wasn't until April 1981 that Durk Pearson and Sandy Shaw completed their manuscript, *Life Extensions*, but the star already had been a devotee of their unusual regimen for some time before. Clint is depicted pseudonymously as 'Mr Smith' in their book, and his real name withheld 'because of his concern that irresponsible tabloids might take quotes out of context and otherwise distort the contents'.

Durk Pearson was an MIT physics graduate who had made the transition from scientific consulting to research 'aimed at enabling a human being to live to one hundred and fifty years with the physical and mental powers of an adult in the prime of life', according to the book's dustjacket; while his co-author, Sandy Shaw, was a UCLA chemistry graduate whose field of expertise was the study of ageing processes.

Life Extensions touted megadoses of nutrients and other boosters as a preventive and cure-all. Although he avoided recreational drugs like the plague – anyone who entered the realm of Malpaso who faintly resembled a 'doper' was swiftly booted out the door – Clint now adopted the complex combination of pharmaceuticals and supplements recommended by Pearson and Shaw.

In their book the authors relate how they met Mr Smith, 'one of our heroes', at a dinner arranged by Merv Griffin, the television personality known to Middle America for his eager-to-please demeanour. (Up in Monterey County, Clint and Merv Griffin were occasional dinner and tennis partners.) All the authors were willing to say was that Mr Smith was a professional actor, well known for his physically vigorous roles.

'He has put together his own experimental life extension formula and has explored various nutrients and prescription drugs for this purpose,' the authors wrote. 'While experimenting with these materials, "Mr Smith" has been careful to have clinical laboratory tests and consultations with a research-oriented physician.'

According to the authors, Mr Smith started out taking two or three '000' gelatine capsules full of choline (about three to four grams) per day, and then maintained that dosage. He also started out by taking one hundred to two hundred micrograms of selenium in yeast (a dosage later upped to three hundred micrograms). 'He says,' Pearson and Shaw wrote, 'that when using this, he feels good and alert.'

Indeed, the choline, along with two hundred and fifty milligrams of Deanol, or Deaner®, a day 'had a beneficial effect on his speaking ability, verbal facility, and recall, so that he could remember to say things during an interview instead of afterward when it was too late. Once, he spoke effortlessly for two hours at an event, whereas ordinarily, he would speak for only a short time like ten minutes. One time he told us, "I couldn't shut myself up!" "Mr Smith" used to be a man of few words in his public appearances, but the elevated levels of brain acetylcholine have brought him a new facility with the spoken word.'

That wasn't all. Mr Smith was a willing guinea pig for other health experiments, the authors reported. '"Mr Smith" has been using Hydergine® as well, about six milligrams a day,' the authors wrote. 'He reports that during the past one and a half years he has had no colds or flu as long as he takes Hydergine'.® Hydergine boasted 'powerful antioxidant effects', according to Pearson and Shaw, said to stimulate the natural immune system.

Their account continued: '"Mr Smith" is physically active and engages in demanding sports such as skiing where minor injuries are inevitable. He says that he has had very good luck using DMSO for skiing bruises, but he has not had the dramatic experiences with it that some others have had, probably due to his tougher skin and capillaries.'

However, tough skin and capillaries required moisturizing, and Clint found a solution for that as well. '"Mr Smith" uses a home-made formula containing NaPCA (the sodium salt of pyrollidone carboxylic acid), the primary natural moisturizer in human skin. He finds it great for an aftershave, for going out in the evening, for skiing, shooting on location, and in other drying environments. He particularly likes its non-oily character'. He also took a 'personal experimental antioxidant formula of nutrients and prescription drugs' to further shield his skin and refresh his hair follicles.

The authors reminded readers that Mr Smith 'works out to keep in good condition' and is in 'excellent shape'.

'We told him,' they continued, 'that he could get much more out of his exercise by using certain nutrients which cause the brain's pituitary gland to release growth hormone . . . "Mr Smith" has been using the growth hormone releasers L-arginine and L-Dopa in conjunction with exercise, usually taking L-Dopa an hour before and L-arginine about twenty minutes before. He reports that, when using L-Dopa, he has *much* greater stamina.'

'"Mr Smith", now fifty years old, says that he can run longer and faster now than he could five years ago, even though he was exercising and taking good care of himself then. He also says that he feels "better than ten years ago maybe"'.

Mr Smith's daily nutrient mix of antioxidants, taken in three or four divided doses, was itemized by Pearson and Shaw: 'Ten thousand IU of vitamin A, two hundred milligrams of vitamin B_2, three grams of vitamin B_3 (niacin), three grams of vitamin B_5 (panthenate), one gram of vitamin B_6, one milligram of vitamin B_{12}, six to seven grams of vitamin C, three thousand IU of vitamin E, one–two grams of PABA, small amounts of biotin and folate, two grams of cysteine, three hundred micrograms of selenium (as sodium selenite), two hundred milligrams of ten per cent beta carotene, and about one gram each of the bioflavinoids rutin and hesperidin complex.'

To this long list was added: 'Extra quantities of C (three to four grams a day), L-arginine (for workouts, six grams a day), and L-Dopa (one-fourth gram per day).'

On top of all this, according to Pearson and Shaw, Mr Smith also ingested canthaxin, a carotenoid ('chemically related to the yellow colouring matter in carrots, beta carotene'), intended to control sensitivity to sunlight and prevent sunburn. First he used about one hundred and twenty milligrams per day; then he switched to every other day. 'He looks as if he has a beautiful golden-bronze sun tan,' the authors gushed.

The daily doses of nutrients and antioxidants even helped this animal-lover with his allergies to horses and household pets. 'Throughout his childhood, "Mr Smith" had frequent contact with animals without noticeable allergic response,' Pearson and Shaw reported. He first detected the development of animal hair allergies 'in his mid to late thirties', they wrote. At first, it was cat hair, then dog hair, then the hair of other animals – including horses. It started with stinging, reddened, itchy eyes, then sneezing and even itchy skin.

'"Mr Smith's" use of the antioxidant nutrients and prescription drugs has almost completely eliminated those allergies. He can now comfortably occupy a room with a cat or ride a horse without eye or skin irritation, antihistamines, or other allergy medications. Indeed, he can now play with cats and even rub cat hair into the sensitive skin on the inside of the elbow without skin itching.'

Although Clint never publicly admitted that he was the famous 'Mr Smith', the link was convincingly made in gossip columns. Insiders also confirm that Clint acted behind the scenes to help the authors obtain their publishing contract from Warner Books, a division of Warner Communications. Clint had percentages and involvement in continuing Malpaso book tie-ins, including a Dirty Harry line of paperback novels.

Of course, the megadoses of nutrients and drugs urged by *Life Extensions* could add up to an expense that was out of the question for ordinary blue-collars. Certainly Clint could afford the costs, but typically he was 'comped' with all the pills and ingredients he desired. In time, he would pay Durk Pearson and Sandy Shaw back.

Sondra Locke was also mentioned in *Life Extensions* as 'Miss Smith', but she didn't have the same consuming fitness concerns. She didn't jog or work out regularly. She played a little tennis, but was a half-hearted skier. Partly because she was much younger than Clint, her involvement with Pearson and Shaw was also half-hearted.

But she had other important health concerns, including two pregnancies with Clint that occurred while the couple were still in their 'honeymoon period', late in the 1970s.

The responsibility for birth control in their relationship, according to Locke, rested primarily with her. However, Clint did espouse ideas about what constituted proper anti-conception measures. When they first got together, the actress had been taking birth control pills, but Clint was worried about the health issues raised by regular use of the pill. So, at his urging, she switched to an IUD, until the star, according to Locke, complained that the IUD interfered with his pleasure during sex.

Then Clint recommended that the actress enrol in a birth control course at Cedar-Sinai Hospital in Los Angeles, which advocated a process of regulation similar to the old-fashioned rhythm method of abstinence on days of high fertility. It was Locke's job to keep track of her daily temperature readings and mark off the high and low days on the calendar.

The system was fallible, however, and their first pregnancy transpired during the summer of 1978, just as they were completing *Every Which Way But Loose*. When Clint learned that the actress was pregnant, the star told Locke he didn't really want any more children, and that he didn't think children would fit into their lifestyle. Clint insisted he was not the type of person who had *ever* wanted children – that was Maggie's impetus. This first pregnancy occurred *before* Maggie had read any published reports about their illicit romance, and *before* Maggie had confronted Clint, so the inopportune timing added to the pressure on Locke to adopt Clint's position.

It was Clint, according to Locke, who made the suggestion that maybe she should consider an abortion. Although the abortion was a 'mutual decision', in her words, Clint played on her uncertainty, and her wish to accommodate 'his desires and needs and happiness'.

'At the time I very much wanted to please him,' Locke recalled.

Clint obtained the name of a doctor at UCLA and drove Locke there to have the procedure. Clint didn't come in, and had someone else pick her up afterwards, because he had a scheduling conflict with one of his important appointments.

After the abortion, Locke returned to the Cedar-Sinai classes. They made a decision to stick with the rhythm-type method, hoping to perfect whatever mistake they had made with the first pregnancy. Then the second pregnancy occurred – almost a year later, during the following summer of 1979. By then Clint had split up with Maggie, and Locke was more than ever conflicted. They were up at the Rising River Ranch when they discussed what to do. Once again Clint was adamant that children did not loom in his future. Once again he encouraged the actress to have an abortion.

'I cried,' said Locke. 'I was upset. I asked him how much he loved me. He said he adored me. I was his Snow White. I was his princess. We would always be together. Not to worry.'

Locke flew down to Los Angeles alone, went to the hospital alone, was picked up and taken home afterwards by friends. Clint had to stay up at the ranch, he said, because he had made a prior commitment to entertain Frank Wells and his wife.

Although these auguries were hardly positive, Clint moved to make amends. Clint's decision to let Locke buy a new house closely coincided with her second abortion and ultimate tubal ligation ('You know, Jane had a surgery to prevent surgery,' Clint mentioned. 'What do you think of that?').

'I don't think I consciously understood it at the time, but finding a house, and building a nest, was also a way of licking my wounds about the tubal ligation,' Locke wrote in her autobiography. 'This home would be my baby.'

With a realtor friend, Locke searched for weeks and weeks. On the handful of occasions when Clint came along, with his usual insistence upon absolute secrecy, he introduced himself as 'Mr Anderson', even when he happened to be wearing a *Thunderbolt and Lightfoot* T-shirt. 'Clint and his six-four frame were so recognizable as Clint Eastwood that the sales agents, trying hard to keep a straight face,' recalled Locke, 'always looked at their feet when they addressed him as "Mr, Anderson".'

Eventually Locke found a large, two-storey house, built around a garden with a central fountain, on a rolling hill in Bel Air on Stradella Road. The back view looked out over the city of Los Angeles and to the west could be glimpsed the Pacific Ocean. The house had been unoccupied for quite some time. The hillside was overgrown. She and Clint would have to install a tennis court and a swimming pool. Roy Kaufman thought it looked too much like a 'fixer-upper'. But Locke loved it. Clint took a look and said fine, Kaufman would handle all the details and sign all the bills, the house would be put in Kaufman's name, but it was hers to own and to fix up, from top to bottom.

When the actress mentioned that she also wanted to buy a house for her husband, Gordon Anderson – so that he might share in her rising fortunes – Clint surprised her by saying that he would buy him one as a gift. It was the least he could do, he liked Anderson so much, and that was something he admired about Locke, her loyalty to her friend from youth. There was a house on Crescent Heights that Anderson had eyed for some time, which was now on the market for $300,000, and Clint bought it – paying for it the same way he paid for many of the houses he bought, all at once, in cash.

Subsequently, the actress was surprised when Roy Kaufman came to her with a lease arrangement for the Crescent Heights place. Kaufman explained that the lease was for Clint's benefit as well as hers, a money-saving device. All the money Locke paid out according to the lease would be channelled back into the house by Kaufman and Bernstein, which owned the property on paper, but represented her best financial interests as well as Clint's. Still, the lease made her very uncomfortable, so she spoke to Clint about it. He assured Locke that it was just a piece of paper, and she was just unsophisticated in money matters. The actress offered to take her salary for *Any Which Way You Can*, and apply it to the lease, buying the house outright. That offended Clint, who said that he wasn't going to take her money. It was a gift. Not to worry.

So Locke took the lease and signed it the same way she signed all of her contracts – that was the kind of person she was – without reading the fine print too closely. Anderson did likewise. Later, Clint's lawyers would be happy to point out the subclauses and actual ownership. Later, Clint's lawyers would be happy to point out that all of Locke's alleged conversations with the star about the Stradella Road and Crescent Heights houses were overheard by no one else, and therefore had no independent corroboration.

Meantime, Clint purchased another house in Carmel on San Antonio Avenue near the ocean. Locke could be expected to visit and stay over, but basically this was Clint's roost where he might 'be alone' away from Hollywood – i.e. for him to entertain other women.

In spite of his apparent commitment to Locke, Clint managed to play the field when the actress wasn't around. There continued to be new 'mystery ladies' in his love life. One of those in the Carmel area, whom he met around 1980, turned out to have the same kind of longevity with the star as Jane Brolin, Roxanne Tunis and others.

Jacelyn Reeves, a pert, slender blonde from Seattle, was an airline hostess who, though she travelled extensively, lived in a rented home in Carmel. Clint was so taken with her, when they were introduced at the Hog's Breath Inn, that he invited her up to the Rising River Ranch. Her polite turndown served both to confuse and intrigue Clint.

At their next meeting, Clint was cool because of the previous rebuff, and Reeves turned aggressive. That launched them into bed and a relationship that would blow hot and cold for the first couple of years. Interestingly, Reeves was in her thirties when she and Clint first got together, and unsure of the identity of her biological father. Because she was born in Seattle during the period when Clint was living there, and because he confided in her his belief that he might be the father of a child born in Seattle around that time, they joked that Reeves might be his daughter. He liked women to call him 'Daddy' anyway, and that was one of Reeves's pet names for him.

Although Reeves had first met Clint at the Hog's Breath, she never turned up there again when Clint was in town unless invited. Most of their late-night rendezvous were arranged at discreet locations or at her home, where she took special care with romantic lighting and touches. And this gave Clint options at his San Antonio address, which in any case was very close to Reeves's residence.

By contrast the house on San Antonio was decidely unromantic. Untidy and uninviting. Clint liked to boast that, when he bought the house from an older couple, it was fully furnished, so he never had to buy a stick of furniture – and he didn't, keeping the same old stuff. The books on the shelves also belonged to the previous occupants, and so the library in the house stayed someone else's books. Clint really didn't care to change (i.e. buy) anything; for years, the kitchen spices still had their 1960s price tags. Visitors to the house were taken aback by the piles and piles of old newspapers, empty water bottles strewn around, dustballs and cobwebs everywhere.

The one part of the house that Clint threw himself into was the Carmel stone front that he had meticulously rebuilt by a local craftsman, who lived on one of Clint's other big properties up the Carmel Valley. Inside, the house was downright funky, but the new exterior was tasteful and impressive. People who knew Clint well joked that the San Antonio house was the perfect metaphor for the star: a great façade.

Bronco Billy – which came along next – arose out of Sondra Locke's belief in the benign Clint as well as the star's need to make amends over her abortions.

Reading the script, Locke instantly saw Clint as the decent, charming Bronco Billy, one of the rare parts in which the star wasn't some swaggering superhero. 'That [*Bronco Billy*] was my pet project,' remembered Locke. 'I begged him to do it. I loved that one so much. It was, I would say, the most *me* of anything I did or was involved with, with Clint.'

Bronco Billy scenarist Dennis Hackin and producer Neal Dobrofsky had first met at the University of Arizona. Dobrofsky drifted into documentaries and commercials, while Hackin concentrated on writing. Their partnership had spawned 1979's *Wanda Nevada*, the only film in which Henry Fonda co-starred with his son Peter, but otherwise

Hackin and Dobrofsky were the type of industry novices Clint preferred.

Their project arrived at Malpaso in the usual circuitous fashion – not through Clint's agent or the studio – but through another 'little blonde gal' (in Richard Schickel's words) acquainted with the star. This blonde stopped by Clint's table at Dan Tana's restaurant one night, and told him she was working for Hackin and Dobrofsky's production company. The writing–producing team had a light comedy that Clint might be interested in; the story was all about a sharp-shooting, knife-throwing cowboy who heads up a ragtag circus troupe that is perpetually mired in crisis and debt.

Clint said to send the script over, although he handed most of those that came into Malpaso to someone else to read first. Fritz Manes read *Bronco Billy*, and admittedly he wasn't crazy about it. Then Locke read the script, and told Clint the story had more warmth than anything he had ever done. Bronco Billy was part fraud, part hero, someone audiences might take to heart and root for. There was also a substantial part for her in the script as the spoiled heiress who joins the circus and falls in love with Bronco Billy.

Clint recently had met Frank Capra, and now, with his growing awareness of film history, he saw the script as an opportunity to 'do a Capra'. *Bronco Billy* 'had some values that were interesting to explore in contrast to the Sixties, Vietnam and Watergate, and so on', the star would later inform the *Los Angeles Times*. 'The guy [the Bronco Billy character] was fun to play because he had to be stripped bare of all his dignity, like the character in *It's A Wonderful Life*, to make the transition and end up all right.'

In August 1979, *Bronco Billy* was announced as the next Malpaso film. Once committed, Clint moved with speed. He would star and direct. Also cast in the film were Scatman Crothers as the ringmaster; Sam Bottoms as a Vietnam draft dodger who performs rope tricks; Dan Vadis as an Indian snake handler; Sierra Pecheur as his wife, a tribal dancer; Geoff Lewis as the runaway heiress's scheming husband; and another Malpaso semi-regular, Bill McKinney, as a one-armed utility man. This troupe of big-tent losers was one of the script's most captivating conceits, although it may be too much to claim, as certain French critics later did, that they represented folk who 'have transcended the boredom of daily life and chosen to live in a universe of poetry and imagination'. What they did represent was the side of Clint that saw himself as the reluctant leader of a motley troop of followers – in essence, Malpaso.

Hackin and Dobrofsky were awarded the customary honorary producer titles, with Bob Daley downgraded to executive producer. Gene Lourie (a.k.a. Eugène Lourié), once one of France's leading art directors, who had worked with Jean Renoir and Chaplin, was hired to create the film's stunning production design.

The hiring of a new director of photography was a sop to Sondra Locke. An editor, photographer and director of 'B' features, David Worth had worked with the actress, pre-*Josey Wales*, in *Death Game,* a horror film about maniacal lesbians. Locke liked Worth and appreciated the way in which he had managed to photograph her under low-budget conditions. Worth was versed in the 'gun and go' style that Clint preferred, and knew how to work rapidly, using natural or low-source lighting.

Actually Worth had been interviewed by Don Siegel first as a possible candidate to act as Bruce Surtees's operator on *Escape from Alcatraz.* But Worth did not enjoy full status in the cameramen's union, and the union had vetoed him. Worth thinks that the union's opposition to him probably consolidated Clint's determination to employ him for *Bronco Billy.* Partly for this reason, a new entity, Robert Daley Productions, a replica of Malpaso, was formed. Robert Daley Productions could sign Worth to a seven-year contract, and then as a 'new' company, it was permitted to make a signatory deal with the union and employ Worth. Incensed union leaders went after Clint, Malpaso and Warner Brothers with all kinds of threats, according to Worth, but Clint's lawyers finessed the situation.

According to Worth, he and Fritz Manes scouted the main locations, choosing the towns and terrain around Boise, Idaho. Clint only had Polaroids to look at before the filming started on 1 October. 'Clint is very much a delegator,' explained the cameraman. 'He never walked on the location until he walked on the set to shoot.'

Clint said little to Worth about the richly-textured look of the photography, which many critics commented on approvingly, afterwards. Clint trusted Worth's instincts. One thing Worth noticed is that the director relied on a conventional method of coverage – shooting distanced master shots, tight over-the-shoulder shots, enough close-ups and even 'reverse masters', so that his editor would have plenty of options. All that coverage didn't slow them down. 'Seventy-five per cent of the time Clint prints either the rehearsal or the first take,' said Worth. 'The most number of takes he'll do is three.'

When Clint himself had dialogue in a scene, according to Worth, he usually shot the other performers first, feeding his own lines to people from behind the camera. The director saved his own close-up for last. This had built-in drawbacks. Describing one key scene, Worth said he noticed that when feeding the lines to people off camera Clint's performance was especially fresh; by the time everyone else had been 'covered' and the angle was switched over to him, however, Clint's energy faltered.

The cameraman pre-lit every set so the director could come in and shoot in any direction, three hundred and sixty degrees, without moving lights. Because they used multiple cameras in the tent scenes, they were able to execute as many as sixty set-ups a day. *Bronco Billy*, widely considered one of Clint's most artistic films, was also one of his fastest. The shoot was scheduled for eight–ten weeks. The photography wrapped inside of six, allowing the studio once again to trumpet Clint's speed and economy. The $5-million-plus budget was 'dirt-cheap, by present standards' noted the *Los Angeles Times*, although as usual there were no specifics about Clint's salary.

Clint singing a song with Merle Haggard was Snuff Garrett's idea. 'CE never made that wish,' said Garrett. 'He never brought it up once, never. I brought it up.'

Garrett was once again supplying the soundtrack. Garrett had first seen the *Bronco Billy* script during his annual summer getaway to Stuart Island north of Vancouver in British Columbia, which was a 'power vacation' that he sponsored for a number of select guests. Clint was one invitee, mixing there with record company executives and celebrities like Roy Rogers. They'd be stuck in the middle of nowhere – all guys, no telephone, no TV – for a week of beers, conversation and great salmon fishing.

Garrett had recruited Merle Haggard to sing one of the songs in the film, and then his hitmakers came up with another, called 'Barroom Buddies', a kind of call-and-response number. Haggard cut his portion at RCA in Hollywood, then Garrett jumped in his van and drove up to Idaho, where Clint was busy filming *Bronco Billy*. In Clint's trailer he buttonholed the star and showed him the sheet music with his part of the lyric. Would he sing a duet with Merle Haggard? Clint said okay, and when he returned to Hollywood they ducked into a recording studio for a few hours.

'He mounted the mike and we put it down,' said Garrett. 'He's not a singer, period, but who is? A lot of them, that's their main gig. CE's got a lot of other stuff to do. All the time I worked with Clint he never had a bad word to say. We had a lot of fun together.'

'Barroom Buddies', with Merle and Clint (who were never in the same room together for the recording), would eventually soar to number one on the country music singles list, while Merle's solo made it to number two. Garrett and Clint realized by now that they had a good thing going. Garrett owned another song he had cut a year earlier and hawked around without success, called 'You're the Reason God Made Oklahoma'. For a half interest in the production costs – $11,000 – Garrett formed with Clint an equal partnership in their own label, Viva Records. 'You're the Reason God Made Oklahoma' then went to number one too, and by their second year of operation, according to Garrett, Viva could boast several of the year's biggest country hits.

Clint was more the silent partner, while Garrett handled the roster and the releases. Garrett would also round up the mainstream country music for the sequel to *Every Which Way But Loose* – *Any Which Way You Can* – and *Honkytonk Man*. Then Garrett suffered a stroke in 1984. When the producer decided to sell his interest in Viva, Clint sold out too, but by then he had made a fortune on his casual investment. Incidentally, the buyer of Viva – the backlist and contract artists – was rock queen Tina Turner.

The music was one of the bargain assets on the profit ledgers of *Bronco Billy*.

Warner Brothers once again threw a lavish party for disc jockeys and music programme directors in New Orleans. The studio announced that it had reserved 1316 theatres for *Bronco Billy*, the highest number yet for a saturation opening. Based on the number of theatres, the substantial advertising and the publicity expenditures (reported as $2,650,000 for pre-opening, and opening, network, radio and print 'buys'), the studio's top sales executive, Barry Reardon, was quoted as predicting that when the film besieged theatres in June 1980, its first-week gross might climb to over $12 million.

So, when the film opened 'soft', which was unprecedented for any Clint Eastwood film in the preceding decade, the studio went into shock. How soft? Terry Semel was quoted in the trades to the effect that the 'opening was not up to par with the high standards of most Eastwood pix'. Alan Friedberg, the president of the National Association of Theater Owners (NATO) and the head of a large chain of theatres in Massachusetts, explained to the *Wall Street Journal*. 'People like to see Clint Eastwood with a cheroot in his mouth and a gun in his hand, preferably a .357 Magnum. But in *Bronco Billy* he's in a comedy and he doesn't even have a chimp . . .'

Clint, up in Jackson Hole, Wyoming, where he was already shooting *Any Which Way You Can*, flew into a rage. Top executives were obliged to hop into a company jet and fly up at the weekend for a tense meeting with Clint, who was threatening to leave the studio. Frank Wells, the supreme diplomat, was there for the occasion, along with Charles Gold, the advertising and publicity consultant who was also one of Clint's close friends. Although the Golds (Charles, his brother Bill, and Charles's wife Kitty) designed much of Malpaso's promotional material – the posters, print and TV spots – there had always been a grey zone between what Malpaso proposed and what the studio would accept.

Although Clint had approved of the initial *Bronco Billy* sales approach, now he oversaw a swift change to a more 'modern motif', according to a published report, 'casting all connection with the Western genre aside'. The original ad illustrations had showed Clint in full costume astride a bucking stallion; the new advertisements would carry a large 'mug shot' of the star, a line drawing of a car caravan, and (unusual for a Clint campaign) favourable critics' quotes. The upshot of the Wyoming showdown was that Clint also gained increased power over Warners' 'ad–pub' division. And advertising and publicity for future Clint films would emphasize his growing acceptance among film critics.

There were favourable critics' quotes aplenty. Kenneth Turan, writing in *New West*, said *Bronco Billy* 'shows enough class to rank as the unexpected joy of the season'. *Variety* found the film 'genuinely funny', while Kevin Thomas of the *Los Angeles Times*, a longtime Clint backer in print, described it as 'thoroughly delightful'. Janet Maslin in the *New York Times* paid the sincere comedy a somewhat backhanded compliment as 'the best and funniest Clint Eastwood movie in quite a while'.

Published reports of the ad–pub reshuffle, and of the film's weak box-office reception, had a way of stirring up critical favour even more. Suddenly, and quite remarkably, Clint took on the aura of an underdog. Some reviewers went back to see *Bronco Billy* and reviewed it again, *after* it had been in theatres for a few weeks. 'At the box-office it's slipping and that hurts,' wrote Ginger Varney in the *Los Angeles Weekly*. 'It hurts me and all the other big and little kids who ever wanted to run away with the circus.'

Bronco Billy was, *is*, a film with charm and vitality. But in spite of strenuous efforts by Clint, Warner Brothers and cooperative critics to elevate it to the status of a Capraesque classic, the film remains more of an appealing oddity. Clint's performance is winning, and he is especially good in the big top scenes, clowning and grandstanding.

But at the same time the star was constantly winking at the camera so that the character resists the credibility or poignancy of a Frank Capra hero. And outside the circus tent, it was the usual Clintisms. The star had to have his barroom brawl (indistinguishable from any other Clint film), his defence of a sexually-assaulted Locke (fourth time in a row for her), his familiar acting riffs (the slow burns and zoom close-ups of vein-bulging).

However at ease in the lead role, where Clint really stumbled was in his broader responsibility as director. In his hands, the character Locke played was cold, off-putting, one-dimensional. All of the subplotting – thin antics involving her husband (Geoff Lewis) and lawyers in New York board room scenes – falls flat. The major setpieces – the circus tent fire, the abortive robbery of the train – never quite gel. The writers had the swell idea of an inspirational ending, with Bronco Billy's circus refurbished with a new big top of American flags stitched by pixilated volunteers. But Capra would have better orchestrated the script, the characters and the thematics. Under Clint the emotion fizzles.

Warners put a saving face on the lean box-office. Although the film's domestic grosses stalled at around $18 million, a studio executive informed the *Wall Street Journal* that 'sale of the film to television networks, pay television and foreign markets' was expected to add substantially to the total revenue. Excluding the sequel to *Every Which Way But Loose*, Clint would stay away from outright comedy in the near future, and another five years would pass before he again donned Western garb.

Nobody had expected *Every Which Way But Loose* to turn such a profit, and weeks went by in 1978, with the ticket-take mounting, before Malpaso warmed to the inevitability of a Philo Beddoe sequel.

Jeremy Joe Kronsberg had got busy in the meantime writing a new orang-utan script called 'Love, Max' – later changed to *Going Ape!* – which he hoped to direct. It was going to star two adult females and a baby orang-utan, *not* Manis, and the script was nearly completed by the time Malpaso got back in touch with Kronsberg, as Clint was obliged to do contractually, to propose the follow-up to *Every Which Way But Loose*. Since in his mind *Going Ape!* was a completely separate property which didn't have a single character from the first film, the writer didn't even mention the project.

Kronsberg went away from his meeting with Clint and Bob Daley at Malpaso and wrote another Philo Beddoe script dropping Clint's character into the desert, in a story that pitted desert-dwellers against invaders in recreational vehicles. He didn't even include the Sondra Locke character, since she had thoroughly spurned Philo Beddoe in *Loose*.

Meanwhile, Clint found out that Kronsberg had his own ape script, and that Paramount was hot to get it made. The star felt betrayed. When Kronsberg delivered his sequel, the script was rejected – whether because Clint hated it, or because Malpaso had commissioned it only as a formality, in accordance with his contract, he never discovered. Another scenarist, Stanford Sherman, who would also crank out the sequel to *Cannonball Run* for Burt Reynolds, was rushed in to concoct a fresh story line.

Sondra Locke's part was restored. The other familiar faces from the first film – Ruth Gordon, Geoffrey Lewis and Clyde the orang-utan – would be augmented by a rival fighter, to be played by Bill Smith, and by a big city better (another negligible character for Harry Guardino) sizing up the odds on the climactic bare-knuckle fight.

Meanwhile Kronsberg, to his astonishment, found himself being sued by Malpaso, which claimed he had usurped its ape-sequel rights. But Paramount didn't flinch, and *Going Ape!* went ahead, with Kronsberg fending off legal attacks while the first-time director guided a cast that included *Play Misty for Me* star Jessica Walter. Then, when Malpaso and Warners began to withhold his profit participations from *Loose*, Kronsberg countersued.

Clint and Kronsberg met again during depositions. The writer remembers the star being friendly and relaxed, even though Kronsberg's life – because of the pressures and mounting debt – had been turned into a hell. Clint disliked depositions and court appearances, and he didn't like to over-rehearse with lawyers, any more than he over-rehearsed for a screen role. The right wardrobe would sometimes give him the right feeling for a film, and it was a funny thing about Clint's court appearances that sometimes he visited the studio costuming department to pick out a suit for his legal appointments.

It was a bad sign, for this particular case, that at one point the court-appointed mediator, a retired judge, asked the star for his autograph. The case against Kronsberg was weak, however, since *Going Ape!* really didn't have anything to do with *Every Which Way But Loose*, and since Kronsberg originally discovered the orang-utans for his first script. Clint could not really claim to have cornered the market on ape-films. There was pressure to come to an understanding, on Kronsberg's part to get his Warners' payments restarted, and on Clint's side, to settle things before the release of *Any Which Way You Can*. As usual with Clint, a gag order was put on the settlement, and all the details were withheld from the press and public.

'By definition,' is all Kronsberg will say, 'any settlement means they pay you more than they want to and less than they owe you.' Kronsberg's name would be credited on screen for *Any Which Way You Can* ('based on the characters created by . . .') but, according to sources, he received only a flat fee and was excluded from any further participation. *Going Ape!* was released to theaters without much ado. And so, for that matter, was *Any Which Way You Can*.

Certainly none of Kronsberg's ideas for the sequel were used. When the creator of *Every Which Way But Loose* saw *Any Which Way You Can*, he was 'shocked and dismayed', Kronsberg admitted.

Sondra Locke had the same name, Lynn Halsey-Taylor, although there was no explanation as to why she is a different person. This time Halsey-Taylor is nice, sweet and amorous (the first and only Clint film where Locke's character wasn't sex- or violence-prone). 'Who *am* I?' the actress kept asking the star during the filming. 'How can I be the same character as before?' 'If they're thinking about that . . .' answered a plainly irritated Clint. He assured her that nobody would notice or care.

The appeal of the original film was sadly watered down, although Clint got to show off his physique, bust up a few barrooms, sing a duet with Ray Charles. Snuff Garrett's forgettable score once again yielded the requisite hits. Warner Brothers threw a gala party for the music industry press and disc jockeys in Nashville, including expensive give-aways. Not only tickets and soundtracks, but the studio, according to *Billboard*, 'sent limited-edition, numbered Clint Eastwood watches to country radio stations and retailers taking part in the *Any Which Way You Can* promotion. The watches were ordered as a thank-you from Eastwood, the film's star, and are also being used as gifts for winning in-store displays in contests sponsored by Warner–Viva Records.'

The studio had booked the film in a new record number of theatres: 1560. The Christmas 1980 opening mandated 'the highest guarantees ever' from exhibitors, according to *Variety*. And it was another feeble Christmas for the other studios; among the films that didn't make waves were *Stir Crazy*, *Seems Like Old Times*, *Popeye*, *The Formula*, *Tribute*, *9 to 5*, *A Change of Season* and *Flash Gordon*.

Even so, *Any Which Way You Can* would barely clear $10 million gross domestically. Its dismal failure ensured the end of the Philo Beddoe series.

Not only in court cases, but behind the scenes at Malpaso there was conflict.

Some people thought Sondra Locke had something to do with caus-ing the trouble and with the 1979–80 changing of the guard that was hardly unprecedented at Malpaso. Locke's image, to some, was cool and crafty, someone who seemed able to manipulate Clint. Others who had known Clint longer – and knew what had happened to Arthur Lubin, Bill Thompkins, Ted Post, Jack Kosslyn, Sonia Chernus and others – believed that it was one of the star's periodic 'down' cycles in which his failures or frustrations were blamed on other people.

One of the winners was the man elevated to director for *Any Which Way You Can*: Buddy Van Horn. Van Horn's father had been a veterinarian on the Universal lot. Bequeathed to Clint by Don Siegel, the one-time stunt man and stand-in had worked on Malpaso productions for a decade. Van Horn was also the star's preferred golf partner on locations. Although stunt man and golf partner might not have been the world's greatest recommendation for a director, Clint wanted someone who was 'not a man with a personal statement to make', in the words of Richard Schickel.

One of the losers was James Fargo, the man who had directed one Dirty Harry film (*The Enforcer*) and the first Philo Beddoe hit, *Every Which Way But Loose*. Fargo had worked for a bargain-basement salary. 'With Clint, if you stay loyal, you work every show,' explained Fargo. 'You are guaranteed X number of hours, usually slightly above scale but not a lot above scale. You may not make as much money on one show as someone else, but if you play the game you keep working.

'Here's the problem,' Fargo continued. 'When you're promoted from within, it's wonderful. But I got scale on *The Enforcer*, and slightly above scale – which had jumped to $100,000 for a guarantee of ten weeks – on *Every Which Way But Loose*. I directed a movie in between and got $300,000 for it, back when $300,000 was a lot of money. On the one hand, you're grateful, and on the other, you have to bite your lip.'

Fargo made the error of thinking his directorial talent might have had something to do with the merits of *The Enforcer* and *Every Which Way But Loose*. When the money for *Loose* started pouring in, Fargo couldn't bite his lip any longer. He instructed his agent to phone Malpaso and ask Clint to throw him a mere fraction of the profits. That may have been the worst thing Fargo could have done. He never again worked for Malpaso. If anyone asked, Fargo had screwed up a number of scenes in *Loose*, and Clint, not Fargo, was responsible for all those deft comic touches.

Rexford Metz, who'd photographed *The Gauntlet* and *Every Which Way But Loose*, also fell out of favour. He was conducting special effects tests for *Firefox* with a small nucleus of crew, including helicopter pilot James Gavin and producer Bob Daley, when 'we did something Clint took offence at' and Clint closed down the operation. With Clint 'unreachable', as was chronically the case between films, Daley had been forced to make a decision the star took issue with; when Clint complained, Daley had made another indiscreet remark. 'Well, next time, stick around and make your own decisions.'

Metz had been scheduled to photograph *Bronco Billy*. The crew, including camera operator Jack Green, was the crew he had hired. When Metz was fired, David Worth was hired. Thinking about it afterwards, Metz figured it could have been because he was always nagging Clint to push up the lighting on scenes. It could have been anything with Clint – even an embarrassing loss at tennis. Metz and his girlfriend had beat Clint and Sondra Locke at doubles one day. 'When it was over,' said Metz, 'and we were talking about it up in our room, my girlfriend said, "That was really cool. We can walk around and say we beat Clint Eastwood at tennis." I said, "I think we made a major mistake. I think we should have let them beat us."'

David Worth, whose photography for *Bronco Billy* was widely admired, would only last two films – the two Robert Daley productions. It must be said that Worth is eternally grateful to Clint for providing 'my Ph.D. in film-making'. Bruce Surtees came back for the next couple of Malpaso films, and behind him, coming up fast and breathing hard, was Jack Green, doing his utmost to emulate Surtees.

Robert Daley Productions then disappeared after *Any Which Way You Can*. The reason is that, after more than twenty years as his friend, and ten as his producer, Daley had been cashiered by Clint. Officially, there were no announcements, and still today people whisper about the reasons. Still today it is vague as to why.

But insiders say that Daley had not proved sufficiently enthusiastic about Sondra Locke. He felt loyal to Maggie. He felt compromised by the other women in Clint's life he knew about. He didn't enjoy the penny-pinching on budget and salaries, and the scrambling for 'complimentary' goods and services, which he knew was unnecessary, especially when Clint was worth hundreds of millions of dollars.

The whole idea of Robert Daley Productions, which was supposed to be a clever business dodge, turned out a kind of sabotage. Daley's name not only became more prominent, he was able, for the first time – the only person, besides Clint – to obtain 'profit points'. Clint might not have liked that precedent, people say.

When Daley didn't show up very much on location for *Bronco Billy*,

Clint grumped. The producer preferred to stay behind in his office, no doubt with the growing feeling that he was swimming at sea without a life preserver. His assistant, Fritz Manes, whom people either loved or hated, was a 'people person' whose energy and ambition seemed indefatigable. Manes was happy to take up the slack.

In addition to which, Manes and Clint hung out together and joked like teenagers. Manes had just separated from his wife and liked to party. He was a wild man with a profane sense of humour. Daley wanted to go home after hours to his wife and 'he'd never go out and get laid or have a few laughs', in Manes's words. Daley was a book-lover, a collector of first editions who could quote poets of the classic age. Manes was a former Marine who could get people marching in unison, dress them down as assholes, in Clint-fashion.

Daley's strengths – budgets and book-keeping – had been mastered by the boss. Clint told Daley he would receive his credit on *Any Which Way You Can* – albeit 'executive producer' – but it would be his last production under Clint's aegis. Clint had a 'we're-closing-the-office-down-for-awhile' routine that usually avoided messy personal confrontation. 'This is where I first saw this routine, but I didn't recognize it when it was my turn,' said Manes. 'He never does it [the firing] himself, see. That's the whole point. He always has someone else do it, or else he "closes" the office. "We're not going to do anything for a year, so we'll close the office."'

Manes took over the producer chores for *Bronco Billy* up in Wyoming, while Daley sat in his office, dazed by the idea that he was supposed to clear off his desk and go home. He awaited further orders. 'Clint would call the office every day,' said Manes, 'and get his secretary, Betty – who had taken over from Judy Hoyt – on the phone. The first thing he would ask is, "Is Daley still there?" She'd lower her voice and go, uh-huh. She had to work with the guy every day and probably he'd be standing right by her desk. Clint'd say, "I can't fucking understand it. Why doesn't he just get out of there? He's through! Why doesn't he just clear his shit out?" He'd be saying all this to Betty, with me in the background. When all this was over he'd say to me, "That asshole. I don't know why he isn't out of there." I'd say, "Clint, why don't you just tell him yourself to get out of there?"'

Manes had been Daley's best man at his wedding. Now he would succeed him as Clint's right-hand man and producer. This was the internecine tradition at Malpaso. 'I know that he [Daley] has blamed me, saying I got him,' insisted Manes. 'But I never got him at all, he got himself. He just rolled over and played dead toward the end.'

Some insiders thought Clint deliberately elevated the least-likely candidate to be his next producer. The choice of Manes, who commonly salted his vocabulary with an endless variety of expletives, would really 'stick it' to sensitive, literate Bob Daley.

'Clint's mind often worked in inverse ways,' explained Paul Lippman, who had his own falling-out with the star, 'for it is my contention that he sometimes went overboard for a friend – maybe even subconsciously – to make up for, or atone for, transgressions on other friendships which, for some strange reason, inwardly seemed to affect him deeply, but which transgressions, also strangely, couldn't be changed or assuaged.'*

For the first time, on *Any Which Way But Loose*, Manes would be credited as producer, although the film was officially a Robert Daley Production. But Manes wouldn't receive that high-sounding title very often. Although Manes would serve in a de facto producer's capacity on nine Malpaso productions – doing all the behind-the-scenes tasks that normally merit the credit – often his card on the screen read, ambiguously, 'executive producer', or even worse, 'unit production manager'.

'With this guy [Clint],' said Manes, 'if you got any credit for anything it was a miracle. He used to choke on the word "producer". "This is my . . . ah . . . uh . . . ahem . . . Fritz Manes . . . he . . . ah . . . uh . . . produces." He couldn't come out and say, "This is my producer."'

On Clint's next film, *Firefox*, a Directors Guild of America strike was threatening, so it was Manes's idea (or maybe Clint planted the suggestion) to get around union rules that kept the director out of the editing room by making the star not only the director but also the *producer*, so Clint could remain at the studio and at work on the editing without crossing picket lines or otherwise jeopardizing his DGA standing. Thus the credits would read, for the first time, 'produced *and* directed by Clint Eastwood'.

'Now, he sort of decided he liked that,' said Manes. 'He used to say,

---

* After accusing Clint of buying a piece of property that he had earmarked for Hog's Breath Inn expansion, Lippman sold out his shares in the Carmel eatery, and finally settled with Clint in court.

"Well, I don't like my name on the screen twice, and three times would be disastrous." He even fought for a long time the credit "A Clint Eastwood Film". He'd say, "You can't have 'A Clint Eastwood Film' starring Clint Eastwood *and* directed by Clint Eastwood". After *Firefox*, he started to say, "I can't put 'produced *and* directed by Clint Eastwood *and* Fritz Manes', can I? So you'll have to take another title: 'Executive producer''.' So I was often "executive producer" or even lower. Isn't that clever? Wasn't I stupid? I said okay.'

Deep down, Manes nursed a hope that his old high school buddy would give him acting breaks. Clint knew Manes had had that yearning since boyhood. The producer was short and funny-looking, with a moptop of hair; he was a hammy guy. But other Malpaso people seemed to have better luck than Manes in getting cute parts from Clint. Clint made fun of Manes's ambitions, setting him up in faceless bits, or giving him brief scenes that were predestined to be left on the cutting-room floor; even, in at least one instance, a scene in which Manes could be counted on to make a fool of himself.

In *Escape from Alcatraz*, Don Siegel and Clint handed Manes a bunch of lines as a prison guard. They told him he had a spotlighted moment in a shower sequence; the room was heavy with steam, as Manes scrunched down on the floor and called out for one of the inmates, 'Wolf! Wolf!' In the dailies the scene played like a dog barking, and everybody had a big laugh. Except Manes, feeling betrayed, who turned crimson.

'He set me up,' said Manes. 'He set me up for everything. He tried to make it out that my acting didn't matter. But he knew because we were friends that – from the time I was this big – acting was important to me. I was always going to get my acting break on the next picture, with him. Meanwhile, I'm out breaking my ass as a producer.'

As for Bob Daley, his name all but disappeared from films. People who encountered him at Malpaso in the 1970s invariably describe the producer as 'a wonderful man', 'super-intelligent', 'a classy guy'. Said to be devastated by what happened to him, he refused an interview for this book. At least he has the satisfaction of knowing that he is not unique. People quoted one of his telling cracks: If they ever called a meeting of all the people Clint has screwed over, they'd have to hold it in the LA Coliseum.

*   *   *

The public would never hear about such internal discord and high-handedness. The image presented by Clint's publicity and largely adopted by the press continued to be that of a man who was, in 'every which way', an anti-Hollywood exemplar of loyalty, generosity and humility. Now, as Clint turned fifty, as Ronald Reagan took the oath of office as the nation's fortieth president, it seemed part of his luck that he could do no wrong.

The two Philo Beddoe films had (almost accidentally) strengthened his hold on fans, and *Bronco Billy*, in spite of weak receipts, cast a spell over critics as never before.

Now some of the savviest critics who had been resisting Clint felt obliged to rethink him. Janet Maslin of the *New York Times* had rejected *Every Which Way But Loose* as a slack, harebrained muddle; yet Maslin found *Any Which Way You Can* 'even better and funnier than its predecessor', although she did add cautiously, 'either that, or intentional jes'-folks stupidity is beginning to look better than the inadvertent kind'.

Tom Allen, holding forth in the normally tough-minded *Village Voice*, hailed *Bronco Billy* as a wonderful film, 'the first movie where he [Eastwood] really puts it all together'. No apparent contradiction if it *was* Clint's first 'together' film, Allen went on to state that 'now it's time to take him [Eastwood] seriously, not just as a popularist phenomenon, but as one of the most honest, influential, personal film-makers in the world today'.

Warner Brothers was thinking along the same lines. John Wayne had died in 1979 – his last film, *The Shootist*, directed by, ironically, Don Siegel. Clint was heir apparent; nobody else had emerged with the Duke's box-office clout. Now the studio's publicity routinely compared Clint the actor not only to Wayne – but to Gable, Cagney, Cooper, Bogart – while also citing him as one of Hollywood's most artistic and personal film-makers.

More Clint interviews were published in which the reader was assured that the star 'rarely gives interviews and hardly ever makes public appearances' (Stephen Schaefer, US magazine). The ballyhoo that passed for journalism continued to extol his common-sense thriftiness, his down-to-earthness, his loyalty, 'a theme common in Eastwood's films and his private life as well' (Gabe Essoe, *The Los Angeles Times*).

No matter the out-of-wedlock children, the abortions, the messy ongoing divorce, some journalists could claim ignorance of the details; others were advised to steer clear of dangerous subjects. No matter that his film's female characters were frequently cutthroat whores, the surging publicity line preferred 'the feminist Clint'.

As Clint told *Cosmopolitan*, 'Macho is probably one of the most misused words in the language' (saying this in his 'hypnotic baritone, a voice that is both soft and strong', according to the correspondent). 'Over the years, I think the most macho guys on the screen were also very sensitive people. I think Bogart and Cagney and Wayne could all portray great sensitivity . . .'

The up-to-date Clint was different from the one once depicted in fan magazines as answerable to no one, including his wife. 'The truth,' Clint now said, 'is that strong men are sensitive and aren't afraid of showing it. It's the people who are insecure about their manliness who are averse to showing their feelings, who have to do the cock-of-the-walk, strut-your-stuff kind of thing. And it's the people who have to go around kicking over furniture all the time who are usually insecure about their manliness. Just like a woman who has to go around acting twitty all the time, flirting and chirping like a canary. A woman like that may be insecure about her femininity.

'Femininity is an inner thing – it's that simple. A woman doesn't have to be a centrefold to be beautiful. She could even have a low voice like Katharine Hepburn's. This culture has too many clichés and stereotypes.'

In the wake of this newfound respect for Clint, the Museum of Modern Art in New York scheduled a one-day tribute to Clint, along with a showing of four of his films. This occasion, in December 1980, anointed Clint artistically for those who hadn't yet picked up on that development. Pierre Rissient knew the museum people and Clint's name came up naturally in conversations. The MOMA tribute just happened to coincide with the nationwide release of *Any Which Way You Can*.

The four films presented to the audiences were *A Fistful of Dollars*, *Escape from Alcatraz*, *Play Misty for Me* and *Bronco Billy*. Clint appeared at the screenings of the two films he directed. Warner Brothers, of course, was helpful in providing new prints of the films as well as contributing to costs of the widely publicized event.

*   *   *

Clint was persuasive, expounding on sensitivity. Listening to himself, perhaps he persuaded himself. He liked to say that he was tired of doing the goddamn Dirty Harrys, but that Warners was always on his back, insisting on another one in the tough-guy series. Listening to himself, Clint flirted with the idea of burying Dirty Harry once and for all.

Sometime in the late Seventies, hanging out with Dennis Shryack, one of the writers of *The Gauntlet*, he learned about a script that Shryack and Michael Butler were working on. This was another full-throttle action picture with a loner cop battling organized crime; only this cop was weary and middle-aged and losing all the battles. The feeling in the script was that this would be the loner cop's last round-up.

'Jesus,' Clint told Shryack, 'that would make a terrific Dirty Harry.'

So Shryack and Butler began to turn the idea around for Clint. 'The theme had to do with Dirty Harry growing older and his preoccupation with death,' said Shryack. 'He visits his wife's grave – all sorts of things like that. It would have been the last Dirty Harry. We felt we could write it that way because he said he didn't want to do another one anyway.'

But Jo Heims died of cancer, in mid-1978, and Clint was shaken by the death of Heims, who was his age. He made a point of attending the funeral of the woman who had written *Play Misty for Me* and *Breezy*. He brooded about her death.

When, later, Shryack and Butler delivered their script, Clint called them up and said, frankly, he hated it. Shryack reminded him that he was well aware of what they were going to write. Clint said yeah, that was true, but the script just didn't work for him anymore. 'I think it probably cut too close to home,' explained Shryack, 'because he was feeling his mortality about himself – and also feeling a mortality about his favourite character . . .'

Clint considerately arranged for Warners to let the rights revert to Shryack and Butler, and later the script would be made into *Code of Silence*, one of the better Chuck Norris vehicles. A short time afterwards, the star phoned Shryack and made the gesture of asking him and Butler to go back to work on another script for him – this one a Western. Clint asked that it be crafted as 'a classic *Shane*-type Western'.

Meanwhile, Clint let it be known that he was on the lookout for another Dirty Harry.

CHAPTER TEN

The Teflon Clint
1980–1984

Clint got his start in Eisenhower's America; he had blossomed during Nixon's presidency; now, in the Ronald Reagan era, he would cement his position in the pantheon of Hollywood immortals. And the political tide during his career would be reflected, now more than ever, in films that slouched towards Republicanism.

Clint had backed Reagan for president in 1980 and supported his re-election in 1984. Reagan, who liked to relax by watching movies, was said to enjoy Clint's films as much as Nixon did. 'Go ahead, make my day!' the one line of dialogue worth reciting from *Sudden Impact* – would become the President's battle cry. Reagan wielded it, memorably, in his March 1983 showdown with Congress over the issue of raising taxes.

Just as there were covert activities in Reagan's White House, there was covert Reaganism in Clint's Malpaso. The hard-working, obscurely titled Fritz Manes finally got credit for something in Richard Schickel's biography of Clint as the man who, in the late 1970s/early 1980s, introduced the star to mercenaries who were working to make the world safe for democracy – a coup here, a bloodbath there, whatever. These included Bob Denard, a French soldier of fortune who had led a successful invasion of the Comoros Islands off the coast of east Africa; Mitchell WerBell III, an international arms dealer 'who specializes in the crafts of assassination and the freelance coup d'état' (Jim Hougan, *Spooks: The Haunting of America: The Private Use of Secret Agents*); and one-time Green Beret James G. 'Bo' Gritz, a freelancer leading the charge on the issue of MIAs ('Missing In Action' soldiers) presumed – never proved – to be held captive in Vietnam.

Denard was flown to Hollywood by Clint, who optioned the rights to his life story, and Bo Gritz took the star on a VIP tour of his counter-terrorist school in northern California. According to one account, Clint lent Gritz and his foot soldiers his ranch for a 'communications check' one day. 'With [Fritz] Manes supervising,' reported Josh Young in *George* magazine, 'the Warner jet in Burbank was flown to the ranch, loaded with M-16s, state-of-the-art communications systems, and camouflage gear. Later that day, Gritz and his men were detained and questioned for testing their equipment.' Manes told *George* that when the local sheriff contacted Clint, he told them the men were testing radio equipment for his next film.

These were dangerous people. Anyone who has read *Soldier of Fortune* magazine or seen a Chuck Norris movie will recognize the species instantly. But Clint identified with such macho soldier-types, he bonded with them, and that led to at least one episode of grievous folly.

Gritz was planning a raid into Laos to ferret out supposed prisoners of war. The US government had encouraged Gritz initially, then his official contacts began to shy away, compromising the prospects of the mission. Gritz couldn't seem to get a definitive go-ahead from Ronald Reagan. Clint, because he and the President conversed now and then – how often and about what precisely has never been revealed – had Reagan's private telephone number at his Santa Barbara ranch. Gritz asked Clint: would he phone the commander of the free world and bring up the topic?

Clint did so, phoning Reagan in late 1982, trying to enlist support for this half-baked scheme. 'The actor told Reagan that the government should be officially involved in POW rescue efforts, according to the testimony of those who briefed the [Senate Intelligence] committee,' the *Los Angeles Times* reported, 'and the federal government ought to help Gritz, not leave the matter up to individuals such as Eastwood.'

Reagan, however, consulted with his advisors, who warned him that Gritz was not to be trusted. That didn't stop Gritz – or Clint. According to subsequent press reports, Clint pledged to contribute $50,000 of his own money to Gritz's errand of patriotism. (Gritz's associates insisted the sum was lower, maybe $30,000.) A few other Hollywood celebrities came up with some of the operating budget, including a contribution from *Star Trek* Captain William Shatner.

His skullduggery partly financed by Clint, Gritz went ahead in November 1982, leading a dozen Americans and anti-Communist guerrillas from Thailand into Laos. Their incursion did not detect any MIAs but they did encounter a hostile patrol, which attacked them, with the result that one guerrilla lost his life. The irrepressible Gritz tried another raid in January 1983, with similarly hapless results: another life lost. When, one month later, the press reported these deeds, Gritz was roundly denounced by all sides as 'less a bloodied hero than an embarrassing nuisance', in the words of *Newsweek*.

Clint knew when to go into his man-of-few-words schtick. He refused to comment publicly on the débâcle he had helped bankroll. It wasn't until a few years later that he felt comfortable saying it was all an ill-advised, patriotically intended gesture.

In truth, his exertions on behalf of Bo Gritz could have been written off as a 'business expense'. With his next Dirty Harry movie on the back burner, Clint was browsing around for a project that would ennoble counter-intelligence agents. The Bob Denard possibility came a cropper when the script Clint had commissioned proved unsatisfactory. Fritz Manes was acquainted with James H. Webb, a decorated Vietnam War veteran, active in veterans' affairs and Republican circles, who had written *Fields of Fire*. Clint also considered adapting one of Webb's novels, which anguished over the mistakes and compromises of Vietnam, before thinking better of it.

Bob Denard was a dubious character: seen as a liberator by some, as a gangster in fatigues by others. It would have been interesting to see how Clint approached that subject. Inevitably, the star preferred his heroes in uniform simplified. When Clint finally found what he was looking for – in British adventure novelist Craig Thomas's 1977 bestseller *Firefox*, and, later on, in *Heartbreak Ridge* – he fell back on comfortable stereotypes.

Thomas was known for his espionage stories pitting Western forces against the iniquities of the Soviet system. *Firefox* was about a retired Air Force special forces expert recruited for a dangerous espionage mission in Moscow. His assignment: steal a Soviet supersonic war plane. This book, the ultimate 'airplane read', had been recommended to Clint by a Carmel lady friend; two others who read *Firefox* and recommended it were friends James W. Gavin and Thomas Friedkin – the former, a pilot who had assisted with second-unit 'aerials' over the years; the latter, the wealthy former president of Pacific Southwest Airlines and CEO of Gulf States Toyota, at whose Colorado residence Clint sometimes 'comped' his skiing vacations.

Clint had been fiddling around with *Firefox* even before *Bronco Billy*. He was filming *Firefox* even as he was shaking hands with the true-life mercenaries. And *Firefox* would be finished and released by the summer of 1982, around the time Gritz was making final preparations for his POW liberation raids. Did Clint think his involvement with Gritz would amount to a publicity tie-in, and is this one of the rare times his usually astute salesmanship backfired?

Some of Clint's Republican movies were subtle in their conservatism. Leaving aside the Philo Beddoe sequel, *Any Which Way You Can*, *Firefox*, the first, new Malpaso production of the Reagan decade, was a blatant Cold War throwback, coming just as Reagan effectively relaunched that era with his denunciations of the Soviet Union as an 'evil empire'.

The film would find ways to refight the Vietnam War, the POW issue slyly introduced via the traumatic flashbacks of Clint's character. Retired from the military because of 'delayed stress syndrome', Mitchell Gant (Clint) is recruited for a 'mission impossible' to Moscow because nobody else could handle the derring-do. One reason it has to be Gant, the film explains, is that, because of his Russian lineage, he can speak the language (though no scenes demonstrate any real fluency).

Because Gant is a lone-wolf, Clint would end up carrying most of the scenes without his customary sidekick, or ragtag band of companions. Two-thirds of the story was an agonizingly tedious build-up to the hijacking of the plane. And although the film was photographed partly on location at Thule Air Force Base in Greenland, they might as well have retired to Warners' soundstages and saved on costs – a budget reported at $18 million, the steepest yet for Clint. The Greenland landscape would be a non-factor on the screen, with most of *Firefox* taking place indoors or up in the sky.

The attraction of the book for the star was undoubtedly the airborne sequences, with Clint the mountain-climber and sky pilot revelling in the aerial acrobatics. But nobody at Malpaso had solved the problem of how to photograph the airborne sequences credibly, the special effects flying was less than riveting, and there were no surprises in the long cloak-and-dagger drama (124 mins).

The film's partisans might point to the humanistic subplot involving the plight of Soviet dissident Jews. This was an unexpected theme, considering that Malpaso was one of the most goyish companies in all of Hollywood, the exception being Clint's accountants, attorneys and agent. (He would boast, in anticipation of a legal battle, 'I'll put my Jews up against theirs any time.')

Many of the Warners executives were Jewish, of course, excluding Clint's friend at the top, Frank Wells. Wells, in any event, would resign from the studio in late 1981, to take a break and fulfil his dream of climbing seven of the world's highest mountains. Clint's constant differences with the studio departments, especially with marketing, led him to gripe sometimes that the way he was treated was owed to the fact he didn't belong to their exclusive club. He and Fritz Manes had their own nicknames for studio officers who happened to be Jewish – 'Wejs' (pronounced 'Wedges') or 'Jews' spelled sort of backwards. 'The Wejs are coming!' is what they'd say to each other, with a wink, when one of the Jewish executives called to say he was coming over for a talk.

Clint sometimes preferred the women in his life to be strong and independent-minded. Other times they were expected to be docile and unquestioning. With more than one woman the star referred to himself as 'Daddy', but some topics were taboo with 'Daddy': especially anything to do with his money or investments.

He had made a point of letting Sondra Locke know that he would take care of her financially. The actress didn't have to worry about money, Clint reassured her more than once. His advice was to put part of her income into the trust of Kaufman and Bernstein, and let them augment her earnings with their far-sighted business moves.*

All the time Locke was playing opposite the world's most bankable movie star, she was probably making less of a salary than any other leading lady in Hollywood. Locke started out at $18,000 for her role in *The Outlaw Josey Wales* – half of what she had earned for her previous film job. By the time of *Any Which Way You Can* – which, unlike the first orang-utan picture, everybody saw as a guaranteed moneymaker

---

* The investments weren't necessarily 'far-sighted', Locke said in an interview. Some were 'bad investments' that she tried hard to back out of, after breaking up with Clint. But Clint – via Kaufman and Bernstein – refused to buy her out of the bad ones, and this became one more way in which she 'lost' with Clint.

– Locke had worked her way up to $100,000 (compared to Clint's salary, before guaranteed percentages, of $3–5 million). Her agent couldn't seem to get a higher price; he happened to be Leonard Hirshan (on the advice of Clint, who liked to have his eggs all in one basket).

Locke had managed to extract a few contractual 'points', but these were always 'net points' to be distributed after a certain level of profits had been attained. Clint himself had switched to 'gross points' a decade before, but he didn't discuss such details with the actress who was his housemate. So Locke, who never gave 'points' any thought, would learn the hard way what many in Hollywood know: Net points rarely yielded pay-outs.

Nor, in the 'honeymoon period' of her relationship with Clint, did Locke give much thought to other contradictions: the rages the supposedly laid-back star was wont to fly into; the one-sided rules that belied his reputation for fairness; the sometimes shabby treatment of old friends and Malpaso employees.

Mechanical failures were one thing that really triggered the anger of the onetime student of motor engines. Clint was always in a hurry, and the slightest malfunction or flaw in design of equipment would slow him down. Video machines, automatic lights, door locks – telephones were the worst. There was one in their home that Clint was forever accidentally knocking over because it was so lightweight, and then forever hurling it furiously across the floor.

One time, frustrated with something that went wrong with his desk phone, Clint got so upset he proceeded to trash his office. Outside the door, his secretary and Fritz Manes heard the crashing and smashing of stuff for long minutes before Clint emerged, pale and tight-lipped, leaving for the day. It was up to the secretary and producer to clean up all the mess, get new and better equipment in there, do it all cheap and fast and, most importantly, pretend that it never happened.

Another time, they were all up at Rising River Ranch – Clint and Sondra Locke and Fritz Manes and his wife. They were having a peaceful evening, Clint was stirring the logs on the fire. Only the fire wasn't cooperating, the poker wasn't doing what it was supposed to do, logs kept rolling out. Clint kept trying to shove the logs back in. Finally, the star blew up. He took the poker and cleared the whole mantel of the figurines and knickknacks that Locke had lined up there, and then turned and started beating on the wall of the fireplace. 'Cocksucker!' he screamed. 'Motherfucker! Piece of shit!'

'Sondra, Audie and I just watched him,' recalled Manes. 'Just sat there. You have no choice. What could you do?'

Arguably, Locke saw less of this than other people, because Clint usually made a point of behaving in gentlemanly fashion around her. And as time went on, she – like other close friends of the star – learned that the best thing to do once any warning signs were noticed was to disappear. The actress believed sympathetically that Clint was under such constant, tremendous pressure from his stardom that these outbursts were understandable, an aberration in his personality.

For most of 1982–3, Locke was happy to keep busy supervising the remodelling of the Stradella Road house. According to her, Clint was interested primarily in the tennis court, swimming pool and hot tub. All of the other details of craftsmanship were left to Locke's taste. She made a point of copying ideas from the Andalusia, one of the first apartment complexes she had lived in in Hollywood, to which she had formed a sentimental attachment. To this end Stradella Road walls were knocked down, stairs rebuilt (wooden handrails carved to order), fireplaces adorned with specially aged bricks, front gates and garage doors replaced, columns changed in the living room, bathrooms torn up and redone with handmade ceramic tiles. (One of the Warners jets flew the actress to Mexico to pick them out.) The courtyard fountain was an exact replica of the one she had loved at the Andalusia.

All the art and ironwork was custom-made. Warners sent craftsmen over from its studio design departments to aid in the renovation. Locke's husband, Gordon Anderson, was often at the house, helping out with tasks. And she was just as often at Anderson's new house, helping him with advice on his decorations and furnishings.

When Clint and Sondra Locke moved into the Bel Air house in late 1982, Fritz Manes bought the Sherman Oaks place. By now marriage had mysteriously receded as an issue between Clint and the actress. The fact that Clint still wasn't divorced, and that there was no end in sight to the negotiations between his lawyers and Maggie's, changed the equation. And Locke agreed with Clint that marriage was 'just another piece of paper'. Regardless of any momentary qualms, and in spite of the two abortions, she already felt 'married' to him, living as 'husband and wife'. And as far as Locke knew, Clint felt the same.

A native Oklahoman, Clancy Carlile was a novelist who was also a journeyman country-and-western musician. Carlile's 1980 novel, *Honkytonk Man*, was a stirring, picaresque tragedy about the dreams and death of a country music singer during the Depression era. When his manuscript sold to Simon & Schuster for publication, Carlile's agent – who worked for the William Morris Agency in New York – took charge of peddling the screen rights, mainly to in-house clients. 'William Morris only submitted that book to William Morris people because they were going to keep it in the family,' Carlile recollected. 'They wanted Clint Eastwood's percentage, they wanted my percentage, and if somebody else got involved, they wanted that percentage too.'

Honkytonk Man is focused on the quest of Red Stovall, a small-time country musician whose ambition it is to record his songs and make an appearance on the Grand Ole Opry. The character, a tubercular alcoholic, is a composite of country music legends Jimmie Rodgers and Hank Williams, both of whom died tragically young. Driving on a cross-country quest from California to Nashville, Stovall passes through dust-plagued Oklahoma and picks up a carful of companions, including his fourteen-year-old nephew, the boy's grandpa, and a teenage girl with her own starry-eyed dreams.

Although the novel was essentially downbeat, with Stovall dying at the end of the story, the narrative had the novelty of being from the fourteen-year-old nephew's point of view. Irene Webb in the West Coast office of William Morris spotted the book's potential for Clint, who 'apparently was looking for a vehicle for his son', according to Carlile.

Red Stovall wasn't often sober and couldn't be trusted to drive. That's where the teenaged Whit came in handy. Relatives delegate the boy to deliver Stovall, alive and sober, to Nashville. The book seemed a natural vehicle for Clint's fourteen-year-old son Kyle. Privately, the star had been voicing hopes that his first-born might follow in his father's footsteps and carry the Eastwood name forward in show business. Now Kyle would be able to spend 'quality time' with his father while receiving a career nudge.

Author Carlile was not a Clint Eastwood fan, however, and thought the star was probably all wrong for the part of Red Stovall, who in the book is age thirty and visibly ill, jaundiced, with cavernous eyes. Not only that, Stovall is blessed with a singing voice which is described as 'a sort of high lonesome sound, a sound that came to be associated with train whistles and piney woods, with wandering and weariness'. When Stovall breaks into song, it is, as Carlile wrote, 'with a feeling of loss so profound that it could break hearts'.

Nonetheless Clint was a leading William Morris Agency client, he had a country music background from *Rawhide* days, and more recent chart status as Merle Haggard and Ray Charles's singing buddy. Plus Clint owned his own music label, which was ongoing with Snuff Garrett. After reading Carlile's book, Clint made it clear. He wanted *Honkytonk Man* as his next film. He wanted to star *and* direct.

Quite apart from the country music angle, Clint might have seen Stovall as someone like himself – a 'people's artist' underappreciated in his time. The book had other elements bound to appeal to him: for one thing, the entire story took place 'on the road', with Stovall tooling around America in a luxurious black Packard, 'a beautiful and powerful and well-made machine', in the words of the book, capable of accelerating up to 110 miles per hour on the highway. *Honkytonk Man* also had one of those goggle-eyed girl tagalongs that followed Clint around in films (just as they sometimes did in real life).

The book had a rather curious scene when the drunken Stovall sleeps with the girl, Marlene, and she becomes pregnant. But the blame is all Marlene's, and Stovall's tirade positively Clint-like: 'Marlene's a star-fucker. You know what that is? Well, I'll tell you. There's a special breed of women that likes to hang around performers and fuck 'em when they get the chance. And the bigger the star you get to be, the more star-fuckers you get. Seems like the only way women like that can feel important is to fuck somebody that's important. Know what I mean? Okay. But you gotta be careful with 'em, 'cause anybody who'd do something like that is crazy to begin with, and they're liable to get you into a whole lotta trouble. Might yell rape at any minute, or hit you with a paternity suit, just so they can show everybody that they got fucked by a star.'

William Morris couldn't keep the book completely a secret, and so the bidding for *Honkytonk Man* in Hollywood was heated. Other producers competed with Clint, upping the price. Though Clint's offer wasn't the best, he was the only one willing to promise Carlile that he could adapt his own novel into a screenplay, and that made all the difference to the author. Carlile had already warmed up to the idea of Clint, when he was invited up to the Rising River Ranch to meet the star for the first time.

Carlile discovered right away that he and Clint had a surprising amount in common. They were both the same age (Carlile was just a few months older). Both had served as firefighters in the California Division of Forestry. Both had hung out at Hambone Kelly's in Oakland – when Clint was living in Piedmont and Carlile in a nearby city.

Sondra Locke was also present for their first meeting. 'She highly influenced him to buy the book, actually,' said Carlile. 'She really liked the book, I think more than he did. I remember her enthusing about the scenes'. Clint was more taciturn, and when Carlile asked the star who he might get to play Whit – mentioning another boy actor of the time – Clint said 'something sort of evasive'. He never mentioned Kyle.

But Carlile liked and was impressed by Clint. Boning up on the star's more recent films, Carlile understood that Clint was trying to get away from his tough-as-nails image in *Bronco Billy* – and now *Honkytonk Man*. The deal was eventually agreed upon, and Carlile began to write the script, his first for motion pictures.

Clint offered no advice, 'nothing at all', in Carlile's words. Just 'Go write the script'. They had dinner a few times, but these talkathons weren't really story conferences.

Sometimes, the talk was peculiar. When Clint learned that Carlile was presently living up in Bend, Oregon, he asked him, 'Are you "getting any" up there?' A little thrown, the writer responded by telling Clint that he had been dating a local bulldozer operator. Clint seemed to be all ears for any salacious titbits. 'He's got this little-boy, lascivious attitude, and he wanted me to tell him some stories,' noted Carlile. 'I thought, "What is this? Can't the guy get any? Why would he be asking me if I was getting any up in Bend, Oregon?" It was almost as if he was asking me to fix him up.'

Clint wanted a couple of small but revealing changes from the book. For example, in the novel it is Red Stovall who offers his nephew Whit a reefer in a juke joint, leading to a comic vignette with the boy getting stoned. Although Clint didn't mind a scene where his character took Whit to a whorehouse, he didn't like the idea of handing a reefer to his own son, even for pretend's sake. The star preferred that a black man in the roadhouse be seen smoking that reefer and then for this man to hold the joint under a table where Whit is sitting; the boy would appear to get an accidental 'contact high'. In this and other ways, Stovall was made less of a rascal, more of a 'good guy'.

Stovall's Packard had been omnipresent in the book, careening through scene after scene. But it was Clint who changed the Packard to the less antique – if equally high-powered luxury car – Lincoln Continental, for the usual reason that he preferred to take a Continental home after the film. 'That really made me mad,' said Carlile, 'because by the end of the story, this car should have been really beat up, but he, because it was going to be his car afterwards, would only ever break a headlight or so.'

The ending of the story was also modified at Clint's behest. The novel ends with Red Stovall's posthumous installation into Country Music's Hall of Fame. In the film, a song he recorded on his death-bed becomes a hit on the radio before his body has mouldered in the grave. It's an instant-gratification ending. 'I would never have put it in,' admitted Carlile. 'The plausibility factor really bothered me there.'

The age and singing ability of Stovall was something that Carlile and Clint understandably never discussed. Writing the script, Carlile 'just left the age [of Stovall] out and hoped for the best', he said. In his modest-sounding interviews Clint would shift attention from the intended 'high lonesome sound'. 'He's not that great a singer,' Clint told *Rolling Stone* about Red Stovall, 'but he writes some interesting things.'

For the 'interesting things' on the soundtrack, Carlile hoped for 'an authentic score with music of that era', people like the Carter Family or Flatt and Scruggs. When Clint muttered something about preferring 'new music', Carlile started to have a queasy feeling. One song in the novel is called 'Pale Rider'. Carlile played for Clint a tape of his bar band performing that number. Clint got extremely excited, and even floated the idea of retitling the film 'Pale Rider'. But Carlile cautioned him. 'If you do that,' the writer commented, 'everybody's going to think it's a Western.' Lo and behold, a couple of films later Clint did borrow Carlile's title – and for a Western.

After listening to 'Pale Rider' and briefly showing enthusiasm for that song, however, Clint never again brought up the subject of music.

The writer eventually learned that the star had given Snuff Garrett carte blanche to manufacture more saleable ditties. *Honkytonk Man* would be weighed down with new 'hit factory' songs that didn't much serve the authenticity of the film, although Clint had the rights sewn up and sales were ensured for the Viva–Warners album featuring the likes of John Anderson, Porter Wagoner and Ray Price.*

'I got the image then,' noted Carlile, 'and I still have that image in my mind – because it's reinforced all the time in Hollywood – of Hollywood being like a little trough full of money with a bunch of piglets surrounding it. You have to fight your way into that money trough, and they're going to try to keep you out every way they can.'

The first draft of the script proved acceptable to Clint. No rewrites required.

Bruce Surtees would return as the Malpaso cameraman, and for the first time Edward Carfagno would serve as production designer of a Malpaso film. Carfagno was a forty-year veteran of the major studios who had been nominated for the Academy Award thirteen times, winning for *The Bad and the Beautiful, Julius Caesar* and *Ben-Hur*. He would stick with Malpaso for the next eight productions, his contribution to pictorial values important to Clint's growing artistic acclamation.

The ensemble recruited by Clint and casting director Phyllis Huffman included Verna Bloom (as Red's sister, Whit's mother), young newcomer Alexa Kenin (as Marlene) and veteran John McIntire (as the cantankerous Grandpa). True-life country legends Ray Price, Porter Wagoner and Marty Robbins would drop by for cameo appearances.

Honkytonk Man would be shot speedily during the summer of 1982, inside of six weeks according to studio publicity, on locations in northern California, Nevada, Oklahoma and Tennessee. The Edward Hopper–Walker Evans evocation of 1930s America was the painstaking collaboration of the production designer and director of photography.

---

* The cross-promotion for *Honkytonk Man* would include simultaneous release of the soundtrack LP and four singles. A $250,000 Warners budget was set 'to promote the film's music at radio and retail, a figure exclusive of supplemental print and TV advertising', according to a report in *Billboard*. Not only would country radio receive 'extensive time buys', according to *Billboard*, but there would be albums, weekend 'all expenses paid' trips awarded as prizes to couples, Warner-distributed Atari video games for giveaways and 'Wallace Beery-styled "Depression jerseys" stamped with the *Honkytonk Man* logo' made available for contests.

All locations were picked out by Edward Carfagno and Fritz Manes; according to Carfagno, Clint hated to look at models of sets, sketches, even Polaroids. By now the director just preferred to show up on the set and trust his instincts.

Although a boon companion of Clint's during preproduction, Clancy Carlile discovered, to his surprise, that he was *persona non grata* once the filming began. Again and again the writer phoned Malpaso and was told that he had to hold off visiting the set until Clint really 'got into his role'. Finally, the author of the novel and script got mad, threatening to contact Clint personally; only then was he permitted to visit the filming.

'There was a very unwelcoming attitude,' said Carlile. 'I don't know why. You tell me. He didn't want me on the set and he didn't want me seeing the rushes. I could tell by his attitude. I'd ask, "Is it okay if I come and see the rushes?" He'd say, "Well, I guess so."'

What might have bothered Clint is that Carlile, more than anyone, knew the built-in compromises. More than anyone, Carlile might be expected to be judgmental about Clint playing Red Stovall, and to know whether the actor measured up to the challenge. It took Carlile by surprise, but suddenly the star seemed defensive around him.

'There were two or three scenes that I watched,' remembered Carlile, 'and you can tell which scenes – when I'm there, behind the camera, and he's looking at me. It amazed me that he would care, or that he would be aware of me being there. But when he was acting in those scenes, he was looking at me as if he was afraid I was going to pull my hair out and scream and say, "That's not the way it's supposed to be done." It surprised me, because he's Clint Eastwood, and who the hell am I?'

For such a fast shoot, *Honkytonk Man* proved another awfully *long* Malpaso production. It is hard to be cynical about a film which for 122 minutes is insufferably earnest and aims so much to please. It is equally hard to be held spellbound.

As an actor, Clint was still half-lazy, and the whole performance was a cheat, with Red Stovall softened up for audiences. He may be scarecrow-gaunt in the book, but in the film Stovall is pretty chipper, letting Clint show himself an undeniably sexy guy 'as some shirtless scenes in the flick will attest', in the words of *People* magazine, with the star evincing 'the tone and musculature of a man twenty years his junior'.

It isn't until the final reel that Stovall shows any ill effects from all the drink and cigarettes. Then the tubercular tragedy kicks in heavily. Though moviegoers have been primed to love him, Clint's deathbed scene seems almost perfunctory, not as moving as it should be, lacking depth from an actor who hedged at playing losers.

The singing was really Clint's, however – obviously so. When the star sang, he made a constipated face, and his numbers do sound strangled. Stovall comes off less like a Hank Williams-type than a walk-in on 'amateur night'. 'Clint can't sing and he can't do that character,' conceded author Carlile. 'He fell down miserably when it came to that character.' The true musical highlight belongs to Marty Robbins, who plays a back-up singer who steps into Stovall's shoes in the recording studio after Stovall is levelled by a spasm. All too fleetingly, the film is transported by Robbins's archetypal baritone.

Although US critics tried to like the 'well-intentioned but weak' (Janet Maslin, *New York Times*) film, not many succeeded. In the main, as Norman Mailer, one of the film's defenders, pointed out, the reviews were cruel. Yet even those who found *Honkytonk Man* 'kitschy bathos' (Joseph Gelmis, *Newsday*) ended up praising Kyle Eastwood.*

The star recently revealed to be an adulterer, and now anxious to be portrayed in the press as a devoted father and a 'more reflective Eastwood', in the words of *People* magazine, deployed Kyle in publicity to illustrate the 'sense of change' that had come over him. Clint made his peace with *People* by appearing on the cover with Kyle.

The experience of the film, in fact, momentarily deluded Clint into thinking his son had a shining future as an actor. Insiders tell the tale of Clint lobbying fiercely for Kyle to star in *The Karate Kid*, which Columbia, then housed on the Burbank lot, was planning to make in 1983. Clint was floated as one possible director, but when the star sought out the film's producer, he was offended that his casting notion wasn't taken seriously. The boy lead went to Ralph Macchio instead. Somebody else directed.

Clint had to have some measure of petty revenge. Because Coca-Cola owned Columbia, henceforth Coca-Cola would be banned from Malpaso. No Coca-Cola on T-shirts or on the set. And if Coke insignia

---

* Sondra Locke, who knew from her own screen debut how to be true to adolescence, had coached Kyle's acting, at Clint's request.

showed up on a dispenser in the background of a shot, filming ground to a halt while the angle was changed, or a Pepsi machine brought in.

Meanwhile, Clint's slow-moving divorce from Maggie finally approached reality.

The divorce was not deemed 'official' until May 1984, when a Monterey court declared 'irreconcilable differences' between the couple. By that time, the Eastwoods had been married for thirty-one years. Disposition of their common property was agreed upon, although the specifics were never made public.

Reports indicated that Maggie received a cash settlement in the neighbourhood of $25 million, along with the Eastwoods' house and waterfront in Pebble Beach. She gained custody of the children, while Clint was granted liberal visiting rights. Apart from the children, the Eastwoods would retain a co-interest in certain businesses, helping to ensure that Maggie would honour the same diplomatic reserve about Clint in the press that she had maintained throughout their marriage. A clause was inserted in Clint's will, just in case, barring his ex-wife from any claims to further inheritance.

Although Clint's wife had become romantically involved with another man (real estate developer Henry Wynberg, who had once squired Elizabeth Taylor around), she was known to be extremely bitter towards Sondra Locke, whom she blamed for the break-up of her marriage. Locke's very name 'visibly distressed' Maggie, according to *People* magazine, which sympathetically profiled Clint's first wife in February 1982.

Sondra Locke meanwhile had stumbled onto something Clint coveted – his next Dirty Harry property. Earl E. Smith and Charles B. Pierce had been partners on the low-budget *Wishbone Cutter*, the last non-Malpaso film Locke had acted in, which was shot after *The Gauntlet*. Now Smith and Pierce came up with a screen story that was meant to provide the actress with a starring vehicle independent of Clint. Since *Any Which Way You Can*, Locke had been growingly anxious about her public image as someone whose career was umbilically attached to the man she lived with.

When Locke showed the story to Clint for his reaction, he surprised her by saying he liked it quite a bit for himself. He was in the market for a Dirty Harry script and thought this scenario, with a little tweaking, would suit the bill. He would keep in the big part for Locke; she would have a chance to climb aboard the Dirty Harry gravy train.

Dean Riesner, the script alchemist, was brought in for a meeting with Clint and Locke – it was still her project, sort of – and Riesner made the same mistake as some others did of thinking the actress was actually in charge. 'She had a lot to contribute,' remembered Riesner. 'She had definite ideas. She was kind of sprawly with her hair in a rubber band, and she looked at you like "fuck-you-Charlie".'

Riesner was not unenthusiastic about another job for Clint, and he dashed off a short treatment retooling the story for the two of them. But Clint was preoccupied with another project – *Firefox* – so Riesner figured there was no urgency; he made time to rewrite *Starman* for Columbia. He didn't seek permission from Clint or notify Malpaso, however, and that might have been his gaffe. Clint probably resented it that his Dirty Harry film had been put on the back burner, and Riesner, who wrote more and better Clint films than anyone else, never again worked for him.

Also, by now Riesner came with an expensive salary. Joseph Stinson, a Clint fan acquainted with Charles Gold and Kitty Dutton – the Malpaso advertising couple – was a bookstore clerk who wanted to break into movie writing. The Golds recommended Stinson heartily. He came cheap and he was eminently available. Clint met him, liked his unpretentiousness, hired Stinson to write the fourth Dirty Harry.

The money he might have saved on Stinson was lost in another category. Producer Fritz Manes argued forcefully that since the project originated with Sondra Locke, the actress should receive $350,000 for the film – three times her previous fee. Clint, who was going to direct as well as star in *Sudden Impact*, grudgingly delivered the raise. But he didn't like to be backed into a corner financially. Was it purely circumstantial that this would be the last time he and Locke co-starred?

The cast would include Pat Hingle and Bradford Dillman, a couple of Dirty Harry veterans. Again the cameraman would be Bruce Surtees. But the editor for the first time in ten years was not Ferris Webster, who finally had trespassed with Clint.

According to nearly everybody, Webster was a crusty type whom Clint tolerated because of his indispensable expertise. A heavy drinker, Webster was getting old, his hands were growing clumsy, his eyesight was beginning to go during *Firefox*. But Webster was also a griper, and one of the things Webster liked to gripe about was Clint's sloppy continuity. Clint had been spoiled by Webster's ability to piece together footage so that it always made sense, but Webster's worst challenge, according to Malpaso insiders, was *Firefox*; not for the first time was the editor tearing his hair out.

The final straw was one of Webster's tirades that Clint happened to overhear during postproduction up at Rising River Ranch. It was late in the morning. Webster was trying to make progress with the samey footage. 'You know, this pisses me off,' the editor complained loudly. 'That cocksucker never shows up until one o'clock and then he expects me to work until midnight. And when he finally shows up . . .'

But Clint *had* shown up. He was right there, standing in the doorway behind Webster. The star didn't say a word, but that was the end of the veteran cutter. Webster wasn't exactly fired, but when the next Malpaso production was organized his name was absent from the crew. Joel Cox, his longtime assistant, had been promoted. Sondra Locke ventured to ask Clint, 'Did you retire Ferris, or even tell him what is happening?' and Clint replied, 'Why? I don't *have* to call him back.' Webster had started out *liking* Clint enormously, had spent much of his career working exclusively for the star. He had even moved up near Burney, thinking he would edit Malpaso films for the rest of his life. 'He died brokenhearted,' said Fritz Manes.

Joel Cox, along with art director Edward Carfagno and director of photography Bruce Surtees – as well as Jack Green, who was patiently waiting in the wings – would anchor the behind-the-camera quality of the Malpaso productions of the 1980s.

Sudden Impact was filmed in the late spring and early summer of 1983.

Apart from 'Go ahead, make my day!' – the line that entered the American lexicon – the script, the first one in the series without a veteran scenarist attached, offered little that was memorable, or intelligent-minded.* And as star, director and producer, Clint moulded this Dirty Harry more to his whims than any of its predecessors.

---

* That catchphrase had been kicking around the American lexicon for years before it caught fire out of Clint's mouth. Some people interviewed for this book guessed the star himself had tossed off the memorable dialogue, one of his ad libs. In fact, scriptwriter Joseph Stinson came up with the line, which was present in his script.

There was the redundant night-time helicopter shot circling San Francisco. There was Harry's lame friction with the bureaucracy and the visit to a diner where crime interrupts a coffee break. There were perfunctory moments showing Harry, deep down inside the same wardrobe and standard grimaces, as the soul of caring. There is the usual tad of comedy relief, mainly, it must be said, jokes about dog flatulence.

Clint's acting grew wearier with each Dirty Harry. The violence grew more preposterous. Harry in San Francisco was only a prelude to the real business, which begins with Harry banished to a small town for a murder investigation. The audience knows the murderer is Jennifer (Sondra Locke), because the film has already offered a close-up of her unzipping a hapless victim, preparatory to fellatio; when the man is thus understandably distracted, she pulls out a gun and shoots him point blank.

But this slinky lady has a list of persons she aims to kill. One of those lurid flashbacks that Clint loves hints as to a gang rape she is avenging. The gang of rapists include the cowardly son of the local police chief and a foul-mouthed lesbian who cheered from the sidelines. This permits Clint the eventual crowd-pleasing moment of decking the bad dyke, although it is Locke who has the privilege of blowing her away.

The finale takes place at the beach, scene of the original crime. The rapists have figured out that Jennifer is stalking them and they take her prisoner near a carousel that provides the backdrop for a messily-staged showdown. Harry comes to the rescue, and when the last punk is extinguished, he topples from a bridge onto the horn of a unicorn. Joel Cox provides three or four shots of same, emphasizing the arty touch.

Jennifer, who has shown herself a cold-blooded serial killer, nonetheless clings to Harry. Harry embraces her back, no matter how illogical that might seem, and decides *not* to turn her in. *Sudden Impact* ends with the two of them heading off together hand in hand!

But Dirty Harry was still a folk hero and Clint was still at the height of his popularity. Audiences liked *Sudden Impact*, and it grossed an astounding $70 million, making it the most successful Dirty Harry to date. And the critics were not unkind.

Some were in fact downright enthusiastic. One faction looked at the Sondra Locke character and thought a strong (no matter how pathological) woman avenging her sister's rape (no matter the violent means) amounted to a philosophical subtext. Once more, people bracketed Clint's name with the unlikely honorific of 'feminist'.

Tom Stempel, a college professor writing in the *Los Angeles Times*, hailed the 'remarkable' range of female characters in Clint's films, and praised Clint's casting, which eschewed 'cutesy, *airhead*, bimbo starlets'. He declared that Clint was probably 'the most important and influential (because of the size of his audience) feminist film-maker working in America today'. This writer went on to praise *Sudden Impact* and excoriate critics who overlooked 'the complexity of the attitudes towards rape that the film shows its characters to have . . . [and] how it shows both the physical and psychological consequences of rape on both the women and the men involved'.

Stempel argued: 'Eastwood suffers from the same lack of intelligent criticism that faced major American directors like Henry King and Howard Hawks during their careers, and for the same reasons: Eastwood is working in the popular genres with a non-flamboyant directorial style' and 'going against the conventions of the genre'.

Several leading critics rushed to lend credence to this breakthrough in Clint-appreciation, writing follow-up pieces to Stempel's article. Many in the 'Clint-as-feminist' camp, ironically, were men. When feminist columnists like Molly Haskell or Ellen Goodman weighed in, their assessment was more equivocal.

Clint probably didn't plan to be hailed as a feminist film-maker, it just worked out that way – more good luck. It was an unexpected publicity boon. 'It's very simple,' Clint humbly informed Roger Ebert in an interview in the *Chicago Sun-Times*. 'I've always been interested in strong women. When I was growing up the female roles were equal to the men, and the actresses were just as strong as the actors. Now, in a lot of movies, you seem to have half a cast. The guy will be a big macho star. The woman will be a wimp. Women in the audience don't like that and I believe men don't either.'

Weak female characters, Clint noted, were the result of weak casting. 'Men do the casting and they cast for looks. They cast an interesting man, and then for the woman they go for a model, a centrefold girl. That's taking the acting profession lightly.'

* * *

As Clint was making films about avengers of rape and expounding on the topic of feminism to wide-eyed members of the entertainment press, he was also, finally, freed of marriage chains and able to return more freely to his habitual womanizing.

Whether or not he was ever monogamous with Sondra Locke, even for a brief span of time, is impossible to say. Some friends say he took 'one-nighters' all along. Other friends insist that his relationship with Locke was a true affair of the heart, and that Clint was devoted to the actress from 1976 to 1980, at the least. 'I marvelled at it,' said Fritz Manes. 'It was absolute total, blind love.' Manes' own friendship with Locke, and his acceptance of her within the Malpaso organization (where backbiting against the woman who had 'captured Clint' was rampant), was one of his pluses with Clint.

Manes conceded that, during the 1976–80 time period, Clint kept up several 'maintenance relationships' – referring to wife Maggie (still in the picture up until 1979); Roxanne Tunis (whom Clint visited irregularly); old friend Jane Brolin (one could never be sure in her case); and new friend Jacelyn Reeves (off and on).

One Malpaso insider says that Clint made an obvious play for the beautiful woman who jumped out of a cake in a gorilla costume at a private party thrown by Warners – whose executives made a show of presenting a $1 million cheque to Clint – celebrating the completion of *Any Which Way You Can*. 'It was as though he had to prove himself by claiming her,' a person who attended the party recalled. 'Clint wasn't subtle about it.'

Another Malpaso insider says that there was an obvious fling with a pretty singing hopeful under contract to Viva, which didn't last very long – the contract or the fling.

Then, in the early 1980s, Clint successfully pursued a young woman he encountered at a Southwest golf tournament (golf tournaments were as propitious for meeting women as casting calls). That is when Clint really fell off the wagon, according to Fritz Manes. It was like one sip to an alcoholic. Like hillside erosion.

There can be doubt about monogamy from 1976–80, but little doubt afterwards. There can be little doubt about Clint's lengthy affair with story analyst Megan Rose.

*   *   *

When, on her 1993 television special, broadcast journalist Barbara Walters asked Clint how he had managed to discover the superb original script for his Oscar-winning Western, *Unforgiven*, his reply was smooth and unhesitating. 'It was a script I had for a number of years,' the star said, squinting in Clint fashion.

The offhand way he said this cut off any further curiosity. One of Clint's specialities has always been avoiding uncomfortable questions by answering with silence or partial truths. There was of course no mention of Megan Rose.

When Megan Rose met Clint in 1982, she was already a fan, a big fan. From Junction City, Kansas, Rose had adored Clint and followed his career since the first time she saw him, on 9 January 1959, when he made his debut as Rowdy in the première of *Rawhide*. Rose says she had a premonition that she would meet this tall, handsome actor and fall in love with him. She was all of fourteen years old.

In the intervening years, between 1959 and 1982, Rose graduated from Kansas State and worked for the Chamber of Commerce in a small town before heading to Hollywood with hopes of landing a job as a reader – reading scripts and analysing their potential merit for producers and studios. A professed bookworm, she had majored in English literature in college, studying the rules and structure of dramaturgy.

Rose did well, working her way up first in the story department at Paramount, then as a reader for actors Tom Selleck and Kevin Costner, before getting a job as a story analyst for Warner Brothers in March 1979. Her speciality was in picking screen material for 'macho' stars; part of her Warners job was to identify those scripts which might be appropriate for Clint or Burt Reynolds, both under studio contract.

At a delayed Christmas party for Warner Brothers staff, in January 1982, Rose fell into a conversation with Marco Barla, who worked with Joe Hyams as a publicity troubleshooter. She mentioned she was a fan of Clint's, and also, it so happened, that she was knowledgeable about country-and-western music. Clint was at that time preparing to film *Honkytonk Man*, and Barla suggested Rose meet Clint and interview him for *Music City News*, Nashville's organ of country music news and articles.

She leapt at the suggestion. Months went by, however, for Clint was busy with the film, and because of the way his separation from Maggie and romance with Sondra Locke had been reported, in one of his 'wary-of-the-press' moods. Finally, in November 1982, Barla was able to arrange an appointment for Rose in Clint's office.

Rose was instructed by Barla to be upfront with her praise of Clint, to put the star at ease. Although Clint was a master of press relationships, the star felt misunderstood and mistreated, Rose was informed, not the least because of some negative reviews accorded recent films – notably, *Any Which Way You Can* and *Firefox*.

Rose wore slacks and one of her eccentric hats. She was a stunning blonde, fifteen years younger than Clint, not bookwormish in her looks; her personality was also bright and effervescent, and she was brimming with New Age notions and ideas.

Later, Rose would muse how interesting it was that Maggie, Sondra Locke, Frances Fisher – even she a little – resembled Clint physically. 'Clint Eastwood is in love with himself,' she would come around to thinking. 'Do you realize that every single relationship that has been serious for him, the woman looks like him? Features like him: the same prominent nose, cheekbones, slim-faced, almost sculptured.'

Rose waited for some time in the outer office of Malpaso, before Clint came out and they were introduced. His eyes took her in. He stepped closer and peered at her like he was examining a bug. She had the distinct impression of intensity but also of surprising vulnerability – of a wild animal, a deer in the forest, who, if she were to move too abruptly, would be frightened away.

Her interview with him went well. Clint spoke softly, intelligently, about his love for country music – how he used to listen to some of the stars, like Red Foley, at redneck bars up in northern California; how his father played in pick-up bands during the Great Depression; how he himself was something of a frustrated musician. All of it was old stuff, recycled in dozens of interviews, but Clint had a way of making it sound fresh.

Afterwards, Megan Rose couldn't help herself. She had prepared for the interview by reading all of the Clint clippings she could lay her hands on. One of them was a *Ladies Home Journal* piece by Rosemary Rogers, the steamy romance novelist who dedicated one of her books to Clint, and who, writing up a 1982 interview with the star, scolded herself after the fact for not having had the gumption to ask him for a smooch.

Standing near the closed door of his office, Rose told Clint she had been in love with him since she was a teenager, and if it wasn't too presumptuous, would he mind giving her a little kiss? He bent down, offering his lips, but when she stretched up to kiss him, he turned away slightly, so that she only brushed the corner of his mouth. Feeling embarrassed, she laughed and said, 'That wasn't very good. Can I try again?'

This time he didn't turn away, and they shared a light peck. She was feeling quite pleased with herself, when, to her astonishment, Clint grabbed her and kissed her again, passionately, leaving her weak in the knees. 'Oh, I like that,' she stammered. 'I think I'd like another.' So he grabbed her, kissed her again. Then they headed towards the door; he opened it a little – looked at her intensely with, this time, transparent bedroom eyes – slammed the door, and they kissed one more time.

All this time, the star had been true to his image; he hadn't said a word. Now Clint did say something. 'I wanted to do that since you first walked in –' he began. And then, because basically there is an honesty at heart with Clint, according to Rose, the star realized he hadn't actually *seen* her walk into the Malpaso offices, so he backpedalled, saying clumsily: ' – since you first walked in *and* I saw your lovely face.'

Clint rubbed his chin ruefully and added, somewhat incongruously, 'I guess I should have shaved today.' After which, Clint escorted Megan Rose out, introduced her to one of his parrots, Meathead (named for the dog in *Sudden Impact*) and said a polite goodbye. This time it felt like more than a premonition that she would see him again.

Megan Rose's office in the story department, on the Warner Brothers lot, was diagonally across and upstairs from Malpaso, on the second floor of one of the studio units. Although she worked directly for Warners executives, not Clint, Clint found personal as well as professional reasons for stopping by her office on a regular basis.

His or her office, it didn't matter where they made love; they did so twelve to fifteen times, Rose estimated, over the course of the next five years. The first time was in August 1983, and the last time, Rose recalled, was approximately in December 1988.

Usually they made love during lunchtime in her office, where she kept a small loveseat. But sometimes their lovemaking took place in the bedroom behind his office, where they were watched over by a huge poster of Sondra Locke from *Sudden Impact* and where there were piles of freebies and gifts. Malpaso people knew about the back door that led into Clint's offices. The chain went up whenever Clint was busy inside with a female visitor. Insiders knew the chain was a signal not to intrude.

Occasionally, their romantic trysts took place at her apartment near the studio, where Clint might linger for several hours afterwards (never, not once, staying overnight). They never went to his house – which, she was given to understand, he was sharing 'happily' with Sondra Locke. That was his 'other' life, none of her business.

The first time Megan Rose mentioned Locke's name, there was a look of positive relief on Clint's face, because she had brought up the actress's name in a professional context. Rose had read a script that she thought was 'perfect for Sondra'. Clint took note.

'Shop talk' was always part of their relationship. They never got together without discussing, in passing, scripts and ongoing films. Megan Rose's ability to diagnose story problems impressed Clint. He encouraged her advice and criticisms.

In May 1984, at which point she had known Clint for about a year and a half, Rose read the script of a Western called 'The William Munny Killings'. She went wild over its prospects. The project had been earmarked for Francis Coppola, the well-known director of *The Godfather*, then under contract to Warner Brothers. Rose, however, thought the script was tailor-made for Clint, for starring and directing. And Clint, she knew, was in the market for another Western somewhere down the road.

The script was marked 'eyes only', which meant that any story analyst employed by Warners was enjoined from discussing it with anyone outside of their immediate superior in the hierarchy. Rose walked the script over to Lucy Fisher, one of the heads of production, and told her that she thought it would make a great vehicle for Clint. Fisher agreed, but neither of them could figure out how to get around the problem that 'The William Munny Killings' had been optioned for Coppola. Both agreed the property was more iffy with Coppola's name attached as director. Coppola, not known for Westerns, would probably turn it into a cost-ineffective 'prestige production'. Worse, Clint would drop out; both suspected that Clint, who had turned down *Apocalypse Now*, would not agree to be directed by Coppola.

Because Megan Rose and Lucy Fisher could not figure out any way around the Coppola problem, they recommended the script with faintly damning praise. Eventually, according to Rose, Warners passed on the property, and the option lapsed. All during 1984 – several months flew by, during which time Rose and Clint were engaged in their affair – the story analyst did not mention the property to the star.

Not until she felt certain that Warners had abandoned 'The William Munny Killings' did Rose pursue the property herself, calling the agent of the writer, David Webb Peoples, to confirm the script's availability. She didn't bring the subject of the script up with Clint until the winter of 1984, on a day close to Christmas, when Clint stopped by her office to say a nice goodbye before taking off on his annual ski vacation to Sun Valley. Clint kept a winter home in Sun Valley, and usually he invited Kyle and Alison up there for the holiday season. In Sun Valley, Clint would ski and socialize with a high-powered circle of Hollywood friends that included producer Richard Zanuck and his wife Lili Fini Zanuck, producer Bud Yoskin and his wife Cynthia, fellow macho star Arnold Schwarzenegger and – the niece of John F. Kennedy, soon to be Mrs Schwarzenegger – TV journalist Maria Shriver.

As usual, Rose had a small Yuletide gift for Clint. Clint himself gave few Christmas presents, she knew; it was a major accomplishment for someone to qualify for one of Malpaso's annual fruit-and-cheese baskets. Clint's own typical gift to friends was a jar of mixed nuts.

The important thing was not her modest present but Rose's stocking stuffer – a copy of 'The William Munny Killings'. She pressed the script into Clint's hands, urging him to read it and insisting it was one of the best Westerns she had ever read – 'Academy Award material'. Clint had grown to have confidence in her script judgment, Rose believed, and his eyes took on a gleam as she uttered those three words.

Clint paused, before heading out the door. He held the script up speculatively, squinting at it. 'Academy Award material? Well, I just want you to know, Megan, that if I ever do this . . . if I do any script that you give me . . . that you'll be rewarded.'

*   *   *

Since Megan Rose knew about Sondra Locke, she wasn't under any illusions.

She didn't dream of marrying Clint one day. But she did think they shared a unique intimacy. Clint was sweet and charming whenever they were together. He would crack jokes and murmur endearments. He had an ability to make people feel special. When she didn't see him for spells – he was away sometimes for weeks or months at a stretch, filming or doing publicity – he wouldn't call, or write. But she didn't worry; she knew he would come back. And then when he was with her, he was totally with *her*.

It was like – at least it seemed this way in retrospect – he was an actor very skilled at playing a certain type of romantic scene. Whatever happened between them, she always felt was truthful. For that day, it was the truth. For that moment. 'I would say I love you and most of the time he would say "Me too",' Rose remembered. 'Which always made me wonder: Is he saying he loves "him" too, or does he love "me"?'

They didn't use birth control. Rose had been married before, and believed she was infertile. Clint assured her that he had had a vasectomy, because he didn't want to have any more children. Rose was lucky not to become pregnant. Considering what transpired elsewhere in Clint's life, it must have been the worst vasectomy in the history of medicine!

She suspected there were Clint-girlfriends in other places: These were his 'separate lives', in her words, which Clint kept secret from her and other people. She had no illusions, and was proud to be the girlfriend at Warners.

Clint had no illusions either. Megan Rose gave him script advice. She brought him healthy desserts that she baked herself. She was available over the lunch hour. He occasionally joked about her, conspiratorially, with Fritz Manes.

According to Fritz Manes, 'There was no romance, no "let's-go-out-to-dinner" [with Rose]. It was strictly in the office. To him, it was a very light, almost funny relationship. He'd say, "Here comes Megan . . ." and snicker. I used to laugh too because we were like brothers. I didn't see there was another human being being hurt. I didn't see that – ever.'

Rose was one of the first to give Fritz Manes a twinge. He liked her free-spiritedness. When Rose suffered a cancer scare, the producer arranged for Clint's salaried driver to take her from the Warners lot to the hospital and then back home again after the tests. Manes let Rose think it was Clint's idea. That was part of his job.

Sondra Locke had no idea what was going on between Clint and Megan Rose. Her path crossed the story analyst's at Malpaso one day, and Clint introduced them, but it must have been his private joke that both women were sleeping with him.

Locke was with Clint flying aboard the Warners jet to Sun Valley when the actor plopped down in front of her to read the script of 'The William Munny Killings'. Afterwards, he passed it around. He tended to focus on what he saw as the surefire comedy scenes. 'Don't you love the part where the guy gets his ass blown off in the shithouse?' he kept asking Fritz Manes, who didn't think the script was all that great. Clint was a little thrown by the style of it. According to Megan Rose, Clint telephoned her from Sun Valley to say either it was the best script he had ever read, or the worst.

Other people went to work, praising the script's virtues. No matter that Malpaso had *Pale Rider* in development, and that Clint wasn't going to make two Westerns back-to-back. Clint could pick up the option to keep 'The William Munny Killings' for very little money, and then put the script in a file drawer while he made up his mind.

CHAPTER ELEVEN

Mid-Life Clint
1984–1986

T*ightrope* was another Richard Tuggle screenplay, inspired by newspaper articles about an elusive Bay Area rapist. Tuggle wrote the script on his own, after *Escape from Alcatraz*, and afterwards went to Don Siegel, hoping Siegel might produce the film with Tuggle directing and Clint starring. Clint liked the script instantly, and committed to doing it; then – a hint of asperity – Siegel withdrew.

Since the last Dirty Harry had taken place in the Bay Area, somebody – Clint or Fritz Manes – suggested relocating the story in New Orleans. Tuggle, from the South, knew New Orleans and liked the idea. This change of scenery was part of the variation for some US film critics, who would later hail the film as a departure from the Dirty Harry norm. The New Orleans details were hastily injected into the script, however, and amounted to cosmetic atmosphere. Julie Salamon of the *Wall Street Journal* was one critic who later noted that 'the script explains away Mr Eastwood's California accent but doesn't account for the absence of a single drawl from anyone else'.

Tuggle's script focused on the mid-life crisis of Clint's character, a just-divorced homicide detective named Wes Block. At home, Block is a decent father, struggling to cope with his two young children. At night, he is a restless soul who seeks escape in booze and anonymous sex. Assigned to investigate a series of brutal killings of strippers and prostitutes, he is drawn into the killer's tortured psychology and develops a fascination for sadomasochism. The killer seems to know Block and manages to stay one step ahead of him, leaving taunting clues at crime scenes.

In *Dirty Harry*, Clint, staking out a rooftop in an attempt to trap a killer, inadvertently spies on a nude girl welcoming a couple to an evening of sex *à trois*. 'Harry,' he murmurs to himself, 'you owe it to yourself to live a little.' *Tightrope* would give Clint's libido that opportunity. A script which put his character into cheap bars, strip clubs and the world of prostitutes had an immediate attraction to a man who sometimes took his own sexual pleasures voyeuristically. In private, Clint had succumbed to the fashionable bedroom sport of home pornography, taking advantage of newly sophisticated and light-weight video equipment to record his lovemaking with Sondra Locke. 'The ultimate turn-on,' the star confided to buddies, though these particular 'Clint Eastwood films', carefully labelled and filed, were restricted viewing.

Just as important, the star, recently divorced in real life, couldn't miss the way in which the script advertised his good fatherhood. Although Maggie had custody of Clint's children, *Tightrope* made Wes Block into the better parent, even granting *him* custody (the absent wife is strangely unaccounted for). The two children in the script were stand-ins for Kyle and Alison; all the better that nine-year-old Alison was the right age to play one of them. If *Honkytonk Man* was made for Kyle, *Tightrope* was for Alison. 'Clint wanted to use his daughter [in the part] and he brought it up to me in a kind of hesitant way,' said Tuggle.

The leading lady's part could be interpreted as a boost to Clint's new, 'sensitive macho' image: Beryl Thibodeaux, the head of a women's rape crisis centre, offers professional advice to Wes Block and gradually succumbs to his magnetism. They have one of those Clint-scenes in a workout gym, turned on by each other's sexiness.

Thibodeaux was supposed to be a part for an actress equal to Clint's stature. Tuggle first lobbied for Jane Fonda, who was also represented by the William Morris Agency. Clint wasn't wild about that idea, either because he felt she was wrong for the part or 'maybe he was afraid of being turned down', said Tuggle. And Susan Sarandon is said to have rejected the role, objecting to the violence towards women in the story.

When casting one of Clint's films, explained Warner publicist Marco Barla in one unguarded interview, 'you'd start talking about Meryl Streep and end up with Patty Clarkson' – later, Clint's co-star in *The Dead Pool*. This time they ended up with Geneviève Bujold. The Mon-treal-born actress, Oscar-nominated for her performance as Anne Boleyn in *Anne of the Thousand Days*, had been on the Malpaso list from the beginning, according to Tuggle. Although Bujold wasn't in Hollywood's top echelon (post-*Anne*, her film appearances had only impacted modestly on US audiences), she did exude an aura of class. ('I like to use gals who bring a substance to the picture,' explained Clint in the publicity interviews.)

Bujold didn't visit the studio. She didn't do any readings with Clint. Clint, Tuggle, producer Fritz Manes and casting director Phyllis Huffman met her for a drink at the Polo Lounge. 'Geneviève and Clint kind of sat at a table next to each other very nervously, and I sat there watching them,' recalled Tuggle. 'He said something like, "What did you think of the script?" And Geneviève said something like, "It's okay." I said a couple of inane things. But since in the script the two of them are opposites – he was this hardbitten cop, she was the feminist rape counsellor – looking at them, this all-American guy and this French Canadian woman, you could just see how they *were* opposites. I remember leaving the meeting and saying, "She's great!" '

Even though Richard Tuggle was directing, it was still Clint's crew and methods. There was, per usual, little rewriting, no rehearsals. Four or five days before they started shooting, Tuggle asked the star, 'Don't you want to talk about the screenplay?' Clint said no, and essentially, therefore, the first draft is the one they shot.

The cameraman was Bruce Surtees, who would lend *Tightrope* his patented black-and-blue look. Buddy Van Horn was around for the action scenes. Clint's passing acquaintance from Fort Ord days, Lennie Niehaus, was hired to compose the jazzy soundtrack. Niehaus had been working as an orchestrator with Jerry Fielding, who had scored *The Enforcer*, *The Outlaw Josey Wales*, *The Gauntlet* and *Escape from Alcatraz*, when he bumped into Clint at one of the recording sessions. They remembered each other, and when Fielding died in 1980, Niehaus eased into position. Niehaus and Joel Cox, back again as editor, would stay with Clint for going on twenty years. The editing of *Tightrope*, Tuggle recalled, took all of eight days.

Down in New Orleans in the fall of 1983, Clint sometimes seemed as pent-up as the character he was portraying. The first signs of a gulf between him and Fritz Manes had begun to surface, resulting in shouting arguments and pushing-shoving matches.

For Wes Block, sex was the outlet for inner turmoil. Off camera, likewise, Clint threw himself into an affair with flame-haired actress Jamie Rose, from TV's *Falcon Crest*. She was playing a small part in *Tightrope* as the first murdered prostitute. Nor, according to production sources, was Rose (no relation to story analyst Megan Rose) the only actress in the film whom the star romanced. He made himself even more obvious and available than usual.

Considering the 'lurid' nature of the script, one incident on the set was amusing. First-time director Tuggle had a habit of not wearing any underwear in muggy New Orleans. One day, standing up on a camera truck, Clint noticed that Tuggle's private parts were hanging out of his shorts. Alison was present, and Clint took umbrage on his daughter's behalf. In front of everybody he ordered Tuggle to go back to his trailer and put on some underwear, pronto. Never mind that Clint himself had cast his underage daughter in the production, which was chock-full of violence and explicit sex.

Writer–director Tuggle viewed Clint as 'a very complex person who had many different facets'. As one example, Tuggle recalled an incident, an old, reliable Clintism: One night they were photographing a sequence in Jackson Square when Alison spotted a beetle or grass-hopper crawling across the set. 'Clint picked it up and put it to the side,' remembered Tuggle. 'Someone asked him what he was doing that for. He said something like, "There's a place on the planet for every living thing."'

Tuggle understood that he was an untried director serving under Clint's goodwill and that 'his clout far out-equalled mine'. The decision-making on the set was sometimes a subtle negotiation. 'Some scenes were done kind of by me,' Tuggie recollected. 'Some scenes were done kind of by him, and most of them were done together. I might come on the set first and look around. He'd show up and I'd say, "Let's do it like this" and he'd say fine. Or I would come out and say, "Let's do this," and Clint might say, "Let's try it this other way". Or we'd have ideas together, but it was his crew and they would basically be listening more to him, than to me.'

At times, some people thought, Clint treated the first-time director, only in his mid-thirties, demeaningly, as a directorial stand-in. 'Time has a way of making people forget some of the pain,' producer Fritz Manes said. 'With people like Jim Fargo and Richard Tuggle, Clint would always do the "what ifs". "What if we . . . ? That's good, but what if . . . ? What if we did it that way?'' If that's not directing, I don't know what is.'

'I never felt that,' insisted Tuggle. 'The politics on the set made me uneasy, but artistically, I liked working with Clint. He was smart, accessible and open to ideas.'

Certain sequences Tuggle more willingly surrendered to Clint's control, especially the ones where Alison was prominent. 'I basically withdrew [from directing those scenes],' explained Tuggle, 'because I could sense the closeness between them, the nervousness Clint had with her. I did not particularly want to get in the middle of that.'

These were among the highlights of the film, with Clint working hard to demonstrate his fatherliness. The scenes that really riveted the critics, however, were those that found the star in unusually graphic sexual situations: in one, an African-American prostitute performs fellatio on detective Wes Block; in another, a blonde, glistening with oils, is handcuffed to a bed while Block brutally sodomizes her.

In another scene, Block searches for the killer in a gay bar, where he is appraised by the customers and propositioned by a hustler. When Block makes it clear that he isn't interested, the gay hustler asks, 'How do you know you don't like it if you haven't tried it?' To which the detective replies: 'Maybe I have.'

A concession to homosexuality, rare in Clint's oeuvre, it came at a time in his life when, privately, his friendship with Sondra Locke's gay husband was at its height. A memorable line (it was in Tuggle's original script), it was nevertheless undercut by Clint's delivery, which edged away from any committed interpretation. In subsequent interviews, the actor would betray himself when asked what the subtext of the remark might be. 'I don't know myself if he's ever had that kind of experience,' Clint hedged. 'Maybe he has or maybe he's just being facetious with the guy.'

With its corny touches and male-oriented montage (ample shots of breasts and buttocks), the film was never as sexy as it wished. Female film critics, generally more dubious about *Tightrope* than their male colleagues, spotted the fake eroticism instantly. Sheila Benson of the *Los Angeles Times* found the kinkiness 'howlingly tame – a little Wesson oil, a back-massage vibrator and too much symbolism with a red Popsicle', while Amy Taubin of the *Village Voice* declared that *Tightrope*'s prurience amounted to 'pimping women's bodies at the box-office'.

Molly Haskell in *Playgirl* noted Clint's determination to 'play it mean and clean simultaneously'.

'This movie was walking a tightrope of its own,' admitted director Tuggle in one interview. 'It's trying to appeal to a wide commercial Clint audience, and at the same time do something different and take chances. And so you never want to go too far in either direction. Everything you do, you wonder if you're turning off the audience. We never knew whether to make it more explicit, less explicit, or whatever.'

Pierre Rissient arranged for *Tightrope* to open the Montreal Film Festival. Warner Brothers then placed the film in a record 1,535 theatres, in the summer of 1984, where it beat the previous Clint total for box-office grosses accumulated during an initial ten-day period. In the long run, *Tightrope* would pass *The Gauntlet* with over $60 million in domestic earnings.

Warner's continued campaign for 'artistic recognition' of Clint was symbolized by the studio's full-page ad for *Tightrope* in the *New York Review of Books*. The calculating sexual content, the directing oneup-manship, the holes in the script,* many US critics were willing to overlook. Especially coming as it did on the heels of *Bronco Billy* and *Honkytonk Man, Tightrope* obliged some prominent hold-outs among the critics to revise their thinking. David Denby, long associated with the Pauline Kael camp, wrote in *New York* magazine that finally the star's acting made sense to him and that Clint was 'beginning to look like the last serious man in Hollywood'. J. Hoberman of the *Village Voice* found *Tightrope* 'Eastwood's finest, most reflexive and reflective film since *Bronco Billy* – and for my money, the best Hollywood movie so far this year'.

Not everyone was won over. A disgusted Pauline Kael wrote that *Tightrope* was 'the opposite of sophisticated movie-making' and that Clint 'seems to be trying to blast through his own lack of courage as an actor'. Kael continued to lead the attack on Clint, even going so far, in a widely quoted 1976 speech to a Filmex (Los Angeles Film Festival) gathering, to link the star with the spread of violence in films – calling it the 'Vietnamization of American movies'. Kael, in that speech, labelled Clint 'the *reductio ad absurdum* of macho today'.

---

* At the climax the killer's ski mask is dramatically yanked off, revealing his identity, but this elicited a blank reaction from audiences, since the man was a complete stranger in the story. His face had never before been glimpsed by the camera!

Kael was one critic Clint did read religiously, fuming over her comments. After Kael's 'Vietnamization' speech was reported, a San Francisco psychiatrist, Dr Ronald Lowell, volunteered himself to the *Los Angeles Times* for a brief interview in which he sought to rebut Kael by diagnosing her as actually feeling 'one hundred and eighty degrees the opposite of what she says and that often a man or woman obsessed with preaching great morality is more interested in amorality'. The newspaper apparently did not know to mention that Dr Lowell, whose credentials as an expert went unspecified, had purchased one of Clint's houses and played tennis with the star.

When Pauline Kael's name came up in interviews, Clint was the rare Hollywood star to dare fire back, saying the film critic took advantage of cynical times to label him simplistically. 'She found an avenue that was going to make her a star,' Clint said on more than one occasion. 'I was just one of the subjects, among many, that helped her along the way.'

One of the tensions on the set of *Tightrope* was the ongoing preparations for Clint's next film, 'Kansas City Jazz', which was going to co-star Burt Reynolds and be directed by Blake Edwards, an accomplished Hollywood veteran with an estimable track record of box-office and critical triumphs. Edwards had directed the Oscar-nominated *Breakfast at Tiffany's* and *Days of Wine and Roses* in the 1960s, the long-running Pink Panther series starring Peter Sellers, and, more recently, hits such as *10* and the cross-dressing musical *Victor/Victoria*, starring his wife, Julie Andrews.

'Kansas City Jazz' was a Blake Edwards script that mixed action and comedy. The two leads were a private eye and his pal on the police force, both of them mixed up in gangster shenanigans in 1930s Kansas City. When Burt Reynolds read the script, he saw it as a great opportunity for something he had always wanted to do: co-star with Clint.

It is hard to say how close a friendship Burt Reynolds really had with Clint (in his autobiography Reynolds states that he never knew exactly where Clint lived and never visited his house until the early 1980s). But they knew each other from early casting calls and from parties around town. They appeared on the cover of *Time* magazine together in 1978 – two of 'Hollywood's honchos' at career crossroads.

They shared the same humour and values, swapped scripts and advice about people and the profession.

Originally, according to Sondra Locke, Reynolds himself couldn't get Clint to read the 'Kansas City Jazz' script. Blake Edwards met with Locke, using her as an intermediary with Clint. She was promised one of the two female leads. Once Clint agreed to star in the film, however, the director mysteriously dropped Locke from the planned cast. Or did Clint provide some tacit indicator? In any event Clint refused to step in and state the case for Locke. It should have been an ominous signal: the first time he had edged away from casting the actress he lived with in one of his films.

As *Tightrope* was being shot, writer–director Edwards was busy guiding Reynolds in *The Man Who Loved Women*, a remake of a François Truffaut film. During lulls in the action Edwards would phone Clint in New Orleans, updating him on the seemingly endless preparations for 'Kansas City Jazz'. More than once Clint stormed out of his trailer, complaining about 'that windy bastard'. He had grown accustomed to working at breakneck speed and in isolation without so much deliberation.

Clint had approved the script and the deal had been announced initially in July 1983. Six months later, Edwards was still engaged in preproduction but also in rewrites to accommodate the 'two superstar egos', according to one published account. Behind the scenes Clint and Burt were competing with each other over script input, then passing the blame for delays.

While Burt Reynolds trusted Blake Edwards, the writer–director and Clint got along like Custer and Geronimo from their first sitdown, according to Reynolds. Edwards was caviar and champagne, while Clint was . . . well, Clint was beer and pretzels. The more Edwards talked about what he was going to do, the more Clint wanted him to 'Just do it.'

The official announcement, explaining why Edwards and producer Tony Adams left the project, came just a few weeks before the cameras were set to roll in February 1984. It stipulated 'creative differences', one of Hollywood's all-purpose descriptions of close-door disagreements. But the bust-up was all about power and control, people say, and about Edwards' painstaking style versus Clint's expeditious one.

Fritz Manes said Edwards and Clint finally had a huge argument, and that Warners was stuck with all the start-up costs, besides ownership of what had become a very expensive property. Reynolds confirmed in his autobiography that Clint 'wanted to get rid of Blake Edwards' and manipulated the hiring of Richard Benjamin, the droll actor, whose first film as a director had been the well-received *My Favorite Year* and who was just finishing up *Racing With the Moon*, which starred Sean Penn.

Fritz Manes was quickly enlisted by Warners as producer. Joseph Stinson was on Clint's current Rolodex and although his sole credit to date was for the dissimilar *Sudden Impact*, he was brought aboard. Edward Carfagno was assigned to handle the art direction, with Lennie Niehaus slotted for the music. The title change to *City Heat* was Clint's final brand.

The sudden massive takeover by Malpaso caused an anxious counter-reaction from Reynolds. He tried horse-trading, demanding his own cameraman. Which he got – in exchange for Bruce Surtees' grip and a Malpaso electrician and special effects crew and stunt coordinator, etc. Reynolds soon understood that he was outflanked, which was a hard lesson in whose career was still on its way up and whose was plummeting.

The cast was promising: Rip Torn, Richard Roundtree, Tony Lo Bianco and Irene Cara were signed for featured roles. Marsha Mason was set to play Burt's private secretary, who is also Clint's romantic interest, until she had to drop out and then was replaced by Jane Alexander. Principal photography was scheduled to begin by late May.

'It didn't take long to figure out why [Richard] Benjamin got the job,' commented Burt Reynolds in his autobiography, *My Life*. 'Not only was he talented, Benjamin was also petrified of Clint. Their exchanges were almost comical, many times better than the picture itself, particularly when imagining Benjamin's monotone voice and Clint's ability to say volumes without uttering a word.'

Reynolds said that whenever Richard Benjamin asked for more coverage of a scene, one-take Clint would cut him off in the middle of his sentence by shaking his head.

Fritz Manes told this anecdote: One night they were scheduled to shoot scenes with explosions on the New York street at Universal. The producer arrived in the late afternoon, with the crew readying the special effects. He noticed that several cameras had been lined up virtually in a row. Manes cornered the director of photography and asked him why the cameras had been positioned so similarly, and the cameraman assured him that Benjamin had ordered an assortment of lenses and that all the angles were subtly different.

Chuckling to himself, Manes strolled into Clint's trailer and told the star to go out and have a look at the set-up. Clint did so, coming back a few minutes later, laughing. Benjamin – Clint always called the director 'Benjamin, as if that was his first name', according to Burt Reynolds – had rushed up to the star, making defensive explanations. 'I told him,' said Clint, 'that I thought it would be nice if there was a camera up on the roof, another on a crane, and if they had at least one coming out of the windows close to the explosion.' Manes walked out half an hour later and the set-up was changed, with cameras scattered around to ensure all variety of 'coverage'.

Adding to the things that went wrong on the film, from start to finish, an actress who had been imported from Europe to play Reynolds' girlfriend passed out during the early days of photography, and Madeline Kahn had to be rushed into the part. Reynolds fell mysteriously ill and had to subsist on various medications throughout the shoot. Clint's co-star was also cursed by a debilitating bout with a kidney stone, he evinced inner-ear problems, and one day fractured his jaw when a stunt man made the mistake of hitting him with a real chair.

Under these circumstances director Benjamin, whose speciality as an actor had been droll comedy, managed to extract intermittently amusing performances from Clint and the wan-looking Reynolds. The two did have a good-humoured, combustible chemistry. The funniest gags had the old friends one-upping each other with phallic pistol-barrels and teasing their own macho mystiques. But the tone of the comedy lurched and foundered, and most of *City Heat* played dead on arrival.

One of Edward Carfagno's most stunning production designs was muted. The supporting cast was sadly wasted. The subplotting was so messy that the line of continuity was difficult to follow. Clint's 'improving' of Blake Edwards' script amounted to scene after scene of weak slapstick and action fireworks.

With the two stars' drawing power, *City Heat* grossed a respectable $50 million when it was released for Christmas 1984. Yet, considering expectations (plus the combined star salaries), it is safe to say the film ended up a disappointment. Although critics uttered courtesies about *City Heat* at the time, it is also safe to say that it is one of the few Clint films to resist cult claims.

Although he had been badly treated, Blake Edwards received a reported pay-off of $3 million, to which the writer–director was entitled by contract, regardless of what eventuated. His name doesn't appear on the screen. Edwards took the pseudonym 'Sam O. Brown', sharing the script credit with Joseph Stinson.

'It broke my heart,' Edwards said in a later interview. 'I had close to a breakdown.' Clint's co-star sympathized with Edwards. 'He [Edwards] never got over it,' Burt Reynolds wrote in *My Life*. 'Thinking back on it, he had a perfect right to be very angry.'

It wasn't any single film that won critical respect for Clint. Individually the productions looked modest, especially compared with the achievements of other major US film-makers during the 1970s and 1980s: Robert Altman, Martin Scorsese, Steven Spielberg, Woody Allen, Francis Coppola, Sidney Lumet, John Cassavetes, even Hal Ashby. Only once, in a survey of 50–100 US critics, done annually, throughout the decade of the 1980s, would a Clint film be ranked in the Top 20 – *Bird,* in 1988, placed as number nineteen that year.

Warner Brothers succeeded not only in focusing critical attention on Clint's 'body of work' as a film-maker, but in narrowing the debate so that Clint was compared mainly to himself. Every move the star made could be touted as artistically adventurous if it was defined within the parameters of limited expectations.

The publicity machine targeted the media nerve centres of New York City and Los Angeles.* The opinions of prestigious critics and the wide reporting of film tributes would, Warners knew, have a trickle-down effect. By the December 1980 Museum of Modern Art tribute to Clint an era of official respectability was launched. This was followed by Robert Mazzocco's 1982 essay in the influential *New York Review of*

---

* Although Clint had influential partisans in critics' organizations in New York City and especially Los Angeles, he did less well when there was a more broad-based survey of the field. The above-cited critics' survey, conducted throughout the 1980s, made a point of including non-New York and Los Angeles reviewers, which took the voting outside of the big-city cliques and camps.

Books, crowning Clint 'The Supply-Side Star', a phrase referring to the economic theories of Ronald Reagan. Then there came Norman Mailer rhapsodizing over Clint in a 1983 issue of *Parade* magazine, stuffed into thousands of Sunday newspapers distributed across America; Mailer hailed Clint as 'the most important small-town artist in America' and reappraised amiable if minor vehicles, for example *Every Which Way But Loose,* as 'a great hunk of Americana'.

The new ardour for Clint and his films would, if anything, burn brighter abroad during the 1980s. Warners was canny about Europe, too. Partly owing to Pierre Rissient, who, on studio retainer, had primed the pump for ten years, the critics who formed the world's largest Clint fan club probably dwelled in France. There *Honkytonk Man,* for example, had been hailed as a masterwork comparable to John Ford's *The Grapes of Wrath.*

Early in 1985, shortly after the release of *City Heat,* Warners put Clint on a plane to France, Germany and England, heralding his 'new film-archives image', in the words of John Vinocur, writing in the *New York Times* magazine. The studio timed the highly publicized trip, which Vinocur dubbed 'The Clint Eastwood Magical Respectability and European Accolade and Adulation Tour', for the early 1985 European distribution of *Tightrope.* The cover of the 24 February 1985 magazine, which displayed Clint in an uncharacteristically elegant suit and tie, said it all: 'Clint Eastwood, Seriously'.

Vinocur, the Paris bureau chief for the *Times,* followed Clint as he country-hopped on the Warners jet with his agent, Warners' publicity executive Joe Hyams and other studio representatives. First there came a twenty-four-film retrospective in January at the Cinémathèque Français in Paris, climaxed by the star's personal appearance and a presentation of *Tightrope.* At a ceremony, held at the Palais de Chaillot – the museum complex that houses the Cinémathèque – speakers extolled the 'abyss of perplexity' which Clint, in his work, had created for critics and students of film.

This was followed by Clint's decoration by the Ministry of Culture as a Chevalier des Arts et Lettres. However, France's Minister of Culture, Jack Lang, was conspicuously absent from the event. 'Some thought that the socialist minister was embarrassed to personally honour a Yank star whose thriller vehicles in the past have frequently been charged with right-wing ideology,' reported *Variety*'s correspond-

ent in the French capital. Steve Ross, chairman of Warner Communications, and studio production head Terry Semel were present, but
it was Leonard Hirshan who threaded the green Chevalier ribbon
through a buttonhole of one of those Dirty Harry corduroy jackets.

Then it was off to Munich for a retrospective at the Filmmuseum
and 'as in France, the deep, wet embrace of at least part of the country's
film intellectuals', in Vinocur's words. Why was there such a Clint vogue
all of a sudden? 'The times, perhaps, caught up to Clint Eastwood,'
hypothesized Vinocur, 'and the critics [have] switched direction on
Eastwood's work like a crowd doing "the wave" at a football game.'

In London the star had been invited to give a lecture at the National
Film Theatre, sponsored by the *Guardian*, the left-wing British newspaper which had hailed *Honktyonk Man* as 'a classic American tragedy'.
'A man from the *Guardian* came, furiously intent on liking Eastwood,
but on his own terms,' wrote Vinocur in the *New York Times* magazine
article. 'At first, he seemed hopeful that Eastwood would say that his
film, *Honkytonk Man*, was about the death of the American Dream. He
did not; it was not. Then, he seemed interested in drawing Eastwood
into confessing that his own youth was hard and bleak, and perhaps,
from there, into some psychopolitical construct: a fifty-four-year-old
man finally coming to terms with his youth and the working class?
Eastwood would not bite; he chewed on an apple instead, and told a
couple of companions later that he saw "that failed American Dream
stuff coming a mile away".'

Critics well disposed towards the star were eager to 'co-opt' his films
with their own complementary ideas, Vinocur observed. If *Honkytonk
Man* was great tragedy, then *Bronco Billy* could be very nearly Capraesque. Yet, analysing the latter film, Vinocur thought that, despite
'different tones and nuances', the 1980 comedy was more like subtle
reinforcement of the same old Clint.

Vinocur noted, for example, that Bronco Billy 'never looks more
angry or less tolerant than when his friend [the Sam Bottoms charac-
ter] tells him he deserted from the Army in Vietnam', thereby
polishing the film's Republican credentials. And Clint is constantly
nudging his fans: 'When a bunch of kids at an orphanage ask him if
he ever kills anybody, Bronco Billy explains "no", and then adds in
what is almost an aside to the theatre audience, well, "not unless it's
absolutely necessary".'

Honkytonk Man may not have been a Republican movie in toto, but in some ways it was Reaganesque. Clint sure sounded like Reagan when he lectured interviewers, 'Today we live in a welfare-oriented society, and people expect more, more from Big Daddy government, more from Big Daddy charity. That philosophy never got you anywhere. I worked for every crust of bread I ever ate.' (In the earlier *Any Which Way You Can*, Philo Beddoe had made a point of endorsing a decidedly Republican position: 'A handout,' he says, 'is what you get from the government, a hand up is what you get from a friend.')

The social context of the Depression, the failed American Dream stuff, were indeed minimal in Clint's adaptation of *Honkytonk Man*. Clint couldn't endorse such a point of view. He saw himself as the embodiment of the American Dream – a hero, a winner.

One result of the Museum of Modern Art retrospective, the French praise, the Munich and London honours, might be that any US film critic not yet won over by Clint would begin to feel weak in the knees. Those who hadn't yet surrendered might feel impelled to reconsider Clint, and then proclaim their retroactive admiration for – if not actual enjoyment of – certain films that originally they had squirmed through.

Unhappy vibrations from *City Heat* would be swiftly discarded and superseded by the happier experience of *Pale Rider*, which Clint had ordered up specifically as a modern-sensibility *Shane*, an artistic Western, with himself as an archetypal stranger similar to the character, who defended homesteaders in the 1953 screen classic.

Dennis Shryack had long wanted to 're-create *Shane*', in the words of his writing partner Michael Butler (whereas 'I, personally, am not in the habit of wanting to re-create anything in the existing canon'). According to Butler, when Clint asked for just such a thing, the two writers came up with 'a new declension of *Shane* that involved 1) The Preacher; (2) the conflict between placer and hydraulic miners,* and 3) a little girl – Megan – instead of a little boy (the late Brandon de Wilde)'.

The Preacher (Clint) would descend magically from the mists of the Sierras to take the side of placer miners against a rapacious hydraulic conglomerate, in the midst of the California gold rush of 1850. Unlike

---

* Placer miners obtained minerals by washing or dredging, versus machine-drilling.

the little boy in *Shane*, the character of fifteen-year-old Megan Wheeler would undergo a 'quasi-erotic trajectory' (Butler's words) in her relationship with the Preacher. Although the Preacher ultimately prefers Megan's mother, young Megan does have one of those well-travelled Clint-scenes in which she is treated brutally and very nearly raped, her clothes ripped off, so that the star can step in and prove her saviour.

Sydney Penny, who had attracted notice in *The Thorn Birds* television series, was cast as Megan. 'The story is basically told from her point of view (as *Shane* was from the boy's),' explained co-scenarist Butler, 'and represents in a sense a rite of passage; a psychosexual and psycho-spiritual bridge between childhood and womanhood.'

Butler, meanwhile, credited Clint with enhancing the mysticism of *Pale Rider* with this idea: 'He [Clint] conceived of and captured the scene in which Megan is reading the Bible at the supper table and – seen through the cabin window – the Preacher rides past just as Megan gets to the passage about (I think it is) the Fourth Horseman,' said Butler. 'I must say that when I saw the movie, that moment gave me chills.'

It must have given novelist Clancy Carlile chills, too. Because that scene was also in *Honkytonk Man*, taking place when an Oklahoma preacher reads the passage from the Bible (Revelations, chapter 6, verse 8: 'And I looked, and behold a pale horse . . .') which inspires Red Stovall to compose the 'Pale Rider' tune. The scene was omitted when *Honkytonk Man* was made into a film and Clint deleted Carlile's songs.

Two in the supporting cast had credentials that mandated critical respect: Carrie Snodgress, Oscar nominated early in her career for *Diary of a Mad Housewife*, would play the somewhat thankless role of Sarah Wheeler, the mother competing with her teenage daughter for the Preacher's affections. (Her performance had to overcome sketchy character development.) The classically trained Michael Moriarty, a Tony and Emmy winner who made occasional appearances in film, would play the bookish leader of the small-time miners. (Moriarty would do his utmost to transcend the burden of playing a weak character cuckolded by Clint.)

Shane had one of the all-time villains in Jack Palance. Clint was still storing up his own screen time – saving money on co-stars – where the bad guys were concerned. Here he had Richard Dysart, Christopher Penn and 7'2" Richard Kiel (the latter best known for lumbering around as the steel-toothed 'Jaws' in the James Bond series). They and the film's personality-free gang of regulators could not really be blamed for fight sequences in which all the script cards were stacked against them. All their mystical evil seemed to evaporate whenever the Preacher stood up against them, knocking them over like ducks in a shooting gallery.

Up in the rugged mountain wilderness of the Sawtooth National Recreation Area, near his home in Sun Valley, Clint shot *Pale Rider* in the fall of 1984. Lennie Niehaus (music), Joel Cox (editing), Edward Carfagno (art direction) and Bruce Surtees (photography) were all on the production, Surtees for the last time on a Clint film.

Owing to these craftsmen and to scenery that was breathtaking, the film did have style and beauty. Even so, arguable beauty; writer Dennis Shryack, after he saw the film, thought Clint's concept of photographing everything in 'available light' led to a 'look' that was 'too dark for my taste'. The scenarist, who likes and admires Clint, didn't mention his quibble to the star, who was also directing. 'I over-all admired what he [Clint] did with that picture so much,' observed Shryack, 'that I didn't want to dwell on the fact that I was squinting, and I think most of the audience was squinting.' (The television networks had to crank up the lighting exposure for later airings at home. 'I actually think it looks better on TV,' commented Shryack.)

Dennis Shryack and Michael Butler insist that virtually every word of their script was filmed. 'In that case I must have been on another picture,' countered producer Fritz Manes, equally insisting that chunks of dialogue and continuity were tossed out when Clint grew impatient on location and announced, 'Action speaks louder than words.'

Although Duane Byrge of the *Hollywood Reporter* would note the film's completion with the chestnut that Clint had a 'nonpareil industry reputation for bringing in his projects on time and for budget', the reality was that Clint rushed scenes if necessary, to beat the schedules. Manes points to the ending of *Pale Rider* where the bad guys are disposed of wholesale and final transitions are jumbled. Filming of the ending was originally scheduled to last several days, according to Manes, until Clint decided he wanted to go home, get out of there. 'That is one of the things that everybody can see in his films', noted

Manes. 'Suddenly they just rush. The details that might have been there in the beginning, or in the midpart, aren't there. So the films are always missing continuity.

'I always called it "the Run for the Roses".* He'd reach a point in the seventh week, then he'd want to get out of there. He loved to shoot stuff in six weeks, seven at the most. If it was going to eight or ten weeks, look out, because everything would just start to go faster. And details would be skipped.'

Pale Rider was eagerly awaited as Clint's first Western in ten years, and by now, the spring of 1985, Clint was ripe for the Cannes Film Festival. Between Pierre Rissient and Warners it was a cinch to get the film entered into official competition at the thirty-eighth of these annual festivities.

Clint had some trepidation. He phoned Dennis Shryack, who had been to Cannes before, and asked what to expect. The writer told the star to relax, it wasn't any big ordeal. Shryack told Clint Cannes was all about schmoozing critics and distributors. 'It's like a rug merchants' convention,' Shryack told him. 'It's all about selling rugs.'

Clint was the leading American rug-seller at Cannes that year, there for the duration. Stationed aboard a yacht leased by Warner Brothers, the star received US and foreign journalists with all the largesse at his command. He made a point of discussing the environmental subtext of *Pale Rider* with Todd McCarthy of *Variety*, thereby adding ecologist to the feminist badges he wore proudly on his chest.

Jean-Luc Godard had dedicated his new film *Détective* to Clint, along with John Cassavetes and Edgar Ulmer. At the press conferences the questions were overly serious, with Clint's replies disarming. However, it was one thing to be promoted as an artist *by* Hollywood and *in* Hollywood, quite another thing to be competing with the finest films and film-makers around the globe. The *Los Angeles Times* reported that some international critics found *Pale Rider* 'too overtly commercial to be in the festival, in or out of competition'. The film did not win any awards, and Clint was said to be disappointed.

He could console himself with the critical reception in the US, when *Pale Rider* was released in the summer of 1985. The majority of

---

* Nickname for the Kentucky Derby, so-called because the winner is presented with a horseshoe-shaped garland of roses.

American film critics swooned. A combination of nostalgia for the Western genre, which had lapsed in fashion and commercial viability since the 1960s, and the rising tide of recognition for Clint-the-artist, gave the film Clint's most unanimous reviews since *Bronco Billy*.

Vincent Canby of the *New York Times* admitted the film had made him scurry 'to revise his thinking about the Eastwood *oeuvre*', noting, 'I'm just now beginning to realize that though Mr Eastwood may have been improving over the years, it's also taken all these years for most of us to recognize his very consistent grace and wit as a film-maker.'

'Easily one of the best films of the year, and one of the best Westerns in a long, long time,' exclaimed Jeffrey Lyons of *Sneak Previews*.

'This year [1985] will go down in film history as the year Clint Eastwood finally earned respect as an artist,' declared Gene Siskel in the *Chicago Tribune*. And to 'artist' *Time* magazine added, 'an American icon'.

Audiences paid nearly $60 million to see the film, its gross earnings topping *The Outlaw Josey Wales* and making it Malpaso's most successful Western to date.

For the sake of publicity, the American icon sat down with Gene Siskel for a chat about things, including the persistent whispers that he avoided leading ladies who might upstage him in the status department and cost too much salary-wise.

Clint huffed a little in his reply. 'There are dozens of fine actresses out there who are as talented – and some more talented – than the three women who were nominated for those ["save-the-farm"] movies this year [Sally Field, Sissy Spacek, and Jessica Lange]. But these other actresses are not the gals of the moment – the fad of the moment – so nobody hires them.'

He mentioned Jessica Walter, Sondra Locke and Carrie Snodgress as examples of his untrendy casting (although two of those three, in fact, were also Oscar nominees). Clint went on to state that Jessica Lange, Academy Award nominated in 1982 for her portrayal of the tragically fated actress Frances Farmer in *Frances*, couldn't 'act in the same league with any of the gals I mentioned', and furthermore, that *Frances* contained 'the worst piece of ham acting I've seen in my life'.

From discussing the underappreciated merits of his distaff co-stars it was a hop, skip and a jump for some journalists to ask Clint to comment on 'what women want in a man'. *Newsweek* did so, and Clint, backtracking a little from the feminist label, responded that he didn't endorse 'the wimp syndrome. No matter how ardent a feminist may be, if she's a heterosexual female, she wants the strength of a male companion as well as the sensitivity. The most gentle people in the world are macho males, people who are confident in their masculinity, and have a feeling of well-being in themselves. They don't have to kick in doors, mistreat women, or make fun of gays.'

In retrospect, this makes for rather interesting reading, considering that in his time, on and off screen, Clint had done all three – kicked in doors, mistreated women, made fun of gays. Indeed, even as he was accepting plaudits for 'strong female relationships' (Charles Champlin, *Los Angeles Times*), the star was coping rather curiously with a strong female making demands on him.

Except for an appearance in 'Vanessa in the Garden', a 1985 episode of NBC's *Amazing Stories* that Clint directed as a favour to Steven Spielberg,* who was serving as the series' executive producer, Sondra Locke had been quiescent as an actress. In fact, she had spent the two years since *Sudden Impact* managing the household while Clint made *Tightrope, City Heat* and *Pale Rider.* As her later court depositions would attest, Clint was stingy about hired help and refused to employ a live-in maid or cook. It was Locke's responsibility to do much of the daily shopping for food, clothing and essentials; cook meals when Clint was in town; handle much of the cleaning.

As those two years went by, the idea grew on Locke that she had backed herself into a corner as an actress, always co-starring with Clint. The idea grew that she might switch gears and become a director. Although Clint would later take credit for Locke's ambition ('I was the one who suggested she direct,' he claimed in one interview), it was, according to her, entirely her goal. Seeking to get around Leonard Hirshan, she asked another William Morris agent, a woman, to help her find the right script.

---

* Spielberg himself wrote this episode, one of the weakest of an erratic series, with Locke the prematurely deceased model of tortured artist Harvey Keitel. Undistinguished artistically, the segment was notable for Clint's casting of secret girlfriend Jamie Rose in one scene with regular girlfriend Locke. The actor continued to have problems attracting an audience as a director only. 'Vanessa in the Garden'. reported the *Los Angeles Times*, attracted 'the smallest audience yet for the NBC series'.

The William Morris agent came up with *Ratboy*, a script by Rob Thompson that had been around for a few years and was stalled in development at Warners. An odd fable about a half-rodent freak of nature, it was, in prospect, a comic cross between *E.T.* and *The Elephant Man*. Its storyline appealed to the whimsical, childlike side of Locke's nature. Clint seemed to think directing *Ratboy* was a creditable idea, and he said that he was happy to help any way he could.

For starters, he and Locke went in to see Terry Semel, and Clint gave a pep talk to Semel that, 'Sondra can do it!' Although Locke was originally going to direct only, Semel wanted her to appear in the film as box-office insurance, and so she agreed to play the role of the window-dresser who tries to exploit the ratboy.

In later interviews to promote *Ratboy*, the actress was somewhat at pains to explain that her relationship with Warners predated Clint's. The fact that she had co-starred in films with Clint, and was currently sharing a residence with the biggest star on the lot, was certainly helpful in obtaining the necessary go-aheads. Still, the actress tried to emphasize in interviews, 'Warner Brothers aren't going to do something crazy and just throw away millions of dollars because someone has a contact. It certainly helps you get to them, and it helps them listen to you. But it doesn't convince them.'

It's impossible to know what Clint was really thinking when Locke made the decision to direct. No doubt he realized that *Ratboy* would keep her busy. It was important that she be kept busy because, apart from his one-night stands, Clint had several ongoing affairs, including those with actress Jamie Rose, story analyst Megan Rose and flight attendant Jacelyn Reeves. By now Locke, although she didn't realize it, was in the same position as Maggie had been during her marriage to Clint, being flown in during Clint's shoots for slotted time, while temporary paramours were shunted to the side.

On some level, Clint must have already made the decision to ditch Locke, because up in Utah for *Pale Rider* his womanizing was transparent. He finally made his interests clear to an attractive crew member who had been platonically flirting with him for several years while working on Malpaso productions. Clint's vaunted patience wore thin; one night in Utah he misread her, and she rebuffed his advances. That was it for this crew member – *Pale Rider* was the last Clint film she ever worked on. To rub it in, the next morning the star took up with another pretty crew member, thirty years his junior, embarrassing the cast and crew by parading around with her, holding hands.

In his nonverbal way, Clint was sending messages to Locke. But the actress had few real allies at Malpaso, and the handful of mutual friends who knew what was going on with Clint were caught between their divided loyalties and at a loss what to say to her.

One mutual friend was Fritz Manes, who was also being sent smoke signals from the star, which he too wasn't reading properly. Starting with *Tightrope*, Clint and Manes had begun to evince more than their customary brinkmanship. Now there seemed never-ending disagreements and friction between the two old buddies.

One Malpaso insider said there was a public incident in New Orleans that was particularly disturbing. Back in the city for *Tightrope*'s première and one of those national publicity events that Clint had mastered, they attended the press party, then adjourned to a local restaurant where a heated exchange ensued. Clint's daughter Alison had been invited along, and she and other diners watched in horror as, after dinner, Clint and Manes spilled outside and began scuffling, shoving each other around and throwing punches.

Manes was perfectly capable of standing up to Clint and, in his words, 'calling Clint's shit'. Manes had balls, even his detractors admit. Clint liked a little of that, especially in private, just between old friends, but it was always on the edge of acceptability with him. Besides, the star hated to be embarrassed publicly.

The tensions between them included, according to insiders, Clint's resentment of Manes's affectionate relationship with the star's children, Kyle and Alison. To them, the producer was invariably amusing, whereas Clint was always grumbling that he had trouble relating to his children and vice versa.

Another subtext was Manes's reconciliation with his spouse. The producer had been estranged from his wife for the first few years he worked for Clint, and recently he and his wife had moved back in together, occupying the Sherman Oaks house once owned by Clint. Therefore Clint's sidekick was less available to romp around after hours. Clint's philandering, of which Manes knew the full extent better than anyone, began to bother the producer, especially when he was forced to lie to Locke.

Probably the biggest cause for mutual aggravation was Manes's pay-cheque. The producer was making $200,000 a year under Clint, while other Hollywood producers were earning four and five times that amount of money for one film. Manes had standard 'points' in some of the productions, but, according to him, he never saw very much additional money. Whenever the producer complained to Clint, the star's response was to throw him another 'comp' or perk. If Manes said he wanted to buy a new car, Clint would say, 'Why do you need a new car? Just take one of the "picture cars", or one of the GM vehicles.' Half the time Manes seemed to be driving around in an unmarked, banged-up ex-police car.

Manes sat up late one night, early in the 1980s, writing out a sum-mary of his merits and responsibilities on a yellow legal pad. It was like a résumé, even though Manes had been working for Clint exclu-sively for almost ten years. It pointed out the duties the producer had performed at Malpaso on a daily basis. It outlined his numerous obligations during the filming of productions. It listed the people Manes had brought into Malpaso who were now valued members of the organization.

But when Manes asked to discuss the issue of his salary with Clint, Clint said, 'I don't really have time to do this now. If you've got something to say to me about money, then say it to Roy Kaufman. I'll tell him to come over here right away.' So Clint called Kaufman, who came over to handle Manes, while Clint went off somewhere. Manes was crushed, having to sit there and review his value to Malpaso under the baleful gaze of Roy Kaufman, who was, after all, just a buffer between people and Clint.

Later, the producer learned from Locke that Clint was furious to be backed against the wall by Manes. Clint figured he had 'made' Manes in Hollywood; without Clint, Manes was a 'nobody'. Clint had sent Roy Kaufman over to teach Manes a lesson, let him know that he had an 'attitude problem'. But Kaufman was more politic and, besides, Manes had a valid case. The producer ended up getting a modest raise, with Kaufman saying he would also bring him in on some of their 'inside' investments.

Against this background Clint came up with a gem of an idea: Manes could make some extra money by producing *Ratboy*. What an inspira-tion: sic Fritz Manes on Sondra Locke! And although originally Clint had said he would stay out of the project, now he proposed that Locke use his regular people – Bruce Surtees as cameraman, Edward Carfagno for art direction, Lennie Niehaus for the music, Joel Cox for the editing. After all, the actress knew and trusted them; the better to keep everything in the Malpaso family. Locke innocently thought this made sense and agreed.

Ever since Ronald Reagan was elected president, people had been asking Clint whether he had any ambitions to run for political office. In 1985 *Rolling Stone* magazine put that question to the star directly, and Clint answered, 'That's something nobody has to worry about.'

Now, quite suddenly, people could worry about it: quite astonishingly, Clint had decided to run for mayor of Carmel, the scenic northern California town where he maintained a separate residence, operated editing facilities, and co-owned the Hog's Breath Inn.

As usual with Clint, he had ulterior motives. One was revenge on the city planning commission that, in June of 1983, had denied his application to build a new, two-storey commercial structure on property adjacent to the Hog's Breath, on San Carlos Avenue, complete with space for offices and downstairs shops. This property, interestingly, had caused the break-up between Clint and original Hog's Breath partner Paul Lippman, who first suggested buying the parcel for business expansion. Clint had demurred, and then, according to Lippman, one day Roy Kaufman materialized in local records as the new owner of the adjacent property. An angry Lippman sold out his interests in the Hog.

The Carmel architectural planning commission, which strictly enforced the city's quaint code of design and construction, had cited the building plans for San Carlos Avenue as relying too extensively on glass and concrete, with not enough wood. Clint hated to be told no, and made an in-person appeal to a hearing board, where his personality usually worked wonders. In this case it didn't.

The appeal was rejected in May 1984, and Clint filed suit against the city, claiming the regulations were vague and subjective. The city offered to mediate a settlement, but it was too late for Clint. It wasn't so much that the proposed new building was so important to his financial future. It was that he hated to be treated in this fashion.

Sitting around, drinking beer with the Carmel barnacles, they all got to talking about the pesky architectural commission. Clint urged one of the barnacles to run for mayor in the upcoming spring 1986 election. He said he'd back any individual among them. The barnacles threw it back in his face: 'Why don't you run, Clint?'

This challenge, along with boredom on the home front, got him to thinking, seriously. Why didn't he run? Well, first of all, he might lose. Gosh, Clint'd hate to lose.

So Clint took every possible insurance against losing. He quietly hired a high-powered election consultant in Eileen Padberg of Costa Mesa-based Nelson–Padberg Communications, which had done some work on Ronald Reagan's two presidential campaigns. Then, covertly, he spent at least seven thousand dollars on a pre-election survey, floating hints of his availability to gauge the possible reaction. 'A man of Clint's stature does not go blind into anything that might end up making him look stupid,' later explained one consultant working on Clint's candidacy for Eileen Padberg.

The survey results were not promising. Fifty-two per cent of the respondents said they were in favour of the incumbent mayor, a two-term, anti-too-much-progress, sixty-one-year-old former librarian named Charlotte Townsend. A fair percentage said they were distinctly hostile to any candidate with a 'Hollywood image'. 'Another problem was that Eastwood's base of support – mainly merchants angry with tough regulations on tourist businesses imposed by the incumbent City Council,' wrote Jeffrey A. Perlman of the *Los Angeles Times*, 'lived outside the city limits and thus could not vote for him.'

If Clint did run for mayor and became elected, the survey indicated he would need a council majority 'to serve effectively', according to Perlman, 'which meant that two Eastwood supporters had to be recruited for council seats'. In other words, the star needed to guarantee not only his own victory, but a council majority.

Clint and Padberg recruited two candidates tacitly allied with Clint, including one of his Carmel neighbours. Padberg would be paid by Clint to handle their campaigns too.

In addition to his pre-candidacy survey, Clint did what salespeople call a 'trial close' when he made a breakfast speech to the Carmel Business Association at the elegant LaPlaya Hotel and was encouraged by the applause. Shortly thereafter, on 30 January 1986, the star took a break after the opening round of the annual Pebble Beach National

Pro-Am Golf Tournament (successor to the Crosby) and showed up at City Hall, forty minutes before the 5 p.m. filing deadline. Clint and his barroom barnacles had managed to round up the requisite thirty signatures in support of his candidacy.

By the time he filed for mayor, Jacelyn Reeves was already pregnant with his son, Scott, born 21 March 1986, a fact corroborated by acquaintances, some of whom heard it from Clint's own mouth. Some years later, a close friend, learning about the child's existence, quizzed Clint as to how and when the pregnancy occurred. The star told her it happened impulsively during a night he spent with Reeves after the West Coast première of *Pale Rider* – scheduled as a benefit at the Golden Bough Theater, a few blocks from Clint's Carmel home, on 20 June 1985.

Since Clint had known Jacelyn Reeves for five years, this explanation was only part of the truth. The flight attendant had more than once expressed her desire to bear Clint's child. Finally the sometimes yup-and-nope actor said, 'yup'. None of this was reported at the time. Clint kept his 'privacy'. Reeves had her baby quietly at the Monterey Community Hospital, and the birth certificate omitted the name of the father.

That was the star's other ulterior motive in running for mayor, for, as some buddies knew, Clint didn't mind the prospect of spending more time in Carmel because of all the women he was involved with up there.

Crosscutting between Carmel and Los Angeles is what would happen in a film now, and that is what happened to Clint from January to April during the 1986 campaign. The Warners jet flew him back and forth between places.

Running for mayor must have seemed a cakewalk compared to the headaches that awaited him whenever he dropped in at Malpaso. As soon as he turned his back, for example, Sondra Locke did an unforgivable thing: she launched into rewriting the *Ratboy* script. Locke had the misimpression that *she* was in charge. Clint had pronounced the script okay, Warners had seconded their approval, and now here she was doing exactly the sort of thing that rubbed Clint the wrong way – working the script over, changing things!

Worse, Gordon Anderson, her husband, was doing some of the

writing! In happier times, Clint had encouraged Anderson to be a writer. In fact, at one point, he became all enthused over the story of Locke's 'Hollywood discovery' and urged Anderson to write it up as a screenplay. He, Clint, might even direct and produce. Now, however, Anderson as writer was anathema.

At first, Clint hadn't realized that Locke was busy 'pepping up' the script. When Fritz Manes caught wind of it, he felt conflicted. He warned Locke that she ought to inform Clint. She didn't do so right away, because, she said, she wanted to wait until she was finished. Then Buddy Van Horn happened to find out, and he told Clint, and Clint hit the roof. Locke *had* to show the script to Clint then, and the star sat up in bed one night reading the new draft, while the actress sat next to him, watching him warily. Yet he seemed to be enjoying it, laughing as he read and scribbling notes in the margins.

The next day, Locke arrived at the Malpaso offices first and told Manes, don't worry, Clint loved the changes. 'Clint comes in the door about noontime because he never came in early and he was purple,' remembered Manes. 'I've never seen him so fucking mad. He takes this thing and he throws it so hard it almost broke the window behind me. He said, "I'm closing this thing down. How could you let her do this?" I said, "I thought you knew." He said, "Well, you don't have to worry about this piece of shit anymore. I'm going out and telling Warners to shut the production down."'

Locke was waiting in the outer office. Clint went out and grabbed her and they went off somewhere and had a huge explosion. Manes went over to the floor and picked up the script. 'It had FUCK – COCKSUCKER – SHIT – across every page,' said Manes. 'Every page had some awful thing on it like some lunatic had scribbled all over it!'

'Clint sort of warmed to my desire to direct because I think he enjoyed the idea that he was going to be a mentor,' recalled Locke. 'It was all about him, and as long as it was about him, it was acceptable. He thought I was going to have the same point of view as he would have. I would be a little carbon copy. Then it became very apparent that he and I were quite different animals when it came to artistic choices. And he hated everything I wanted to do on the script.

'I don't know how else to explain it to you other than to give you an example of a scene. I felt my character was a quirky person and

Above: Inger Stevens nursing Clint in *Hang 'Em High*, his first, post-Leone American film. Their off-camera chemistry fuelled their on-camera lovemaking.

Below: Clint found a perfect match in Don Siegel. Here Siegel directs the star in one of those shirt-off, bathtub scenes Clint liked, in their first film, *Coogan's Bluff*.

Above: Clint, Richard Burton, Ingrid Pitt (left) and Mary Ure (right) are all smiles in this scene from *Where Eagles Dare*, otherwise sober derring-do from an Alistair MacLean story.

Below: Jean Seberg's love affair with Clint, which took place during the filming of *Paint Your Wagon*, was cut short when Maggie came to visit.

One shining moment: gathered under the studio logo for an unusual group portrait, in 1969, were these luminaries active on the lot. In the front row are Lee Marvin, producer Robert Evans, Barbra Streisand, studio executive Charles Bluhdorn, and Clint; the back row includes Rock Hudson, John Wayne and Yves Montand.

Above: Joanne Harris was another one of Clint's 'beguiled', and their relationship, which continued beyond *The Beguiled*, was so torrid that pals thought she would be the one, finally, to break up his marriage.

Left: Iconic Clint as Dirty Harry, a modern-day lawman whose popularity with audiences would grow to equal that of the Man with No Name.

Above: With fame and success came more responsibilities as well as leisure opportunities. Up in Carmel Clint had his own tennis tournament in the early 1970s.

Right: Skiing was a long-time passion. Aspen was another playground. Here Clint is seen on the slopes with two friends and, in the background, Hog's Breath co-owner Paul Lippman.

Left: Birthday party: Kyle is blowing out the candles for Clint's 40th. Next to Maggie is Malpaso story editor Sonia Chernus, who helped Clint get his break on *Rawhide*. Holding Kyle is Columbia producer George LaMerier, a family friend.

Below: At home with producer Bob Daley (left), Maggie and long-time friend Brett Halsey.

Clint, seen here with co-star Donna Mills, impressed critics with his directing debut, *Play 'Misty' for Me*, with himself as a disc jockey stalked by a pathological fan.

Roxanne Tunis (seen here with Clint on the set of *Hang 'Em High*) and her daughter Kimber continued to exist on the periphery of the star's life.

Above: *Thunderbolt and Lightfoot* was one of Clint's best vehicles of the 1970s, the first production written and directed by Michael Cimino. Clint is seen here with Jeff Bridges and George Kennedy, two co-stars who added to the film's free-wheeling quality.

Below: Clint as Josey Wales from the Bicentennial Western, *The Outlaw Josey Wales,* widely considered one of his best films.

there was one scene in the beginning, which is cut out of the finished film, where my character had gone into the ladies' room. She was very frustrated, nothing was going right, she had just been fired, and she sat on the floor of the bathroom and pulled a Butterfinger out of her purse and started to eat it. I didn't think there was anything so unusual about that scene, which I had written in.

'He was so threatened by it, so upset. "What are you doing? You can't have her *sit* on the floor of the *bathroom?* And eating a *candy bar?*" I had gone so far left-field that he didn't have any control over me, and that was very terrifying to him.

'All of a sudden, because it was my job and I had a point of view, I was arguing with him. And do you know that we had never had any real fights until I started to direct.'

Clint put his foot down: No changes in the script! Locke had no recourse but to acquiesce. She went back to the old script, with only small concessions to what she had wanted to do.

Then Clint turned his back a little too long again – probably one of those flying trips to Carmel – and yikes! Now it emerged that Locke was planning to cast Gordon Anderson in one of the featured roles, playing one of her character's brothers. Anderson once had been an actor; Locke thought he could handle the role, and that his highly mischievous personality would lend itself to the film. In happier times, Clint, after seeing some of Anderson's stage reviews, had encouraged him to return to his first love of acting. Now he cried, 'That's nepotism!' Although Clint could hire his own buddies, cast his children and mistresses, this was going too far.

Once again, Clint put his foot down: Gordon Anderson absolutely could not be in *Ratboy!*

Again, the novice director dared not rebel against the boss. What Locke didn't yet realize is that, behind her back, Clint wasn't calmed by his defeat of her notions. Instead he was working himself into a froth against Anderson, developing a kind of 'dossier' against him. For the first time people overheard the star referring to Locke's long-time best friend and legal spouse as 'that fucking faggot'.

Around this time, Clint pointedly asked Locke to stop hanging out so much at Anderson's house when he was out of town – which was more and more frequently – and to please stay home at the Stradella place. (Whether he said 'our home' or '*my* home' would later be a source of discussion among lawyers.) Locke, expressing amazement that Clint would show any hostility towards Anderson, whom he had always treated warmly, agreed to his wishes. Although she hated to be in a house alone at night, she stopped staying occasional overnights at Anderson's, and for the first time wondered what was wrong with Clint. He was so disagreeable all of the time. What was happening to him? Was it the mayoral campaign? Or some kind of mid-life crisis?

Some years later, in court depositions, Clint would date the deterioration of his relationship with Locke to late 1985 and early 1986. During that period the actress had proved just too attached to her husband. She hardly had any time for Clint. And it was worse once he was elected mayor: she only infrequently deigned to visit him up in Carmel, where, in the Maggie years, she had felt only half-welcome.

Years later, Locke grew to believe that, if there was ever a chance for the two of them, that chance was lost when she announced her ambition to become a director. As long as the actress treated Clint as Daddy, everything was hunky-dory. But the minute she stepped out of his cocoon and sought to be perceived on equal terms – challenging him on his own turf – his attitude towards her changed and hardened.

Cut to Carmel, where the mayoral campaign was more exciting than some Clint films.

Reports that the star had thrown his candidacy into the ring had electrified the press around the world. News media from Finland to Fiji sent correspondents to cover the small-town contest, the hype reaching a saturation point on election night with two hundred journalists gathered from around the globe to report on the tabulated results.

Norman Mailer had once likened Dirty Harry to a young politico with a promising future who, when seen striding down the street, looked as though he were making campaign stops. Now, this particular campaign and all the stops would be carefully orchestrated.

During the campaign, the paid political operatives working on the star's behalf kept out of the limelight, the better to pretend Clint's race was a grassroots affair. In fact, more than once Clint went so far as to deny that he had commissioned a preeelection survey; even among voters who ended up casting their ballots for him, and later counted themselves among his supporters, this falsehood lingered in the air.

Clint adopted the advice of professionals to keep the campaign 'as low profile as possible, because the obvious thing we wanted to avoid was the image that he already had', in the words of political consultant Sue Hutchinson. Bumper stickers asked voters to 'Go Ahead . . . Make Me Mayor', and the campaign headquarters was hung with Hollywood posters, but otherwise he was presented as average-guy Clint.

Ironically, considering what eventuated, he vowed to keep the 'circus atmosphere' out of city politics. His approach was relentlessly humble, with a smile: Clint attended dozens of teas and coffees held in people's homes, where he could personally meet virtually every 'undecided' voter and let his 'in-person' charm triumph. He devoted himself to local media outlets, rather than representatives from the national or world press. (He was pleased to give interviews to the *Carmel Pine Cone*, but declined the *Wall Street Journal*! – a national newspaper whose critics had not always been complimentary to his films.) Autographs were frowned upon (although Clint usually turned people down gently, saying, 'Thank you for asking').

The political debate in the pocket-size town usually revolved around the dread prospect of commercial development, the chronic tourist overflow, shortages of parking and water. In brief speeches and newspaper comments, Clint positioned himself as a moderate alternative to the city's perceived 'anti-business' ethic and adopted the same 'let's-get-government-off-our-backs' theme as Ronald Reagan. Progress wasn't such a bad thing; the incumbent city government, Clint insisted, had a 'kill-joy mentality'.

His strategy tapped into the mood of local citizens already irked by some of Carmel's more dubious governmental measures, which included restriction of parking along popular beachfront drives and the widely publicized denial of a permit for an outdoor ice cream stand. (This latter was a controversial gesture towards minimizing trash and sticky sidewalks.)

It wasn't until *after* the campaign that the survey and consultants were revealed, and only afterwards did Eileen Padberg explain how Clint learned to master the smooth regurgitation of his stands on issues by using an actor's device straight out of President Reagan's book. 'He sat down with me,' Padberg was quoted in the *Los Angeles Times*, 'and said he knew he would have to repeat the same message thousands of times, which is what is required in political campaigns. And he said that he didn't want to hear himself repeat things so often.

He was already getting tired of it. So he said to me: "I'll use an old actor's trick and change the order and the emphasis [of the issues] each time."'

'His manner of speaking is extremely deliberate,' political operative Sue Hutchinson elaborated. 'It's an art to learn how to do that, and it is especially useful when either you don't know an answer or are reaching for an answer. His mode of speech lent itself.'

Incumbent mayor Charlotte Townsend never quite got over the shock of who she was running against. One of Clint's local nicknames was 'The Phantom of Carmel', because, except for appearances in bars, he was usually only glimpsed *leaving* town. 'He [Clint] has shown absolutely no interest in anything in this town,' the Mayor charged.

Although she was a Stanford graduate, Townsend, who had lived in Carmel since the late 1930s, was straight from Central Casting as a small-town mayor. She made a point of referring to Clint as 'our cinema star'. She herself had only ever seen one of his movies, *The Eiger Sanction*. 'It starts with a man in Zurich getting his throat slit,' Mayor Townsend told the *Wall Street Journal*. 'I disliked it terrifically right away.'

Described in nearly all press accounts as earnest, friendly, concerned and hard-working, the ex-librarian went one to one with Clint knocking on doors, addressing public forums, debating with him live on tele-vision. Everywhere Mayor Townsend went, questions were lobbed at her by dozens of reporters with foreign accents. She nervously over-rehearsed her prepared statements while Clint seemed to be 'winging' his. ('Despite dozens of films,' reported the *San Jose Mercury News* after their 29 March televised debate, 'Eastwood stumbled over his words – "parking spaces" became "parking splaces" – and peppered his on-air comments with "ahs".')

Carmel, in short order, became twice as circus-like as *Bronco Billy*. 'Poor little town,' the anti-progress incumbent told journalists at one point. 'We don't need this.'

On election day, 10 April, Clint arrived to vote early, before break-fast, driving 'a funky, ageing, pale-yellow Volkswagen convertible', according to wire service accounts. By the end of the day, 2,166 votes had been counted for Clint against 799 for Townsend (with a small number scattered among other candidates). The two council candid-ates who had been recruited by Clint and supported by his paid pro-fessionals also won.

At his final coffee klatch, Clint had handed out jelly beans, reminding people of his ties to America's jelly-bean president. Now President Reagan was quick to phone, congratulating the winner and declaring himself 'envious' of Clint's 72 per cent margin of victory. 'What's an actor who's played in a movie with a monkey doing in politics?' the President wisecracked.

The new mayor would be sworn in five days later, on 15 April, surrounded by friends and family, and a thousand tourists and reporters. In brief remarks Clint announced that he would launch his two-year term by engaging in 'philosophical discussions' with the city hall staff. 'The crowd cheered when Eastwood arrived, when he took his oath, when he spoke, when he waved and when he left', reported the *Los Angeles Times*.

Post-campaign records indicated the movie star had spent $40,000 compared with $3,000 for Charlotte Townsend, or slightly more than $100 for every person who voted in the election. Previous to Clint, no one had ever spent more than a few hundred dollars during a Carmel campaign. The mayoral post paid only $200 a month. At that rate, Clint would have to stay in office almost twenty years to break even.

Back at Malpaso, *Ratboy* was finished by the time Clint was sworn in.

Because of the mayoral campaign, Clint wasn't around much during the photography of *Ratboy*, which took place during the spring of 1986. After blocking rewrites and vetoing Gordon Anderson as an actor, Clint stayed aloof from the production.

Manes thought it was just another movie. True, it was Locke's directorial debut, and she seemed tense, under a lot of pressure, but that was to be expected. True, there had been some craziness during pre-production, and snafus during filming, but there was always craziness and snafus. It hadn't yet dawned on the producer that *Ratboy* might be some kind of test for Locke, and not only for her but also for him.

Even though Clint only visited the set once or twice, one of his closest confederates, Jack Green, was there. It was Green, serving as Bruce Surtees' camera assistant, who came up to Locke one day and let her know, confidentially, that Manes had been bad-mouthing and second-guessing her behind her back. Locke was flabbergasted, since Manes had been her friend from day one.

She decided to confront the producer. Manes denied undercutting

391

her. He felt betrayed by such accusations. Even though the two smoothed the misunderstanding over, from then on Manes stepped back from his wholehearted endorsement of Locke. He started distancing himself from her, and let her dangle a little more with Clint.

And Locke distanced herself from Manes. Later, the actress grew to believe that Jack Green had made it all up, or perhaps had exaggerated things to cultivate a rift between her and Manes. Green was ambitious, he wanted to move up in the Malpaso organization; he wanted to succeed Surtees as director of photography and maybe direct some day. One person standing between him and Clint was Manes.

Nor was Green alone in disliking the tough-talking producer. Judy Hoyt, who had returned in the early 1980s as Clint's secretary, was a keeper of Malpaso secrets, and therefore a power of sorts behind the throne. Hoyt too had ambitions to move up in the organization, maybe become a producer. She too had endured friction with Manes. Now all of a sudden Locke looked under a cloud and Clint's boyhood friend seemed surprisingly vulnerable. And Judy Hoyt kept Clint apprised.

Enter Jane Brolin, poison to the brew. Clint's on-and-off paramour, dating from the late 1950s, was breaking up with her husband, actor James Brolin, after twenty years of marriage. Fritz Manes and his wife had stayed friendly with James Brolin, and were still seeing the actor socially, along with his new wife-to-be, actress Jan Smithers. That marked Manes for doom, as far as Jane Brolin was concerned. She began to whisper petty things about Manes in Clint's ear, adding to the growing chorus.

If all that wasn't enough, around this time Malpaso began to receive a series of strange, threatening letters addressed to Clint, mailed from various California locations. The messages were sometimes cut-out words, with crude, very specific language, often mentioning Sondra Locke. 'Get that bitch out of your life!' That sort of thing.

Clint had received death threats before. Yet these were particularly vile and seemed to come from someone with inside knowledge of Clint's life and Malpaso operations. Because of his Dirty Harry role, Clint was a hero to many policemen, and had gone out of his way to do favours for police organizations. He even had a collection of police badges of which he was proud. Now he called on the services of a friend who was a detective on the Los Angeles police force.

The detective, helped by the US Postal Service, began to investigate the letters. The trouble was, the detective had an extremely long list of possible Clint enemies and ex-girlfriends but no real clues as to who might be the culprit. While people at Malpaso pointed fingers at each other over *Ratboy*, the detective was trying to figure out if any of them could be the anonymous pen-pal. After a while suspicion focused on Jane Brolin.

Clint scoffed at the idea it was Jane Brolin. He thought it might be an actress friend of Roxanne Tunis, seeking some kind of revenge on him. One night he drove around the Hollywood hills with Fritz Manes, trying to find this lady's address. He tried to convince Manes that they should burgle her place, and see if the lady's typewriter matched up with any of the letters. Manes said no; another mark against him.

Even in the best of times, Malpaso was a paranoid place, but now, as the vile letters waxed and waned, the atmosphere of distrust and suspicion grew.

During the time when the threatening letters first appeared Clint was running for mayor. The star had first taken out a gun permit in 1983. Now Mayor Clint began to carry a .38 calibre handgun wherever he went, including Carmel, or Clintville, as it had been swiftly dubbed by the press corps.

The Mayor possessed few official powers. Clint's primary responsibilities would be to preside at the monthly council sessions (first Tuesday of each month), attend department and agency meetings, represent the city at important functions and events.

At his first council meeting, Clint brought back the Pledge of Allegiance, which had lapsed from tradition. At his second meeting, Clint ousted the planning commissioners who had impeded his downtown building expansion, replacing them with appointees of his own. Among Clint's appointees was the publisher of the *Carmel Pine Cone*, a clever move which thereby helped to encourage friendly coverage of his tenure.*

The meetings had to be moved out of the traditional fifty-seat council

* The funny thing was that even Clint's hand-picked Planning Commission didn't approve the glass and concrete design for his annex building. The design dispute dragged on into the 1990s, beyond Clint's mayoral tenure, until finally the plans were officially accepted. Today the building is mostly faced with wood, 'still ugly and modern, but not *as* ugly', in the words of one political opponent.

chambers and into the roomier Carmel Women's Club in order to accommodate crowds of tourists and reporters. For a time, a closed-circuit telecast with loudspeakers was set up for the overflow in a parking lot. Clint said he hoped all the ballyhoo would fade away.

People joked that Clint was the only mayor in America who kept an unlisted telephone number. His office phone was certainly listed, but he maintained fast and loose hours and wasn't expected to be there, always, on site. He had many 'helpers', including a young, ambitious college graduate named Tom Rooker, who had volunteered on the campaign and continued to lend a hand. Rooker, a big admirer of Clint's who wrote him fan letters, would eventually carve a future at Malpaso.

When Clint wasn't in the office, the phone was answered and emergency requests handled by aide Sue Hutchinson, the professional political consultant who had come up to Carmel to organize the star's mayoral campaign, and then moved there for the duration of his term.

Originally from Pasadena, Hutchinson had started out in politics working as a volunteer in the first state assembly campaign of George Deukmejian. (Deukmejian, a rising star among conservatives, had gone on to become California's governor.) Hutchinson only ever toiled on behalf of Republican candidacies or causes; one of her accomplishments was the defeat of a rent-control initiative in Long Beach, and another was the turning back of anti-offshore oil forces in a Santa Barbara election.

When she was first introduced to Clint over at Malpaso, the star had exclaimed, 'Perfect typecasting!' 'What he meant by that probably,' Hutchinson explained, 'is that I was the median age of a Carmel citizen. I fit right in there.' Her motherly appearance, however, belied her energy, dedication, organized mind and will of steel. When the campaign was over, Clint invited her to stay on as his executive assistant.

Clint claimed hiring Hutchinson would 'save the city money', though in fact she occupied a position that didn't exist under previous administrations and did things other mayors did as part of their accepted obligations. In the event, people were dismayed by a stranger – an outsider – in the mayor's office, who was viewed as a 'surrogate mayor'. (Her nickname locally was 'the Stunt Mayor'.) Clint expanded his staff with other helpers never seen before or since, who treated City Hall as their temporary turf.

Probably the most important part of Hutchinson's job was to wall off the world-famous small-town mayor from unwanted approaches. Hutchinson was answerable only to Clint, who took care of her salary – the exact amount never revealed. Actually, her cheques were issued by Warner Brothers, as they had been throughout the campaign. Meanwhile, the Mayor continued to fly back and forth from Malpaso, often on a Warners jet.

Ratboy was still in postproduction, the weird death threats were still under investigation, and Fritz Manes was playing catch-up with all the problems plaguing Clint's next project, *Heartbreak Ridge*, as the summer of 1986 approached.

Heartbreak Ridge had come into the office via Warner Brothers back in 1984 after Clint let it be known that he was open to doing another military subject. The original script had been written by James Carabatsos, a Vietnam War veteran, whose best-known prior credit was *Heroes*, starring Henry Winkler. Warners optioned the script 'naked', without a bankable star attached, then convened a month of executive-level story conferences which went nowhere, until, according to Carabatsos, he got a call at home from Clint, 'who said in his inimitable way, "Why don't you mosey on over?"'

Carabatsos found Clint very precise in his script suggestions. Clint had fallen in love with the main character – an ageing army sergeant named Tom Highway, whose service record includes heroism in Korea at Heartbreak Ridge. Highway was depicted as a foul-mouthed relic of the army's glorious past – a drinker and brawler. The screen story gives him one last chance to recoup his honour by training a platoon of young misfits. All the while he is trying to patch things up with his divorced wife.

The 'film-archives image' put pressure on Clint to live up to his mystique among critics. He was as anxious now to be seen as a striving actor as he was a director. Around Malpaso, he kept talking about the 'shades' of Sgt Highway, a character he described in one interview as 'very hard-boiled, but at the same time searching for the sensitivities of his own soul'.

'He was just beginning to use that word: "shades",' said Fritz Manes. 'He thought he had never done anything that had that much dimension in the role.'

Originally, in the script there was a young woman character but her role would be combined with that of the divorced wife to create more of a leading lady's part. Originally, the character Mario Van Peebles plays was a civilian, but in the revision he ended up in uniform. Originally, there was no slam-bang finale, but Clint wanted one set during the October 1983 invasion of Grenada by US troops.

One of President Reagan's sabre-rattling exercises, the war in Grenada – a small West Indies island, north of Venezuela – was meant to displace an internal military coup leadership and establish a so-called peacekeeping force in the region to counter growing Cuban influence. In Clint's eyes the real-life events would form a glorious capstone to Sgt Highway's career, and a Republican capstone to a film already thick with flag-waving.

Carabatsos supplied all these things in his rewrite, before moving on to pressing commitments on two other scripts of his about to be filmed, *Hamburger Hill* and *No Mercy*. Once Carabatsos was gone, however, the script tinkering continued.

Clint wanted more action and more comedy and more oomph at the climax. First Dennis Hackin, the guy who had written the dissimilar *Bronco Billy*, was brought in to execute a new version of the script. Then, when Hackin's version failed to gratify Clint, Joseph Stinson was asked to try another draft. The characters were perhaps more in-depth in the Stinson variation, but the story didn't move, it just lay there. The Hackin draft was more lightweight, but also faster-moving.

The rewriting went on longer than usual, during late 1985 and early 1986. Clint asked the opinion of Megan Rose, with whom he continued to carry on a sexual liaison. The story analyst took a look at the Hackin and Stinson drafts, and said, 'It's too bad you can't weave them together.'

'You think that might work?' Clint asked.

So Clint and Megan Rose got together in his office with a pair of scissors and Scotch tape, cutting scenes out of one script and pasting them into the other. Clint vowed to reward Rose, since such activity was above and beyond the call of duty for a story analyst (and in any case, she was employed by Warners, not Malpaso). Rose said she was happy to help out any way she could. The one project she did want to be rewarded for was 'The William Munny Killings', which was still on Clint's plate for the future. 'No, I owe you a lot,' Clint insisted, according to Megan Rose. 'I promise to reward you, and I want you to know that I'm a man who keeps his promises.'

The two worked on splicing the two scripts together for a short time before Clint's energy waned. 'Oh, you do the rest of it,' he suggested. Rose went home and finished up a 'hybrid', typing it herself. When she brought it back, Rose suggested that either Hackin or Stinson be brought back into the project to create linkage scenes in the same style as the rest of the script. Clint wanted Rose to write them herself; when she refused, insisting she was a story editor not a writer, Clint got mad at Rose.

Producer Fritz Manes insisted in an interview that Megan Rose couldn't have made any real contribution to the script, and that Clint was shining her on, which was one of his techniques with people. Behind Rose's back, according to Manes, Clint used to make denigrating jokes about the script judgment of the woman who discovered 'The William Munny Killings'. 'He used to say something like, "I wish she could pick projects like she can bake cookies",' recalled Manes. 'It was a real shitty thing to say.'

Anyway, Clint brought both Hackin and Stinson back, and asked them to work together as a team. Thrown together in this old-Hollywood fashion, the duo did their best to craft a shooting script, but they were an odd couple, and their unsuitability aggravated what was already a mish-mash. The comedy became increasingly sophomoric, the drama felt more and more contrived. Fritz Manes couldn't see the point. 'I was reading it as these guys were pumping it out,' recalled Manes. 'I kept saying to myself, "This whole film is the biggest waste of time."'

The defects of the script certainly seemed manifest to the army. Clint could have shot *Heartbreak Ridge* without official Department of Defense endorsement (directors Oliver Stone and Stanley Kubrick both made highly praised Vietnam War films without the army's seal of approval). But with the army's goodwill came all of the actual locales and free-of-cost vintage ships and helicopters and jets – the major hardware important to Clint's psychology – with which to dress up the film.

Indeed, Clint and Manes had spent a lot of time wooing the army for approval of the script. They visited the Pentagon and Army Airborne bases and schmoozed the brass. Clint never suspected that he,

Clint Eastwood, would receive a turndown. Therefore he was furious when the army formally rejected *Heartbreak Ridge* on the grounds that Sgt Highway – that character of many shades! – was an outdated stereotype.

Manes came up with an idea to salvage the production. The army was actually the most conservative branch of the military when it came to backing Hollywood projects. The most liberal, ironically, was probably the Marine Corps, which took a 'whole-script' approach to a film, and didn't mind a little profanity and sex. The Marine Corps had sanctioned the hard-hitting *The Great Santini* and assisted with *An Officer and a Gentleman* (with its scene of a failed officer candidate committing suicide). The Marines felt their rough-and-tumble image could withstand Hollywood warts and blemishes.

If *Heartbreak Ridge* could be converted into a Marines film, argued Manes, then maybe Malpaso could get help from Lt Col. Fred Peck, who liaised with the film industry and ran the Public Affairs branch of the Marine Corps from an office in downtown Los Angeles. Clint was intrigued, but wary. He and Manes had a longstanding rift between them over which division of the service was the toughest. Clint had been in the army, so he always took the army's side. Manes was a proud former Marine, who had been decorated with a Purple Heart for being wounded in action in Korea (while Clint was tending the swimming pool at Fort Ord).

The problem with Manes's idea, countered Clint, was that the army had won the battle of Heartbreak Ridge. There weren't any Marines there. Yes, there sure were Marines, responded Manes, plenty of them in the vicinity known as 'the Punchbowl'. Indeed, a handful of Marines were decorated as heroes. Clint was sceptical, but Manes said he would bring Peck over to Malpaso to state the case.

A Naval Academy double-master's graduate, Lt Col. Fred Peck was a Marine 'lifer' who had served a short stint as an aide to President-elect Reagan before being posted to Los Angeles. He took a gander at the script of *Heartbreak Ridge* which Manes sent over, and decided that with very little effort the film could be retrofitted into a Marines context.

Peck also thought Clint's character was 'Hollywood's stereotypical, hard-ass sergeant who knows better than the upper brass'. Therefore: 'I wasn't expecting *Play Misty for Me* or *The Beguiled*, where Clint demonstrated good acting capability.' He thought the other characters and most of the plot was just as cardboard. His passion for *Heartbreak Ridge* came from his belief that Clint Eastwood in dress blues would amount to a tremendous recruiting poster. 'I saw it as a good opportunity for the Marine Corps,' Peck said. 'I saw Clint as the John Wayne of his generation.'

It would be easy enough to translate the army jargon and rigmarole into Marine jargon and rigmarole. The 82nd Airborne platoon would have to be changed to a recon. platoon, Peck told Clint, where it was plausible to find a 'gunny', or gunnery sergeant, as a platoon leader. A recon. platoon was also more of a crisis unit, which gave the story more action potential, although Peck knew that it was absurd that Sgt Highway, a man Clint's age, would ever be put in command of a recon. unit.

Even more absurd, a gunnery sergeant would be God to a recon. unit, and the post-Carabatsos drafts had played up the *Animal House*-type comedy of the rebellious misfits moulded into men under Highway's leadership. This was intended to leaven the serious drama about a man at a critical crossroads in his life and career. But some scenes were ridiculous, with the young soldiers defying Sgt Highway to such an extent that in one scene they even threaten to punch him out.

The major contradiction – that a guy Clint's age, a Korean veteran, was still in the Marines and drilling a recon. platoon – was irreconcilable. 'Clint was way too old to play that character,' Peck realized. But nobody dared mention that to the youth-conscious Clint. Later on, watching the filming of one of the Grenada scenes, Peck worried about Clint scampering up a wall alongside the young studs and real Marines among the cast. 'We were afraid that Clint was going to fall from the rope and kill himself or break his ankle or something,' said Peck. 'He did it, but they had to use good camera angles so he wouldn't look as clumsy as he did, actually going up.'

Clint couldn't let go of the issue of whether there truly were Marines at Heartbreak Ridge. Peck sided with Manes, assuring the star that Marines were present, but even so, Clint insisted upon a new scene that made laborious mention of the fact that Sgt Highway had served in the army back in Korea days, before *transferring over* to the Marines.

Peck couldn't help but notice the Marines-army rivalry between Clint and Manes that simmered beneath all of their discussions. 'It was a little joke between them,' Peck recalled. 'It ended up becoming a bit more of a rivalry as time went on.'

The masterstroke was Manes's idea, but he didn't take any credit for it with Clint, or it might have boomeranged, coming from the former Marine. The producer asked Peck to put together a dress uniform decorated with a rack of ribbons, including gold jump wings, a scuba badge, and the Medal of Honor. They hung the dress uniform in Clint's office so he could stare at it during their meetings and get 'a feeling for the character'. The impressive costume was the decisive factor in favour of going ahead.

'Clint, smart guy that he is, worked the uniform into a scene when he first reports into the battalion,' recalled Peck, 'and bumps into a lieutenant who does a double take at his ribbon rack.'

Joe Stinson went to work on a fix-it draft to be sent through proper Marine channels.

Originally, Clint had hoped to start filming in the spring, but because of his election as mayor the principal photography had to be delayed until summer. Fritz Manes began to scout military bases and locations in the San Juan Capistrano and San Clemente area, the latter familiar to Clint from beach time during his Arch Drive days. Everything would be scheduled so that Clint never would have to miss a city council meeting.

Up in Carmel, Clint was getting mixed reviews, early on. He couldn't walk around as mayor in his preferred T-shirt and slacks, so he tended to show up in one of his movie suits. The tweed sports jackets were straight from *Dirty Harry*. Clint also wore reading glasses, which he had eschewed during the campaign, while presiding over the council meetings. Long-winded and fractious, these sometimes lasted up to six hours.

His initial style was impatient, 'mean and hostile', in the words of one political opponent, also reminiscent of *Dirty Harry*. Wielding his gavel freely, Clint sometimes rode roughshod over speakers who tried to disagree with him, gavelling one woman to silence, he explained, because 'absolutely nothing constructive [was] being offered'. A number of his most avid political opponents, Clint said, were wolves and coyotes ('pack animals that tear their victims apart').

The packed crowds and press attention lingered. Souvenir sales, propelled by Clint's election, boomed. Trash in the streets increased, some say doubled. Carmel, long in the tourist guides, was well on its way to must-see status, with many of the camera-carrying visitors from afar making a point of attending a council meeting, or stopping for lunch or dinner at the Hog's Breath Inn.

The other casting for *Heartbreak Ridge* was arranged. Marsha Mason, left over from *City Heat*, would play Clint's estranged wife Aggie (rhymes with Maggie). Because Clint was playing Sgt Highway, his platoon rival would have to be a contemporary in age – actor Moses Gunn (b. 1929). ('My God,' thought Lt Col. Peck, 'the guy's old enough to be my grandfather.') Bo Svenson and Eileen Heckart would take featured roles. Mario Van Peebles, cast as a jive-ass recruit, would provide son–father conflict with Sgt Highway and pander to more of a 'youth audience'.

Edward Carfagno would again bring impeccable detailing to the production design. Jack Green would be rewarded for years of faithful service to Malpaso by promotion to director of photography. Joel Cox would do the editing, Lennie Niehaus the music.

Manes arranged for the actors impersonating recruits to go through a day of rigorous drill with senior Marine Corps instructors. Peck arranged for Clint to meet and observe his counterparts. That kind of preparation was always minimized time-wise for Clint, but he did have an ability to soak up details. Peck recalled watching the star do a scene one day in which the actor was about to deliver his first salute, an act in which Marines take fastidious pride. 'I felt angst,' said Peck. 'I hadn't shown him how to salute correctly. The cameras were rolling, a guy walked up to him, and Eastwood popped the most perfect Marine Corps salute I ever could have hoped for.'

The Marine-conscious Manes thought Clint needed more than his usual walk-through grounding. There was another film that Manes and Peck both admired – which Peck had consulted on – *Death Before Dishonor*, in which Fred Dreyer, the former defensive end for the Los Angeles Rams, also played a hardass gunnery sergeant. 'It is the best movie I've ever seen for capturing the right feel for the gunny, his relationship with his troops and his commanding officer,' noted Peck. 'It's human, not cardboard.'

Fred Dreyer's poster was pasted up wherever they went on military bases. Dreyer, or younger action stars such as Bruce Willis or Sylvester Stallone (who played a one-man army in the *Rambo* series), rarely Clint. Manes made the mistake of urging Clint to go down and visit the recruiting depot in San Diego and then spend time at Camp Pendleton with a real recon. outfit. 'That's what Fred Dreyer did,' the producer told Clint. 'I don't give a fuck what Dreyer did,' Clint replied, getting angry. 'Fuck Dreyer. I don't have all that time to waste.'

All the preparations were ongoing when, at the eleventh hour, the momentum nearly ground to a halt. The Department of Defense came in over the Marines with a surprise veto of the script. The Assistant Secretary of Defense for Public Affairs, Bob Simms, had read the shooting script and pinpointed concerns. Simms hated the overall profanity, but also took issue with the authenticity of certain incidents taking place during Clint's pet sequence – the finale in Grenada.

The military higher-ups would have preferred to delete any reference to Grenada because the whole script was so artificial. But Clint's writers had borrowed actual events from Grenada and incorporated them into the script. These included a scene where a radio operator is killed (the Department of Defense argued that this was false history, since no Marines were killed in ground combat); and another scene where Marines rescue the American medical students who had given President Reagan the pretext for his decision to invade (more false history, since it was the army, *not* the Marines, that actually rescued the students). There were several sticking-points in all.

Clint was furious about the fresh complaints. Here he had changed everything on behalf of the Marines, and still the script was being shot down by the Department of Defense. Lt Col. Fred Peck was on Clint's side, believing that 'the army was objecting to the film because the Marines had taken it away from them', and that the script was absolutely 'in the realm of dramatic licence'. A high-level conference call had to be arranged between Clint, Manes, Peck and officials in Washington, DC. Clint was indignant, yet he promised to work with the DoD concerns 'and to change things, if possible', in the words of Peck. Photography was okayed to proceed on schedule.

But Manes knew that Clint hated to be told what to do. By now so did Peck, who was personally tested on the first day of shooting at Camp Pendleton. Peck had negotiated out of the script a scene where Sgt Highway and a sergeant major arrive at a party on a military base, and Highway reaches into his back pocket, brings out a flask, takes a swig, and passes it on to his superior. In story conferences Peck had pointed out to Clint that the characters were going to a party with a free bar, so why would they be standing around outside, drinking from a flask? Not to mention, no gunnery sergeant would offer a drink from a flask to a sergeant major.

As crew members prepared for that scene, Peck was startled to hear a set dresser call out, 'Hey, where's the flask?' 'What do you mean flask?' asked Peck. 'There's supposed to be a flask in the scene,' the set dresser answered. 'No, there isn't!' exclaimed Peck, and went looking for Clint, banging first on Fritz Manes's trailer door.

'Clint thinks the flask should still be in there,' the producer told Peck. 'It's *not*,' said Peck, who hated to be double-crossed. 'We negotiated that out. This is going to be the shortest goddamn production that ever hit Camp Pendleton, because I'm going to close you down right now.' Manes went running off to find Clint in his trailer.

Clint came out a few minutes later, all dressed up in his uniform ('looked dynamite,' said Peck, 'with his big stack of ribbons that I personally had done up with my two little hands to make sure they were perfect'). Clint came up to the public affairs officer and said, 'Fred, I don't think we need a flask in this scene.' Peck said, 'That's right. You don't.' Clint said, 'Because it doesn't really make sense to me. The next set-up is at the bar. Why would he have a flask anyway?' Peck said, 'That's right, Clint.' Clint said, 'So we won't have that flask. Don't worry about it.' And the flask was out.

'It takes twenty years to develop a friendship with Eastwood,' Peck said later, 'and twenty seconds to destroy it. Everybody in the Hollywood tradition calls him "Clint". But they walk on eggshells around him and they're really trying to think, "What does he want? What does he *really* want?" And they're afraid to ask him. Certainly everybody's afraid to tell him no.'

There were really two dramas ongoing behind the scenes: the attempt by the Department of Defense to police Clint had its corollary in the growing gulf between two old friends – the star and the film's producer. Fritz Manes thought Lt Col. Fred Peck's position would be jeopardized if Clint didn't compromise, adhering to some of his promises to the DoD. He also thought Clint was laughable, playing a tough Marine.

The real-life 7th Regiment Marines they met on location appeared to agree with the producer. Rather than flocking around Clint, instead they gravitated to the genuine Marine in their midst – Fritz Manes.

Not only the grunts ('They'd go to Clint for his autograph,' said Peck, 'but then they'd come and *talk* to Fritz because Fritz was a Marine'), but also the commanding officers. After word about 'one of our own' circulated, then a steady stream of regimental officers and commanders came to eat lunch with Manes, making presentations of stick pins, shoulder patches, decals for his car. Clint, sitting next to Manes, would be watching stonily as all of this unaccustomed praise was showered on his boyhood friend.

One day the colonel heading the 7th Regiment came by to give Manes a plaque. He volunteered a little speech. 'We're so pleased to see that one of our own has made it into such a lofty position in the entertainment industry...' The colonel glanced over at Clint, glowering over his lunch tray, and added, 'We'd like to give you one of these too, Mr Eastwood, excepting we only reward our own...' Clint stood up, took his tray and dumped it in a garbage can. The colonel looked at Manes and asked, 'Did I say something wrong?' Manes said, 'No, Clint's just got something on his mind.'

Things reached a low point one evening when Clint and Manes were invited to a military base social event, during which they were expected to drink endless toasts to the honourableness and bravery of the Marine Corps. The whole idea of such all-out parties, from Manes's point of view – from the Marine point of view (it surely would have been Sgt Highway's point of view) – was to get ripped and rowdy, if possible finalizing the evening with a slugfest.

Sure enough Manes got bombed 'and by the time this night was over I was farting in the back of station wagons and laughing and ready to punch everybody out. The Marines thought that was the greatest thing they ever saw because I was one of their own. They thought Eastwood was a pussy, because all night long he pretended like he was drinking wine, but he wasn't drinking at all. The level of his glass never changed.'

The next day, driving to the set, Clint made a point of upbraiding Manes in front of Lt Col. Peck. 'I thought I told you to watch yourself and not get drunk!' Clint chastized. 'You're embarrassing me!' That was one thing Clint often said to bring people down, 'You're embarrassing me!' By now, however, Manes was fed up. 'I was driving the car,' recalled Manes, 'so hung over I could barely see. I turned around and said, "Hey, go fuck yourself!"'

That's the way it went throughout the filming of *Heartbreak Ridge*.

Clint dropped a couple of the scenes that bothered the DoD and left a couple intact.

The profanity only got worse. Clint and Lt Col. Peck had talked about profanity in films; according to Peck, a champion boxer at the Naval Academy, Martin Scorsese's *Raging Bull* had been ruined for both of them by its excessive foul language. Peck had taken on the mission of reducing the profanity in *Heartbreak Ridge*, but wherever they went on location, the recon. commanders and ordinary Marines talked saltier than the script. Everybody adopted the patois, and the dialogue blossomed with F-words and extra-added oaths. Peck thought profanity was the most ludicrous DoD objection.

The production had a crisis towards the end of the schedule when Clint was shooting the medical school scene at a private school in Solano Beach. Peck called the Division of Public Affairs in Washington, DC from where they were filming, just to check in. When Lt Col. John Shotwell casually asked him what was being photographed that day, Peck told him. Shotwell got upset because he thought that scene was supposed to be deleted from the script. Peck told him Clint never agreed to do anything specific, only to 'make changes, where possible'. Rescuing the medical students was integral to the film's plot – besides, that's what most Americans remembered about Grenada. Shotwell informed his superior officer, Brig. Gen. Walt Boomer, who had assumed his Public Affairs post in mid-production and was unaware of all the preceding discussions.

At four that morning, Peck received a blistering phone call from Brig. Gen. Boomer in Washington, DC. Boomer read him the riot act. Boomer wanted to close the production down. Peck, who was performing a tightrope act throughout the filming, asked to be relieved if the General didn't have confidence in him; Peck reminded him that there was only one scene left which required cooperation from the Marines – a shipboard scene utilizing an amphibious assault ship. The DoD would only be hurting itself at this point. Why not stay calm, and take a look at the finished film?

'I want to talk to Eastwood,' declared Gen. Boomer. Knowing Clint, Peck said he'd better try to reach the star first So Peck phoned Clint, waking him up at 4:30 a.m., and telling him that the DoD was insisting that he drop the medical school scene. Clint was outraged. 'I'm calling Ronald Reagan!' he announced. 'Goddamn it, I'm not going to put up with this!' Peck called Boomer back and said, 'Clint is calling the White House. He's willing to go to the mat on this.' Both Peck and Fritz Manes tried to reason with Boomer.

Whether or not Clint got through to President Reagan no one knows, but finally Gen. Boomer got Clint on the phone and digested the fact that it really was too late to do anything. What was done was done. Proceed, the General reluctantly told Peck.

All this bad blood was still in the air when Warners moved up the release date of *Heartbreak Ridge* to Christmas, 1986. Lt Col. Peck told Clint he ought to take the film back and show it to the DoD himself, because the DoD wouldn't have the balls to say no to Clint Eastwood personally. According to Fritz Manes, it was the other way around; Clint didn't have the guts to face the DoD, so Manes got stuck with the unwelcome assignment of taking the finished film to DC for a high-level screening.

A whole DoD entourage was in the room. They never recovered from the first scene, which was Sgt Highway, drying out in a jail cell after one of his sprees, exclaiming, 'I've been pumping pussy since Christ was a corporal and I'm here to tell you the best goddamn poontang I ever paid for was in a place on Duc Lop Street in the beautiful city of Da Nang . . .' Ironically, James Carabatsos had written that scene in the first draft, and Lt Col. Peck had authenticated the dialogue.

Assistant Secretary of Defense for Public Affairs Robert Simms branded the film as blasphemous pornography. All of the Grenada stuff was deemed inaccurate. Clint's filming of scenes that had been targeted for removal was duly noted. After all the support that had been given, Simms ordered that the DoD would have nothing further to do with the movie and thus the Marine Corps was obliged to put out a press release, repudiating *Heartbreak Ridge* and withdrawing any and all association ex post facto.

Lt Col. Peck thought the film turned out okay, all things considered, and that the DoD overreacted. He ended up having mixed feelings about Clint. 'Many people have asked me, "What's Clint Eastwood like?'' Peck mused, 'and I've always answered, he's probably more like Dirty Harry in real life than even he realizes. He's a strange character. He would be carrying a gun in his glove compartment, but then slam on the brakes not to run over some squirrel that scampers across the road in front of him. He is a very interesting man who could sometimes act like a fifty-nine-year-old spoiled brat.'

As for James Carabatsos, the original writer left behind, he received sole credit on the screen, but not without a skirmish of his own with Clint. Clint phoned one day to say that he wanted to give one of the Malpaso writers, Joe Stinson, a co-credit, because he felt Stinson deserved it. Clint was taken aback when Carabatsos replied that he didn't think anyone else earned a credit, and besides, such decisions weren't up to him or to Clint. The apportioning of credits was strictly regulated by the Writers' Guild.

Nonetheless, Clint, as the film's producer, put forth Stinson's name, and therefore the credit had to be arbitrated. Carabatsos was awarded sole credit. Later, according to Carabatsos, Clint made statements in interviews that implied the script had been heavily revised under Malpaso supervision, and a Guild officer had to step forward and intercede, advising Clint to back off from any such comments in the future.

When *Heartbreak Ridge* was released, it went into 1,470 theatres and ended up doing very well in the US ($70 million gross) before adding revenue overseas. The reviews were enthusiastic about Clint's acting; the star got additional feminist mileage out of his apologetic relationship with Marsha Mason as Sgt Highway's ex-wife.

Warners, overly optimistic, mounted its most intensive campaign intended to reward Clint with a Best Actor Oscar nomination. Scant hope; as a whole *Heartbreak Ridge* was a draggy 130 minutes, with few 'shades' in Clint's character or anywhere in the film.

The whole experience was a touchy subject with Clint. He felt betrayed by the DoD. He felt betrayed by Fritz Manes, who was supposed to have threaded the needle with the Marine Corps. Clint began to compile one of his 'dossiers' on Manes: everything that went wrong with *Ratboy* was translated as, 'Fritz can't handle Sondra.' Everything that went wrong with *Heartbreak Ridge* was translated as, 'Fritz fucked up, major league.'

*   *   *

Earlier in the year, *Ratboy* had had a limited release in the US.

Postproduction had continued a tug-of-war. Clint stepped in to take more of a role; he took pride in his postproduction savvy. Fritz Manes thought the star was trying to do his best to help the actress–director. Locke thought, in retrospect, that Clint's advice and insistences were 'controlling for the sake of controlling'.

'Clint has much more of a flat-footed approach to things,' Locke explained. 'The film needed reworking all along, but I wanted to do something quite different than him, and the two of us made for an impossible combination. Ratboy became a mish-mash. The things about the script that needed to be changed I was never allowed to change, and so suddenly, as the film goes along, there are these odd, flatfooted sections. That's what I really resented about his input, and still resent.'

Lt Col. Fred Peck, the technical advisor of *Heartbreak Ridge*, which was being filmed at the same time that *Ratboy* was in postproduction, couldn't help but notice how some people at Malpaso sneered at Locke behind her back. 'They put her down,' recalled Peck. 'There were comments like, "What's he see in her? She can't act. She's not very pretty." So I went out of my way to be nice to her.'

All along their mutual friends had urged Clint to leave his name off the picture, so that nothing would take away from Locke's achievement. He was torn. He was not really the producer; on the other hand, Locke had 'borrowed' his producer and crew (at his insistence). What if the picture was a big flop? What if it was a success? In the end Clint hedged his bets, leaving his name off but putting Malpaso's on.

Warners wasn't sure what to do with the film, despite at least one important review, Michael Wilmington in the *Los Angeles Times* describing it as 'something really unusual: Grimm Brothers-style, mixing wonder with rough edges, undertones of pain beneath the fantasy'. *Ratboy* only did well overseas, especially in France, where it received its world première at the Deauville Film Festival in September 1986. *Le Monde, Liberation, Le Figaro, Pariscope* and *Cahiers du Cinéma,* among other major French publications, gave rhapsodic notices to Sondra Locke's directorial debut. She was kept busy for weeks, flying on a Warners jet to festivals and events.

*   *   *

Sondra Locke thought the mayoral gig was a manifestation of Clint's mid-life crisis. None of his recent films had done as well as he hoped. 'I guess they don't like your old Dad anymore,' Clint had told Locke wistfully after *Honkytonk Man* died in theatres. Around this time, the mid-1980s, is when the star had secret hair transplants. And, worried about ageing, he started eating red meat again, telling one friend it was because he found out 'all of the higher intelligence mammals of the world were meat eaters'.

Being mayor did rejuvenate him, people say. The reviews up in Carmel were getting better. Clint began to run meetings with a more casual touch. His old, self-deprecating humour returned, although the wheels of his government spun too fast for some.

His *beau geste*, the purchase of Carmel's Mission Ranch, came in December 1986. Disposition of the historic Mission Ranch property, twenty acres of ranch and wetlands lying just south of Carmel's city limits, had preoccupied the municipal government for years. The long-time owners preferred to build new townhouses on the property, while Carmel wanted to modify development and ensure the site's future preservation.

The city had made an offer of $3.75 million for the Mission Ranch, which included cottages, a well-known restaurant and a large barn where dances used to be held. But the owners had refused to budge from their higher asking price of $6.5 million, which the city was unable to afford. Litigation between the two parties had tied up the issue in court.

Clint, saying he could find no other investors willing to step in, came to the rescue with a reported $5.5 million of his own money. Clint said that he had a fondness for the place, dating back to his days as a soldier at nearby Fort Ord. His purchase would keep the Mission Ranch 'out of hostile hands' who might develop for profit. 'I will do the best I can to keep it like it is,' Clint said. 'It is a historic piece of property.' Asked at a Carmel Heritage meeting to put this pledge on paper, Clint ducked and dodged and finally politely refused.

So the news, reported across the country, was greeted sceptically by some Carmel area preservationists. Coincidentally or not, the widely publicized act of generosity dovetailed with the nationwide opening of *Heartbreak Ridge*.

* * *

At least one Marine would 'die' at Clint's Heartbreak Ridge: Fritz Manes.

Hampered by his 'attitude problem', disliked by Judy Hoyt and Jane Brolin, left to twist in the wind by Sondra Locke, and tainted by what had happened over *Ratboy* and *Heartbreak Ridge*, Manes was already mortally wounded, although he didn't know it. He understood that Clint was mad at him, but he never thought he was about to be canned.

Clint was busy seeking everyone's opinion. Everybody was glad to help. They told him what he wanted to hear. Many of them had some axe to grind against Manes anyway.

The list of criticisms against Manes was long. He abused his power. He played loose with company money. He embarrassed Clint with his behaviour. Worst of all, Manes didn't know his history and had got Clint into that mess with the Marines.

Clint was spending more and more time up north, in Carmel, San Francisco, or at the Rising River Ranch. It was natural that he be absent from the office for long spells. It wasn't quite as natural that nothing loomed on the horizon as the next Malpaso production. Manes had things to do in the office, however. He didn't take Clint's hints that it might be a *long* time between films.

'I don't know if we're going to make a picture next year or not,' Clint told Manes. 'What do you feel like doing?'

On the side, Manes was talking almost every day to one of the court intrigants, good-health Dr Harry Demoupoulis.* Manes thought the tension between him and Clint would blow over, but he wanted Demoupoulis's advice. Demoupoulis presented himself as a mediator between two old friends, and since he also spoke with Clint on a regular basis, Manes valued his perspective. Demoupoulis said that what Manes should do was go in to see Clint, the next time he was in the office, clear the air.

So Manes did. He was set up like a bowling pin. 'What the fuck do you want?' were the first words out of Clint's mouth when he walked in. Manes said, 'What do you mean "What the fuck do I want?" I want to get this thing between us cleared up.'

---

* Dr Demoupoulis, cited in Durk Pearson and Sandy Shaw's *Life Extensions*, had become one of Clint's health and nutrition advisers. He would play bit parts in several Clint films.

Clint said Manes' attitude was negative and that he embarrassed him all the time by screaming and yelling at people. Manes pointed out that Clint was screaming and yelling at him. Manes said he wanted to know what the hell was bugging Clint. They screamed and yelled at each other for twenty minutes. 'The mind has a kind way of making you forget some of what happened,' said Manes. 'The stuff that he was accusing me of, and the stuff that I yelled back at him, was stupid. Finally it died away.'

Clint got on an airplane and went to San Francisco and from there down to Carmel. Then for two months, nothing happened. Clint didn't even show up in the office.

Finally one day Roy Kaufman called Manes and said his cheques were no longer being issued by Warners. Manes called the head of accounting, who told him that instructions had come directly from Terry Semel, so he'd better get hold of Clint. It still hadn't quite hit home. He asked Judy Hoyt to find Clint for him. She said, 'Find him yourself.'

Manes got in his car and drove home, feeling dazed. He sat down and told his wife. She couldn't believe such a thing had happened, and urged him to speak to Clint.

It took him several days to reach Clint. Finally Manes trapped him on the phone and Clint said, 'The deal is this. We're going to close down the office for a while. I'm not going to do anything for a year or so. It would be a good time for you to go to work with somebody else and get some other experience.'

'What is the time frame?' Manes asked, feeling queasy.

'What do you mean, what is the time frame?' Clint responded.

'You know that my wife and I have planned a trip to Europe. She's going to a cooking school in Florence and then we're heading for Venice. It's been planned for months.'

'Fuck all that. I don't want to hear about that.'

'I mean, is it still okay to go? Or will something be scheduled while I'm away?'

'I don't give a damn,' said Clint. 'Do whatever you want.'

Manes still wasn't sure what was happening. About a week went by, with him showing up in the office every day. Judy Hoyt wasn't even speaking to him. Everybody thought he was toughing it out, but really, he was just trying to figure out what was going on.

According to Sondra Locke, Clint was deliberately evading Manes, trying to forestall any confrontation. Coming into Los Angeles on the Warners jet, Clint wouldn't even call Judy Hoyt on his private line because he didn't want the producer, who was still at his desk, to see the line light up and know it was Clint. So he would call on the public line and demand to know why Manes was still there. Manes just didn't get the hints.

Finally, Manes's phone rang, and it was Clint.

'What the fuck are you doing hanging out in there?' his old friend wanted to know.

'I beg your pardon?' said Manes. ('I thought he was being funny, at first.')

'Get all your shit out of there,' said the star. 'Sonia Chernus is moving in.'

'She's what?' asked Manes, still on another planet.

'She's moving in,' repeated Clint. 'I'm bringing her back into the company and she's going to be using your office.'

That was certainly clear enough. Somebody whom Clint had always spoken of as a 'bottom feeder' would be taking over the producer's office.

'I'll be out of here in an hour,' said Manes. After thirteen years of helping to produce seventeen Malpaso productions, Manes left the offices, never to return.

That wasn't the end of it. Roy Kaufman called and tried to retrieve Manes's GM 'Jimmy' truck. He said it belonged to Clint, to Malpaso. An angry Manes said the truck didn't belong to Clint, it belonged to GM and was leased to him for a year. He reminded Kaufman that the accountant also represented *him*. Look up the Jimmy in my file, said Manes.

When Kaufman called back, it was to say that the Jimmy might belong to Manes, but the car phone mounted in the console did belong to Malpaso. It had been mounted in the console of three leased Jimmys before this one. Manes told Kaufman it would cost several hundred dollars to take the car phone out and that it would virtually wreck the console. Kaufman said Clint would pay for the removal. He wanted that car phone back. It was his, by rights.

There was one more Kaufman phone call. 'You have something else that Clint needs back,' Kaufman told Manes, 'a VCR.' Manes had forgotten all about the VCR: removed from Clint's old motor home when Warners ponied up for a new, customized recreational vehicle, it sat in the company conference room for a long time before everyone got new matching systems at Malpaso. Then the old VCR became superfluous. Manes had asked to take it home, to supplement his Beta machine.

'Would you mind unplugging that,' asked Kaufman, 'and we'll send someone over to pick it up?'

Manes told him it would cost more than the machine was worth to have it picked up and fixed. Its technology was virtually obsolete. 'Look at it this way,' Kaufman told him, 'you can easily find a replacement. It's not worth it to argue with Clint . . .'

Kaufman stayed Manes's business manager only a short while longer. Like other little fish associated with Malpaso (director Ted Post, cameraman Rexford Metz, Sondra Locke), and others in the Hollywood community (director Stanley Kramer) Manes lost money on his investments there.

Starting over in Hollywood, Manes would have to fight the impression that Clint produces his own films and that he was naught but a spear-carrier for the great man. He would have to fight the innuendo against him. 'Clint does a destruction derby on everyone who leaves,' said Manes, 'and it's never traceable.' Since 1986, Manes has endeavoured to produce his own films. He is still trying.

CHAPTER TWELVE

Shades of Clint
1986–1989

Clint the film-maker did take off much of 1987, concentrating his energies elsewhere.

Up in Carmel he was conscientious about the council meetings and civic events a mayor was expected to attend. With briefings by Sue Hutchinson and other experts, he seemed genuinely conversant with the diverse issues and conflicting opinions in the wider community. He surprised himself; being Mayor was a broadening experience for him, and he found himself enjoying it.

Not only did Clint settle the fate of Mission Ranch by taking it off the market, but he was credited with the resolution of other long-standing issues. He accelerated construction of new beach stairways and public toilets, sped up completion of pathways along the bluffs, helped finalize a decades-old plan for a new library annex.

Some letters to the *Pine Cone* continued to complain that Mayor Clint was rude and arrogant to people who didn't tumble for his ideas, or expedient methods. Equal time – payback for appointing the *Pine Cone* publisher to the planning commission – came in the form of an intermittent Mayor's Column in which Clint commented on public affairs and derided his enemies.

Some enemies were marked for worse than derision. On one occasion, Mayor Clint led the council in overturning a planning commission decision granting former councilman David Maradei a variance to construct a gable on his roof, which would have risen one and a half feet higher than permitted by home restrictions. The Mayor 'appeared to take particular pleasure in reading aloud from a letter he received from Maradei and late Councilwoman Helen Arnold four years ago,' according to local newspaper accounts, 'which denied his design for an elevator shaft that would stick up one and a half feet higher than the city allows at his proposed building on San Carlos Street because of a 1983 moratorium on second storeys'.

Announcing that 'this [variance] stinks of the worst type of cynicism', Clint said he was going 'to do something that he [Maradei] never did for me', abstain from voting on whether to deny the variance. 'It was perhaps the loudest abstention in recent memory,' according to the *Pine Cone*, since Clint's prefabricated council majority could be depended upon to side with him in overturning the planning commission.

Another more amusing contretemps involved Clint's attempt to bring sky-sweeping klieg lights to Carmel for a local film festival tribute to fellow screen legend Jimmy Stewart. The council turned the proposal down. Objecting to the klieg lights, Councilman Robert Evans explained, 'It's kind of a Hollywood atmosphere, if you'll forgive the expression.' That really ticked off Mayor Clint. 'For one hour, I don't see what the big deal is,' he said.

Behind the local controversies and rapid-fire style were policies that many residents considered 'pro-development', and actions that in the long run 'could unalterably change the character of Carmel', in the words of the *Los Angeles Times*. In this category were proposals by Clint and his supporters to build parking garages in residential districts, rezone chunks of city land for higher-density building, sell city-owned parkland for development. Also worrisome was 'a shift in the allocation of water permits'. Clint's opponents believed that under previous administrations residents received first consideration, 'but under Eastwood, downtown businesses got top priority'.

Much of the best reporting on Clint's tenure appeared in the *Los Angeles Times*, where the reportorial staff were sometimes at odds with the entertainment writers. While *Los Angeles Times* entertainment writers tended to idealize Clint, the reportorial staff began to regard him sceptically as Mayor of Carmel, and increasingly had to fight for space to cover political activities which the film pages treated in Capraesque terms.

Los Angeles Times reporters dug deep, noting several 'potential conflict-of-interest situations' during his 1986–8 mayoral tenure. In one instance, an architect employed by Clint applied for a water meter permit for a 'commercial building site Eastwood owned, only hours before a building moratorium was slapped on the city by the local water board'. The former chairman of the Water Management District board was quoted as saying he thought Clint should have withdrawn the application, since the timing hinted at inside information. Yet Mayor Clint withdrew nothing.

Meanwhile, the Pope made a Carmel stopover in 1987 and shook Clint's hand. So did King Juan Carlos I of Spain. The tourists continued to multiply, as did sales of Mayor Clint souvenirs.

All this time away from Hollywood was probably needed respite from the *Sturm und Drang* of Malpaso and Stradella Road. Locke didn't visit Carmel often, but when she did she was thrown by the half-burned candles at Clint's house, and the throaty messages on his phone machine, the stains on bed sheets. Clint always had a good explanation: 'There was an electrical blackout and . . .' The actress grew so suspicious of one local muralist, who slipped mash notes to Clint under his door, that she attended a Carmel gallery show, trying to catch a glimpse of her imagined rival. In the end, Locke believed and trusted Clint because she *wanted* to believe and trust him.

All this time Clint was carrying on with other women. His notches on the belt included onetime political opponents in Carmel then spectacularly won over to his side on civic issues. The reporters who wrote about how charming and down-to-earth Mayor Clint was, living alone 'in a modest, comfortable stone house he recently purchased complete with furniture', not to mention 'stacks of newspapers and books', missed the fact that Clint still hated to be alone.

Not one of those reporters from all around the world noticed that Mayor Clint was still avidly carrying on his affair with Jacelyn Reeves, who lived only a couple of blocks away from him. This relationship led to the conception of their second child, Kathryn Ann Reeves, also born at Monterey Community Hospital on 2 February 1988.

Maybe rough-around-the-edges producer Fritz Manes didn't suit Clint's upgraded image of himself as an Oscar-calibre actor and film-maker exploring tones and shades.

Clint's next production would be his toniest yet. Indeed, it would be the riskiest, least commercial film project he had ever undertaken.

Clint's love of jazz had been established in publicity and articles for years; it was a virtue that was guaranteed mention. More than once Clint had sponsored strong, jazz-inflected scores for his films. (Although Gary Giddins of the *Village Voice*, one of the nation's leading jazz critics, might have gone overboard in declaring that soundtracks for Malpaso productions – by Jerry Fielding, Lalo Schifrin and Lennie Niehaus – constituted 'some of the finest jazz scores of the past 25 years'.)

Now Clint would embark on a biographical film about alto saxophonist Charlie Parker, one of the visionaries of the bebop era who was also, tragically, a heroin addict. The film would give him an opportunity to explore the art of jazz through the life story of a musical giant; and, for the second time in his career, to dare all by directing only – to express himself with the camera, playing down his name and face.

Clint came around to the project by degrees. First came his backstage assistance on Bertrand Tavernier's *'Round Midnight*, a 1986 Oscar-nominated homage to Paris jazz expatriates, which starred Dexter Gordon. Clint's aid to Tavernier is cited so routinely in complimentary accounts of his career that it is worth noting that Tavernier was a former press attaché partner of Pierre Rissient's, is still Rissient's close friend, and as one of France's foremost film-makers, was also, on his own, a figure with whom Clint might value a 'power relationship'.

Tavernier honestly admires Clint's work. This is his account of what happened:

In 1985 *'Round Midnight* had been rejected even for partial financing by nearly every major studio in Hollywood, with producer Irwin Winkler taking courage from the turndowns and sticking to his belief in the film. 'The fact that they all refuse it proves that we are right,' Winkler kept saying. 'There was a tiny hope at Warners,' explained Tavernier. 'But [head of production] Mark Rosenberg, in spite of all his demonstrations of admiration and love, was reluctant.'

Through Pierre Rissient, Clint was made aware of Tavernier's problems, and knowing that the French film-maker had an appointment one day with Rosenberg, Clint told Tavernier he would phone him there to let him know the hour and the day of a *Pale Rider* screening in New York, to which Tavernier was invited. 'When the secretary said that Mr Eastwood wanted to talk to Bertrand Tavernier,' Tavernier recounted, 'Mark had a shock, as if he was struck by lightning. His attitude changed. During the conversation he kept asking very softly and kindly: "Can I talk to him?" He did and told Clint how much he loved *Pale Rider*. When it was over he said, "I did not know you knew Clint so well . . ."'

'I don't think Clint said one word about *'Round Midnight*,' continued Tavernier, 'but he knew his phone call was going to impress Mark and make me feel important. It did. But Rosenberg did not like the tests I made of Dexter Gordon, thinking he was homosexual "because of the way he moved his hands".' Rosenberg tried to convince Tavernier to cast Christopher Lambert as Francis, the jazzman's most fervent admirer, a role eventually taken by François Cluzet. 'That would have been terrible,' said Tavernier. 'Lambert, not a great actor, was too strong, too healthy. I refused.'

A few weeks later Tavernier learned that Rosenberg had turned down the project, but that Richard Fox, president of Warner Brothers International, which oversaw all aspects of Warners' foreign theatrical distribution, had made a bid of one million dollars for the foreign-language markets. In Paris shortly thereafter, following Cannes and the showing of *Pale Rider* there, a dinner was held at Maxim's, with Clint as guest of honour. Tavernier was also present and there he was introduced to Richard Fox. He heatedly confronted the studio's foreign distribution executive. Tavernier told Fox that one million dollars for all foreign territories was absurd. In France alone, Tavernier said, he could expect a guarantee of $2 million.

That is when Clint made a point of speaking up, saying 'a few nice words about the project. He said how much he loved jazz, how much he respected Dexter Gordon. He was the only one in the whole group who knew him, having heard him twice in concert. And I think he added that it was not a great risk, considering the budget of the movie. His kind words, maybe combined with my violent "charge", and Irwin's determination, influenced Richard Fox who, a few days after, said he was giving three million dollars for the foreign territories. And we made the film with that money. We got nothing, zero, for the domestic market.'

Tavernier added forthrightly: 'To this day I do not know the real effect of Clint's words. He did not say much, but it came at a good moment. The fact that he knew Dexter was reassuring, but you must not underestimate the fights done by Irwin (and me, too) who always cared for the project, loved it and protected me.'

Another French connection for Clint arose when, in the course of preparation for the Charlie Parker project, Malpaso people stumbled across a documentary, obscure except to aficionados, called *The Last of the Blue Devils*. Made by lawyer-turned-film-maker Bruce Ricker in the mid-1970s, it featured rare footage of jazz legends Joe Turner, Count Basie, Jay McShann and Jo Jones, as well as Charlie Parker, all key figures in the Kansas City scene of the 1930s and 1940s. Although *The Last of the Blue Devils* had been shown theatrically in the US and England, and also on German and Scandinavian television, it had never had a French-language release. At Clint's urging, Warners picked up the documentary for new markets, ordered a new 35mm print, subtitled it in French, and released *The Last of the Blue Devils* in Paris in the spring of 1988 – preceding *Bird* – under the logo 'Clint Eastwood Presents'.

Ricker also had another, uncompleted, jazz documentary, long in the works, celebrating the life and art of pianist Thelonious Monk. Clint talked to Warners about that film too, arranged some financing, and *Thelonious Monk: Straight No Chaser* became a Warners–Malpaso 'negative pick-up' whose fall 1989 release would follow *Bird*'s.

Of course Sonia Chernus did not take up residency in Fritz Manes's old office; effectively, Malpaso's story department was moribund, and for the next, most celebrated, stretch of his career Clint – for all his vaunted independence – would repeatedly fall back on script material developed, and channelled to him, by Warners.

Bird had a long prehistory outside of Clint's purview. The writer, Joel Oliansky, was a Hofstra and Yale Drama School graduate, who had concentrated much of his career in television, where he did Emmy-winning work as a scenarist. In 1980 Oliansky made his feature directing debut with *The Competition*, whose script, another musical opus, starring Richard Dreyfuss and Amy Irving as two competing classical pianists, he also wrote. The following year, his eight-hour epic, *Masada*, starring Peter O'Toole, played on ABC.

Shortly after *Masada*, Oliansky received the go-ahead from Columbia, where he was under contract, to write a biographical film about Charlie ('Yardbird', or 'Bird') Parker, the legendary jazz musician, under the supervision of producer–partner Bill Sackheim. Oliansky, a lifelong bebop fan, sought out and brought over from France Charlie Parker's surviving widow, Chan. The script was fashioned as a love story between the jazz musician and Chan, their relationship doomed by Parker's Faustian pact with his art.

Although later articles gave Clint credit for involving trumpeter Red Rodney and Chan in the project, they were in fact consulted from the beginning by Oliansky. Their alternating perspectives informed his script, which began with Charlie Parker's death in 1955 at the age of thirty-four, and then in complex fashion, unwound in flashback over the course of Parker's life and career, his marriage with Chan, his self-destructive heroin habit.

In a meeting with Columbia executives, Oliansky was solemnly informed that, even more than *The Competition*, the Charlie Parker project was going to be his picture, he alone should direct it. '*That afternoon*, they sent it to Bob Fosse,' Oliansky recalled, with a certain unavoidable relish. It's a good joke, even if it's on him: Fosse passed.

The script Oliansky crafted was intended for Richard Pryor, the black comedy star who had played a supporting part in a similar project, *Lady Sings the Blues*, about the life of jazz vocalist Billie Holiday. Pryor, at the apogee of his popularity, was under contract to Columbia. But in 1980, Pryor had sustained third-degree burns over half his body, while attempting to 'freebase' cocaine; other misfortune followed, and his health and career never recovered. So 'Yardbird Suite' (Oliansky's tentative title) languished on the shelf.

Fast forward five years, to mid-1987: now Oliansky was busy in epi-sodic television, again on the Columbia lot. The Charlie Parker script had a terrific word-of-mouth in Hollywood, but he and producer Bill Sackheim were under no illusions that the script would ever be pro-duced. Who would have the guts to tackle such a serious, downbeat subject?

Warners, however, had Prince under contract, and rumours began to swirl that Terry Semel and Bob Daly were interested in Oliansky's script as a possible vehicle for the multi-talented musician. Through Semel and Daly, Clint caught wind of what was going on; he was interested in Charlie Parker. When Columbia aggressively sought to buy a hot Warners script called *Revenge*, Semel and Daly offered a trade: 'Yardbird Suite' for *Revenge*.

Clint was maybe interested in directing. There were no formal announcements to that effect and zero publicity as Clint went through discreet warm-up motions. Oliansky had heard the Prince rumours. His agent tried to find out what was happening with the script, but for weeks nothing was said. Nothing was definite.

Oliansky and Clint had passed each other by in jazz circles; they had a mutual acquaintance in Lalo Schifrin, and hung out at the same Los Angeles jazz joints. 'I knew he [Clint] was a serious jazz person,' said Oliansky. 'He didn't just go to a Spyro Gyra concert.' Although they were on the same Burbank lot, it wasn't until the late summer of 1987 that Oliansky received a phone call from Clint telling him he had done a bang-up job on the script.

'What script?' asked Oliansky, drawing a momentary blank.

'Charlie Parker,' said Clint. 'We're going to make it.'

Oliansky asked when.

'Oh,' replied Clint. 'About six weeks.'

Clint strolled over for a sit-down with the writer. They talked for roughly two hours, comparing notes on jazz albums they owned, and dates of concerts and club appearances at which they had glimpsed musical legends. They were kindred beboppers. Little by little Clint worked around to stipulating that he was going to direct.

'I'm sure you think the script needs work,' said Oliansky. 'After all, it's just a first draft.'

'Oh, absolutely,' said Clint.

'When do you think you might need a second draft?'

'Yesterday.'

'I know it's long – 139 pages,' said Oliansky. 'It needs cutting.'

'I'd love to shoot 105,' agreed Clint.

'Great,' said the scenarist. 'Let's call my agent.'

Oliansky could tell by the look on Clint's face that he had made some kind of unforgivable faux pax. So he quickly offered to do a rewrite for nothing. It was too late. That was the first, longest, and only genuine conversation Oliansky had with Clint.

Weeks later, after phoning Malpaso repeatedly, Oliansky was told through an intermediary to send Clint his revision suggestions. He did. 'A couple of them actually made it into the film,' Oliansky said. The writer tried to re-establish contact with Clint. And tried. Finally Judy Hoyt called with a message from Clint. In effect: 'Clint has received your notes. Thank you. If he needs anything more from you, he'll contact you.' 'Well, I know what "fuck you" means, so I didn't want to be told that twice,' said Oliansky. 'I didn't bother him again.'

After setting up these parameters, Clint kept Oliansky apprised. He sent the writer the shooting script, which had twenty pages excised – down to 119 – and a brief note saying he hoped the writer liked the cuts. 'You know what?' recalled Oliansky. 'It was fine. He made the same cuts I would have made, scenes he didn't need, scenes where the point had been made elsewhere. The only thing is, when you cut twenty pages from a script there are little jagged edges that occur, that you want to fix. Well, none of them was fixed.

'By not being able to go beyond the first draft,' Oliansky continued, 'I became the only person connected to the project, from the director to the hairdresser to the actors to the craft service people, who wasn't able to ask for Take Two.'

Clint did invite Oliansky to the prerecording of the jazz numbers, where for the first time the writer encountered the cast members, who included Michael Zelniker (playing Red Rodney), Diane Venora (Chan), and Forest Whitaker (Charlie Parker).

The stage-trained Whitaker had already proven himself a stand-out in *The Color of Money*, *Platoon* and *Good Morning Vietnam*. Lennie Niehaus, who had begun his career as a saxophone sideman with Stan Kenton, and whose own early alto work had been influenced by Charlie Parker, would teach Whitaker Bird's fingering.

Venora had made striking appearances in *FX* and *Wolfen*. Oliansky took the actress aside and engaged her in a long, heartfelt discussion about jazz and the character she was going to play in the film, learning that Venora wasn't much farther along the chain of information than him. 'Are you directing?' she asked Oliansky innocently.

Oliansky informed her, no, Clint was the director. But Clint was approaching this task cautiously, like a man trying out the new inflections of a foreign tongue. Everything about how he proceeded was more ambiguous than usual, more muted and studied.

The soundtrack offered a particular challenge. After being urged to do so by Oliansky, Clint went to France to meet Chan and she told him about a cache of long-rumoured reel-to-reel tapes she possessed of Parker playing at gigs and parties. Whereas for *Honkytonk Man*,

Clint had eschewed musical authenticity, here he would do his best to recreate Charlie Parker's 'sound'. As he had first done with *Play Misty for Me*, where he rerecorded Erroll Garner, he would 'recreate' classic jazz. With the help of modern technology, Parker's solo lines would be isolated from the old tapes, and then fresh accompaniment mixed in, using rhythm sections composed of some of Bird's onetime bandmates mixed with 'new generation' studio musicians.

Besides Lennie Niehaus, Malpaso regulars Edward Carfagno, Jack Green and Joel Cox were all on tap. Clint's new producer was David Valdes, hired and trained by Fritz Manes and now promoted in the wake of Manes's firing. Parts of *Bird* would be photographed in old sections of Los Angeles, Pasadena and the Sacramento Valley, while the crucial New York scenes were mocked up on the Burbank back-lot. Carfagno's nuanced recreations of the 1930s, 1940s and 1950s would be a highlight of the film.

The production designer was not the only one to notice that Clint's approach was more consuming than usual, during filming in late 1987 and early 1988. 'He did more takes when he was doing that picture than I'd ever seen him do,' said Carfagno. 'He would go eight, nine, ten takes, or even sometimes more than that, to try to get what he wanted.'

Scriptwriter Oliansky had the Felliniesque experience of seeing the characters he had created on the page, now costumed, parade past his office on the way to the set. He wasn't invited to watch dailies, nor did he observe the filming. In the winter, however, he was asked to the film's preview on the Warners lot, and subsequently he learned from an item in the newspaper that the film he had written had been invited to the Cannes Film Festival. That worried him a little.

'I thought the film needed some work in the cutting,' explained Oliansky. 'If you think about it, Clint shot 119 pages and the picture is six minutes shorter than *Raintree County*. You'd have to say the pace is a little deliberate. I didn't know how much of it was locked in. Was the print really going to be that dark? I couldn't see anybody. Also, even though I wrote the dialogue, the guy [Forest Whitaker] was so garbled, I didn't know what he was saying.'

Although Oliansky had differences with Clint's approach (feeling Clint had missed the hectic, urban sensibility of bebop, which was 'a great mixture of the Jew and the black with this Puerto Rican sauce on top'), he nonetheless tried to accept Clint's vision while hoping that maybe he could make a few postproduction suggestions.

This time he managed to reach Clint himself, who, perhaps thinking kudos were in order, accepted his phone call. They had a brief, strained conversation during which Oliansky diplomatically made his critique. 'Clint had a little hissy-fit,' recalled Oliansky. 'He said, "Well! Apparently you've learned more after directing one film than I have after directing fourteen." A small voice inside me said, "Why not?"'

Then it was off to the forty-first annual Cannes Film Festival.

Clint took with him a script to read, an adaptation of Peter Viertel's 1953 novel *White Hunter, Black Heart*, a famous *roman à clef* about director John Huston, the stalking of an elephant, and the eventful filming of *The African Queen* on location in Kenya.

Although the standard publicity would later claim that Clint 'lifted the story from the dusty shelves of unproduced projects' (Jack Mathews, *Los Angeles Times*), the property was brought to Malpaso by Stanley Rubin. Rubin, who had produced one of Clint's earliest films, *Francis Joins the Navy*, was now working for Ray Stark and Rastar Productions in offices on the Columbia part of the Burbank lot. As Rubin was engaged in preproduction for *Revenge* – the film traded to Columbia for *Bird* – he also was going through dormant scripts to determine what he might work on next. He came across a Columbia-financed adaptation of *White Hunter, Black Heart* which Viertel and writer–director James Bridges had teamed up on years earlier. The Western writer–director, Burt Kennedy, had followed Bridges and Viertel on the script, making revisions. But Columbia and Rastar had tried and failed to interest a big enough star, which was necessary to make the expensive project a 'go'.

A Phi Beta Kappa, Rubin had started out as a studio messenger boy; he had written his first Hollywood film in 1940. He knew the novel and loved it; loved the adaptation, although he thought parts needed revision. He also knew Clint. He took the Viertel–Kennedy script into a meeting of Rastar executives and sang its praises. He was told that they all thought somebody like Clint Eastwood would make the project 'bankable', only Rastar had not been able to get the script to Clint, past the high stone walls of Malpaso.

Dating back to their days at Universal, Clint had always been cordial with Rubin. They had 'a long, thin relationship', in the producer's words. Rubin made a call to Clint, and got through. The producer told Clint that the script contained four or five of the best scenes he had ever read in his life, and that playing John Huston would provide an exciting change of pace for the star. Would Clint read the script? Clint had never read the book; he had never met Huston (he was already fifteen years older than Huston was when he directed *The African Queen*). Yet he was intrigued.

Rubin walked across the lot to Malpaso and delivered the script to Clint in person, sitting down and having a chat about the past, their mutual interest in golf, and the merits of *White Hunter, Black Heart.* In fact they discussed the project in some detail, with Rubin stating that, although the script was quite strong, it did require additional work. The producer said he would be glad to discuss the fine points with Clint later if the star confirmed his interest. Clint said he would have a little free time at Cannes to read the script and make up his mind.

The conversation was very friendly, and since both were golf enthusiasts, Clint even mentioned that the two ought to get together to play some golf, one of these days.

This time at the festival, Clint stayed at a hotel, mingled with press and public, and hoped – badly wanted – to give *Bird* the canonization of a Cannes prize.

William Goldman, who won Academy Awards for his scripts for *Butch Cassidy and the Sundance Kid* and *All the President's Men* – the latter a Warners film – was the sole US representative of the international jury that included Italian film-maker Ettore Scola (president of the jury), actress Nastassja Kinski (vice-president), actress Elena Sofonova (whose fame was largely restricted to her native Soviet Union), Dutch-born cameraman Robby Müller, French composer Philippe Sarde, Australian-born director George Miller (who, like Robby Müller, worked frequently in Hollywood), and Argentinian producer–director Hector Olivera.

Goldman had helped write the Academy Awards jokes in 1973, the year Clint subbed at the last minute for an absent Charlton Heston, whose car was stuck on the freeway. (Clint showed special aplomb, since all the cue-cards played off jokes at the expense of the man who had impersonated Moses in *The Ten Commandments*.) In his first book about Hollywood, *Adventures in the Screen Trade*, Goldman expressed his appreciation for Clint as a man 'more at ease with himself than any other star'. Goldman regarded Clint as 'the most consistently durable popular star in the history of American films'; and after seeing *Bird*, he found Clint's jazz biography 'a spectacular piece of work . . . something rare – an intimate epic'.

Besides *Bird* the major contenders for Best Film that year at Cannes were *A World Apart*, a British film about the South African racial gulf; *Pelle the Conqueror*, a Danish–Swedish nineteenth-century drama; and *Le Sud*, directed by Argentinian Fernando Solanas, a film which certain critics considered deeply philosophical, although Goldman regarded it as 'full of dead people not being dead and time blending into time and phrases rich with meaning' plus a lot of shots of newspapers blowing along the streets.

There was heavy jury sentiment for *Pelle the Conqueror* (which went on to win Hollywood's Best Foreign-Language Film Oscar that year). Best Actor voting took place first, however, and the initial round of balloting came up strong for Forest Whitaker's intense, showy Charlie Parker impersonation. As Goldman explained things, in his book *Hype & Glory*, this induced him to launch a forceful countercampaign on behalf of Max Von Sydow, star of *Pelle the Conqueror*. Why?

'I thought Whitaker was also brilliant,' Goldman explained. 'But I knew if he won as actor, my man Eastwood didn't have a prayer for director. The jury would never give two [major] awards to one picture in the same year. So, although I believed every sentence about Von Sydow, I also had my motives. If Von Sydow won, Eastwood would get director. I was sure of it.'

After everybody voted again, Forest Whitaker still won handily. 'Eastwood was dead in the water,' Goldman surmised. Best Director went to Fernando Solanas for *Le Sud*, the one with all the newspapers blowing. Wrote *Time* magazine sympathetically, 'Eastwood dutifully mounted the Palais stage [for the awards ceremony] and though he stood tall, his dignity was stooped. The ceiling of expectations for his film was too high, the reward for lending his easy magnetism to Cannes too low.'

Although Clint was once again disappointed by Cannes, he would remember William Goldman's militance on his behalf and reward the writer in the future.

*   *   *

When he returned from Cannes, Clint's secretary phoned Stanley Rubin and set up a meeting. Clint told the producer that he had found *White Hunter, Black Heart* to be everything Rubin had promised. He wanted to make the film. Rubin made it clear that he intended to work closely with Clint, serving as co-producer on behalf of Rastar, and he reiterated his concerns that the script be improved. Clint said fine.

During the next few weeks, while Rastar worked out intricacies of the financial partnership with Leonard Hirshan and Bruce Ramer, Clint and Rubin had several meetings, usually with David Valdes in tow. The meetings seemed very positive to Rubin. He and Clint discussed locations, casting, scheduling, script alterations.

Rubin pointed out two particular weaknesses in the script. The character of Paul Landers, the wheeler-dealer producer, needed to be strengthened, in order to make him closer to the celebrated figure on whom the character was based – independent producer Sam Spiegel; also, that would heighten the tensions between the producer and the John Huston character, director John Wilson. Clint nodded his agreement.

Also, in Rubin's opinion, the continuity lacked drive, especially the first third of the script. The opening sequences, set in London and involving Wilson's dealings with Landers and British financiers, ought to be tightened and condensed. Again Clint nodded his agreement, and Rubin went away from the meetings feeling optimistic.

Then the Rastar–Malpaso contract was signed, the partnership became official, and both Clint and Rubin had to turn their attention to more immediate problems. *White Hunter, Black Heart* was placed on the back burner, and they dropped out of touch.

What about Sondra Locke? She had two new properties in development at Warners, and was doing her best to cope at home with the loose ends of Clint's personal life.

Jane Brolin had become a regular house guest at Stradella Road. Not only was Brolin undergoing an acrimonious divorce, but she had been hit with a diagnosis of breast cancer. These days she seemed to be constantly in Los Angeles, coming down from Paso Robles, where she lived, keeping appointments with lawyers and physicians. Locke felt sorry for her, and they began to develop a cosy friendship.

It was Brolin who told Locke some of Clint's longtime secrets (his purported vasectomy, details of his 'understanding' with Roxanne Tunis). She gave Locke an earful about how ungenerous Clint could be, and how it was too bad that the rich, successful star didn't buy his live-in lover expensive gifts – jewellery and clothing. Locke listened patiently, although everyone says that if there was anything she didn't expect or *receive* from Clint it was . . . expensive gifts. Little did Locke suspect that everything she did and said to Brolin was reported back to Clint.

Then, in mid-1987, Kyle Eastwood moved into Stradella Road. He had received poor grades at USC, where he was majoring in cinema studies, and the hope was that he might turn his life around over the summer and re-enroll in the fall. Locke was annoyed that Clint didn't even discuss the matter with her. He simply said, 'Kyle is moving in,' and then within a few days, 'Clint promptly left town', according to Locke.

Locke had tried to reach out to Clint's children. She felt genuinely fond of Kyle, a sweet kid as low-key as his dad, and now she tried to make the best of the awkward situation. While Clint was in Cannes, up in Carmel, at Rising River Ranch, at his golf tournaments, whenever and wherever Clint roamed, Locke and Kyle lived together as a make-shift family unit. Tensions increased when one of Kyle's friends moved in; his pals showed up, and also their girlfriends. One night Locke woke up to find one of Kyle's friends in her bedroom, staring down at her. She ordered him out.

When she complained to Clint, Clint got mad. 'I don't know what your problem is,' the star told her. 'Kyle's my son. I want him there. I haven't had a chance to be with him all these years.' Locke was thinking, 'Excuse me – you're not *here, now*'; and, 'Hey, whose fault is *that*?' But she held her tongue and instead said, 'That's fine, Clint. We're not talking just about Kyle. We're talking about all his friends.' Clint responded, 'You're not at home half the time anyway. You're always visiting Gordon.'

They were starting to have circular conversations and arguments. So they talked less. That wasn't hard to arrange, because Clint was out of town so much.

Why was Clint being so cold and uncommunicative? Locke talked it over with Jane Brolin. Brolin was sympathetic. Clint went through 'down cycles'. Brolin explained. Locke griped a little about Kyle and his friends, who had started up a country-rock band and now were rehearsing at odd hours at Stradella. This was translated back to Clint and right down the line (Maggie, still friendly with Brolin, began quoting it to friends) as, 'Sondra hates Kyle'.

One of the few times Mayor Clint ventured into political controversies outside Carmel, he lent his name and donated a cheque to the successful electoral campaign to oust California State Supreme Court Justice Rose Bird, a crusading liberal jurist who was opposed to the death penalty. He was more sought after than ever in Republican circles, and national figures such as Republican majority leader, Senator Bob Dole, stopped in Carmel to meet him and talk about his future. There was speculation his political stock was rising, and Clint did flirt with the idea of running for another office (one time, in Washington, DC for a lunch at the White House with President Reagan, he whispered to Sondra Locke, as their limo passed the White House, 'Look, sweetie, all this could be ours'). But it was only flirtation, and more than once Clint had reassured local citizens, 'My political ambitions start and stop with Carmel.'

In February of 1988, Clint announced that he wasn't going to attempt a sequel to his two-year mayoral term, owing to his desire to spend more time with his children while they were still in their formative years. 'Raising children in the present atmosphere of drugs and teen suicide is frightening,' Clint declared. Clint's announcement was taken at face value by the press, although Kyle was almost twenty and Alison nearly sixteen – Clint himself was fifty-seven. His children were *beyond* their formative years. 'I don't think that [raising his children] had much to do with it,' his daughter Alison conceded in an interview some years later.

Although he had been touted for higher office, Clint knew his limitations. As he admitted in an interview a few years later, 'I would never have been able to pass the Bill Clinton–Gary Hart test, the scrutiny [politicians] are put through nowadays – no one short of Mother Teresa could pass.' Only his closest friends knew, way back in 1988, how short of Mother Teresa he truly was.

His mayoral term had marked Carmel for ever as Clintville, and the verdict on his leadership was mixed. The *Carmel Pine Cone* gave him high marks. The Democratic-controlled California state legislature passed a resolution in his honour. Eleven Monterey County mayors signed a plaque citing his 'refreshing, regular-guy attitude'.

Clint's reign bequeathed a different legacy to others. Citizens talked of reforms that would preclude celebrities from commandeering local elections. Others formed 'an unusually committed opposition', according to the *Los Angeles Times*, 'who swore that they would never again take preservation for granted. They joined forces with fishermen and environmentalists and others concerned about rampant development.'

Tom Rooker moved down to southern California and began working at Malpaso. Some months after Clint's term ended, his former campaign manager and assistant, Sue Hutchinson, would also move down from Carmel to take over from Judy Hoyt, who retired as Clint's secretary. Hutchinson was well-schooled in the art of walling Clint off, but she found that Hollywood already knew the rules. Most days she was all alone at Malpaso, and the phone didn't even ring. Clint was good to her, but she found it one of the most boring jobs she ever had and would only stay for about a year before gladly leaving her glamorous post.

A couple of weeks after Clint announced he wasn't going to seek a second term, he rushed off to nearby San Francisco to shoot the last of the Dirty Harry series (so far).

The film originated with his health and nutrition consultants Durk Pearson and Sandy Shaw. They had 'comped' him with a mountain of pills and nutrients, now he 'comped' them back by buying their script idea.

Their story would thrust Detective Callahan into a milieu of disgusting rock stars, satanic music videos and obsessed know-it-all fans, with the detective challenged by a string of macabre celebrity murders – including a scene with a vapid film critic, a Pauline-Kael-type, terrorized by a knife-wielding intruder. Eventually Harry himself becomes a target of the mysterious killer.

With its final script by Steve Sharon, *The Dead Pool* did have a patina of 'seriousness'. Musings about 'the price of fame' hinted at a thoughtful intent. But there was never any philosophical consistency or depth to the Dirty Harry films.

Richard Schickel wrote that Clint was attracted to *The Dead Pool* partly because of the darkly comic sequence where Harry and his partner are pursued by a toy car loaded with a bomb. This augured, in Clint's mind, 'a nifty parody of the famous *Bullitt* car chase'. The trouble, even with toy car chases in Clint's films, was that they looked as though they were directed by the second unit after being diagrammed by the stunt buddies. The only way to judge is to watch the film. *Bullitt* it's not.

Apart from the modest contributions of Patrice Clarkson (a Locke-alike damsel in distress) and Liam Neeson (a schlock horror director), *The Dead Pool* is the worst, most egregious Dirty Harry. It has become axiomatic to cite comic Jim Carrey, in one of his first screen appearances here, as representative of Clint's knack for picking newcomers. Carrey would gush about Clint at the American Film Institute special and Hollywood Walk of Fame ceremonies; and no doubt he was eternally grateful. One has only to watch Carrey, playing a devil-worshipping rock singer (and do watch closely, it's a fleeting part), to realize that nobody behind the camera had the slightest concept of his true potential.

It seems unfair to overly blame Buddy Van Horn, who is listed as director of *The Dead Pool*, when Clint, already worth several hundred million dollars, felt compelled to make the film as a sure-fire, money-making hedge against the real gamble of *Bird*.

Even though *Bird* had failed to win top honours at Cannes, film festival showings tended to breed more film festival showings, and for the first time, in the fall of 1988, a Clint film was invited to the New York Film Festival. This would position *Bird* for artistic acclaim in the US, which was essential, since Warners could not strong-arm its customary wide bookings for a two-hour-and-forty-one-minute film that did not even boast the familiar face of Clint.

Bill Gold shaped the artistic campaign with his moody poster promising 'A Film by Clint Eastwood', adorned with a portentous quote from F. Scott Fitzgerald: 'There are no second acts in American lives.'

Among US critics, however, there was severely divided opinion. There were scathing fault-finders such as Stanley Crouch in the *New Republic* (who called *Bird* a 'very bad film') and Pauline Kael in the *New Yorker* (who wrote that 'the picture looks as if [Eastwood] hasn't paid his Con Edison bill'); while even those inclined to be sympathetic, such as Charles Champlin of the *Los Angeles Times*, thought the film 'relentlessly underlit' with 'surprisingly few glimpses of the inner man'. But Clint's audacious tackling of the subject matter won many over.

Hal Hinson of the *Washington Post* commented, 'Eastwood has succeeded so thoroughly in communicating his love of his subject, and there's such vitality in the performances, that we walk out elated, juiced on the actors and the music. In *Bird*, Eastwood shows talents that were never even hinted at in his earlier pictures.'

The studio had coast-to-coast quotes for its advertisements. Yet, once again, the customary Clint fans stayed away in droves, nor did *Bird* build a constituency at the arthouses. Clint had tried harder, but his old habits were ingrained, and it must be said that the film was hobbled by entertainment as well as 'artistic' weaknesses. *Bird* lacked narrative drive; it lacked emotional revelation from its lead character – and director.

Letting the music run on was one excuse for the length of the film. Yet even the well-intentioned soundtrack of *Bird* was debatable. The sound quality of the 'lost' tapes was crude, and half the film-making effort seemed devoted towards refining the sound. Purists thought Lennie Niehaus overstepped his bounds, comparing what he did with the strings to 'colourizing' black-and-white movies. Even Red Rodney was quoted as criticizing the choice of contemporary drummers for the soundtrack, when Roy Haynes and Max Roach were still eminently available.

First and foremost the music in the film was an engineering feat. No wonder the only prize besides Forest Whitaker's that *Bird* brought home from Cannes was a special one for technical achievement. Likewise the only Academy Award nomination would go to Les Fresholtz, Dick Alexander, Verne Poore and Willie D. Burton, who won the Oscar for their 'remastering' genius.*

Many jazz aficionados, impressed as were film reviewers by Clint's willingness to attempt such a project, overcame their scepticism. Clint won some of them over in person. Gary Giddins, whose jazz writing appeared in the *Village Voice*, entertained apprehensions about Clint based on 'two widespread assumptions: that country was his musical sphere and that (incidentally, if not consequently) he was a fascist'.

---

* Fresholtz, Alexander, Poore and Burton won in their Best Sound category.

But a summit meeting was arranged between the influential Giddins and Clint: Warners invited Giddins to Malpaso in early summer, so that he could interview Clint and time his *Esquire* cover piece ('A Tough Guy's Soul Revealed') for the fall release.

After meeting Clint, Giddins decided the star was a reticent, surprisingly warm man, who, sitting on his office couch, displayed the 'awkwardness of Henry Fonda in *Young Mr Lincoln* in trying to find a place to store his long legs'. Thinking it over, Giddins compared Clint to one of the foremost novelists of the twentieth century, Graham Greene, who in his career also alternated popular works with more searching ones. Clint's long, underrated filmography was 'something of an affront to profligate Hollywood', wrote Giddins, and *Bird* was 'remarkably adult and manifestly European in style'.

Fellow film-maker Spike Lee (his father is jazz bass player Bill Lee) is one of the handful who grumbled about *Bird* in print, prompting a sharp retort from Clint. Another jazz musician who expressed reservations about the film was Stan Levey, a one-time drummer with Parker, who noted, 'The guy [Charlie Parker] was humorous, and that side of him was missing.' And alto saxophonist Jackie McLean, one of Parker's protégès in the late 1940s, complained, 'It wasn't about the Charlie Parker I knew.'

Even McLean said, however, he could see *Bird* a thousand times, because 'there was that great sound coming off the screen'. Jazz-lovers everywhere were eternally grateful for that, as was the National Association for the Advancement of Colored People (NAACP), which bestowed a special Dedication to Excellence Award on Clint at its twenty-first annual Image Awards in late 1988, supposedly for his career-long efforts to use African–Americans in positive roles in films. Only a sceptic would note Clint's value to the awards telecast on NBC; the tie-in publicity for the film; the sometimes stereotypical roles for blacks in Clint films (pimps, criminals and terrorists); or the longtime dearth of African–American personnel behind the scenes at Malpaso.

Pink Cadillac would have a soundtrack as painfully middle-of-the-road and countryish as *Bird* was authentic bebop. Where the prejudice experienced by Charlie Parker was treated solemnly, if in passing, the Birthright militia of *Pink Cadillac* were a jokey depiction of ugly, real-life racists. *Pink Cadillac*, like *The Dead Pool*, would have Jim Carrey stumbling among the cast, Buddy Van Horn behind the camera, and a surfeit of stunts and crashes, building to a car-chase climax that was a hectic mess.

Clint, as a 'skip tracer' mixed up with a brassy dame (played by Bernadette Peters), a kidnapped baby and a white supremacist gang, was obliged to don various guises in the film, at moments taking on the voice and mannerisms of a redneck, a clown, a disc jockey. At a time when his private life was about to explode, he was surprisingly playful on camera. This may have been because *Pink Cadillac* was filmed in the fall of 1988 in the vicinity of the Rising River Ranch, and around Sacramento, where Clint had lived as a boy. This may have been because of a certain actress among the cast.

First, according to observers on the set, Clint had made a somewhat obvious play for Bernadette Peters, the offbeat, bubbly actress who worked more often in the musical theatre than in Hollywood. On camera, Clint and his leading lady evinced a feisty chemistry, but off camera Peters proved oblivious to the star's smooth advances. Getting up early most mornings to work out, it didn't take Clint long to turn his gaze to strawberry-blonde actress Frances Fisher, then in her late thirties, also jogging and lifting weights.

Although she was born in England, Fisher's father had been in construction and she had lived in cities all over the world before graduating from high school in Texas. Her first paying job in show business was sneezing in a Dristan commercial. After fourteen years of theatre and two soap opera roles in New York, along with appearances in Norman Mailer's *Tough Guys Don't Dance* and Paul Schrader's *Patty Hearst*, she had moved to the West Coast to expand her career. In *Pink Cadillac*, her first part in Hollywood, Fisher was playing the small supporting role of Bernadette Peters' sister.

Clint and she began a more-torrid-than-usual relationship. Fisher said later that, because she was a relative newcomer to Hollywood, she had no idea Clint was involved with, in fact living with, Sondra Locke. When she asked the star about other women in his life, he issued his usual disclaimer, 'I've been with someone – but it hasn't been happening for about three years.' According to sympathetic friends of Fisher, she persisted in asking, 'Is that it?' and Clint added, 'And I'm seeing a *few* other people.'

Back in Los Angeles after filming, Clint and Fisher continued to see each other on the q.t. She did think it odd, however, that Clint never invited her up to visit his house.

Locke hadn't been expressly informed that it wasn't 'happening' anymore. She and Clint had last slept together in October 1988, just before filming of *Pink Cadillac* started. But Locke was busy planning her next directing foray, a suspense film involving a lady cop working undercover as a prostitute. And wasn't Clint just busy, working and travelling? Busy was normal for Clint. Locke was looking forward to their annual Christmas trip to Sun Valley, when Clint could let his hair down and relax.

Nineteen eighty-eight had been filled by four feature films in assorted stages of production; public ceremonies, private hanky-panky; new-born children; indeed, as Richard Schickel wrote, Clint's life was sometimes 'a masterpiece of compartmentalization'.

Sometimes the pressures made Clint careen out of control. Sometimes innocent folk got in his way – as happened in a Dirty Harry film, with all those bullets flying.

There had been more than a few violent occurrences concealed from the public: one time, Clint and Fritz Manes were waiting for the arm of the entrance gate to open at Paramount. The gatekeeper was bent over talking to a *Star Trek* cast member. Clint didn't like to wait, and his mood darkened. The gatekeeper took his time, and had just looked up and finally recognized Clint, when the star angrily gunned the truck and tore through the gate. Steel, concrete and wood flew all over the place, as Clint drove on, squealing into his parking space, getting out of the car, locking the door, stomping off to his appointment. The studios were fiefdoms; nobody at Paramount questioned the incident.

Since Universal days, Clint had behaved strangely about cars and parking spaces, which were part of his psychological turf. Parking spaces for Malpaso employees were notoriously inviolate. Fritz Manes remembered once when Clint found a choreographer's Cord in a company space, he drove into it and pushed it up against a fence, got out, rolled up his windows and locked the door, so the classic car couldn't be budged. And there was another time, according to Manes, when Clint yanked open the hood of someone's car that had strayed into the wrong spot and tried to rip out the wiring. Later, the woman driver came out, managed to get the car started, and drove away. Clint admitted to a twinge of regret, because the woman turned out to be kind of . . . gorgeous.

Stacy McLaughlin was also a pretty young woman, although Clint couldn't have known that when he rammed her car. On 16 December 1988, McLaughlin, an animation producer, drove onto the Warners lot to keep an appointment with producer Paul Maslansky, for whom she was working on the *Police Academy* cartoon series. It was late on a Friday afternoon, and she was in a hurry. McLaughlin drove up in her year-old white Nissan Maxima, noted that five out of the six spaces set aside for Malpaso were empty, and thinking she would only be a few minutes – besides, it was past 5 p.m. – eased into one.

Clint arrived in his GM pickup a brief time later, and although there were four other spaces available to him, he bulldozed his truck into McLaughlin's Nissan Maxima and shoved the car aside. Then he rushed into the Malpaso offices where Jane Brolin, waiting for him, kindly handed him a ballpeen hammer. According to onlookers, Clint rushed back out, hammer in hand, intending to pound on McLaughlin's car.

Malpaso underlings, accustomed to such incidents, were only a few feet behind and managed to grab Clint and pull him away. A studio guard rushed off to find Stacy McLaughlin. She arrived, with Clint long gone, quite mystified as to why a crowd had gathered – *Murphy Brown* crew members, on break from shooting for television. Mystified as to why her car was angled weirdly. Mystified as to why the guard insisted she drive her car away as fast as possible and park it in a nearby garage.

Since McLaughlin was not finished with her appointment, she went back to her meeting. Only an hour later, as she walked to her car, did she notice that her car was smashed in on the passenger side. Monday morning, she phoned Paul Maslansky and learned that everybody at Warners was talking about the incident. Only then did she phone Malpaso and ask, rather politely under the circumstances, if Clint's insurance might assume the cost of her repairs. She was still under the assumption that it was all somehow an accident.

At first Tom Rooker, who was answering the phone at Malpaso, was very sympathetic, giving indications that such mishaps were not unfamiliar to him. At first she was told that Malpaso would cover the necessary costs. She was told to go round to Keith Dillin, Clint's transportation captain, who had his offices elsewhere on the Warners lot. But Dillon snickered at her and told her that she'd better round up some reliable witnesses.

She thought that was pretty strange. McLaughlin sought out *Murphy Brown* crew members and started taking depositions. Only then did she learn that people believed Clint had rammed her car on purpose. Suddenly, whenever she phoned Malpaso, people hung up on her. She was informed that no one was allowed to talk to her anymore.

Malpaso people figured she'd get the point and move on. Didn't McLaughlin realize that Warners was a place with its own laws and justice? Didn't she understand that Clint was a stubborn guy? That he would never admit wrongdoing? And that Clint was a very busy guy, too; busy with preparations for the release of *Bird*, and busy completing postproduction for *Pink Cadillac*, a film *full* of cars careening out of control.

No question that *Bird* performed disappointingly at the box-office: $11 million gross. *The Dead Pool*, geared to Clint's core base of fans, followed for Christmas 1988, and did much better: $59.8 million. But US critics were finally turned off by the fifth Dirty Harry. And $59.8 million was less than any other Clint film of the decade, except *City Heat*. There was anxiety at Warners that Clint had peaked and was faltering at the box-office.

Grosses are always illusory, however, and especially so in Clint's case. Some industry experts prefer to measure a film's success by its 'rentals', which is the money paid by exhibitors to the companies distributing a film. 'Grosses' are frequently reported to make a film seem more successful than it really is, whereas a film's actual profits are determined from 'rentals'.

During the 1970s, the only Clint films besides the Dirty Harrys to end up among the Top Ten Rentals of any year was *Every Which Way But Loose*. During the 1980s, the only one to place in the Top Ten was *Sudden Impact*, another Dirty Harry. Excluding *Honkytonk Man* and *Bird*, however, the others did reasonably well, and in 1984, thanks to the combined revenue of *Tightrope*, *City Heat* and *Pale Rider* – another of Clint's hat tricks – the star had again been ranked number one at the box-office.

Warners' terms for a Clint film kept rising, and the exhibitors were still willing to pay. Clint still brought customers in. And since international rentals could contribute as much as another seventy per cent to the total, the outlook was always bright outside the US. Around the world, especially with films like *The Dead Pool*, Clint continued to do business.

Christmas 1988 approached, with Clint probably let down by the reaction to *Bird* and *The Dead Pool*. That, plus he prided himself on his willpower, and Sondra Locke wasn't getting his messages. He had clashed with her on *Ratboy*. He was spending more and more time away from Stradella Road. He philandered almost brazenly. Still, Locke hung on. Was she dense?

Clint surprised Locke on the day before Christmas Eve by saying that he had decided to go up to Carmel and play golf. 'I feel like hitting some golf balls, that's all.' They had always made a point of spending Christmas Eve and Day together (usually with Gordon Anderson and his longtime companion), but not this year. Clint promised they would still go to Sun Valley on the day after Christmas. Crushed and angry, Locke spent Christmas with Anderson and his friends.

Jane Brolin called at Christmas to say that Clint wanted her to come to Sun Valley with them. Locke, feeling that she and Clint badly needed some time alone, asked Brolin not to come. 'Well,' said Brolin, 'what could I say? If Clint wants you to do something, you just do it. You know that. Of course, I have to wonder what he has up his sleeve.'

The awkward threesome, along with Kyle and Alison, took a Warners jet to Sun Valley. There, on the morning before New Year's Eve, Brolin cornered the actress in the kitchen and told her that it had become apparent to her that Clint was alienated from Locke; didn't want to be with her anymore. Locke should recognize the relationship was at an end. Locke was aghast, and she and Brolin started to quarrel. Quickly the argument escalated, with Brolin dragging in the issue of Kyle and Alison and claiming that Locke didn't really like Clint's children.

Clint wandered in, closing the argument with, 'There's a Warner plane leaving for LA today, and I think you should *both* be on it.' Locke left; Brolin stayed.

A sobbing Locke was driven to the airport by Lili Zanuck, the wife of Richard Zanuck, one of the Sun Valley skiing circle who had known Clint since *The Eiger Sanction*. Lili Zanuck urged Locke to confer with a lawyer. She told Locke all of her girlfriends were talking about Clint. The star seemed to be behaving irrationally.

Subsequently, Locke made contact with Norman Oberstein, a well-known divorce lawyer whose name she was familiar with because he was also representing Jane Brolin in her split-up with James Brolin. Oberstein advised the actress to watch and wait.

'In my head, I knew it was over,' said Locke. 'In my heart I kept thinking, "This isn't happening. Somehow, some miracle is going to occur and it's going to turn around." A part of me was glad and wanted out. A part of me was beginning to feel sick. Another part of me wanted things to be the way they were, even though they weren't ever really that way.'

For a short while Clint stayed behind in Sun Valley. When he left Sun Valley, and where he stayed when he did, it is hard to say. In later court depositions, Norman Oberstein would be thwarted in his attempts to find out. The caretaker of the Stradella Road house told Locke that Clint was 'creeping in and out of the house when I was not home, careful not to disturb anything'. But where was he sleeping at night?

Clint's lawyers would object to any line of questioning that inquired as to Clint's other personal relationships, and Clint himself was vague, insisting that he occasionally sneaked onto the Stradella Road premises without alerting Locke and then he tucked himself away quietly some nights in a spare room in the caretaker's quarters – off the courtyard next to the garage – or the guest bedroom, down the hall from where Locke slept every night.

In fact, this was when Clint was heavily wooing Frances Fisher. When he wasn't staying up in Carmel or at the Rising River Ranch, he was probably staying in his reliable pad at Malpaso, or at the place Fisher shared with her brother at the beach.

Fisher herself was still in the dark as to Locke's precise circumstances. One night Clint and Fisher drove up to Stradella Road, because the star said he had to retrieve something. He advised her to wait in the car. She watched as he went in, leaving the door ajar. Inside, a light or two went on. The minutes ticked by, curiosity overcame her. She got out of the car and walked up to the door, intending to peek in. But the moment Fisher got there, the door swung open and there was Clint, urging her to get back inside the car. He was in a big hurry. That is the closest Fisher came to meeting Sondra Locke.

If Locke was there. Since her film *Impulse* was in preproduction, Clint would have had access to the studio schedule. He would have known her office hours and when she would or would not be at home. This might have been the night, some time in March, when, as he later admitted, Clint placed a recording device on his own telephone. He didn't inform Locke, who was still living there and who was the only person using the home phone on a daily basis from January to April.

Locke only laid eyes on Clint in the flesh three times during that period. The first two occasions were interesting: both were for public appearances. Clint had a long-scheduled commitment to attend the foreign press association's Golden Globe Awards in January (the previous year, he had taken home the Cecil B. DeMille Award for outstanding contribution to the world of entertainment) and also to show up at the American Cinema Awards programme that same month (he was one of the honorees).

For both events, Clint materialized first at Stradella. He took Leonard Hirshan with him to the Golden Globes, but he and Locke went with Kyle to the American Cinema Awards. Clint and Locke sat together and didn't say two words to each other, although they were sighted and photographed for the columns. Afterwards, they came home and slept in the same bed without sharing any physical intimacies. The next morning, Clint got up and left, without ever broaching the impasse.

The only possible explanation for Clint's behaviour, considering what happened next, is that either he still hadn't made up his mind to act, or that he was waiting for Sondra Locke to act first – get out of his life voluntarily. He was still trying to exert his willpower.

As for Locke, she was mystified. By now she realized she and Clint had their deep problems but she was also heavily into denial. She thought Clint was doing all these things because he wasn't number one at the box-office anymore, or because he was facing his mortality. She thought there was still a chance they might work things out, but decided that the next move – communication and reconciliation – was up to him.

The worst thing that could happen, she believed, was that Clint's lawyer, Bruce Ramer, would ring her up and say Clint wanted to initiate talks for a mutually-agreeable separation.

Therefore, the third time she saw Clint was shocking. On 4 April Clint asked Locke's production secretary to phone her in the morning and wake her up, and then he turned up at Stradella Road to greet her as she came downstairs in her robe. He opened up by telling her that he had just washed a dirty dish in the sink. ('Is he trying to tell me how neat and thoughtful he is,' Locke wondered, 'or is he saying I am a slob for having left a dirty dish in the sink?') Standing in the dining room, his arms crossed, gently swaying from side to side, the star gave a little prepared speech. 'I hestitated to bring it up while you were shooting this film,' Clint began. 'But I was . . . uh . . . thinking, it's come to my attention that you . . . uh . . . and Gordon are sitting on my only *real estate* in Los Angeles.'

When Locke got her powers of speech back, she told Clint that it was hard for her to deal with the crisis now. She had just launched into directing *Impulse*. But, she continued, she wasn't going anywhere. Stradella Road was every bit *her* house. She had shopped long and hard for it, had renovated and furnished it to her taste. She had lived there for eight years. If Clint was uncomfortable being around her, then he should stay in one of his other houses, or wherever it was that he had been staying. 'And where *is* that, Clint?' Which the star did not answer, for he was busy staring out the window. Instead Clint mumbled, 'Well, maybe you could just put it on the back burner until you finish your film.' Then, with nothing more to say, Clint left.

Clint *knew* that Locke was in the midst of shooting *Impulse*. 'The timing was calculated,' said Locke. 'Clint knew the pressure I was under. He also was jealous that I was doing something away from him. He didn't want me to be able to succeed at all away from him. He didn't like that for one second.'

He didn't give her much time. On 10 April Locke was engaged in directing one of the film's most challenging scenes – the one towards the end ('a nightmare to choreograph', in Locke's words) in which everyone converges on the safe house where the undercover prostitute–policewoman (played by Theresa Russell) is hiding in wait for the killer. Clint would know this from the phone tapes, if he didn't know it from daily logs circulated at Warners.

Clint showed up at Stradella Road. The first thing he did was change the locks. He was aided by Malpaso underlings, whose job descriptions this day included stuffing Sondra Locke's belongings into some fourteen Bekins boxes and then stacking the boxes in the driveway for a mover to transport over to Gordon Anderson's house.

Anderson phoned Locke on the set and read her a letter which had just arrived, directed to Mrs Gordon Anderson at the Crescent Heights address. The letter, signed by Bruce Ramer, stated that on behalf of Clint Eastwood and Roy Kaufman, Locke was being duly notified that in the past the Stradella Road house had been utilized by her 'free of rent, on a nonexclusive basis', and that 'this accommodation may be terminated by Mr Eastwood at any time. Mr Eastwood now wishes to take possession of the Stradella Road house on an exclusive basis. Mr Eastwood has asked you to vacate the premises. You have refused to do so.'

Therefore, because of Locke's 'intransigence', the locks were being replaced, and all of her possessions were being packed up and taken to the Crescent Heights house which 'you and your husband rent and occupy'.

Locke fainted dead away in front of cast and crew. The next day, the tabloids, the legitimate dailies and the broadcast media were full of the news, competing amongst themselves for details of Clint and Locke's sensational break-up.

Pink Cadillac opened on 26 May. 'Mediocre,' *Variety* opined. 'A 122-minute dozer,' concurred Richard Freedman of the Newhouse News Service. Although block-booked by Warners into more than 2000 theatres, the film, crushed by the weight of such negative reviews – Clint's worst of the 1980s – quickly sank out of sight, and ended up one of the lowest-grossing Malpaso productions of the decade.

All during the spring of 1989 *White Hunter, Black Heart* was in preproduction, and Rastar co-producer Stanley Rubin had been trying without much luck to get Clint on the phone.

Rubin had called twice since Christmas, when he returned from location work on *Revenge*. Both times he reached producer David Valdes, who told him the star was unavailable and that Valdes would take any message. Rubin said he was eager to speak personally with

Clint because he wanted to discuss casting and location possibilities, and, most of all, he wanted to discuss the much-bruited-about script improvements.

'I can characterize David Valdes by his very words to me, which I've never forgotten,' said Rubin. 'At one point, when I said something about wanting to get together with Clint, Valdes said, "Well, you know Clint is very busy." I said, "Would you convey to Clint that I'm eager to talk to him about things that I think are important to making this script better, before he starts to shoot it?" He said, "Yes, I'll pass it on to him," adding, "but remember, Stanley, that while I am called executive producer at Malpaso Productions, I am here to service Clint Eastwood, and what I do is simply to smooth the path for Clint on any of the roads he travels." That's his characterization of himself, pretty much a verbatim quote.'

Nonetheless, Rubin stayed optimistic. He prepared a breakdown of the demographics of various countries in Africa where it might be feasible to shoot *White Hunter, Black Heart.* He took his preventive shots from a physician on the Burbank lot. He was all ready to go to work and still waiting to hear from Clint when he received a phone call from his boss, Rastar chief executive Ray Stark.

'This was kind of interesting,' said Rubin. 'Ray Stark said, "Stanley, Clint called me and told me that he really wants to be left alone. You're nagging him about *White Hunter, Black Heart* and it's upsetting him. For God's sake, pal, get off his back.'

Rubin got out his daily calendar book, checked it, phoned Stark back. 'Ray,' the producer said, 'I hardly think I've been on Clint's back. I've called him exactly twice since I've got back from Mexico. If that's nagging him, when we're supposed to be co-producing the picture, then I don't know what to make of it.' Ray Stark's attitude was, they were lucky to have a big star like Clint, leave him alone. 'Stanley, for God's sake,' Stark told Rubin, 'Clint knows how to shoot a picture.'

Rubin promised Stark he would not phone Clint again. He would wait until Clint called him. He was still waiting when he heard the scuttlebutt that David Valdes was off in Africa, scouting locations; still waiting when he heard the news that Clint and Malpaso had packed up and left for Africa to shoot *White Hunter, Black Heart.* Not only did Rubin not so much as receive a courtesy phone call from Clint, the 'co-producer' actually never heard directly from the star again. Nor did they ever play golf.

Ray Stark told Rubin to look on the bright side: they were partners on a Clint Eastwood film.

Before Clint left for Africa, he had some pressing legal problems.

Sondra Locke had refused to accept her public humiliation and physical ejection from the Stradella Road house. Her lawyer, Norman Oberstein, had contacted Clint's lawyers, threatening suit and asking for step-term compensation amounting to $1.3 million and ownership of the Stradella Road and Crescent Heights houses. Only when Clint, through his lawyers, said no, absolutely not, did Locke file a suit against him for $70 million.

The lawsuit, which was filed on 26 April, stated Locke's case for 'financial support, breach of contract, emotional distress, forcible entry, possession of personal property and other claims', in the words of the *Los Angeles Times*. The case was widely referred to as a 'palimony suit', because it sought to prove that certain common-law agreements between Clint and Locke had been violated. 'The suit is a potentially precedent-setting legal case,' noted the *Los Angeles Times*, 'because it raises the question of whether a woman, who is legally married to one man, can claim palimony rights from another.'

The lawsuit riveted Hollywood, because few in the film industry would have dared to make a public enemy of Clint (and through him, Warner Brothers). Also, Locke's sworn declaration, leaked to the press, hinted, for the first time, at the hidden personality of the 'intensely private' (*Los Angeles Times*) star. Maggie, in their divorce, had agreed to seal the public record; now, however, leaks to the press painted Clint as a sometimes distant, manipulative, volatile man with an abusive temper. The public learned for the first time that Clint helped persuade Locke to have two abortions and the sterilization operation of a tubal ligation.

Clint felt the need to convince mutual friends and possible Sondra Locke allies that he had been wounded by the drastic turn of events. Privately he explained himself, weeping, especially, on the shoulders of female friends – Lili Zanuck, Kitty Dutton, the omnipresent Jane Brolin. His line, echoed in later court depositions, would be that he had been forced to act the way he did by Locke's unwillingness to separate amicably and also by her betrayal of him when she consulted a lawyer behind his back.

Publicly, at first, and for a long time, there was 'no comment' from Clint himself. His publicists released a prepared statement claiming that Locke's suit was 'unfounded and without merit', while, behind the scenes, the team at Gang, Tyre, Ramer & Brown prepared a legal counterpunch, taking the usual Clint precaution of asking the court to seal any 'discovery' documents from press scrutiny. Locke's lawyer went along with this, agreeing to a private hearing with a judge, because the actress naively trusted 'that if it were completely private, my high-profile friends might participate' on her side.

Because Clint was heading off to Africa, depositions of the two main principals would be expedited for the last week of May. Sondra Locke would go first, under questioning from Howard King, a senior partner of Bruce Ramer's. Then Clint would be interrogated by Norman Oberstein, in the presence of Locke. Roy Kaufman would be there in the room, watching and saying nothing, on both occasions.

Clint's legal team pressed to establish several motifs: that Clint, through Roy Kaufman, paid for all costs and expenses at Stradella Road; that no significant purchase or household decision was ever made without Clint's approval; that nothing in writing, no witnesses, could corroborate Locke's assertion that the house was in any way co-owned by her; that Locke was, in fact, married, and beholden to her husband.

In the deposition sessions Clint's lawyers tried to assert that Locke had fairy-tale hangups and saw Clint, in some delusional way, as a Prince Charming. They inquired about her long-term devotion to Gordon Anderson, asserted that she often had visited Anderson or stayed overnight at the Crescent Heights address, wondered if she and Anderson ever had sex or were still in the habit of having sex. Locke gladly admitted her affection for Anderson, but denied any sexual relationship with him.

They did their best to raise suspicions that Locke had sexual relations with others while living with Clint, but to little avail; she came off poignantly as the monogamous partner. They even inquired if she had engaged in sex with one of the cameramen of *Impulse*, although this activity would have taken place *after* the lock-out. (Anyway, Locke replied no, she and the cameraman had merely gone to dinner, during which time the man in question had been kind enough to express sympathy with her plight.)

Locke's longtime marriage to Anderson, convenient for Clint at one time, was now one of the principal grievances stacked against her. As he had done in conversations with his close friends, now Clint, in sworn statements, advanced the argument that he felt in a losing competition with Anderson; that his feeling for Locke was eroded by her first loyalty to her childhood sweetheart. He wanted Locke to spend more time at Stradella Road; she hung out too much with Anderson. He wanted Locke to go places with him; she preferred to stay home, near Anderson.

'I don't think he was at all threatened or jealous of Gordon until he decided he wanted to end the relationship,' commented Locke in an interview, 'and then I think he, in moments, might even have convinced himself that he *was* jealous.'

Clint's fear and jealousy of Locke's husband dominated the star's lengthy deposition, taken two days after Locke's. Norman Oberstein was permitted to question Clint for six hours. Clint wore a suit and tie straight out of Dirty Harry's closet. With his hair thinning and mussed, with his sleepy expression, the tough-guy star looked more like Stan Laurel.

Clint used the formal language of his eviction notice to explain that Locke had always resided at Stradella Road on a 'non-exclusive basis'. Locke's lawyer pointed out that, in his will dated 18 April 1980, Clint had set aside the Sherman Oaks home for Locke; and an 8 March 1985 codicil gave her the Stradella Road house. Why had Clint, who was always rewriting his will, revoked those clauses in a more recent 17 June 1987 codicil?

He, uh, didn't remember. He explained that at one point in the past he had truly loved Locke and wanted her to be happy. Then a gulf opened up between them. This gulf was worsened by Clint's 'feeling that she had spoken to a litigator to attack my finances and estate, and I considered that to be an act of hostility not to be rewarded in case of my death'.

Asked to characterize his precise relationship with Locke in the past, Clint reverted to teenage lingo to note they had been 'going together'. He refused to concede that they ever really lived together. He didn't care to describe Locke as a 'live-in' lover, explaining that they were lovers but 'not necessarily live-in', because after all Locke was married. He was more wont to describe Locke as someone who helped out with the decorating and then stayed overnight occasionally – more like a 'part-time roommate'. Asked to define a part-time roommate, Clint explained, 'Anytime a person spends one night it's part time.'

Sensing an opening, Norman Oberstein asked Clint if he had had any other 'part-time roommates' during the time he was 'going together' with Locke. But Clint's lawyers objected to that question, and Clint refused to answer on the grounds of privacy. Asked where, for example, he had been sleeping from January to March 1989, Clint said he didn't recall staying anywhere other than his official residences.

Locke's lawyer then unaccountably backed off that line of questioning. Locke and Norman Oberstein were at odds over this strategy. Oberstein was reluctant to probe into Clint's other relationships, believing that Clint's womanizing was a double-edged sword for his client. If it could be proven that Clint had other mistresses in his life, it might weaken Locke's claim to being any kind of de facto Mrs Clint Eastwood.

As for Locke, she knew about Roxanne Tunis (Clint's daughter Kimber had worked briefly in the Malpaso office) but still did not know about any of the other ongoing inamoratas; she did not know about actress Frances Fisher, whose continuing relationship with Clint would not become public knowledge until the end of 1989.

It was one of the peculiarities of Clint's deposition that Locke herself was present for the whole time and observing his interrogation, though the star never once made eye contact with her or offered any reference to her proximity. Another peculiarity, missing from the transcript, is that at one point Locke left the room to take a phone call. This phone call, ironically, turned out to be from a reporter representing a tabloid weekly, asking the actress for her reaction to rumours they were investigating, that a woman living up in Carmel, Jacelyn Reeves, had given birth to two illegitimate children fathered by Clint. That was the first time Locke had ever heard Jacelyn Reeves's name, and when the actress returned to the deposition room, she was shaken.

Clint's confession that he had wiretapped his own telephone was directly linked in this hearing to the perceived threat of Gordon Anderson. The confession was all the more surprising since Clint had not mentioned any wiretapping in his earlier, sworn declarations. Knowing

Clint, Locke had entertained suspicions that her phone was tapped. He always seemed to *know* what she said and did. Asked directly if there were any transcripts related to her claims that Locke's attorneys hadn't seen, Clint admitted that he had placed a tape-recording device on the Stradella Road phone, without Locke's knowledge, some time early in March.

Back in 1972, *Playboy* asked Clint, apropos of the Watergate revelations then in the headlines, how he felt about wiretapping and electronic surveillance. The star had replied, 'I just don't think it's morally right. Same as I think the morality of President Nixon's making those tapes in the Oval Office was bad. Innocent people were in there talking with him – like the prime minister of some country – very frankly stating their points of view with no idea that their conversations were being taped.'

Clint added, 'President Nixon knew. They didn't. If I knew I was bugging a room and I was going to keep the tapes for history, I sure as hell wouldn't say anything on tape that might convict me.'

Nor in this instance did Clint say anything that would convict Clint. In fact, Clint's voice wasn't even *on* the tapes, which amounted to six or seven hours of conversation in total. The transcripts were limited to Sondra Locke and her friends (including her lawyer), because this was during the period of time when Clint was rarely glimpsed on the Stradella Road premises; the wiretaps were removed shortly after Locke was expelled. Nonetheless Clint's argument for why it was suddenly 'morally right' for him to engage in wiretapping was that it was *his* phone, *his* home. Only he and his lawyer, Clint noted, had listened to them (although Jane Brolin, discussing the tapes with friends, indicated *she* also had listened to them).

Clint further explained that he had been receiving harassing phone calls, both at home and at Malpaso, since the mid-1980s. These calls he characterized as coming from a voice not unlike his own – a whispery male – saying, 'I am going to kill you! I am going to kill you! I am going to fuck you!' This combination of threatened violence with homosexual overtones might have been the reason why, without any concrete evidence, Clint insisted, in his deposition, that the likely culprit was Anderson. Taping his calls, went the theory, would catch Anderson in the act.

No such evidence was provided by the transcripts. However, Clint was able to point to a conversation between Locke and Anderson, in which the two of them rehashed Clint's increasingly bizarre behaviour. The little pistol Locke owned, which had been given to her as a present by Clint, she kept in a leather case in her purse. On one tape, Anderson asked Locke what she would do if Clint showed up on the set of *Impulse* to bad-vibe her, and she responded that she'd dig in her purse, get out her gun, and shoot him in the fucking head!

There: evidence of threat to Clint's life and limb. It's important to keep in mind that these were Clint's transcriptions, and that Locke's side never accepted their accuracy. And even so, this remark was made in a joking context. Above all, it did nothing to support Clint's original motive for the wiretapping: it proved nothing about Anderson. It was Locke who made the so-called threat!

This was the highlight of Clint's deposition. Mostly Clint said that he didn't remember; or a favourite phrase, 'I have no records on that' – about seventy-nine times during the six-hour session. Clint's lawyers refused to let him answer many queries; they went off the record in several instances to complain about the line of attack. Finally, as the clock neared 7 p.m., Clint and his lawyers got up and left the room, over the protests of Norman Oberstein, who still had a list of unanswered questions.

An interesting footnote, for film buffs, is that the whole deposition was videotaped. Even more than the X-rated home movies, this is the great, unseen Clint film. The visual style is radical, almost Godardian – one long take, an unvarying medium close-up of Clint, whose face is the only one in the frame. The performance is deeply unsettling. There is baffling lack of emotion. A hint of smugness. Absurdist comedy. Siskel and Ebert, if they ever saw the deposition film, would surely agree: both thumbs up!

One week later, there was another, closed-door preliminary hearing which further illuminated Clint's legal strategy. If and when the Sondra Locke lawsuit ever reached a jury, they would hear the rather astonishing contention that Locke really didn't live at Stradella Road; she kept a separate set of clothing at Gordon Anderson's house and frequently stayed overnight at Crescent Heights, according to Clint's lawyers.

Deserted by her celebrity friends Maria Shriver ('Maria was in New York and "couldn't possibly return in time"') and Lili Zanuck (busy filming in Florida and 'quite unable to be away from the set for even one day'), Locke had a painfully short witness list, consisting of Gordon Anderson, one of Anderson's close friends (who said he had witnessed an incident up in Carmel when animal-lover Clint, in a pique, had hurled his pet parrot Rosanna to the floor), and the Guatemalan caretaker of Stradella Road ('the only person from my life with Clint who dared to come forward and tell the truth').

The Stradella Road realtor, plumber and electrical contractors were questioned by both sides, eliciting the fact that Locke had employed and given them their instructions, but that all cheques were signed by Roy Kaufman. None of the contractors, including those who did simultaneous work at Crescent Heights, could affirm the contention of Clint's lawyers that Locke kept a second wardrobe in the closets at Anderson's house. Indeed, the contractors said they never noticed any quantity of women's clothing at Crescent Heights.

A psychiatrist testified that in his expert opinion Locke had been authentically traumatized and plunged into genuine depression by ejection from Stradella Road.

Clint didn't muster a very long list either; he counted only two witnesses on his behalf. The first was Jane Brolin, whose testimony was intended to buttress the notion that Locke actually lived with Gordon Anderson the whole time she *appeared* to be living with Clint. Brolin insisted that whenever she visited Crescent Heights she observed extensive wardrobe and cosmetics belonging to Locke strewn around, in drawers, and inside closets.

Brolin's testimony, so intense, so ardent on Clint's behalf, might have backfired. What was she doing poking around in drawers and closets anyway? Plainly irritated, Brolin was forced to note, under questioning from Locke's lawyer, Norman Oberstein, that Oberstein had represented her in her own recent divorce case, adding that she only wished Oberstein had proven half as devoted to her and *her* litigation.

Brolin also admitted that she had tipped off the *National Enquirer* with insider details about the rift between Clint and Locke, because, as she explained, 'Clint is not good at giving interviews. He doesn't give interviews.' It was unclear whether Clint, the sworn enemy of tabloids, had sanctioned this gesture on his behalf, but he certainly did sanction Brolin, who, according to sources, was paid in cash by at least one tabloid for her 'insider information'.

Cross-examination elicited the fact that Brolin was due to accompany Clint to Africa, where he was headed to shoot *Black Hunter, White Heart*, and that for the first time, in the 17 June 1987 codicil to his will, Brolin had become one of Clint's inheritors, entitled upon his death to the not inconsiderable sum of one million dollars.

The other witness was Clint's ace in the hole. Kyle Eastwood came forward, saying absolutely nothing against Sondra Locke, but testifying to the fact that, after living elsewhere for a while, he had decided to move back into Stradella Road, where he had every expectation of sharing the house with his father. Cross-examination elicited the fact that Kyle actually had moved back in a couple of days before the preliminary hearing. That familial grace note pretty much sealed Locke's hopes to get the house back, even though very shortly after the hearing, Clint left the country for two months of filming in Africa. The much-disputed Stradella Road property then was left empty, according to sources, for Kyle promptly moved back in with a room-mate in the San Fernando Valley.

Clint's travelling companion to Africa was indeed Jane Brolin, who boasted to friends that the longtime, on-and-off affair between her and Clint was . . . definitely 'on'.

In this time of personal crisis, Clint would make his bravest film as an actor, playing another Hollywood icon, John Huston, in a film that was as much a naked bid for respect in the category of acting as *Bird* was intended to garner accolades for his directing.

Huston was Hollywood's Charlie Parker. The writer–director of *The Maltese Falcon, Treasure of the Sierra Madre, The Asphalt Jungle* and many other memorable films made over the span of a lengthy career, was a legend as a film-maker. Off the set, Huston was also a legend as a man, indulging his massive appetite for life in egocentric behaviour, expensive gambling and sporting activities, and incessant womanizing.

Creatively, he had periods of boom or bust. Peter Viertel had written John Wilson, the Huston character of his novel, as both a glorification and vilification. Clint insisted, in interviews, that he saw little of himself in Huston, who died in 1987. But one of the themes in Viertel's novel might have intrigued Clint: the John Wilson character viewed directing as a sometimes tedious business upon which he hated to focus his energy. The recreation and socializing of making films were every bit as important to him.

On location in Zimbabwe, during the summer of 1989, Clint's regulars assembled, mixing with a veteran British crew. Lennie Niehaus and Joel Cox were part of the production, but Edward Carfagno had been replaced by British designer John Graysmark, who had contributed to *Firefox*.

In an interview, Carfagno, who had crafted the Malpaso 'house style' for nine films, expressed some bitterness about the circumstances. Clint thought Carfagno (b. 1907) was getting too old for the assignment; what Clint actually told some people was that Carfagno was getting 'senile'. The way in which Clint handled the changeover was characteristically aloof; Carfagno simply didn't get a call-back. Carfagno himself dated the internal strife at Malpaso to *Ratboy*, on which he had served – perhaps too dutifully – as Sondra Locke's production designer.

David Valdes was on location as 'executive producer'. Clint had grown into the 'producer *and* director' credit he once eschewed. Jack Green, the director of photography, had also grown into his promotion. With the unstable health of Bruce Surtees, Green had become Clint's right-hand man. He had mastered Surtees' dark shadings, and improved on Clint's set-ups. Now he was the only person on a Malpaso set who, after a take, might venture a substantial criticism, or suggestion, to Clint.

The cast that was rounded up included Marisa Berenson as Kay Gibson (the Katharine Hepburn character), Richard Vanstone as Phil Duncan (the Humphrey Bogart character), George Dzundza as Paul Landers (the Sam Spiegel character) and Jeff Fahey as Peter Verrill (the Peter Viertel character). Dzundza and Fahey, the latter a young, former professional dancer first seen in *Silverado*, were particularly curious choices, given that they had appeared before the cameras, earlier in 1989, in Sondra Locke's film *Impulse*.

'I had seen a small film that Jeff had done called *Split Decisions*,' recalled Sondra Locke, 'and I liked Jeff a lot, so I cast him. When Clint asked me who I had decided on, I showed him his picture and he said, "Well, I don't know what you want with that pretty boy." I just said nothing because I knew what he was doing. Then, lo and behold, while I'm shooting *Impulse* and am in the middle of production

– after he's locked me out of my house – he then puts an offer out not only to Jeff Fahey but to another actor I had hired for *Impulse* – George Dzundza – and hired them out of my movie to do his next movie, the "more important" movie. It was a weird psychological move.'

Novelist–screenwriter Viertel, who lived in Marbella, Spain, with his wife, actress Deborah Kerr, was invited on location. He found Clint, at least in their personal interaction, quite unlike the John Huston he had known. Clint didn't play cruel practical jokes on people, nor did he appear to evince any of the deviousness or flamboyant madness. Although the star was embroiled in an ungentlemanly scandal back in the US, he couldn't have seemed more reasonable in Africa. 'In his relations with me,' noted Viertel, 'he was a true gentleman. Although, like all famous actors, he's surrounded by people who are dependent on him – or, what I should say, in awe of him.'

Viertel did have some qualms about the script, which was his draft, but as revamped by Burt Kennedy. The shooting script (and film) began with a vignette of John Wilson galloping on a horse across the English countryside, providing audiences with, in Viertel's view, a none-too-subtle reminder of Clint's cowboy image. And there had to be a tacked-on white-water scene with the boat, the *African Queen*, stuck in the middle of the film, because, Viertel said, 'Clint felt he needed an action sequence somewhere.'

Since Viertel knew the source material better than anyone, and since he realized that nobody had toiled on the script *after* Burt Kennedy, he ventured at one point to ask Clint whether he might add a small yet crucial transition sequence. Clint was gracious in turning him down and telling him that there was no time left for any revisions.

In the end, Viertel was duly impressed by the actor *and* director. Clint took on Huston's vocal timbre, expansive gestures, his avuncularity and condescension. Viertel thought the star caught Huston's gleam of madness in the scene where John Wilson enunciates his film-making credo ('We're lousy little gods who control the lives of the people we create . . .'), and just the right tone in the scene where Wilson brutally humiliates a society snob complaining about London 'kikes'. One of the best scenes in *Bird*, with Charlie Parker blowing wild at a wedding, also touched on the culture of Jews and, along with *Firefox*, augured a surprising new propensity in Clint's work.

The only radical change from the novel to the film was Clint's prescribed ending. The book was predicated on the narrator's disgust with John Wilson's obsessive desire to stalk and kill an elephant, which is carried through to a sorry conclusion. In Africa, Clint began to rethink the ending, discussing it with author Viertel. Huston himself had changed his mind by the time he wrote his autobiography, *An Open Book*, declaring, 'I've never killed an elephant, although I surely tried. I never got a shot at one whose trophies were worth the crime. No, not crime – sin. I wouldn't dream of shooting an elephant today – in fact, I've given up all shooting with a rifle . . .'

To Viertel, Clint confided his hesitation about shooting one of Africa's tuskers, even for pretend purposes. Jane Brolin, an animal rights crusader, may have been whispering in his ear. (She raised chimpanzees on her ninety-seven-acre Dover Canyon ranch.) The ending Clint came up with was distinctly his own.

After several disappointing hunting trips, Wilson finally has managed to track and corner a small herd. When one of the largest of the elephants charges Wilson, he lifts his gun and aims to fire. The beast slows to a halt, trumpeting his challenge from just a few yards away. Wilson finds himself mesmerized, deeply touched despite himself, and gradually he lowers his gun. Then (as happens in the book) the small herd is spooked, and Wilson's native guide, Kivu (played by Boy Mathias Chuma), dashes forward to save Wilson, only to be trampled by the elephants. The death of the only man he admires is Wilson's reward for his folly.

This is followed by a coda, which was always the ending of the script. After the death of Kivu, Wilson returns to the set, where cast and crew are waiting for the cameras to be turned on for the first time. Looking around, the director sees the grief spread among the villagers, who bear Kivu's body away. He overhears their whispered reproaches, which translate as 'White hunter, black heart'. As accusing eyes envelop him, Wilson slumps into the director's chair and calls out, 'Action!'

This stark note of personal censure was and still is unique in Clint's cinema.

After the filming of *White Hunter, Black Heart*, Clint stopped over in London and met up with his ex-wife, Maggie.

In 1985, Maggie had married Henry Wynberg, but now her second marriage was on the verge of divorce, and Maggie and Clint had reason to effect a platonic *rapprochement*. Maggie hated Sondra Locke, whom she blamed for wrecking her marriage, and Locke was now out of Clint's life. Maggie and Clint had several ongoing financial partnerships, as a result of their divorce settlement; she was a co-owner of certain companies and properties.

Most importantly, they had Kyle and Alison in common, and Maggie had always put the interests of the children above her own feelings. Kyle was doing well. Although he had dropped out of college, music had developed into an avid pursuit. After studying with French bassist Bunny Brunel, who had performed with Chick Corea, Kyle would take up the acoustic bass and gravitate towards jazz. Kyle was in the process of forming one of the first of his quartets which would gig in clubs around Los Angeles, playing jazz standards as well as Kyle Eastwood compositions.

Alison, the pretty blonde youngster from *Tightrope*, was the wild scion and the family question mark. Around Carmel, Alison was known for dyed hair, a partying lifestyle, older boyfriends and fast cars. Alison too dropped out of college. In 1991, she would be arrested for drunk driving – although not quite twenty, she carried a fake ID. Detained overnight, she was bailed out by her mother. Clint took away her BMW as punishment. The judge gave her three years' probation, restricting her licence.

Admittedly, she and her father had a stormy relationship. Clint's separation from Maggie had come when Alison was six years old. She told *Good Housekeeping*, 'I didn't know him too well as a kid. He was very enthralled with work.' Now, when her father lectured her about college, her lifestyle or the age of one of her boyfriends, she laughed.

A sibling Kyle and Alison had never met was Kimber Tunis.

Ironically, Kimber and her mother, Roxanne Tunis, became peripheral victims of the Sondra Locke 'palimony' story. Clint's divorce had given gossip columnists and the supermarket weeklies an excuse to report the disparity between the publicity version of the star's life and the reality. The break-up with Locke really opened the floodgates to snoop journalism about Clint.

For the first time, in July of 1989, the tabloids revealed the identity of Clint's 'love child' born in 1964. Clint had managed to keep his out-of-wedlock daughter secret from the public for almost twenty years.

Almost certainly, his career would have suffered had this become known in the 1960s. Almost certainly, knowledge of this – and other out-of-wedlock children – would have hampered his mayoral campaign.

Because the tabloid articles were linked to 'dirty laundry' lurking among court documents in the Locke lawsuit, the Tunis family believed that Locke had tipped off the supermarket newspapers. However, it is just as likely that Jane Brolin, who knew all the inside stuff about Clint's paternity arrangements, did the tipping off.

Many people knew about Kimber anyway. Some of Clint's drinking buddies knew. Malpaso people who worked in the office at the same time as Kimber knew. Sometimes it appeared that the only three people in the world who didn't know about Kimber – learning about her existence for the first time from the tabloids – were Kyle, Alison and Maggie.

Kimber had long since dropped the 'Tunis' and adopted the name 'Eastwood', in school and other records, although she didn't legally change her last name to her famous father's until 1983. When the tabloids located Kimber, she was working as a waitress in Denver, supporting herself and Clinton Eastwood Gaddie, her baby son from a first marriage. Soon after, in the early 1990s, Kimber would move from Denver to the Los Angeles area, choosing to pursue a career as an actress. According to sources sympathetic to the Tunis family, Clint encouraged his daughter, saying he would consider her for one of his films when the right part came along.

Kimber's attitude about her celebrity father seemed to shift under the media glare. In one publication Kimber was quoted as saying she and her dad had an excellent relationship, and that the star had arranged to see her 'every three or four months' of her life. Other times Kimber was quoted as expressing frustration that Clint and she were not closer ('I've begged and begged for a relationship,' she reportedly said) and as referring to her father as 'His Highness'.

Sources sympathetic to the Tunis family say that the media has been cruel to Kimber, fabricating its quotes or quoting her out of context. Though she has been offered thousands of dollars by the tabloids, Kimber's mother has refused to give a single interview on the subject of Clint, ever. Family friends insist that Roxanne Tunis feels Clint was always there for her and her daughter, emotionally and financially. Content in her life as a teacher of Transcendental Meditation, she never would have divulged his secret, hated the press attention.

Clint stayed fond of Tunis, according to these friends, and visited her periodically. She always welcomed him with open arms. For him, her house was a guaranteed retreat from the outside world; for her, he was always Clint of the Rowdy years.

Back in America after the filming of *White Hunter, Black Heart*, Clint was rumoured to be on the rebound romantically with various women. The tabloids reported that he was carrying on an affair with Carmel Mayor Jean Grace, who succeeded him as mayor and whose successful candidacy Clint had backed. He was also reported to be dating Barbra Streisand, and seeing the ex-wife of Steve McQueen. Or maybe Clint was dallying with Dani Crayne, the ex-wife of David Janssen and stunt-man–director Hal Needham, whose infatuation with Clint harked back to the 1950s. The tabloids went so far as to suggest that the star had fallen in love again – with Jane Brolin! But Clint didn't appreciate this particular gossip – considering that Brolin herself was on record as a pipeline to the tabloids – so Brolin flew into print with a denial.

One woman definitely back in his life was Frances Fisher. According to Richard Schickel, Clint had put some emotional distance between himself and the actress from the cast of *Pink Cadillac*. Clint never wooed Fisher 'exclusively' and it was 'always on his timetable'. Their summer break from each other was also convenient for Clint's depo-sitions in the Sondra Locke lawsuit, in which Frances Fisher's name was never acknowledged, and for the weeks of filming *White Hunter, Black Heart* in Africa.

Now, in the late summer of 1989, Clint and the actress resumed contact, and over the next few months 'drifted into what would soon become an exclusive relationship', in Schickel's words. 'She was living then in Manhattan Beach, a long drive from his house and from working rounds. It made sense for her to stay over in Bel-Air, to begin leaving a few clothes there, and this seemed perfectly agreeable to him. Pretty soon, without their ever formally discussing it, they were living together . . .'

Soon Fisher was introduced to Clint's older buddies and to members of his family, to Arnold and Maria and the rest of the Sun Valley crowd. Soon she was spending time with Clint up at Rising River Ranch.

*　　*　　*

Two other women stubbornly remained part of Clint's world, in adversarial fashion.

The young woman whose car Clint had damaged because it was parked in his favourite space kept phoning Malpaso, wouldn't go away. Finally, Stacy McLaughlin grew fed up at the stonewalling and consulted a lawyer about filing a suit for damages.

Sondra Locke was also keeping lawyers busy. Her attorneys were exchanging heated letters with Clint's lawyers, with both sides filing motions preparatory to trial.

Although all of Locke's belongings had purportedly been placed in Bekins boxes, no one had accepted them when the truck drove the boxes over to the Crescent Heights place. Anderson, because Locke did not live there and because he suspected Clint was up to something, refused to answer the door. Therefore, her belongings had been transported to Bekins Storage and deposited in the West Jefferson Boulevard warehouse. 'Our client will pay for the first month of storage and handling fees,' Clint's lawyers advised Locke. 'Should these items remain in storage for longer than one month, you must bear the additional costs.'

When she got the fourteen boxes out of storage, things were missing. Clint, unilaterally, had decided what Locke would get and he would keep. The lawyers drew up lists of what each side claimed as possessions. Clint took special interest in the lists, and worked as hard to prove claim for small treasures as he did for the grand prize of the house.

Some of these battles he lost. One old acquaintance was taken aback when Clint called to ask him about a white, old-fashioned telephone. Locke had claimed the phone. It had been a gift, but Clint couldn't remember – to him or Sondra? Clint couldn't conceal his disappointment at the answer: it was a gift to the actress.

Others he won. The household boasted two parrots, Rosanna and Putty, but only Putty was contested. Locke insisted that Putty, a Yellow Nape Amazon parrot, was hers, a gift from Jane Brolin back in the days when they were friendly. She had named Putty, fed and taken care of Putty. Clint insisted Putty was his, a *house* gift from Brolin, not a personal gift to Locke. Naturally, Brolin backed Clint up, and Clint instructed his lawyers not to budge, for Putty, an emotional issue with Locke, was a proprietary issue for him. And Clint won. Indeed, Putty lived on at Stradella Road and Clint renamed him Paco.

Meanwhile, *White Hunter, Black Heart* went through stages of postproduction.

Stanley Rubin, who saw the film at a screening at Ray Stark's house, thought Clint had adhered faithfully to the material, and that the key moments of the film turned out very exciting. The next day, Rubin phoned Clint and left a message; this time the star called him back. Rubin began by praising the film, but the conversation grew cold very quickly when he ventured to suggest a small, constructive change – 're-editing' the climactic elephant charge to build more emotion into the scene. 'Clint said he liked it the way it was, there were no other takes and no way to improve it,' said Rubin.

For the third time in seven years Clint trooped off to Cannes in the spring of 1990. Jack Mathews of the *Los Angeles Times* was there to interview Clint and write about the film. He reported that critical reaction was 'subdued, even though dozens of journalists jostled for position to get the director's autograph after the hour-long press conference'.

Bruce Bawer, with the *American Spectator* in Cannes, also attended Clint's press conference and reported on it somewhat incredulously: 'Eastwood avers that he didn't base his performance on Huston (!) and says he shares Wilson's disdain for Hollywood's cautiousness. (*Quel rebelle!*) He discusses Zimbabwe, where the picture was filmed: "You'd never know there's been a war there. The people were very up." And he fields questions. A Swedish woman complains about the film's females; Eastwood cites his feminist credentials. Another journalist asks if the film's message is partly environmental; Eastwood says that, yes, thanks to environmentalism, Viertel's story has taken on new meaning. This pleases him. It seems to please the press, too: that the movie has a trendy political angle apparently makes for more interesting copy.'

Another, more sympathetic film festival showing was arranged by Pierre Rissient. Clint had his own tribute at the Telluride Film Festival in Colorado that September, coinciding with a preview screening of *White Hunter, Black Heart*. However, even there, the film got a 'somewhat mixed reaction' from festival-goers, according to the *Hollywood Reporter*.

The film festival auguries may be why, preparatory to the autumn 1990 release of *White Hunter, Black Heart*, Clint hastened back to work on another, more populist film. Quickly and quietly, around San Jose locations, he shot *The Rookie*, a buddy-buddy cop script by Boaz Yakin and Scott Spiegel that was a regrettable Dirty Harry pastiche.

Clint, here, was an ageing cop chasing auto theft racketeers. Charlie Sheen was his young blood partner. Others in the cast included Sonia Braga (whom Clint had met at his first Cannes Film Festival), playing the lady-satan girlfriend of crime boss Raul Julia.

The Rookie would be another orgy of vehicle crashes, Clint's enemies as sheer assholes, and old-enough-to-be-your-father routines with 'the kid'. Clint's character has an ex-wife, a cigar as a running prop, and a wardrobe of T-shirts. Not only did Clint star, but he also directed. As kinky as anything in *Tightrope*, one scene has Sonia Braga fucking a bruised and handcuffed Clint as she memorializes the occasion on video camera. She's clothed alluringly, he's baring his pecs: shot above the waist for wide audiences. Despite his predicament, Clint's character appears to enjoy himself. He just can't help it that women fall for him, and the sex is good.

The improbable plot peregrinations end with an airport shoot-out and bloodletting that sees innocent bystanders and airport guards idiotically stepping in front of whizzing bullets. Clint then gives Sonia a final *coup de grâce* in the forehead. Although badly wounded, Clint crawls over a moving conveyor belt of luggage to give Raul Julia a forehead venting too.

Although a few critics were caught with starry eyes (new convert Gary Giddins hailed *The Rookie* as 'A knockout!' in the *Village Voice*, describing it as 'the best action film since *Lethal Weapon 2*'), most couldn't figure out how a man who tried to evoke the spirit of John Huston in *White Hunter, Black Heart* could, the same year, produce something so 'astonishingly empty' (Vincent Canby, *the New York Times*).

Glenn Lovell of the *San Jose Mercury News*, in whose city *The Rookie* was shot, pointed out that the film was riddled with 'blatant racial stereotyping'. All the killer car thieves were Hispanic, the ringleader was a Puerto Rican with a comic German accent, and his bodyguard a Brazilian sex kitten; all the heroes were 'Anglo archetypes'.

In this way, too, *The Rookie* was the opposite of *Bird* and *White Hunter*,

Black Heart. For *The Rookie* brought in $43 million in the US alone, while Clint's diligent adaptation of Peter Viertel's novel took in only $8.4 million before vanishing from theatres.

CHAPTER THIRTEEN

Clint's New Clothes
1990–1995

'The William Munny Killings' would quietly undergo a title change to *Unforgiven*, but not until August of 1991 would the Western be announced as Clint's next film, first in trade publications and then confirmed by Jack Mathews in the *Los Angeles Times*.

Megan Rose, the Warners story analyst who had discovered the script, last slept with the star around December 1987. He was making *Bird*, his elegy to Charlie Parker, and their lovemaking took place within the confines of Clint's forty-foot customized silver recreational vehicle, purchased for him by the studio, which was then parked on the lot.

She had no idea it would be the last time. 'I'm the one who ended it,' Rose said in an interview. 'It probably would have lasted longer. In fact, Clint wasn't aware that it was different until we started fighting over *Unforgiven*. That is when I flat out told him it was different [between us]. I told him, "I will always love you, but not the same way."'

Their relationship deteriorated when she insisted that she be credited, professionally and financially, for 'finding' the script. One time, discussing 'The William Munny Killings' with Clint, she was surprised to hear him say, 'You gave me the script for the *writer*' – meaning, she gave him the script to consider the writer for future assignments, but Clint had fallen in love with the *script*. 'No,' Rose corrected the star, 'I gave it to you for the *project* – not the writer.' Clint then dropped the subject, but the seeds were planted.

Throughout the second half of the 1980s, Rose feels, she helped to keep *Unforgiven* alive. The story analyst communicated with the writer, David Webb Peoples, and made script suggestions to him and to Clint. She had other irons in the fire, and continued to advise on scripts tailored for masculine stars. Away from Warners, Rose was instrumental in finding a property for Tom Selleck, an 'Australian Western' called *Quigley Down Under*, which became a 1992 film. Rose received co-producer credit.

In the late 1980s she came down with a mysterious illness, later diagnosed as Lyme disease. She dropped out of circulation for a while. But she continued to stop by Malpaso with her fat-free, healthy desserts, including a family recipe for Southern-style pan-fried apple pie, which Clint especially loved. Although Rose knew about some of the unfair things that happened around Malpaso, she continued to adore Clint and right up to the start of photography never dreamed she would not be credited and compensated for *Unforgiven*.

Sondra Locke's 'palimony' suit dragged on, with motions, delays, legal communiqués back and forth. *Impulse* was released to favourable reviews in the spring of 1990 but the taut, well-made crime film 'was pretty much dumped by Warner Brothers', in Locke's words. The studio was also in the process of dumping other projects she had in development.

By May 1990, Locke had had enough of the legal manoeuvring and thought to intercede personally with Clint. She tried to make an appointment with the star, 'hoping that if he felt I'd "come begging" he'd feel he had won and would settle fairly with me'. She hoped 'enough time had passed that I could remind him of all the good that had been in our relationship and that we could end this ugly battle'.

Clint agreed to see her alone, in his offices at Malpaso. The first thing Clint said was, 'The whole world thinks what you've done to me is terrible. The *whole* world.' What *she'd* done to him. The actress, Clint explained, had embarrassed him publicly. No longer, as one of his buddies later informed *GQ* magazine, was the fourth estate treating him 'like Mother Teresa'.

'You just *want* something like everybody else,' Clint told Locke. 'I don't owe you anything. How much do you want for each time we did it? Huh?'

Locke pleaded with him. 'Look, Clint, do we *have* to be enemies? For your own good, if you don't stop distrusting everybody's every move, you're never going to be happy . . . ever. No matter who you put in your bed, you're going to be miserable.'

'I *am* happy! I'm ecstatic!' he screamed. 'I have lots of friends and lots of people I trust.'

At times, during the brief meeting, Clint acted warmly, even flirtatiously, at one point kissing the actress on the cheek and holding her hand. The truly scary part, Locke reflects nowadays, was that, with everything that had happened between them, he seemed the same old Clint. It was as if he was sending her a subliminal message: they could go back to the way they were, if she only would behave the way he wanted; if she could content herself with being, in effect, one of his 'other women'.

When Clint lowered his voice and asked, in a super-sincere tone, if she really, honestly, believed he owed her anything, Locke had to say, yes, honestly, she believed he did. So they couldn't come to any agreement, and shook hands goodbye. Clint's farewell words rang in the actress's ears, 'I'll be your friend! No strings attached. Drop your suit, come back, and I'll see what I can do for you, but it has to be no strings attached.'

The legal shenanigans continued. Then, in August 1990, Locke was suddenly diagnosed with breast cancer. Her surgery followed immediately, the second week of September – a double mastectomy.

While still in chemotherapy, she was contacted by Al Ruddy, her producer on *Impulse* and a longtime member of Clint's social circle. Ruddy asked her to come and see him at his office in Beverly Hills. There, Ruddy explained that he had decided to exercise a little 'shuttle diplomacy'. Was there any way the actress would agree to settle peaceably with Clint?

By now Locke wanted nothing more than to repair her life and get on with her career; put all the bad karma behind her. What if, Ruddy suggested, Clint was to arrange a directing contract at Warner Brothers, in lieu of all this destructive litigation?

Locke believed she had damaged her acting respectability in Clint's films. She believed her future lay in directing. She believed Ruddy had good intentions; although in retrospect, she also believes he was a spear-carrier for Clint, who feared that her recent breast cancer was bound to influence any jury.

The basic idea was that Locke would drop all claims against Clint in return for a multi-year directing–development contract with the studio. Gordon Anderson would get the Crescent Heights house;

Locke would receive $450,000 cash owed for 'past employment' at Malpaso, and a $1.5 million directing deal. Locke accepted the terms, even though it meant she gave up all claims on Stradella Road and was left in questionable health and with an uncertain future. All in order to get back to work.

Another nagging issue in Clint's life was Stacy McLaughlin and her quest for the kind of justice without bureaucratic entanglement that Dirty Harry stood up for in the movies.

Prodded by friends and relatives who sympathized with the manner in which she had been treated, McLaughlin had filed a civil lawsuit against Clint in May 1989. A few weeks later, the studio insurance company finally paid her $960 bill for car damages, but McLaughlin, angry at how she had been treated, decided to proceed with the suit. Her complaint sought punitive remuneration from Clint, but because of California law, the amount of any settlement would have to be determined after the verdict, by a judge or jury. Her real goal, she says, was to extract an admission of guilt.

The motions and referrals would eat up another two years. Finally, in the summer of 1991, Clint's lawyers succeeded in having the case quietly transferred to a municipal branch of the Burbank Judicial District, ensuring that the star would go to court in his professional backyard. Stacy McLaughlin was informed that Clint had an opening in his schedule for an immediate arraignment. Take it or leave it, Clint's lawyers said, for the star's numerous commitments might keep him busy for months ahead.

Although, originally, she had sought a jury trial, McLaughlin and her lawyer agreed to go forward. A Burbank judge who normally occupied himself handling routine traffic violations presided over the high-profile hearing, which took place on 31 July 1991.

Only it wasn't high-profile. When the car-ramming incident had first happened, there had been a few leaks to gossip columns, with the implication that McLaughlin was some kind of crazed Clint fan. Again and again she had refused interview requests from the tabloids and other media, hoping to settle the matter swiftly and with dignity. The many delays in the case and final switch of jurisdiction had left the reporters behind. No representatives of the press were present for the concluding hearing.

The judge opened the 1991 hearing by inviting the attorneys for both sides into his chambers where he stated that, even if he found in favour of Stacy McLaughlin, he didn't foresee any big monetary judgement. Maybe three thousand dollars, tops. McLaughlin's attorney said that was fine with McLaughlin; it was a matter of principle with the plaintiff. That being the situation, the judge ordered the attorneys to confer one more time and see if they could come to some mutually satisfactory arrangement.

Clint was wearing one of his nondescript, Dirty Harry suits. This was the first time Stacy McLaughlin ever glimpsed him, although the star didn't so much as glance over at her. His attorneys huddled with Clint for several minutes, until McLaughlin's lawyer was beckoned over. After speaking to Clint's attorneys, he returned to McLaughlin with an amazed expression. Clint did not want to offer any financial settlement, but he was willing to offer McLaughlin a free weekend up at his Mission Ranch and 'access to his personal video library', according to McLaughlin. This proposal, with its inference that, after all was said and done, McLaughlin must be, at heart, some kind of Clint cultist, made the plaintiff all the more angry. McLaughlin said 'no'.

The testimony went forward. Clint's lawyer, Denise Georges – the civil case had been jobbed out by Gang, Tyre, Ramer & Brown – worked hard to establish the fact that the parking spaces were well marked for Malpaso use. They brought forward photographs showing Clint's own name emblazoned there; McLaughlin's lawyer countered that this emblazoning had taken place in the weeks before the hearing.

When Clint himself took the stand, his testimony was surprising. He admitted he had done the car-ramming, saying he just hated it when somebody took his favourite parking space and he was a busy man in a hurry who had reacted accordingly. He knew he might cause a little damage to McLaughlin's car, and didn't care. He knew he had alternatives, like studio towing, if McLaughlin couldn't be located. What was the big deal? The insurance company had finally paid for everything, hadn't it?

Stacy McLaughlin and her lawyer were jubilant. It appeared they had won. Until the judge got out a book and began to read from it the strict, legal definition of malice. Even then McLaughlin and her lawyer did not catch the drift until the judge ruled that Clint had done precisely what was alleged, but there really didn't seem to be any actual *malice* involved. The ruling, incredibly, went in favour of the defendant. Clint's attorney said they'd waive McLaughlin paying court costs, if she agreed not to appeal.

Stacy McLaughlin was in shock. Well and truly beaten, she agreed to accept the verdict. Clint pumped his attorney's hand and left in a trice, wearing a big grin.

These legal distractions were why Clint did not work as an actor or director in 1990, and why 1991 was only the third year in twenty without one of his films in theatres. The very next year, however, a new president would be sworn into the nation's highest office, and the star would rebound dramatically, finally capturing his Oscar. Nineteen ninety-two would be a very good year for Clintons.

From the courtroom Clint headed straight to locations for his next film – *Unforgiven.*

The writer of *Unforgiven*, David Webb Peoples, was the son of a geology professor who had grown up partly in the Philippines. After graduating in English from Berkeley, Peoples worked for years as a news and documentary editor. He wrote and directed the Oscar-nominated *The Day After Trinity*, about the development of the A-bomb. In 1982, he achieved his breakthrough as a scenarist with his co-script for *Blade Runner.*

Peoples had finished his Western, originally entitled 'The Cut-Whore Killings', way back in 1976. Retitled 'The William Munny Killings', the script had been optioned many times, and there were times when it looked as though it would never be filmed.

Even with Clint, it took six years. Warners' publicity chief Joe Hyams later explained the lag time by saying that the star had waited until he was *old* enough to play the lead character. Clint himself said, 'I was kind of savouring it as the last of that genre, maybe the last film of that type for me.' But *Pale Rider*, which was supposed to have been Clint's *Shane*, had taken up the Western slack in the 1980s. And by 1991 Malpaso had no real story department, no producer entrusted with creative decisions, little else in development.

In spite of owning the script from 1985 to 1990, there was, true to Malpaso form, only minimal revision. Peoples later said that Clint shot his script 'straightforwardly and uncompromisingly'. Clint and the writer never had a face-to-face discussion, however, the writer never set foot on the set, and indeed Peoples didn't meet Clint for the first time until the film was done, edited, and previewed at Warners.

In subsequent articles, it became pro forma for people to refer to *Unforgiven* as a 'revisionist Western'. Critics said something of the sort ('a neat piece of revisionism, a violent film that is determined to demythologize killing', in Ken Turan's words), and then Clint picked up on that in interviews ('it demythologizes idolizing people for violent behaviour', the star explained). Or maybe it was the other way around, you never knew with Clint.

Yet Peoples' script was as traditional as it was revisionist, steeped as much in the old lore of Hollywood Westerns as in the new lore of Leone's 'paella trilogy'. Any revisionism, any demythologizing of violence, was modest and formulaic, although it was exaggerated for the sake of publicity.

The script did supply surprisingly generous screen time for the other characters, besides the star. Peoples had crafted a showman's part in English Bob, the dead-eye, dime-fiction legend. Irish actor Richard Harris was up to that challenge, and every bit deserved the Best Supporting Actor nomination that went to another actor in the cast. Harris was never in the same frame as Clint; English Bob never meets William Munny, a marked difference from past films where Clint had to dominate his co-stars.

The scribe that tags along after English Bob, W. W. Beauchamp (played by Saul Rubinek), was also a substantial role. The script's scornful attitude towards him dovetailed with Clint's new wariness towards the press. *The Dead Pool* had targeted vapid film critics and now *Unforgiven* would question the integrity of ghost writers.

The script gave a lot of importance to a thick-headed young gunslinger (Canadian actor Jaimz Woolvett) and even more weight to Ned Logan, William Munny's retired outlaw partner, an African–American who has lost his stomach for violence. That character would be portrayed with quiet eloquence by Morgan Freeman, one of Hollywood's foremost character leads (his two Oscar nominations included Best Supporting Actor for 1987's *Street Smart*, and Best Actor for 1989's *Driving Miss Daisy*).

The town sheriff loomed as a figure second only to William Munny. Little Billy Daggett runs Big Whiskey, Wyoming with cynicism and an iron fist. When not on duty, Daggett's busy constructing his 'dream house'. When wearing his badge, he brutally dispenses frontier justice. Only Daggett stands between the trio of bounty hunters and the drovers (*Rawhide* cast-offs) marked for death by the vengeful town whores.

The sheriff's part called for an actor who could stand up to Clint. The script went out to Gene Hackman, widely regarded as a virtuoso star, although he was often reduced to second leads. Hackman, winner of an Oscar for his gritty performance in *The French Connection,* turned the part down, as he had once before, when Francis Ford Coppola had talked about it with him. Later, Hackman was candid in telling journalists that 'I didn't see what Clint saw in it at the time', and that 'I thought it was too violent'. His agent urged the actor to reconsider, and Clint was persuasive. Hackman's involvement was crucial to the growing significance of the project.

The cast was rounded out by two actresses: Frances Fisher, at the height of her romance with the star–director, would play Strawberry Alice, who forges the feminist solidarity of the town whores, maintaining the peculiar Clint tradition of a real-life girlfriend playing a prostitute in his films. Fisher said in subsequent interviews that she had the option of playing the whore–victim savagely disfigured in the film's opening sequence. That character would be played affectingly by Anna Thomson.

Especially with the star support of Richard Harris, Morgan Freeman and Gene Hackman, *Unforgiven* loomed as a shift from the Malpaso norm. On location in Alberta, Canada in August 1991, composer Lennie Niehaus, editor Joel Cox and director of photography Jack Green would anchor the production unit. Green, once Bruce Surtees' acolyte, continued his rise, working 'almost telepathically' with Clint, in Frances Fisher's words. Surtees had been fast and loose, so was Green; but Green's greater emphasis on composition and an intimacy in the framing – he was always inching the camera in closer – marked an improvement in Clint's visual style.

Adding his prestige to the film would be production designer Henry Bumstead, who had last worked for Clint on *High Plains Drifter* twenty years earlier. Two-time Oscar-winner Bumstead would now build Big Whiskey for *Unforgiven,* and, along with Jack Green, create the impressive, over-all 'drained, wintry look' of the Western, in David Thomson's words.

Warners invited key journalists to the set, encouraging early Oscar whispering. Jack Mathews of the *Los Angeles Times* flew in and reported from location. Richard Schickel was underfoot, filming a behind-the-scenes documentary. Peter Biskind of *Première*, the glossy monthly film magazine, was there for a cover story, timed for the release, in which he would compare Clint's Westerns – not to John Ford – but to Elizabethan tragedy.

The shooting schedule was 'twice as long as *Pale Rider*'s', in Schickel's words. It was, Schickel reported, a 'sunny shoot – literally', Clint's weather. 'The many Eastwood veterans on the set sensed a slight mood shift in their director,' Schickel noted, 'a willingness to rehearse a little longer than usual, make more takes, do more coverage of complex scenes, and wondered, some of them, if this might be a farewell of sorts.'

By mid-January, Joel Cox had already completed his rough cut, and Warners could begin to push the film at Sho-West, the annual convention in Las Vegas, which Clint visited to mix and mingle with the nation's exhibitors. According to Schickel, the pre-release campaign had to be 'low-key', at Clint's insistence. 'He did not want to stir excessive expectations for the movie, or openly acknowledge his own,' the biographer wrote.

In truth, this low-key campaign was one of Warners' most aggressive promotions. The generally repeated belief about the Warners' hierarchy is that they pushed Clint into quick, lowest-common-denominator vehicles, and that they fretted over his more 'artistic' efforts. Terry Semel and Bob Daly don't give interviews, and they probably don't mind reading about themselves in this negative light, over and over, since what they most enjoy reading are the studio's financial ledgers.

Clint appreciated that Semel and Daly were outstanding salesmen. They, in turn, were smart enough to recognize that Clint's 'youth appeal' was fading, and that his name as a director was essential to the long-term strategy for a diversified audience bloc. *Unforgiven* was not such a big gamble; *Pale Rider* had chalked up nearly $60 million in US box-office. The real test of *Unforgiven* would come with the critics and Academy Awards. And Semel and Daly were, early on, in on the Oscar fever.

For the first time in fifteen years, Charles Gold and Kitty Dutton would not be involved in the advertising campaign. Although they had been his close friends for more than a decade, dining out and attending jazz concerts together, Clint let them go, without any explanation other than 'Warners has some better ideas', As he often did when he switched professionally, he also cut all personal ties to the Golds.

In the Frank Wells era, Clint felt he needed the marketing input – Wells was a lawyer, not a salesman. But Clint had learned to trust Semel and Daly (the studio heads were notorious for approving the design and exact wording of every poster Warner churned out) and he could save a little money and bother by ceding this function to the studio. One insider's theory is that Warners superseded the Golds as part of a closed-door arrangement for which the studio would pay Sondra Locke's 'palimony' (i.e. her directing deal). Others believe the Golds simply had made the mistake of staying on too-friendly terms with Clint's former live-in lover. No couple in Hollywood knew him and Locke better as a couple; nobody double-dated with them more frequently.

Warners swung into action, in the spring of 1992. 'Well in advance of the opening,' wrote Kirk Honeycutt in the *Hollywood Reporter*, '[Joe] Hyams and Marco Barla, the film's unit publicist, toured key media centres and showed it [*Unforgiven*] to influential journalists.' This 'low-key' sally was followed by a New York City junket, covering 150 media outlets, whose representatives were treated to an advance showing of the film, wined and dined, introduced to the stars.

Two different television spots aired repeatedly around the country: one spotlighting Clint, and another with more of a 'women's angle', emphasizing the moral conflict of the film. Two different teaser posters went out, one with Clint alone, the other featuring the four male stars.

The first trailer went out to theatres with *Lethal Weapon 3*, in May. After that it was also attached to *Batman Returns* and *Patriot Games*, two of the summer's guaranteed hits. Warners estimated fifteen thousand *Unforgiven* trailers were distributed.

Tie-in contests were arranged for interested theatre-owners. Major circuits, including General Cinema, AMC and Laemmle, offered cash prizes, travel rewards and other promotional gifts subsidized by Warner Brothers.

Clint did a record number of interviews for newspapers and magazines, including an unusual, 'live', nationally-televised appearance on

The Tonight Show, with Jay Leno. 'This is the first time I can remember in a long time that Clint went out and hustled for a movie all over the place,' a Warners executive was quoted in the trades. This was gilding the lily; amazingly, it was still part of his image that Clint, who hustled heroically on behalf of his films, shunned interviews.

The ballyhoo was capped by a special 'Great Westerns Week', hosted by Clint, on seventy TV stations across the US. *Unforgiven*'s opening had been slated for August, after the summer hits died down. Remember the time when dozens of films competed for theatres, and *The Beguiled* led with 50 bookings? *Unforgiven* would be thrust onto more than two thousand screens. Barry Reardon, the studio's distribution chief, was quoted in the *Hollywood Reporter* as saying the Western was preordained to be a 'home run', but, the *Reporter* added, 'Nevertheless, Warners marketing executives want to make sure this home run happens with the bases loaded.'

A minor irritant during this Oscar foreplay was Megan Rose, the story analyst who had slept with Clint and handed him the script of *Unforgiven*. Angry at seeing the film she had been crucially responsible for in the process of being positioned for the Academy Award she had predicted, she hired a lawyer and threatened to sue.

All she wanted was her 'finder's fee' and a modest screen credit. Rose's lawyer spoke to Clint's lawyer, who informed him that Clint could not justify giving her a fee and credit. The offer came back that Clint would pay her $10,000 to act as story editor on his next production, *A Perfect World*, which might be especially attractive to Rose because she had once worked as a reader for Kevin Costner. Rose said no, she felt she had already done the work for which she ought to be compensated.

Rose threatened to go public with her story – and the revelation of her affair with Clint. Before she could do so, however, she found herself exposed in the *New York Post* of 8 March 1993, where the 'Page Six' gossip column reported her claims of having discovered the *Unforgiven* script, along with her story of romantic involvement with Clint. Warners Vice President of Worldwide Advertising and Publicity Robert Friedman was quoted, stepping outside his customary purview to note that Rose was 'just a low-level exec in the story department'. Friedman conceded Rose may have championed the script, but insisted that she didn't work directly for Clint, and that Warners employees were not entitled to any financial rewards for recommending scripts. She wasn't even owed, the column noted, 'a spent .44 Magnum bullet casing'.

That was harsh enough, but Friedman was also quoted as stating that Rose once told another Warners executive 'that she'd had an affair with Eastwood six hundred years ago in a previous life'. Since Rose had apprised Clint of her belief in reincarnation, she took this as coming directly from the star, and felt crushed. A few lawyer manoeuvres followed, then Rose dropped her pursuit of payment and credit.

To this day, poignantly, she doesn't hold a grudge, and like many people once enamoured of Clint, she would be happy for a phone call and another chance in his life.

The August 'bases-loaded' release of *Unforgiven* exceeded studio expectations, pulling in somewhere between $13 and $14 million in ticket sales in its opening weekend, the best-ever opening for a Clint film, the best-ever August opening for a Warner Brothers production. In one weekend alone, Clint's Western out-tallied the combined domestic gross of *White Hunter, Black Heart* and *Pink Cadillac*.

The critics tried to top each other with superlatives. 'A classic Western for the ages,' opined Todd McCarthy in *Variety*. 'The finest classical Western to come along since perhaps John Ford's 1956 *The Searchers*', said Jack Mathews of the *Los Angeles Times* in a feature piece extolling Clint. 'One of the best films of the year', exclaimed Rex Reed in the *New York Observer*, hailing *Unforgiven* as 'a profound work of art'. Richard Corliss in *Time* wrote that the new film was 'Eastwood's meditation on age, repute, courage, heroism – on all those burdens he has been carrying with such grace for decades'.

The uncharacteristic time, money and care taken in the crafting of *Unforgiven* had resulted in a richness and roundness, a grandeur, that other Clint films often lacked. Although the film was a directorial triumph, Clint also rose to the occasion as actor. He was always evocative in Western costume, and the intimations of mortality in the dialogue ('I'm scared of dying,' Munny confesses at one point) could be interpreted to have personal meaning for the ageing star. However, the deceased-wife-good-father routine (with two frontier children as stand-ins for Kyle and Alison), the falling off horses into pig slop, the through-the-past-darkly backstory, were old Clintisms. When, at the end, the previously rusty William Munny rides into Big Whiskey alone to avenge Ned Logan, the film shrugs and abandons its brooding thoughtfulness.

In the end, Clint manages to dispatch a half dozen bad'uns while barely stubbing his toe – a finale which harks back to 'the magisterial deliverer of death that Sergio Leone cherished', as David Thomson has noted. And if that Leone-borrowing was demythological revisionism, demonstrating the haunting consequences of violence, then what was the film's final scroll, which informed audiences that Munny had moved to San Francisco, where (like Eastwoods of yore) he prosperously lived out his days selling dry goods?

But film critics were as grateful for a stylish Western as the NAACP was for a jazzman's biography. *Unforgiven* earned Clint the year's Best Director award from the National Society of Film Critics. The film was named the best of the year by the Boston Society of Film Critics, while notching Best Director *and* Actor for Clint from the Los Angeles film critics' association. Across the nation, *Unforgiven* would crop up on more than two hundred of the annual Ten Best lists.

Clint's luck also held for the competition, and 1992 was one of the worst years in memory for studio-financed, Hollywood-produced films. This circumstantial element of good timing was made clear by the Directors Guild of America, which announced its five nominations for Best Director in January of 1993. The five: Neil Jordan (*The Crying Game*), James Ivory (*Howard's End*), Robert Altman (*The Player*), Rob Reiner (*A Few Good Men*) and Clint (*Unforgiven*).

Neil Jordan was foreign-born (his film foreign-made); James Ivory was a true independent based on the East Coast (his film also foreign-made); Altman was the perennial Hollywood outsider (his film an independent production which was in fact a scathing attack on the studio bureaucracy). That left only Clint and another actor-turned-director, Rob Reiner and *A Few Good Men*, in the category of 'home-grown success'.

The DGA nomination, which was voted on by the Guild's nine thousand members, was Clint's first. The trade papers noted that East Coast DGA members were pulling for Altman to win; but Altman, unlike Clint, did no compaigning, and the West Coast (with its higher numbers) was sure to prevail. When, in March, Clint topped the DGA balloting, he then became the odds-on favourite to repeat as Best Director at the Academy Awards one month later.

Unforgiven was Oscar-nominated for Best Picture. And Clint was not only nominated for Best Director, but also Best Actor. *Unforgiven*'s other Oscar nominations included Best Supporting Actor (Gene Hackman), Editing (Joel Cox), Original Screenplay (David Webb Peoples), Art Direction–Set Decoration (Henry Bumstead, Janice Blackie-Goodine), Cinematography (Jack Green), and Sound (Les Fresholtz, Vern Poore, Dick Alexander, Rob Young). Nine in all, a singular accomplishment.

The *Los Angeles Times* published an article handicapping the nominees, explaining why Clint was a shoo-in as Best Director and a strong candidate for Best Actor. First of all, for his body of work; secondly, because of *Unforgiven* 'being in the tradition of a classic'; and thirdly, because he was a local boy made good (as opposed to all those genuine industry outsiders). The critics had embraced *Unforgiven*, but equally important, Clint's Western was produced and distributed by 'one of the industry's giants', Warner Brothers. 'No film has ever been named Best Picture by the Academy of Motion Picture Arts and Sciences', the *Los Angeles Times* noted, 'without some affiliation with a major Hollywood studio or to a mainstream Hollywood-based producer.'

'Moreover,' the *Los Angeles Times* added, Clint was notoriously 'likeable, as evidenced by his apparent pleasure in making the rounds of the many pre-Oscar festivities during the past few weeks – always with a wide grin on his face and only funny, self-deprecating comments to say about his current favourite-son status.'

The only true surprise on Oscar night, 19 March, was that Clint did not collect the Best Actor prize, too. There his competition was mild: Robert Downey Jr in *Chaplin*, Stephen Rea in *The Crying Game*, Denzel Washington in *Malcolm X*, Al Pacino in *Scent of a Woman*. But Academy members balked at voting for Clint as Best Actor, and Pacino, nominated six times in past years without having won, finally took the coveted honour.

Joel Cox won Best Editing and Gene Hackman accepted Best Supporting Actor, with the evening building towards Clint's moment. When his name was announced as Best Director, Clint took the podium and accepted sustained applause from the audience. He delivered a brief speech, thanking cast and crew – and, because it was the year of the woman – 'the women of Big Whiskey' and (a tacit nod to Megan Rose?) 'all the gals who really were the catalyst to getting this story off the ground'. The Best Director made a point of acknowledging 'the film critics for discovering this film', saying *Unforgiven* 'wasn't a highly touted film when it came out, but they sort of stayed with it throughout the year'; especially French critics, the Museum of Modern Art and British Film Institute which 'embraced some of my work' before it became fashionable.

He returned to the podium to receive the Best Picture statuette from Jack Nicholson, this time expressing gratitude to Warners publicists Joe Hyams and Marco Barla, executives Terry Semel and Bob Daly ('the whole executive strata' of the studio), 'the whole marketing department', and especially Warners CEO Steve Ross, who had died of prostate cancer earlier in 1992. 'In the year of the woman,' Clint added, 'the greatest woman on the planet is here tonight and that's my mother, Ruth.' The television cameras flashed to eighty-three-year-old Ruth Eastwood, beaming in the audience.

Clint himself was a few weeks shy of sixty-two, the same age as John Wayne when he won his Oscar for *True Grit*. Hollywood columnists remarked on Clint's elegant formal wear and noted that the Oscar winner was one of the last to leave the celebration parties that night. *Unforgiven* would go on to sell $160 million worth of tickets in America alone. It was box-office and it was art. The greening of Clint was complete.

To say that Clint had made an amazing comeback is not quite right; he had never gone away. But by the mid-1980s, his films had begun to wobble, younger stars were charging the box-office, and Sondra Locke's 'palimony' case had tarnished his once-pure image. *Unforgiven* regenerated a career that looked as though it had peaked.

The Nino Cerruti suit he wore on Oscar night was indicative of the new Clint and was also his costume from his next film, for by Oscar night Clint already had *In the Line of Fire* – destined to rival the success of *Unforgiven* – done and ready for release.

In the Line of Fire was another of those scripts that had bounced around Hollywood for years. The initial concept of a film about Secret Service agents dedicated to protecting the President had been the brainchild of producer Jeff Apple, with Dustin Hoffman tentatively set as lead character Frank Horrigan. Hoffman had dropped out when the script versions proliferated. Then Jeff Maguire came along to write the final draft, which placed Horrigan on the running board of John F. Kennedy's ill-fated motorcade through Dallas in 1963, evoking Clint Hill, the real-life Secret Service agent who bravely shielded the First Lady in Dallas and whose guilt over his failure to prevent Kennedy's assassination later caused him to break down on national television.

The Jeff Maguire script was sold to Castle Rock for $1.4 million in April 1992. The independent company, which was headed by Rob Reiner, had packaged *A Few Good Men*, with Reiner directing Demi Moore, Tom Cruise and Jack Nicholson. Now Castle Rock set out to package *In the Line of Fire* with Clint as Frank Horrigan and German-born Wolfgang Petersen as director. Petersen was best-known for his gripping Oscar-nominated German-language film, *Das Boot (The Boat)*.

All the later publicity emphasized that, with *In the Line of Fire*, Clint was stepping outside the Warner Brothers umbrella for the first time in nearly twenty years. This was partly true, although Castle Rock films were released by Columbia, whose parent company, Sony, owned about forty four per cent of Castle Rock. Terry Semel and Bob Daly knew that it behoved Clint to work with directors other than Buddy Van Horn. Besides, as was true of *Absolute Power* – another Castle Rock production a couple of years later – Warners, as part of the deal, probably retained a healthy percentage of foreign and home-video rights.

The part of a Secret Service man haunted by his failures had not been shaped expressly for Clint. But the piano-playing, jazz-loving background of Frank Horrigan was an 'accidental' detail that the star could appreciate. Accidental, too, were Horrigan's background of divorce; the young, doomed sidekick (played by Dylan McDermott); the female agent whom Horrigan initially dismisses as 'window-dressing'; the FBI and CIA higher-ups not dissimilar to thick-headed Dirty Harry-series bureaucrats. These Clintisms were in the script, and the star warmed to them.

At one point a line in the film describes Horrigan as a 'border-line burnout with questionable social skills'. His boss tells him he's a dinosaur, too old for the job. When jogging alongside the motorcade, he is left gasping. Ironically, after all those years playing characters younger than himself, now Clint would have to *fake* his vulnerabilities, going through the film with a runny nose and a cough left over from *Honkytonk Man*. In Hollywood fashion, however, Horrigan is able to outrun all the young bucks when the emergency demands it; just as in *The Dead Pool*, ageing Detective Callahan, butt of jokes, has a scene where he outjogs his young Asian partner.

Director Petersen met Clint just before the summer 1992 release of *Unforgiven*. 'We sat together for two hours,' the director explained, 'and it was just wonderful. We talked and talked and talked, not only about this script, but about movies, about how we approach things as film-makers. It was a wonderfully in-sync conversation.'

After Clint's commitment came John Malkovich's. Malkovich, another Leonard Hirshan client, would play the psychopathic stalker obsessed with creating a second failure for Horrigan by another assassination of a sitting president. According to the film's director, Clint previously had tried to hire Malkovich, a meticulous actor from Chicago's Steppenwolf Ensemble, for Malpaso productions. But he 'was never able to', in Petersen's words.

Rene Russo was Columbia executive Mark Canton's idea for the female Secret Service agent who spars verbally with Frank Horrigan before falling in love with him. Although in *Lethal Weapon 3* Russo had had a romance with Mel Gibson, the actress was more thrilled to be kissing Clint, whom she had adored from afar, dating from a childhood crush on Rowdy. 'I wasn't at all nervous with Mel,' Russo commented to one interviewer. 'To tell you the truth, I have loved Clint Eastwood for years and years and years, and I had to go out and rent *Lethal Weapon 1* and *2* before I did *3*, just to see what they were about, so I think that's what the difference was.'

Think of the project as 'Dirty Harry Goes to Washington', or as Clint's *JFK*. Clint had been glancing over his shoulder at Kevin Costner the same way John Wayne had once watched him nervously. *Dances with Wolves* had paved the way for *Unforgiven*. Costner had played the conspiracy DA Jim Garrison in Oliver Stone's *JFK* in 1991. Now *In the Line of Fire* would present a Republican's one-man theory of Kennedy's Dallas death, with Malkovich the Lee Harvey Oswald-type lone nut.

If *In the Line of Fire* was half a potboiler, the director was an intelligent man widely respected for his visual mastery, his handling of atmosphere and tension, his conscientious craftsmanship in all departments. Wolfgang Petersen would be the first film-maker since Don Siegel to establish any real independence from Clint.

The first thing Petersen managed to do was limit the Malpaso input. As cameraman Jack Green later explained, Petersen 'didn't want too many of Clint's support team'. So instead of Jack Green, the director of photography would be John Bailey; the editor was Anne V. Coates, production designer Lilly Kilvert, and costumer Erica Edell Phillips (who coaxed Clint into Cerruti); and the music would be composed by Ennio Morricone, who hadn't scored a film of Clint's for twenty years. The Malpaso 'support team' on location in Washington, DC, when *In the Line of Fire* went before the cameras in late 1992, were relative 'non-creatives': stunt coordinator Buddy Van Horn (with Clint's artistic image in ascendancy, Van Horn's directing days appeared over) and executive producer David Valdes (sharing the producer's credit with others).

Petersen began by treating Clint as an actor, not as a standby director or god. He urged Clint to think about the leitmotif of a profession in which someone is trained to step in front of a bullet, if necessary, to save the life of another person. Clint said in one interview that he remembered meeting a few Secret Service agents back in the days when he played golf with President Gerald Ford. He knew that they were trained not just to protect the President, but other visiting dignitaries. That put a limit on Clint's empathy with the character. 'Suppose it's Fidel Castro?' Clint mused, indicating he would stop short of taking a bullet for someone most conservatives considered a political enemy. 'Would you jump in front of a bullet for Fidel Castro? I sure as hell wouldn't.'

Petersen had ways of tweaking Clint's acting. He encouraged Malkovich to 'mess with Clint', quietly telling Clint's co-star, 'Go ahead, befuddle him.' Malkovich's chilling, free-wheeling performance (he would later be nominated for a Best Supporting Actor Oscar) caught Clint off guard, startled him. Malkovich was always driving things up a notch – for example, sucking on the barrel of a gun Clint pointed at him during the rooftop chase, one of the film's highlights. 'This notion of dissing him [Clint], you know,' said Malkovich in one interview, 'seemed to come up a lot.'

Take a look at the scene where Frank Horrigan fights back tears, recounting his guilt over the JFK assassination. Then take a look at the scene in *The Bridges of Madison County*, where Robert Kincaid, facing separation from Francesca, similarly breaks down. In the latter film, Kincaid (Clint) turns his back to the audience, while the camera swiftly cuts away to Francesca (Meryl Streep). Clint couldn't handle the revelatory tears when directing himself, whereas the scene from *In the Line of Fire* showed his acting at its best. 'He's a better actor than I thought before I started the film,' Petersen said in interviews, 'and the more we shot, the more I enjoyed seeing how many layers he had to show.'

Except for John Malkovich, *In the Line of Fire* was not really an acting forum. It was a director's showcase of superbly paced plotting and cross-orchestrated tension, drawing on a $40 million budget and state-of-the-art computer animation that replicated presidential events, digitally superimposing Clint's face at rallies and in Dallas, 1963. Never was any Clint vehicle better timed than this one, released in the summer of 1993, after the *Unforgiven* Oscars.

Critics and audiences were vastly entertained, and *In the Line of Fire* went on to become the most profitable Clint film of all time, with a reported gross of $200 million in the US alone. That makes it one of two Clint films included on *Variety*'s list of the Top 200 all-time box-office hits. The other is *Unforgiven*.

Incredibly, Clint had already got busy, during the late spring and summer, directing another film. Others might slow down, but something spurred the sixty-two-year-old star on. Now an Oscar winner as a director, he was making films as quickly and as searchingly as at any time in his career.

A Perfect World had been scheduled to begin location photography in February, but was delayed by the Oscar events. The project had begun with a script by John Lee Hancock, a Texas native and law graduate of Baylor University, who had practised law for four years before turning to theatre and film. Hancock had written and directed plays for a small Los Angeles theatre company, before his first film script was optioned by producer Mark Johnson. The property had a short dalliance with Steven Spielberg, until Spielberg found he wasn't able to juggle his commitments. Clint had read the script when looking for writers; he said parts of it reminded him of Kirk Douglas's 1962 film *Lonely Are the Brave*. When Clint expressed interest in directing, *A Perfect World* was set up at Warner Brothers.

Similar to *Lonely Are the Brave*, the story was set in the 1960s with a lead, doomed character pursued by state police using modern means of transportation and communication. Spielberg thought Clint might play the lead, Butch Haynes, who takes a seven-year-old boy hostage during his flight. But for the first time in his career Clint was heard to say, 'I'm too old.' He would direct only; he was trying to wean himself away from starring *and* directing, he told interviewers, to alleviate the stress of double duties.

Producer Mark Johnson had Kevin Costner on the hook, and would Clint, the Oscar-winning director of *Unforgiven*, be willing to direct Costner, similarly Oscar-honoured for *Dances With Wolves?* Clint was intrigued. 'I started thinking, "Well, this doesn't seem like his [Costner's] cup of tea, normally",' Clint explained in an interview. 'But maybe that's when actors get their best breaks.' As Richard Schickel wrote, Butch Haynes was 'a part he [Clint] would have loved to have played twenty years earlier' – an unloved, unloving character – never mind that he could have and never did.

Costner was amenable, but he wanted Clint as his co-star to boost the film's box-office chances. Costner wondered if Clint might play the secondary part of Texas lawman Red Garnett, the leader of the posse chasing Haynes. Clint didn't think the Red Garnett part had much substance; plus, in the script, the lawman only had one brief encounter with the fugitive. So Costner went to work with John Lee Hancock, making suggestions to bulk up the character 'so, in a sense, he [Costner] could seduce Clint by giving him more to do', in producer Mark Johnson's words.

The revamped script would stipulate a 'backstory' connecting Clint and Costner. Not until the climax would it be revealed that Red Garnett arrested Butch Haynes as a juvenile, then convinced the judge to throw the book at him to 'save' him from bad influences; the harsh punishment had the reverse effect of triggering a life of crime.

The script changes convinced Clint that his character would have a 'vested interest' in the drama, and he said yes. At the back of everyone's minds, during the preproduction meetings, were the differences between how Clint and Costner operated. Clint was well known for minimum takes and maximum speed, while Costner was a niggling perfectionist. All of the decisions had to be delicately negotiated. Clint and Costner 'danced around one another for a bit', said producer Johnson.

Once the two stars felt comfortable with each other, the rest of the cast was lined up. Laura Dern would play the spunky criminologist dogging Red Garnett's heels whose part, too reminiscent of other Clint-distaff sidekicks, from *The Enforcer* to *In the Line of Fire*, got padded along with Clint's. Utah-born newcomer T. J. Lowther would play the kidnapped boy who sees the hardened convict through sympathetic eyes.

Regardless of the diplomacy that had brought about the Clint–Costner pairing, there was tension on the set, once the filming began in the summer in Texas. Partly this was because the child actor required unique attention and partly this was because Costner proved a 'carefully calculating' performer who endlessly debated the right prop and the most 'minuscule movement', according to Richard Schickel. Clint was quoted in one interview as grumping about it: 'He'll [Costner] garnish for ever.'

Costner came to the location with his own directorial ideas. These were 'respected and talked out', according to Schickel, but even so the production fell behind schedule, almost unprecedented for Clint. There was one incident, where Costner walked off the set and then the director photographed his stand-in to show who was the boss. But crowned by Oscar, and still on top after forty years in show business, now more than ever Clint could afford to stay calm and good-natured, and he did.

Clint was still in Texas come mid-July, giving interviews to promote *In the Line of Fire* from the big silver bus that bore Red Garnett on his pursuit. The hi-tech mobile home had grown as a plot device throughout the rewrite, a symbol of futuristic law-enforcement which nonetheless proves futile in the story. The bus mirrored Clint's own trailer van, a familiar sight on his sets, and known to Malpaso regulars as 'the Shrine' or 'Popemobile'. The 'Popemobile' was as much home for the footloose Clint as any of his houses. Its interiors were just as nondescript, although the gadgets and technology were kept up to date. 'Inside,' a correspondent from *Vogue* wrote, 'it is totally style-free, not even particularly comfortable, a functional piece of privacy.'

Nineteen ninety-three was something of an *annus mirabilis* for Clint: the Oscars for *Unforgiven, In the Line of Fire* was a box-office smash, *A Perfect World* was put in the hopper, and by the end of summer, there

Cute kids: Alison, Kyle and the family dog in the mid 1970s.

Below: The 'forever house': while it was being built, Clint's marriage was crumbling.

Left: Sondra Locke and Clint in the 1970s. On- and off-camera his favourite 'squirts' rarely came up past his shoulders.

Left: On the set of *Every Which Way But Loose* with scriptwriter Jeremy Joe Kronsberg (third from left), director James Fargo (sunglasses) and cinematographer Rexford Metz (back to camera).

Right: Clint and his cheapest, most profitable co-star, Manis the ape.

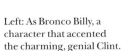

Left: As Bronco Billy, a character that accented the charming, genial Clint.

Left: From all appearances, Clint and Sondra Locke were still a happy couple. They are seen here with Dani Crayne, the actor's old friend from Universal contract days.

Above: Locke was put in charge of renovating the house Clint bought on Stradella Road. All of the re-design and details of décor were closely modelled after an apartment house she had lived in before they met.

Left: While Locke was occupied, Clint was busy romancing other women, including story analyst Megan Rose, who first handed him the script for *Unforgiven*.

Left: Friends say that being Mayor opened him up to people. Political enemies say he favoured business and developers and nurtured his own interests with contacts.

Below: The director with Forest Whitaker, accepting his Best Actor award at the 41st Cannes film festival for playing Charlie Parker in *Bird*.

The 1992 Western, *Unforgiven*, came at a propitious moment in a long, popular career. It would be declared Clint's masterwork as actor and director.

Backstage, on his night of triumph, with Oscar presenters Jack Nicholson and Barbra Streisand.

Here, on Oscar night, Clint is seen with his mother Ruth and her husband John Belden Wood, and actress Frances Fisher. Fisher, who appeared in *Unforgiven*, was now co-starring in Clint's private life, but she was under strict orders not to tell people that she was pregnant.

Clint's break-up with Sondra Locke led to some unpleasant newspaper stories and revelations in the tabloids that for the first time mentioned the existence of his out-of-wedlock daughter Kimber Tunis Eastwood. Later Kimber Eastwood would play a small part in one of her father's films, *Absolute Power.*

Above from left: Alison Eastwood, Clint, The Lady Chablis and John Cusack at the studio premiere of *Midnight in the Garden of Good and Evil.*

Below: When *Bridges of Madison County* was over, so was the relationship between Frances Fisher and Clint. A young news anchorwoman, Dina Ruiz, materialized to capture his heart – and sealed their declarations of love with marriage and a baby.

Gentleman Clint: approaching the millennium and still going strong.

was another baby, this one a girl with the last name Fisher-Eastwood.

Accompanying Clint to events, throughout late 1992 and 1993, was Frances Fisher, the actress from *Pink Cadillac* and *Unforgiven* who now was publicly acknowledged to be starring in Clint's private life. According to an interview with Fisher in *Redbook*, she and Clint conceived a baby in December 1992, just as they were starting their critics' rounds, accepting year-end honours on behalf of *Unforgiven*. 'The decision to have a baby had been percolating in the back of my mind for years,' Fisher told *Redbook*, 'and we were coming close to it anyway. He wasn't opposed. He knew that I wanted to have children – everybody knows that about me. It was part of the package.'

This is what she said in print. In actuality, according to sympathetic friends of Fisher, she had made it clear to Clint that she was interested in a life partner, husband and father. He, typically, remained elusive. When she became pregnant, his reaction was to make a joke about her womanly figure going to hell. When she asked Clint if he wanted the baby, he said, in his noncommittal way, that it was up to her.

This was a period of inner turmoil for Fisher, despite the smiles she displayed to the press whenever she and Clint were out and about. She did decide to have the baby, and even then Clint sent her negative signals. He didn't want her to tell anyone, especially before the Academy Awards, because as the star told her flatly, he didn't want anything to detract from his Oscar campaign. So the actress was forbidden to tell her closest friends, and she went to the Oscars, four months pregnant, trying to feel that the congratulations they received that night were partly for the baby growing inside her.

Clint still refused to tell people, and it wasn't until a couple of months later, when Fisher visited the set of *A Perfect World* in Texas, that he started to acknowledge the pregnancy to friends and the press. People on the set recall what a glowering mood he was in that day, when Buddy Van Horn commented to him that Fisher was 'showing'. It's probably relevant that her visit also interrupted his flirtations with a young assistant, according to people behind the scenes of that film.

The baby was not due until September. After the filming of *A Perfect World*, Clint and Fisher travelled up to Rising River Ranch, where the editing and postproduction would take place. On the afternoon of August 6, her water broke, and they left, with Clint piloting his own helicopter, for the hospital some sixty miles away in Redding. At

5:38 a.m. the next day, after twenty-two hours of labour, the baby was born, and named Francesca Ruth Fisher-Eastwood.

Clint was there throughout the labour, though he had been absent from the births of Kyle and Alison. They went home together for five weeks, a 'miraculous time', in Fisher's words, in which the couple nurtured each other and lavished attention on the newborn. 'He became the person I knew was in him,' Fisher later said. 'He was there. He cooked breakfast, lunch and dinner for me. I'd be nursing the baby and he'd be feeding me so I could hold the baby.'

During those weeks Clint was also consulting with Joel Cox trying to complete the editing of *A Perfect World* in time for a pre-Christmas release. If possible, Warner Brothers wanted to have a Clint Eastwood film at holiday time to capitalize on the heady year of *Unforgiven* and *In the Line of Fire*. 'A tone was established [between Clint and Frances Fisher] in those weeks that persisted for months,' noted Richard Schickel. 'The three of them were constantly together, and on the rare occasions when they were apart Clint always stayed punctiliously in touch.'

Later, the actress admitted she entertained some misgivings, right from the hospital table. 'A nurse whispered something to Clint, something I couldn't hear,' Fisher told a London newspaper later. 'I heard him reply, "It's not appropriate," and I knew she'd asked for his autograph. I loved him for that moment when he said no. But suddenly, he seemed to change his mind. He turned to the doctor, and said, "Do you have a pen?"' That's when Fisher started cursing at Clint to stop talking about autographs.

She believed Clint's philandering days were past. When Fisher had asked him about other women in his life, Clint reportedly quoted his *Unforgiven* character: 'I ain't like that no more.' The same month that baby Francesca was born, however, the *Ladies Home Journal* published an interview with Clint in which the same question was asked differently. Was Frances Fisher the only woman in his life right now? Clint always hated that question, because it raised all sorts of bogeys in his mind, and because, if answered truthfully, it would open the door to skeletons.

'He [Clint] thinks,' the interviewer wrote in the August 1993 *Ladies Home Journal*, 'for a long time.'

'"My mother is still alive. She is a very special lady," he finally replies. "A lot of untruths have been printed about my . . . about Frances and me. But we do get around a lot. That *is* the truth." '

'Has she made many alterations to your house?' the interviewer asked ('thinking that if she has, she'll probably stick around for a while').

That was a more easily-parried question. ' "Uh . . . she's been dealing with the workmen," he says reluctantly. His eyes scan the horizon, avoiding mine. "I don't interfere . . . much. I leave it to her."

' "Does that mean you prefer a woman who is willing to stay at home once she is married?"

'Another dreadful silence.'

Just as the interviewer began to wonder 'if I should cut my losses and make a graceful exit', Clint's 'eyelids flicker and he ventures a reply: "Women who are homemakers work harder than most. Their services are vastly underrated. But I don't mind career women either – I love all women. I especially love my mother. Took her with me to the Academy Awards [this year]." '

In September Clint was made a fellow of the British Film Institute in London and the next month he was conspicuous at a New York Museum of Modern Art gala in his honour. The Clint Eastwood collection was being installed in MOMA archives, and a MOMA series of Clint's films showed in the fall. The kick-off benefit, to aid MOMA's Film Preservation Center, was chaired by the chief executive officer of the Warners parent corporation, which had donated 35mm copies of all the Warners–Malpaso films.

Meanwhile, *A Perfect World* moved forward towards release. Richard Schickel complained on Clint's behalf about 'long postproduction hours', a rating boards squabble, and negotiations with Kevin Costner's agent, Michael Ovitz, over the film's publicity and advertising. Although Clint was known for editing his films speedily, this one was rushed, in his view, because of the studio's desired November release.

The bleak, relentlessly downbeat, overlong (138 minutes) film did okay with US audiences, while eventually bringing in a reported $150 million worldwide. And American critics applauded *A Perfect World*, with Janet Maslin of the *New York Times* going so far as to call it 'the high point of Mr Eastwood's directing career so far', a work which, in sensitively treating lost childhood and in the convict's fatherly feeling for his kidnap victim, gave 'real meaning' to the subject of 'men's legacies to their children'.

Indeed, *A Perfect World* was Clint's most harrowing work as a director. The fundamental brutality of the piece was mingled with lyrical flights of imagery. Costner's performance was a revelation, the boy actor held his own, and Clint's directing was at home with racing cars, swooping helicopters, and the beauty of landscape and skies.

Think of *A Perfect World* as Clint's attack on the family unit. The film weeps tears for Butch Haynes's boyhood abuse by cruel parents, while the all-American family the fugitive meets on the road becomes the object of simple-minded humour. Violence and alienation are seen to lurk within the most innocent-seeming family, even that of the poor black farmer who befriends the criminal. This man turns out to be a child-walloper just like other no-good fathers. In the film's most difficult moment, directed unblinkingly by Clint, an angry Haynes nearly kills the Samaritan and his family.

Think of it as Clint's *JFK 2*. At this crossroads of his life, in the twilight of his career, Clint made an informal, dark trilogy mired in the early 1960s: *In the Line of Fire, A Perfect World,* and (still to come) *The Bridges of Madison County*. There is referential dialogue in *A Perfect World* about JFK coming to Dallas; the film's governor, a hollow grandstander, would have been the Texas Democrat, John Connally, who was a wounded survivor of the same motorcade poorly protected by Frank Horrigan.

John Kennedy looked golden before the November 1963 tragedy. Clint's road was the one really paved with gold. Time would only magnify the luck of Rowdy. Curious that, in this and other films which Clint was now making, he was expressing not only a nostalgia for but a distrust of the past. As if Clint was questioning some of his own choices, and losers and winners aren't always that clear cut.

The ending was as well done as could be, with Butch slain by over-eager FBI agents and Red Garnett muttering, 'I don't know nothing. I don't know a damn thing.' Once again, as with only a few films – *The Beguiled, Honkytonk Man* and *White Hunter, Black Heart* – Clint triumphed with an ending that was the opposite of expected, demonstrating nothing so much as his own impotence.

*　　*　　*

The more than respectable figures for *A Perfect World*, added to the spillover box-office for *Unforgiven* and the audience totals for *In the Line of Fire*, made Clint the number one box-office star of 1993. It was his old stunt of three films in release in the same calendar year, all the more satisfying considering Clint's age and the fact that the last time he had achieved the top position was a decade earlier, in 1984.

The critics were never as united on his behalf. Certain unregenerate members of the old guard – Pauline Kael, for example – had retired. She had hung around long enough to review *Bird*, calling the film 'excruciatingly bad' and Clint a 'perfectly atrocious' director. She thought the star had seduced the press because many critics wanted to *be* Clint Eastwood. 'It is basically as silly as that,' Kael explained in one interview. 'I mean, he is tall and his stardom is very sexy and a lot of people in magazines who lead lives that are not very exciting imagine him to have a terrific time.'

Even in retirement, Kael continued to snipe at Clint, saying that the Museum of Modern Art should be ashamed for throwing retrospectives in his honour and that critics had been 'hornswoggled' on the subject of *Unforgiven*. ('It was another Western in which you were pacifist until it's necessary for you to start shooting. I always see Eastwood following the script slavishly; I never see him taking off as a director.') But Kael stopped writing regular reviews in 1991, and as Clint himself said, there were few among the old guard who hadn't come around. 'I've mellowed,' he told one interviewer, 'and maybe they [critics] have too.'

The younger guard had grown up with Clint an established icon – acclaimed by museums as an artist – and they were among his staunchest allies. And Clint was their ally when the occasion demanded it. One of the best and most influential of the young critics, working for a major newspaper in New York City, had always been a Clint aficionado, going so far as to provide a defence of such lesser works as *Pink Cadillac* and *The Rookie*. However, this iconoclastic critic was in lonely company when finding fault with Steven Spielberg's generally acclaimed *Schindler's List* in 1993. The word went around the newspaper office that he was going to be fired for his critique of the film. In desperation, this critic did the only thing he could think of: he phoned Richard Schickel, asking him to bring the crisis to the attention of Clint.

The scuttlebutt is that Clint personally intervened, phoning the publisher. No one knows if Clint truly made such a call. The critic in question pleaded that his name be kept anonymous, since he did keep his job, which remains a precarious perch today.

The holiday season of 1993 brought Clint, Frances Fisher and four-month-old Francesca Fisher-Eastwood on their annual vacation to Sun Valley. Hollywood columnists assured readers that the star was acting like an indulgent father, doing his share of bottle-time.

Clint rarely filmed in winter and early spring, when the mountain slopes were firm with snow. One of the people Clint often went skiing with was Frank Wells. Wells, Clint's lawyer at the outset of his career, then the executive at Warner Brothers responsible for bringing Clint to the studio, had become an officer of Walt Disney corporation in 1984. There Wells was credited, along with chairman Michael Eisner, for Disney's return to profits with reinvigorated animation, feature films, theme parks and merchandising.

On Easter weekend 1994, Clint accompanied Wells and others on a helicopter ski trip to the rugged Ruby Mountains in northeastern Nevada. They flew into high-altitude virgin snow country, beyond the reach of ordinary skiers. Clint chopper-skied along with Wells on Saturday and Sunday, before he left the area aboard his own 'copter.

Only an hour after Clint's departure an accident took the life of Wells and others aboard Wells's helicopter. Apparently the aircraft malfunctioned and crashed into a mountainside at 7,500 feet. Passenger Mike Hoover, Clint's climbing mentor for *The Eiger Sanction*, survived in serious condition; Hoover's wife was listed among the fatalities.

Wells was Clint's age, only sixty-two. His death stunned the Hollywood community. 'I'll miss you, pal,' Clint said at a tribute to Wells, held on a soundstage of the Disney studios. Reportedly, Clint also sang a snatch of 'Hey Jude', the Beatles song that, he explained, Wells liked to sing full-throatedly while hurtling down the slopes.

Wells had made the occasional stab at luring Clint over to Disney. *Turner and Hooch*, written by Dennis Shryack and new writing partner Michael Blodgett, was an offbeat cop drama tailored for Clint at Disney, until Clint turned it down, and it was retailored as a comedy for Tom Hanks. Wells had continued as Clint's friend ('as close to a soulmate as Clint had ever known', in Richard Schickel's words), but he couldn't prise Clint out of Warners. Although Clint might like to blame the studio for things that went wrong – most recently the mishandling of *A Perfect World* – he was comfortable at Warners, and knew that he was worshipped by Terry Semel and Bob Daly.

May brought the Cannes Film Festival, with Clint making his fourth trip to the international event, this time without having one of his films entered in competition. He had agreed to serve as president of the jury, a rare honour for an American.

Cannes organizer Gilles Jacob admitted that Clint was invited to head up the jury as part of the festival's effort to broaden its image and, in the words of the *Hollywood Reporter*, 'dispel the notion that Cannes is a private club that favours European jurors'. Said Jacobs: 'We need to alternate the offerings between auteur-type films and light-entertaining films, so people can catch their breath and relax.' Although Pierre Rissient was no longer acting as Clint's publicist outside the US (he finally had gone off the Warners payroll after the *Unforgiven* Oscars), he still served as a paid consultant to the Cannes event, and he played a role in arranging this prestigious position for a film-maker whose works were once thought to be too commercial and 'light-entertaining' for artistic contention.

Around this time Clint's relationship with Frances Fisher was reverting to 'its former troubled state', according to Richard Schickel. Since giving birth to Francesca, Fisher had become more demanding. 'He, in his turn, was beginning to find some of her "New Age" ideas – which included strong reformist impulses about traditional masculine modes as well as theories of feminism – puzzling, irritating and, as they applied to his own ways of thinking and being, impossible to adopt,' explained Schickel. 'He also says he found himself once again under pressure to find roles for an actress who had a large personal claim on him.' Clint's mother took the actress aside and warned Fisher that she loved her son too much.

At the time of Frank Wells's death, Fisher was on location in Texas appearing in a Malpaso film, which had been initiated as her project. *The Stars Fell on Henrietta* began when Fisher met James Keach, the actor–brother of Stacy Keach; he had an oil-boom script, set in Texas in the 1930s, that he wanted to direct. Fisher loved the script and championed Keach as its director to Clint. Malpaso, in almost thirty

years of existence, would make only two feature films without Clint –
Ratboy and *The Stars Fell on Henrietta*.

Robert Duvall and Aidan Quinn were the marquee names in *The
Stars Fell on Henrietta*. Fisher's featured role as Aidan Quinn's wife
kept mysteriously shrinking during the course of production. Baby
Francesca Fisher-Eastwood also had a cameo on the screen. Cameraman Bruce Surtees was among the Malpaso veterans recruited for the
filming.

One night on location, Fisher did something that would come back
to haunt her. She was summoned to Los Angeles to perform publicity
chores for *Baby Fever*, a Henry Jaglom film in which she acted. Actress
Jane Seymour (married to James Keach) had a private plane on location, and Fisher decided to 'borrow' it for a round trip to Hollywood.
She put the charter service on Clint's credit card, which was handy,
and asked the private plane company to hold the billing until she was
able to arrange payment. In any case, she expected to be reimbursed
by the *Baby Fever* company.

Then *The Stars Fell on Henrietta* wrapped up photography. Even
though there were undiscussed 'bad feelings' between them, in
Richard Schickel's words, Fisher and Francesca were due to accompany
Clint to Cannes. The actress was nervous, flying on her first transatlan-
tic flight with a baby. She didn't get much advice from Clint. Perhaps
she overcompensated with too much luggage and infant para-
phernalia.

How could Fisher guess that Clint was almost phobic about carrying
too much luggage? He prided himself on 'travelling light' with the
smallest possible carry-on; never mind that everything was always taken
care of for him, wherever he was headed.

In France, Clint, Frances Fisher and nine-month-old Francesca were
joined by Kyle, his new wife Laura, and their infant son Graylen. Clint
was installed in a villa in Mougins, replete with swimming pool and
high walls; the star's elegant wardrobe was reported as a gift from
fashion designer Nino Cerruti; the jury president was accompanied
to all interviews and screenings by bodyguards furnished by Warner
Brothers.

Clint arrived a cultural hero. Indeed, during the festival, he was
presented with France's medal of the Comandeur de L'Ordre des Arts
et des Lettres (a more exalted level than the previous Chevalier).

Everyone agreed the new Minister of Culture's speech was too long and boring. Clint, at the end, said only, 'Merci beaucoup', before adding, 'I am really delighted by the enthusiasm that the French have always shown for my work, a long time before the Americans did.' This was undoubtedly a nod to Pierre Rissient, who had done his job exceedingly well over the years.

'It is a miracle,' said actress Jeanne Moreau about Clint in welcoming remarks at the opening ceremonies, 'that a man so important in the European cinema has found the time to come here and spend twelve days watching movies with us'.

The 1994 jury included two people with whom Clint was well acquainted: actress Catherine Deneuve (with whom he had had a long-ago tryst), who was serving as vice-president, and Lalo Schifrin, the Argentina-born composer who had composed the background music for *Kelly's Heroes*, *The Beguiled*, *Dirty Harry*, *Magnum Force*, *Sudden Impact* and *The Dead Pool*. Others on the distinguished panel were veteran Italian director Pupi Avati, Cuban-born writer G. Cabrera Infante, novelist Kazuo Ishiguro, Russian actor Alexander Kaidanovksy, journalist Marie-Françoise Leclière, South Korean director Shin Sang-Okk and French producer Alain Terzian.

The competition that year was 'distinguished and ultra-serious', in the words of Todd McCarthy, the first-string film critic of *Daily Variety*. The leading contenders for the Palme d'Or included Krzysztof Kies-lowski's *Three Colours: Red* (Poland), Zhang Yimou's *To Live* (China), Abbas Kiarostami's *Through the Olive Trees* (Iran), Nikita Mikhalkov's *Burnt By the Sun* (Russia) and Nanni Moretti's *Dear Diary* (Italy).

The meetings to debate the festival award were extremely long, with Clint, in his 'yup-nope' mode, deferring to those with unquestioned stature in their fields. He allowed jurors to talk and talk, and mostly listened himself, but some suspected he was being cleverly noncommit-tal. There was grumbling among European cineastes when Quentin Tarantino's wild, comic, super-violent *Pulp Fiction* won the top prize. A 'horrendous' decision, noted *Le Parisien*, blaming the American win partly on an American jury president 'who took an awful lot of time to make a decision'. The bitter fruit of a powerful man, complained *France-Soir*, who went to great lengths to defend his home country.

So Clint left Cannes a tad tainted. Pupi Avati tried to defend the jury selections, but in doing so he tended to reinforce the anti-Clint whispers. 'Behind the apparent shell of the "tough guy" and the "hero",' the Italian film-maker was quoted, 'Eastwood is a very emotional man – sometimes fragile – with a certain, deep insecurity towards European culture.'

Things went no better in Paris, to which Clint repaired for an overnight with Frances Fisher and Francesca, before taking off with them for a Scottish golfing vacation. There Fisher made another luggage mistake. She realized she was hauling around too many bags, and asked Clint's permission to send all of the Cannes suitcases and boxes back to America, while purchasing smaller bags to tide her over in Scotland.

There was a Louis Vuitton shop nearby. Fisher had started her own collection of Louis Vuitton baggage – known for its durability and cost – while a struggling actress. Now she splurged on ten thousand dollars' worth of Louis Vuitton travel equipment. Again, she happened to use Clint's credit card. 'Clint, who is not much of a comparison shopper – or for that matter any kind of shopper – said nothing,' according to Richard Schickel.

Not only did the star say nothing, according to sympathetic friends of Fisher, he probably wasn't even aware of the fancy brand name. He glanced at the luggage that Fisher brought back, grunted his approval, then went back to what he was doing. Clint was notorious while visiting Paris for wanting to do little in the normal sightseeing, shopping or bistro-hopping vein, instead preferring to stay in his hotel room and flick channels on the TV.

Back in America, the Louis Vuitton tab arrived on the same day as the earlier plane charter bill, which had been marked to Clint's account because of their prolonged European stay. Fisher had made the fatal mistake of appearing to be reckless with Clint's money. Clint went ballistic.

His rage abided even after Fisher explained everything and paid both bills herself.

Confirming the rumours in Hollywood, Clint announced at his Cannes press conference that he had agreed to star in an adaptation of the hugely popular best-seller, *The Bridges of Madison County*. Adding to the excitement, the director of the film was announced as Bruce Beresford, the Australian who had been Oscar-nominated for *Tender Mercies*.

Therefore it appeared that Clint would continue the positive trend evidenced by *In the Line of Fire*, submitting himself to a strong-minded outside force.

The name 'Francesca' might have encouraged him. That was the name of Clint's daughter, who was actually given that name by Frances Fisher. After amniocentesis, when they found out that the child was going to be a girl, Fisher and Clint had begun to call the baby, in the womb, 'Little Franny'. Clint liked to call Fisher 'Big Franny'.

Clint liked name coincidences. The two Bob Daleys (spelled differently) in his career, the Shiffrin and Schifrin, the two Lennies (Hirshan and Niehaus), the two Fargos (no relation to each other); two Kittys (who had never met each other) and Roses (ditto); and now, two Francescas.

'Francesca' was also the name of the middle-aged Iowa farm wife in Robert James Waller's novel, who is smitten by Robert Kincaid, a free spirit assigned to photograph covered bridges for the *National Geographic*. While her family is away at the state fair, Francesca and Robert Kincaid have a four-day love affair. An Italian war bride, Francesca hates the drudgery that has come to define her life. She aches for romance; Robert Kincaid offers to take her along on his adventures. Starting with his physical description ('at fifty-two, his body was all lean muscle'), Kincaid was a character bound to reflect favourably on any actor who played him. He is presented as the ideal man, a sexual athlete and sensitive artist who can cook as well as quote Yeats.

The decidedly lonely-heartish novel was derided by critics ('an insipid, fatuous, mealymouthed, third-rate soap opera', one reviewer called it), but *The Bridges of Madison County* sold close to ten million copies in hardcover after its 1992 publication in the US, becoming a genuine literary phenomenon. Lili Zanuck was one of the people who called Clint up and advised him to read the book, pointing out a resemblance between the star and the sensitive–macho lone-wolf Robert Kincaid. No doubt his home studio was also urging him to consider the project. *The Bridges of Madison County* had been published by Warner Books, and the Warners corporation had a collateral interest in making sure that the best-seller was successfully transferred to the screen.

Again, Steven Spielberg was involved, because his company, Amblin Entertainment, had bought the screen rights to the book before publication. For a while director Sydney Pollack was tentatively mentioned as director, with Robert Redford as everyone's preferred Robert Kincaid. Pollack and Redford came and went, as did various screenwriters who foundered on transposing the book's 171 pages of pseudo-mystical prose. Spielberg seriously considered directing *The Bridges of Madison County*, before he moved on to the more daunting task of *Schindler's List.*

It was Spielberg who championed Clint for the lead. They were quite friendly, although Spielberg was Clint's opposite in many ways. Spielberg admired Clint; he was as susceptible as anybody to the Clint mythology. And Spielberg also felt he knew the real man. Robert Kincaid would draw on 'the part of Clint that friends of his know well but have never seen acted', Spielberg was quoted as saying. Many of Clint's friends believed the same: *The Bridges of Madison County* would exploit his charm, sense of humour, the attractiveness to women. This campaign to win over Clint flattered him, even if he didn't need much convincing to play the Rhett Butler part in a Warners literary property that was stirring as much advance expectation as had *Gone With the Wind.*

By early summer Clint was committed. Richard LaGravenese, Oscar-nominated in 1991 for *The Fisher King*, had become the latest batter-up on the script, while designated director Beresford busied himself with casting and location decisions.

That Clint and Beresford were ill-matched became clear over the issue of Francesca. Clint wanted an American actress, while Beresford leaned towards a more exotic candidate, such as Pernilla August (the Scandinavian actress closely associated with Ingmar Bergman) or Swedish-born Lena Olin (Oscar-nominated for Best Supporting Actress in *Enemies, A Love Story*). Isabella Rossellini (Ingrid Bergman's daughter, riveting in *Blue Velvet*) eventually emerged as the director's preference, but Clint didn't fancy Rossellini, and he was choosey about his leading ladies. All the more so in this case with the whole story a love match.

Optimism (and Clint's pushing) had set the start date for September. Only people removed from the reality of Hollywood were surprised, the first week of August, by the announcement that Beresford – like Philip Kaufman and Blake Edwards, other directors with careful approaches – was leaving the production. According to the trade papers, 'The Academy Award-winning Beresford had been butting heads with Warner Brothers over the casting of the lead female, with the Australian-born helmer pushing for a European actress, as true to the novel, and the studio standing strong for an American.'

Fortunately, there was another Academy Award-winning director available, and that was Clint. Within days, the new Numero Uno was announced. Beresford never uttered a public comment about what transpired behind the scenes, but colleagues say he was bitter over the valuable preproduction work he had done, the manner of his dismissal, and the amount of money that was negotiated for his compensation.

'You guys have blown enough time,' Clint reportedly told Terry Semel. Clint then took a Warners jet to Winterset, Iowa, where on 7 August he made a whirlwind tour of the sites Beresford had mapped out. According to press accounts, on the spot Clint scrapped plans to build a new Roseman Bridge (the main covered bridge in the story), thereby lopping $1.5 million off the budget. Instead, the actual Roseman Bridge, which because of recent renovations had looked too spiffy for Beresford, would be aged by the studio craft departments, then returned to unweathered form after the filming.

Clint also moved swiftly to resolve the co-star debate. 'They were testing all these thirty-year-old women,' Clint explained.* 'And it just shocked me. I said, "You know, the best actresses in this world are somewhere probably between forty and sixty. I said, "What about Meryl Streep?" And they said, "Well, she's not Italian, and she'd just hate doing another accent." And I said, "Yeah, but she does them so marvellously."'

Streep, the premier screen actress of her generation, had an East Coast pedigree: Vassar, Yale Drama School, Shakespearean theatre. Only age forty-three (two years younger than Francesca in the book), Streep's two Academy Awards and five nominations to date already placed her in the same immortal niche as Bette Davis and Katharine Hepburn. Streep had even had a modest commercial hit, the year before, when, as Clint might have noticed, she buffed up and shot the rapids in *The River Wild.*

Who better to make the point that Clint had arrived, artistically? Who better to make Clint the actor and director look artistic than the

* Although, incidentally, August, Olin and Rossellini were all in their forties.

artistically certified Streep? There could be no safer choice; she was like a Louis Vuitton label on luggage.

Streep lived in Connecticut with her husband, sculptor Don Gummer, and four children. Her name must have come up before, since she confessed in one interview that Bruce Beresford wasn't one of her fans. She didn't care; she didn't think much of *The Bridges of Madison County* anyway, and, removed from Hollywood, didn't even realize she was in Clint's world. She had met the star only once (he was wearing a 'boxy' suit, she recalled). The only one of his movies the actress had seen was *Play Misty For Me* – she had never seen any of the Dirty Harrys – until she caved into the more recent, universally approved *In the Line of Fire* and *A Perfect World*.

Clint put in a call to Streep. He told her he heard she wasn't really interested in the project, and didn't like the book. But the Richard LaGravenese script minimized the high-flown dialogue, and Clint really wanted her for the part. Would she read the script? It came by courier, Streep read it in the morning, and in the afternoon called back to say yes.

Streep would have to be paid a salary of $4 million, plus a share of the revenue, but she would more than balance the expense with her power to attract a different segment of female moviegoers – not Clint's usual fans – reassured by her presence. Streep and the director would not talk very much about her characterization, prior to the first take. Although she was known for her foreign pronunciations, Clint did ask her to refrain from an accent (her character had lived in Italy for the first twenty years of her life). That was about it; get ready, report to the set in Iowa in two weeks.

'It intrigued me that he would want to do something so emotional that a lot of actors would be afraid to touch,' Streep explained in interviews. 'And that he had the nerve to think that he could direct it, too. I was very intrigued by that level of confidence.' Asked to speculate why Clint would want to portray Robert Kincaid, Streep mused, 'Part of it is that there are resonances in the writing that refer obliquely to something he's felt about being an artist, or not regarded as one for a while in his career.'

The script needed a last-minute polish. Spielberg and Clint phoned and faxed each other daily for a week. Spielberg's speciality – the heightening of emotion; Clint's, crossing out dialogue. At Spielberg's urging, LaGravenese had added the extended frame-flashback sequences of Francesca's son and daughter, reading her last testament. Francesca's children are taken aback by her wish to be cremated and have her ashes scattered off Roseman Bridge, and they discover her past affair with Kincaid by reading diary accounts. This is also in the book, but the film makes it a more elaborate device.

Spielberg left the day-to-day to his Amblin partner, Kathleen Kennedy. As for Malpaso, David Valdes had left Clint's employ after *The Stars Fell on Henrietta*. According to sources, Valdes went the way of Bob Daley and Fritz Manes after hearing that a higher salary and better-sounding producer's credit was not in his future (Valdes had often been stuck with 'executive producer', so that Clint could keep 'producer and director'.)

With Malpaso increasingly partnered with other companies, the role of producer was perhaps downgraded. Tom Rooker, after having started out licking envelopes on Clint's mayoral campaign, had ascended in Hollywood. Early on, as a production assistant on *The Dead Pool*, he passed an acid test. One day on the set, the crew was waiting to photograph a major special effects sequence, and the cameras were still being rigged, when all of a sudden the explosions went off prematurely. All of the preparation was ruined. Oh-oh, everybody thought, catastrophe. They all waited to see who was going to get their bowels ripped out by Clint.

That is when Tom Rooker stepped into the middle of the street with a megaphone and said, 'I have an announcement to make. I screwed up. I accidentally gave a cue. It's entirely my fault.' Rooker went up to Clint, whose veins were bulging. They all tried not to watch as the young man took massive amounts of verbal abuse. Tom Rooker proved himself that day – proved he was willing to take the blame – and ever since, Clint had moulded and promoted him. With Valdes gone, the 'associate producers' on *The Bridges of Madison County* were Rooker and Michael Maurer, the Malpaso accountant.

Clint, with his cigarette and beer props, T-shirt and pick-up truck left over from other films, was ready on time. Cast and crew assembled in Des Moines, Iowa for a kick-off party on 14 September. Lennie Niehaus, Joel Cox and Jack Green were there. And Kyle Eastwood would be on hand for one scene in the film, when Francesca and

Kincaid visit a roadhouse, playing the bass in the James Rivers combo.

Nearby Winterset would serve as the centre of filming operations. The small town of 4,200, which was spotlighted in Robert James Waller's novel, was enjoying a 'cult popularity heretofore reserved for Graceland and the grassy knoll', according to the *New York Times*. It also happens to be the birthplace of John Wayne.

Streep was at the kick-off celebration. She had put on weight to look doughy and dyed her hair to chestnut brown, and, ignoring Clint, she had worked up a formidable Italian accent. Again the director mentioned he hoped she wasn't going to do 'a big accent thing'. Having done the preparation, however, the actress felt she had no choice but to plough ahead.

With no rehearsals, they shot the next morning, with the first scene of Francesca sweeping off the porch of her farm house and looking off into the distance as Kincaid (Clint) drives up in his pick-up to ask directions to the Roseman Bridge. Clint didn't bat an eye when out of Streep's mouth flew an Italian accent. Nor did he say anything director-like to her during much of the first half of the filming. Streep was beginning to grow alarmed. Was she meeting expectations? Finally, Clint sidled up to her. 'You know,' her director and co-star told her, 'I don't say much unless I don't like it.'

In subsequent publicity-oriented interviews, Clint explained that he tried to allow 'a lot of real time between people' in directing *The Bridges of Madison County*, as opposed to 'our MTV mentality' of cutting to the action and chase. 'I tried to be more in the [John] Ford and [Howard] Hawks tradition,' Clint explained, linking his name with two of America's greatest directors, 'of allowing things to happen on the screen.'

Clint said he wanted Kincaid and Francesca – he and Streep – to get to know each other for the first time, however awkwardly, on camera. The star for whom action and chase were career touchstones now talked about 'free-painting' improvisationally and the 'inner-life energy' that resulted from his one-take philosophy. Once again, as he did when climbing Mount Eiger, Clint talked about the higher level of reality-based work.

Putting himself in Streep's class showed how his self-image and self-esteem had evolved. 'Perhaps by reshaping Mr Waller's New Age cowboy in his own lean image,' astutely observed Maureen Dowd, profiling Clint for the *New York Times*, 'Mr Eastwood is hoping to capture the one honour that has eluded him – an Oscar for acting.' Perhaps holding his own with Meryl Streep would help clinch the elusive trophy.

According to all accounts, Clint and Streep got along famously. *The Ladies Home Journal* noted, 'More than professional respect, an intense friendship blossomed between the two stars.' The *Los Angeles Times* reported widespread rumours that the two 'had carried on the intense romance of the script off camera. Both scoff at the suggestions.' Streep was quoted: 'It's not even worth responding to. It's like, "I can't *act* this?"'

Nobody can say for sure what transpired between them. Only director of photography Jack Green was present when they filmed their love scenes, which in the film are presented – decorously – in flickering, muted PG-13 style.

'Their real affair took place off camera,' insisted one well-placed industry source. 'I was told by several people at Warners that it's true. If it isn't true, people like Joe Hyams certainly believed it to be true, or at least took great delight in spreading the story.'

Certainly, The *Bridges of Madison County* spelled the end of Clint's relationship with Frances Fisher, who like Sondra Locke – and others – couldn't decode the subliminal messages Clint was sending. According to Richard Schickel, the actress who was also the mother of Clint's daughter made her last error by proposing herself for a role as Francesca's daughter. That was rejected by Clint. 'Personal issues aside,' wrote Schickel, 'she had just finished another Malpaso picture, and he was more than ever determined not to repeat the Sondra Locke scenario.'

According to Schickel's book, Clint also was not very encouraging when Fisher proposed a visit to the Iowa set. Definitely not encouraging, agree friends of Fisher. Although, indeed, Fisher had hoped to play a part in *The Bridges of Madison County*, she had said, '*Any* part'. She revered Meryl Streep and simply wanted to be part of any film that starred the foremost actress of her generation; she wanted to observe Streep at work. Clint knew this. So he kept saying, 'Next week . . .' whenever Fisher asked to visit. Finally, when Fisher and Francesca arrived in Iowa, they discovered Streep had already gone. 'Oh,' Clint informed her, 'she's done with her scenes.'

*   *   *

Frances Fisher knew about Roxanne and Kimber Tunis. But it didn't help the tensions between her and Clint when the actress also learned about Jacelyn Reeves and her two children. According to sources sympathetic to Fisher, the actress was up at Clint's Carmel house, tidying around one day, when she noticed a children's-type birthday card inscribed to 'Daddy'. Glancing at it, thinking how sweet it was of Kyle and Alison to send Clint such a children's card, she was perplexed to discover two names she had never heard of: 'Scott and Katie'.

Confronted with her discovery, Clint first clammed up, angry that, from his point of view, Fisher had been snooping around. Later he explained that he and Reeves had got together at the première of *Pale Rider*; they had slept together on impulse, she had got pregnant, and since she made no great demands on Clint, he later repeated the experience. Fisher was sworn to secrecy. It was only later that she learned that Clint had been carrying on with Reeves for over ten years; half of Carmel and all of Clint's barnacles knew about Reeves; not to mention, after February of 1990, when the first articles about Reeves appeared, in the tabloids, America's inquiring readers.

Fisher finally met Jacelyn Reeves at the funeral of one of Clint's golf buddies, where Jane Brolin, loving the drama of it, took her aside and told her the mother of two of Clint's children was *there*. Clint, with a frozen look, ducked away, roaming the room and making small talk, while Fisher eventually came face to face with Reeves. They politely introduced themselves to each other, these two women with Clint and babies in common.

Nor did it help that more mothers and offspring seemed to be forever popping up. In mid-1993, Clint was confronted with the claims of a woman in her late thirties, originally from Washington State, who had researched her adoption and ascertained that Clint was her biological father. She was the pregnancy left behind in 1953, when Clint went to Hollywood for the first time. Clint sometimes talked about the possibility that he was the father of someone living in Washington. Now this lady appeared genuine.

Clint had his lawyers and business managers check her out, before agreeing to meet her. The woman was married to a rich man, had no designs on Clint's money. Happy to guard her anonymity, she desired only to meet her father. Clint had a cordial if awkward dinner with the woman and her husband, and promised to stay in touch.

This is the first published mention of her existence. For years Clint successfully cruised along on his all-American image, and kept his sideline affairs out of the press. Apart from Kyle and Alison, it turns out he has fathered at least five children out of wedlock, which is some kind of not-quite-all-American record, even in Hollywood. The people who know Clint best suspect there are other families in his closet. And if Kimber Tunis was kept secret for twenty-five years, and the Washington woman for forty, might there not be others?

The Bridges of Madison County, which had been scheduled for ten weeks of filming, wrapped after six, according to studio publicity. A sixty-day shoot had been accomplished in forty-two. Postproduction began, with June 1995 the target release date.

Back at Stradella Road, the house Clint still shared with Frances Fisher was 'alternately silent and quarrelsome', in Richard Schickel's words, with Fisher trying desperately to figure out the relationship, and Clint projecting ambivalence.

According to Schickel, the last straw was Jane Brolin's death, which came on 13 February 1995. Brolin was fifty-five when she died from injuries sustained in a late-night auto accident near her home in Templeton, California. A phone call awakened Fisher and Clint with the news. When Fisher tried to console Clint, he turned away from her. 'He cried, the first and only time Frances saw him in tears,' wrote Schickel.

Clint and Jane Brolin had had a falling out after *White Hunter, Black Heart*. Maybe Brolin, whose role had always been as one of Clint's sidekicks, had turned around and become too clingy. The word went around that a resentful Brolin was writing a tell-all book about Clint. Maggie tipped off Clint, and then fresh word went around that Clint and Warner Brothers had come to some kind of understanding with Brolin. Brolin's *Variety* obituary concluded with this titbit of information: 'She had recently negotiated a contract with Warner Brothers to film a television series starring chimpanzees.'

Brolin's will, scrawled just a few months before her death because she knew her habit of taking too many sleeping pills, officially declared her undying love for Clint. It also stipulated that the star would receive payment of all monies she owed him before any other debts or bequests were honoured.

Clint did seem upset, so Fisher proposed that they spend the coming weekend together. But Clint thought it would be more healing and relaxing for him to spend the weekend with a few of his buddies, playing in the Bob Hope Golf Classic at the Bermuda Dunes Country Club in Indian Wells.

So Fisher, who had also become friendly with Brolin, threw herself into helping to organize a memorial service for the following Monday. Clint showed up in Paso Robles, where the service was being held, looking appropriately distraught. It was only a couple of weeks later that Fisher first saw the tabloid newspaper with a photograph of Clint and a young woman named Dina Ruiz, nuzzling each other at the golf tournament on the weekend following Jane Brolin's death.

Looking forward to the upcoming release of *The Bridges of Madison County*, Warner Brothers might have been helpful in proposing Clint as the 1995 recipient of the Irving Thalberg Award, guaranteeing that he would make a personal appearance at the internationally-televised Academy Awards for the second year in a row.

The Irving Thalberg Award is an honorary Academy Award, named for the onetime production head of MGM in the 1930s. It is periodically voted to a leading producer by the Board of Governors of the Academy of Motion Picture Arts and Sciences. Nominations are submitted annually, a secret ballot is held, and the winner must claim a majority of the votes cast by the board members, who in 1995 included Warners executive Robert Daly, Kathleen Kennedy (Steven Spielberg's partner), and Richard Zanuck (Clint's skiing partner and the co-producer of *The Eiger Sanction*).

'Eastwood is widely acknowledged to be a hands-on film-maker,' explained Academy of Motion Picture Arts and Sciences President Arthur Hiller, in announcing the award, 'even on those pictures for which he does not receive producer credit.'

A short list of the high-calibre producers – more maverick, East Coast-oriented, or simply independent of the studios – still waiting for their Irving Thalberg Award: directors Francis Coppola and Robert Altman; Ismael Merchant (producer of James Ivory's films); Robert Chartoff and Irwin Winkler; Robert Redford (sponsor of many independent films through his Sundance Institute); Charles H. Joffe (for that matter, Woody Allen). The Irving Thalberg is reserved especially for Hollywood insiders.

The emphases among the film clips compiled by Richard Schickel, that evening, were on the critical favourites and more tasteful hits. Sun Valley skiiing friend Arnold Schwarzenegger handed the honorary Oscar to Clint, who wore another Nino Cerruti suit, and accepted the warm applause with brief remarks. He mentioned Darryl Zanuck (Richard Zanuck's father), Hal Wallis, William Wyler, Billy Wilder and Alfred Hitchcock, 'people that I grew up idolizing', in his brief remarks. The names of Malpaso producers Robert Daley, Fritz Manes or David Valdes were not uttered.

Wags noted that Clint attended the most important social occasion of the year alone, without Frances Fisher. Alone, too, he attended the Los Angeles première of *The Bridges of Madison County* in May. When an interviewer for the *Los Angeles Times*, doing one of those ritually complimentary articles timed for the film's release, dared to ask Clint if he was still 'with' Fisher, the star snapped, 'I'm not *with* anybody.'

The scepticism of theatre-owners might be reflected in the number of theatres in which *Bridges* was booked, 1805, compared, for example, to 2518 monopolized at the same time for Bruce Willis's *Die Hard With a Vengeance*. But the seats quickly filled up for Clint's film, and at the end of the summer *The Bridges of Madison County* was still playing in one thousand theatres, edging towards its final domestic gross of $70 million.

Not only were large audiences captivated, but critics were more than pleasantly surprised. Janet Maslin of the *New York Times* wrote that Clint had managed to locate 'a moving, elegiac love story at the heart of Mr Waller's self-congratulatory overkill'. Dave Kehr of the *New York Daily News* said, 'There are moments here . . . that are as powerful as anything the movies have given us.' Joe Morgenstern of the *Wall Street Journal* called *Bridges* 'one of the most pleasurable films in recent memory'.

Apart from his standard cut of the grosses, Clint had a profitable sideline in the soundtrack, which featured jazz greats Dinah Washington and Johnny Hartman, along with Clint's wistful piano composition 'Doe Eyes' subtitled 'Love Theme from *The Bridges of Madison County*'. The music from the film went to the top of the jazz music charts, becoming as much of a sales phenomenon as the book. Its popularity prompted Clint to announce, with appropriate fanfare, the formation of Malpaso Records, distributed by Warner Records. The new label would nurture neglected jazz while introducing handpicked acts.*

The film *was* handsomely mounted, Streep was wonderfully effacing, and Clint's performance was good. He did the flirtation stuff well, and the camera filled in where his emotions balked.

The final scene, where Francesca sees Kincaid in town for the last time, was a small masterpiece of construction. Kincaid is glimpsed in the middle of a street, off in the distance, rain pouring off him. Clint may or may not be weeping; the camera placement and set design have already conveyed that implication. Francesca and her husband get into their car and pull out in traffic, finding themselves stalled at a traffic light behind Kincaid's pick-up. The light takes for ever to change, as Francesca agonizes over her decision to stay behind and say nothing. Long close-up of the back of the truck with Clint's product placement: the GMC insignia.† And by the time Kincaid's truck swings out in one direction, and Francesca's husband turns to drive off in another, the audience is also sopping wet . . . with tears.

All of the interviews for the film focused on the hitherto-neglected romantic side of Clint's persona. Especially considering that he was in the process of unceremoniously discarding Frances Fisher, this was nervy, although at times Clint did sound defensive about his 'romantic nature'. 'There are a lot more men that are romantics than I think people give them credit for,' Clint told the *New York Times*.

In more than one interview, Clint said that what interested him about the project was depicting a love story through a woman's eyes. Those are certainly the best scenes, the ones centring on Francesca. Clint skimped on Kincaid, allowing audiences, as ever, to fill in the blanks. But the film has another perspective which is important, the one that constitutes the only major deviation from the book: Francesca's two grown-up children (Victor Slezak and Annie Corley), opening and closing the story, interrupting it laboriously, with their deepening understanding of their mother.

If *A Perfect World* was partly about a father's legacy to his children,

---

* Four years later, with the *Bridges* soundtrack still strong on the charts, the other releases of Clint's new record company included *Remembering Madison County* (additional film-inspired music) and a live recording of the 17 October 1996 jazz tribute held for Clint at Carnegie Hall, *Eastwood After Hours*.

† The first shot of the film was also a gradually approaching GMC vehicle, with clearly legible insignia.

The Bridges of Madison County was also about heirs and entitlements. One can see Clint reading himself into the scene where relatives hover around Francesca's will wondering about the 'secret millions'. A daughter-in-law is depicted as grasping. The two siblings are unpleasant, fractious, harshly filmed. They say moronic things (the older brother looks at an old Kincaid photo of Francesca and exclaims, 'She isn't wearing a bra!') and react like Puritans to the notion of cremation. Although their whining is partly done to set up their uplifting 'conversion', they add too much to the 135 minutes running time and too little uplift.

Clearly, as Kincaid expressly states it in the film, 'the American family ethic' is again under attack. Clint upholds his own individualist banner: the loner, the reluctant leader, the self-important man on a self-important mission. After twenty-five years as a star and film-maker, this was one of his personal, persistent, unadmirable themes.

Starting wth the theme song for *Pale Rider,* Clint had begun to do composing for his film soundtracks. Generally, the actor worked out the melodies on a computerized keyboard which printed out a lead sheet as he played, then, when the composition was completed, he turned it over to professionals who knew how to augment the music properly.

He told Megan Rose that 'Megan's Theme' for *Pale Rider,* which refers to the girl character in the film, was also a secret allusion to their relationship. The lilting 'Claudia's Theme' for *Unforgiven* was also the star's composition (uncredited). 'Big Fran's Baby', the music which Clint wrote for *A Perfect World,* also had personal connotations, referring to his newborn daughter Francesca and her mother, actress Frances Fisher.

'Doe Eyes', heard at the end of *The Bridges of Madison County,* Clint had written as a simple piano number but Lennie Niehaus envisioned it as needing a large string orchestra. 'Clint thought that the piano should be the only solo instrument,' said Niehaus in one interview, 'but I thought that something additional was required.' Niehaus orchestrated the lush romantic theme using an EVI, or Electronic Valve Instrument.

That theme song also had hidden meaning. The real 'Doe Eyes' was of course Dina Ruiz of Salinas television station KSWB-Channel 8, who anchored the six and eleven p.m. weekday newscasts, and who, just as *The Bridges of Madison County* arrived in the nation's theatres, was observed behaving affectionately with Clint at northern California social occasions.

By then Frances Fisher had moved out of Stradella Road, taken up single parenthood, and resumed a busy career, where every one of her acting jobs wouldn't be ascribed to Clint's influence.* Whereas thirty years of publicity and articles had depicted Clint as unwaveringly loyal to friends, family and employees, more recently, his behaviour had begun to make him look the very opposite, a man who, in the words of Josh Young in *George*, constantly renewed himself 'by shedding people close to him'.

Fisher, like other mothers of Clint's children, probably received a carefully negotiated settlement. A house and regular financial instalments were part of the standard agreement. Usually the houses would be designated as remaining under Roy Kaufman's name until Clint's death, a not-so-subtle enforcement of Clint's preference that the women he left behind avoid any statements about him to the press.

The regular financial instalments would vary in each case. Some (like Roxanne Tunis) never cared about the money and tried to stress their independence. In all cases, the financial flow was strictly controlled by Clint. Sometimes, according to sources, emergency requests were answered by the star carrying cash in paper bags. Most times, the expenditures were strictly agreed upon in advance and closely monitored by Roy Kaufman, who dunned the mothers back for the difference, even for as little as one dollar. Low budgets for mothers and children were as sacrosanct as those of Malpaso films.

Regardless of the cooing and diaper-changing that went on in the press after Clint had one of the babies to which he admitted, the reality was usually starkly different in the long run. Mothers and children were left to their daily struggles. Inevitably, Clint, with his super-hyped-up schedule, became what one of the mothers calls 'a five-minute Daddy', seeing his out-of-wedlock children only infrequently as the years flew by.

Just like Francesca in *Bridges*, Clint had a will, and he would make

---

* Fisher was pivotal in the supporting role of the social-climbing mother in 1997's smash hit, *Titanic*.

stipulations for all of his admitted children in this document. The star revised his terms and legatees periodically, and the wills provided by discovery motions in the Sondra Locke case no doubt have been superseded by updated versions. Every personal upheaval in Clint's life mandated changes.

Clint's 1980s wills, interestingly, provided no charitable bequests. To each of the out-of-wedlock families – at least those mothers and children Clint was willing to concede – he offered a lump sum of money that would be considered sizeable by the average American household, although stingy when set against the vastness of his total wealth. In any event, this liberating sum would, it must be remembered, come to the mothers only upon Clint's death; in the meantime they would do well to be patient.

The great bulk of Clint's net worth was assigned to be divided equally between Kyle and Alison upon his death. With Kyle and Alison, Clint had always been financially generous, buying them, over the years, IBM and other blue-ribbon stock. As indicated by his will, these were the two for whom Clint felt the most responsibility, love and perhaps – though everyone says it isn't a strong emotion with him – guilt.

'There is no guilt with Clint,' noted one of the mothers of his children, speaking on condition of anonymity. 'Anything that vaguely resembles guilt is channelled into anger. His anger is always intended to prove people wrong, or prove their behaviour bad. And if people are wrong or bad, there is nothing for him to feel guilty about.'

CHAPTER FOURTEEN

Clint's World
1995–Today

Although now he was alone at Stradella Road, in the the future Clint would stay less often at the house he had gone to such lengths to wrest from Sondra Locke. He would spend less time in southern California. Malpaso was the phone in his hand, Burbank stops were minimized, the productions of the 1990s would be shot largely on locations outside of the Los Angeles area and then edited, mostly, at his Rising River Ranch.

Monterey County was increasingly the place for him, because of Dina Ruiz. Clint moved into the Mission Ranch, and divided time between there and his San Antonio address in Carmel, where substantial and cosmetic renovations were made to improve the house.

According to most accounts, Clint first met Ruiz when she interviewed him for her television station in April 1993. But, according to one published interview with Ruiz, the two actually had an earlier encounter at a Carmel council meeting, to which Ruiz had taken her divorced mother. Ruiz thought Clint and her mother, a Montgomery Ward saleswoman, might hit it off. But Clint would turn out to have eyes more for the daughter.

In the spring of 1993, Clint had just won his *Unforgiven* Oscars. Ruiz, a 1989 graduate of San Francisco State, had apprenticed in broadcasting in Arizona and just taken her 'on-air' job at the NBC affiliate in Salinas. Clint was almost sixty-three; Ruiz was a twenty-seven-year-old brunette 'slim enough to qualify as a trophy wife', in the words of the *San Francisco Chronicle*.

Her roots were humble: she was raised in Fremont, California, near Oakland. Her father, part African–American, part Japanese, was a high school teacher. She and Clint had 'similar working-class backgrounds', according to an article syndicated for the Knight–Ridder chain. Their romance blossomed when they 'found themselves chatting about places familiar to them both', according to the *San Francisco Chronicle*, 'Sunol, Mission, San Jose, San Francisco, Fenton's, the old-timey ice-cream parlour in Piedmont'.

Ruiz admitted to interviewers that she had seen 'zero of his movies' and in the spring of 1993 was 'ga-ga in love' with another boyfriend. Clint was 'seeing someone else too', Ruiz said.

Ruiz's interview with Clint for local television ran on so pleasantly that it was expanded into a series. Ruiz might have found an ally when she included Clint's mother in the programme, because afterwards Ruth Eastwood wrote her a complimentary note, saying she had never seen footage of her son in which he appeared so relaxed and amusing.

The 'someone else' Clint was seeing, in 1993, was of course Frances Fisher, who in August of that year gave birth to Clint's baby, followed by the 'miraculous time'. According to most accounts, after inter-viewing the movie star, the young anchorwoman and Clint did not run into each other again for almost a year when they found themselves seated next to each other (quelle coincidence!) 'at a local function'. That rough chronology would lead to April 1994, with Clint, Frances Fisher and baby Francesca just about to leave for Cannes, Paris and the Louis Vuitton incident.

Back in the US, Clint saw Ruiz furtively over the summer of 1994, even as he prepared to film *The Bridges of Madison County*, about another restless, secretive man lucky with the ladies. According to the Knight–Ridder article, Clint and Ruiz occasionally shared drinks up in Carmel, 'usually with groups of friends', going out alone only 'a few times'. The last time was shortly before Clint left for Iowa, when they stayed up until five in the morning, 'smooching and talking', in Ruiz's words. Nonetheless, according to Ruiz, 'We didn't become a couple . . . until he was free.'

Clint was thoroughly hooked by the fall of 1994, and from Iowa bombarded Dina Ruiz with phone calls. After the filming of *The Bridges of Madison County* was over, although Clint continued to cohabit with Frances Fisher, he had places to go – shuttling up to Carmel and editing at the Rising River Ranch. For a long time Fisher didn't have a clue the star was also wooing Ruiz. 'After he came back from *Bridges*,' the *San Francisco Chronicle* later quoted Ruiz, 'we were inseparable.'

Clint felt 'free' enough by February 1995 – the week of Jane Brolin's death; the week he 'came out' on the golf links, kissing Ruiz. By the time *The Bridges of Madison County* was released, the romance had begun to trickle into the mainstream press. At the local Emmy awards in Oakland in mid-May, Clint and Ruiz went public, and the anchorwoman 'couldn't seem to keep her hands off Eastwood all night', according to Bay Area columns; within weeks, newspapers, magazines and wire services felt confident in announcing Ruiz as Clint's 'new love'.

In September, a more astonishing development: the *San Francisco Chronicle* reported that the star had proposed marriage, buying Ruiz an 'oval-shaped ruby ring', which, though modest-sized, was 'visible at twenty paces'.

By 1995, some of the press had begun to question Clint's once-unassailable mythology. The majority of film critics and journalists were still cooperative and admiring. But the tabloids especially – which had led the media in reporting his split-up with Maggie, his acrimonious parting with Sondra Locke, the existence of Kimber Tunis and Clint's 'secret' brood with Jacelyn Reeves – were perceived as a threat to his image. So Clint directed his lawyers to attack their mistakes.

Clint had first sued the nation's largest-circulation weekly, the *National Enquirer*, in 1984, contesting an article that alleged without proof his romantic involvement with country-and-western singer Tanya Tucker. That suit, which sought $10 million in damages for exploiting Clint's name and invading his privacy, was settled for undisclosed terms out of court. In 1994, ten years later, Clint again filed suit against the *Enquirer*, this time complaining about an alleged interview with him that was flagged as an 'exclusive' on the cover of the weekly's 21 December 1993 issue.

The interview was actually a version of a previously published piece from London's *Today*, which had been picked up by the *Enquirer* for circulation in the US. Although this practice is widespread in journalism, Clint claimed the transplanted article, condensed and reworded by an *Enquirer* staff member, falsely implied his endorsement of the tabloid and constituted a 'misappropriation' of his name.

The article quoted Clint on fatherhood, new baby Francesca, diaper-changing and the possibility of him marrying Frances Fisher ('I propose marriage to her from time to time and sometimes she says yes and sometimes she says no'). As the *National Enquirer* pointed out in its legal brief, Clint had also discussed fatherhood and diaper-changing with *Variety, Ladies Home Journal, Rolling Stone, Playboy*. Although both versions of the published piece contained inaccuracies (quoting Clint: 'I drink a lot of scotch'), most of it was not only 'inherently believable' but 'unabashedly positive'. The *National Enquirer* had even gone to the lengths of contacting the original interviewer, Cameron Docherty, to ascertain to its satisfaction that the quotes were legitimate.

But Clint, who was quoted in the article as saying that he didn't really care to edify the public as to 'what kind of relationship I have with Frances', certainly didn't want the public edified via the *National Enquirer*. Moreover, the tabloid had printed one of the first photographs of Francesca, which Clint's lawyers insisted was 'purloined'. This claim would be omitted from the lawsuit, however, as would any claim against the interview's authenticity. Whether or not the interview actually took place was never proven, particularly after Docherty, a British citizen, refused to be deposed or appear at the trial, which took place in Los Angeles in October 1995.

At the hearing, Clint's lawyers conceded that the *National Enquirer* article was not fundamentally derogatory, but argued that linking Clint's name with a publication he was known to loathe constituted a form of malice. The hearing climaxed with Clint on the witness stand calling the tabloid trashy and parasitical. 'I think it's detrimental to the whole legal profession,' Clint stated, 'to sit there and be able to get away with lying about people and exploit children, exploit people in order to sell magazines. It's plain and simple like that, is that they are just lying . . . the fact is they do it all the time. They are doing it here to me, and I don't think it's fair.'

But Clint was in a winning position. He knew he had a sympathetic jury in Hollywood, where other stars felt oppressed by tabloid reportage. In the men's room during a break, he noticed he was in line next to Senior Editor Steve Plamann, one of the witnesses who took the stand for the *Enquirer*. 'He looked up at me, grinned, and said, "I guess we're pissed off at each other",' said Plamann.

Clint had asked for $10–15 million in damages. The jury was sequestered for three and a half days before awarding the star a mere $75,000 for damage to his reputation and another $75,000 for the estimated profits the *National Enquirer* had accrued by exploiting his name. Taking a swipe at O. J. Simpson jurors ('The jury worked very hard, unlike a lot of juries we've seen lately'), Clint declared the decision a 'win' and shook the hands of jury members. Reportedly, he also offered to sign autographs. 'I don't think that's appropriate,' noted jury foreman Michael Mallon, who took a pass. The foreman told the press that the main problem with what the *Enquirer* had done was the word 'exclusive'. 'If they said "fantastic interview", we would not be here,' the jury foreman was quoted. 'There would be no case.'

Clint announced he would donate his court award of $150,000 to a charity, whose identity has never been announced. His lawyers made no such public vow, and in 1996, after further courtroom haggling, a federal judge awarded them $653,156.38 in legal fees and expenses, or more than four times the amount of the settlement.

The *Enquirer* hastened to file an appeal and stated its confidence that the verdict would be overturned on constitutional grounds at a higher court level. 'What is at stake here,' argued the tabloid lawyers in their brief, 'is the actual malice standard – and how it will govern the relationship between all publishers and all public figures who wish to exert greater control over their press coverage than is allowed by the First Amendment.'

But Clint, backed by his powerful lawyers, was rarely beaten in court. In 1998, the Ninth US Circuit Court of Appeals would uphold the jury award and the lawyer's fees, noting that the tabloid should have known better than to cross the line of legality with a star who was known even by the justices, as stated in the ruling, for his 'litigiousness'.

The tabloids were nothing if not dogged. It was the *Star*, another publication owned by the *National Enquirer*, which broke the news, early in 1996, that Clint had filled out a marriage licence. Clint reportedly strolled into Blaine County Court House in Hailey, Idaho, thirty minutes before closing time on 29 December 1995, and took out a $28 application, valid for one year. He used his Sun Valley vacation address on the form.

The Idaho permit was either a ruse or a whim, because when Clint finally did marry Ruiz, the event took place somewhere else without much advance notice. Richard Schickel had the inside scoop on the nuptials, which took place on 31 March 1996, timed to coincide with an annual 'girls-only' outing Ruiz and her school chums made to Las Vegas, a place that had long been one of Clint's favourite playgrounds too.

'Clint showed an unusual interest in the affair,' wrote Schickel, 'and on Friday, lounging at the pool of the Mirage Hotel, Dina heard herself being paged. The occasion had proved irresistible to him. All her old friends were gathered around her; his friend Steve Wynn, the casino magnate, had a perfect venue for a wedding, the patio of his home just outside his Shadow Creek golf course; it would be easy to fly both their families in from northern California on short notice. What better moment for a marriage?

'And so, in forty-eight hours, it was done – flowers ordered, menus set, music chosen. Just in case word leaked out, the control tower at nearby Nellis Air Force Base, which commands the air space over Wynn's property, was alerted to be on guard against low-flying planes. With everything in hand, Clint decided to pass the afternoon on the golf course . . .'

Thus, on 31 March 1996, a small number of privileged guests assembled on the lily- and orchid-decorated lawn of Shadow Creek for a ceremony presided over by a Reverend Judy, who usually worked the wedding chapel of one of the big hotels.

Wynn, the owner of the Mirage, the Treasure Island and the Golden Nugget, and probably the single most powerful man in the Las Vegas casino business, was a longtime Clint friend. Kyle Eastwood served as Clint's best man (Alison was also present among the guests). The sixty-five-year-old groom wore a dark blue Nino Cerruti suit. The thirty-year-old bride also wore Cerruti – an ivory silk dress with a long train. The band struck up Clint's composition, 'Doe Eyes'.

Clint reportedly told the guests, 'I'm proud to make this lady my wife. She's the one I've been waiting for.' Later, the new Mrs Clint Eastwood would tell an interviewer, 'The fact that I'm only the second woman he has married really touches me.'

For their honeymoon they went to Hawaii where, according to the ever-vigilant tabloids, they spent two days visiting Jacelyn Reeves, who had moved into a house there, owned by Clint under Roy Kaufman's name. According to the *National Enquirer*, which felt obliged to soft-pedal its report with complimentary remarks about 'the bighearted star', the newly-marrieds brought presents to Clint's two children by

Reeves while Clint attended the private school play of his eight-year-old daughter. Afterwards, the daughter announced to the crowd that she was grateful for the presence of her Dad, Clint Eastwood. A 'sheepish Clint' beamed at everyone.

Reeves, who cooperated with the *Enquirer* reporters, was quoted as saying she and Clint had a 'good relationship'. She and her children were said to be living in a $550,000 golf course home with three bedrooms, a pool and jacuzzi. Clint made sure to send her a new car every year, gifted her with four thousand dollars monthly, paid expensive private school tuition, and 'showers the youngsters with presents'.

The intrepid *National Enquirer* even reported that it was during this trip that Ruiz became pregnant, hence her desire to meet other Clint offspring. Reeves, according to the *Enquirer*, gave Ruiz valuable 'mommy advice'. This time the tabloid was not sued.

The love first heralded in the tabloids was one of the weddings of the year. *People* magazine headlined its 15 April 1996 report: 'Making His Day: Clint Eastwood weds a 30-year-old TV anchor – and not at gunpoint.' Indicating the degree to which more mainstream publications were also beginning to regard Clint sceptically, the magazine alluded negatively to the star's 'moral fibre' and his previous love affairs gone awry, even contacting Sondra Locke for her reaction. 'The only thing that's sad,' the actress was quoted, 'is that there are several women in his life who are the mothers of his children, and he chose to marry one who is not.'

The line drawn in the sand by the *National Enquirer* lawsuit was also meant to intimidate others. Clint was particularly infuriated by the *People* article, considering that *People* was owned by Time–Warner, the parent company of Warner Brothers, where Malpaso had been housed for the past twenty years.

Gang, Tyre, Ramer & Brown did its duty, dashing off a sharp note to *People* complaining about the article's 'snide tone' and dubious Clint-quotes which the magazine had lifted from the *National Enquirer*. The lawyers demanded an apology 'for an article which was a marriage, in its own right, of bad journalism and bad taste'.

Behind the scenes, according to sources, Clint made noises about dropping out of his next project, a film based on the Warner Books' best-seller *Absolute Power*. The *People* apology had to be swift and it was forthcoming in the magazine's 13 May issue. Even so, according to a subsequent article by Patricia Bosworth in the *Ladies Home Journal*, 'Eastwood remained so ticked off, he refused to meet with Time–Warner honcho Norman Pearlstine at the company's Rockefeller Center offices to hear the editor-in-chief's *mea culpas* in person. Instead, Pearlstine was kept waiting in the lobby of Eastwood's hotel while the star attended to other business.'

Clint, interviewed by Patricia Bosworth, said that he didn't read everything about himself. 'Just read stuff that could be upsetting to me or the people I care about.'

In spite of an intensive ad campaign by Warner Brothers, and supportive buzz by friendly journalists (Bernard Weinraub in the *New York Times* listed Clint as a legitimate contender for either his acting or directing of *The Bridges of Madison County*), Clint's name was missing from the spring announcement of Academy Award nominations. Meryl Streep received a Best Actress nomination, her seventh Oscar nomination, although she ultimately lost to Susan Sarandon for *Dead Man Walking*.

The American Film Institute Life Achievement Award would have to substitute for Oscar. Clint was announced as the twenty-third recipient of the annual honour, which is, in effect, a tribute dinner filmed as a one-hour special for television to benefit the AFI's education and preservation programmes. Previous award-winners have included directors John Ford and Alfred Hitchcock, and actors James Cagney and James Stewart. In recent years the AFI, in order to attract a younger generation of viewers, had gravitated towards post-1960s screen luminaries such as Jack Nicholson and Steven Spielberg. The honoree must agree to participate in the evening-long ceremony.

Under these conditions Clint was a natural choice, in 1996, to attract the highest conceivable TV ratings and the highest possible network sale (reportedly a $1.25 million cheque to the AFI). Clint was now known to enjoy these gala occasions, and as Army Archerd reported apropos of the AFI event, 'If you invite Clint Eastwood to a party, be prepared to stay until closing. That's when he leaves.' According to one Malpaso insider, that is also when Clint and staff roam the room and make a collection of the freebies – gifts and souvenirs – guests inadvertently have left behind.

One might note how impersonal the whole affair seemed to be, how striking was the absence of genuine close friends. Steven Spielberg, the previous year's honoree, was the choice to confer the AFI award. Rene Russo and Jim Carrey shared the hosting chores. Clint, in the audience, was flanked by his mother and Dina Ruiz. The man of the hour made his acceptance speech 'with just the kind of low-voltage, intense embarrassment you'd expect from him', according to the *New York Times*.

This was followed by a Film Society of Lincoln Center tribute in May 1996, timed to coincide with a Museum of Modern Art series of Don Siegel films, a few starring Clint. Bernard Weinraub capped the season of honours with an article in the *New York Times* exclaiming that 'Mr Eastwood's work as a director equals and, at times, transcends his acting'. For his cover profile of Clint in *GQ* magazine for March of 1993, Weinraub had gone even further, proclaiming, 'With the exception of [Woody] Allen, no American actor–director has turned out such a variety of films of such consistently high quality.'

After having reached such an apogee, *Absolute Power* was an appropriate title for Clint's next production, scheduled for principal photography in the summer of 1996.

Absolute Power was a political thriller based on a 1995 novel about an ageing professional thief named Luther Whitney who, while burgling a mansion in a Washington, DC suburb, witnesses a sadomasochistic tryst turned savage killing. Only the thief knows who is to blame: the President of the United States. He takes away from the scene of the crime evidence implicating the Commander-in-Chief. The thief becomes the chief suspect; then he must somehow clear himself, while eluding Secret Service agents determined to 'eliminate' him. His estranged daughter, a prosecuting attorney, is drawn into his plan to lead detectives to the real culprit.

Washington, DC lawyer David Baldacci wrote the novel, his first. Hollywood producers interested in the film rights helped Baldacci through his rewrites and then with placing the manuscript in the hands of a top New York agent, who was able to sell it for $2 million to Warner Books. The first printing of 350,000 hardcover copies landed the book on Top Ten sales lists, and the book was sold to Castle Rock for $1 million.

Obviously from the word go it was a high-octane project, and more fuel was poured on expectations when Castle Rock employed William Goldman, he of *All the President's Men* and Clint-in-Cannes fame, to adapt the book into a screenplay.

Goldman thought there were maybe too many characters in the book, and worse, no obvious starring part. But he was struck by three sensational sequences: the opening seventy-page 'rough sex' involving the President; a setpiece involving a 'double attempt' (by Secret Service agents and a gunman hired by the victim's husband) on Luther Whitney's life; and Whitney's surprise death, just when readers finally think he is safe.

Most film critics, commenting later on Clint's adaptation, hadn't read the novel, so they didn't realize that, yes, Luther Whitney *died* in the book, while Seth Frank (played by Ed Harris in the film), the police detective assigned to investigate the crime, gradually assumes centre stage. 'He [Luther Whitney] had to die,' explained scenarist Goldman in his introduction to the published screenplay of *Absolute Power*. 'Not just because it provided a wonderful chance for a strong scene. Luther's death provided the impact the story needed to sustain itself. Morally and viscerally. Because he was the most decent person in the story in spite of his occupation.'

While Goldman went to work on a draft, Castle Rock went to work on Clint. *Absolute Power* could be a kind of oval-office bookend with *In the Line of Fire*. Clint could star and direct. Castle Rock thought Clint might play Seth Frank, although the detective's age would have to be cheated and the role might be a tad reminiscent of other Clint-detectives. If Clint chose to play Luther Whitney, he would be taking a rare acting risk, killing off one of his screen heroes and doing so, in this instance, halfway through the story. Perhaps he would decide to play the sadomasochistic President – an evil, hollow creep – the most artistically risky proposition. What was Clint's pleasure?

When Clint read Goldman's script, the word came back. Clint would prefer to play Luther Whitney, the good guy, the stealth hero; in addition, he wanted Luther 'to live and bring down the President'. Goldman was 'rocked' by this demand. But Goldman was admittedly 'desperate to work with Eastwood, had been for decades'.

'One other problem,' Goldman noted, 'it was now November, I was literally starting from scratch again and I knew this: I had to get it in before Christmas. His agent had indicated as much, because Eastwood, who had taken time off after *The Bridges of Madison County*, was ready to go to work again. After Christmas he would be gone to something else.'

What Goldman came up with, however far-fetched, suited Clint's need, always, to be the hero. Luther Whitney would somehow manage to elude the double assassins and the Secret Service and find and confront cuckolded billionaire Walter Sullivan with the truth about his wife's killer. This revelation spurs Sullivan to visit the White House after dark and kill the President (with the nation led to believe it is a presidential suicide).

Gone were two of three sequences that appealed to Goldman in the first instance. Gone was the narrative logic of the Luther Whitney character.

Film critics would bend over to credit the father–daughter sentiment of *Absolute Power* to Clint, although that is one thing about the film preserved intact from the novel. It was also more moving in the book. There Luther's alienated daughter helps to betray him, causes his killing, and then risks all to vindicate her father after his death.

The $40 million-plus budget of the production would take into account the added prestige and higher salaries of a cast that was in keeping with the new Clint of the 1990s. Clint's *Unforgiven* co-star Gene Hackman would return as the President. Two-time Oscar-nominee Judy Davis would play the President's slutty Chief of Staff.* Ed Harris (another previous Oscar-nominee) would play the police detective who, in Goldman's adaptation, forfeited character development. Scott Glenn and Dennis Haysbert would play the Secret Service agents. Veteran E. G. Marshall would play the rich man whose wife's death is caused by the President. Laura Linney, who had been noticed by critics in *Primal Fear* with Richard Gere, would play Whitney's daughter.

Alison Eastwood would be given a small part as the willowy blonde artist eyeing Whitney's sketchwork in the opening scene. An even smaller part was awarded to Kimber Eastwood, for the first time in one of her father's films, glimpsed here as a tour guide in the White House.

---

* Clint was always cleaning up the sex for broader audiences. In the novel, the Chief of Staff is an even sluttier character; in the opening sequence, she has sex with the President *after* he has killed his mistress and passed out.

Bumped from *In the Line of Fire*, Lennie Niehaus, Joel Cox, Henry Bumstead and Jack Green were back for this 'Clint goes to Washington'. *Absolute Power* went on location in June and July, with ever-fast-efficient director Clint wrapping, according to Army Archerd, 'seventeen days ahead of schedule and substantially under-budget'.

In September of 1996, Clint was back in court, with, of all people, Sondra Locke.

Clint's former live-in lover, recovered from her bout with cancer, had spent three years at Warners, unable to persuade the studio to develop a single story or idea out of the thirty or so projects she brought to the table. Frustrated and angry, the actress filed suit, alleging the studio had treated her fraudulently, giving her a directing deal upon Clint's say-so without any intention of making good on the contract.

In the discovery stages of her lawsuit, Locke discovered paperwork that indicated Clint was in on the deception. So she filed a $2 million suit against the star, too. Friends warned her against such action. It was dangerous to take on the corporate giant, Warner Brothers. It was stupid to go after Clint once again. The actress would be destroyed in the courtroom by Clint's lawyers ... if she ever got that far.

Locke was determined to try to bring Clint to justice. Clint was just as determined to evade her, at one point calling in the studio police on a professional process server, having the man handcuffed and then held for interrogation on the Warners lot. After months of legal stalling – with Clint and Warners choosing to separate themselves in the litigation – the case arrived in the Burbank Superior Court in September 1996.

A jury was picked. Since it was a civil case, only nine of the twelve jurors would have to side with Locke in order for her to gain a verdict against Clint. The presiding judge was David M. Schachter. Locke was represented by attorney Peggy Garrity.

For two weeks witnesses were heard. Locke explained affectingly how the star, known far and wide for his warmth, generosity, loyalty, etc., had operated behind the scenes, in collusion with Warner Brothers, to deceive her and ruin her career. And how the studio deal was in reality the star's secret, cut-rate pay-off of her 1989 'palimony' lawsuit against him.

Clint was called as Locke's final witness. His time on the witness stand would be covered by media from around the world. The star was tense, uncomfortable. Under questioning from Peggy Garrity, he reverted to his Gary Cooper-mode, saying only about fifteen words. These included, as itemized in one account, five 'Yes' responses, three 'No's, and an occasional, 'That's true'. His most verbose reply, according to one press account, was 'Part of it, yes'.

Speaking in a 'barely audible voice', Clint admitted that it was he who covertly had paid Locke the $1.5 million of her Warners salary during her three-year dead-end deal. He had little choice but to confess, since, in the discovery phase of the trial, the actress had unearthed a bookkeeping print-out from Warner Brothers which recorded the figure of $975,000, part payment to Locke, as being written off to the budget for *Unforgiven*, with the remainder of her salaries and expenses amortized to Malpaso.*

Back on the witness stand later, in the defence phase of the trial, the 'previously laconic' Clint now 'grew animated on the witness stand', in the words of the *Los Angeles Times*, claiming, 'I never intended to defraud anyone. I didn't discourage them from making movies with Sondra Locke.' He insisted he underwrote Locke's directing pact as 'icing on the cake' to convince Terry Semel to accept the arrangement.

Filmdom's much-honoured star borrowed language from the Dirty Harry genre to say that Locke's palimony suit and the resultant publicity made him feel as though she and her lawyers 'were holding a gun to my head'. Clint denied any malfeasance. But when asked by his lawyer, Raymond Fisher, if he ever told Warners *not* to make a film with Locke, Clint couldn't restrain a chuckle, saying, 'No, not at all.'

After giving his testimony and leaving the courtroom, Clint was 'unusually loquacious' to outside reporters, quipping: 'No good deed goes unpunished.'

Warner Brothers executives also paraded to the stand to testify that Clint had never spoken ill of Locke and in fact had recommended

---

* The judge refused to allow the records showing the charging of Locke's costs to *Unforgiven* to be admitted to the court record. Locke's lawyer Peggy Garrity argued that this was 'the heart of the fraud. It was hidden, it was concealed, and it was concealed in the payment and the costs on *Unforgiven*.' But Warner Brothers 'fought hard' to keep those documents out of the public eye, and the judge decided in the studio's favour because 'that's between them and their investors'. According to Sondra Locke in her book, *The Good, the Bad and the Very Ugly*, 'We were allowed to say that Eastwood paid but now *how* he paid.'

her for projects as a director. But the damage had been done by the bookkeeping records and by Clint's transparently dismissive attitude towards Locke while he was on the stand, which, according to published reports, visibly swayed jury members as well as the press.

When, on 23 September, the jury went into deliberation, the betting odds had switched to Locke. Ten of the twelve jurors were believed to be solidly in her corner, with the only real issue being how much money ultimately would be awarded.

Since before the trial, Clint's friends had been lobbying him to settle once and for all with the actress. According to sources, even his own legal team argued against the messy courtroom showdown. But Clint's mind was stubbornly set.

Now, at the eleventh hour, the friends and lawyers began to lobby him again. Clint was bound to lose. An out-of-court settlement was bound to be less costly than a judgement. Also, if he moved swiftly, Clint would seem the generous spirit, acting to end all this misunderstanding and hostility. Clint liked that side of the argument.

At the back of everyone's minds, no doubt, were those financial ledgers showing Clint had paid Locke partly out of the *Unforgiven* budget. Although Clint later gave interviews in which he specifically noted that part of the Locke pay-off was borne by *profits* from *Unforgiven*, the records appear to show that the money was charged against the *operating* budget. In a film industry where 'creative bookkeeping' is rife, it would be prudent not to linger on this subtlety in a court of law, now or ever, on appeal.

Therefore, on the morning in which jurors were set to begin a second day of deliberation, a surprise announcement was made. Locke had agreed to drop her suit against Clint in return for an unspecified monetary settlement. 'I just hope she got a good deal,' jury forewoman Brenda Williams was quoted in the press.

The actress stated for the public record that her cause would have been vindicated by the award of one dollar. Her victory over Clint was meant for 'the little person' everywhere, the outcome a 'loud and clear' message to Hollywood 'that people cannot get away with whatever they want to, just because they're powerful'.

That is how a sympathetic press also covered the conclusion of the case, with smiling photos of a triumphant Locke. The settlement was, as usual, sealed from public scrutiny, and technically, no verdict had come down, but any hopes Clint might have had of looking magnanimous were dashed by the coverage. Any hopes that he might look the winner – keeping his perfect court record – were dashed by the public perception. It was a bitter experience to have lost in front of the whole world.

Any hopes Clint might have had of looking magnanimous were also dashed by interviews he gave, shortly following, in which his anger and bitterness were vented.

Gordon Anderson, Locke's husband, came in for especially nasty sniping. The fact that Anderson is homosexual had been acknowledged openly for the first time by Sondra Locke in the courtroom during the trial. But the press, rightly considering Anderson a private individual who did not court any public recognition, did not cite his sexual orientation in print.

Now Clint, in a March 1997 interview with Bernard Weinraub in *Playboy* – a heterosexual venue for the occasion – 'outed' Anderson in print, then disparaged him publicly, as he had sometimes disparaged gay characters in his films. Soon after, in another interview for *George*, John Kennedy Jr's glossy magazine, Clint added to the disparagement, claiming Locke and Anderson were 'macabre' people, saying, 'Jeffrey Daumer is right up their alley', an astonishing allusion – unchallenged in print – to the Milwaukee, Wisconsin serial murderer who preyed on postpubescent boys.

Clint's callous remarks were more the type he usually reserved for his 'barroom barnacles'. In *Playboy*, he went so far as to accuse Locke of playing the card of victim by currying sympathy with people with her breast cancer and double mastectomy.

Clint also played cards with the public. In the months following the Sondra Locke settlement, he gave many interviews to promote *Absolute Power* and effect damage control. Apart from *Playboy* and *George*, there were two separate Clint pieces in the *Los Angeles Times* (spaced a few weeks apart), a *Parade* magazine cover, and full-length articles in *Cosmopolitan* ('Hollywood's Most Private Star') and *Men's Journal* ('A subplot in *Absolute Power* reminds me of myself,' commented Clint. 'This guy has led a thrill life, and there's a big regret in his heart').

Capping all this was Richard Schickel's biography, *Clint Eastwood*, published by Alfred A. Knopf in time for Christmas gift-giving, 1996.

Clint made appearances on behalf of the book, upholding the Schickel version of his life in a lecture at the 92nd Street Y in New York City and on Charlie Rose's nationally televised interview show.

The author (with Clint the silent partner) could not have been pleased when the Sunday *New York Times* review was assigned to Michael Sragow, a San Francisco-based critic long associated with the Pauline Kael camp. Not for that reason alone (the book, taking its cue from Clint, harped on Kael's misunderstanding of Clint's work) did Sragow accuse Schickel of having become a tortured evangelist for Clint, his book a labour to read, written as if Dirty Harry held a Magnum .44 to the author's head.

Clint himself was Schickel's principal source. Although certain estranged people from his past, such as Ted Post, Bob Daley and Fritz Manes, were quoted, their use was selective. 'Schickel spent more time shutting his tape recorder off and sort of looking around furtively as if Clint was going to come around the corner to answer something that I said,' Fritz Manes reported. 'I probably asked him more questions than he asked me. We spent three hours together and he said, "I'll be back." I never heard from him again.'

The book was less a journalistic effort than a strenuous argument on behalf of Clint's greatness as an actor and film-maker, and his fundamentally decent complexity as a man. As such, it not only defined Clint's appeal to film critics, but epitomized his seduction of them.

Ironically, the book prompted some soul-searching on the part of critics once firmly in Clint's corner. David Thomson, an iconoclastic essayist, and acknowledged friend of Schickel's, was provoked to take after the book in his 'Cinéma Vérité' column in *Esquire*. Thomson drubbed *Clint Eastwood* as 'a helpless piece of star polishing', which even if Clint 'had no contractual say over the text', was influenced by his friendship with the author.

Thomson excoriated Alfred A. Knopf – publisher of several of his own books! – for having underwritten joint appearances by the two men, likely because the publisher 'hoped for better sales than it got'. Complaining that Schickel's biography 'skirts much that is grubby, mean and selfish' about Clint, Thomson pointed out how unaware the author seemed to be 'of how steadily Eastwood has campaigned – first in Europe, then at home – for respectability, esteem and "life achievement" awards'.

Thomson, himself a veteran of Clint-interviews, commented: 'Being with Clint can make you feel very privileged – and it is a reward he handles carefully.'

If the first thirty years of Clint in film can be measured by his campaign for respect and recognition, Schickel's overpraising book, intended to seal the artistic acclaim, may have had the paradoxical effect of raising doubts and signalling a reappraisal. Clint, as Thomson reassessed, was perhaps 'an impersonal director and an actor of narrow range', and the intended Schickel valedictory 'a kind of *coup de grâce*'.

Owing to lawsuits, public appearances and *Absolute Power*, Clint pretty much sat out the 1996 presidential election. He had supported George Bush in the 1988 campaign, but declined to campaign for the Republicans in 1992. Clint said later that he had voted for third party candidate Ross Perot rather than for the Democrat whose last name was the same as his first. Without his vote, Bill Clinton won both elections, America's first Democratic president in twelve years and the first two-termer since World War II.

Absolute Power, with its sexually swashbuckling president, would be as implicitly 'anti-Clinton' as most of Clint's 1980s films were subtly 'pro-Reagan'. Not as comfortable as he was under previous administrations, Clint sniped at Clinton in interviews; on at least one occasion he lobbed a verbal hand grenade at First Lady Hillary Rodham Clinton – even more of a target for diehard right-wingers than her husband – informing the fashion magazine *W*, 'She's not an unattractive woman, but for some reason, it's like there's a pit bull in the background ready to bite your leg.'

In general, however, Clint receded from public political activism, while behind the scenes he vigorously promoted pro-growth initiatives in the Carmel area. The onetime mayor was fairly adept at using channels that had opened up to him in office to expand and consolidate the holdings that make him one of Hollywood's wealthiest citizens.

The Mission Ranch, where he lived much of the time, came in for enhancements. After purchasing the historic place and vowing that it would 'stay as it is', Clint nonetheless made a few controversial 'improvements'. He tore down nine cabins and built four large buildings with guest units. And another application is on file to revamp the tennis courts and tear down and rebuild the clubhouse.

Even more disputed is Clint's Cañada Woods development. This is actually two separate projects, Cañada Woods East and Cañada Woods North. In the case of the former, one of Clint's local land parcels, the star angered conservationists when he managed to get a 'permanent' scenic easement removed in order to develop further housing on the site. Cañada Woods East is now in the process of being bulldozed for subdivision.

Cañada Woods North will be a more exclusive enclave. It is a planned development on a pristine mountaintop overlooking Carmel Valley, south of the Monterey–Salinas Highway and east of Monterey Peninsula Airport. Carmel Valley is a semi-rural, semi-pine-forested that is home to golden eagles, peacocks, turkeys, wild boar, bobcats and mountain lions. Throughout much of 1996, Clint pushed ahead his plans to top his 1,060 acres of mountain real estate with an eighteen-hole golf course, a clubhouse with suites, a fitness and equestrian centre and anywhere from thirty-four to eighty-eight estate-style homes. This would be Monterey Peninsula's nineteenth golf course, Mark Arax noted in the *Los Angeles Times*, with all eighteen holes 'more or less the private reserve of Eastwood and his friends'.

Because of the environmental issues, and because water is so scarce in the vicinity, Clint needed government permits. The *Los Angeles Times* noted that Monterey County planners and elected officials, 'awed by Eastwood's immense celebrity and wealth', failed to sufficiently investigate the project's impact on wildlife and the water supply, instead fast-tracking the star's applications. Investigation revealed that Clint's permit to draw water from 'the overworked Carmel River' was granted in 'record time', after Clint showed up in Sacramento, 'shook hands with water board executives and staff and signed autographs for starry-eyed secretaries'. A state Water Quality Board official said preferential treatment saved at least two years of ordinary procedure.

High school activists ended up picketing the local première of *Absolute Power*. The newspaper columns filled with debate. The Sierra Club sued for a fresh environmental impact report, and in late 1997, a Monterey County judge ruled that Clint could go ahead.

One of the project's biggest boosters, a Monterey County supervisor named Sam Karas, was a longtime Clint buddy and fellow jazz buff who

merited several lines of dialogue as Thirsty Thurston in *Unforgiven*.*
Karas defended Clint on the grounds that he was a generous citizen
who had given of himself to the Carmel area, including land donations
to the county and weights and equipment to local boys' organizations.

Local cynics believed that when Clint gave away fitness equipment
to community groups, it was a sure sign that he was upgrading his
personal gym and remaindering old stuff. Local cynics understood
that Clint was available for high-society charity functions, but was not
a donor of big money behind the scenes. 'Generosity' was part of the
image, not always the reality.

Clint's opponents charge, for example, that when, in 1995, Clint
appeared to 'give away' 283 acres to the county – this was Mal Paso,
the land for which his film company was named, and one of Clint's
first properties, a five-parcel lot located south of the Carmel Highlands
– it was actually a cunning business transaction intended to profit from
taxpayers' funds set aside for open land acquisition by State Prop. 70.
Although the giveaway did take the land off the commercial market,
Clint received $3.08 million of public monies for property last assessed
at $308,682, and furthermore, part of the arrangement gave Clint
permission to buy other valuable, set-aside land.

The land Clint bought with an undisclosed portion of the money
was the historic, 134-acre Odello artichoke ranch, located along the
Carmel River mouth, long recognized for its scenic value and development potential. In 1997 – a gesture that coincided with the nationwide
release of *Midnight in the Garden of Good and Evil* – Clint and Maggie
'donated' the Odello property to the county and the Big Sur Land
Trust (BSLJ). On the face of it, this looked like more largesse. However 'complex and labyrinthine manoeuvring' behind the scenes,
according to local reporters, showed that Clint had 'swapped' water
and development rights from one property to another, and again was
permitted to buy a tract of set-aside land, known locally as the Cusack
property, which had been marked for scenic easement in perpetuity.
The new land came with development permissions and happened to
be adjacent to Clint's Cañada Woods East subdivision.

The belief among some Monterey County planners was that securing

---

* According to sources, Karas and his wife were also given small speaking parts in
Midnight in the Garden of Good and Evil, although they found out, on the night of the
première, that Clint had left them on the cutting-room floor.

ownership and preservation of the Odello Ranch was of greater value than preserving the adjacent Cañada Woods land, but this 'swap' of open spaces bothered many in and out of government. A comprehensive investigation by the *Coast Weekly* 'suggests Eastwood took economic advantage of the [Cusack] property's additional development rights and scenic value, as well as a healthy tax deduction' of an estimated $6 million.

In 1996 Mark Arax closed his *Los Angeles Times* report with this musing: 'Some wonder why an American icon – who has earned more than $500 million over the span of his forty-year career, collected the highest acting awards and even had his best line stolen by a president – would even play the California development game.'

Clint couldn't be reached by this news reporter for the *Los Angeles Times*, was not quoted in the *Coast Weekly*. Interviews were for friendly film-buff journalists. His supporters, his architect and development partners, were available to speak on Clint's behalf. On business matters, the Hollywood star was terse.

The master of compartmentalization also found time as a new husband and father-to-be.

Throughout the fall of 1996, Dina Ruiz, hitherto primarily a Monterey County celebrity, had a kind of coming-out in Hollywood, where she was introduced to the film industry's top echelon at parties such as the one hosted by old Clint friend Dani Crayne and attended by Shirley MacLaine and David Geffen, the James Coburns, the Dennis Hoppers, the Don Rickles, the Jim Carreys, the Pierce Brosnans.

Ruiz's pregnancy was officially announced in September. Initial reports noted that the baby was due in January, although this was amended to late December.

Reporters for various media sometimes interviewed the pregnant Ruiz at the office where she kept up her news-anchoring, sometimes at the San Antonio address. One article reported, 'The pair appeared to be living a very normal lifestyle. They share a house with no hired help except for a cleaning woman who comes once a week. They go out to dinner and the movies. They stay up late and channel-surf. Both are avid readers; Ruiz subscribes to about six magazines.'

Ruiz told the *San Francisco Chronicle*, 'We go to the movies, dinner, jogging. He's teaching me golf.'

She told another interviewer: 'He has a gun permit but wouldn't even kill a spider. When we see a bug in our house, we coax it out the window.'

The *San Francisco Chronicle* noted that Ruiz 'politely declines to discuss their prenuptial agreement'. The new Mrs Clint Eastwood told *Cosmopolitan*, 'I'm still getting to know him. I just found out about another house he owns.' The Knight–Ridder article explained that Ruiz maintained her own current account, Visa bill, cell phone and home phone accounts. 'Keeping separate accounts was her idea,' the Knight–Ridder reporter added.

'What I bring to the marriage,' Ruiz told the *San Francisco Chronicle*, 'is that I have no agenda.'

Clint shared her sentiments – and language. 'We sure are happy,' Clint told the *Ladies Home Journal*. 'Also, Dina has no agenda.'

The star informed *George* magazine. 'She's younger than I am, but she's more mature than a lot of older women. To me, she's just perfect. This is it. As far as I'm concerned, this is the woman I like monogamy with. She's quirky but fun, and she's got a really good soul. I never had the feeling that she is there for monetary gain'.

While visiting Los Angeles, Ruiz had her pregnancy check-ups at Cedars–Sinai, although she and Clint intended to have their baby in a hospital up in the Carmel area. However, on December 10, the doctor examining her thought that she had suffered a significant decrease in amniotic fluid, and decided Ruiz should check into Cedars–Sinai right away. She did so, under the name Dina Morgan, the 'Morgan' her mother's maiden name.

After a reported forty-five hours of labour, Morgan Colette Eastwood was born at 11.55 a.m. on 12 December, weighing a healthy eight pounds, four ounces. A month later, Army Archerd was in print assuring *Variety* readers that Clint was taking the baby in her bassinet to his Athletic Club in Sun Valley while he worked out. A month after that, at the première of *Absolute Power*, Dina Ruiz told the press, 'Clint is great at changing diapers.'

Absolute Power opened 'wide' at 2568 theatres in a month – February – that hadn't seen the première of a Clint film for decades. This was less an indication of behind-the-scenes jitters than an acknowledgement that the preceding Christmas season was packed with younger stars and surefire crowd-pleasers. Warners had to wait for enough theatres to open up after the box-office rush for *Jerry Maguire, Michael, Ransom, Star Trek: First Contact* and *Scream. Absolute Power* would end up grossing close to $50 million, although this had to be disappointing, considering that $1 million wasn't what it used to be, considering Clint's and the other salaries, and considering that 1997 was a banner year for Hollywood, with over thirty films accumulating higher grosses. As always, however, Clint's name was strong in foreign markets and the film could be counted on to nearly double the domestic figures outside US borders.

Artistically, *Absolute Power* was a step backward from the smooth expertise of *Unforgiven, In the Line of Fire, A Perfect World,* even *The Bridges of Madison County.* Indeed, the plot seemed 'quietly berserk', in the words of Janet Maslin of the *New York Times.* A superb cast looked adrift.

The film was more lurid than *Tightrope,* with Luther Whitney (Clint) a voyeur in the 'rough sex' scene that so captivated writer William Goldman. Whitney hides in a closet behind a two-way mirror and watches as the President of the United States achieves a turn-on by beating up a pretty young thing. The sordid violence goes on for ever (with the camera cutting away to a grimacing Clint, so the audience understands that he is just as disgusted as them).

The 'rough sex' ends with the unfortunate day player having her brains blown out in slow motion, the kind of slow-motion blood-spurting Clint once swore he would never resort to in his films. Well, it was probably an artistic requirement of the scene.

The other moment that sums up *Absolute Power* takes place before the s & m *guignol*; this scene, not in the book, was added by William Goldman expressly for Clint.

It is the opening sequence, which has Luther Whitney sketching Old Masters in a museum. Sidling up next to him, peering over his shoulder, is a fetching art student (Alison Eastwood), who may or may not be flirting with him. Clint and Alison reunited on screen hammered home the film's emotional subtext – an absentee father's love for children who perhaps misunderstand him. Since this might be lost on some people, Alison (and Kimber Tunis) were incorporated into publicity-article interviews. 'Alison and Eastwood had a stormy relationship,' noted *Men's Journal,* 'accounting for the resonance he [Clint] felt with the subplot of *Absolute Power*.'

Just as important, the scene alerts viewers to the notion that Luther Whitney is something of an artist – translation: Clint himself is sort of an Old Master. Although the 'old' with Clint was always sliding in and out like a slipshod accent. In the museum scene Luther wears eyeglasses and appears to be a duffer; later, in total darkness, without his eyeglasses and carrying a heavy backpack, he manages to rappel down from the second storey of his burgle and to outjog through a forest two perfect physical specimens equipped with night vision goggles.

Although a few stubborn critics remained oblivious to Clint's artistry (Peter Rainer in Los Angeles's *New Times* decried the film's blankness and 'audio-animatronic' heartfeltness), others had long since joined the wave, with Ken Turan of the *Los Angeles Times*, for example, noting in his review that Clint was 'the last Old Master in Hollywood, just as reliable in his sphere (at least when he's not co-starring with orangutans) as Rembrandt and Rubens were in theirs'.

In advance of its US opening, *Absolute Power* had been scheduled for the prestigious closing night slot of the Cannes Film Festival, with the idea being that Clint himself would appear at the spring festivities in the south of France for the fifth time in ten years. But at the last moment, perhaps fearing a negative reaction to his new film, Clint bowed out, disappointing festival organizers. His understandable excuse was that he was already on location in the South, immersed in directing his next film, an adaptation of the best-seller *Midnight in the Garden of Good and Evil.*

He need not have feared the French critics. Those who did not like *Absolute Power* politely recounted the plot, without passing judgement on the work's merits, or else, as was the case with the man from *Libération*, they spoke respectfully of 'the Carmel master's quiet schizophrenia', consisting of 'the troubled and troubling', personal filmmaker on the one hand, and 'on the other, the man of big-budget cinema'.

Most unabashedly wrote love letters to Clint. Especially the cineastes from the specialized film journals – *Positif* and *Cahiers du Cinéma* – which had acclaimed Clint early on. The two-page review in *Cahiers du Cinéma* spoke of the film's truth and beauty, its subtle reflection on power, a sophistication bordering on poetry. It was a reminder that Clint still exerted remarkable charisma overseas and that, if ever there was doubt, now his name was recognized as actor *and* film-maker in France, held up there as artistically akin to such other neglected Hollywood figures as Nicholas Ray and Jerry Lewis.

Midnight in the Garden of Good and Evil, by former *Esquire* columnist John Berendt, was another publishing-industry phenomenon, a fluke success to rival *The Bridges of Madison County*. The non-fiction book was a unique amalgam of travelogue, social gossip and crime story, focusing on the Southern charm and idiosyncratic denizens of the antebellum city of Savannah in southeastern Georgia. The centrepiece of the book was a murder mystery that began in 1981 when a locally prominent gay antiques dealer named Jim Williams shot to death his street-hustler lover. Published in 1994, the book went on the best-seller list and was still selling strong in hardcover three years later, as the film went into release.

It was a Random House, not a Warners, book but the manuscript had been optioned before publication by agent-manager Arnold Stiefel, who had a 'first look' deal with the Warners studio. Stiefel, a gay man who had been a force in the careers of Bette Midler and Rod Stewart, hired John Lee Hancock, who had scripted the well-received *A Perfect World*; the producer might have been thinking ahead to Clint. When Warners took over the rights from Stiefel in 1994, the studio picked up the overhead costs and placed the project under the steward-ship of Joel Silver's Silver Pictures.

Everyone concedes that the digressive book had inherent problems as a movie. Unlike *The Bridges of Madison County*, there was no clear-cut structure, no easily-recounted story, no obvious leading man and woman among an eccentric roster of characters that included a local voodoo priestess and an African–American drag queen. The book was short on plot, heavy on atmosphere. Hancock hoped to solve this in his script by turning the author into a lead character, John Kelso, who is trying to make sense of the strange people and mysterious events by following everybody around with his pencil and notebook.

Warners found fault with Hancock's submission draft, and put the script into a holding pattern while debating how to proceed. Hancock then slipped it under Clint's door, asking the star's opinion. 'He called back a couple of days later, and said, "What's going on with this?"' Hancock explained: 'Which, in Clint-speak, means he's interested.' Clint called Terry Semel and Bob Daly, and told the studio executives he wanted to direct *Midnight in the Garden of Good and Evil*. They were happy he was interested, and in February 1996 Clint was announced as the film's director.

He hadn't read the book, just the script; later he read the book. For his final rewrite, Clint asked Hancock to emphasize all the 'weird' vignettes, and streamline the courtroom marathon (all four trials, reported in the book, narrowed down to one in the shooting script). This was one project where Clint intended to prove his quirky sense of humour.

The casting of Clint's 1990s films continued to be a major factor in their perceived quality (by now casting director Phyllis Huffman was receiving a prominent screen credit). John Kelso would be played by John Cusack, a clean-cut actor who had graduated from teenager parts to sincere, sometimes offbeat young leads. Kevin Spacey, hot from his Best Supporting Oscar in *The Usual Suspects*, would portray Jim Williams. There was much press speculation as to who would play the trash-talking drag queen Lady Chablis, and after some internal deliberation – and a three-hour meeting with Clint – the answer was Lady Chablis her/himself.

The part of Mandy, a flower-shop flirt, had been built up in John Lee Hancock's adaptation. Mandy was also in the book, but not as the author's girlfriend or in quite so many scenes. No real surprise, Alison Eastwood was auditioned by Huffman and then put on tape for Clint. After putting her toe back in the water in *Absolute Power*, the star's daughter had developed serious acting ambitions. No real surprise, Alison got the part, undoubtedly one of Clint's reasons for doing the film.

Warners, Clint, cast and crew and press descended on Savannah in May. 'All along, Clint was quite fearless in understanding and knowing the movie he wanted to make, in terms of having it feel like Savannah,' said John Lee Hancock. 'Sometimes it is a divergent movie, and sometimes it isn't commonly plotted. He had a real understanding that that was part of Savannah, and part of the beauty of the book.

'Clint's very much a Zen film-maker, even though he wouldn't describe himself that way. He goes to a location and says, "Here's what we're bringing – actors, the script, the camera equipment, now, what is this location going to bring to us?" A lot of directors force their vision of a production onto a script, and then it doesn't feel organic.'

The filming was swift, with photography accomplished inside six weeks, and the postproduction was equally swift, with *Midnight in the Garden of Good and Evil* readied for a pre-Thanksgiving release. Clint would have two films in theatres in 1997, both based on best-selling books.

Clint had been first in Hollywood with his own websites and digital press kits.

Now, to coincide with the nationwide release of *Midnight in the Garden of Good and Evil,* he threw himself into one of those intensive press campaigns in which his reluctance to do publicity was rotely mentioned. Although he had to make an appearance in an organ of the political right, *The American Enterprise,* reassuring readers as to his basic conservative values, Warners concentrated its campaign on the liberal media which was thought to be vital to the prospects of a film that was in part a homosexual murder mystery. To this end, Clint was featured on the cover of *The Advocate,* which is geared to a gay constituency, with a provocative headline ('Why did this macho gun-slinger make a film about closeted gays and drag queens?') and inside, with an extremely brief, gushing interview by one of Clint's pre-approved writers. Not once did the article mention the star's 'outing' of Sondra Locke's gay husband, or Clint's track record of gay-bashing in earlier films. (And a sidebar profiling producer Arnold Stiefel reminded *Advocate* readers, 'It wasn't only a macho producer who got this film made. It was a big fag.')

The campaign climaxed with Clint's two-part appearance on day-time's *The Oprah Winfrey Show,* a beloved programme of thoughtful housewives, with the star's presence augmented by his mother and wife and baby. Warners' only mistake may have been in handing Clint over to Sunday night's venerable *60 Minutes* investigative programme. Correspondent Steve Kroft, preparing his profile, did research and discovered the astonishing fact, something he was unaware of (since it was only first admitted to in Richard Schickel's 1996 biography), that Clint had numerous children by several different women. 'I like kids a lot,' a clearly dismayed and caught-off-guard Clint had to explain to Kroft, when confronted, on camera, with this information.

Kroft then asked Clint directly how many children did he have. 'I have a few,' replied Clint, stonily adding that he was 'in touch' with all of them. 'Seven kids with five women?' persisted Kroft, and Clint gave him a look that Kroft interpreted as a real, 'intimidating' Dirty Harry look. ('I don't think I've had anybody look at me like that before,' said a taken-aback Kroft.) Actually, the look was more of a 'caught-in-the-headlights' one, since Clint was aghast that such a man had been let in the door with such a question, one that all of his life he had carefully arranged never to be asked. 'It's almost never been an issue in your career,' continued the intrepid TV reporter, 'and you have managed to get away with it . . .' Kroft fumbled for words. 'Managed to get away with it is the wrong term because I'm not . . . you're not a politician . . .'

Clint had nothing to say to that unprecedented statement, nor did he directly reply to Kroft's question about the actual number of his children. He couldn't really, since Kroft's estimate was conservative. Mumbled explanations were enough for Kroft, who meekly backed off and that was the end of *60 Minutes'* vaunted hard-hittingness. Clint might have signalled the end to the interview, because that was pretty much the end of the questions and answers. After that, it was off to the Mission Inn, a visit with Dina, shots of Clint cooing over the baby, and a helicopter trip over his planned mountaintop golf course (with nary a mention of controversy or opposition). With Clint's luck even the *60 Minutes* segment probably turned out good publicity; certainly it was good advertising, since one of the paid spots in Warners' national advertising budget for *Midnight in the Garden of Good and Evil* closed the show.

Clint's version of *Midnight in the Garden of Good and Evil* didn't turn out as bad as detractors said ('It's incredible how bad it is,' declared Elvis Mitchell on National Public Radio), nor was it as good as Warners wished when taking out double-truck ads of quotes from Chicago and Boston critics and stalwart enthusiasts like Jack Mathews.

Scriptwriter Hancock made some arguable decisions, but the one that probably hurt the film most was making John Kelso a witness to everything, a kind of hero even in the courtroom, and a romeo for Clint's daughter. John Cusack, normally an appealing actor, couldn't deliver. It was partly Clint's fault, his direction of Cusack; the film tries hard to identify with the journalist–protagonist, and make him 'fun'. He isn't.

Identifying with Jim Williams (Kevin Spacey) was the more obvious – and, for Clint, radical – alternative. To the extent the film works, it does so because of Kevin Spacey. But however compelling Spacey is, his character is never allowed to dominate the film. Clint keeps edging back to Cusack, who exaggerates the film's 'quirky' humour, telegraphing the clues and jokes with his eye-rolling and hammy expressions.

Alison Eastwood is certainly perky in her part. Her father did her a disservice, however, indulging her at inordinate length. He even indulges her musically: in one scene she gets to sing one of the film's tunes by Savannah native son Johnny Mercer. Although Clint stayed behind the camera, he likewise indulged himself on the soundtrack, performing 'Ac-cent-tchu-ate the Positive'. (Clint's performance was reviewed as 'flat and joyless' by *New York Times* music critic Jon Pareles, and singled out as a must-to-be-avoided on an otherwise outstanding recording.)

Clint, the 'Zen film-maker' who kept his location time brief, never succeeded in conjuring any Savannah reality. In spite of the actual places and smattering of local faces, 'there is seldom enough context,' Janet Maslin wrote, 'to make these [film] characters seem anything but adorably whimsical to excess.'

The best scenes, ironically, were within the four walls of the courtroom. There, Alison, Cusack and Clint the director had the least to do. There, the scriptwriter, an ex-attorney, knew his territory best. There, Jack Thompson, an Australian known for his role in *Breaker Morant*, playing a flamboyant defence attorney, saved the film.

Clint erred worse than usual in the film's exhausting, 155-minute length. Exhibitors were forced to accept one less showing on their daily schedules. *Midnight in the Garden of Good and Evil* was in and out of the nation's theatres between Thanksgiving and Christmas. By all accounts it was one of Hollywood's disasters of 1997, partly accounting for a year considered by *Variety* to be 'the weakest in modern memory' for Warner Brothers. The film everyone expected to duplicate the success of a best-selling book earned less than $25 million, prompting a reassessment at the studio's top levels, and the sudden firing of one of Warners' chief marketing executives.

Word went around Hollywood that the star was looking for another Dirty Harry – his sixth. Clint approached an old friend and said he had a sketchy idea for a plot that the man might consider developing into a script. Dirty Harry retires from the San Francisco force and moves down the coast, closer to Clint's own stomping ground of Monterey County. Against his wishes, he is drawn into the investigation of a series of mysterious crimes. His life is imperilled. In more ways than one, this could be his last case . . .

While a new Dirty Harry gestated, Clint took basic insurance on two other crime stories. Paul Nathan in *Publisher's Weekly* announced an unusual $1 million pre-publication option on a new book. Although Clint himself 'couldn't be pinned down to reading' Michael Connelly's *Blood Work*, according to Nathan, the star had committed to the project based on the enthusiasm shown by Malpaso associates, the William Morris Agency and Warner Brothers.

The story line was about a former FBI expert on serial killers who finds himself in need of a heart transplant because of job stress. When recovering from his operation, he learns that his heart donor was mysteriously slain, and that the culprit is still at large.

After the option was announced, Clint did get around to reading the novel, according to author Connelly, a former police reporter whose previous works had been acclaimed by critics. The star summoned him to a meeting. 'He's a wonderful storyteller,' Connelly recounted. 'And [he has] influenced me as a writer, [with] some of his earlier films. And so when we met, before I was done with the book, he was telling me what his take on the book [was] and what he would probably want to change if he made it into a movie. And the main thing he wanted to change [was] he wanted to amp up or raise the stakes of the ending.'

So that is exactly what Connelly did, 'amp up' the ending of the novel. Down the road Clint was expected to direct (but not necessarily star in) *Blood Work*. The star was formally thanked in the acknowledgements for the book, published by Little, Brown, part of Time-Warners' corporate empire – providing a singular example of the vertical integration of publishing and show business, of literature and Hollywood.

Clint needed something more immediate. As *Blood Work* was shipped to bookstores, another crime story was announced as his next film, his forty-second since *Rawhide* as a star, his twenty-first as director. *True Crime* was a best-seller from Andrew Klavan about a dissolute newspaper reporter who must race the clock to uncover the necessary evidence to stop a Death Row execution. Although the book was not a Warners product, the screen rights had been optioned by Clint's old pal Richard Zanuck, who set up the production at Clint's home studio in partnership with his wife Lili.

The novel had been set in St Louis; at Clint's behest, the script relocated the story in and around Oakland. The cast included Isaiah Washington as the condemned killer who stubbornly protests his innocence, James Woods as Clint's editor, Diane Venora from *Bird* as Clint's estranged wife, and Frances Fisher as the prosecutor of the case. Fisher's casting, however inconsequential her part, raised eyebrows in Hollywood and among Clint's friends; either he was mending fences, purchasing some good will, or both.

In the book Clint's character, Steve Everett, has a wife and young child; but Everett is also half Clint's age – thirty-five years old. The script would have to rationalize this somehow. One way was to cast Fisher's and Clint's real-life daughter, five-year-old Francesca, as Everett's daughter. They could have quality time together on screen.

Apart from several film projects that would keep him busy into the future, there were new business moves: announcement of a Clint brand of beer, and a Clint line of golfwear that would be stocked by WalMart, one of the nation's largest retail chain. Inevitably, there were more prestigious honours and public relations exercises.

One might think the French, with their suspicious attitude towards cultural imperialism, would recognize Clint as being as American a brand name as any soft drink or hamburger chain. It might seem that the star had already received every possible accolade in France, but in the spring of 1998 the film establishment there came up with another – a César d'Honneur for Clint's directing career.

A journalist from the London *Times*, Ginny Dougary, was in Paris for the occasion. Clint surprised her by attempting his acceptance speech in the native tongue. 'He is wearing shiny patent shoes with his Cerruti tuxedo,' Dougary reported, 'and neither the style nor the size seems to fit. He stumbles as he comes down the steps which flank the stage. When he takes his handwritten speech out of his breast pocket, he is unable to reconnect his mike and M C Antoine de Caunes – oh, humiliation – has to come to his rescue. The speech is clearly an ordeal. He doesn't seem to have a clue what the words mean, and his pronunciation is appalling. Several times he has to stop and take a deep breath before continuing. Once he has a fit of the giggles.'

Once, Clint's press image was loyal husband and family man. Now, the press had to adjust their rose-coloured spectacles to depict a man on record as having fathered at least seven children by five different women – four out of wedlock. Maybe because they were in Paris, Dougary proved somewhat more successful than America's *60 Minutes* in getting an answer out of the star when she asked him why so many women had his babies.

'Is it catching?' she asked in print. 'Should I get out of here immediately?'

'Well,' Clint was quoted, 'sometimes – ughh ... arghh ... I ... I don't ... ahh ... know why it is that I'm any more of a sire than anyone else. Um ... er ... something to do with the genes, I guess.'

Accompanying her husband in Paris, Dina Ruiz, herself a journalist, had slid comfortably into coping with the press. She had learned to expect questions about Clint's past history with women. Profiled for America's *Access Hollywood* for television in April, Ruiz maintained, 'He's a philanthropist, but not a philanderer. He's home all the time and devoted.' She added that Clint was a doting father to their one-year-old daughter, Morgan, whom he had nicknamed 'Googles', and even did the shopping for diapers.

Clint had first invited the press into his marriage back during *Rawhide* days. Now, any topic was open for discussion. The *Access Hollywood* host wondered if, considering their age difference, Clint was still energetic enough for sex most evenings. Yes, said Ruiz, laughing and blushing, saying Clint was a veritable 'love bug'.

Clint's friends fretted when, in December 1997, it was announced that Ruiz had left her job at the NBC affiliate in Monterey–Salinas to devote herself to staying at home and taking care of their child. How would the star adjust to a stay-at-home wife?

Not to worry; four months later, the retirement was ended with the news that Ruiz would host a television magazine programme called 'Quest for Excellence', intended to spotlight California public schools. *Access Hollywood* noted that Ruiz's show would include a segment in which celebrities recalled their favourite teachers. Among her first guests would be Kevin Costner (offices are on the Warners lot), George

Clooney (who had been announced as Warners' next Batman) and Clint himself.

The spring of 1999 saw the nationwide release of *True Crime*, mild reviews and disappointing box-office sales. The film was easily Clint's least successful of the decade, earning less than $17 million dom-estically in spite of its placement on 1852 screens.

The Sondra Locke case continued to haunt the star. In May the actress achieved another, last-minute out-of-court settlement, this time with Warner Brothers, for its part in alleged collusion with Clint, dating back to the 1989 break-up. After ten years of battling her former lover and Warners in the courts, the agreement awarded Locke with undisclosed financial compensation and a new business arrangement with the studio.

In July, in a precedent-setting decision, the California Supreme Court also reacted to the Sondra Locke dispute, upholding the public's right to be present during civil trials and setting out guidelines advising judges of the limited circumstances in which such proceedings may be held in private. The judgement arose from the 1996 civil trial between Eastwood and his former companion, and the successful attempt by Clint's lawyers to bar the public and news media from arguments which took place away from the jury. Those rulings had been appealed by the *Los Angeles Times* and other media.

Also in July, Warners and the entire film industry were stunned by the unexpected resignations of co-chairmen Robert Daly and Terry Semel. Daly and Semel, protégés of the original management that had lured Clint to the studio, had run Warner Brothers for nineteen years of stability and profits. The failure of *True Crime* and the Sondra Locke dénouement had nothing to do with their decision; according to news accounts, Daly and Semel merely wanted to strike out on their own, producing films.

Clint may fear ageing and mortality, but he need not fear his legacy. His face is guaranteed to be enshrined for ever on Hollywood's Mount Rushmore. The films will never perish. One may attempt to separate his image from the reality, but one can't argue with a lifetime of success and popularity. Hollywood has always loved a hero that turns a profit, and America likewise loves a winner at any cost.

Afterword

Clint Eastwood's name first appeared on my list of proposed subjects over fifteen years ago. He was repeatedly passed over by publishers who preferred the sales potential of other film personalities. It wasn't until *Unforgiven* and the Oscars and other honours began to mount up that a New York editor who had previously rejected Clint as a subject, saying he was unfamiliar with many of his films and not particularly disposed towards him anyway, resurrected the idea. Clint, he thought, was 'hot'.

By then, however, it was me who was diffident. Was there anything left to be said about Clint after all the acclaim, all the articles, interviews and a dozen books? I wasn't sure. But this editor was determined to have a book about him, and in short order he came up with the necessary money to start the research and interviews.

My proposal was modest, saying something to the effect that beneath the surface of an actor who plays the Man With No Name and Dirty Harry so tough and convincingly must be a man who is different and more complicated than the warm-fuzzy image projected by his publicity. I had met Clint once, interviewed him at some length, liked him well enough, but still maintained reservations about him and many of his films.

On my first trip to Los Angeles after signing the contract, I had dinner with Richard Schickel, who was also working on a book about Clint Eastwood. It was our first meeting, although I have admired Schickel's work over the years and flatteringly reviewed some of his books for the *Boston Globe*. (We share Wisconsin roots and both worked for the same college newspaper.) Schickel's book was going to be an authorized one, written with Clint's approval. Schickel had phoned me to ask if I would send him a copy of the Clint interview I had done back in 1976, for possible citation in his book. After telling him that I would mail the piece to him straightaway, I mentioned that, coincidentally, I too had just agreed to write a book about Clint's life and career.

'What kind of a book will it be?' he asked. Frankly, I didn't know at that stage (I rarely do). I told Schickel that I intended to do massive research, as many interviews as possible, and that, as usual, I was most interested in the secrets of my subject, the kinds of issues Clint evaded or refused to talk about in previously published interviews: sex, politics, religion, attitudes or traits that, while they may be kept hidden from the public, might reflect on his films – and personal character. Schickel said, very graciously, that he would look forward to reading my book, and I said, partly tongue in cheek, that I hoped he finished his first because I looked forward to reading his and incorporating it into mine.

At dinner, he was again very gracious, not only making a point of complimenting other books of mine but picking up the bill. I remember he asked me, with a somewhat horrified expression, if I was going to be phoning up 'people like Sondra Locke'. I told him I wasn't looking forward to it, but that it would seem to be required under the circumstances. (My impression of Locke, at that early stage, was that she was some kind of wounded bird flapping around on one wing.) He said he could never do that sort of thing, but fortunately his book had the benefit of Clint's total cooperation and wonderful memory.

Certainly I thought he had not only the higher advance, but the better job, and I went away from dinner dismayed to think how excellent Clint's memory must be and how far ahead of me Schickel was. As I usually do, I phoned my agent and editor, pleading to change the contract to another subject. But the editor still wanted his Clint book, and so I went to work, starting out, as I usually do, by looking into Clint's family tree and delving, first, into persons and incidents from hundreds of years before his birth.

I knew almost nothing of what, after nearly four years of investigation – a lot of time logged in northern California, library work and interviews in Paris, Rome, London, New York and Los Angeles – I was to find out. Right from the beginning, and delving into Clint's genealogy, there was surprising, new information. In Hollywood I uncovered much that contradicted the previously published accounts. Although I have, in my office, a floor-to-ceiling stack of Clint interviews and clippings (a vast number for a guy supposedly wary of publicity), I discovered in the course of my work much that, inadvertently or not, had been left out of, or treated erroneously in, past articles and books. The puzzle pieces began to fit into a portrait of Clint that was very different from what had gone before.

When I wrote my book about Jack Nicholson, Jack neither helped nor hindered me. Some people associated with him refused to see me, but most were happy to, and I had only a small number of off the record conversations with key people. With Clint, it was clear from the outset that his imprimatur was necessary to gain admission to his world. People were worried about talking to me without his go-ahead, and therefore many people, especially those currently employed by Malpaso (the people quoted in most articles and books), shied away from me, sometimes without replying to letters or phone calls, other times as politely as possible. The people who did talk to me on the record either did not work in the film industry or, if they did, felt secure in their careers independent of Malpaso and didn't fear for their livelihoods. They didn't fear Clint.

The sister of one long-deceased Clint friend pleaded to be excused from an interview, because, even though she had 'nothing really bad' to say about Clint, she feared Clint's wrath and, worse, being sued; even Clint's grade-school principal had to call Malpaso first before deciding. (Whoever answered the phone at Malpaso advised him against talking to me, and he didn't.) One lady friend of Clint's was perfectly forthcoming about the star in phone calls and letters, but insisted on anonymity in print. 'I love Clint dearly,' she told me, 'but I also know him very well. And he's vindictive.'

Unlike the Nicholson book, I was confronted with numerous, reputable sources who believed in Clint's vindictiveness and wished to remain unidentified as sources. I am pledged to conceal their names. I was struck by how many people I encountered who really hated Clint and made no bones about it. 'People like Sondra Locke' – who felt that he had betrayed or mistreated them. In the case of the Nicholson book, I would be hard-pressed to name a single such source; almost everybody loved Jack, felt obliged to defend and protect and *explain* him against the violations of a biographer. Not so with Clint, who, contrary to his decent–loyal image, has left many broken friends and outright enemies in his wake. He has left many 'unidentified sources'.

'Hatred', in the case of some, is too strong a word. 'When someone defends Clint too much, I feel like attacking him,' explained one director (off the record) who has been associated with Malpaso in the past. 'When someone attacks him, I feel like defending him. In some ways I hate him, but I also love him. Can you understand that?'

I have tried to understand that. However, in the end I was left with a Clint who is in many ways the antithesis of his legend and certainly the antithesis of his authorized biography. Looking back over Clint's career, I find that his life is partly a triumph of publicity, and his beguilement of the press and critics an unavoidable part of the story.

'In the end,' a distinguished French film critic said to me, wary of what I told him about Clint, 'you are left with his films. If you love the films, nothing else matters.' I trust the findings of my work will shed light on those films and on his larger place in film history. In the end, there are (as there always are) missing puzzle pieces in Clint's life story, but I have tried my best to arrive at a certain truth about the man who remains, even to closest colleagues, friends and family, a stubborn enigma.

Acknowledgements

Sources and Letters: Joan Akeyson, William Alland, Fred Amsel, Chrystine Austin, David Bakish, Ben Brady, Ria Brown, Michael Butler, Ken Chernus, John Cleare, Duncan Cooper, David Dilworth, Louis Ferry, Alexander Golitzen, Charles F. Haas, Geneviève Hersent-Koevoets, Ed Hocking, Val Holley, Ross W. Hughes, Dudley Knowles, Craig J. Lane, Ron Lofman, Sylvia Loomis, Ron Lowell, Warren Murphy, Bob Quinn, Lyle Ritz, Wilton Schiller, Carole Siegel, Judy Stone, Marianna Thompkins, Robert E. Thompson, Lindy Warren, Frank Weldon.

Interviews: Buckley Angell, Julian Blaustein, Hilda Bohem, Paul Brinegar, Bridget Byrne, James Carabatsos, Henry Cauthen, Clancy Carlile, Lou Cutell, Peter Cuttita, Edward Dmytryk, Bob Donner, John Dunkel, James Fargo, Jamie Farr, Gene Fowler Jr., Fred Freiberger, James Frew, Snuff Garrett, Hal Gefsky, Race Gentry, Mel Goldberg, Charles Gray, Alberto Grimaldi, John Lee Hancock, Estelle Harmon, Elaine Hollingsworth (a.k.a. Sara Shane), Betty Jane Howarth, Kathleen Hughes, Sue Hutchinson, Elliott Kastner, Mickey Knox, Charlotte Hunter Kornder, Jeremy Joe Kronsberg, Elmore Leonard, Paul Lippman, Sondra Locke, Don Loomis, Arthur Lubin, Fritz Manes, Kal Mann, Ruth Marsh, Stacy McLaughlin, Rexford Metz, Herman Miller, Martin Milner, Edward Muhl, Al Naudain, Sally Rinehart Nero, Joel Oliansky, Fred Peck, Donald Pooley, Ted Post, Rex Reason, Dean Riesner, Megan Rose, Stanley Rubin, John Saxon, Karen Sharpe, Wayne A. Shirley, Stirling Silliphant, Floyd Simmons, Conard Schweitzer, Dennis Shryack, Michael Straight, Duccio Tessari, Bertrand Tavernier, Richard Tuggle, Peter Viertel, Luciano Vincenzoni, Chuck Waldo, Eli Wallach, Bobs Watson, David Worth, Glenn Wright, George D. Wyse.

Tonino Delli Colli was interviewed in Paris by Eve-Marine Dauvergne; a transcript of Frank Stanley's cinematography seminar in Maine was provided courtesy of Rob Draper.

Genealogical research: I owe a debt of thanks to Helen Imburgia and Ryta M. Kroeger; also Harley R. Jones Jr, Lenore and Richard Oyler and Meredith N. Runner.

Collegial advice and assistance: Steven Bach, Pat H. Broeske, Bill Cappello, Crystal Chow, Duane and Paula DeJoie, Bernadette Fay, C. David Heymann, Charles Higham, Richard Lamparski, Vincent LoBrutto, Glenn Lovell, Todd McCarthy, James Robert Parish, Gerald Peary, Nat Segaloff, Harry Wasserman, Michael Wilmington.

Especially: Ken Mate, for pro bono detective work.

Insights and critiques: David Thomson and John Baxter.

Hospitality and friendship: Marie-Dominique and John Baxter in Paris; Mary and Brian Troath in London; Regula Ehrlich and William B. Winburne in New York and New Jersey; and Ken Mate in Los Angeles.

Extra-curricular activity: Thank you to the magazine and newspaper editors who sponsored my occasional piece work, which helped to pay the bills: Richard Jameson of *Film Comment*; David Mehegan of the *Boston Globe*; Barry Gewen of the *New York Times*.

Screenings and films: I watched Ziv programmes at the State Historical Society in Madison, Wisconsin, and caught rare television episodes at the Museum of Broadcasting in Chicago. Boyd Magers provided *Rawhide* and other Western shows; and the good people at Video Visions, Milwaukee, tracked down all available films.

Clint's musical recordings: Ron Lofman.

Research and supplementary interviews: Eve-Marine Dauvergne in France and Italy; Kristi Jaas in Paris; Marcy Coon and Kitajima A. Yuji in Japan; Mary Troath in London; Hayley Buchbinder in Boston, where she looked into the Don Siegel papers at Boston University; Jeffrey P. Hearn in Washington, DC, where he investigated the campaign records of Richard Nixon and other Republican Party candidates, and also tracked down National Council for the Arts documents; and Jake Epstine in Los Angeles, where he performed numerous research tasks at the Academy of Motion Picture Arts and Sciences library and other area archives and local courthouses.

Archives and organizations: Ellis T. Hull, Town Historian, Allentown, New Jersey; Jim Hickson, Reference Librarian, Auburn-Placer County Library (California); Sayre Van Young, Reference Librarian, Berkeley Public Library (Ca.); Karen Mix, Archivist, Special Collections, Mugar Memorial Library, Boston University; Lona Flynn, Cicero Town Historian, Cicero, New York; Karen Miles, Elmwood Library, Elmwood, Illinois; Dr Stephen Payne, Defense Language Institute, Fort Ord Archives (Presidio of Monterey, Ca.); Mrs Eleanor Tandowsky, Reference Services, Fremont Main Library (Ca.); Larry L. Murphy, Director, Human Resources, Containerboard and Packaging, Georgia-Pacific Corporation; Janet Bombard and Arlene Hess, Harrison Memorial Library, Carmel-by-the-Sea (Ca.); Miles Kreuger, Institute of the American Musical, Los Angeles; Penny Wade, Chief, Budget, Finance and Personnel, Department of Parks, Planning and Resources, King County (Washington); Casey Lewis, Las Vegas-Clark County Library District, Interlibrary Loan Department; Ola May Earnest, President, Linn County Historical and Genealogical Society, Pleasanton, Kansas; Memorial Library, Marquette University (especially Interlibrary Loan and Reference), Milwaukee, Wisconsin; Milwaukee Public Library; Barbara Carver Smith, Monmouth County Historical Association, Freehold, New Jersey; Rosy Brewer, Reference Librarian, Monterey Bay Area Cooperative Library System (Ca.); Victor H. Bausch, Reference Librarian, Monterey Public Library (Ca.); Ron Magliozzi, Film Study Center, Museum of Modern Art, New York City; Steve Plamann, *National Enquirer*; Norman Rasmussen, *New Horizons*; Ruth A. Carr, Chief, US History, Local History and Genealogy, New York Public Library; William W. Sturm, Librarian, Oakland History Room, Oakland Public Library; Esther Din, Library Services, Oakland Public Schools; Dorothy Rogers, Librarian, Oakland Technical High School; Steven Lavois, *Oakland Tribune*; Mark E. Allnatt, Librarian, and Jean B. Palmer,

Local History/Special Collections, Onondaga County Public Library (NY); Babs Brower, Registrar, Piedmont High School; Don McConnell, *The Piedmonter*; Noreen Riffe, Special Collections Librarian, Pueblo Library District, Pueblo, Colorado; Cathy Brownell and Barbara Pozner, Reference Librarian, Renton Public Library (Wash.); Ruth Ellis and Teddy Lehner, Sacramento Room, Sacramento Public Library (Ca.); Claudia Davis and Alice LaCentra, St Helena Public Library (Ca.); Richard Geiger, *San Francisco Chronicle*; Judy Cantor, *San Francisco Examiner*; Matthew W. Buff, Reference Assistant, San Francisco Performing Arts Library and Museum; Virginia M. Crook, Head Reference Librarian, San Luis Obispo City County Library; William D. Rawson, Reference Coordinator, Seaside Branch Library (Ca.); Kathleen Harvey, Fine and Performing Arts Dept, Seattle Public Library; Judith Munns, Library Director, and Dr Bruce Weber, Skagway Museum, Skagway, Alaska; Joyce Siniscal, Reference Librarian, Sno-Isle Regional Library System (Oak Harbor, Washington); Dorothy Hendricks, Solano County Library (Ca.); Kay Bost, Curator, DeGolyer Library, Southern Methodist University Oral History Program; Mark Garber, *Springfield News* (Oregon); George Arents Research Library, Manuscript Collection, Syracuse University Library (NY); Robert Jones, Editor, *Valley Daily News* (Kent, Washington); Maradee Girt, Weyerhaeuser Corporation.

Especially: Ned Comstock, who goes the extra mile for me and other researchers, at the Cinema–Television Archives of the University of Southern California.

Unlike my previous books, this one had to rely on more than a dozen key sources who cannot be named. They gave me valuable interviews, but many went further, supplying crucial leads, documentation of facts and photographs for the book, and in several instances, reading and critiquing the manuscript. I thank them, above all, for taking the risks and believing in the value of an honest book about Clint.

My HarperCollins editor, Richard Johnson, never wavered in his civility and support. My agent, Gloria Loomis, always tried to keep me on the correct path. Finally, thanks to Tina, Clancy, Bowie and Sky, who for a number of years had to reside in Clint's world.

Notes

Books about Clint Eastwood that I read and referred to include *Clint Eastwood* by Stuart M. Kaminsky (Signet, New York, 1974), *Clint Eastwood: Movin' On* by Peter Douglas (Henry Regnery Books, Chicago, 1974), *Clint Eastwood: The Man Behind the Myth* by Patrick Agan (Coronet Books, London, 1975), *Clint Eastwood* by Noël Simsolo (Éditions de l'Étoile/Cahiers du Cinéma, Paris, (1990), *The Man With No Name* by Iain Johnstone (Plexus, London, 1981), *Clint Eastwood/Malpaso* by Fuensanta Plaza (Ex Libris, Carmel Valley, California, 1991), *Clint Eastwood* by Christopher Frayling (Virgin, London, 1992), *Clint Eastwood: Riding High* by Douglas Thompson (Contemporary Books Chicago, 1992), *Clint Eastwood: Hollywood's Loner* by Michael Munn (Robson Books, London, 1992), *Clint Eastwood: A Cultural Production* by Paul Smith UCL Press, London, 1993), *The Films of Clint Eastwood* by Boris Zmijewsky and Lee Pfeiffer (Citadel Press, New York, 1993), *Clint Eastwood* by Minty Clinch (Hodder & Stoughton, London, 1994), *Clint Eastwood: Filmmaker and Star* by Edward Gallafent (Continuum, New York, 1994), *Clint Eastwood* by Robert Tanitch (Studio Vista, London, 1995), *Clint Eastwood* by Neil Sinyard (Crescent Books, Greenwich, Connecticut, 1995), *Clint Eastwood: 'Quote Unquote'* by Bob McCabe (Crescent Books, Avenel, New Jersey, 1996), *Clint Eastwood* by Richard Schickel (Alfred A. Knopf, New York, 1996). I found something worthwhile in the least of them.

Budget and box-office statistics are notoriously unreliable. For this book, I used Malpaso's own figures, as cited in the special 27 March 1995 issue of *Variety* honouring Clint Eastwood, with updated or corrected information, where available. In all instances, only domestic grosses are indicated; international earnings are rarely reported. In order to explain the relationship between grosses and rentals, which is important in understanding box-office figures, I consulted *The 1990 Survival Guide to Film* by Richard Sean Lyon (LyonHeart, West Los Angeles, California, 1995).

Only principal non-interview quotations are noted below. Film reviews are not sourced. I consulted countless newspaper and magazine clippings, local history pamphlets, census records, court documents and transcripts, city directories, phone books, and other written materials. Wherever possible, I tried to trace Clint's quotes, recycled from previous books or articles, back to their origin. Some sources – the first *Playboy* interview, for example – are endlessly reused in articles and books; transcripted interviews are always particularly reassuring. When quoting Clint, my intention was usually to find a 'representative' quote – echoed in more than one source – rather than an 'unusual' one that might not reflect fairly his characteristic utterances.

CHAPTER ONE
The Tree of Clint

Barbara Carver-Smith of Lakewood, NJ, supplied deeds, documents and archival materials from New Jersey, including the 18th century land and tax transactions of Lewis Eastwood, drawing on resources from local history organizations, including the Monmouth County Historical Association Library of Freehold, NJ. Useful reading included *A History of Monmouth County* by Franklin Ellis (1885) and *The History of Allentown Presbyterian Church, Allentown, New Jersey, 1720–1970* by F. Dean Storms (1970).

Ruth A. Carr supplied many New York City and State references. Books consulted included *The Encylopedia of New York City* edited by Kenneth T. Jackson (Yale University Press, New Haven, Conn., 1995), *The Eastwood Family in America* (typescript by Sidney Kingman Eastwood, 1967), *New York City Cartmen* by Graham Russell Hodges (New York University Press, New York, 1986), *The New York Police, Colonial Times to 1901* by James F. Richardson (Oxford University Press, New York, 1970), *New York: An American City, 1783–1803. A Study of Urban Life* by Sidney I. Pomerantz (Columbia University Press, New York, 1938) and *Minutes of the Common Council of the City of New York, 1784–1831, Volume XII, September 3, 1821 to March 31, 1823* (City of New York, 1917).

Also consulted were numerous newspaper clippings supplied by the Onondaga County Public Library, Local History/Special Collections Department, *Onondaga's Centennial: Gleanings of a Century, Vol. II* edited by Dwight H. Bruce (Boston History Company, Boston, 1896) and *History of Onondaga County, New York* by Professor W. W. Clayton (D. Mason and Co., Syracuse, NY, 1878). Asa Eastwood's frontier journals are cited from an undated Onondaga County newspaper article, circa September 1908, and from a perusal of the journals themselves, as furnished by Syracuse University. Also helpful was 'Scenes of Yesteryear' by Lona Flynn from the 9 March 1988 *Cicero Star-News*.

Asa B. Eastwood's obituaries appear in the *Placer Herald*, 4 April 1908, and the *Placer County Republican*, 11 April 1908. Also consulted was 'Placer County' by J. B. Hobson in the *Report of the State Mineralogist* (California, 1890).

The Kelloggs, Franklins and Bartholomews are traced in *A Genealogical Dictionary of the First Settlers of New England, Showing Three Generations of Those Who Came Before May, 1692, On the Basis of Farmers' Register* by James Savage (Genealogical Publishing Company, Baltimore, 1969), *The Abridged Compendium of American Genealogy* by Frederick Adams Virkus (F. A. Virkus & Co., Chicago, 1925–42), *The Kelloggs in the Old World and New* by Timothy Hopkins (Sunset Press and Photo Engraving Co., San Franciso, California, 1903), and *Record of the Bartholomew Family: Historical, Genealogical and Biographical* by G. W. Bartholomew Jr. (Austin, Texas, 1885).

The family's migration to the Midwest is documented in *The Historical Encyclopedia of Illinois* edited by Newton Bateman and Paul Selby (Munsell Publishing Co., Chicago, 1902–1916), and especially in 'J. B. Bartholomew' by David McCulluch in *Vol. II, The History of Peoria County, Illinois* by R. G. Ingersoll (Johnson and Co., Chicago, 1880), 'Elmwood, 1831–1976' by the Elmwood Historical Society, and *The Girlhood Story of Jennie Bartholomew*, privately published by Harley R. Jones Jr. (1986).

To chronicle the adventures of the Jayhawkers, I consulted 'Goodbye, Death Valley! The 1849 Jayhawker Escape' by L. Burr Belden (Death Valley '49ers, Inc.). The story of 'Bartholomew's Bear' comes from an undated article by Charles E. Reed that appeared in *Sports Afield*, supplied to the author by Meredith Runner.

The Kansas–Colorado period of the family history is chronicled in *History of the State of Kansas* (A. T. Andreas, Chicago, 1883), *History of Kansas* by William E. Connelley (American Historical Society, Chicago/New York, 1978), *Linn County, Kansas: A History* by William Ansel Mitchell (Kansas City, Mo., 1928) and 'Federated Church Centennial of Mound City, Kansas' (MSLS publication, 1966).

Eastwood forebears are notably mentioned in the 20 February 1881, 18 April 1884, 9 May 1884, 13 June 1884, 27 February 1885, 3 April 1885, 16 October 1885, 6 November 1885, 12 March 1887 and 4 May 1888 editions of the *Mound City Progress* (Kansas). Also pertinent: the *Linn County Republic* 18 April 1910.

Meredith Runner graciously shared his family research, including his own 'Pioneers During the Last Half of the 19th Century' essay. Relevant citations from 1889–1908 editions of the *Skagway Daily Alaskan* were forwarded by Bruce Weber.

Lenore Oyler shared her family research on the Boyles and McLanahans and volunteered a facsimile copy of the frontier journal of Henry Green Boyle.

For background on Piedmont I read *Queen of the Hills: The Story of Piedmont, A California City* by Evelyn Craig Pattiani (Fresno: The Academy Libary Guild, 1953).

Details of Clint's birth are from Ruth Eastwood's interview in 'My Daughter, My Son' in *Family Circle*, 18 May 1982, and 'How Clint Makes My Day' by Ruth Eastwood as told to Leon Wagener in the Sunday *News of the World* magazine, 11 July 1993.

CHAPTER TWO
'The Shitty Years'

Clint discusses his penchant for using the word 'asshole' in 'A Fistful of Critics' by Robert Ward in *Crawdaddy*, April 1978. 'In a mix of Oakies' is from 'All the Pirates and People' by Norman Mailer in *Parade* magazine, 23 October 1983. 'We knew the house very well . . .' is from Richard Schickel, *Clint Eastwood*. 'Those were shitty years . . .' is from 'Clint's Not Cute When He's Angry' by Larry Cole in the *Village Voice*, 24 May 1976. 'We weren't itinerant . . .' is from 'Clint Eastwood: The *Rolling Stone* Interview' by Tim Cahill in *Rolling Stone*, 4 July 1985. 'Occasionally times were so hard . . .' and 'Grandma had more to do . . .' are from *News of the World* magazine, 11 July 1993. 'Is it [religion] important to you . . . ?' is from 'Clint Eastwood . . . Talking With David Frost', a transcript of the television interview supplied by the David Paradine Group of Companies. 'Clint enjoyed his own company . . .' is from *News of the World* magazine, 11 July 1993. 'Since I was almost always the new boy . . .' is from 'Charismatic Clint' by Ric Gentry in *McCall's*, June 1987. 'Disastrous' and 'We muffed a lot . . .' is from 'Playboy Interview: Clint Eastwood' by Arthur Knight in *Playboy*, February 1974. Clint mistakes Cukor for Mamoulian in 'Clint Eastwood: "Let's Go to Lunch and BS for Awhile"' by Chris Hodenfield in *Look*, July 1979. 'His eyes reflecting the mesmerization . . .' is from 'Eastwood: The Man Behind the Image' by John L. Wasserman in the *San Francisco Chronicle*, 28 May 1975. 'I was such a backward kid . . .' is from *Rolling Stone*, 4 July 1985. 'I didn't really get involved in team sports . . .' is from *Rolling Stone*, 4 July 1985. 'Better cars than my parents . . .' is from Richard Schickel, *Clint Eastwood*. 'Clint not only wrote an obscene suggestion . . .' is from an untitled item from the *Oakland Tribune*, 15 April 1986. Perhaps the item, found in the newspaper's archives, meant Clint *burned* someone in effigy, but no correction was issued.

'Fast cars and easy women' is from Richard Schickel, *Clint Eastwood*. 'I rebuilt one plane engine' is from *Crawdaddy*, April 1978. 'He cites Mr Hawks . . .' is from 'Make His Day? Museum Does That for Eastwood' by Janet Maslin in the *New York Times*, 27 October 1993. 'Pretty much on my own . . .' is from *Crawdaddy*, April 1978. 'Unlike most country bands . . .' is from *Rolling Stone*, 4 July 1985. 'Up to speed . . .' is from Richard Schickel, *Clint Eastwood*. 'It's a little like a platoon . . .' is from 'Down a New Road With a Family Man' by Paul A. Witteman in *People*, 10 January 1983. 'That particular year . . .' is from *No Minor Chords: My Days in Hollywood* by André Previn (Doubleday, New York, 1991). 'He [Clint] used to be a bartender . . .' is from 'Cherokee to Madison County' by David Meeker and M. Salmi in *Sight and Sound*, September 1995. 'I had had a similar experience . . .' is from *US*, 26 January 1987. 'Someone stalking me . . .' is from a profile of Clint by Ginny Dougary in *The Times* (London) 28 March 1998. 'Like four-star movie reviews' is from *Playboy*, February 1974. 'Everything seemed to go wrong . . .' is from 'Ord Swimming Instructor Paddles Two Miles On Last Lap Of Furlough' in the 12 October 1951 edition of the *Fort Ord Panorama*.

Also consulted for background and details about Clint's airplane crash and swim ashore were 'Torpedo Bomber Down in Sea Near SF, Pilot, Hitch-Hiking Soldier Swim Ashore' in the *San Francisco Examiner*, 1 October 1951; 'Swimming Teacher Paddled 2 Miles After Plane Crash' in the *San Francisco Examiner*, 2 October, 1951; 'Bomber Ditched, 2 Swim Ashore' in the *Oakland Tribune*, 1 October 1951; 'Plane Crash Blamed on Radio, Clouds' in the *San Francisco Chronicle*, 2 October 1951; and 'Pilot, Rider Swim 2 Miles After Crash' in the *Salinas Californian*, 1 October 1951.

Earl Leaf wrote about Clint and Seattle in 'The Way We Were', an (undated) 1972 clipping from *Rona Barrett's Hollywood*, on file in the Constance McCormick Collection of the Cinema–Television Archives at the University of Southern California. Apart from my own interview with Arthur Lubin, I consulted the Southern Methodist University Oral History of Lubin by Ronald L. Davis from 1985, and the Directors Guild of America Oral History of Lubin by James Desmarais on deposit at the Margaret Herrick Library of the Academy of Motion Picture Arts and Sciences. 'We hit it off right away . . .' is from Richard Schickel, *Clint Eastwood*. 'My beloved lifeguarding' is from *Reagan's America* by Garry Wills (Doubleday, New York, 1987). 'There are stories . . .' is from 'It WAS Clint, and He Was Gorgeous' by Mary Swift in the *Valley Daily News* (Kent, Washington), 2 April 1993. 'To please a girl he dug . . .' is from 'The Way We Were', *Rona Barrett's Hollywood*.

Clint's engagement was announced in the *San Francisco Chronicle*, 14 November 1953, and the *San Francisco Examiner*, 6 December 1953.

CHAPTER THREE
Clint's Luck

All Universal Talent School citations are from studio records and clippings in the archives of the Cinema–Television Library at the University of Southern California.

I also consulted the following articles: 'Hollywood Holiday' in *Movie Life*, November 1951; 'Train for Movies at Home' by Sophie Rosenstein in *Movie Land*, February 1952; 'More Than Talent' by Edwin Miller and Sara Salzer in *Seventeen*, March 1953, 'Louella Parsons' Good News' in *Modern Screen*, March 1954; 'Puttin' on an Act' in *Photoplay*, March 1954; 'Inside UI' in *Movie Life*, March 1954; 'Their Homework is Making Love' in *Prevue*, June, 1954; 'New Faces Coming Up' in *Pageant*, c. May 1954, 'Learning to be Movie Stars' in *The American Weekly* of the *San Francisco Examiner*, 17 October 1954; 'Hollywood's 3Rs' by Richard G. Hubler in *Redbook*, January 1955; 'Fundamentals Stressed at New School of Motion Picture Drama in Hollywood' in *Kansas City Times*, 14 October 1955; 'Stardom's Students' in the *New York World-Telegram*, 25 November 1955; 'Talent School Develops Film Stars of Tomorrow' in *Los Angeles Herald & Express*, 20 February 1956; 'Hollywood Talent School' in *The Queen* (UK), 7 March 1956; and UI's Talent School Comes to You . . .' in *True Magazine* (UK), June 1954.

Also useful for background on Clint's contract years at Universal: *Playing the Field: My Story* by Mamie Van Doren with Art Aveilhe (Putnam's, New York, 1987), *David Janssen: My Fugitive* by Ellie Janssen (Lifetime Books, Hollywood, Fla., 1994) and *Jimmy Durante: His Show Business Career* by David Bakish (McFarland, Jefferson, North Carolina, 1995).

Apart from my own interview with John Saxon, I also drew on the Southern Methodist University Oral History by Ronald L. Davis from 1985. 'One of the inventories of our trade . . .' is from the *Kansas City Times*, 14 October 1955. All dialogue from Clint's 1950s films is quoted from Christopher Frayling, *Clint Eastwood*. 'The first year of marriage was terrible . . .' is from *Photoplay*, 1963, as cited in *Clint Eastwood: Hollywood's Loner*. 'One day I got fired . . .' is from 'Who Can Stand 32,580 seconds of Clint Eastwood? Just About Everybody' by Judy Fayard in *Life*, 23 July 1971.

Apart from my own interview with Jamie Farr, I read his book, *Just Farr Fun* (Eubanks/Donizetti Inc., Clearwater, Florida, 1994) for background on Jack Kosslyn and the Mercury Stage group. 'Really, it [acting study] was sort of a pseudointellectual . . .' is from Richard Schickel, *Clint Eastwood*. Clint is 'Cliff Eastwood' in 'Actress On a Budget' from *TV Guide*, 6–12 July 1957. 'Really depressed' is from *Crawdaddy*, April 1978. 'It was a difficult period . . .'

is from 'Clint Eastwood: Hollywood's Most Private Star' by Patricia Bosworth in *Cosmopolitan*, January 1997. 'I auditioned for it; hundreds of guys did . . .' is from 'Clint Eastwood: Long-overdue Respect Makes His Year' by Gene Siskel in the *Chicago Tribune*, 9 June 1985. 'It was *sooo* bad . . .' and 'Coffee or tea or something . . .' are from *Crawdaddy*, April 1978.

There are many versions of Clint getting cast in *Rawhide*. I have relied principally upon Arthur Lubin's, the February 1974 *Playboy* and April 1978 *Crawdaddy*. In addition, I consulted Ronald L. Davis's 1980 interview with Charles Marquis Warren from the Southern Methodist University Oral History Project. The original *Rawhide* press releases are on file among Hal Humphrey's papers in the USC archives.

'I thought, "Oh, my God" . . .' is from *Crawdaddy* April, 1978. 'So Mag and I did a little champagne trick . . .' is from *Playboy*, February 1974.

CHAPTER FOUR
The Rowdy Years

'A miserable human being' is from the Southern Methodist University Oral History interview with Charles Marquis Warren. 'Fleming was stiff . . .' is from *Storytellers to the Nation* by Tom Stempel (Continuum, New York, 1992).

Apart from my own interviews with *Rawhide* personnel, I consulted a number of *TV Guide* articles, including 'Clint Eastwood of *Rawhide* Advises Diet, Rest, Exercise' from 15–21 August 1959; 'This Cowboy Feels He's Got It Made' from the 4–10 February 1961 issue; 'Dynamite on Horseback' by Dwight Whitney from 1–7 December 1962; and 'How to Revive a Dead Horse' by Arnold Hano from the 2–8 October 1965 issue. 'You have to keep selling yourself . . .' is cited from a 1959 interview with Clint in a syndicated interview by Gene Siskel, from January 1973. 'It wasn't one of those promotional things . . .' is from 'A Mellow Eastwood Keeps His Edge' by Charles Champlin in the *Los Angeles Times*, 30 June 1984. 'With *Rawhide*, everything changed . . .' is from Douglas Thompson, *Clint Eastwood: Riding High*. 'Lazy' and 'He always cost you a morning . . .' is from *The Box: An Oral History of Television, 1920–1961* by Jeff Kisseloff (Viking, New York, 1995).

Apart from my own interview with Ted Post, I consulted the published interview with Post in *The Live Television Generation of Hollywood Film Directors: Interviews With Seven Directors* by Gorham Kindem (McFarland & Co., Jefferson, North Carolina, 1994).

For information about Clint's early recording career, I am indebted to Ron

Lofman and his book *Goldmine's Celebrity Vocals* (Krause Publications, Iola, Wisconsin, 1994).

'A juvenile delinquent or better yet . . .' is from 'Piedmont's Clint Eastwood Wins Success on TV Cattle Range' by James Bacon in the *Oakland Tribune*, 19 November 1961.

All Japanese articles were translated by Kitajima A. Yuji.

'To tell you the truth . . .' is from *Clint Eastwood: Hollywood's Loner*. 'Rap sessions, beer busts . . .' and 'Nobody ever made me laugh . . .' are from 'The Way We Were', *Rona Barrett's Hollywood*. 'Amiable young giant' is from *TV Guide*, 4–10 February 1961. 'Walking volcano', 'Cloak of boyish vulnerability . . .' and 'I like women . . .' are from *TV Guide*, 1–7 December, 1962. 'I was never very realistic . . .' is from 'Life Without Clint' by Terri Lee Robbe in *US* magazine, 16 February 1982. 'Calm on the outside . . .' is from Hank Grant's 'On the Air' column in the *Hollywood Reporter*, 13 July 1961. 'When the show was good . . .' is from *TV Guide*, 2–8 October 1965.

All Italian and French publications relating to Sergio Leone and the 'spaghetti Westerns' were translated by Eve-Marine Dauvergne. Especially important were *Directed by Sergio Leone* by Gianni Di Claudio (Libreria Universitaria Editrice, 1990), *Conversations avec Sergio Leone* by Noël Simsolo (Editions Stock, Paris, 1987) and 'Sergio Leone' by Francesco Mininni in *Il Castoro Cinema* (special issue, January–February 1989). Leone is quoted from these sources, unless otherwise noted.

Among the English-language texts discussing Leone, *Once Upon A Time: The Films of Sergio Leone* by Robert C. Cumbow (The Scarecrow Press, Metuchen, New Jersey, 1987) was recommended by Luciano Vincenzoni as the most accurate and insightful.

'What fascinated me about Clint . . .' is from Christopher Frayling, *Clint Eastwood*. 'Atrocious' and 'intelligently laid out' are from Patrick Agan, Clint Eastwood. 'I was tired of playing the nice . . .' is from *Playboy*, February 1974. 'Clint says I'm good at spotting . . .' is from *Clint Eastwood: Hollywood's Loner*. 'He arrived, dressed with exactly . . .' is from Noël Simsolo, *Conversations Avec Sergio Leone*. 'While I organized chariot races . . .' is from Christopher Frayling, *Clint Eastwood*. 'The truth is that I needed . . .' is from 'Sergio Leone' by Francesco Mininni in *Il Castoro Cinema* (special issue, January–February 1989). 'Endless pages of dialogue' and 'I wanted to play it with an economy . . .' are from *McCall's*, June 1987. 'As soon as I got into his flat . . .' is Leone from Noël Simsolo's *Conversations Avec Sergio Leone*. 'When we were working together . . .' is from Christopher Frayling's *Clint Eastwood*. 'Only the big arc lamps standing there . . .' and 'Maybe I hurt too easily inside . . .' are from Douglas Thompson, *Clint Eastwood: Riding High*.

CHAPTER FIVE

The Greening of Clint

'I'd like to take an Arriflex . . .' is from 'The Real Clint Eastwood' by Patrick McGilligan in the *Boston Globe*, 9 May 1976. The complete text of this interview was published as 'Clint Eastwood' in *Focus on Film*, Summer–Autumn, 1976.

'I wanted to direct, way back when . . .' and 'Some trailers and various . . .' are from Bob McCabe's *Clint Eastwood: Quote Unquote*. 'The only advantage was that . . .' is from Gianni Di Claudio, *Directed by Sergio Leone*. 'Not only was there a movie prejudice . . .' is from *Playboy*, February 1974. 'The biggest male star in Italy . . .' and 'But this time I was mobbed . . .' are from 'In Italy, Clint Goes Over Big' by Doris Klein, a syndicated article from 15 August 1965. 'Mired so deeply . . .', 'They were paying me . . .', 'Why should I be pleased?', 'Utter shock' and 'Mediocre' are from *TV Guide*, 2–8 October 1965. 'CBS just said go to work . . .' is from 'If *Rawhide* Fails, He's Big in Europe' by Hal Humphrey in the *Los Angeles Times*, 16 September 1965. 'An ad budget several times more . . .' is from '*Hang 'Em High* Is Top Eastwood Western to Land in US Market' by Robert B. Frederick in *Variety*, 28 August 1968. 'The first is a mask of wax . . .' is from Christopher Frayling, *Clint Eastwood*. 'Unique formula for getting rich' is from 'Clint Eastwood Formula for Jumping His Take' in the *Hollywood Reporter*, 16 June 1969. 'If the hero talks too much . . .' is from 'Clint Eastwood Making It Big in Year of Reckoning' by Joyce Haber in the *Los Angeles Times*, 7 June 1970. 'The biggest UA opening day . . .' is from *Variety*, 28 August 1968.

All Don Siegel quotes, unless otherwise noted, are from *Don Siegel, Director* by Stuart M. Kaminsky (Curtis Books, New York, 1974) and the director's autobiography, *A Siegel Film* by Don Siegel (Faber & Faber, London, 1993). Extremely useful to my portrait of Siegel's collaborations with Clint were production files, script drafts, records and correspondence in the Special Collections department of Mugar Memorial Library at Boston University. Also consulted was Stuart M. Kaminsky's *Clint Eastwood* which amply quotes Siegel, producer Jennings Lang and writer Dean Riesner. Background on Riesner came from my interview with him and his profile in *The Making of Rich Man, Poor Man* by Richard Anobile (Berkeley, New York, 1976).

All material about Kyle Eastwood's birth is from 'How They Had a Baby After 14 Childless Years' by Favius Friedman in *Modern Screen*, February 1969. 'Terrible . . .', 'All exposition and complications . . .' and 'We sat down one day in Austria . . .' are from 'Clint Eastwood on Clint Eastwood' by Dick Lochte in the *Los Angeles Free Press*, 20 April 1973.

Helpful background on *Paint Your Wagon* came from *Alan Jay Lerner* by

Edward Jablonski (Henry Holt, New York, 1996). Jean Seberg's ill-fated affair with Clint is reported in depth in *Played Out: The Jean Seberg Story* by David Richards (Random House, New York, 1981). 'I want Clint to get better acquainted . . .' is from *Modern Screen*, February 1969.

CHAPTER SIX
Blue-Collar Clint

'Flown in to Cocoyoc . . .' and the anecdote about a moth invading the set of *Two Mules for Sister Sara* are from *Clint Eastwood: Hollywood's Loner*. 'I guess I have too much . . .' is from *Playboy*, February 1974. 'I can't stand long locations . . .' is from 'Clint Eastwood: *Play Misty for Me*' in *Action*, March– April, 1973. 'Our styles were inconsistent . . .' is from the *Los Angeles Free Press*, 20 April 1973. 'Because he doesn't feel . . .' is from 'He's Clint Eastwood!' by Arthur Knight in *Film International*, June 1975.

Albert Maltz is quoted on the subject of *The Beguiled* in Don Siegel's memoir. Irene Kamp's papers, on file at the Margaret Herrick Library of the Academy of Motion Picture Arts and Sciences, also shed light on the evolution of the script.

'I thought Geraldine Page was out of my league . . .' is from 'No Tumbleweed Ties for Clint' by Rex Reed in the *Los Angeles Times*, 4 April 1971. 'Maybe a lot of people just don't . . .' is from Stuart M. Kaminsky, *Clint Eastwood*. 'Emasculated' is from *Playboy*, February 1974. 'To judge his own performance . . .' is from an untitled article by 'Mack' in *Variety*, 28 October 1975, found in the Margaret Herrick Library files. 'Nervous and not very talkative . . .' is from 'Some Early and Recent Eastwood' by Dennis Hunt in the *San Francisco Chronicle*, 18 October 1971. 'Misinterpretation of commitment' is from *Action*, March–April 1973. 'I've got a six-pack of beer . . .' is from *Playboy*, February 1974. 'Zero presumption, zero arrogance . . .' is from *Clint Eastwood/ Malpaso*.

For background on Steve Ross, I relied upon *Master of the Game: Steve Ross and the Creation of Time Warner* by Connie Bruck (Simon & Schuster, New York, 1994). 'A sadness about him . . .' is from Richard Schickel, *Clint Eastwood*. 'All of Harry's partners looked up to him . . .' is from *Clint Eastwood/Malpaso*. 'Well, I don't have any political affiliations . . .' is from Richard Schickel, *Clint Eastwood*. 'Vengeance' and 'a great feeling of impotence and guilt' is from the *Village Voice*, 24 May 1976. 'Jesus, some people are so politically oriented . . .' is from the *Los Angeles Free Press*, 26 April 1973. 'People even said I was a racist . . .' is from the *Village Voice*, 24 May 1976. 'A rebel lying deep . . .' is from 'Rebel in My Soul' by Gerald Lubenow in *Newsweek*, 22 July 1985.

Key newspaper and magazine articles tracing the relationship between Clint, Richard Nixon and the Republican Party include: 'Hollywood' by Peter Bogdanovich in *Esquire*, December 1972; 'Hollywood in San Clemente As Nixon Hosts Film Stars' by Robert B. Semple Jr in the *New York Times*, fall, 1972 (syndicated version from the Margaret Herrick Library files); 'Celebrities Find There's No Biz Like Election Biz' by Gregg Kilday in the *Los Angeles Times*, 29 October 1972; and 'The Night Those Stars Came Out' by Hugh Sidey in 'The Presidency' column from *Life*, 8 September 1972.

In addition, I examined numerous documents held by the Federal Election Commission, and Celebrities for the President records and memoranda from the Nixon Presidential Material Project of the National Archives at College Park, Maryland.

Clint notes that he was 'against' the war in Vietnam in 'The Man Behind the Eastwood Mystique' by Ian Markham-Smith in *US*, 25 March 1985. 'But I'm not among the people who say . . .' is from *Clint Eastwood: Hollywood's Loner*. 'Tough man' needed for 'where the world is going . . .' is from 'Eastwood's Star: Risen' by Tom Shales in the *Washington Post*, 24 April 1973.

All National Council for the Arts citations are from the official minutes of meetings.

'Westerns – a period gone by . . .' is from *Clint Eastwood: Hollywood's Loner*. Glenn Lovell graciously provided a transcribed portion of his unpublished interview with director John Sturges, relating to Clint and the making of *Joe Kidd*. 'Without sounding exactly like Morricone' is from *Clint Eastwood/Malpaso*. 'It surprises me . . .' is from 'Good Ole Burt; Cool-Eyed Clint' by Richard Schickel in *Time*, 9 January 1978. 'Not quite willing to believe her good luck . . .' is from 'Maggie's Back on the Courts' from the *Monterey Herald*, 1 July 1972. 'Why They Call Clint Eastwood the Worst Husband in Hollywood' is the headline of the July, 1969 *Modern Screen* article. 'Only if I was sure I could convince people . . .' is from 'Man More in Demand Than Burton' by Stanley Eichelbaum from the *San Francisco Chronicle*, 16 February 1969. 'I understood the [Frank Harmon] character . . .' and 'Rejuvenation of a cynic' are from 'Clint Eastwood: The Interview' by Henry Sheehan in the *Hollywood Reporter*, 11 March 1993.

CHAPTER SEVEN
Clint's Weather

On the subject of *Magnum Force*, I also consulted Ted Post's published remarks in *Them Ordinary Mitchum Boys* by John Mitchum (Creatures at Large Press, Pacifica, California, 1989).

My portrait of Leonard Hirshan is informed by *The Agency: William Morris and the Hidden History of Show Business* by Frank Rose (HarperCollins, New York, 1995).

For my profile of Michael Cimino, I have relied upon published information from *Who's Who in America*, 1981's *Current Biography* and 'Michael Cimino's Battle to Make a Great Movie' by Jean Valley from *Esquire*, 2 January 1979. Steven Bach in his book *Final Cut: Dreams and Disaster in the Making of Heaven's Gate* (Morrow, New York, 1985) also writes about United Artists, *Thunderbolt and Lightfoot*, and Clint.

David Brown wrote about Clint and *The Eiger Sanction* in his book *Let Me Entertain You* (Morrow, New York, 1990). Apart from correspondence and interviews with people who shared the Eiger experience with Clint, I drew on 'The Eiger Sanction' by Mike Hoover in *American Cinematographer*, August 1975, and 'Clint Eastwood Faces the Ultimate Challenge, The White Spider of the Eiger' by Eddie Kafafian in *Stars in Sports*. December 1974. I am particularly indebted to Rob Draper of Camden, Maine for providing a transcript of Frank Stanley's cinematography seminar held at the Maine Photographic Workshop in June of 1980. 'Without question the most hazardous film . . .' is from James Bacon's column 'Clint's Cliff Hanger' in the *Los Angeles Herald-Examiner*, 22 October 1974. 'What's the most exciting part? . . .' is from 'Action Hero Clint Eastwood: "I'm Just Doing What I Dreamed of as a Kid" ' by Peter J. Oppenheimer in *Family Weekly*, 29 December 1974.

Trevanian's footnote about the film of *The Eiger Sanction* appears in *Shibumi* (Ballantine, New York, 1979). Making mention of exotic assassination tactics, Trevanian notes 'these will never be described in detail. In an early book, the author portrayed a dangerous ascent of a mountain. In the process of converting this novel into a vapid film, a fine young climber was killed.'

'The guy had a story sense . . .' is from 'Any Which Way He Can' by Peter Biskind in *Première*, April 1993. 'Wells reportedly wrote checks . . .' is from 'Wells Recalled As Exec, Sportsman' by Dan Cox in *Variety*, 5 April 1994.

Apart from interviews with cast and crew of *The Outlaw Josey Wales*. I quoted Phil Kaufman from 'Are We Pods . . . Yet?' by Ralph Appelbaum in *Films and Filming*, April 1979.

Apart from my own extensive interviews with Sondra Locke, I consulted her book *The Good, the Bad & the Very Ugly* (William Morrow, New York, 1997). In addition, I drew on, and sometimes quoted, many useful and illuminating articles, including: 'A Searching Kind of Person' by Edwin Miller in *Seventeen*, April 1968; 'Sondra Locke – They Call Her "The Beautiful Flake" ' by Peter J. Oppenheimer in *Family Weekly*, 24 November 1968; 'An Eastwood Co-star Finally Is Visible' by Vernon Scott, a December 1977 UPI dispatch; 'Sondra Locke Starring With And Directed by Clint Eastwood' by Catherine Guiness in *Interview,* January 1978; 'Sondra Locke's Stock Rises in Surviving Eastwood's Mayhem and Hollywood's Whispers' by Lois Armstrong in *People*, 13 February 1978; 'Southern Belle Sondra Locke is Ready to Stand on Her Own' by Rana Arons in *US*, 19 August 1980; 'Locke Turns to *Ratboy* to Escape Clint's Maze' by Roderick Mann in the *Los Angeles Times*, 23 March 1986; 'Locke Exercises Control Over *Ratboy*. Her Career' by Nancy Mills in the *Los Angeles Times*, 19 August 1987; 'In the Matter of Locke Vs. Eastwood' by Claudia Puig in the *Los Angeles Times*, 8 May 1989; 'Sondra Locke Says Life With Eastwood Was a Tough Battle' by Claudia Puig in the *Los Angeles Times*, 10 May 1989; 'Suing Clint Eastwood, Sondra Locke Strikes With Magnum Force' by Joanne Kaufman, Elizabeth McNeil and Jacqueline Savaiano in *People*, 15 May 1989; 'Judge to Hear Eastwood Dispute Today' by Claudia Puig in the *Los Angeles Times*, 31 May 1989; and 'The Best Little Girl in Town' by Rachel Abramowitz in *Première*, July 1995.

'I like to swing with what's happening . . .' is from *US*, 26 January 1987. 'Never answered' is from 'Hollywood's Quiet Conservative' by John Meroney in *The American Enterprise*, January–February 1998. 'I hate the thought of spending weeks . . .' is from Herb Caen's column in the *San Francisco Chronicle*, 26 July 1976.

Apart from Stirling Silliphant answering my questions by fax from Thailand, I also consulted Nat Segaloff's interview with him in *Backstory 3: Interviews With Screenwriters of the 1960s* edited by Patrick McGilligan (University of California Press, Berkeley, 1997).

'Eastwood touch and magic' is from 'Silliphant *Harry* Work Fine: Daley' in the *Hollywood Reporter*, 4 March 1976. 'Seriously involved . . .', 'Otherwise, you're putting . . .' and 'I haven't added them up . . .' are from Marilyn Beck's 'No Love on the Force' column in the *San Francisco Examiner*, 20 December 1978. 'We live in a violent society . . .' is from 'Clint Eastwood: Macho Hero to Middle America' by Lee Grant in the *Los Angeles Times*, 30 December 1976.

CHAPTER EIGHT
The Sondra Years

'Clint looking for someone special . . .' is from an untitled item in the Margaret Herrick Library files from the *Los Angeles Herald-Examiner*, 26 January 1977. 'Happy couple' is from *Time*, 9 January 1978. 'More than just co-stars . . .' is from *People*, 13 February 1978. 'Mizz Beck, or whatever you call her . . .' is from one of Herb Caen's 'It Takes All Kinds' columns in February 1978, found in *San Francisco Chronicle* files. 'Manager, attorney, agent and producer . . .' is from 'Bare-Knuckle Culture Okays "Comedy" – Providing It's Clint Eastwood's?' by Dale Pollock in *Variety*, 24 January 1979. 'As a cynical attempt to muscle . . .' is from *Look*, July 1979. 'Basically, I can't interview actors . . .' is from 'Clint Eastwood: Tough Talk With a Movie Legend About Love, Politics and Heartbreak Ridge' by Ric Gentry in *US*, 26 January 1987. 'Sag in the dog days . . .' and 'Clint Eastwood's most successful picture . . .' are from *Variety*, 24 January 1979.

CHAPTER NINE
The Feminist Clint

'Clint would get like a little boy . . .' is from 'In Like Clint' by Josh Young in *George*, March 1997. Material about Clint's nutritional regimen is cited from *Life Extensions: A Practical Scientific Approach* by Durk Pearson and Sandy Shaw (Warner Books, New York, 1982). 'Opening was not up to par . . .' is from '*Moses* Looks to Be Strongest of 5 Weekend Openings' in *Variety*, 17 June 1980. 'People like to see Clint Eastwood . . .' is from 'Theater Owners Blame Box Office Blues This Summer on Lower Quality of Movies' by Earl C. Gottschalk Jr in the *Wall Street Journal*, 8 July 1980. 'Sale of the film to television networks . . .' is from the *Wall Street Journal*, 8 July 1980. 'A theme common in Eastwood's films . . .' is from 'Eastwood Stays Loose With *Billy*' by Gabe Essoe in the *Los Angeles Times*, 8 June 1980. 'Macho is probably one of the most misused words . . .' is from 'Clint Eastwood: A Sexy Legend at Fifty' by John Love in *Cosmopolitan*, July 1980.

CHAPTER TEN
The Teflon Clint

'With Fritz Manes supervising . . .' is from *George*, March 1997. Clint's involvement with Bo Gritz is pieced together from several accounts, including 'The POWs: starring Bo Gritz, Dirty Harry and Ronald Reagan', an Associated Press dispatch of 25 February 1983; 'Eastwood Told Reagan of Planned POW Raid' by Richard E. Meyer and Mark Gladstone from the *Los Angeles Times*, 25 February 1983; and 'A Tale of True Gritz' from *Newsweek*, 14 February 1983.

'He's not that great a singer . . .' is from *Rolling Stone*, 4 July 1985. 'To promote the film's music . . .' is from 'Triple Promotion Set for *Honkytonk Man* S'track' by Kip Kirby in *Billboard*, 13 November 1982. 'As some shirtless scenes will attest . . .' and 'More reflective Eastwood' are from *People*, 10 January 1983. 'Visibly distressed' is from 'Life Without Clint' by Terri Lee Robbe in *US*, 16 February, 1982. 'Remarkable' and 'Cutesy, airhead, bimbo starlets . . .' is from 'Let's Hear It for Eastwood's "Strong" Women' by Tom Stempel in the *Los Angeles Times*, 11 March 1984. 'It's very simple . . .' is from an undated profile of Clint by Roger Ebert in the *Chicago Sun-Times*, in Margaret Herrick Library files.

Rosemary Rogers wrote about 'Sweet Savage Clint' in the *Ladies Home Journal.* June 1982.

CHAPTER ELEVEN
Mid-Life Clint

Footnote: The nationwide film critics' survey mentioned in text was conducted by Patrick McGilligan and Mark Rowland, first in 1981 for the *Los Angeles Times*, and then annually until 1994, and published in the *Washington Post*, *Chicago Tribune, San Francisco Chronicle, Philadelphia Inquirer* and *American Film* magazine.

'Today we live in a welfare-oriented . . .' is from an item in *People*, 9 September 1976. 'You'd start talking . . .' is from *Première*, April 1993. 'I like to use gals . . .' and 'I don't know myself . . .' are from 'Cool Clint Eastwood Moves On, Again' by Sean Mitchell in the *Los Angeles Herald-Examiner*, 17 August 1984.

'This movie was walking a tightrope . . .' is from 'He Directed Clint and Happily Lived to Tell the Tale' by Elaine Warren in the *Los Angeles Herald-Examiner*, 17 August 1984. 'One hundred and eighty degrees the opposite . . .' is from 'Searching for the Right Combination' by Mary Murphy in the *Los Angeles Times*, 12 April 1976. 'She found an avenue . . .' is from *Video*, May 1985.

For background on *City Heat*, I have drawn on material from 'Burt Reynolds *IS* the Comeback Kid' by Craig Modderno in the *Los Angeles Times*, 4 January 1987, as well as from the book *My Life* by Burt Reynolds (Hyperion, New York, 1994). 'It broke my heart . . .' is from 'Survival Is the Best Revenge' by Anthony Cook in *Gentleman's Quarterly*, April 1989.

'The most important small-town artist . . .' is from *Parade*, 23 October 1983. John Vinocur is quoted on the subject of Clint's European tour from his article 'Clint Eastwood, Seriously' in the Sunday *New York Times* magazine, 24 February 1985. 'Some thought that the socialist minister . . .' is from 'France Awards Eastwood With an Official Arts Honor' by Lenny Borger in *Variety*, 9 January 1985. 'Nonpareil industry reputation . . .' is from 'Eastwood Readies Next Feature' by Duane Byrge in the *Hollywood Reporter*, 18 January 1985. Clint touches on the ecological theme of *Pale Rider* with Todd McCarthy in 'Eastwood Chases Classical Western With *Pale Rider*' in *Variety*, 10 May 1985.

'Too overtly commercial . . .' is from 'Cannes Fest: It's Hard to Figure' by Charles Champlin in the *Los Angeles Times*, 20 May 1985.

'There are dozens of fine actresses . . .' is from 'Eastwood, a Hollywood Rebel, Takes on His Critics' by Gene Siskel in the *Chicago Tribune*, 8 July 1985. 'The wimp syndrome . . .' is from *Newsweek*, 22 July 1985. 'Strong female relationships' is from an undated profile of Clint by Charles Champlin in the *Los Angeles Times* in Margaret Herrick Library files. 'The smallest audience . . .' is from 'Upsies, Downsies' by Lee Margulies in the *Los Angeles Times*, 12 January 1986. 'Warner Brothers aren't going to . . .' is from the *Los Angeles Times*, 10 August 1986. 'That's something nobody has to worry about . . .' is from *Rolling Stone*, 4 July 1985.

I read and drew from numerous articles about Clint's mayoral campaign, including 'Clint to Carmel Council: Make My Day' by Harold Gilliam in the *San Francisco Chronicle*, 1 December 1985; 'Eastwood Asks Carmel to Make His Day, Elect Him Mayor' by Mark A. Stein in the *Los Angeles Times*, 31 January 1986; 'Who Wants Dirty Harry for Mayor?' by Patricia Freeman in the *Los Angeles Herald-Examiner*, 3 February 1966; 'Promising a New Spirit – And Freedom of Ice Cream – Clint Eastwood Tackles His Toughest Role: Mayoral Candidate' by Eric Levin in *People*, 17 March 1986; 'Quiet Little Carmel Is Suddenly Having A Very Noisy Race' by Michael W. Miller in the *Wall Street Journal*, 19 March 1986; 'As Clint Eastwood Runs for Mayor, Small-Town Race Hangs on Big Issue' by Robert Lindsey from the *New York Times*, 25 March 1986; 'Campaigning With Clint' by Mark Stein in the *Los Angeles Times*, 30 March 1986; 'Eastwood Opponents Face Him on His Turf – the TV Screen' by Alicia C. Shepard in the *San Jose Mercury News*, 30 March 1986; 'Clint's Carmel Campaign Heating Up' from the *Los Angeles Herald-Examiner*, 3 April 1986; 'Go Ahead, Voters, Make My Day' by Paul A. Witteman in *Time*, 7 April 1986; 'Clint Eastwood Runs For Office in Carmel, California' by Jeff Silverman in *US*, 7 April 1986; ' "Feeling Good", Eastwood Cites Need to Avoid Dewey Image' from the *Los Angeles Times*, 8 April 1986; 'Eastwood Wins Easy Victory in Carmel Vote' by Mark A. Stein in the *Los Angeles Times*, 9 April 1986; 'His Honor, "Dirty Harry" ' by Patricia Freeman in the *Los Angeles Herald-Examiner*, 9 April 1986; 'Clint Gets a Call From Central Casting' by Mark A. Stein in the *Los Angeles Times*, 10 April 1986; 'Guiding Eastwood to Victory Was a "Fun" Job' by Jeffrey A. Perlman in the *Los Angeles Times*, 10 April 1986; 'Eastwood Gets Revenge With a Landslide Victory as Mayor' by Robert Lindsey in the *New York Times*, 10 April 1986; ' "Eastwood's Inauguration Rained On But Not Out" ' by Mark Stein in the *Los Angeles Times*, 16 April 1986; 'Ice Cream Is In Again Under Eastwood Rule' by Mark A. Stein in the *Los Angeles Times*, 1 October 1986; 'Aide Guards Eastwood From Cranks' by David Leland in the *Salinas Californian*, 12 December 1986;

'In Like Clint' from *Newsweek*, 21 April 1987; ''Eastwood Cool in First Act as Mayor of Carmel'' ' from the *Los Angeles Herald-Examiner*, 7 May 1986; 'Eastwood Moves to Shoot Down Ice Cream Ban' in the *Los Angeles Times*, 8 May 1987; 'Eastwood's Building Is Approved' by Ann O'Neill and Lee Quarnstrom in the *San Jose Mercury News*, 27 February 1988; 'Clint Eastwood the Columnist' by Thomas G. Keane in the *San Francisco Chronicle*, 21 November 1986; 'Sue Hutchinson, Eastwood's Right-Hand Man' by David Leland, *Carmel Pine Cone*, 4 December 1986; 'Mayor Eastwood Solves Another Thorny Issue' by Mark A. Stein in the *Los Angeles Times*, 19 December 1986; 'Clint Eastwood: Small-Town Mayor' by Walter Roessing in the *Saturday Evening Post*, September 1987; 'It's Tit-For-Tat Zoning in Carmel' by Ann W. O'Neill in the *San Jose Mercury News*, 8 January 1988; 'Eastwood Won't Seek a Repeat Role As Mayor' in the *Los Angeles Times*, 4 February 1988; and 'Eastwood No ''Dirty Harry'' in Last Scene as Mr Mayor' by Miles Corwin in the *Los Angeles Times*, 10 April 1988.

'Very hard-boiled, but at the same time searching . . .' is from *US*, 26 January 1987.

CHAPTER TWELVE
Shades of Clint

A vast number of often undated and sometimes untitled local newspaper articles chronicling Clint's stint as Mayor of Carmel were supplied by the Monterey Public Library from the library clipfile. In particular I have cited: 'Appeared to take particular pleasure in reading aloud . . .' from 'Eastwood Settles an Old Score With Maradei' by David Leland in the *Carmel Pine Cone*, 'This [variance] stinks of the worst . . .' also from the *Carmel Pine Cone* and 'It's kind of a Hollywood atmosphere . . .' from 'Carmel Council Turns Off Jimmy Stewart's Lights' by Thom Akerman from the *Monterey Herald*. 'Potential conflict-of-interest situations . . .' is from the *Los Angeles Times*, 10 April 1988.

'Some of the finest jazz scores . . .' is from 'Clint Eastwood Shoots Us the *Bird*' by Gary Giddins from *Esquire*, October 1988. 'He did more takes . . .' (and all other Edward Carfagno quotes) are from the oral history with Carfagno by Barbara Hall, on deposit at the Margaret Herrick Library. 'Lifted the story from the dusty shelves . . .' is from 'The Hunt for John Huston' by Jack Mathews in the *Los Angeles Times*, 9 September 1990.

William Goldman's books, cited in the text, include *Adventures in the Screen Trade* (Warner, New York, 1983), *Hype & Glory* (Villard Books, New York, 1990) and the Introduction to and Screenplay of *Absolute Power* (Applause Books, New York, 1997). 'Eastwood dutifully mounted the Palais stage . . .' is from 'Clint, Brits and Kids at Cannes' in *Time*, 6 June 1988.

'I don't think that [raising his children] had much . . .' is from 'Eastwood Exposure' by Louise Farr from *WWD* [*Women's Wear Daily*], 17 August 1997. 'I would never have been able to pass . . .' is from an Internet chat on 'Mr Showbiz', as quoted in the *Los Angeles Times* from its 'Morning Report' of 9 December 1995.

Gary Giddins wrote about Clint and *Bird* in *Esquire*, October 1988, and his article was reprinted in *Faces in the Crowd* (Oxford University Press, New York, 1992). Stan Levey and Jackie McLean are quoted in 'Bird's Men Sound Off' by Zan Stewart in the *Los Angeles Times*, 19 October 1988. Red Rodney is quoted from 'Lennie Niehaus on *Bird*' by Michael Lipton in *International Musician*, March 1989.

'The suit is a potentially precedent-setting . . .' and 'Intensely private' are from the *Los Angeles Times*, 8 May 1989. 'I just don't think it's morally right . . .' is from *Playboy*, February 1974. 'I didn't know him too well . . .' is from 'Clint Eastwood and His Daughter Alison Talk About Rebellion, Reunion, and Their Renewed Love' by James Grant in *Good Housekeeping*, July 1995. Clint's relationship to Kimber Tunis was first revealed in print in 'Clint's Bombshell Secret Illegitimate Daughter' in the *National Enquirer*, 11 July 1989. I also drew on several articles which feature Kimber as their subject, including 'Clint Eastwood Disowns Love Child He's Kept Secret for 25 Years' by Kate Caldwell in the *Star*, 1 May 1990, 'Clint's Kid' in *People*, 15 November 1993, and the article in *George*, March 1997.

'Subdued, even though dozens of journalists . . .' is from 'Cannes Makes His Day' by Jack Mathews in the *Los Angeles Times*, 12 May 1990. 'Eastwood avers that he didn't base . . .' is from Bruce Bawer's book *The Screenplay's the Thing: Movie Criticism, 1986–1990* (Archon Books, Hamden, Connecticut, 1992). 'Somewhat mixed reaction' is from 'Telluride Makes Eastwood's Weekend' by Robert Denerstein in the *Hollywood Reporter*, 7 September 1990.

CHAPTER THIRTEEN
Clint's New Clothes

'Like Mother Teresa' is from 'Even Cowboys Get Their Due' by Bernard Weinraub in *Gentleman's Quarterly*, March 1993. 'A more enduring star . . .' is from 'Clint, Closing In on El Dorado' by Jack Mathews in the *Los Angeles Times*, 28 March 1993. Background on David Webb Peoples from 'A Screenwriter Whose Life's Script Stars Privacy' by Bernard Weinraub in the *New York Times*, 6 October 1992, and 'A Reluctant Hollywood Hero' by Elaine Dutka in the *Los Angeles Times*, 5 October 1992. 'Almost telepathically' is from 'Working With Eastwood' by Jerry Roberts in the *Hollywood Reporter*, 11 March

1993. 'A neat piece of revisionism . . .' is from 'Back With a Vengeance' by Kenneth Turan in the *Los Angeles Times*, 7 August 1992. 'It demythologizes idolizing people . . .' is from the speech Clint made when he accepted the Directors Guild of America award as Best Director of 1992. 'I didn't see what Clint saw . . .' is from 'A Few Good Words Behind Scenes' by Elaine Dutka and Robert W. Welkos in the *Los Angeles Times*, 30 March 1993.

I consulted the following articles about the advertising–publicity campaign for *Unforgiven*: 'WB Hunting BO Bounty With *Unforgiven* Push' by Kirk Honeycutt in the *Hollywood Reporter*, 6 August 1992, '*Unforgiven* Hits Target: Hottest August Opening' by Leonard Klady in the *Hollywood Reporter*, 10 August 1992, 'Giving the Public What It Wants . . .' by David J. Fox in the *Los Angeles Times*, 12 August 1992, and *Unforgiven* Success Shoots Down Skeptics' by Martin A. Grove in the *Hollywood Reporter*, 12 August 1992.

Megan Rose's claim to have discovered the *Unforgiven* script is rebutted by Warners executives in Frank DiGiacomo, Florence Anthony and Timothy McDarrah's 'Page Six' column, 'Is She Clint's *Unforgiven* Gal?' from the *New York Post*, 8 March 1993.

Clint's DGA and Oscar campaigns are chronicled in 'Eastwood, Altman Key Awards Players' by Martin A. Grove in the *Hollywood Reporter*, 7 January 1993; 'Laying Down Bets in Oscar Town' by Kenneth Turan in the *Los Angeles Times*, 10 January 1993; 'A Surprise Oscar *Scent* at Globes' by David J. Fox in the *Los Angeles Times*, 25 January 1993; 'DGA Declares Independents' by Anita M. Busch and Kirk Honeycutt in the *Hollywood Reporter*, 26 January 1993; 'Oscar May Make His Day Next' by David J. Fox in the *Los Angeles Times*, 8 March 1993; 'DGA Rides With Eastwood' by Kirk Honeycutt in the *Hollywood Reporter*, 8 March 1993; 'New York Pulls for Altman' by Doris Toumarkine in the *Hollywood Reporter*, 8 March 1993; 'An Honor to Be Nominated' by Kirk Honeycutt in the *Hollywood Reporter*, 17 March 1993; 'Oscar Forecast Favors *Unforgiven*, Eastwood' by Martin A. Grove in the *Hollywood Reporter*, 26 March 1993; 'Most Big Players Are Sticking With Clint' by Jane Galbraith in the *Los Angeles Times*, 28 March 1993; 'Eastwood's *Unforgiven* Is Best Film' by David J. Fox in the *Los Angeles Times*, 30 March 1993; 'In the End, All Is *Unforgiven*' by Kenneth Turan in the *Los Angeles Times*, 30 March 1993; and 'Unforgettable *Unforgiven*' by Anita M. Busch and Kirk Honeycutt in the *Hollywood Reporter*, 30 March 1993.

Transcripts of Clint's acceptance speeches, at the Oscar awards and on the occasion of his Irving Thalberg honour, are to be found among the official records of the Academy of Motion Picture Arts and Sciences at the Margaret Herrick Library.

'We sat together for two hours . . .' is from 'Eastwood–Petersen Chemistry Sparks "Fire" ' by Martin A. Grove in the *Hollywood Reporter*, 14 June 1993. 'I wasn't at all nervous with Mel . . .' is from 'You Only Live Twice' by Jenny Cooney in an undated article in *Empire* in Margaret Herrick Library files.

'Suppose it's Fidel Castro? . . .' is from *Empire*. 'Mess with Clint . . .' and 'This notion of dissing him . . .' is from 'The Touch of Evil' by Jess Cagle in *Entertainment Weekly*, undated article in Margaret Herrick Library files. 'He's a better actor . . .' is from *Empire*.

For background and on-set reportage about *A Perfect World*, I have relied upon 'One Directs, the Other Doesn't' by Joe Leydon from the *Los Angeles Times*, 11 July 1993. 'Inside, it is totally style-free . . .' is from 'Cool Clint' by Georgina Howell in *Vogue*, February 1993.

'The decision to have a baby had been percolating . . .' is from 'She's Having Clint's Baby' by Jennet Conant from *Redbook*, October 1993. 'A nurse whispered something to Clint . . .' is from 'Clint's Ex Spills the Beans' from the *Globe*, 27 May 1997. 'Miraculous time' and 'He became the person . . .' is from Richard Schickel, *Clint Eastwood*. 'He [Clint] thinks . . .' is from 'Clint Eastwood: Riding High' by Gil Gibson in the *Ladies Home Journal*, August 1993. 'Excruciatingly bad . . .' and 'It is basically as silly . . .' are from 'Go Ahead, Make My Lecture!' by Christopher Tricarico in the *Los Angeles Times*, 16 October 1988. 'Hornswoggled' and 'It was another Western . . .' are from 'Idol Chatter' in *Première*, October 1995. 'Dispel the notion that Cannes is . . .' is from 'Eastwood Set for Cannes Jury' by Pia Farrell in the *Hollywood Reporter*, 21 June 1993. My account of Clint at Cannes in 1993, and all quotes from French sources, are indebted to research and translations by Eve-Marine Dauvergne. 'Distinguised and ultra-serious' is from Todd McCarthy's Introduction to *Cannes: Fifty Years of Sun, Sex & Celluloid: Behind the Scenes at the World's Most Famous Film Festival* (Hyperion, New York, 1997), which contains a Foreword by Clint.

I drew on many articles about the filming of *The Bridges of Madison County*, including 'Eastwood May Fill Beresford *Bridges* Gap' by Donna Parker in the *Hollywood Reporter*, 4 August 1994; 'Her Peculiar Career' by Bernard Weinraub in the *New York Times*, 18 September 1994; 'Go Ahead, Make Him Cry' by Maureen Dowd in the *New York Times*, 26 March 1995; 'Clint by Candlelight' by Sean Mitchell in the *Los Angeles Times*, 28 May 1995; 'Clint Eastwood Plays *Misty*' by Doug Stanton in *Esquire*, June 1995; 'Bridges on the River Cry' by Anne Thompson in *Esquire*, June 1995; 'Giving Good Clint' by Derek Malcolm in the *Guardian*, 1 September 1995; 'When Clint Called Meryl' by Claudia Glenn Dowling in the *Sydney Morning Herald* (Australia), 30 September 1995; as well as the official commemorative book *The Bridges of Madison County: The Film* (Warner Books, New York, 1995).

'They were testing all these thirty-year-old women . . .' and 'not a fan' are from the *New York Times*, 26 March 1995. 'It intrigued me that he would want . . .' and 'A lot of real time between people . . .' are from the *Los Angeles Times*, 28 May 1995. 'More than professional respect . . .' is from an undated article in *Ladies' Homes Journal*. 'Had carried on the intense romance . . .' is from the *Los Angeles Times*, 28 May 1995.

Jacelyn Reeves's relationship with Clint was first reported in 'Clint Eastwood's Secret 4–Year Love Comes Out of Hiding' by Stephen Viens and Bob Smith from the *Star*, 27 February 1990, with additional details revealed in 'Clint's Amazing Love Life' by Alan Smith and Tony Brenna from the *National Enquirer*, 12 September 1996. Dina Ruiz's romance with Clint was first reported in 'Clint Flips for TV News Beauty' in the *Star*, 14 March 1995. 'Eastwood is widely acknowledged . . .' is from 'Oscar Makes His Day' by Kathleen O'Steen in *Variety*, 19 January 1995. 'I'm not *with* anybody' is from the *Los Angeles Times*, 28 May 1995. 'There are a lot more men . . .' is from 'Go Ahead, Make Him Cry' by Maureen Dowd in the *New York Times*, 26 March 1995. 'Clint thought that the piano . . .' is from *Sight and Sound*, September 1995. 'Shedding people close to him . . .' is from *George*, March 1997.

CHAPTER FOURTEEN
Clint's World

'Slim enough to qualify . . .' is from 'She Makes His Day' by Sylvia Rubin in the *San Francisco Chronicle*, 9 April 1996. 'Similar working-class backgrounds . . .' is from 'Dirty Harry's Better Half' by Lynn Carey for the Knight-Ridder Newspapers, as published 2 October 1996 in the *Long Beach Press-Telegram*. 'Found themselves chatting . . .', 'Zero of his movies' and 'ga-ga in love' are from the *San Francisco Chronicle*, 9 April 1996. 'Usually with groups of friends . . .' is from the Knight-Ridder article. 'After he came back from *Bridges* . . .' is from the *San Francisco Chronicle*, 9 April 1996. 'Couldn't seem to keep her hands off . . .' is from 'Actor Clint Eastwood Makes Emmy's Day' by Susan Young in the *Oakland Tribune*, 15 May 1995. 'Yearlong courtship . . .' is from the *San Francisco Chronicle*, 9 April 1996. 'I propose marriage to her . . .' is from 'Clint Eastwood at 63: Being a New Dad Has Made My Day' by Don Gentile in the *National Enquirer*, 21 December 1993. 'The jury worked very hard . . .' and 'I don't think that's appropriate . . .' are from 'Eastwood Whips Enquirer' by Matt Krasnowski for the Copley News Service as published in the *Outlook Weeklies*, 26 October 1995. 'Litigiousness' is from 'The Court Files' by Ann O'Neill in the *Los Angeles Times*, 31 August 1997.

Articles I consulted that reported details of Clint's marriage to Dina Ruiz include 'Making His Day' by Paula Yoo and Penelope Rowlands in *People*, 15 April 1996; 'Clint Weds "The Girl I've Been Waiting For" – And There's Not a Dry Eye in the House' by Peter Kent in the *Star*, 16 April 1996; and 'Clint Eastwood's Secret Wedding' by William Keck, Marc Cetner, Suzanne Ely and Tony Brenna in the *National Enquirer*, 16 April 1996.

A letter to the editor from Clint's lawyers appears in the 'Mail' section of *People*, 13 May 1996. 'Eastwood remained so ticked off . . .' and 'Just read stuff that could be upsetting . . .' are from 'Clint Eastwood: Hollywood's Most Private Star' by Patricia Bosworth in *Cosmopolitan*, January 1997. 'If you invite Clint Eastwood to a party . . .' is from Army Archerd's 'Just For *Variety*' column in *Variety*, 4 March 1996. 'Just the kind of low-voltage . . .' is from 'Honor and Embarassment for Eastwood' by John J. O'Connor in the *New York Times*, 27 May 1996. 'Mr Eastwood's work as a director . . .' is from 'Fistful of Praise and Clips For Clint Eastwood Tribute' by Bernard Weinraub in the *New York Times*, 6 May 1996. 'With the exception of [Woody] Allen . . .' is from *GQ*, March 1993.

I relied upon the following reportage concerning Sondra Locke's lawsuit: 'Clint Eastwood Ruined Movie Career of Former Girlfriend, Court Is Told' in the *Los Angeles Times*, 12 September 1996; 'Clint Eastwood Testifies He Funded Ex-Lover's Deal' by Ann W. O'Neill in the *Los Angeles Times*, 17 September 1996; 'Eastwood Denies Fraud in Film Deal for Former Lover' by Ann W. O'Neill in the *Los Angeles Times*, 18 September 1996; 'Eastwood: No Attempt Made to Defraud Locke' in the *Hollywood Reporter*, 18 September 1996; 'Eastwood Has His Say in 15 Words' by Giles Whittell in *The Times* (London), 19 September 1996; and 'Eastwood, Locke Settle Fraud Suit for Undisclosed Sum' by Ann W. O'Neill and Efrain Hernandez Jr in the *Los Angeles Times*, 25 September 1996.

Clint's second interview with *Playboy* by Bernard Weinraub was featured in its March 1997 issue. 'Macabre' and 'Jeffrey Daumer is right up . . .' are from *George*, March 1997.

'A subplot in *Absolute Power* . . .' is from 'The Hoarse Whisperer: Eastwood in One Take' by Bob Drury in *Men's Journal*, April 1997. Michael Sragow's review of the Richard Schickel book, 'Go Ahead, Make My Day', was published in the *New York Times* Sunday Book Review, 1 December 1996. David Thomson wrote about Clint and the Richard Schickel biography in 'The Overachievers' in *Esquire*, April 1997. 'She's not an unattractive woman . . .' is from *W* magazine, as quoted in *The Times* (London), 24 August 1996.

For background on Clint's land development deals, I consulted 'Cañada Woods Project Up for Final Approval' by Calvin Demmon in the *Monterey Herald*, 16 December 1996; 'Golf Course Would Make His Day' by Mark Arax in the *Los Angeles Times*, 15 December 1996; 'Youth Protest Dirty Harry's Planned Eagle-Tree Destruction', a news release of the Community Against Dirty Harry (CAD) Organization; 'Foes Give Golf Plan Thumbs Down' by

Patrick May in the *San Jose Mercury News*, 30 March 1997; and 'In the Horses' Mouth: Eastwood's Odello Donation Helped the Movie Mogul and the County' by Richard Pitnick in the 29 January 1998 *Coast Weekly*.

'The pair appeared to be living . . .' is from the Knight-Ridder article. 'We go to the movies . . .' is from the *San Francisco Chronicle*, 9 April 1996. 'He has a gun permit . . .' is from *Cosmopolitan*, January 1997. 'She's certainly the light of my life . . .' is from *George*, March 1997. 'Alison and Eastwood had a stormy relationship . . .' is from *Men's Journal*, April 1997.

For translation of articles reporting the reaction to *Absolute Power* in France, I am indebted to Kristi Jaas.

Clint is interviewed on the subject of his conservative politics in *The American Enterprise*, January–February 1998. Clint can be found on the cover of the 11 November 1997 issue of *The Advocate*. Inside the magazine he is profiled in 'In Like Clint' by Edward Guthmann. 'The weakest in modern memory' is from 'WB Loses Luster: Lauded *Confidential* Brightens Studio's Slump' by Paul Karon in *Daily Variety*, 7 January 1998. 'Couldn't be pinned down to reading . . .' is from Paul S. Nathan's 'Rights & Permissions' column in *Publisher's Weekly*, 15 August 1980. 'He's a wonderful storyteller . . .' is from Donald Van De Mark and Beverly Schuch's interview with Michael Connelly from 'Show Biz Buzz' on the Cable News Network, 25 March 1998. 'He is wearing shiny patent shoes . . .' is from *The Times* (London), 28 March 1998.

Television

1955
'Allen in Movieland', The Steve Allen Show

1956
'Cochise, Greatest of the Apaches', *TV Readers Digest*
'Motorcycle', *Highway Patrol*

1957
'White Fury', *West Point*
'The Charles Avery Story', *Wagon Train*

1958
'The Lonely Watch', *Navy Log*
'The Last Letter', *Death Valley Days*

1959
'Duel at Sundown', *Maverick*

1959–1966
'Multiple Episodes', *Rawhide*

1962
'Clint Eastwood Meets Mr Ed', *Mr Ed*

1985
'Vanessa in the Garden', *Amazing Stories*
Director: Clint Eastwood. Sc: Steven Spielberg.
Cast: Harvey Keitel, Sondra Locke, Beau Bridges.

Filmography

Key: Sc: Screenwriter; Ph: Photography; Art Dir: Art Director; Ed: Editor. Producer and approximate running time appear in parentheses. Cast listings are partial.

1955

Revenge of the Creature

Unbilled as Jennings, a lab technician. Director: Jack Arnold. Sc: Martin Berkeley. Ph: Charles S. Wellbourne. Art Dirs: Alexander Golitzen, Alfred Sweeney. Ed: Paul Weatherwax. Cast: John Agar (Clete Ferguson), Lori Nelson (Helen Dobson), John Bromfield (Joe Hayes), Nestor Paiva (Lucas), Grandon Rhodes (Foster), Dave Willock (Gibson), Robert B. Williams (George Johnson), Charles Crane (police captain). (William Alland for Universal Pictures, 82 mins.)

'*While* Revenge of the Creature *may lack the thematic purity and gothic atmosphere of the original, it is nonetheless a creditable effort that enjoyed such popularity that the studio wanted yet another sequel.*'

DANA M. REEMES, *Directed by Jack Arnold*

Francis in the Navy

As Jonesy. Director: Arthur Lubin. Sc: Devery Freeman, based on the character created by David Stern. Ph: Carl Guthrie. Art Dirs: Alexander Golitzen, Bill Newberry. Eds: Milton Carruth, Ray Snyder. Cast: Donald O'Connor (Lt Peter Stirling and Bosun's Mate Slicker Donevan), Martha Hyer (Betsy Donevan), Richard Erdman (Murph), Jim Backus (Commander Hutch), David Janssen (Lt Anders), Leigh Snowden (Appleby), Martin Milner (Rick), Paul Burke (Tate), Phil Garris (Stover), Chill Wills (voice of Francis). (Stanley Rubin for Universal, 80 mins.)

'*Not only did he get listed in the credits (he played Jonesy, a sailor), but he was also noticed by the critics. He was variously described as "handsome", "engaging" or simply as "shows promise".*'

PETER DOUGLAS, *Clint Eastwood: Movin' On*

Lady Godiva

As First Saxon. Director: Arthur Lubin. Sc: Oscar Brodney, Harry Ruskin. Ph: Carl Guthrie. Art Dirs: Alexander Golitzen, Robert Boyle. Ed: Paul Weatherwax. Cast: Maureen O'Hara (Lady Godiva), George Nader (Lord Leofric), Eduard Franz (King Edward), Leslie Bradlie (Count Eustace), Victor McLaglen (Grimald), Torin Thatcher (Lord Godwin), Rex Reason (Harold), Grant Withers (Pendar). (Robert Arthur for Universal, 88 mins.)

'*Cardboard costumer involving famed lady and her horseback ride set in Middle Ages England . . . and what a dull ride!*'

LEONARD MALTIN, *TV Movies and Video Guide*

Tarantula!

Unbilled, as first bomber pilot. Director: Jack Arnold. Sc: Robert M. Fresco, Martin Berkeley. Ph: George Robinson. Art Dirs: Alexander Golitzen, Alfred Sweeney. Ed: William M. Morgan. Cast: John Agar (Dr Matt Hastings), Mara Corday (Stephanie Clayton), Leo G. Carroll (Prof. Deemer), Nestor Paiva (Sheriff), Ross Elliott (John Burch), Edwin Rand (Lt John Nolan), Raymond Bailey (Townsend). (William Alland for Universal, 80 mins.)

'*You can't get a good look at him as he sits there in a studio cockpit ordering his fellow pilots to drop the napalm that finally kills the giant spider. An undistinguished quickie,* Tarantula *is a very funny movie that wasn't meant to be so.*'

PATRICK AGAN, *Clint Eastwood*

1956

Never Say Goodbye

Unbilled as Will, a lab assistant. Director: Jerry Hopper. Sc: Charles Hoffman. Ph: Maury Gertsman. Art Dirs: Alexander Golitzen, Robert Boyle. Ed: Paul Weatherwax. Cast: Rock Hudson (Dr Michael Parker), Cornell Borchers (Lisa), George Sanders (Victor), Ray Collins (Dr Bailey), David Janssen (Dave), Shelley Fabares (Suzy Parker), Raymond Greenleaf (Dr Kelly Andrews). (Albert J. Cohen for Universal, 96 mins.)

'*Highly lachrymose.*'

CLIVE HIRSCHHORN, *The Universal Story*

Away All Boats

Unbilled, as a sailor. Director: Joseph Pevney. Sc: Ted Sherdeman. Ph: William Daniels. Ed: Ted Kent. Cast: Jeff Chandler (Capt Jedediah Hawks), George Nader (Lt Dave MacDougall), Julie Adams (Nadine MacDougall), Lex Barker (Commander Quigley), Keith Andes (Dr Ball), Richard Boone (Lt Fraser), William Reynolds (Ensign Kruger), Charles McGraw (Lt Mike O'Bannion), Jock Mahoney (Alvick), John McIntire (Old Man). (Howard Christie for Universal, 114 mins.)

'Lacklustre war film.'

MICK MARTIN *and* MARSHA PORTER, *Video Movie Guide*

The First Traveling Saleslady

As Jack Rice. Director: Arthur Lubin. Sc: Devery Freeman, Stephen Longstreet. Ph: William Snyder. Ed: Otto Ludwig. Cast: Ginger Rogers (Rose Rillray), Barry Nelson (Charles Masters), Carol Channing (Molly Wade), David Brian (James Carter), James Arness (Joel Kingdom), Robert Simon (Cal), Frank Wilcox (Marshal Duncan). (Arthur Lubin for RKO, 92 mins.)

'Quite dreadful.'

IAIN JOHNSTONE, *The Man with No Name*

Star in the Dust

Unbilled, as a ranch hand, Director: Charles Haas. Sc: Oscar Brodney, based on the novel *Law Man* by Lee Deighton. Ph: John L. Russell Jr. Art Dir: Alexander Golitzen. Ed: Ray Snyder. Music: Frank Skinner. Cast: John Agar (Bill Jordan), Mamie Van Doren (Ellen Ballard), Richard Boone (Sam Hall), Leif Erickson (George Ballard), Coleen Gray (Nellie Mason). (Albert Zugsmith for Universal, 80 mins.)

'A superior B Western, this is one of the best of a number of Westerns that set lawmen against the people they were elected to protect.'

PHIL HARDY, *The Western*

1957

Escapade in Japan

Unbilled, as a rescue pilot. Director: Arthur Lubin. Sc: Winston Miller. Ph: William Snyder. Art Dir: Walter Holscher. Ed: Otto Ludwig. Cast: Teresa Wright (Mary Saunders), Cameron Mitchell (Dick Saunders), Philip Ober (Lt Col. Hargrave), Jon Provost (Tony Saunders), Roger Nakagawa (Hiko), Susumu Fujita (Kei Tanaka), Kuniko Miyake (Michiko), Tatsuo Saito (Mr Fushimi). (Arthur Lubin for RKO–Universal, 93 mins.)

'If you looked away you missed him completely. He played an air force pilot searching for a downed plane. He has but one brief scene in the film, and two lines, one of which was simply, "Pilot to radio operator".'

STUART KAMINSKY, Clint Eastwood

1958

Lafayette Escadrille
(UK: Hell Bent for Glory)

As George Moseley. Director: William A. Wellman. Sc: A. S. Fleischman, from a story by Wellman. Ph: William Clothier. Ed: Owen Marks. Cast: Tab Hunter (Thad Walker), Etchika Choureau (Renée), Marcel Dalio (Drillmaster), David Janssen (Duke Sinclair), Paul Fix (US General), Bill Wellman Jr (Bill Wellman), Jody McCrea (Tom Hitchcock), Dennis Devine (Red Scanlon). (William Wellman for Warner Bros., 93 mins.)

'All the script required of Eastwood was to lend his taciturn presence and he had no significant dialogue.'

MICHAEL MUNN, Clint Eastwood: Hollywood's Loner

Ambush at Cimarron Pass

As Keith Williams. Director: Jodie Copeland. Sc: Richard G. Taylor and John K. Butler, based on a story by Robert A. Reeds and Robert W. Woods. Ph: John M. Nickolaus Jr. Ed: Carl L. Pierson. Cast: Scott Brady (Sgt Matt Blake), Margia Dean (Teresa), Frank Gerstle (Sam Prescott), Dirk London (Johnny Willows), Baynes Barron (Corbin), William Vaughan (Henry), Ken Mayer (Corporal Schwitzer), John Manier (Private Zach), Keith Richards (Private Lasky), John Merrick (Private Nathan), Irving Bacon (Stanfield), Desmond Slattery (Cobb). (Herbert E. Mendelson for Regal–20th Century-Fox, 73 mins.)

'Clint Eastwood, who has a small part here, has described this contrived yam about a cavalry patrol riding into an Apache ambush as the low point of his movie career; he has been heard to call it "the worst Western ever made". In any case, it's bad..

BRIAN GARFIELD, Western Films

1964

Per Un Pugno Di Dollari
US (1967): A Fistful of Dollars

As the Stranger (Joe). Director: Sergio Leone. Sc: Leone and Duccio Tessari, adapted from *Yojimbo* by Akiro Kurosawa. Ph: Massimo Dallamano. Art Dir: Carlo Simi. Ed: Robert Cinquin. Music: Ennio Morricone. Cast: Gian Maria

Volonté (Ramon Rojo), Marianne Koch (Marisol), Pepe Calvo (Silvanito), Wolfgang Lukschy (John Baxter), Sieghardt Rupp (Esteban Rojo), Antonio Prieto (Don Miguel Rojo), Margherita Lozano (Consuela Baxter), Daniel Martin (Julio), Bruno Carotenuto (Antonio Baxter), Benito Stefanelli (Rubio), Mario Brega (Chico), Josef Egger (Piripero). (Harry Colombo and George Papi for Jolly Film–Constantin–Ocean–United Artists, 100 mins.)

'A Fistful of Dollars, *together with* For A Few Dollars More *and* The Good, the Bad and the Ugly, *introduced a new kind of hero in a new kind of setting. From the moment The Man With No Name rode into the town of San Miguel on his mule – like a mercenary version of Henry Fonda at the beginning of John Ford's* Young Mr Lincoln *– and ignored the slob in a sombrero who was roughing up a small Mexican child, it was clear to audiences all over the world that something very different was going on; that a new style of Western was being created.'*

CHRISTOPHER FRAYLING, *Clint Eastwood*

1965

Per Qualche Dollari in Più
US (1967): For a Few Dollars More

As the Stranger (The Man With No Name). Director: Sergio Leone. Sc: Leone and Luciano Vincenzoni, based on a story by Leone and Fulvio Morsella. Ph: Massimo Dallamano. Art Dir: Carlo Simi. Eds: Giorgio Ferralonga, Eugenio Alabiso. Music: Ennio Morricone. Cast: Lee Van Cleef (Colonel Douglas Mortimer), Gian Maria Volonté (El Indio), Klaus Kinski (Juan, the hunchback), Josef Egger (Prophet), Rosemarie Dexter (Mortimer's sister in flashbacks), Mara Krup (Mary, the hotel landlady), Mario Brega (Nino), Benito Stefanelli (Rocky), Aldo Sambrel, Luigi Pistilli, Giovanni Tarallo, Mario Meniconi, Lorenzo Robledo (Indio's gang). (Alberto Grimaldi for Produzioni Europee Associates–Constantin–Arturo Gonzales–United Artists, 130 mins.)

'*Showier and more baroque than its predecessor.*'

ROBERT C. CUMBOW, *Once Upon a Time: The Films of Sergio Leone*

1966

Le Streghe
US (1969): The Witches
(Part Five only: 'A Night Like Any Other')

As Mario, the husband. Director: Vittorio De Sica. Sc: Cesare Zavatinni, Fabio Carpi, Enzio Muzii. Ph: Giuseppe Rotunno. Ed: Adriana Novelli. Music: Pierto Piccinoi. Cast (Part Five only): Silvana Mangano (Giovanna). (Dino De Laurentiis for Les Productions Artistes Associés, 110 mins., 'A Night Like Any Other' segment, 19 mins.)

'*Here the director's attempt to spin off a Felliniesque fantasia on the frustrated wife's daydreams is only slightly less laboured than Eastwood's embarrassed stab at light comedy.*'

J. HOBERMAN, *The Village Voice*

Il Buono, Il Brutto, Il Cattivo
US (1968): The Good, the Bad and the Ugly

As the Stranger (Blondie). Director: Sergio Leone. Sc: Leone and Luciano Vincenzoni, based on a story by Age-Scarpelli, Leone and Vincenzoni. English Adaptation: Mickey Knox. Ph: Tonnio Delli Colli. Art Dir: Carlo Simi. Eds: Nino Baragli, Eugenio Alabiso. Music: Ennio Morricone. Cast: Lee Van Cleef (Angel Eyes), Eli Wallach (Tuco), Aldo Giuffre (Northern officer), Mario Brega (Corporal Wallace), Luigi Pistilli (Padre Ramirez), Al Mulloch (Tuco's nemesis). (Alberto Grimaldi for Produzioni Europee Associates–United Artists, 161 mins.)

'The Good, the Bad and the Ugly *could never have been made in America. For one thing, it is too long and plot-heavy for the generally single-point-of-view Hollywood Westerns. Leone, far from being glossy, seems to revel in the texture of Death Valley dustiness. When Eli Wallach (the Ugly) drags Clint Eastwood (the Good) across a desert, the suffering becomes so intensely vivid and the framing so consciously poetic that the audience is subjected to a kind of Cactus Cavalry. No American Western would ever wallow so ecstatically in pain and privation worthy of the most masochistic Messiah, and he will be rewarded in this world long before the next. Leone knows this, and Leone's audience knows this. Then, why is the mercenary's reward so long deferred? Simply because the sheer duration of the suffering makes Eastwood a plausible lower-class hero whose physical redemption is the contemporary correlative of Christ's spiritual redemption. Leone's longueurs are thus part of a ritual alien to the American's traditional confidence in his ability to conquer nature. Leone's characters require more than strength and determination to survive. They require also a guile and reason more European than American. That Eastwood does not kill Wallach at the final fade-out is due not so much to Eastwood's being moral as to his being civilized by an ancient code of resignation that is hardly the code of the West.*'

ANDREW SARRIS, *Confessions of a Cultist*

1968

Hang 'Em High

As Jed Cooper. Director: Ted Post. Sc: Leonard Freeman, Mel Goldberg. Ph: Richard Kline, Lennie South. Art Dir: John B. Goodman. Ed: Gene Fowler Jr. Music: Dominic Frontiere. Cast: Inger Stevens (Rachel), Ed Begley (Captain Wilson), Pat Hingle (Judge Adam Fenton), Arlene Golonka (Jennifer), James MacArthur (Priest), Ben Johnson (Bliss), Bruce Dern (Miller), Dennis Hopper (The Prophet). Also: Charles McGraw, L. Q. Jones, Ruth White, James Westerfield, Alan Hale Jr, Jack Ging, Bob Steele, Bert Freed. (Leonard Freeman for United Artists–Malpaso Company, 114 mins.)

'*Hang 'Em High is a film of distinctive and original qualities. Director Ted Post (a film-maker who has not since had the projects he deserves) gives the film a commanding, dreamlike cast, playing on spatial compression (the run-down Main Street set, dominated by a whoppingly out-of-scale red brick courthouse) and surrealistic imagery (Dennis Hopper as a messianic madman coolly shot down in the opening reel, a prison set that is lit to look like a medieval dungeon) to give the action a primal accent. This is a Western-as-moral-nightmare; seen today, it is a sharp reminder of the artistic seriousness that could once be found (and even expected) in a modest genre piece.*'

DAVE KEHR, *American Film*

Coogan's Bluff

As Walt Coogan. Director: Don Siegel. Sc: Herman Miller, Dean Reisner, Howard Rodman, based on a story by Miller. Ph: Bud Thackery. Art Dirs: Alexander Golitzen, Robert McKichan. Ed: Sam E. Waxman. Music: Lalo Schifrin. Cast: Lee J. Cobb (McElroy), Susan Clark (Julie), Tisha Sterling (Linny Raven), Don Stroud (Ringerman), Betty Field (Mrs Ringerman), Tom Tully (Sheriff McCrea), Melodie Johnson (Millie), James Edwards (Jackson), Rudy Diaz (Running Bear), David F. Doyle (Pushie), Louis Zorich (Taxi Driver), Meg Myles (Big Red), Marjorie Bennett (Mrs Fowler), Seymour Cassell (Young Hood), Skip Battyn (Omega), Albert Popwell (Wonderful Digby). (Don Siegel and Richard E. Lyons for Universal, 94 mins.)

'*Another evocative action cop film from Don Siegel. This time Clint Eastwood is a Western lawman who shows up the big city cops in New York. Siegel has an unparalleled ability to breathe life and interest into simple stories like this one.*'

JAMES MONACO, *The Connoisseur's Guide to the Movies*

Where Eagles Dare

As Lieutenant Morris Schaffer. Director: Brian G. Hutton. Story and sc: Alistair MacLean. Ph: Arthur Ibbetson. Art Dir: Peter Mullins. Ed: John Jympson.

Music: Ron Goodwin. Cast: Richard Burton (John Smith), Mary Ure (Mary Ellison), Michael Hordern (Vice-Admiral Rolland), Patrick Wymark (Colonel Turner), Robert Beatty (Cartwright Jones), Derren Nesbitt (Major von Hapen), Anton Diffring (Colonel Kramer), Donald Houston (Christiansen), Ferdy Mayne (Reichsmarschal Rosemeyer), Neil McCarthy (MacPherson), Vincent Ball (Carpenter), Peter Barkworth (Berkeley), William Squire (Thomas), Brook Williams (Sgt Harrod), Ingrid Pitt (Heidi). (Elliott Kastner for Metro-Goldwyn–Mayer, 155 mins.)

'*Archetypal schoolboy adventure, rather unattractively photographed but containing a sufficient variety of excitement.*'

LESLIE HALLIWELL, *Halliwell's Film Guide*

1969

Paint Your Wagon

As Pardner. Director: Joshua Logan. Lyrics and sc: Alan Jay Lerner, based on his and Frederick Loewe's musical play. Adaptation: Paddy Chayefsky. Ph: William Fraker. Production Design: John Truscott. Art Dir: Carl Braunger. Ed: Robert Jones. Music: Frederick Loewe, André Previn, orchestrated and conducted by Nelson Riddle. Cast: Lee Marvin (Ben Rumson), Jean Seberg (Elizabeth), Harve Presnell (Rotten Luck Willie), Ray Walston (Mad Jack Duncan), Tom Ligon (Horton Fenty), Alan Dexter (Parson), William O'Connell (Horace Tabor), Ben Baker (Haywood Holbrook), Alan Baxter (Mr Fenty), Paula Trueman (Mrs Fenty), Robert Easton (Atwell), Geoffrey Norman (Foster), H. B. Haggerty (Steve Bull), Terry Jenkins (Joe Mooney), Karl Bruck (Schermerhorn), John Mitchum (Jacob Woodling), Sue Casey (Sarah Woodling), Eddie Little Sky (Indian), Harvey Parry (Higgins), H. W. Gim (Wong), William Mims (Frock-coated man), Roy Jenson (Hennessey), Pat Hawley (Clendennon) and the Nitty Gritty Dirt Band. (Alan Jay Lerner for Paramount, 164 mins.)

'*Just when we're peacefully nodding off, someone breaks into song . . .*'

MICHAEL SAUTER, *The Worst Movies of All Time*

1970

Kelly's Heroes

As Kelly. Director: Brian G. Hutton. Sc: Troy Kennedy Martin. Ph: Gabriel Figueroa. Art Dir: Jonathan Berry. Ed: John Jympson. Music: Lalo Schifrin. Cast: Telly Savalas (Big Joe), Don Rickles (Crapgame), Carroll O'Connor (Gen. Colt), Donald Sutherland (Oddball), Gavin MacLeod (Moriarty), Fred

Pearlman (Mitchell), Tom Troupe (Job), George Savalas (Mulligan), Hal Buckley (Maitland), Stuart Margolin (Little Joe), Gene Collins (Babra), Perry Lopez (Petchuko), Dick Balduzzi (Fisher), Harry Stanton (Willard), Dick Davalos (Gutkowski), Len Lesser (Bellamy), Jeff Morris (Cowboy), Michael Clark (Grace), David Hurst (Col. Dankhopf), Robert McNamara (Roach), James McHale (Guest), Ross Elliott (Booker), Tom Signorelli (Bonsor), John Heller (German Lieutenant), George Fargo (Penn), Karl Otto Alberty (German Tank Commander), Hugo de Vernier (French Mayor), Harry Goines (Supply Sergeant), David Gross (German Captain), Donald Waugh (Roamer), Vincent Maracecchi (Old Man in Town). (Gabriel Katzka and Sidney Beckerman for MGM, 146 mins.)

'*It's a superbly acted, exquisitely photographed, howling spoof of wartime heroics*'.

Argory

Two Mules for Sister Sara

As Hogan. Director: Don Siegel. Sc: Albert Maltz, based on a story by Budd Boetticher. Ph: Gabriel Figueroa. Art Dir: José Rodriguez Granada. Eds: Robert Shugrue, Juan José Marino. Music: Ennio Morricone. Cast: Shirley MacLaine (Sara), Manolo Fábregas (Colonel Beltran), Alberto Morín (General LeClaire), Armando Silvestre (First American), John Kelly (Second American), Enrique Lucero (Third American), Pedro Armendariz (Young French Officer) David Estuardo (Juan), Ada Carrasco (Juan's Mother), Pancho Córdoba (Juan's Father), José Chavez (Horacio). (Martin Rackin and Carroll Case for Universal–Malpaso, 105 mins.)

'*This almost makes the grade as high-quality movie-making, but just never quite gets there.*'

JAY ROBERT NASH AND STANLEY RALPH ROSS, *The Motion Picture Guide*

1971

The Beguiled

As John McBurney. Director: Don Siegel. Sc: John B. Sherry (Albert Maltz) and Grimes Grice (Irene Kamp), based on the Thomas Cullinan novel. Ph: Bruce Surtees. Production designer: Ted Haworth. Art Dir: Alexander Golitzen. Ed: Carl Pingitore. Music: Lalo Schifrin. Cast: Geraldine Page (Martha Farnsworth), Elizabeth Hartman (Edwina Dabney), Jo Ann Harris (Carol), Darleen Carr (Doris), Mae Mercer (Hallie), Pamelyn Ferdin (Amy), Melody Thomas (Abigail), Peggy Drier (Lizzie), Pattye Mattick (Janie). (Don Siegel for Universal–Malpaso, 105 mins.)

'*As has been pointed out, the film both looks back to Ford's* Seven Women *and forward to Eastwood's* Play "Misty" for Me, *but the style is full-blown Southern Gothic larded with all the atmospherics and sexual tensions of a Carson McCullers story. A mixture of psychodrama and Western,* The Beguiled *invokes throughout its length a sustained, overt stylization that normally erupts only occasionally in either Siegel's or Eastwood's work. If much of the film is reminiscent of* Reflections in a Golden Eye, *the climax is worthy of John Webster.*'

JULIAN PETLEY, *The BFI Companion to the Western*

Play Misty for Me

As Dave Garland. Director: Clint Eastwood. Sc: Jo Heims, Dean Riesner. Ph: Bruce Surtees. Art Dir: Alexander Golitzen. Ed: Carl Pingitore. Music: Dee Barton. Cast: Jessica Walter (Evelyn Draper), Donna Mills (Tobie Williams), John Larch, (Sgt McCallum), Clarice Taylor (Birdie), Irene Hervey (Madge Brenner), Jack Ging (Frank Dewan), James McEachin, (Al Monte), Don Siegel (Murphy), Duke Everts (Jay Jay), George Fargo (Man), Mervin W. Frates (Locksmith), Tim Frawley (Deputy Sheriff), Otis Kadani (Policeman), Brit Lind (Angelica), Paul E. Lippman (Second Man), Jack Kosslyn (Cab Driver), Ginna Paterson (Madelyn), Malcolm Moran (Man in Window), the Johnny Otis Show and the Cannonball Adderly Quintet. (Robert Daley for Universal–Malpaso, 102 mins.)

'*The film is exciting, weirdly amusing, and scary (many critics compare the knife scenes to* Psycho), *but the most enjoyable thing about it is watching Eastwood's cool-talking disc jockey become increasingly confused, perturbed, and terrified by this lunatic he has no control over.*'

DANNY PEARY, *Guide for the Film Fanatic*

Dirty Harry

As Detective Harry Callahan. Director: Don Siegel. Sc: Harry Julian Fink, Rita M. Fink, Dean Riesner, based on a story by Harry Julian Fink and Rita M. Fink. Ph: Bruce Surtees. Art Dir: Dale Hennessy. Ed: Carl Pingitore. Music: Lalo Schifrin. Cast: Harry Guardino (Lt Bressler), Reni Santoni (Chico), John Vernon (The Mayor), Andy Robinson (Scorpio), John Larch (Chief), John Mitchum (DiGeorgio), Mae Mercer (Mrs Russell), Lyn Edgington (Norma), Ruth Kobart (Bus Driver), Woodrow Parfrey (Mr Jaffe), Josef Sommer (Rothko), William Paterson (Bannerman), James Nolan (Liquor Proprietor), Maurice S. Argent (Sid Kleinman), Jo de Winter (Miss Willis), Craig G. Kelly (Sgt Reineke). (Robert Daley for Warner Bros–Malpaso, 102 mins.)

'*Despite its violence, the beat of the film is laconic. The movie is almost as open in its space as a Western. Maybe that is why the violence works. For the movie, when seen,*' *is considerably less graphic than this description of it. The violence is not so much unendurable as frequent and successful – like a cruise with many ports of call. Dirty Harry looks as clean and well turned out as any young Senator with a promising future. In scenes where we see him striding down the street, he could be walking from one campaign spot to another. Eastwood knows the buried buttons in his audience as well as any film-maker around. Is it out of measure to call him the most important small-town artist in America?'*

NORMAN MAILER, *'All the Pirates and People'*, Parade

1972

Joe Kidd

As Joe Kidd. Director: John Sturges. Sc: Elmore Leonard. Ph: Bruce Surtees. Art Dirs: Alexander Golitzen, Henry Bumstead. Ed: Ferris Webster. Music: Lalo Schifrin. Cast: Robert Duvall (Frank Harlan), John Saxon (Luis Chama), Don Stroud (Lamarr), Stella Garcia (Helen Sanchez), James Wainwright (Mango), Paul Koslo (Roy), Gregory Walcott (Mitchell), Dick Van Patten (Hotel Manager), Lynne Marta (Elma), John Carter (Judge), Pepe Hern (Priest), Joaquin Martinez (Manolo), Ron Soble (Ramon), Pepe Callahan (Naco), Clint Ritchie (Calvin), Gil Barreto (Emilio), Ed Deemer (Bartender), Maria Val (Vita), Chuck Hayward (Eljay), Michael R. Horst (Deputy). (Robert Daley and Sidney Beckerman for Universal–Malpaso, 88 mins.)

'A curiously strangled Western which can't make up its mind whether it wants to wring straight action out of the range war between poor Mexicans and a tycoon rancher (Duvall), or to explore the moral standing of the disreputable character (Eastwood) who takes law and order into his hands.'

TOM MILNE, *The Timeout Film Guide*

1973

High Plains Drifter

As the Stranger. Director: Clint Eastwood. Sc: Ernest Tidyman. Ph: Bruce Surtees. Art Dir: Henry Bumstead. Ed: Ferris Webster. Music: Dee Barton. Cast: Verna Bloom (Sarah Belding), Marianna Hill (Callie Travers), Mitchell Ryan (Dave Drake), Jack Ging (Morgan Allen), Stefan Gierasch (Mayor Jason Hobart), Ted Hartley (Lewis Belding), Billy Curtis (Mordecai), Geoffrey Lewis (Stacy Bridges), Scott Walker (Bill Borders), Walter Barnes (Sheriff Sam Shaw), Paul Brinegar (Lutie Naylor), Richard Bull (Asa Godwin), Robert Donner (Preacher), John Hillerman (Bootmaker), Anthony James (Cole Carlin), William O'Connell (Barber), John Quade (Jake Ross), Jane Aull

(Townswoman), Dan Vadis (Dan Carlin), Reid Cruikshanks (Gunsmith), James Gosa (Tommy Morris), Jack Kosslyn (Saddlemaker), Russ McCubbin (Fred Short), Belle Mitchell (Mrs Lake), John Mitchum (Warden), Carl C. Pitti (Teamster), Chuck Waters (Stableman), Buddy Van Horn (Marshal Jim Duncan). (Jennings Lang and Robert Daley for Universal–Malpaso, 105 mins.)

'*Clint Eastwood seems to have absorbed the approaches of two of his former directors, Sergio Leone and Don Siegel, and fused them with his own paranoid vision of society. Whether we like it or not, Eastwood is a formidable new talent on the directorial scene – a man who not only knows his own mind, but knows how to make that knowledge pay off.*'

ARTHUR KNIGHT, *Saturday Review*

Breezy

As director only. Director: Clint Eastwood. Sc: Jo Heims. Ph: Frank Stanley. Art Dir: Alexander Golitzen. Ed: Ferris Webster. Music: Michel Legrand. Cast: William Holden (Frank Harmon), Kay Lenz (Breezy), Roger C. Carmel (Bob Henderson), Marj Dusay (Betty Tobin), Joan Hotchkis (Paula Harmon), Jamie Smith Jackson (Marcy), Norman Bartold (Man in Car), Lynn Borden (Overnight Date), Shelley Morrison (Nancy Henderson), Dennis Olivieri (Bruno), Eugene Peterson (Charlie), Lew Brown (Police Officer), Richard Bull (Doctor), Johnnie Collins III (Norman), Don Diamond (Maitre D'), Scott Holden (Veterinarian), Sandy Kenyon (Real Estate Agent), Jack Kosslyn (Driver), Mary Munday (Waitress), Frances Stevenson (Saleswoman), Buck Young (Paula's Escort), Priscilla Morrill (Dress Customer). (Jennings Lang and Robert Daley for Universal–Malpaso, 106 mins.)

'Breezy *is a little jewel, full of sweetness, yet pared of sentimentalism.*'

FUENSANTA PLAZA, *Clint Eastwood–Malpaso*

Magnum Force

As Detective Harry Callahan. Director: Ted Post. Sc: John Milius and Michael Cimino, based on a story by Milius and characters by Harry Julian Fink and Rita M. Fink. Ph: Frank Stanley. Art Dir: Jack Collis. Ed: Ferris Webster. Music: Lalo Schifrin. Cast: Hal Holbrook (Lieutenant Neil Briggs), Mitchell Ryan (Charlie McCoy), David Soul (Ben Davis), Tim Matheson (Phil Sweet), Kip Niven (Red Astrachan), Robert Urich (John Grimes), Felton Perry (Early Smith), Margaret Avery (Prostitute), Richard Devon (Carmine Ricca), Tony Giorgio (Frank Palancio), Jack Kosslyn (Walter), John Mitchum (DiGeorgio), Clifford A. Pellow (Lou Guzman), Albert Popwell (Pimp), Christine White (Carol McCoy), Adele Yoshioka (Sunny), Maurice S. Argent

(Nat Weinstein), Bob March (Estabrook), Bob McClurg (Cab Driver), Russ Moro (Ricca's Driver). (Robert Daley for Universal–Warners–Malpaso, 122 mins.)

'This is one of those movies that are interesting only as social litmus. Post's shooting is needlessly fancy – why photograph head-on when you can film from the floor or the roof? John Milius's gun-worshipping, junior-macho script tries to substitute synthetic toughness for style. The sexual material – pretty girls begging Eastwood for his body – is of the Penthouse *variety. And gratuitous vulgarity is everywhere . . .'*

PAUL D. ZIMMERMAN, *Newsweek*

1974

Thunderbolt and Lightfoot

As John 'Thunderbolt' Doherty. Director and screenwriter: Michael Cimino. Ph: Frank Stanley. Art Dir: Tambi Larsen. Ed: Ferris Webster. Music: Dee Barton. Cast: Jeff Bridges (Lightfoot), George Kennedy (Red Leary), Geoffrey Lewis (Goody), Catherine Bach (Melody), Gary Busey (Curly), Jack Dodson (Vault Manager), Gene Elman and Lila Teigh (Tourists), Burton Gilliam (Welder), Roy Jenson (Dunlop), Claudia Lennear (Secretary), Bill McKinney (Crazy Driver), Vic Tayback (Mario), Dub Taylor (Gas Station Attendant), Gregory Walcott (Used Car Salesman), Erica Hagen (Waitress), Alvin Childress (Janitor), Virginia Baker and Stuart Nisbet (Couple at Gas Station), Irene K. Cooper (Cashier), Cliff Emmich (Fat Man), June Fairchild (Gloria), Ted Foulkes (Little Boy), Leslie Olvier and Mark Montgomery (Teenagers), Karen Lamm (Girl on Motorcycle), Luanne Roberts (Suburban Housewife), Tito Vandis (Counterman). (Robert Daley for Malpaso–United Artists, 115 mins.)

'All the performers are excellent, and Eastwood unwinds a little from his customary characterization of a terse, razor-eyed stranger, breaking through to a kind of boyish affability. Cimino himself renders most of the movie with enough cunning to make it one of the most ebullient and eccentric diversions around.'

JAY COCKS, *Time*

1975

The Eiger Sanction

As Jonathan Hemlock. Director: Clint Eastwood. Sc: Warren B. Murphy, Hal Dresner and Rod Whitaker, based on the novel by Trevanian. Ph: Frank Stanley. Art Dirs: George Webb, Aurelio Crugnola. Ed: Ferris Webster. Music: John Williams. Cast: George Kennedy (Ben Bowman), Vonetta McGee (Jemima Brown), Jack Cassidy (Miles McHough), Heidi Bruhl (Anna Montaigne), Thayer David (Dragon), Reiner Schoene (Freytag), Michael Grimm (Meyer), Jean-Pierre Bernard (Montaigne), Brenda Venus (George), Gregory Walcott (Pope), Candice Rialson (Art Student), Elaine Shore (Miss Cerberus), Dan Howard (Dewayne), Jack Kosslyn (Reporter), Walter Kraus (Kruger), Frank Redmond (Wormwood), Siegfried Wallach (Hotel Manager), Susan Morgan (Burns), Jack Frey (Cab Driver). (Richard D. Zanuck, David Brown and Robert Daley for Universal–Malpaso, 125 mins.)

'A total travesty of the James Bond books, stilted, self-conscious, belaboured, and boring, its only novelty a mountain-climbing sequence that, for all its slips, slides and thrills on actual Monument Valley and Swiss Alps locations, left me as cold as the icy slopes.'

JUDITH CRIST, *New York*

1976

The Outlaw Josey Wales

As *Josey Wales*. Director: Clint Eastwood. Sc: Philip Kaufman and Sonia Chernus, based on the novel *Gone to Texas* by Forrest Carter. Ph: Bruce Surtees. Production Design: Tambi Larsen. Ed: Ferris Webster. Music: Jerry Fielding. Cast: Chief Dan George (Lone Watie), Sondra Locke (Laura Lee), Bill McKinney (Terrill), Paula Trueman (Grandma Sarah), Sam Bottoms (Jamie), Geraldine Keams (Little Moonlight), Woodrow Parfrey (Carpetbagger), Joyce Jameson (Rose), Sheb Wooley (Travis Cobb), Royal Dano (Ten Spot), Matt Clarke (Kelly), John Verros (Chato), Will Sampson (Ten Bears), William O'Connell (Sim Carstairs), John Quade (Comanchero Leader), Frank Schofield (Senator Land), Buck Kartalian (Shopkeeper), Len Lesser (Abe), Douglas McGrath (Lige), John Russell (Bloody Bill Anderson), Charles Tyner (Zukie Limmer), Bruce M. Fisher (Yoke), John Mitchum (Al), John Chandler (First Bounty Hunter), Tom Roy Lowe (Second Bounty Hunter), Clay Tanner (First Texas Ranger), Madeline T. Holmes (Grannie Hawkins), Erik Holland (Union Army Sergeant), Cissy Wellman (Josey's Wife), Faye Hamblin (Grandpa), Danny Green (Lemuel). (Robert Daley for Warner Bros–Malpaso, 136 mins.)

'Orson Welles said that if Eastwood had not directed The Outlaw Josey Wales, *everyone would have called it a classic. Everyone would probably have been right. The film hangs in the mind for all kinds of reasons, and it gathers, as only the best movies do, its style and its preoccupations into a single thought. America here is not a place people die for, it's a vast, beautiful, shifting landscape that people keep dying in, killing each other out of sheer smallness of mind, or for reasons they can't remember.'*

MICHAEL WOOD, *London Review of Books*

The Enforcer

As Detective Harry Callahan. Director: James Fargo. Sc: Stirling Silliphant and Dean Riesner, from a story by Gail Morgan Hickman and S. W. Schurr, based on characters created by Harry Julian Fink and Rita M. Fink. Ph: Charles W. Short. Art Dir: Allen E. Smith. Eds: Ferris Webster, Joel Cox. Music: Jerry Fielding. Cast: Tyne Daly (Kate Moore), Harry Guardino (Lt Bressler), Bradford Dillman (Capt McKay), John Mitchum (DiGeorgio), DeVeren Brookwalter (Bobby Maxwell), John Crawford (Mayor), Samantha Doane (Wanda), Robert Hoy (Buchinski), Jocelyn Jones (Miki), M. G. Kelly (Father John), Nick Pellegrino (Martin), Albert Popwell (Big Ed Mustapha), Rudy Ramos (Mendez), Bill Ackridge (Andy), Bill Jelliffe (Johnny), Joe Bellan (Freddie the Painter), Tim O'Neill (Police Sergeant), Jan Stratton (Mrs Grey), Will MacMillan (Lt Dobbs), Jerry Walter (Krause), Steve Boss (Bustanoby), Tim Burrus (Henry Lee), Michael Cavanaugh (Lalo), Dick Durock (Karl), Ronald Manning (Tex), Adele Proom (Irene DiGiorgio), Glenn Leigh Marshall (Army Sergeant), Robert Behling (Autopsy Surgeon), Terry McGovern (Disc Jockey), Stan Richie (Bridge Operator), John Roselims (Mayor's Driver), Brian Fong (Scoutmaster), Art Rimdzius (Porno Director), Chuck Hicks (Huey), Ann Macy (Madam), Gloria Prince (Massage Girl), Kenneth Boyd (Abdul), Bernard Glin (Koblo), Fritz Manes (First Detective). (Robert Daley for Warner Bros–Malpaso, 96 mins.)

The movie is laced with jokes about Harry's humiliation at having to work with a lousy broad, but his prejudice is made to seem so Neanderthal that the routine backfires enough to be funny. The movie has other coarsely comic moments, but not enough of them to make it seem a deliberate self-parody instead of an inadvertent one.'

JANET MASLIN, *Newsweek*

1977

The Gauntlet

As Ben Shockley. Director: Clint Eastwood. Sc: Michael Butler, Dennis Shryack. Ph: Rexford Metz. Art Dir: Allen E. Smith. Eds: Ferris Webster, Joel Cox. Music: Jerry Fielding. Cast: Sondra Locke (Gus Mally), Pat Hingle (Josephson), William Prince (Blakelock), Bill McKinney (Constable), Michael Cavanaugh (Feyderspiel), Carole Cook (Waitress), Mara Corday (Jail Matron), Douglas McGrath (Bookie), Jeff Morris (Desk Sergeant), Samantha Doane, Roy Jenson and Dan Vadis (Bikers), Carver Barnes (Bus Driver), Robert Barrett (Paramedic), Teddy Bear (Lieutenant), Mildred J. Brion (Old Lady on Bus), Ron Chapman (Veteran Cop), Don Circle (Bus Clerk), James W. Gavin and Tom Friedkin (Helicopter Pilots), Darwin Lamb (Police

Captain), Roger Lowe (Paramedic Driver), Fritz Manes (Helicopter Gunman), John Quiroga (Cab Driver), Joe Rainer (Rookie Cop), Art Rimdzius (Judge), Al Silvani (Police Sergeant). (Robert Daley for Warner Bros–Malpaso, 109 mins.)

'It is a movie without a single thought in its head, but its action sequences are so ferociously staged that it's impossible not to pay attention most of the time. It's not simply that the film is noisy. It has a kind of violent grace . . .'

VINCENT CANBY, The New York Times

1978

Every Which Way But Loose

As Philo Beddoe. Director: James Fargo. Sc: Jeremy Joe Kronsberg. Ph: Rexford Metz. Art Dir: Elayne Ceder. Ed: Ferris Webster. Music: Snuff Garrett. Cast: Sondra Locke (Lynn Halsey-Taylor), Ruth Gordon (Ma Boggs), Geoffrey Lewis (Orville Boggs), Beverly D'Angelo (Echo), Walter Barnes (Tank Murdock), George Chandler (Clerk at DMV), Roy Jenson (Woody), James McEachin (Herb), Bill McKinney (Dallas), William O'Connell (Elmo), John Quade (Cholla), Dan Vadis (Frank), Gregory Walcott (Putnam), Hank Worden (Trailer Court Manager), Jerry Brutsche (Sweeper Driver), Cary Michael Cheifer (Kincaid's Manager), Janet Louise Cole (Girl at Palomino), Sam Gilman (Fat Man's Friend), Chuck Hicks (Trucker), Timothy P. Irwin (MC at Zanzabar), Tim Irwin (Bandleader), Billy Jackson (Better), Joyce Jameson (Sybil), Richard Jamison (Harlan), Jackson D. Kane (Man at Bowling Alley), Jeremy Kronsberg (Bruno), Fritz Manes (Bartender at Zanzabar), Michael Mann (Church's Manager), Lloyd Nelson (Bartender), George Orrison (Fight Spectator), Thelma Pelish (Lady Customer), William J. Quinn (Kincaid), Tom Runyon (Bartender at Palomino), Bruce Scott (Schyler), Al Silvani (Tank Murdock's Manager), Hartley Silver (Bartender), Al Stellone (Fat Man), Jan Stratton (Waitress), Mike Wagner (Trucker), Guy Way (Bartender), George Wilbur (Church) and Manis (Clyde). (Robert Daley for Warner Bros–Malpaso, 114 mins.)

'Because, in Every Which Way But Loose, *Clint Eastwood plays the kind of thick lunkhead his detractors have always assumed him to be, I am tempted to call it the Clint Eastwood movie for people who don't like Clint Eastwood movies. In actuality, this new film will probably confirm the prejudices of Eastwood-haters and Eastwood-avoiders. Unlike the movies featuring Dirty Harry and other cops, the appeal to a redneck audience here is not merely ideological. It's absolutely direct. This is a redneck comedy with no stops pulled. If I could persuade my friends to see it, they'd probably detest it. I loved it.'*

STUART BYRON, The Village Voice

1979

Escape from Alcatraz

As Frank Morris. Director: Don Siegel. Sc: Richard Tuggle, based on the book by J. Campbell Bruce. Ph: Bruce Surtees. Production Design: Allen E. Smith. Ed: Ferris Webster. Music: Jerry Fielding. Cast: Patrick McGoohan (Warden), Roberts Blossom (Chester Dalton), Jack Thibeau (Clarence Anglin), Fred Ward (John Anglin), Paul Benjamin (English), Larry Hankin (Charley Butts), Bruce M. Fischer (Wolf), Frank Ronzio (Litmus), Fred Stuthman (Johnson), David Cryer (Wagner), Madison Arnold (Zimmerman), Blair Burrows (Fight Guard), Bob Balhatchet (Medical Technical Assistant), Matthew J. Locricchio and Stephen Bradley (Exam Guards), Don Michaelian (Beck), Ray K. Goman (Cellblock Captain), Jason Ronard (Bobs), Ed Vasgersian (Cranston), Ron Vernan (Stone), Regie Bagg (Lucy), Hank Brandt (Associate Warden), Candace Bowen (English's Daughter), Joseph Miksak (Police Segeant), Garry Goodrow (Weston), Ross Reynolds (Helicopter Pilot), Al Dunlap (Visitor's Guard), Donald Siegel (Doctor), Fritz Manes and Lloyd Nelson (Guards), Danny Glover and Glenn Wright (Inmates). (Donald Siegel and Robert Daley for Malpaso–Siegel Film–Paramount, 112 mins.)

'*In the past, Eastwood has played killers, and his lack of emotion was eerie. In* Alcatraz, *however, Siegel has gotten him to discard the scary, chic murderousness of his old character. He's close to a traditional movie hero here, a man with a private code, loathing authority and bullies and instinctively protecting the weak. He's more appealing now, but he's still far from a complete man because he gives so little of himself. Who is this convict? What are his feelings? What's the source of his strength? Eastwood is too tight to be even an interesting enigma. Siegel makes the pace of* Alcatraz *weighty and deliberate as Eastwood's movements, but the movie doesn't gain in significance, only in emphasis. Its sullen force is finally baffling; it feels blocked – a simple movie, heavy with unexpressed meanings.*'

DAVID DENBY, *New York*

1980

Bronco Billy

As 'Bronco Billy' McCoy. Director: Clint Eastwood. Sc: Dennis Hackin. Ph: David Worth. Production Design: Gene Lourie. Ed: Ferris Webster. Music: Snuff Garrett. Cast: Sondra Locke (Antoinette Lily), Geoffrey Lewis (John Arlington), Scatman Crothers ('Doc' Lynch), Bill McKinney ('Lefty' LeBow), Sam Bottoms (Leonard James), Dan Vadis (Chief Big Eagle), Sierra Pecheur (Lorraine Running Water), Walter Barnes (Sheriff Dix), Woodrow Parfrey (Dr

Canterbury), Beverlee McKinsey (Irene Lily), Douglas McGrath (Lt Wiecker), Hank Worden (Station Mechanic), William Prince (Edgar Lipton), Pam Abbas (Mother Superior), Edye Byrde (Maid, Eloise), Douglas Copsey and Roger Dale Simmons (Reporters at Bank), John Wesley Elliott Jr (Sanatorium Attendant), Chuck Hicks and Bobby Hoy (Cowboys at Bar), Jefferson Jewell (Boy at Bank), Dawneen Lee (Bank Teller), Don Mummert (Chauffeur), Lloyd Nelson (Sanatorium Policeman), George Orrison (Cowboy in Bar), Michael Reinbold (King), Tessa Richarde (Mitzi Fritts), Tanya Russell (Doris Duke), Valerie Shanks (Sister Maria), Sharon Sherlock (Licence Clerk), James Simmerhan (Bank Manager), Jenny Sternling (Reporter at Sanatorium), Chuck Waters and Jerry Wills (Bank Robbers). (Dennis Hackin, Neal Dobrofsky and Robert Daley for Warner Bros–Second Street Films–Malpaso, 116 mins.)

'*Clint Eastwood has done something extraordinary in* Bronco Billy. *He has made a film that deftly lampoons his own strapping image while retaining the essence of its appeal, a film that emphasizes how secure a place the Western tradition has in our dreams and fantasies even as it demonstrates its irrevocable passing. As a director, Eastwood shows a surprising flair for sly comedy, and as a star he gives what looks to be the performance of his career, a piece of work that may yet earn him serious attention as an actor.*'

KENNETH TURAN, *New West*

Any Which Way You Can

As Philo Beddoe. Director: Buddy Van Horn. Sc: Stanford Sherman. Ph: David Worth. Production Design: William J. Creber. Eds. Ferris Webster, Ron Spang. Music: Snuff Garrett. Cast: Sondra Locke (Lynn Halsey-Taylor), Geoffrey Lewis (Orville Boggs), William Smith (Jack Wilson), Harry Guardino (James Beekman), Ruth Gordon (Ma Boggs), Michael Cavanaugh (Patrick Scarfe), Barry Corbin (Fat Zack), Roy Jenson (Moody), Bill McKinney (Dallas), William O'Connell (Elmo), John Quade (Cholla), Al Ruscio (Tony Paoli Sr), Dan Vadis (Frank), Camilla Ashlend (Hattie), Dan Barrows (Baggage Man), Michael Brockman (Moustache Officer), Julie Brown (Candy), Glen Campbell (Himself), Dick Christie (Jackson Officer), Rebecca Clemons (Buxom Bess), Reid Cruikshanks (Bald-Headed Trucker), Michael Currie (Wyoming Officer), Gary Lee Davis (Husky Officer), Dick Durock (Joe Casey), Michael Fairman (CHP Captain), James Gammon (Bartender), Weston Gavin (Beekman's Butler), Lance Gordon (Biceps), Lynn Hallowell (Honey Bun), Peter Hobbs (Motel Clerk), Art La Fleur (Second Baggage Man), Ken Lerner (Tony Paoli Jr), John McKinney (Officer), Robin Menken (Tall Woman), George Murdock (Sgt Cooley), Jack Murdock (Little Melvin), Ann Nelson (Harriet),

Sunshine Parke (Old Codger), Kent Perkins (Trucker), Ann Ramsey (Loretta Quince), Logan Ramsey (Luther Quince), Michael Reinbold (Officer With Glasses), Tessa Richarde (Sweet Sue), Jeremy Smith (Intern), Bill Sorrels (Bakersfield Officer), Jim Stafford (Long John), Michael Talbott (Officer Morgan), Mark Taylor (Desk Clerk), Jack Thibeau (Head Muscle), Charles Walker (Officer). (Fritz Manes and Robert Daley for Warner Bros–Malpaso, 117 mins.)

'*Eastwood looms as a sort of Orange County redneck Peter Pan. He offers his fans a fantasy of prolonged prepubescence carried into adult life with grown-up sex tacked on but all sense of responsibility ignored ... Fights are started, songs are sung and brew is consumed – often simultaneously. But all this, fascinating though it might be to anthropologists, is sheer torture to film lovers. No one behind the camera or in front of it seems much to care how things are done. Everyone seems to be sleepwalking – lost in a hard-hat dream. Let's hope Eastwood wakes up next time and sends his "lost boys" out to face the harsh reality his other films show so well.*'

DAVID EHRENSTEIN, *Los Angeles Herald-Examiner*

1982

Firefox

As Mitchell Gant. Director: Clint Eastwood. Sc: Alex Lasker and Wendell Wellman, based on the Craig Thomas novel. Ph: Bruce Surtees. Art Dirs: John Graysmark, Elayne Cedar. Eds: Ferris Webster, Ron Spang. Music: Maurice Jarre. Cast: Freddie Jones (Kenneth Aubrey), David Huffman (Buckholz), Warren Clarke (Pavel Upenskoy), Ronald Lacey (Semelovsky), Kenneth Colley (Colonel Kontarsky), Klaus Löwitsch (General Vladimirov), Nigel Hawthorne (Pyotr Baranovich), Stefan Schnabel (First Secretary), Thomas Hill (General Brown), Clive Merrison (Major Lanyev), Kai Wulff (Lt Col. Voskov), Dimitra Arliss (Natalia), Austin Willis (Walters), Michael Currie (Capt. Seerbacker), James Staley (Lt Commander Fleischer), Ward Costello (General Rogers), Alan Tilvern (Air Marshal Kutuzov), Oliver Cotton (Dimitri Priabin), Bernard Behrens (William Saltonstall), Richard Derr (Admiral Curtis), Woody Eney (Major Dietz), Bernard Erhard (KGB Guard), Hugh Fraser (Police Inspector Tortyev), David Gant (KGB Official), John Grillo (Customs Officer), Czeslaw Grocholski (Old Man), Barrie Houghton (Boris Glazunov), Neil Hunt (Richard Cunningham), Vincent J. Isaacs (Sub Radio Operator), Alexei Jawdokimov and Phillip Littell (Code Operators), Wolf Kahler (KGB Chairman Andropov), Eugene Lipinsky (KGB Agent), Curt Lowens (Dr Schuller), Lev Mailer (Guard at Shower), Fritz Manes (Captain), David Meyers (Grosch), Alfredo Michelson (Interrogator), Tony Pappenfuss (GRU Officer), Olivier

Pierre (Borkh), Zenno Nahayevsk (Officer at Plane), George Orrison (Leon Sprague), Grisha Plotkin (GRU Officer), George Pravda (General Borov), John Ratzenberger (Chief Peck), Alex Rodine (Captain of the Riga), Lance Rosen (Agent), Eugene Scherer (Russian Captain), Warrick Sims (Shelley), Mike Spero (Russian Guard), Malcolm Storry (KGB Agent), Chris Winfield (RAF Operator), John Yates (Admiral Pearson), Alexander Zale (Riga Fire Control Chief), Igor Zatsepin (Flight Engineer), Konstantin Zlatev (Riga Technician). (Clint Eastwood and Fritz Manes for Warner Bros–Malpaso, 136 mins.)

'*None of it makes much sense, but the movie moves fast and foolishly in a direction that strikes me as doggedly right wing.*'

BRUCE WILLIAMSON, *Playboy*

1982

Honkytonk Man

As Red Stovall. Director: Clint Eastwood. Sc: Clancy Carlile, based on his novel. Ph: Bruce Surtees. Production Design: Edward Carfagno. Eds: Ferris Webster, Michael Kelly, Joel Cox. Music: Snuff Garrett. Cast: Kyle Eastwood (Whit), John McIntire (Grandpa), Alexa Kenin (Marlene), Verna Bloom (Emmy), Matt Clark (Virgil), Barry Corbin (Derwood Arnspringer), Jerry Hardin (Snuffy), Tim Thomerson (Highway Patrolman), Macon McCalman (Dr Hines), Joe Regalbuto (Henry Axle), Gary Grubbs (Jim Bob), Rebecca Clemons (Belle), Johnny Gimble (Bob Wills), Linda Hopkins (Flossie), Bette Ford (Lulu), Jim Boelson (Junior), Tracey Walter (Pooch), Susan Peretz (Miss Maud), John Russell (Jack Wade), Charles Cyphers (Stubbs), Marty Robbins (Smoky), Ray Price (Bob Wills Singer), Shelley West and David Frizzell (Opry Singers), Porter Wagoner (Dusty), Bob Ferrera (Oldest Son), Tracy Shults (Daughter), R. J. Ganzert (Rancher), Hugh Warden (Grocer), Kelsie Blades (Veteran), Jim Ahart (Waiter), Steve Autry (Mechanic), Peter Griggs (Mr Vogel), Julie Hoopman (Whore), Rozelle Gayle (Club Manager), Robert V. Barron (Undertaker), DeForest Covan (Gravedigger), Lloyd Nelson (Radio Announcer), George Orrison and Glenn Wright (Jailbirds), Roy Jenson (Dub), Sherry Allurd (Dub's Wife), Gordon Terry, Tommy Alsup and Merle Travis (Texas Playboys), Robert D. Carver (First Bus Driver), Thomas Powels (Second Bus Driver). (Clint Eastwood and Fritz Manes for Warner Bros–Malpaso, 123 mins.)

'*In the role of Red Stovall, Eastwood might have given a great performance if he'd had another director there to pull it out of him. But Eastwood the director isn't hard enough on Eastwood the actor, who appears uncomfortable with emotional material (or, in fact, anything out of a somewhat limited range) . . . The music aside, a certain unifying, bedrock authenticity is gone, leaving the film with a sense of what might have been. It's a great pity since this story could have lent itself to a raffish, original memorable work with its own, lovely dying fall.'*

SHEILA BENSON, *The Los Angeles Times*

1983

Sudden Impact

As Detective Harry Callahan. Director: Clint Eastwood. Sc: Joseph C. Stinson, based on a story by Earl Smith and Charles B. Pierce, based on the characters created by Harry Julian Fink and Rita M. Fink. Ph: Bruce Surtees. Production Design: Edward Carfagno. Ed: Joel Cox. Music: Lalo Schifrin. Cast: Sondra Locke (Jennifer Spencer), Pat Hingle (Chief Jannings), Bradford Dillman (Captain Briggs), Paul Drake (Micky), Audrie J. Neenan (Ray Parkins), Jack Thibeau (Kruger), Michael Currie (Lt Donnelly), Albert Popwell (Horace King), Mark Keyloun (Officer Bennett), Kevyn Major Howard (Hawkins), Bette Ford (Leah), Nancy Parsons (Mrs Kruger), Joe Bellan (Burly Detective), Wendell Wellman (Tyrone), Mara Corday (Coffee Shop Waitress), Russ McCubbin (Eddie), Robert Sutton (Carl), Nancy Fish (Historical Society Woman), Carmen Argenziano (D'Ambrosia), Liza Britt (Elizabeth Spencer), Bill Reddick (Police Commissioner), Lois de Banzie (Judge), Matthew Child (Alby), Michael Johnson and Nick Dimitri (Assassins), Michael Maurer (George Wilburn), Pat Du Val (Bailiff), Christian Phillips and Steven Kravitz (Hawkins' Cronies), Dennis Royston, Melvin Thompson, Jophery Brown and Bill Upton (Young Guys), Lloyd Nelson (Desk Sergeant), Christopher Pray (Detective Jacobs), James McEachin (Detective Barnes), Maria Lynch (Hostess), Ken Lee (Loomis), Morgan Upton (Bartender), John X. Heart (Uniformed Policeman), David Gonzales, Albert Martinez, David Rivers and Robert Rivers (Gang Members), Harry Demopoulos (Dr Barton), Lisa London (Young Hooker), Tom Spratley (Senior Man), Eileen Wiggins (Hysterical Female Customer), John Nowak (Bank Robber). (Clint Eastwood and Fritz Manes for Warner Bros–Malpaso, 117 mins.)

'The picture is like a slightly psychopathic version of an old Saturday afternoon serial, with Harry sneering at the scum and cursing them before he shoots them with his "king-size, custom-made .44 Auto Mag". He takes particular pleasure in kicking and bashing a foul-mouthed lesbian; we get the idea – in his eyes, she's worse than her male associates, because women are supposed to be ladies.'

PAULINE KAEL, *State of the Art*

1984

Tightrope

As Wes Block. Director and screenwriter: Richard Tuggle. Ph: Bruce Surtees. Production Design: Edward Carfagno. Ed: Joel Cox. Music: Lennie Niehaus. Cast: Geneviève Bujold (Beryl Thibodeaux), Dan Hedaya (Detective Molinari), Alison Eastwood (Amanda Block), Jennifer Beck (Penny Block), Marco St John (Leander Rolfe), Rebecca Pearl (Becky Jacklin), Regina Richardson (Sarita), Randi Brooks (Jamie Cory), Jamie Rose (Melanie Silber), Margaret Howell (Judy Harper), Rebecca Clemons (Girl with Whip), Janet MacLachlan (Dr Yarlofsky), Graham Paul (Luther), Bill Holliday (Police Chief), John Wilmot (Medical Examiner), Margie O'Dair (Mrs Holstein), Joy N. Houck Jr (Swap Meet Owner), Stewart Baker-Bergen (Blond Surfer), Donald Barber (Shorty), Robert Harvey (Lonesome Alice), Ron Gural (Coroner Dudley), Layton Martens (Sergeant Surtees), Richard Charles Boyle (Dr Fitzpatrick), Becki Davis (Nurse), Jonathan Sacher (Gay Boy), Valerie Thibodeaux (Black Hooker), Lionel Ferbos (Plainclothes Gus), Eliott Keener (Sandoval), Cary Wilmot Alden (Secretary), David Valdes (Manes), James Borders (Carfagno), Fritz Manes (Valdes), Jonathan Shaw (Quono), Don Lutenbacher (Dixie President), George Wood (Conventioneer), Kimberley Georgoulis (Sam), Glenda Byars (Lucy Davis), John Schluter Jr (Piazza Cop), Nick Krieger (Rannigan), Lloyd Nelson (Patrolman Restic), Rod Masterson (Patrolman Gallo), David Dahlgren (Patrolman Julio), Glenn Wright (Patrolman Redfish), Angela Hill (Woman Reporter), Ted Saari (TV News Technician). (Clint Eastwood and Fritz Manes for Warner Bros–Malpaso, 118 mins.)

'*A startling treatment of sexual dysfunction in the hard cop, and an altogether impressive, if disconcerting, picture.*'

DAVID THOMSON, *A Biographical Dictionary of Film*

City Heat

As Lieutenant Speer. Director: Richard Benjamin. Sc: Sam O. Brown (Blake Edwards) and Joseph C. Stinson. Ph: Nick McLean. Production Design: Edward Carfagno. Ed: Jacqueline Cambas. Music: Lennie Niehaus. Cast: Burt Reynolds (Mike Murphy), Jane Alexander (Addy), Madeline Kahn (Caroline Howley), Rip Torn (Primo Pitt), Irene Cara (Ginny Lee), Richard Roundtree (Dehl Swift), Tony Lo Bianco (Leon Coll), William Sanderson (Lonnie Ash), Nicholas Worth (Troy Roker), Robert Davi (Nino), Jude Farese (Dub Slack), John Hancock (Fat Freddie), Tab Thacker (Tuck), Gerald S. O'Loughlin (Counterman Louie), Jack Nance (Adam Strossell), Dallas Cole (Redhead Sherry), Lou Filippo (Referee), Michael Maurer (Vint Diestock), Preston

Sparks (Keith Stoddard), Ernie Sabella (Ballistics Expert), Christopher Michael Moore (Roxy Cop), Carey Loftin (Roxy Driver), Harry Caesar (Locker Room Attendant), Charles Parks (Dr Breslin), Hamilton Camp (Garage Attendant), Arthur Malet (Doc Loomis), Fred Lerner (Pitt Roof Sniper), George Orrison (Pitt Doorway Thug), Beau Starr (Pitt Lookout), Joan Shawlee (Peggy Barker), Minnie Lindse (Bordello Maid), Darwyn Swalve (Bordello Bouncer), Wiley Harker and Bob Maxwell ('Mr Smiths'), Tom Spratley (Chauffeur), Bob Terhune (Billiard Soldier), Holgie Forrester (Little Red), Harry Demopoulos (Roman Orgy Patron), Jim Lewis (Roxy Patron), Edwin Prevost (Butler), Alfie Wise (Short Man), Hank Calia (Shorter Friend), Alex Plasschaert (Shortest Friend), Daphne Eckler (Agnes), Lonna Montrose (Didi), Bruce M. Fischer and Art La Fleur (Bruisers). (Fritz Manes for Warner Bros–Malpaso–Deliverance, 99 mins.)

'*Too often, it's like watching a couple of cash-registers upstaging each other.*'
ALEXANDER WALKER, *Evening Standard* (UK)

1985

Pale Rider

As Preacher. Director: Clint Eastwood. Sc: Michael Butler, Dennis Shryack. Ph: Bruce Surtees. Production Design: Edward Carfagno. Ed: Joel Cox. Music: Lennie Niehaus. Cast: Michael Moriarty (Hull Barret), Carrie Snodgress (Sarah Wheeler), Christopher Penn (Josh LaHood), Richard Dysart (Coy LaHood), Sydney Penny (Megan Wheeler), Richard Kiel (Club), Doug McGrath (Spider Conway), John Russell (Marshal Stockburn), Charles Hallahan (McGill), Marvin J. McIntyre (Jagou), Fran Ryan (Ma Blankenship), Richard Hamilton (Jed Blankenship), Graham Paul (Ev Gossage), Chuck LaFont (Eddie Conway), Jeffrey Weissman (Teddy Conway), Allen Keller (Tyson), Tom Oglesby (Elam), Herman Poppe (Ulrik Lindquist), Kathleen Wygle (Bess Gossage), Terrence Evans (Jake Henderson), Jim Hitson (Biggs), Loren Adkins (Bossy), Tom Friedkin (Miner Tom), S. A. Griffin (Deputy Folke), Jack Radosta (Deputy Grissom), Robert Winley (Deputy Kobold), Billy Drago (Deputy Mather), Jeffrey Josephson (Deputy Sedge), John Dennis Johnson (Deputy Tucker), Mike Adams, Clay Lilley, Gene Hartline. R. I. Tolbert, Cliff Happy, Ross Loney, Larry Randles, Mike McGaughy and Gerry Gatlin (Horsemen), Lloyd Nelson (Bank Teller), J. K. Fishburn (Telegrapher), George Orrison (Stationmaster Whitey), Milton Murrill (Porter), Mike Munsey (Dentist–Barber), Keith Dillin (Blacksmith), Wayne Van Horn (Stage Driver), Fritz Manes and Glenn Wright (Stage Riders). (Clint Eastwood and Fritz Manes for Warner Bros–Malpaso, 116 mins.)

'*Many of the greatest Westerns grew out of a director's profound understanding of the screen presence of his actors; consider, for example, John Ford's films with John Wayne and Henry Fonda. In* Pale Rider, *Clint Eastwood is the director, and having directed himself in nine previous films, he understands so well how he works on the screen that the movie has a resonance that probably was not even there in the screenplay.*'

ROGER EBERT, *Roger Ebert's Video Companion*

1986

Heartbreak Ridge

As Sgt. Tom Highway. Director: Clint Eastwood. Sc: James Carabatsos. Ph: Jack N. Green. Production Design: Edward Carfagno. Ed: Joel Cox. Music: Lennie Niehaus. Cast: Marsha Mason (Aggie), Moses Gunn (Sgt Webster), Eileen Heckart (Little Mary), Bo Svenson (Roy Jennings), Everett McGill (Maj. Powers), Boyd Gaines (Lt Ring), Mario Van Peebles ('Stitch' Jones), Arlen Dean Snyder (Master Sgt Choozoo), Vincent Irizarr (Fragetti), Ramon Franco (Aponte), Tom Villard (Profile), Mike Gomez (Quinones), Rodney Hill (Collins), Peter Koch ('Swede' Johanson), Richard Venture (Col Meyers), Peter Jason (Maj. Devin), J. C. Quinn (Quartermaster), Begoña Plaza (Mrs Aponte), John Eames (Judge Zane), Thom Sharp and Jack Gallagher (Emcees), John Hostetter (Reese), Holly Shelton-Foy (Sarita Dwayne), Nicholas Worth (Jail Binger), Timothy Fall (Kid in Jail), John Pennell (Jail Crier), Trish Garland (Woman Marine Officer), Dutch Mann and Darwin Swalve (Bar Tough Guys), Christopher Lee Michael and Alex M. Bello (Marines), Steve Halsey and John Sasse (Bus Drivers), Rebecca Perle (Student in Shower), Annie O'Donnell (Telephone Operator), Elisabeth Ruscio (Waitress), Lloyd Nelson (Deputy), Sgt Maj. John H. Brewer (Sergeant Major in Court), Michael Maurer (Bouncer in Bar), Tom Ellison (Marine Corporal). (Clint Eastwood and Fritz Manes for Warner Bros–Malpaso, 130 mins.)

'Heartbreak Ridge *is not what one might expect the film to be. For all but about twenty of the film's much-too-long 130 minutes,* Heartbreak Ridge *is really a comedy. The combat-action sequences that the film's title (along with the newsreel footage of Korean War battles which runs behind the opening credits) seems to promise arrive only after three quarters of the film is over; and even the combat sequences are a perfunctory, gag-riddled charade. Producer-director Clint Eastwood and writer James Carabatsos do seem to want to say something thought-provoking about the state of American military readiness, but even the eventual substance of their statement is laughably jingoistic.*'

GORDON WALTERS, *Magill's Cinema Annual 1987*

1988

Bird

As director only. Director: Clint Eastwood. Sc: Joel Oliansky. Ph: Jack N. Green. Production Design: Edward Carfagno. Ed: Joel Cox. Music: Lennie Niehaus. Cast: Forest Whitaker (Charlie 'Yardbird' Parker), Diane Venora (Chan Richardson), Michael Zelnicker (Red Rodney), Samuel E. Wright (Dizzy Gillespie), Keith David (Buster Franklin), Michael McGuire (Brewster), James Handy (Esteves), Damon Whitaker (Young Bird), Morgan Nagler (Kim), Arlen Dean Snyder (Dr Heath), Sam Robards (Moscowitz), Penelope Windust (Bellevue Nurse), Glenn Wright (Alcoholic Patient), George Orrison (Patient with Checkers), Bill Cobbs (Dr Caulfield), Hamilton Camp (Mayor of 52nd Street), Chris Bosley (First Doorman), George T. Bruce (Second Doorman), Joey Green (Gene), John Witherspoon (Sid), Tony Todd (Frog), Jo deWinter (Mildred Berg), Richard Zavaglia (Ralph the Narc), Anna Levine (Audrey), Al Pugliese (Owner, Three Deuces), Hubert Kelly (John Wilson), Billy Mitchell (Billy Prince), Karl Vincent (Stratton), Lou Cutell (Bride's Father), Roger Etienne (Parisian MC), Jason Bernard (Benny Tate), Gretchen Oehler (Southern Nurse), Richard McKenzie (Southern Doctor), Tony Cox (Pee Wee Marquette), Diane Salinger (Baroness Nica), Johnny Adams (Bartender), Natalia Silverwood (Red's Girlfriend), Duane Matthews (Engineer), Slim Jim Phantom (Grainger), Matthew Faison (Judge), Peter Crook (Bird's Lawyer), Alec Paul Rubinstein (Recording Producer), Patricia Herd (Hun), Steve Zettler (Owner, Oasis Club), Ann Weldon (Violet Welles), Charley Lang (DJ at the Paramount), Tim Russ (Harris), Richard Jeni (Chummy Morello), Don Starr (Doctor at Nica's), Richard Mawe (Medical Examiner). (Clint Eastwood and David Valdes for Warner Bros–Malpaso, 161 mins.)

'*Up to a point, this is a defensible interpretation of a man who was a junkie from his teens until his death at thirty-four, and who had gargantuan appentites for alcohol, food and sex. Beyond that point, however, one has to consider other factors, especially Parker's embattled status as an avant-garde innovator and his extreme sensitivity to racism – two factors the film pays lip service to, but hasn't the room or inclination to explore. Parker's life was an authentic tragedy, and Eastwood regards it as such, but he can't tell us much about what it meant to be a radical artist or a rebellious black man in the 1940s and early 1950s.*'

JONATHAN ROSENBAUM, *Placing Movies: The Practice of Film Criticism*

The Dead Pool

As Detective Harry Callahan. Director: Buddy Van Horn. Sc: Steve Sharon, from a story by Sharon, Durk Pearson and Sandy Shaw, based on the characters created by Harry Julian Fink and Rita M. Fink. Ph: Jack N. Green. Production Design: Edward Carfagno. Eds: Joel Cox, Ron Spang. Music: Lalo Schifrin. Cast: Patricia Clarkson (Samantha Walker), Liam Neeson (Peter Swan), Evan C. Kim (Al Quan), David Hunt (Harlan Rook), Michael Currie (Capt. Donnelly), Michael Goodwin (Lt Ackerman), Darwin Gillett (Patrick Snow), Anthony Charnota (Lou Janero), Christopher Beale (DA Thomas McSherry), John Allen Vick (Lt Ruskowski), Jeff Richmond (First Freeway Reporter), Patrick Van Horn (Second Freeway Reporter), Singrid Wurschmidt (Third Freeway Reporter), James Carrey (Johnny Squares), Deborah A. Bryan (Girl in Rock Video), Nicholas Love (Jeff Howsker), Maureen McVerry (Vicky Owens), John X. Heart (Samantha's Cameraman), Victoria Bastel (Suzanne Dayton), Kathleen Turco-Lyon (Officer at Trailer), Michael Fagi (Sergeant at Trailer), Ronnie Claire Edwards (Molly Fisher), Wallace Cho (Chinese Store Manager), Melodie Soe (Chinese Restaurant Hostess), Kristopher Logan (First Gunman), Scott Vance (Second Gunman), Glenn T. Wright (Detective Hindmark), Stu Klitsner (Minister), Karen Kahn (TV Associate Producer), Shawn Elliott (Chester Docksteder), Ren Reynolds (Perry), Ed Hodson (Paramedic at Elevator), Edward Hocking (Warden Hocking), Diego Chairs (Butcher Hicks), Patrick Valentino (Pirate Captain), Calvin Jones (First Pirate Tug Reporter), Melissa Martin (Second Pirate Tug Reporter), Phil Dace (Detective Dacey), Louis Giambalvo (Gus Wheeler), Peter Anthony Jacobs (Sgt Holloway), Bill Wattenburg (Nolan Kennard), Hugh McCann (Young Man on Talk Show), Suzanne Sterling (Young Woman on Talk Show), Lloyd Nelson (Sgt Waldman), Charles Martinet (First Police Station Reporter), Taylor Gilbert (Second Police Station Reporter), George Orrison (First Embarcadero Bodyguard), Marc Alaimo (Second Embarcadero Bodyguard), Justin Whalin (Jason), Kris LeFan (Carl), Katie Bruce (Girl on Sidewalk), Harry Demopoulos (Doctor in Hospital Room), John Frederick Jones (Dr Friedman), Martin Ganepoler (Reporter at Pier). (David Valdes for Warner Bros–Malpaso, 91 mins.)

'It's possible that Clint Eastwood and crew are just enjoying a bit of self-mockery on this one. If not, and any one of them took this thing seriously for a moment, then the failure is monumental.'

HAR, *Variety*

1989

Pink Cadillac

As Tommy Nowak. Director: Buddy Van Horn. Sc: John Eskow. Ph: Jack N. Green. Production Design: Edward Carfagno. Editor: Joel Cox. Music: Steve Dorff. Cast: Bernadette Peters (Lou Ann McGuinn), Timothy Carhart (Roy McGuinn), John Dennis Johnston (Waycross), Michael Des Barres (Alex), Jimmie F. Skaggs (Billy Dunston), Bill Moseley (Darrell), Michael Champion (Ken Lee), William Hickey (Mr Burton), Geoffrey Lewis (Ricky Zee), Bill McKinney (Bartender), Gary Klar (Randy Bates), Gary Leffew (John Captshaw), Julie Hoopman (Waitress), Paul Benjamin (Judge), Cliff Remis (Jeff), Frances Fisher (Dina), Mara Corday (Stick Lady), Bob Feist (Rodeo Announcer), Wayne Storm (Jack Bass), Richie Allen (Derelict), Roy Conrad (Barker). (David Valdes and Michael Gruskoff for Warner Bros–Malpaso, 121 mins.)

There's little that's new in the material, and nobody seems to have asked whether the emotional charge of blatant racism belongs in a lightweight story like this.'

ROGER EBERT, *Chicago Sun-Times*

1990

White Hunter, Black Heart

As John Wilson. Director: Clint Eastwood. Sc: Peter Viertel, James Bridges and Burt Kennedy, based on the novel by Viertel. Ph: Jack N. Green. Production Design: John Graysmark. Ed: Joel Cox. Music: Lennie Niehaus. Cast: Jeff Fahey (Pete Verrill), Charlotte Cornwell (Miss Wilding), Norman Lumsden (Butler George), George Dznudza (Paul Landers), Edward Tudor Pole (Reissar), Roddy Maude-Roxby (Thompson), Richard Warwick (Basil Fields), John Raple (Gun Shop Salesman), Catherine Neilson (Irene Saunders), Marisa Berenson (Kay Gibson), Richard Vanstone (Phil Duncan), Jamie Koss (Mrs Duncan), Anne Dunkle (Scarf Girl), David Danns (Bongo Man), Myles Freeman (Ape Man), Geoffrey Hutchins (Alec Laing), Christopher Fairbank (Tom Harrison), Alun Armstrong (Ralph Lockhart), Clive Mantle (Harry), Mel Martin (Margaret MacGregor), Martin Jacobs (Dickie Marlowe), Norman Malunga (Desk Clerk), Timothy Spall (Hodkins), Alex Norton (Zibelinsky), Eleanor David (Dorshka), Boy Mathias Chuma (Kivu), Andrew Whalley (Photographer), Conrad Asquith (Ogilvy). (Clint Eastwood and David Valdes for Warner Bros–Malpaso, 112 mins.)

'It's a movie that's about something: the contradictions of the artist and American macho, the evils of racism, the byzantine madness of some big-time movies. It's about

exploitation and betrayal, man's attacks on nature and the dark side of the adventurous spirit. It's a fine film in many ways – even if Huston's persona becomes Eastwood's own big tusker: the prey he can't quite shoot. He doesn't bring back the Big One, but he doesn't return empty-handed; intellectually and morally, there's plenty of game for the pot.'

MICHAEL WILMINGTON, *The Los Angeles Times*

The Rookie

As Nick Pulovski. Director: Clint Eastwood. Sc: Boaz Yakin and Scott Spiegel. Ph: Jack N. Green. Production Design: Judy Cammer. Ed: Joel Cox. Music: Lennie Niehaus. Cast: Charlie Sheen (David Ackerman), Raul Julia (Strom), Sonia Braga (Liesl), Tom Skerritt (Eugene Ackerman), Lara Flynn Boyle (Sarah), Pepe Serna (Lieutenant Ray Garcia), Marco Rodriguez (Loco), Pete Randall (Cruz), Donna Mitchell (Laura Ackerman), Xander Berkeley (Blackwell), Tony Plana (Moralles), David Sherrill (Max), Hal Williams (Powell), Lloyd Nelson (Freeway Motorist), Pat Duval, Mara Corday and Jerry Schumacher (Interrogators), Matt McKenzie (Wang), Joel Polis (Lance), Roger LaRue (Maître d'), Robert Dubac (Waiter), Anthony Charnota (Romano), Jordan Lund (Bartender), Paul Ben-Victor (Little Felix), Jeanne Mori (Connie Ling), Anthony Alexander (Alphonse), Paul Butler (Captain Hargate), Seth Allen (David as a child), Coleby Lombardo (David's Brother), Roberta Vasquez (Heather Torres), Joe Farago (Anchorman), Robert Harvey (Whalen), Nick Ballo (Vito), Jay Boryea (Sal), Mary Lou Kenworthy (Receptionist), George Orrison (Detective Orrison). (Howard Kazanjian, Steven Siebert and David Valdes for Warner Bros–Malpaso, 121 mins.)

'This box-office flop was a low point for Eastwood. Sonia Braga and Raul Julia play the German (?!) villains. There are lots of car chases.'

MICHAEL J. WELDON, *The Psychotronic Video Guide*

1992

Unforgiven

As William Munny. Director: Clint Eastwood. Sc: David Webb Peoples. Ph: Jack N. Green. Production Design: Henry Bumstead. Ed: Joel Cox. Music: Lennie Niehaus. Cast: Gene Hackman ('Little Bill' Daggett), Morgan Freeman (Ned Logan), Richard Harris (English Bob), Jaimz Woolvett (the 'Schofield Kid'), Saul Rubinek (W. W. Beauchamp), Frances Fisher (Strawberry Alice), Anna Thomson (Delilah), David Mucci (Quick Mike), Rob Campbell (Davey Bunting), Anthony James (Skinny Dubois), Tara Dawn Frederick (Little Sue), Beverley Elliott (Silky), Lisa Repo-Martell (Faith), Josie Smith

(Crow Creek Kate), Shane Meier (Will Munny), Aline Levasseur (Penny Munny), Cherrilene Cardinal (Sally Two Trees), Robert Koons (Crocker), Ron White (Clyde Ledbetter), Mina E. Mina (Muddy Chandler), Henry Kope (German Joe Schultz), Jeremy Rathford (Deputy Andy Russell), John Pyper-Ferguson (Charley Hecker), Jefferson Mappin (Fatty Rossiter), Walter Marsh (Barber), George Orrison (The Shadow). (Clint Eastwood and David Valdes for Warner Bros–Malpaso, 127 mins.)

'*Most of Clint Eastwood's early Westerns* (The Outlaw Josey Wales, Pale Rider) *were in a postmodern, post-Leone mode: their settings, both natural and stylized, resembled nothing so much as a vast game reserve for that now endangered species, the American cowboy. What was extraordinary about* Unforgiven *by contrast, was that it gave us a unique foretaste of what not only the genre in question but the American cinema as a whole might look like when they re-emerged on the other side of postmodernism. It was, in a sense, the first authentically post-postmodern Hollywood movie. Leone's baroque manners and mannerisms, once sedulously mimicked, were now completely assimilated, thereby enabling Eastwood to return the Western, its mythopaeic potency intact, to its proper habitat.*'

GILBERT ADAIR, *Flickers*

1993

In the Line of Fire

As Frank Horrigan. Director: Wolfgang Petersen. Sc: Jeff Maguire. Ph: John Bailey. Production Design: Lilly Kilvert. Ed: Anne V. Coates. Music: Ennio Morricone. Cast: John Malkovich (Mitch Leary), Rene Russo (Lilly Raines), Dylan McDermott (Al D'Andrea), Gary Cole (Bill Watts), Fred Dalton Thompson (Harry Sargent), John Mahoney (Sam Campagna), Greg Alan-Williams (Matt Wilder), Jim Curley (the President), Sally Hughes (the First Lady), Clyde Kusatsu (Jack Okura), Steve Hytner (Tony Carducci), Tobin Bell, (Mendoza), Bob Schott (Jimmy Hendrickson), Juan A. Riojas (Raul), Elsa Raven (Leary's Landlady), Patrika Darbo (Pam Magnus), Mary Van Arsdel (Sally), John Heard (Professor Riger), Alan Toy (Walter Wickland). (Wolfgang Petersen, Gail Katz and David Valdes for Castle Rock–Apple–Rose–Columbia, 129 mins.)

'*To its credit,* In the Line of Fire *squirms onto eerie psychological terrain: it gets into the suppressed neurosis – the morbid blend of nobility and masochism – at the heart of the Secret Service ethos. Yet the way most of this plays out feels flat and familiar. The whole notion of making the killer Eastwood's Doppelgänger is lifted directly from his 1984 film* Tightrope, *another film that paid lip service to dark inner states. Eastwood's bantering romance with a feminist agent (Rene Russo) recalls his (platonic) sparring with Tyne Daly in* The Enforcer. *And Malkovich, enjoyable as he is, seems less a creepy, believable nut than a pure movie concoction . . .'*

OWEN GLEIBERMAN, Entertainment Weekly

A Perfect World

As Red Garnett. Director: Clint Eastwood. Sc: John Lee Hancock. Ph: Jack N. Green. Production Design: Henry Bumstead. Ed: Joel Cox. Music: Lennie Niehaus. Cast: Kevin Costner (Butch Haynes), Laura Dern (Sally Gerber), T. J. Lowther (Phillip Perry), Leo Burmester (Tom Adler), Keith Szarabajka, Wayne Dehart, Paul Hewitt (Dick Suttle), Bradley Whitford (Bobby Lee), Ray McKinnon (Bradley), Jennifer Griffin (Gladys Perry), Leslie Flowers (Naomi Perry), Belinda Flowers (Ruth Perry), Darryl Cox (Mr Hughes), Jay Whiteaker (Superman), Taylor Suzanna McBride (Tinkerbell), Christopher Reagan Ammons (Dancing Skeleton), Mark Voges (Larry), John M. Jackson (Bob Fielder), Connie Cooper (Bob's Wife), George Orrison (Officer Orrison). (Mark Johnson and David Valdes for Warner Bros–Malpaso, 138 mins.)

'He [director Eastwood] gives the picture an easy spirit, a wayward mischievousness that seems surprising after the soberly mythological Unforgiven. *He has a wonderful eye; and, not surprisingly, the movie is paced and framed like a Western. Nothing is rushed. And the picture has a classic Western's feeling of innocence in all kinds of ways, without losing its modern appearance.'*

JULIE SALAMON, The Wall Street Journal

1995

The Bridges of Madison County

As Robert Kincaid. Director: Clint Eastwood. Sc: Richard LaGravenese, based on the Robert James Waller novel. Ph: Jack N. Green. Art Dir: Jeannine Oppewall Ed: Joel Cox. Music: Lennie Niehaus. Cast: Meryl Streep (Francesca Johnson), Annie Corley (Carolyn), Victor Slezak (Michael), Jim Haynie (Richard), Sarah Kathryn Schmitt (Young Carolyn), Christopher Kroon (Young Michael), Phyllis Lyons (Betty), Debra Monk (Madge), Richard Lage (Lawyer), Michelle Benes (Lucy Redfield), Child #1 (Alison Wiegert), Brandon Bobst (Child #2), Pearl Faessler (Wife), R. E. 'Stick' Faessler (Husband), Tania Mishler (Waitress #1), Billie McNabb (Waitress #2), Art Breese (Cashier), Lana Schwab (Saleswoman), Larry Loury (UPS Driver), and James Rivers, Mark A. Brooks, Peter Cho, Eddie DeJean Sr., Jason C. Brewer and Kyle Eastwood (James Rivers Band). (Clint Eastwood and Kathleen Kennedy for Warner Bros–Malpaso, 135 mins.)

'Terribly tasteful, long-winded adaptation of North America's record-selling hardback

novel, lovingly and sensitively brought to the screen by director–producer–star Clint Eastwood. Carefully avoiding the pitfalls of heavy-handed emotional manipulation, Clint has produced a good-looking, heartfelt drama from Richard LaGravenese's literate, well-crafted adaptation. But with Clint and Meryl Streep in the roles of the bewildered lovers, it's hard to forget that they're Clint and Meryl. Maybe it's this fact that stems the flow of tears.'

JAMES CAMERON-WILSON, *Film Review 1997*

The Stars Fell on Henrietta

As producer only. Director: James Keach. Sc: Philip Railsback. Ph: Bruce Surtees. Production Design: Henry Bumstead. Ed: Joel Cox. Music: David Benoit. Cast: Robert Duvall (McCoy), Aidan Quinn (Don Day), Frances Fisher (Cora Day), Brian Dennehy (Big Dave), Lexi Randall (Beatrice Day), Kaytlyn Knowles (Pauline Day), Francesca Ruth Eastwood (Mary Day), Joe Stevens (Big Dave's Driver), Billy Bob Thornton (Roy), Victor Wong (Henry Nakal), Paul Lazar (Seymour), Spencer Garrett (Delbert Tims), Park Overall (Shirl the Waitress), Zach Grenier (Larry Ligstow), Wayne DeHart (Robert), Woody Watson (Jack Sterling), Rodger Boyce (P. G. Pratt), George Haynes (Stratmeyer). (Clint Eastwood and David Valdes for Warner Bros–Malpaso, 110 mins.)

'A leisurely-paced – just this side of poky, really – Depression-era drama about a colorful codger's seemingly quixotic quest for black gold.'

RITA KEMPLEY, *Washington Post*

1996

Absolute Power

As Luther Whitney. Director: Clint Eastwood. Sc: William Goldman, based on the David Baldacci novel. Ph: Jack N. Green. Production Design: Henry Bumstead. Ed: Joel Cox. Music: Lennie Niehaus, Clint Eastwood. Cast: Gene Hackman (President Alan Richmond), E. G. Marshall, (Walter Sullivan) Scott Glenn (Bill Burton), Ed Harris (Seth Frank), Dennis Haysbert (Tim Collin), Judy Davis (Gloria Russell), Laura Linney (Kate Whitney), Melora Hardin (Christy Sullivan), Kenneth Welsh (Sandy Lord), Penny Johnson (Laura Simon), Richard Jenkins (Michael McCarty), Mark Margolis (Baltimore Bartender), Elaine Kagain (Valerie), Alison Eastwood (Art Student), Yau-Gene Chan (Waiter), George Orrison (Airport Bartender), Charles McDaniel (Medical Examiner), John Lyle Campbell (Repairman), Kimber Eastwood (White House Tour Guide), Eric Dahlquist Jr (Oval Office Agent), Jack Stewart Taylor (Watergate Doorman), Joy Ehrlich (Reporter) and Robert Harvey (Cop). (Clint Eastwood and Karen Spiegel for Castle Rock–Malpaso, 121 mins.)

'*Eastwood understands, as a director, what his star's face is worth – a testament of life lived, of victories missed and defeats redeemed, of a worn but persistent beauty. Everything that Eastwood does is helpful, but his face is in itself the film's true foundation.*'

STANLEY KAUFFMAN, *The New Republic*

1997

Midnight in the Garden of Good and Evil

As director only. Director: Clint Eastwood. Sc: John Lee Hancock, based on the book by John Berendt. Ph: Jack N. Green. Production Design: Henry Bumstead. Ed: Joel Cox. Music: Lennie Niehaus. Cast: Kevin Spacey (Jim Williams), John Cusack (John Kelso), Jack Thompson (Sonny Seiler), Jude Law (Billy Hanson), the Lady Chablis (Herself), Alison Eastwood, (Mandy Nichols), Irma P. Hall (Minerva), Paul Hipp (Joe Odom), Dorothy Loudon (Serena Dawes), Anne Haney (Margaret Williams), Kim Hunter (Betty Harty), Geoffrey Lewis (Luther Driggers), Richard Herd (Henry Skerridge), Leon Rippy (Detective Boone), Bob Gunton (Finley Largent), Michael O'Hagan (Geza Von Habsburg), Gary Anthony Williams (Bus Driver), Tim Black (Jeff Braswell), Muriel Moore (Mrs Baxter), Sonny Seiler (Judge White), Terry Rhoads (Assistant DA), Victor Brandt (Bailiff), Patricia Herd (Juror #1), Nick Gillie (Juror #20), Patrika Darbo (Sara Warren), J. Patrick McCormack (Doctor), Emma Kelly (Herself), Tyrone Lee Weaver (Ellis), Greg Goossen (Cell Mate), Shannon Eubanks (Mrs Hamilton), Virginia Duncan (Card Club Woman), Rhoda Griffis (Card Club Woman), Judith Robinson (Card Club Woman), Jo Ann Pflug (Cynthia Vaughn), James Moody (William Simon Glover), John Duncan (Gentleman in Park), Bess S. Thompson (Pretty Girl), Jin Hi Soucy (Receptionist), Michael Rosenbaum (George Tucker), Dan Biggers (Harry Cramm), Georgia Allen (Lucille Wright), Collin Wilcox Paxton (Woman at Party), Charles Black (Alpha), Aleta Mitchell (Alphabette), Michael Kevin Harry (Phillip), Dorothy Kingery (Jim Williams's Sister), Amanda Kingery (Amanda, Jim Williams's Niece), Susan Kingery (Susan, Jim Williams's Niece), Ted Manson (Passerby). (Clint Eastwood and Arnold Stiefel for Warner Bros–Malpaso, 155 mins.)

'Midnight in the Garden of Good and Evil *is an outstanding lean film trapped in a fat film's body. Clint Eastwood's screen version of John Berendt's phenomenally successful nonfiction tome, about a sensational murder case in genteel, eccentric old Savannah, Ga., vividly captures the atmosphere and memorable characters of the book. But the picture's aimless, sprawling structure and exceedingly leisurely pace finally come to weigh too heavily upon its virtues.*'

TODD MCCARTHY, *Variety*

1999

True Crime

As Steve Everett. Director: Clint Eastwood. Sc: Larry Gross, Paul Brickman and Stephen Schiff, based on the Andrew Klavan novel. Ph: Jack N. Green. Production Design: Henry Bumstead. Ed: Joel Cox. Music: Lennie Niehaus. Cast: Isaiah Washington (Frank Beachum), Denis Leary (Bob Findley), Lisa Gay Hamilton (Bonnie Beachum), James Woods (Alan Mann), Bernard Hill (Luther Plunkitt), Diane Venora (Barbara Everett), Michael McKean (Reverend Shillerman), Michael Jeter (Dale Porterhouse), Mary McCormack (Michelle Ziegler), Penny Bae Bridges (Gail Beachum), Francesca Ruth Fisher-Eastwood (Kate Everett), John Finn (Reedy), Laila Robins (Patricia Findley), Sydney Poitier (Jane March), Erik King (Pussy Man), Graham Beckel (Arnold McCardle), Frances Fishes (Cecilia Nussbaum), Marissa Ribisi (Amy Wilson), Christine Ebersole (Bridget Rossiter), Anthony Zerbe (Henry Lowenstein), Colman Domingo (Wally Cartwright), Karl Dahlquist, Kathryn Howell, Lucy Alexis Liu, John B. Scott, William Windom, Hattie Winston and Kelvin Han Yee. (Clint Eastwood and Tom Rooker for Malpaso and Lili Fini Zanuck and Richard D. Zanuck for Warner Bros., 127 mins.)

'This is a very old movie formula – the little guy against the system – and Eastwood, directing his 21st film, doesn't apologize for the creakiness of the concept or the gaps in logic that leap out of the script. What the hell, he seems to be saying, it's a juicy part and I've earned the right to goof off.'

EDWARD GUTHMANN, *San Francisco Chronicle*

2000

Space Cowboys

(Tentative credits)
Director: Clint Eastwood. Sc: Ken Kaufman and Howard Klausner. Cast: Tommy Lee Jones, James Garner, James Cromwell, Donald Sutherland, William Devane, Marcia Gay Harden, Georgia Emelini, Renee Olstead.

Index

Steven Spielberg

The Unauthorised Biography

John Baxter

'John Baxter has applied considerable scholarship in his quest to discover what makes Steven Spielberg tick . . . It is a success story Baxter tells with relish . . . He has got beneath the skin of his subject for a detailed and eminently readable biography of an enigmatic and complex personality . . . I found this book a most intelligent piece of detection work, totally engrossing.'

BRYAN FORBES, *Daily Telegraph*

Steven Spielberg dominates the cinema of the nineties. He is one of the screen's greatest enchanters, with a spellbinding capacity – and a box-office record – matched by very few. His power now exceeds that of the greatest moguls of Hollywood's golden era, and films like *Jaws*, *ET*, *Close Encounters of The Third Kind* and *Jurassic Park* have been seen by billions around the world, and have changed forever the way movies are made. How was it that this 'movie brat', from an unhappy and rootless adolescence on the fringes of American society, became one of the most formidable players on the global entertainment scene?

John Baxter charts the director's career from his first 8mm home movies to the Oscar-winning *Schindler's List* and beyond, in a full, frank and entertaining account based on extensive interviews with those important in Spielberg's life.

'Absorbing . . . Baxter is a shrewd, witty and very readable writer.'
J.G. BALLARD, *Independent*

'A very valuable book . . . Baxter's success is beyond question.'
DAVID THOMSON, *Independent on Sunday*

0 00 638444 7

Stanley Kubrick

A Biography

John Baxter

'In this superbly readable biography, John Baxter traces Kubrick's career from the day this spoilt Jewish boy from the Bronx was given a camera for his thirteenth birthday to his present situation as an eccentric hiding away in a remote Hertfordshire mansion.'

GERALD KAUFMAN, *Sunday Telegraph*

'John Baxter's highly readable biography makes Kubrick maddening, endearing and paranoid in equal proportions . . . Many of the stories are riveting.'

NIGEL ANDREWS, *Financial Times*

'Judicious and well-researched.'   PHILLIP FRENCH, *Observer*

'John Baxter's superb biography sets out with enormous relish to unravel this mystery [of Kubrick's reclusiveness]. His earlier biographies, of Buñuel, Fellini, Ken Russell and Spielberg, are among the best in their field, and his account of Kubrick's somewhat tortured soul is written in the same vivid prose.'

J.G. BALLARD, *New Statesman*

'*Stanley Kubrick* is the sharpest book on cinema since Jake Eberts and Terry Ilott's *My Indecision Is Final*, the history of Goldcrest Films.'   BRIAN ALDISS, *Daily Telegraph*

ISBN: 0 00 638445 5